HUMAN MEMORY
Basic Processes

Selected reprints, with new commentaries,
from *The Psychology of Learning and Motivation*

Edited by
GORDON BOWER

Department of Psychology
Stanford University
Stanford, California

1977

ACADEMIC PRESS   New York · London · San Francisco
A Subsidiary of Harcourt Brace Jovanovich, Publishers

The chapters of this book, reprinted with new commentaries, appeared originally in the 1967, 1968, 1972, 1973, and 1974 issues (Volumes 1, 2, 6, 7, and 8) of *The Psychology of Learning and Motivation* published by ACADEMIC PRESS, INC., edited by K. W. Spence and J. T. Spence (Volumes 1 and 2), and by Gordon Bower.

ACADEMIC PRESS, INC.
111 Fifth Avenue, New York, New York 10003

United Kingdom Edition published by
ACADEMIC PRESS, INC. (LONDON) LTD.
24/28 Oval Road, London NW1

Library of Congress Cataloging in Publication Data

Main entry under title:

Human memory.

     Includes bibliographies and index.
     1.   Memory—Addresses, essays, lectures.   I.   Bower, Gordon
BF371.H76   153.1'2'08   77-74024
ISBN 0-12-121050-2

PRINTED IN THE UNITED STATES OF AMERICA

6.2.80

CONTENTS

HUMAN MEMORY: A PROPOSED SYSTEM AND ITS CONTROL PROCESSES

R. C. Atkinson and R. M. Shiffrin

STORAGE MECHANISMS IN RECALL

Murray Glanzer

3. *Commentary on "Working Memory"*   **191**

ALAN D. BADDELEY AND GRAHAM HITCH

WORKING MEMORY

Alan D. Baddeley and Graham Hitch

4. *Commentary on "Reaction Time Measurements in the Study of Memory Processes: Theory and Data"*   **243**

JOHN THEIOS

REACTION TIME MEASUREMENTS IN THE STUDY OF MEMORY PROCESSES: THEORY AND DATA

John Theios

ORGANIZATION AND MEMORY

George Mandler

ELABORATIVE STRATEGIES IN VERBAL LEARNING AND MEMORY

William E. Montague

A MULTICOMPONENT THEORY OF THE MEMORY TRACE
Gordon Bower

PREFACE

This volume brings together the more seminal and frequently cited papers on human memory from 10 years of *The Psychology of Learning and Motivation*. Those volumes are published annually and contain papers on diverse topics within learning and motivation. However, this book reprints some of the more visible papers on a highly focused topic—basic processes of human memory. It fulfills the students' need by collecting in one place the most influential articles on memory scattered throughout the 10 annual volumes. The book can serve as a textbook for advanced students in experimental psychology as well as a resource reference for the psychological researcher. The collection gives a selective overview of important developments in theories of memory since the late 1960s. The four chapters by Atkinson and Shiffrin, Glanzer, Theios, and Baddeley and Hitch deal primarily with short-term memory—evidence for it, and how to conceive of it. The chapters by Montague and Mandler deal primarily with how new information is transferred from short-term to long-term memory by the use of mnemonic, organizing methods. The chapter by Bower proposes a structural representation for a memory trace and investigates implications of that representation for many memory-guided performances.

These papers comprise a relatively coherent cluster of theoretical positions that have been influential in research on memory during the past 10 years. The papers continue to be read and to have influence. In order to increase their contemporary contacts, each author has provided a brief commentary on his paper in which he updates the paper on relevant points and comments on later extensions or elaborations of the ideas. In some instances, the commentary can be appreciated most fully after the main paper has been read. Authors were asked to be brief, so the reader should expect a selective rather than comprehensive commentary on research since the paper originally appeared.

Each paper is self-contained, making it a useful text for the student or researcher wishing a summary of important research findings. The authors typically provide a lengthy, integrative treatment of their subject matter, weaving together their own research with that of others working on their particular problem. This integrative motif makes the papers informative surveys as well as provocative presentations of new research and theorizing.

1

COMMENTARY ON "HUMAN MEMORY:

A PROPOSED SYSTEM

AND ITS CONTROL PROCESSES"[1]

R. M. Shiffrin

DEPARTMENT OF PSYCHOLOGY, INDIANA UNIVERSITY

There were two main thrusts of the Atkinson and Shiffrin (1968) chapter. The first was the construction of a general theoretical framework for human memory, information processing, and re-trieval—a framework with primary divisions into sensory registers, short-term store, and long-term store. The second was the careful, even quantitative, delineation of the important role played by con-trol processes in human memory. Each of these contributions has had important influences upon work over the last 10 years, and both these influences and the state of current work will be discussed briefly.

Probably the most salient (but not the most important) aspect of our theory was the division of memory into three stores: the sensory registers, short-term store, and long-term store. In more recent writings (Atkinson & Shiffrin, 1971; Shiffrin & Geisler, 1973; Shif-frin, 1975, 1976) the sensory registers (i.e., icons) have been com-bined with short-term store into a single component, also termed short-term store. One of the major reasons for this change was the rapidly accumulating evidence that information arriving at the sense organs undergoes many stages of recoding, and the stages persist for varying durations (e.g., see Sperling, 1960; Hogben & DiLollo, 1974; Posner, 1969 [in vision] ; Crowder & Morton, 1969; Massaro, 1972 [in audition]). Therefore, we decided to treat the various products of processing within active memory as part of a single continuum. Since we continued to recognize the differing characteristics of retention for different stages, however, the new version of the theory is not substantially different from the original.

---

[1] Richard Atkinson was unable to write this preface due to his duties as Acting Director of the National Science Foundation. He is in substantial agreement, however, with the remarks prepared by Professor Shiffrin, who coauthored the original chapter.

It is interesting to note that some alternatives to the three-store approach have been willing to accept the existence of sensory registers but have instead presented arguments that short- and long-term stores may better be viewed as a single store (e.g., Murdock, 1974; Wickelgren, 1970), while other theorists have proposed a considerable increase in the number of stores (e.g., Baddeley & Hitch, 1974; Baddeley, 1976). The single-store theorists have argued that no conclusive evidence for the existence of two different stores exists, since the rules governing information stored in the two modes appear to be more similar than different. Indeed, it would have been convenient if the rules governing information storage and retention in the two stores had differed radically. Even in the original treatment, however, it was recognized that the information in the two stores would obey similar rules because of the nature of the long-term storage process: What is stored in permanent long-term memory is (some subset of) the information that has been rehearsed, coded, or otherwise attended in short-term store. Thus, it is a bit naive to expect to find any simple distinguishing characteristic, and it is not even sensible to ask for a "proof" that two separate stores exist. Instead, the theory must be evaluated in light of its entire set of major assumptions, and it must be judged in light of its ability to organize previous findings, to predict new results, and to give rise to new experiments. On these grounds, the theory has been quite successful.

Our theory was, of course, certainly not the first theory to propose several memory stores nor the first to predict memory phenomena in a quantitative fashion. It had a considerable impact on the field, however, because it presented a global framework within which precisely stated models could be constructed for many different memory phenomena and could be tested in quantitative fashion. We believed that a theory could not be tested adequately by the results of any single experiment, since any global theory would be sufficiently complex and have sufficient freedom to predict any one set of results.

Prior memory models tended to consist of qualitatively stated general principles or of precisely and quantitatively stated sets of axioms meant to apply to very limited paradigms. Thus, it was an important step forward for psychologists to realize that global theories could be constructed and tested in quantitative fashion with a reasonable degree of success. Estes' (1955a, b) stimulus sampling theory and our later paper helped to establish the validity of this contention. Norman and Rumelhart's (1970) paper and Shiffrin and

Geisler's (1973) paper were later attempts to create general models with greater emphasis upon the early stages of information processing, while Anderson and Bower (1973) provide an example of an attempt to construct a general theory with greater emphasis upon the role of language related phenomena. Even today, however, our original theory remains an accurate enough representation to engender useful and pertinent experimental explorations.

Probably the most important contribution of our chapter, however, and that aspect which will have the greatest long-range impact was its specification of subject control processes. The idea that the subject is an active agent deeply involved in governing all aspects of his information processing and retrieval is an ancient concept. In practice, however, such concepts had not been incorporated in most memory theories because it seemed to be too difficult to specify processes that could change at the whim of the subject and that could appear in a bewildering variety of manifestations in any one experimental task. By utilizing a carefully designed set of tasks, we were able to induce subjects to adopt a common set of control processes (in particular, a rehearsal process called a "buffer"); we were then able to specify the nature of those processes and to test their characteristics quantitatively. Our success in this area led us to present theories concerning the role of control processes in information processing in general and to distinguish carefully between such processes and those structural processes that do *not* change from one moment to the next at the whim of the subject.

Having demonstrated in our chapter that control processes were subject to the same sort of scientific investigations as the more permanent facets of memory, we opened the door to a cornucopia of new ideas and investigations that spread across the entire range of investigations in cognitive psychology. Even those papers that attacked the validity of our original model, implicitly accepted our views of control processes and helped to verify them. For example, the influential paper of Craik and Lockhart (1972), while ostensibly offering an alternative to the short- and long-term memory approach of our chapter, in fact provided a powerful demonstration of the role of control processes in coding and in the transfer from short- to long-term store. They were able to devise an experimental method by means of which one could control the nature of the coding given by subjects to various inputs. They then found that retrievability from long-term store was closely related to the type of coding that subjects had been induced to utilize. In a similar vein, Bjork (1975) induced subjects to utilize rote rehearsal or elaborative coding and showed that retrieval from short-term store was better following rote rehearsal, while retrieval from long-term store was superior following elaborative coding.

A dramatic new demonstration of the value of distinguishing controlled processes from structural characteristics of the system may be found in Schneider and Shiffrin (1977) and Shiffrin and Schneider (1977). Schneider and Schiffrin examined a variety of search, detection, and attention situations. The results distinguished controlled search (a serial comparison process) from automatic detection (a learned automatic response that calls attention to any consistently trained target, thereby by-passing the need for a serial search). Having established the basic differences between the two forms of detection in these tasks, the next step was to link together search and attention phenomena and to construct a common quantitative model for both.

Even more important, our results enabled us to set forth, in much greater detail and much more clearly, the defining characteristics of processes that are, and are not, under control of the subject. Whereas our chapter referred vaguely to "permanent structural" features of the system, we now propose that information processing may be divided into two qualitatively differing classes: "automatic" and "controlled." Automatic processing is built into the system or learned after much training, does not require capacity or attention, is not under subject control once initiated by appropriate inputs, and operates in parallel with other automatic and controlled processing. Examples range from the many varieties of perceptual encoding (such as those involved in the reading process) to well-learned motor response sequences (such as those utilized in sports). Controlled processing is initiated easily, is highly flexible and may be altered from trial to trial, demands attention and uses up available capacity, is serial in nature, and does not operate in parallel with other controlled processes. Examples include those discussed in our 1968 chapter. Automatic sequences are assumed to be learned following the prior utilization of identically constitued controlled sequences.

I expect that the next 10 years will see an increasingly detailed examination of the role of control processes in information processing and memory. This area of study was initiated in the 1968 chapter, but, despite the considerable influence of this chapter, I think the most important consequences of this approach remain to be seen.

REFERENCES

Anderson, J. R., & Bower, G. H. *Human associative memory.* Washington, D.C.: Winston, 1973.

Atkinson, R. C., & Shiffrin, R. M. Human memory: A proposed system and its control processes. In K. W. Spence & J. T. Spence (Eds.), *The psychology of learning and motivation: Advances in research and theory.* Vol. 2. New York: Academic Press, 1968.

Atkinson, R. C., & Shiffrin, R. M. The control of short-term memory. *Scientific American,* 1971, **225**, 82–90.

Baddeley, A. D. *The psychology of memory.* New York: Basic Books, 1976.

Baddeley, A. D., & Hitch, G. Working memory. In G. H. Bower (Ed.), *The psychology of learning and motivation.* Vol. 8. New York: Academic Press, Pp. 47–90.

Bjork, R. A. Short-term storage: The ordered output of a central processor. In F. Restle, R. M. Shiffrin, N. J. Castellan, H. Lindman, & D. B. Pisoni (Eds.), *Cognitive theory.* Vol. 1. Hillsdale, New Jersey: Erlbaum, 1975.

Craik, F. I. M., & Lockhart, R. S. Levels of processing: A framework for memory research. *Journal of Verbal Learning and Verbal Behavior,* 1972, **11**, 671–684.

Crowder, R. G., & Morton, J. Precategorical acoustic storage (PAS). *Perception and Psychophysics,* 1969, **5**, 365–373.

Estes, W. K. Statistical theory of distributional phenomena in learning. *Psychological Review,* 1955, **62**, 369–377. (a)

Estes, W. K. Statistical theory of spontaneous recovery and regression. *Psychological Review,* 1955, **62**, 145–154. (b)

Hogben, J. H., & DiLollo, V. Perceptual integration and perceptual segregation of brief visual stimuli. *Vision Research,* 1974, **14**, 1059–1070.

Massaro, D. W. Preperceptual images, processing time, and perceptual units in auditory perception. *Psychological Review,* 1972, **79**, 124–145.

Murdock, B. B., Jr. *Human memory: Theory and data.* Potomac, Maryland: Erlbaum, 1974.

Norman, D. A., & Rumelhart, D. E. A system for perception and memory. In D. A. Norman (Ed.), *Models of human memory.* New York: Academic Press, 1970.

Posner, M. I. Abstraction and the process of recognition. In G. H. Bower & J. T. Spence (Eds.), *The psychology of learning and motivation.* Vol. 3. New York: Academic Press, 1969.

Schneider, W., & Shiffrin, R. M. Controlled and automatic human information processing: I. Detection, search and attention. *Psychological Review,* 1977, **84**, 1–66.

Shiffrin, R. M. Short-term store: The basis for a memory system. In F. Restle, R. M. Shiffrin, N. J. Castellan, H. Lindman, & D. B. Pisoni (Eds.), *Cognitive theory.* Vol. 1. Hillsdale, New Jersey: Erlbaum, 1975. (b)

Shiffrin, R. M. Capacity limitations in information processing, attention, and memory. In W. K. Estes (Ed.), *Handbook of learning and cognitive processes.* Vol. 4: *Memory processes.* Hillsdale, New Jersey: Erlbaum, 1976.

Shiffrin, R. M., & Geisler, W. S. Visual recognition in a theory of information processing. In R. L. Solso (Ed.), *Contemporary issues in cognitive psychology: The Loyola Symposium.* Washington, D.C.: Winston, 1973.

Shiffrin, R. M. & Schneider, W. Controlled and automatic human information processing: II. Perceptual learning, automatic attending, and a general theory. *Psychological Review,* 1977, **84**, 127–190.

Sperling, G. The information available in brief visual presentations. *Psychological Monographs,* 1960, **74**.

Wickelgren, W. A. Multitrace strength theory. In D. A. Norman (Ed.), *Models of human memory.* New York: Academic Press, 1970.

Reprinted from *The Psychology of Learning and Motivation*, 1968, **2**, 89–195.

HUMAN MEMORY: A PROPOSED SYSTEM

AND ITS CONTROL PROCESSES[1]

R. C. Atkinson and R. M. Shiffrin

STANFORD UNIVERSITY
STANFORD, CALIFORNIA

[1] This research was supported by the National Aeronautics and Space Administration, Grant No. NGR-05-020-036. The authors are indebted to W. K. Estes and G. H. Bower who provided many valuable suggestions and comments at various stages of the work. Special credit is due J. W. Brelsford who was instrumental in carrying out the research discussed in Section IV and whose overall contributions are too numerous to report in detail. We should also like to thank those co-workers who carried out a number of the experiments discussed in the latter half of the paper; rather than list them here, each will be acknowledged at the appropriate place.

I. Introduction

This paper is divided into two major portions; the first outlines a general theoretical framework in which to view human memory, and the second describes the results of a number of experiments designed to test specific models that can be derived from the overall theory.

The general theoretical framework, set forth in Sections II and III, categorizes the memory system along two major dimensions. One categorization distinguishes permanent, structural features of the system from control processes that can be readily modified or reprogrammed at the will of the subject. Because we feel that this distinction helps clarify a number of results, we will take time to elaborate it at the outset. The permanent features of memory, which will be referred to as the memory structure, include both the physical system and the built-in processes that are unvarying and fixed from one situation to another. Control processes, on the other hand, are selected, constructed, and used at the option of the subject and may vary dramatically from one task to another even though superficially the tasks may appear very similar. The use of a particular control process in a given situation will depend upon such factors as the nature of the instructions, the meaningfulness of the material, and the individual subject's history.

A computer analogy might help illustrate the distinction between memory structure and control processes. If the memory system is viewed as a computer under the direction of a programmer at a remote console, then both the computer hardware and those programs built into the system that cannot be modified by the programmer are analogous to our structural features; those programs and instruction sequences which the programmer can write at his console and which determine the operation of the computer, are analogous to our control processes. In the sense that the computer's method of processing a given batch of data depends on the operating program, so the way a stimulus input is processed depends on the particular control processes the subject brings into play. The structural components include the basic memory stores; examples of control processes are coding procedures, rehearsal operations, and search strategies.

Our second categorization divides memory into three structural components: the sensory register, the short-term store, and the long-term store. Incoming sensory information first enters the sensory register, where it resides for a very brief period of time, then decays and is lost. The short-term store is the subject's working memory; it receives selected inputs from the sensory register and also from long-term store. Information in the short-term store decays completely and is lost within a period of about 30 seconds, but a control process called rehearsal can maintain a limited amount of information in this store as long as the subject desires. The long-term store is a fairly permanent repository for information, information which is transferred from the short-term store. Note that "transfer" is not meant to imply that information is removed from one store and placed in the next; we use transfer to mean the copying of selected information from one store into the next without removing this information from the original store.

In presenting our theoretical framework we will consider first the structural features of the system (Section II) and then some of the more generally used control processes (Section III). In both of these sections the discussion is organized first around the sensory register, then the short-term store, and finally the long-term store. Thus, the outline of Sections II and III can be represented as follows:

	Sensory register	Short-term store	Long-term store
Structure	Sec. II,A	Sec. II,B	Sec. II,C
Control processes	Sec. III,A	Sec. III,B	Sec. III,C

These first sections of the paper do not present a finished theory; instead they set forth a general framework within which specific models can be formulated. We attempt to demonstrate that a large number of results may be handled parsimoniously within this framework, even without coming to final decisions at many of the choice points that occur. At some of the choice points several hypotheses will be presented, and the evidence that is available to help make the choice will be reviewed. The primary goal of Sections II and III is to justify our theoretical framework and to demonstrate that it is a useful way of viewing a wide variety of memory phenomena.

The remaining sections of the paper present a number of precise models that satisfy the conditions imposed by our general theoretical framework. These sections also present data from a series of experiments designed to evaluate the models. Section IV is concerned with an analysis of short-term memory; the model used to analyze the data emphasizes a control process based in the short-term store which we designate a rehearsal buffer. Section V presents several experiments that shed some light upon processes in the long-term store, especially subject-controlled search processes. Some of the experiments in Sections IV and V have been reported by us and our co-workers in previous publications, but the earlier treatments were primarily mathematical whereas the present emphasis is upon discussion and overall synthesis.

If the reader is willing to accept our overall framework on a provisional basis and wishes to proceed at once to the specific models and experiments, then he may begin with Section IV and as a prerequisite need only read that portion of Section III,B concerned with the rehearsal buffer.

II. Structural Features of the Memory System

This section of the paper will describe the permanent, structural features of the memory system. The basic structural division is into the three components diagrammed in Fig. 1: the sensory register, the short-term store, and the long-term store.

When a stimulus is presented there is an immediate registration of that stimulus within the appropriate sensory dimensions. The form of this registration is fairly well understood in the case of the visual system (Sperling, 1960); in fact, the particular features of visual registration (including a several hundred millisecond decay of an initially accurate visual image) allow us positively to identify this system as a distinct component of memory. It is obvious that incoming information in other sense modalities also receives an initial registration, but it is not clear whether these other registrations have an appreciable decay period or any other features which would enable us to refer to them as components of memory.

The second basic component of our system is the short-term store. This store may be regarded as the subject's "working memory." Information entering the short-term store is assumed to decay and disappear completely, but the time required for the information to be lost is considerably longer than for the sensory register. The character of the information in the short-term store does not depend necessarily upon the form of the sensory input. For example, a word presented visually may be encoded from the visual sensory register into an auditory short-term store. Since the auditory short-term system will play a major role in subsequent discussions, we shall use the abbreviation a-v-l to stand for auditory-verbal-linguistic store. The triple term is used because, as we shall see, it is not easy to separate these three functions.

The exact rate of decay of information in the short-term store is difficult to estimate because it is greatly influenced by subject-controlled processes. In the a-v-l mode, for example, the subject can invoke rehearsal mechanisms that maintain the information in STS and thereby complicate the problem of measuring the structural characteristics of the decay process. However, the available evidence suggests that information represented in the a-v-l mode decays and is lost within a period of about 15–30 seconds. Storage of information in other modalities is less well understood and, for reasons to be discussed later, it is difficult to assign values to their decay rates.

The last major component of our system is the long-term store. This store differs from the preceding ones in that information stored here does not decay and become lost in the same manner. All information eventually is completely lost from the sensory register and the short-term store,

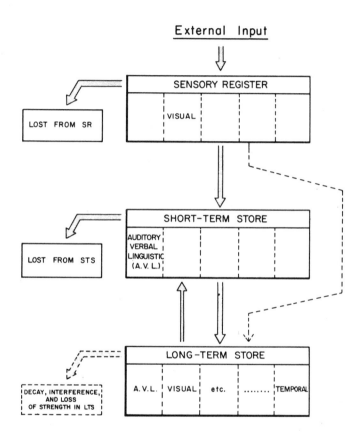

FIG. 1. Structure of the memory system.

whereas information in the long-term store is relatively permanent (although it may be modified or rendered temporarily irretrievable as the result of other incoming information). Most experiments in the literature dealing with long-term store have been concerned with storage in the a-v-l mode, but it is clear that there is long-term memory in each of the other sensory modalities, as demonstrated by an ability to recognize stimuli presented to these senses. There may even be information in the long-term store which is not classifiable into any of the sensory modalities, the prime example being temporal memory.

The flow of information among the three systems is to a large degree under the control of the subject. Note that by information flow and transfer between stores we refer to the same process: the copying of selected information from one store into the next. This copying takes place without the transferred information being removed from its original store. The information remains in the store from which it is transferred and decays according to the decay characteristics of that store. In considering information flow in the system, we start with its initial input into the sensory register. The next step is a subject-controlled scan of the information in the register; as a result of this scan and an associated search of long-term store, selected information is introduced into short-term store. We assume that transfer to the long-term store takes place throughout the period that information resides in the short-term store, although the amount and form of the transferred information is markedly influenced by control processes. The possibility that there may be direct transfer to the long-term store from the sensory register is represented by the dashed line in Fig. 1; we do not know whether such transfer occurs. Finally, there is transfer from the long-term store to the short-term store, mostly under the control of the subject; such transfer occurs, for example, in problem solving, hypothesis testing, and "thinking" in general.

This brief encapsulation of the system raises more questions than it answers. Not yet mentioned are such features as the cause of the decay in each memory store and the form of the transfer functions between the stores. In an attempt to specify these aspects of the system, we now turn to a more detailed outline, including a review of some relevant literature.

A. SENSORY REGISTER

The prime example of a sensory register is the short-term visual image investigated by Sperling (1960, 1963), Averbach and Coriell (1961), Estes and Taylor (1964, 1966), and others. As reported by Sperling (1967), if an array of letters is presented tachistoscopically and the subject is instructed to write out as many letters as possible, usually about six letters are reported. Further, a 30-second delay between presentation and report does not cause a decrement in performance. This fact (plus the facts that confusions tend to be based on auditory rather than visual similarities, and that subjects report rehearsing and subvocalizing the letters) indicates that the process being examined is in the a-v-l short-term store; i.e., subjects scan the visual image and transfer a number of letters to the a-v-l short-term store for rehearsal and output.

In order to study the registered visual image itself, partial-report procedures (Averbach & Coriell, 1961; Averbach & Sperling, 1961; Sperling, 1960, 1963) and forced-choice detection procedures (Estes, 1965; Estes & Taylor, 1964, 1966; Estes & Wessel, 1966) have been employed. The partial-report method typically involves presenting a display (usually a 3×4 matrix of letters and numbers) tachistoscopically for a very brief period. After the presentation the subject is given a signal that tells him which row to report. If the signal is given almost immediately after stimulus offset, the requested information is reported with good precision, otherwise considerable loss occurs. Thus we infer that a highly accurate visual image lasts for a short period of time and then decays. It has also been established that succeeding visual stimulation can modify or possibly even erase prior stimulation. By using a number of different methods, the decay period of the image has been estimated to take several hundred milliseconds, or a little more, depending on experimental conditions; that is, information cannot be recovered from this store after a period of several hundred milliseconds.

Using the detection method, in which the subject must report which of two critical letters was presented in a display, Estes and Taylor (1964, 1966) and Estes and Wessel (1966) have examined some models for the scanning process. Although no completely satisfactory models have yet been proposed, it seems reasonably certain that the letters are scanned serially (which letters are scanned seems to be a momentary decision of the subject), and a figure of about 10 msec to scan one letter seems generally satisfactory.

Thus it appears fairly well established that a visual stimulus leaves a more or less photographic trace which decays during a period of several hundred milliseconds and is subject to masking and replacement by succeeding stimulation. Not known at present is the form of the decay, that is, whether letters in a display decay together or individually, probabilistically or temporally, all-or-none, or continuously. The reader may ask whether these results are specific to extremely brief visual presentations; although presentations of long duration complicate analysis (because of eye movements and physical scanning of the stimulus), there is no reason to believe that the basic fact of a highly veridical image quickly decaying after stimulus offset does not hold also for longer visual presentations. It is interesting that the stimulation seems to be transferred from the visual image to the a-v-l short-term store, rather than to a visual short-term store. The fact that a written report was requested may provide the explanation, or it may be that the visual short-term store lacks rehearsal capacity.

There is not much one can say about registers in sensory modalities other than the visual. A fair amount of work has been carried out on the auditory system without isolating a registration mechanism comparable to the visual one. On the other hand, the widely differing structures of the different sensory systems makes it questionable whether we should expect similar systems for registration.

Before leaving the sensory register, it is worth adding a few comments about the transfer to higher order systems. In the case of the transfer from the visual image to the a-v-l short-term store, it seems likely that a selective scan is made at the discretion of the subject.[2] As each element in the register is scanned, a matching program of some sort is carried out against information in long-term store and the verbal "name" of the element is recovered from long-term memory and fed into the short-term store. Other information might also be recovered in the long-term search; for example, if the scanned element was a pineapple, the word, its associates, the taste, smell, and feel of a pineapple might all be recovered and transferred to various short-term stores. This communication between the sensory register and long-term store does not, however, permit us to infer that information is transferred directly to long-term store from the register. Another interesting theoretical question is whether the search into long-term store is necessary to transfer information from the sensory register to the short-term store within a modality. We see no a priori theoretical reason to exclude nonmediated transfer. (For example, why should a scan or match be necessary to transfer a spoken word to the a-v-l short-term store?) For lack of evidence, we leave these matters unspecified.

B. SHORT-TERM STORE

The first point to be examined in this section is the validity of the division of memory into short- and long-term stores. Workers of a traditional bent have argued against dichotomizing memory (e.g., Melton, 1963; Postman, 1964). However, we feel there is much evidence indicating the parsimony and usefulness of such a division. The argument is often given that one memory is somehow "simpler" than two; but quite the opposite is usually the case. A good example may be found in a comparison of the model for free recall presented in this paper and the model proposed by Postman and Phillips (1965). Any single-process system making a fair attempt to explain the mass of data currently available must, of necessity, be sufficiently complex that the term *single process* becomes a misnomer. We do not wish, however, to engage in the controversy here. We ask the reader to accept our model provisionally until its power to deal with data becomes clear. Still, some justification

[2] Sperling (1960) has presented evidence relating the type of scan used to the subject's performance level.

of our decision would seem indicated at this point. For this reason, we turn to what is perhaps the single most convincing demonstration of a dichotomy in the memory system: the effects of hippocampal lesions reported by Milner (1959, 1966, 1968). In her words:

"Bilateral surgical lesions in the hippocampal region, on the mesial aspect of the temporal lobes, produce a remarkably severe and persistent memory disorder in human patients, the pattern of breakdown providing valuable clues to the cerebral organization of memory. Patients with these lesions show no loss of pre-operatively acquired skills, and intelligence as measured by formal tests is unimpaired, but, with the possible exception of acquiring motor skill, they seem largely incapable of adding new information to the long-term store. This is true whether acquisition is measured by free recall, recognition, or learning with savings. Nevertheless, the immediate registration of new input (as measured, for example, by digit span and dichotic listening tests) appears to take place normally and material which can be encompassed by verbal rehearsal is held for many minutes without further loss than that entailed in the initial verbalization. Interruption of rehearsal, regardless of the nature of the distracting task, produces immediate forgetting of what went before, and some quite simple material which cannot be categorized in verbal terms decays in 30 seconds or so, even without an interpolated distraction. Material already in long-term store is unaffected by the lesion, except for a certain amount of retrograde amnesia for preoperative events" (Milner, 1966).

Apparently, a short-term store remains to the patients, but the lesions have produced a breakdown either in the ability to store new information in long-term store or to retrieve new information from it. These patients appear to be incapable of retaining new material on a long-term basis.[3]

As with most clinical research, however, there are several problems that should be considered. First, the patients were in a general sense abnormal to begin with; second, once the memory defect had been discovered, the operations were discontinued, leaving only a few subjects for observation; third, the results of the lesions seem to be somewhat variable, depending for one thing upon the size of the lesion, the larger lesions giving rise to the full syndrome. Thus there are only a few patients who exhibit the deficit described above in full detail. As startling as these patients are, there might be a temptation to discount them as anomalies but for the following additional findings. Patients who had

[3] A related defect, called Korsakoff's syndrome, has been known for many years. Patients suffering from this abnormal condition are unable to retain new events for longer than a few seconds or minutes (e.g., they cannot recall the meal they have just eaten or recognize the face of the doctor who treated them a few minutes earlier), but their memory for events and people prior to their illness remains largely unimpaired and they can perform adequately on tests of immediate memory span. Recent evidence suggests that Korsakoff's syndrome is related to damage of brain tissue, frequently as the result of chronic alcoholism, in the hippocampal region and the mammillary body (Barbizet, 1963).

known damage to the hippocampal area in one hemisphere were tested for memory deficit after an intracarotid injection of sodium amytal temporarily inactivated the other hemisphere. Controls were patients without known damage, and patients who received injections inactivating their damaged side. A number of memory tests were used as a criterion for memory deficit; the easiest consisted of presenting four pictures, distracting the patient, and then presenting nine pictures containing the original four. If the patient cannot identify the critical four pictures then evidence of memory deficit is assumed. The results showed that in almost all cases memory deficit occurs only after bilateral damage; if side A is damaged and side B inactivated, memory deficit appears, but if the inactivated side is the damaged side, no deficit occurs. These results suggest that the patients described above by Milner were not anomalous cases and their memory deficits therefore give strong support to the hypothesis of distinct short- and long-term memory stores.

1. *Mechanisms Involved in Short-Term Store*

We now turn to a discussion of some of the mechanisms involved in the short-term store. The purpose of this section is not to review the extensive literature on short-term memory, but rather to describe a few experiments which have been important in providing a basis for our model. The first study in this category is that of Peterson and Peterson (1959). In their experiment subjects attempted to recall a single trigram of three consonants after intervals of 3, 6, 9, 12, 15, and 18 seconds. The trigram, presented auditorily, was followed immediately by a number, and the subject was instructed to count backward by three's from that number until he received a cue to recall the trigram. The probability of a correct answer was nearly perfect at 3 seconds, then dropped off rapidly and seemed to reach an asymptote of about .08 at 15–18 seconds. Under the assumption that the arithmetic task played the role of preventing rehearsal and had no direct interfering effect, it may be concluded that a consonant trigram decays from short-term store within a period of about 15 seconds. In terms of the model, the following events are assumed to occur in this situation: the consonant trigram enters the visual register and is at once transferred to the a-v-l short-term store where an attempt is made to code or otherwise "memorize" the item. Such attempts terminate when attention is given to the task of counting backward. In this initial period a trace of some sort is built up in long-term store and it is this long-term trace which accounts for the .08 probability correct at long intervals. Although discussion of the long-term system will come later, one point should be noted in this context; namely, that the long-term trace should be more powerful the more repetitions of the trigram before arithmetic, or the longer the time before arithmetic. These effects were found by Hellyer (1962); that is, the model predicts the probability correct curve will reach an asymptote that reflects long-term strength, and in the aforementioned experiment, the more repetitions before arithmetic, the higher the asymptote.

It should be noted that these findings tie in nicely with the results from a similar experiment that Milner (1968) carried out on her patients. Stimuli that could not be easily coded verbally were used; for example, clicks, light flashes, and nonsense figures. Five values were assigned to each stimulus; a test consisted of presenting a particular value of one stimulus, followed by a distracting task, followed by another value of the stimulus. The subject was required to state whether the two stimuli were the same or different. The patient with the most complete memory deficit was performing at a chance level after 60 seconds, whether or not a distracting task was given. In terms of the model, the reduction to chance level is due to the lack of a long-term store. That the reduction occurred even without a distracting task indicates that the patient could not readily verbalize the stimuli, and that rehearsal in modes other than the verbal one was either not possible or of no value. From this view, the better asymptotic performance demonstrated by normal subjects on the same tasks (with or without distraction) would be attributed to a long-term trace. At the moment, however, the conclusion that rehearsal is lacking in nonverbal modes can only be considered a highly tentative hypothesis.

We next ask whether or not there are short-term stores other than in the a-v-l mode, and if so, whether they have a comparable structure. A natural approach to this problem would use stimuli in different sense modalities and compare the decay curves found with or without a distracting task. If there was reason to believe that the subjects were not verbally encoding the stimuli, and if a relatively fast decay curve was found, then there would be evidence for a short-term memory in that modality. Furthermore, any difference between the control group and the group with a distracting task should indicate the existence of a rehearsal mechanism. Posner (1966) has undertaken several experiments of this sort. In one experiment the subject saw the position of a circle on a 180-mm line and later had to reproduce it; in another the subject moved a lever in a covered box a certain distance with only kinesthetic feedback and later tried to reproduce it. In both cases, testing was performed at 0, 5, 10, and 20 seconds; the interval was filled with either rest, or one of three intervening tasks of varying difficulty. These tasks, in order of increasing difficulty, consisted of reading numbers, adding numbers, and classifying numbers into categories. For the kinesthetic task there was a decline in performance over 30 seconds, but with no obvious differences among the different intervening conditions. This could be taken as evidence for a short-term kinesthetic memory without a rehearsal capability. For the visual task, on the other hand, there was a decline in performance over the 30 seconds only for the two most difficult intervening tasks; performance was essentially constant over time for the other conditions. One possibility, difficult to rule out, is that the subjects' performance was based on a verbal encoding of the visual stimulus. Posner tends to doubt this possibility for reasons that include the accuracy of the performance. Another possibility is that there is a short-term visual memory with a rehearsal component; this hypothesis seems somewhat at variance with the results from Milner's patient who performed at chance level in the experiment cited above. Inasmuch as the data reported by Posner (1966) seem to be rather variable, it would probably be best to hold off a decision on the question of rehearsal capability until further evidence is in.

2. *Characteristics of the a-v-l Short-Term Store*

We restrict ourselves in the remainder of this section to a discussion of the characteristics of the a-v-l short-term store. Work by Conrad (1964) is particularly interesting in this regard. He showed that confusions among visually presented letters in a short-term memory task are correlated with the confusions that subjects make when the same letters are read aloud in a noise background; that is, the letters most confused are those sounding alike. This might suggest an auditory short-term store, essentially the auditory portion of what has been called to this point an a-v-l store. In fact, it is very difficult to separate the verbal and linguistic aspects from the auditory ones. Hintzman (1965, 1967) has argued that the confusions are based upon similar kinesthetic feedback patterns during subvocal rehearsal. When subjects were given white noise on certain trials, several could be heard rehearsing the items aloud, suggesting subvocal rehearsal as the usual process. In addition, Hintzman found that confusions were based upon both the voicing qualities of the letters and the place of articulation. The place-of-articulation errors indicate confusion in kinesthetic feedback, rather than in hearing. Nevertheless, the errors found cannot be definitely assigned to a verbal rather than an auditory cause until the range of auditory confusions is examined more thoroughly. This discussion should make it clear that it is difficult to distinguish between the verbal, auditory, and linguistic aspects of short-term memory; for the purposes of this paper, then, we group the three together into one short-term memory, which we have called the a-v-l short-term store. This store will henceforth be labeled STS. (Restricting the term STS to the a-v-l mode does not imply that there are not other short-term memories with similar properties.)

The notation system should be made clear at this point. As just noted, STS refers to the auditory-verbal-linguistic short-term store. LTS will refer to the comparable memory in long-term store. It is important not to confuse our theoretical constructs STS and LTS (or the more general terms short-term store and long-term store) with the terms short-term memory (STM) and long-term memory (LTM) used in much of the psychological literature. These latter terms have come to take on an operational definition in the literature; STM refers to the memory examined in experiments with short durations or single trials, and LTM to the memory examined in long-duration experiments, typically list learning, or multiple-list learning experiments. According to our general theory, both STS and LTS are active in both STM and LTM experiments. It is important to keep these terms clear lest confusion results. For example, the Keppel and Underwood (1962) finding that performance in the Peterson situation is better on the first trials of a session has been appropriately interpreted as evidence for proactive interference in short-term memory (STM). The model we propose, however, attributes the effect to changes in the long-term store over the session, hence placing the cause in LTS and not STS.

At this point a finished model would set forth the structural characteristics of STS. Unfortunately, despite a large and growing body of experiments concerned with short-term memory, our knowledge about its structure is very limited. Control processes and structural features are so complexly interrelated that it is difficult to isolate those aspects of the data that are due solely to the structure of the memory system. Consequently, this paper presumes only a minimal structure for STS; we assume a trace in STS with auditory or verbal components which decays fairly rapidly in the absence of rehearsal, perhaps within 30 seconds. A few of the more promising possibilities concerning the precise nature of the trace will be considered next. Because most workers in this area make no particular distinction between traces in the two systems, the comments to follow are relevant to the memory trace in the long-term as well as the short-term store.

Bower (1967a) has made a significant exploration of the nature of the trace. In his paper, he has demonstrated the usefulness of models based on the assumption that the memory trace consists of a number of pieces of information (possibly redundant, correlated, or in error, as the case may be), and that the information ensemble may be construed as a multicomponent vector. While Bower makes a strong case for such a viewpoint, the details are too lengthy to review here. A somewhat different approach has been proposed by Wickelgren and Norman (1966) who view the trace as a unidimensional strength measure varying over time. They demonstrate that such a model fits the results of certain types of recognition-memory experiments if the appropriate decay and retrieval assumptions are made. A third approach is based upon a phenomenon reported by Murdock (1966), which has been given a theoretical analysis by Bernbach (1967). Using methods derived from the theory of signal detectability, Bernbach found that there was an all-or-none aspect to the confidence ratings that subjects gave regarding the correctness of their response. The confidence ratings indicated that an answer was either "correct" or "in error" as far as the subject could tell; if intermediate trace strengths existed, the subject was not able to distinguish between them. The locus of this all-or-none feature, however, may lie in the retrieval process rather than in the trace; that is, even if trace strengths vary, the result of a retrieval attempt might always be one of two distinct outcomes: a success or a failure. Thus, one cannot rule out models that assume varying trace strengths. Our preference is to consider the trace as a multicomponent array of information (which we shall often represent in experimental models by a unidimensional strength measure), and reserve judgment on the locus of the all-or-none aspect revealed by an analysis of confidence ratings.

There are two experimental procedures which might be expected to shed some light on the decay characteristics of STS and both depend upon controlling rehearsal; one is similar to the Peterson paradigm in which rehearsal is controlled by an intervening activity and the other involves a very rapid presentation of items followed by an immediate test. An example of the former procedure is Posner's (1966) experiment in which the difficulty of the intervening activity was varied. He found that as the difficulty of an intervening task increased, accuracy of recall decreased.

Although this result might be regarded as evidence that decay from STS is affected by the kind of intervening activity, an alternative hypothesis would ascribe the result to a reduction in rehearsal with more difficult intervening tasks. It would be desirable to measure STS decay when rehearsal is completely eliminated, but it has proved difficult to establish how much rehearsal takes place during various intervening tasks.

Similar problems arise when attempts are made to control rehearsal by increasing presentation rates. Even at the fastest conceivable presentation rates subjects can rehearse during presentation if they attend to only a portion of the incoming items. In general, experiments manipulating presentation rate have not proved of value in determining decay characteristics for STS, primarily because of the control processes the subject brings into play. Thus Waugh and Norman (1965) found no difference between 1-second and 4-second rates in their probe digit experiment; Conrad and Hille (1958) found improvement with faster rates; and Buschke and Lim (1967) found increases in the amount of primacy in their missing-span serial position curves as input rate increased from one item per second to four items per second. Complex results of this sort make it difficult to determine the structural decay characteristics of STS. Eventually, models that include the control processes involved in these situations should help clarify the STS structure.

3. *Transfer from STS to LTS*

The amount and form of information transferred from STS to LTS is primarily a function of control processes. We will assume, however, that transfer itself is an unvarying feature of the system; throughout the period that information resides in the short-term store, transfer takes place to long-term store. Support for such an assumption is given by studies on incidental learning which indicate that learning takes place even when the subject is not trying to store material in the long-term store. Better examples may be the experiments reported by Hebb (1961) and Melton (1963). In these experiments subjects had to repeat sequences of digits. If a particular sequence was presented every several trials, it was gradually learned. It may be assumed that subjects in this situation attempt to perform solely by rehearsal of the sequence within STS; nevertheless, transfer to LTS clearly takes place. This Hebb-Melton procedure is currently being used to explore transfer characteristics in some detail. R. L. Cohen and Johansson (1967), for example, have found that an overt response to the repeated sequence was necessary for improvement in performance to occur in this situation; thus information transfer is accentuated by overt responses and appears to be quite weak if no response is demanded.

The form of the STS-LTS transfer may be probabilistic, continuous, or some combination; neither the literature nor our own data provide a firm basis for making a decision. Often the form of the information to be remembered and the type of test used may dictate a particular transfer process, as for example in Bower's (1961) research on an all-or-none paired-associate learning model, but the issue is nevertheless far from settled. In fact, the changes in the transfer process induced by the subject effectively alter the transfer function form experiment to experiment, making a search for a universal, unchanging process unproductive.

C. LONG-TERM STORE

Because it is easiest to test for recall in the a-v-l mode, this part of long-term store has been the most extensively studied. It is clear, however, that long-term memory exists in each of the sensory modalities; this is shown by subjects' recognition capability for smells, taste, and so on. Other long-term information may be stored which is not necessarily related to any of the sensory modalities. Yntema and Trask (1963), for example, have proposed that temporal memory is stored in the form of "time-tags." Once again, however, lack of data forces us to restrict our attention primarily to the a-v-l mode, which we have designated LTS.

First a number of possible formulations of the LTS trace will be considered. The simplest hypothesis is to assume that the trace is all-or-none; if a trace is placed in memory, then a correct retrieval and response will occur. Second-guessing experiments provide evidence concerning an hypothesis of this sort.

Binford and Gettys (1965) presented the subject with a number of alternatives, one of which was the correct answer. If his first response is incorrect, he picks again from the remaining alternatives. The results indicate that second guesses are correct well above the chance level to be expected if the subject were guessing randomly from the remaining alternatives. This result rules out the simple trace model described above because an all-or-none trace would predict second guesses to be at the chance level. Actually, the above model was a model of both the form of the trace and the type of retrieval. We can expand the retrieval hypothesis and still leave open the possibility of an all-or-none trace. For example, in searching for a correct all-or-none trace in LTS, the subject might find a similar but different trace and mistakenly terminate the search and generate an answer; upon being told that the answer is wrong the subject renews the search and may find the correct trace the next time. Given this hypothesis, it would be instructive to know whether the results differ if the subject must rank the response alternatives without being given feedback after each choice. In this case all the alternatives would be ranked on the basis of the same search of LTS; if the response ranked second was still above chance, then it would become difficult to defend an all-or-none trace.

A second source of information about the nature of the trace comes from the tip-of-the-tongue phenomenon examined by Hart (1965), R. Brown and McNeill (1966), and Freedman and Landauer (1966). This phenomenon refers to a person's ability to predict accurately that he will be able to recognize a correct answer even though he cannot recall it at the moment. He feels as if the correct answer were on the "tip of the tongue." Experiments have shown that if subjects who cannot recall an answer are asked to estimate whether they will be able to choose the correct answer from a set of alternatives, they often show good accuracy in predicting their success in recognition. One explanation might be that the subject recalls some information, but not enough to generate an answer and feels that this partial information is likely to be sufficient to choose among a set of alternatives. Indeed, Brown and McNeill found that the initial sound of the word to be retrieved was often correctly recalled in cases where a correct identification was later made. On the other hand, the subject often is absolutely certain upon seeing the correct response that it is indeed correct. This might indicate that some new, relevant information has become available after recognition. In any case, a simple trace model can probably not handle these results. A class of models for the trace which can explain the tip-of-the-tongue phenomenon are the multiple-copy models suggested by Atkinson and Shiffrin (1965). In these schemes there are many traces or copies of information laid in long-term store, each of which may be either partial or complete. In a particular search of LTS perhaps only a small number or just one of these copies is retrieved, none complete enough to generate the correct answer; upon recognition, however, access is gained to the other copies, presumably through some associative process. Some of these other copies contain enough information to make the subject certain of his choice. These multiple-copy memory models are described more fully in Atkinson and Shiffrin (1965).

The decay and/or interference characteristics of LTS have been studied more intensively over the past 50 years than any other aspect of memory. Partly for this reason a considerable body of theory has been advanced known as interference theory.[4] We tend to regard this theory as descriptive rather than explanatory; this statement is not meant to detract from the value of the theory as a whole, but to indicate that a search for mechanisms at a deeper level might prove to be of value. Thus, for example, if the interfering effect of a previously learned list upon recall of a second list increases over time until the second list is retested, it is not enough to accept "proactive interference increasing over time" as an explanation of the effect; rather one should look for the underlying search, storage, and retrieval mechanisms responsible.

We are going to use a very restricted definition of interference in the rest of this paper; interference will be considered a structural feature of memory not under the control of the subject. It will refer to such possibilities as disruption and loss of information. On the other hand, there are search mechanisms which generate effects like those of structural interference, but which are control processes. Interference theory, of course, includes both types of possibilities, but we prefer to break down interference effects into those which are structurally based, and those under the control of the subject. Therefore the term *interference* is used henceforth to designate a structural feature of the long-term system.

---

[4] For an overview of interference theory see Postman (1961).

It is important to realize that often it is possible to explain a given phenomenon with either interference or search notions. Although both factors will usually be present, the experimental situation sometimes indicates which is more important. For example, as we shall see in Section V, the decrease in the percentage of words recalled in a free verbal-recall experiment with increases in list length could be due either to interference between items or to a search of decreasing effectiveness as the number of items increase. The typical free recall situation, however, forces the subject to engage in a search of memory at test and indicates to us that the search process is the major factor. Finally, note that the interference effect itself may take many forms and arise in a number of ways. Information within a trace may be destroyed, replaced, or lessened in value by subsequent information. Alternatively, information may never be destroyed but may become irretrievable, temporarily or permanently.

In this section an attempt has been made to establish a reasonable basis for at least three systems—the sensory register, the short-term store, and the long-term store; to indicate the transfer characteristics between the various stores; and to consider possible decay and interference functions within each store.

III. Control Processes in Memory

The term *control process* refers to those processes that are not permanent features of memory, but are instead transient phenomena under the control of the subject; their appearance depends on such factors as instructional set, the experimental task, and the past history of the subject. A simple example of a control process can be demonstrated in a paired-associate learning task involving a list of stimuli each paired with either an A or B response (Bower, 1961). The subject may try to learn each stimulus-response pair as a separate, integral unit or he may adopt the more efficient strategy of answering B to any item not remembered and attempting to remember only the stimuli paired with the A response. This latter scheme will yield a radically different pattern of performance than the former; it exemplifies one rather limited control process. The various rehearsal strategies, on the other hand, are examples of control processes with almost universal applicability.

Since subject-controlled memory processes include any schemes, coding techniques, or mnemonics used by the subject in his effort to remember, their variety is virtually unlimited and classification becomes difficult. Such classification as is possible arises because these processes, while under the voluntary control of the subject, are nevertheless dependent upon the permanent memory structures described in the previous section. This section therefore will follow the format of Section II, organizing the control processes into those primarily associated with the sensory register, STS, and LTS. Apart from this, the presentation will be somewhat fragmentary, drawing upon examples from many disparate experiments in an attempt to emphasize the variety, pervasiveness, and importance of the subject-controlled processes.

A. CONTROL PROCESSES IN THE SENSORY REGISTER

Because a large amount of information enters the sensory register and then decays very quickly, the primary function of control processes at this level is the selection of particular portions of this information for transfer to the short-term store. The first decision the subject must make concerns which sensory register to attend to. Thus, in experiments with simultaneous inputs from several sensory channels, the subject can readily report information from a given sense modality if so instructed in advance, but his accuracy is greatly reduced if instructions are delayed until after presentation. A related attention process is the transfer to STS of a selected portion of a large information display within a sensory modality. An example to keep in mind here is the scanning process in the visual registration system. Letters in a tachistoscopically presented display may be scanned at a rate of about 10 msec a letter, the form of the scan being under the control of the subject. Sperling (1960) found the following result. When the signal identifying which row to report from a matrix of letters was delayed for an interval of time following stimulus offset, the subjects developed two observing strategies. One strategy consisted of obeying the experimenter's instructions to pay equal attention to all rows; this strategy resulted in evenly distributed errors and quite poor performance at long delays. The other strategy consisted of anticipating which row would be tested and attending to only that row; in this case the error variance is increased but performance is better at longer delay intervals than for the other strategy. The subjects were aware of and reported using these strategies. For example, one experienced subject reported switching from the first to the second strategy in an effort to maximize performance when the delay between presentation and report rose above .15 seconds. The graph of his probability of a correct response plotted against delay interval, while generally decreasing with delay, showed a dip at about .15 seconds, indicating that he did not switch strategies soon enough for optimal performance.

The decisions as to which sensory register to attend to, and where and what to scan within the system, are not the only choices that must be made at this level. There are a number of strategies available to the subject for matching information in the register against the long-term store and thereby identifying the input. In an experiment by Estes and Taylor (1966) for example, the subject had to decide whether an F or B was embedded in a matrix display of letters. One strategy would have the subject scan the letters in order, generating the "name" of each letter and checking to see whether it is a B or an F. If the scan ends before all letters are processed, and no B or F has been found, the subject would presumably guess according to some bias. Another strategy might have the subject do a features match on each letter against B and then F, moving on as soon as a difference is found; in this strategy it would not be necessary to scan all features of each letter (i.e., it would not be necessary to generate the name of each letter). A third strategy might have the subject compare with only one of the crucial letters, guessing the other if a match is not found by the time the scan terminates.

B. CONTROL PROCESSES IN SHORT-TERM STORE

1. *Storage, Search, and Retrieval Strategies*

Search processes in STS, while not as elaborate as those in LTS because of the smaller amount of information in STS through which the search must take place, are nevertheless important. Since information in STS in excess of the rehearsal capability is decaying at a rapid rate, a search for a particular datum must be performed quickly and efficiently. One indirect method of examining the search process consists of comparing the results of recognition and recall experiments in which STS plays the major role. Presumably there is a search component in the recall situation that is absent in the recognition situation. It is difficult to come to strong conclusions on this basis, but recognition studies such as Wickelgren and Norman (1966) have usually given rise to less complicated models than comparable recall experiments, indicating that the search component in STS might be playing a large role.

One result indicating that the STS search occurs along ordered dimensions is based upon binaural stimulus presentation (Broadbent, 1954, 1956, 1958). A pair of items is presented, one to each ear simultaneously. Three such pairs are given, one every half second. Subjects perform best if asked to report the items first from one ear and then the other, rather than, say, in pairs. While Broadbent interprets these results in terms of a postulated time needed to switch attention from one ear to the other (a control process in itself), other interpretations are possible. In particular, part of the information stored with each item might include which ear was used for input. This information might then provide a simple dimension along which to search STS and report during recall. Another related possibility would have the subject group the items along this dimension during presentation. In any case we would expect similar results if another dimension other than "sides" (which ear) were provided. Yntema and Trask (1963) used three word-number pairs presented sequentially, one every half second; one member of a pair was presented to one ear and the other member to the other ear. There were three conditions: the first in which three words were presented consecutively on one side (and therefore the three numbers on the other), the second in which two words and one number were presented consecutively on one side, the third in which a number separated the two words on one side. Three test conditions were used: the subject was asked to report words, the numbers (types); or to report one ear followed by the other (sides); or the simultaneous pairs in order (pairs). The results are easy to describe. In terms of probability correct, presentation condition one was best, condition two next, and condition three worst. For the test conditions, "types" yielded the highest probability of correct response, followed by "sides" and then "pairs." "Sides" being better than "pairs" was one of the results found by Broadbent, but "types" being even better than "sides" suggests that the organization along available dimensions, with the concomitant increase of efficiency in the search process, is the dominant factor in the situation.

One difficulty in studying the search process in STS is the fact that the subject will perform perfectly if the number of items presented is within his rehearsal span. Sternberg (1966) has overcome this difficulty by examining the latency of responses within the rehearsal span. His typical experiment consists of presenting from one to six digits to the subject at the rate of 1.2 seconds each. Following a 2-second delay, a single digit is presented and the subjects must respond "yes" or "no" depending on whether or not the test digit was a member of the set just presented. Following this response the subject is required to recall the complete set in order. Since the subjects were 98.7 % correct on the recognition test and 98.6 % correct on the recall test, it may be assumed that the task was within their rehearsal span. Interesting results were found in the latencies of the recognition responses: there was a linear increase in latency as the set size increased from one to six digits. The fact that there was no difference in latencies for "yes" versus "no" responses indicates that the search process in this situation is exhaustive and does not terminate the moment a match is found. Sternberg concludes that the subject engages in an exhaustive serial comparison process which evaluates elements at the rate of 25 to 30 per second. The high processing rate makes it seem likely that the rehearsal the subjects report is not an integral part of the scanning process, but instead maintains the image in STS so that it may be scanned at the time of the test. This conclusion depends upon accepting as a reasonable rehearsal rate for digits the values reported by Landauer (1962) which were never higher than six per second.

Buschke's (1963) missing-span method provides additional insight into search and retrieval processes in STS. The missing-span procedure consists of presenting in a random order all but one of a previously specified set of digits; the subject is then asked to report the missing digit. This technique eliminates the output interference associated with the usual digit-span studies in which the entire presented set must be reported. Buschke found that subjects had superior performance on a missing-span task as compared with an identical digit-span task in which all of the presented items were to be reported in any order. A natural hypothesis would explain the difference in performance as being caused by output interference; that is, the multiple recalls in the digit-span procedure produce interference not seen in the single test procedure of the missing span. An alternative explanation would hold that different storage and search strategies were being employed in the two situations. Madsen and Drucker (1966) examined this question by comparing test instructions given just prior to or immediately following each presentation sequence; the instructions specify whether the subject is to report the set of presented digits or simply to report the missing digit. Output interference would imply that the difference between missing-span and digit-span would hold up in both cases. The results showed that the missing-span procedure with prior instructions was superior to both missing-span and digit-span with instructions following presentation; the latter two conditions produced equal results and were superior to digit-span with prior instructions. It seems clear, then, that two storage and search strategies are being used: a missing-span type, and a digit-span type. Prior instructions (specifying the form of the subject's report) lead the subject to use one or the other of these strategies, but instructions following presentation are associated with a mixture of the two strategies. It appeared in this case that the strategies differed in terms of the type of storage during presentation; the digit-span group with prior instructions tended to report their digits in their presentation order, while the digit-span group with instructions after presentation more often reported the digits in their numerical order. This indicates that the missing-span strategy involved checking off the numbers as they were presented against a fixed, numerically ordered list, while the digit-span strategy involved rehearsing the items in their presented order. It is interesting to note that if the subjects had been aware of the superiority of the missing-span strategy, they could have used it in the digit-span task also, since the two types of tests called for the same information.

It should be noted that retrieval from STS depends upon a number of factors, some under the control of the subject and some depending upon the decay characteristics of STS. If the decay is partial in some sense, so that the trace contains only part of the information necessary for direct output, then the problem arises of how the partial information should be used to generate a response. In this case, it would be expected that the subject would then engage in a search of LTS in an effort to match or recognize the partial information. On the other hand, even though traces may decay in a partial manner, the rehearsal capability can hold a select set of items in a state of immediate recall availability and thereby impart to these items what is essentially an all-or-none status. It is to this rehearsal process that we now turn.

2. *Rehearsal Processes*

Rehearsal is one of the most important factors in experiments on human memory. This is particularly true in the laboratory because the concentrated, often meaningless, memory tasks used increase the relative efficacy of rehearsal as compared with the longer term coding and associative processes. Rehearsal may be less pervasive in everyday memory, but nevertheless has many uses, as Broadbent (1958) and others have pointed out. Such examples as remembering a telephone number or table-tennis score serve to illustrate the primary purpose of rehearsal, the lengthening of the time period information stays in the short-term store. A second purpose of rehearsal is illustrated by the fact that even if one wishes to remember a telephone number permanently, one will often rehearse the number several times. This rehearsal serves the purpose of increasing the strength built up in a long-term store, both by increasing the length of stay in STS (during which time a trace is built up in LTS) and by giving coding and other storage processes time to operate. Indeed, almost any kind of operation on an array of information (such as coding) can be viewed as a form of rehearsal, but this paper reserves the term only for the duration-lengthening repetition process.

In terms of STS structure, we can imagine that each rehearsal regenerates the STS trace and thereby prolongs the decay. This does not imply that the entire information ensemble available in STS immediately after presentation is regenerated and maintained at each rehearsal. Only that information selected by the subject, often a small proportion of the initial ensemble, is maintained. If the word "cow" is presented, for example, the sound of the word cow will enter STS; in addition, associates of cow, like milk, may be retrieved from LTS and also entered in STS; furthermore, an image of a cow may be entered into a short-term visual store. In succeeding rehearsals, however, the subject may rehearse only the word "cow" and the initial associates will decay and be lost. The process may be similar to the loss of meaningfulness that occurs when a word is repeated over and over (Lambert & Jakobovitz, 1960).

An interesting question concerns the maximum number of items that can be maintained via rehearsal. This number will depend upon the rate of STS decay and the form of the trace regenerated in STS by rehearsal. With almost any reasonable assumptions about either of these processes, however, an ordered rehearsal will allow the greatest number of items to be maintained. To give a simple example, suppose that individual items take 1.1 seconds to decay and may be restarted if rehearsal begins before decay is complete. Suppose further that each rehearsal takes .25 seconds. It is then clear that five items may be maintained indefinitely if they are rehearsed in a fixed order over and over. On the other hand, a rehearsal scheme in which items are chosen for rehearsal on a random basis will quickly result in one or more items decaying and becoming lost. It would be expected, therefore, that in situations where subjects are relying primarily upon their rehearsal capability in STS, rehearsal will take place in an ordered fashion. One such situation, from which we can derive an estimate of rehearsal capability, is the digit-span task. A series of numbers is read to the subject who is then required to recall them, usually in the forward or backward order. Because the subject has a long-term store which sometimes can be used to supplement the short-term rehearsal memory, the length of a series which can be correctly recalled may exceed the rehearsal capacity. A lower limit on this capacity can be found by identifying the series length at which a subject never errs; this series length is usually in the range of five to eight numbers.[5]

The above estimates of rehearsal capability are obtained in a discrete-trial situation where the requirement is to remember every item of a small input. A very similar rehearsal strategy can be employed, however, in situations such as free recall where a much greater number of items is input than rehearsal can possibly encompass. One strategy in this case would be to replace one of the items currently being rehearsed by each new item input. In this case every item would receive at least some rehearsal. Because of input and reorganization factors, which undoubtedly consume some time, the rehearsal capacity would probably be reduced. It should be clear that under this scheme a constant number of items will be undergoing rehearsal at any one moment. As an analogy, one might think of a bin always containing exactly n items; each new item enters the bin and knocks out an item already there. This process has been called in earlier reports a "rehearsal buffer," or simply a "buffer," and we will use this terminology here (Atkinson & Shiffrin, 1965).

---

[5] Wickelgren (1965) has examined rehearsal in the digit-span task in greater detail and found that rehearsal capacity is a function of the groupings engaged in by the subject; in particular, rehearsal in distinct groups of three was superior to rehearsal in four's and five's.

In our view, the maintenance and use of the buffer is a process entirely under the control of the subject. Presumably a buffer is set up and used in an attempt to maximize performance in certain situations. In setting up a maximal-sized buffer, however, the subject is devoting all his effort to rehearsal and not engaging in other processes such as coding and hypothesis testing. In situations, therefore, where coding, long-term search, hypothesis testing, and other mechanisms appreciably improve performance, it is likely that a trade-off will occur in which the buffer size will be reduced and rehearsal may even become somewhat random while coding and other strategies increase.

At this point we want to discuss various buffer operations in greater detail. Figure 2 illustrates a fixed-size buffer and its relation to the rest

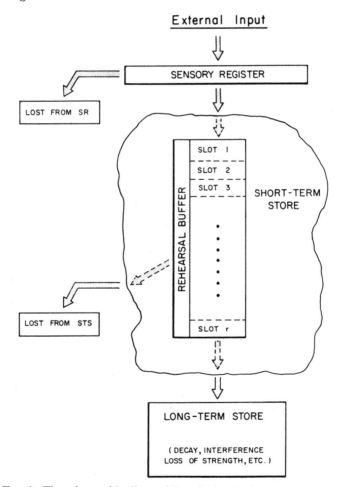

FIG. 2. The rehearsal buffer and its relation to the memory system.

of the memory system. The content of the buffer is constructed from items that have entered STS, items which have been input from the sensory register or from LTS. The arrow going toward LTS indicates that some long-term trace is being built up during an item's stay in the buffer. The other arrow from the buffer indicates that the input of a new item into the buffer causes an item currently in the buffer to be bumped out; this item then decays from STS and is lost (except for any trace which has accumulated in LTS during its stay). An item dropped from the buffer is likely to decay more quickly in STS than a newly presented item which has just entered STS. There are several reasons for this. For one thing, the item is probably already in some state of partial decay when dropped; in addition, the information making up an item in the buffer is likely to be only a partial copy of the ensemble present immediately following stimulus input.

There are two additional processes not shown in Fig. 2 that the subject can use on appropriate occasions. First, the subject may decide not to enter every item into the buffer; the reasons are manifold. For example, the items may be presented at a very fast rate so that input and re-organization time encroach too far upon rehearsal time. Another possibility is that some combinations of items are particularly easy to rehearse, making the subject loath to break up the combination. In fact, the work involved in introducing a new item into the buffer and deleting an old one may alone give the subject incentive to keep the buffer unchanged. Judging from these remarks, the choice of which items to enter into the buffer is based on momentary characteristics of the current string of input items and may appear at times to be essentially random.

The second process not diagrammed in Fig. 2 is the choice of which item to eliminate from the buffer when a new item is entered. There are several possibilities. The choice could be random; it could be based upon the state of decay of the current items; it could depend upon the ease of rehearsing the various items; most important, it could be based upon the length of time the various items have resided in the buffer. It is not unreasonable that the subject knows which items he has been rehearsing the longest, as he might if rehearsal takes place in a fixed order. It is for this reason that the slots or positions of the buffer have been numbered consecutively in Fig. 2; that is, to indicate that the subject might have some notion of the relative recency of the various items in the buffer.

The experimental justification for these various buffer mechanisms will be presented in Section IV. It should be emphasized that the subject will use a fixed-size buffer of the sort described here only in select situations, primarily those in which he feels that trading off rehearsal time for coding and other longer term control processes would not be fruitful. To the extent that long-term storage operations prove to be successful as compared with rehearsal, the structure of the rehearsal mechanism will tend to become impoverished. One other point concerning the buffer should be noted. While this paper consistently considers a fixed-size short-term buffer as a rehearsal strategy of the subject, it is possible to apply a fixed-size model of a similar kind to the structure of the short-term system as a whole, that is, to consider a short-term buffer as a permanent feature of memory. Waugh and Norman (1965), for example, have done this in their paper on primary memory. The data on the structure of STS is currently so nebulous that such an hypothesis can be neither firmly supported nor rejected.

3. Coding Processes and Transfer between Short- and Long-Term Store

It should be evident that there is a close relationship between the short- and long-term store. In general, information entering STS comes directly from LTS and only indirectly from the sensory register. For example, a visually presented word cannot be entered into STS as an auditory-verbal unit until a long-term search and match has identified the verbal representation of the visual image. For words, letters, and highly familiar stimuli, this long-term search and match process may be executed very quickly, but one can imagine unfamiliar stimuli, such as, say, a nonsense scribble, where considerable search might be necessary before a suitable verbal representation is found to enter into STS. In such cases, the subject might enter the visual image directly into his short-term visual memory and not attempt a verbal coding operation.

Transfer from STS to LTS may be considered a permanent feature of memory; any information in STS is transferred to LTS to some degree throughout its stay in the short-term store. The important aspect of this transfer, however, is the wide variance in the amount and form of the transferred information that may be induced by control processes. When the subject is concentrating upon rehearsal, the information transferred would be in a relatively weak state and easily subject to interference. On the other hand, the subject may divert his effort from rehearsal to various coding operations which will increase the strength of the stored information. In answer to the question of what is a coding process, we can most generally state that a coding process is a select alteration and/or addition to the information in the short-term store as the result of a search of the long-term store. This change may take a number of forms, often using strong preexisting associations already in long-term store. A number of these coding possibilities will be considered later.

Experiments may be roughly classified in terms of the control operations the subject will be led to use. Concept formation problems or tasks where there is a clear solution will lead the subject to strategy selection and hypothesis-testing procedures (Restle, 1964). Experiments which do not involve problem solving, where there are a large number of easily coded items, and where there is a long period between presentation and test, will prompt the subject to expend his efforts on long-term coding operations. Finally, experiments in which memory is required, but long-term memory is not efficacious, will lead the subject to adopt rehearsal strategies that maintain the information the limited period needed for the task. Several examples of the latter experiment will be examined in this paper; they are characterized by the fact that the responses assigned to particular stimuli are continually changing, so that coding of a specific stimulus-response pair will prove harmful to succeeding pairs using the same stimulus. There are experiments, of course, for which it will not be possible to decide on a priori grounds which control processes are being used. In these cases the usual identification procedures must be used, including model fits and careful questioning of the subjects.

There are other short-term processes that do not fit easily into the above classification. They include grouping, organizing, and chunking strategies. One form that organizing may take is the selection of a subset of presented items for special attention, coding and/or rehearsal. This selection process is clearly illustrated in a series of studies on magnitude of reward by Harley (1965a, 1965b). Items in a paired-associate list were given two monetary incentives, one high and one low. In one experiment the subjects learned two paired-associate lists, one consisting of all high incentive items, the other consisting of all low incentive items; there were no differences in the learning rates for these lists. In a second experiment, subjects learned a list which included both high and low incentive items; in this case learning was faster for the high than the low incentive items. However, the overall rate of learning for the mixed list was about the same as for the two previous lists. It seems clear that when the high and low incentive items are mixed, the subject selectively attends to, codes, and rehearses those items with the higher payoffs. A second kind of organizing that occurs is the grouping of items into small sets, often with the object of memorizing the set as a whole, rather than as individual items. Typically in this case the grouped items will have some common factor. A good example may be found in the series of studies by Battig (1966) and his colleagues. He found a tendency to group items according to difficulty and according to degree of prior learning; this tendency was found even in paired-associate tasks where an extensive effort had been made to eliminate any basis for such grouping. A third type of information organization is found in the "chunking" process suggested by Miller (1956). In his view there is some optimal size that a set of information should have in order to best facilitate remembering. The incoming information is therefore organized into chunks of the desired magnitude.

C. Control Processes in Long-Term Store

Control processes to be considered in this section fall roughly into two categories: those concerned with transfer between short-term and long-term store and those concerned with search for and retrieval of information from LTS.

1. *Storage in Long-Term Store*

It was stated earlier that some information is transferred to LTS throughout an item's stay in STS, but that its amount and form is determined by control processes. This proposition will now be examined in greater detail. First of all, it would be helpful to consider a few simple examples where long-term storage is differentially affected by the coding strategy adopted. One example is found in a study on mediators performed by Montague, Adams, and Kiess (1966). Pairs of nonsense syllables were presented to the subject who had to write down any natural language mediator (word, phrase, or sentence associated with a pair) which occurred to him. At test 24 hours later the subject attempted to give the response member of each pair and the natural language mediator (NLM) that had been used in acquisition. Proportion correct for items on which the NLM was retained was 70 %, while the proportion correct was negligible for items where the NLM was forgotten or significantly changed. Taken in conjunction with earlier studies showing that a group using NLMs was superior to a group learning by rote (Runquist & Farley, 1964), this result indicates a strong dependence of recall upon natural language mediators. A somewhat different encoding technique has been examined by Clark and Bower (personal communication). Subjects were required to learn several lists of paired-associate items, in which each item was a pair of familiar words. Two groups of subjects were given identical instructions, except for an extra section read to the experimental group explaining that the best method of learning the pairs was to form an elaborate visual image containing the objects designated by the two words. This experimental group was then given a few examples of the technique. There was a marked difference in performance between the groups on both immediate and delayed tests, the experimental group outperforming the control group by better than 40 % in terms of probability correct. In fact, postexperimental questioning of the subjects revealed that the occasional high performers in the control group were often using the experimental technique even in the absence of instructions to do so. This technique of associating through the use of visual images is a very old one; it has been described in considerable detail, for example, by Cicero in *De Oratore* when he discusses memory as one of the five parts of rhetoric, and is clearly very effective.

We now consider the question of how these encoding techniques improve performance. The answer depends to a degree upon the fine structure of long-term store, and therefore cannot be stated precisely. Nevertheless, a number of possibilities should be mentioned. First, the encoding may make use of strong preexisting associations, eliminating the necessity of making new ones. Thus in mediating a word pair in a paired-associate task, word A might elicit word A' which in turn elicits the response. This merely moves the question back a level: how does the subject know which associates are the correct ones? It may be that the appropriate associations are identified by temporal position; that is, the subject may search through the associations looking for one which has been elicited recently. Alternatively, information could be stored with the appropriate association identifying it as having been used in the current paired-associates task. Second, the encoding might greatly decrease the effective area of memory which must be searched at the time of test. A response word not encoded must be in the set of all English words, or perhaps in the set of all words presented "recently," while a code may allow a smaller search through the associates of one or two items. One could use further search-limiting techniques such as restricting the mediator to the same first letter as the stimulus. A third possibility, related to the second, is that encoding might give some order to an otherwise random search. Fourth, encoding might greatly increase the amount of information stored. Finally, and perhaps most important, the encoding might protect a fledgling association from interference by succeeding items. Thus if one encodes a particular pair through an image of, say, a specific room in one's home, it is unlikely that future inputs will have any relation to that image; hence they will not interfere with it. In most cases coding probably works well for all of the above reasons.

There is another possible set of effects of the coding process which should be mentioned here. As background, we need to consider the results of several recent experiments which examine the effect of spacing between study and test in paired-associate learning (Bjork, 1966; Young, 1966). The result of primary interest to us is the decrease in probability correct as the number of other paired-associate items presented between study and test increases. This decrease seems to reach asymptote only after a fairly large number (e.g., 20) of intervening items. There are several possible explanations for this "short-term" effect. Although the effect probably occurs over too great an interval to consider direct decay from STS as an explanation, any of several rehearsal strategies could give rise to an appropriate-looking curve. Since a paired-associate task usually requires coding, a fixed-size rehearsal buffer may not be a reasonable hypothesis, unless the buffer size is fairly small; on the other hand, a variable rehearsal set with semirandomly spaced rehearsals may be both reasonable and accurate. If, on the other hand, one decides that almost no continuing rehearsal occurs in this task, what other hypotheses are available? One could appeal to retroactive interference but this does little more than name the phenomenon. Greeno (1967) has proposed a coding model which can explain the effect. In his view, the subject may select one of several possible codes at the time of study. In particular, he might select a "permanent" code, which will not be disturbed by any other items or codes in the experiment; if this occurs, the item is said to be learned. On the other hand, a "transitory" code might be selected, one which is disturbed or eliminated as succeeding items are presented. This transitory code will last for a probabilistically determined number of trials before becoming useless or lost. The important point to note here is the fact that a decreasing "short-term" effect can occur as a result of solely long-term operations. In experiments emphasizing long-term coding, therefore, the decision concerning which decay process, or combination of decay processes, is operative will not be easy to make in an a priori manner; rather the decision would have to be based upon such a posteriori grounds as goodness-of-fit results for a particular model and introspective reports from the subject.

2. Long-Term Search Processes

One of the most fascinating features of memory is the long-term search process. We have all, at one time or another, been asked for information which we once knew, but which is momentarily unavailable, and we are aware of the ensuing period (often lasting for hours) during which memory was searched, occasionally resulting in the correct answer. Nevertheless, there has been a marked lack of experimental work dealing with this rather common phenomenon. For this reason, our discussion of search processes will be primarily theoretical, but the absence of a large experimental literature should not lead us to underestimate the importance of the search mechanism.

The primary component of the search process is locating the sought-for trace (or one of the traces) in long-term store. This process is seen in operation via several examples. The occasionally very long latencies prior to a correct response for well-known information indicates a non-perfect search. A subject reporting that he will think "of it the moment he thinks about something else" indicates a prior fixation on an unsuccessful search procedure. Similarly, the tip-of-the-tongue phenomenon mentioned earlier indicates a failure to find an otherwise very strong trace. We have also observed the following while quizzing a graduate student on the names of state capitals. The student gave up trying to remember the capital of the state of Washington after pondering for a long time. Later this student quickly identified the capital of Oregon as Salem and then said at once that the capital of Washington was Olympia. When asked how he suddenly remembered, he replied that he had learned the two capitals together. Presumably this information would have been available during the first search if the student had known where to look: namely in conjunction with the capital of Oregon. Such descriptive examples are numerous and serve to indicate that a search can sometimes fail to uncover a very strong trace. One of the decisions the subject must make is when to terminate an unsuccessful search. An important determiner of the length of search is the amount of order imposed during the search; if one is asked to name all the states and does so strictly geographically, one is likely to do better than someone who spews out names in a haphazard fashion. The person naming states in a haphazard fashion will presently encounter in his search for new names those which he has already given; if this occurs repeatedly, the search will be terminated as being unfruitful. The problem of terminating the search is especially acute in the case of recalling a set of items without a good natural ordering. Such a case is found in free-verbal-recall experiments in which a list of words is presented to the subject who must then recall as many as possible. The subject presumably searches along some sort of temporal dimension, a dimension which lets the subject know when he finds a word whether or not it was on the list presented most recently. The temporal ordering is by no means perfect, however, and the search must therefore be carried out with a degree of randomness. This procedure may lead to missing an item which has a fairly strong trace. It has been found in free-verbal-recall experiments, for example, that repeated recall tests on a given list sometimes result in the inclusion on the second test of items left out on the first test. In our own experiments we have even observed intrusions from an earlier list that had not been recalled during the test of that list.

It would be illustrative at this point to consider an experiment carried out by Norma Graham at Stanford University. Subjects were asked to name the capitals of the states. If a correct answer was not given within 5 seconds following presentation of the state name, the subjects were then given a hint and allowed 30 seconds more to search their memory. The hint consisted of either 1, 2, 4, 12, or 24 consecutive letters of the alphabet, one of which was the first letter in the name of the state capital. The probability correct dropped steadily as the hint size increased from 1 to 24 letters. The average response latencies for correct answers, however, showed a different effect; the 1-letter hint was associated with the fastest response time, the 2-letter hint was slower, the 4-letter hint was slower yet, but the 12- and 24-letter hints were faster than the 4-letter hint. One simple hypothesis that can explain why latencies were slower after the 4-letter hint than after the 12- and 24-letter hints depends upon differing search processes. Suppose the subject in the absence of a hint engages in "normal" search, or N search. When given the first letter, however, we will assume the subject switches to a first letter search, or L search, consisting of a deeper exploration of memory based upon the first letter. This L search might consist of forming possible sounds beginning with the appropriate letter, and matching them against possible city names. When the size of the hint increases, the subject must apply the L search to each of the letters in turn, obviously a time-consuming procedure. In fact, for 12- or 24-letter hints the probability is high that the subject would use up the entire 30-second search period without carrying out an L search on the correct first letter. Clearly a stage is reached, in terms of hint size, where the subject will switch from an L search to N search in order to maximize performance. In the present experiment it seems clear that the switch in strategy occurred between the 4- and 12-letter hints.

In the above experiment there were two search-stopping events, one subject-controlled and the other determined by the 30-second time limit. It is instructive to consider some of the possible subject-controlled stopping rules. One possibility is simply an internal time limit, beyond which the subject decides further search is useless. Related to this would be an event-counter stopping rule that would halt the subject when a fixed number of prespecified events had occurred. The events could be total number of distinct "searches," total number of incorrect traces found, and so on. A third possibility is dependent on a consecutive-events counter. For example, search could be stopped whenever x consecutive searches recovered traces that had been found in previous searches.

It was noted earlier that searches may vary in their apparent orderliness. Since long-term memory is extremely large, any truly random search would invariably be doomed to failure. The search must always be made along some dimension, or on the basis of some available cues. Nevertheless, searches do vary in their degree of order; a letter-by-letter search is highly structured, whereas a free associative search that proceeds from point to point in a seemingly arbitrary manner will be considerably less restrained, even to the point where the same ground may be covered many times. One other possible feature of the search process is not as desirable as the ones previously mentioned. The search itself might prove destructive to the sought-after trace. That is, just as new information transferred to the long-term store might interfere with previous material stored there, the generation of traces during the search might prove to have a similar interfering effect.

A somewhat different perspective on search procedures is obtained by considering the types of experimental tests that typically are used. Sometimes the very nature of the task presumes a specific search procedure. An example is found in the free-verbal-recall task in which the subject must identify a subset of a larger well-learned group of words. A search of smaller scope is made in a paired-associate task; when the set of possible responses is large, the search for the answer is similar to that made in free recall, with a search component and a recognition component to identify the recovered trace as the appropriate one. When the set of responses in a paired-associate task is quite small, the task becomes one of recognition alone: the subject can generate each possible response in order and perform a recognition test on each. The recognition test presumably probes the trace for information identifying it as being from the correct list and being associated with the correct stimulus.

It was said that the primary component of the search process is locating the desired memory trace in LTS. The secondary component is the recovery of the trace once found. It has been more or less assumed for simplicity in the above discussions that the trace is all-or-none. This may not be the case, and the result of a search might be the recovery of a partial trace. Retrieval would then depend either upon correctly guessing the missing information or performing a further search to match the partial trace with known responses. It is possible, therefore, to divide the recovery processes into a search component and retrieval component, both of which must be successfully concluded in order to output the correct response. The two components undoubtedly are correlated in the sense that stronger, more complete traces will both be easier to find and easier to retrieve, having been found.

One final problem of some importance should be mentioned at this time. The effects of trace interference may be quite difficult to separate from those of search failure. Trace interference here refers either to loss of information in the trace due to succeeding inputs or to confusions caused by competition among multiple traces at the moment of test. Search failure refers to an inability to find the trace at all. Thus a decrease in the probability of a correct response as the number of items intervening between study and test increases could be due to trace interference generated by those items. It could also be due to an increased likelihood of failing to find the trace because of the increasing number of items that have to be searched in memory. One way these processes might be separated experimentally would be in a comparison of recognition and recall measures, assuming that a failure to find the trace is less likely in the case of recognition than in the case of recall. At the present, research along these lines has not given us a definitive answer to this question.

IV. Experiments Concerned with Short-Term Processes

Sections II and III of this paper have outlined a theoretical framework for human memory. As we have seen, the framework is extremely general, and there are many alternative choices that can be made in formulating models for particular experimental situations. The many choice points make it impossible for us to examine each process experimentally. Instead we shall devote our attention to a number of processes universally agreed to occur in experiments on memory, namely rehearsal and search processes. In Section V the LTS search processes will be examined in detail; in the present section the major emphasis will be on STS mechanisms, particularly the control process designated as the rehearsal buffer. The sensory registration system is not an important factor in these models; the experiments are designed so that all items enter the sensory register and then are transferred to STS. The long-term store will be presented in the models of this section but only in the simplest possible manner. We now turn to a series of experiments designed to establish in some detail the workings of the buffer mechanism.

A. A Continuous Paired-Associate Memory Task (Experiment 1)

This study is the prototype for a series of experiments reported in this section designed specifically to study buffer processes. The buffer is a fixed-size rehearsal scheme in STS; conditions which prompt the subject to make use of a buffer include difficulty in using long-term store, a large number of short study-test intervals, and a presentation rate slow enough that cognitive manipulations in STS are not excessively rushed. The task that was developed to establish these conditions is described below.[6]

The subject was required to keep track of constantly changing responses associated with a fixed set of stimuli.[7] The stimuli were 2-digit numbers chosen from the set 00–99; the responses were letters of the alphabet. At the start of a particular subject-session a set of s stimuli was chosen randomly from the numbers 00 to 99; these stimuli were not changed over the course of that day's session. To begin the session each stimulus was paired with a letter chosen randomly from the alphabet. Following this initial period, a continuous sequence of trials made up the rest of the session, each trial consisting of a test phase followed by a

---

[6] The reader may consult Atkinson, Brelsford, and Shiffrin (1967) for details of the experimental procedure and theoretical analyses that are not covered in the present discussion. Also presented there is an account of the mathematics of the model.

[7] The task is similar to those used by Yntema and Mueser (1960, 1962), Brelsford *et al.* (1966), and Katz (1966).

study phase. During the test phase, one of the s stimuli was randomly selected and presented alone for test. The subject was required to respond with the most recent response paired with that stimulus. No feedback was given to the subject. Following his response the study portion of the trial began. During the study portion the stimulus just presented for test was paired with a new response selected randomly from the alphabet; the only restriction was that the previous response (the correct response during the immediately preceding test phase) was not used during the study phase of the same trial. The subject was instructed to forget the previous pairing and try to remember the new pairing currently being presented for study. Following the study period, a stimulus was again selected randomly from the set of s stimuli and the test portion of the next trial began.

The result of this procedure is as follows: a particular stimulus-response pair is presented for study, followed by a randomly determined number of trials involving other stimuli, and then tested. Having been tested, the pair is broken up and the stimulus is paired with a different response; in other words, no stimulus-response pair is presented for study twice in succession. It is easy to imagine the effects of this procedure on the subject's long-term memory processes. If any particular pair is strongly stored in long-term memory, it will interfere with subsequent pairings involving that same stimulus. In addition, the nature of the stimuli and responses used makes coding a difficult task. For these reasons, the subject soon learns that the usual long-term storage operations, such as coding, are not particularly useful; in fact, the subject is forced to rely heavily on his short-term store and his rehearsal capacity. The experimental procedure also was designed so that it would be possible to carry out extensive parametric analyses on data from individual subjects. This was accomplished by running each subject for 12 or more days and collecting the data on a system under the control of a time-sharing computer, a procedure which made the precise sequence of events during each session available for analysis.

1. *Method*

The subjects were nine students from Stanford University who received $2 per experimental session. This experiment, and most of the others reported in this paper, was conducted in the Computer-Based Learning Laboratory at Stanford University. The control functions were performed by computer programs run on a modified PDP-1 computer manufactured by the Digital Equipment Corp., and under control of a time-sharing system. The subject was seated at a cathode-ray-tube display terminal; there were six terminals, each located in a separate 7×8 foot sound-shielded room. Stimuli were displayed on the face of the cathode ray tube (CRT); responses were made on an electric type-writer keyboard located immediately below the lower edge of the CRT.

For each session the subject was assigned to one of the three experimental conditions. The three conditions were defined in terms of s, the size of the set of stimuli to be remembered, which took on the values 4, 6, or 8. An attempt was made to assign subjects to each condition once in consecutive three-session blocks. Every session began with a series of study trials: one study trial for each stimulus to be used in the session. On a study trial the word "study" appeared on the upper face of the CRT. Beneath the word "study" one of the stimuli (a 2-digit number) appeared along with a randomly selected letter from the alphabet. Subjects were instructed to try to remember the stimulus-response pairs. Each of these initial study trials lasted for 3 seconds with a 3-second intertrial interval. As soon as there had been an initial study trial for each stimulus to be used in the session, the session proper began.

Each subsequent trial involved a fixed series of events. (1) The word "test" appeared on the upper face of the CRT. Beneath the word "test" a randomly selected member of the stimulus set appeared. Subjects were instructed that when the word "test" and a stimulus appeared on the CRT, they were to respond with the last response that had been associated with that simulus, guessing if necessary. This test portion of a trial lasted for 3 seconds. (2) The CRT was blacked out for 2 seconds. (3) The word "study" appeared on the upper face of the CRT for 3 seconds. Below the word "study" a stimulus-response pair appeared. The stimulus was the same one used in the preceding test portion of the trial. The response was randomly selected from the letters of the alphabet, with the stipulation that it be different from the immediately preceding response assigned to that stimulus. (4) There was a 3-second intertrial interval before the next trial. Thus a complete trial (test plus study) took 11 seconds. A subject was run for 220 such trials during each experimental session.

2. *Theoretical Analysis*

In order that the reader may visualize the sequence of events which occurs in this situation, a sample sequence of 18 trials is illustrated in Fig. 3. Within the boxes are the displays seen on the CRT screen. In this session the stimulus set includes the four stimuli 20, 31, 42, and 53 (i.e., $s = 4$). On trial n, item 31-Q is presented for study. On trial $n + 1$, 42 is tested and 42-B presented for study. Then on trial $n + 2$, 31 is tested; the correct answer is Q as is seen by referring to trial n. After the subject answers he is given 31-S to study. He is instructed to forget the previous pair, 31-Q, and remember only the new pair, 31-S. The response letter S was selected randomly from the alphabet, with the restriction that the

previous response, Q, could not be used. A previously used response may
through chance, however, be chosen again later in the session; for
example, on trial $n + 7$, 31-Q is again presented for study. It is also
possible that two or more stimuli might be paired with the same response
concurrently; as an example, on trial $n + 15$, 20 is paired with C and on
trial $n + 16$, 42 also is paired with C. The stimulus presented on each
trial is chosen randomly; for this reason the number of trials intervening

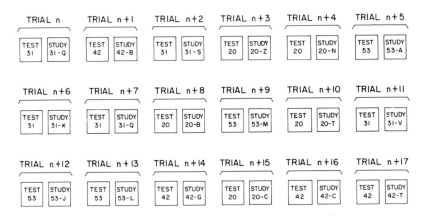

Fig. 3. A sample sequence of trials for Experiment 1.

between study and test is a random variable distributed geometrically.
In the analysis of the results, a very important variable is the number of
trials intervening between study and test on a particular stimulus-
response pair; this variable is called the *lag*. Thus 20 is tested on trial
$n + 4$ at a lag of 0 because it was studied on trial $n + 3$. On the other
hand, 42 is tested on trial $n + 14$ at a lag of 12, because it was last studied
on trial $n + 1$.

Consider now the processes the subject will tend to adopt in this
situation. The obvious difficulties involved in the use of LTS force the
subject to rely heavily upon rehearsal mechanisms in STS for optimal
performance.[8] A strategy making effective use of STS is an ordered
rehearsal scheme of fixed size called the buffer in Section III,B. The
fixed-size requirement may not be necessary for maximal utilization of

---

[8] The usual examples given for the usefulness of a distinct short-term store do
not stress the positive benefits of a memory decaying quickly and completely.
Without such a memory, many minor tasks such as adding a long column of
numbers might become far more difficult. The current experiment, in which
associative bonds are frequently broken and re-formed, is an example of a class
of operations for which a short-term store is almost essential.

STS, but is indicated by the following considerations. Keeping the size of the rehearsal set constant gives the subject a great deal of control over the situation; each rehearsal cycle will take about the same amount of time, and it is easier to reorganize the buffer when a new item is introduced. Furthermore, an attempt to stretch the rehearsal capacity to its limit may result in confusion which causes the entire rehearsal set to be disrupted; the confusion results from the variable time that must be allowed for operations such as responding at the keyboard and processing the new incoming items. The hypothesis of an ordered fixed-size buffer is given support by the subjects' reports and the authors' observations while acting as subjects. The reader is not asked, however, to take our word on this matter; the analysis of the results will provide the strongest support for the hypothesis.

It must be decided next just what is being rehearsed. The obvious candidate, and the one reported by subjects, is the stimulus-response pair to be remembered. That is, the unit of rehearsal is the two-digit stimulus number plus the associated response letter. Under certain conditions, however, the subject may adopt a more optimal strategy in which only the responses are rehearsed. This strategy will clearly be more effective because many more items may be encompassed with the same rehearsal effort. The strategy depends upon ordering the stimuli (usually in numerical order in the present case) and rehearsing the responses in an order corresponding to the stimulus order; in this way the subject may keep track of which response goes with which stimulus. For a number of reasons, the scheme is most effective when the size of the stimulus set is small; for a large set the subject may have difficulty ordering the stimuli, and difficulty reorganizing the rehearsal as each new item is presented. When the number of stimulus-response pairs to be remembered is large, the subject may alter this scheme in order to make it feasible. The alteration might consist of rehearsing only the responses associated with a portion of the ordered stimuli. In a previous experiment (Brelsford *et al.*, 1966) with a similar design, several subjects reported using such a strategy when the stimulus set size was four, and an examination of their results showed better performance than the other subjects. Subject reports lead us to believe that this strategy is used infrequently in the present experiment; consequently, our model assumes that the unit of rehearsal is the stimulus-response pair, henceforth called an "item."

Figure 2 outlines the structure of the model to be applied to the data. Despite the emphasis on rehearsal, a small amount of long-term storage occurs during the period that an item resides in the buffer. The information stored in LTS is comparatively weak and decays rapidly as succeeding items are presented. In accord with the argument that the long-term process is uncomplicated, we assume here that information stored in LTS increases linearly with the time an item resides in the buffer. Once an item leaves the buffer, the LTS trace is assumed to decrease as each succeeding item is presented for study.

Every item is assumed to enter first the sensory register and then STS. At that point the subject must decide whether or not to place the new item in the rehearsal buffer. There are a number of reasons why every incoming item may not be placed in the buffer. For one thing, the effort involved in reorganizing the buffer on every trial may not always appear worthwhile, especially when the gains from doing so are not immediately evident; for another, the buffer at some particular time may consist of a combination of items especially easy to rehearse and the subject may not wish to destroy the combination. In order to be more specific about which items enter the buffer and which do not, two kinds of items must be distinguished. An O item is an incoming stimulus-response pair whose stimulus is currently in the buffer. Thus if 52-L is currently in the buffer, 52 is tested, and 52-G is presented for study, then 52-G is said to be an O item. Whenever an O item is presented it is automatically entered into the buffer; this entry, of course, involves replacing the old response by the appropriate new response. Indeed, if an O item did not enter the buffer, the subject would be forced to rehearse the now incorrect previous response, or to leave a useless blank spot in the buffer; for these reasons, the assumption that O items are always entered into the buffer seems reasonable. The other kind of item that may be presented is an N item. An N item is a stimulus-response pair whose stimulus currently is not in the buffer. Whenever an N item is entered into the buffer, one item currently in the buffer must be removed to make room the new item (i.e., the buffer is assumed to be of fixed size, r, meaning that the number of items being rehearsed at any one time is constant). The assumption is made that an N item enters into the buffer with probability α; whenever an N item is entered, one of the items currently in the buffer is randomly selected and removed to make room for it.

The model used to describe the present experiment is now almost complete. A factor still not specified is the response rule. At the moment of test any item which is in the buffer is responded to correctly. If the stimulus tested is not in the buffer, a search is carried out in LTS with the hope of finding the trace. The probability of retrieving the correct response from LTS depends upon the current trace strength, which in turn, depends on the amount of information transferred to LTS. Specifically we assume that information is transferred to LTS at a constant rate θ during the entire period an item resides in the buffer; θ is the transfer rate per trial. Thus, if an item remains in the rehearsal buffer for exactly j trials, then that item accumulated an amount of information equal to $j\theta$. We also assume that each trial following the trial on which an item is knocked out of the buffer causes the information stored in LTS for that item to decrease by a constant proportion τ. Thus, if an item were knocked out of the buffer at trial j, and i trials intervened between the original study and test on that item, then the amount of information in LTS at the time of the test would be $j\theta\tau^{i-j}$. We now want to specify the probability of a correct retrieval of an item from LTS. If the amount of information in LTS at the moment of test is zero, then the probability of a correct retrieval should be at the guessing level. As the amount of information increases, the probability of a correct retrieval should increase toward unity. We define ρ_{ij} as the probability of a correct response from LTS for an item that was tested at lag i, and resided in the buffer for exactly j trials. Considering the above specifications on the retrieval process,

$$\rho_{ij} = 1 - (1 - g)\exp[-j\theta(\tau^{i-j})]$$

where g is the guessing probability, which is 1/26 since there were 26 response alternatives.[9]

The basic dependent variable in the present experiment is the probability of a correct response at the time of a test, given lag i. In order to derive this probability we need to know the length of time that an item resides in the memory buffer. Therefore, define $\beta_j =$ probability that an item resides in the buffer for exactly j trials, given that it is tested at a lag greater than j. The probability of a correct response to an item tested at lag i can now be written in terms of the β_j's. Let "C_i" represent the occurrence of a correct response to an item tested at lag i. Then

$$\Pr(C_i) = \left[1 - \sum_{k=0}^{i} \beta_k\right] + \left[\sum_{k=0}^{i} \beta_k \rho_{ik}\right]$$

The first bracketed term is the probability that the item is in the buffer at the time of the test. The second bracket contains a sum of probabilities, each term representing the probability of a correct retrieval

---

[9] Lest the use of an exponential function seem entirely arbitrary, it should be noted that this function bears a close relation to the familiar linear model of learning theory. If we ignore for the moment the decay feature, then

$$\rho_{ij} = 1 - (1 - g)\exp(-j\theta).$$

It is easily seen that this is the linear model expression for the probability of a correct response after j reinforcements with parameter $e^{-\theta}$. Thus, the retrieval function ρ_{ij} can be viewed as a linear model with time in the buffer as the independent variable. To be sure, the decay process complicates matters, but the reason for choosing the exponential function becomes somewhat less arbitrary. A decay process is needed so that the probability of a correct retrieval from LTS will approach chance as the lag tends toward infinity.

from LTS of an item which remained in the buffer for exactly k trials and was then lost.[10] There are four parameters in the model: r, the buffer size which must be an integer; α, the probability of entering an N item into the buffer; θ, the transfer rate of information to LTS; and τ, the decay rate of information from LTS after an item has left the buffer.

One final process must be considered before the model is complete. This process is the recovery of information from STS which is not in the buffer. It will be assumed that the decay of an item which has entered and then left the buffer is very rapid, so rapid that an item which has left the buffer cannot be recovered from STS on the succeeding test.[11] The only time in which a recovery is made from STS, apart from the buffer, occurs if an item is tested immediately following its study (i.e., at a lag of 0). In this case there is virtually no time between study and test and it is assumed therefore that the recovery probability is one, regardless of whether the item was entered into the buffer or not. In other words, the probability correct is one when the lag is zero.

3. *Data Analysis*

Figure 4 presents the probability of a correct response as a function of lag for each of the three stimulus set sizes examined. It can be seen that the smaller the stimulus set size, the better the overall performance. It is important to note that the theory predicts such a difference on the following basis: the larger the size of the stimulus set, the more often an N item will be presented; and the more often N items will be presented, the more often items in the buffer will be knocked out. Recall that only N items can knock items from the buffer; O items merely replace themselves.

It can be seen that performance is almost perfect for lag 0 in all three conditions. This was expected because lag 0 means that the item was tested immediately following its study, and was therefore available in STS. The curves drop sharply at first and slowly thereafter, but have not yet reached the chance level at lag 17, the largest lag plotted. The chance level should be 1/26 since there were 26 response alternatives.

The four parameters of the model were estimated by fitting the model to the lag curves in Fig. 4 using a minimum chi-square as a best fit

[10] One factor which the model as outlined ignores is the probability of recovering from LTS an old, incorrect trace. In the interest of simplicity this process has not been introduced into the model, although it could be appended with no major changes.

[11] Clearly this assumption depends on the time intervals involved. In the present experiment the trials were quite slow; in experiments where a faster presentation rate is used, the model probably would need to be modified slightly to allow a nonzero probability of recovery of an item from STS on the test following its removal from the buffer.

criterion.[12] The solid lines in Fig. 5 give the best fit of the model, which occurred when the parameter values were: $r = 2$, $\alpha = .39$, $\theta = .40$, and $\tau = .93$. It can be seen that the observed data and the predictions from the model are in close agreement. It should be emphasized that the three curves are fit simultaneously using the same parameter values, and the differences between the curves depend only on the value of s (the stimulus

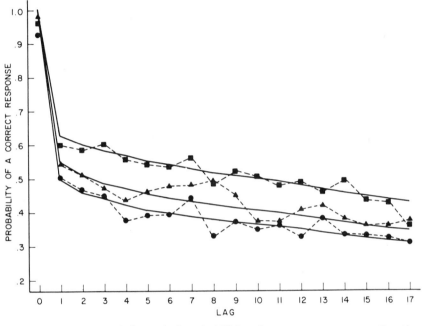

FIG. 4. Observed and theoretical probabilities of a correct response as a function of lag (Experiment 1). $--\blacksquare-- s = 4$; $--\blacktriangle-- s = 6$; $--\bullet-- s = 8$;—theory.

set size) which, of course, is determined by the experimenter. The predicted probabilities of a correct response weighted and summed over all lag positions are .562, .469, and .426 for s equal to 4, 6, and 8, respectively; the observed values are .548, .472, and .421.

The estimated value of r might seem surprising at first glance; two items appear to be a rather small buffer capacity. But there are a number of considerations that render this estimate reasonable. It seems clear that the capacity estimated in a task where the subject is constantly interrupted for tests must be lower than the capacity estimated, for example, in a typical digit-span task. This is so because part of the attention time that would be otherwise allotted to rehearsal must be used to search memory in order to respond to the continuous sequence

[12] See Atkinson, Brelsford, and Shiffrin (1967) for details of the estimation procedure and a statistical evaluation of the goodness-of-fit.

of tests. Considering that two items in this situation consist of four numbers and two letters, an estimate of r equal to two is not particularly surprising. The estimated value of α indicates that only 39% of the N items actually enter the buffer (remember that O items always enter the buffer). This low value may indicate that a good deal of mental effort is involved in keeping an item in the buffer via rehearsal, leading to a reluctance to discard an item from the buffer that has not yet been tested. A similar reluctance to discard items would be found if certain

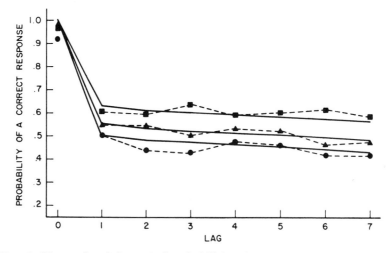

FIG. 5. Observed and theoretical probabilities of a correct response as a function of lag when every intervening item uses the same stimulus (Experiment 1). $--\blacksquare-- s = 4; --\blacktriangle-- s = 6; --\bullet-- s = 8;$—theory.

combinations of items were particularly easy to rehearse. Finally, note that the theory predicts that, if there were no long-term storage, the subject's overall probability of a correct response would be independent of α. Thus it might be expected that α would be higher the greater the effectiveness of long-term storage. In accord with this reasoning, the low value of α found would result from the weak long-term storage associated with the present situation.

In addition to the lag curves in Fig. 4, there are a number of other predictions that can be examined. One aspect of the theory maintains that O items always enter the buffer and replace themselves, while N items enter the buffer with probability α and knock an item out of the buffer whenever they do so. The effects of different stimulus-set sizes displayed in Fig. 5 are due to this assumption. The assumption, however, may be examined in other ways; if it is true, then an item's probability of being correct will be affected by the specific items that intervene

between its initial study and its later test. If every intervening trial uses
the same stimulus, then the probability of knocking the item of interest
from the buffer is minimized. This is so because once any intervening
item enters the buffer, every succeeding intervening item is an O item
(since it uses the same stimulus), and hence also enters the buffer. Indeed,
if α were one, then every intervening item after the first would be an O

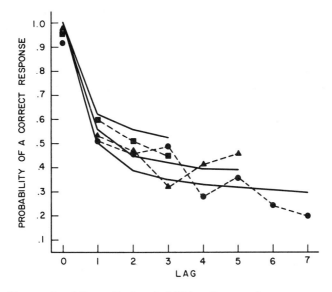

FIG. 6. Observed and theoretical probabilities of a correct response as a function
of lag when every intervening item uses a different stimulus (Experiment 1).
$--\blacksquare-- \ s = 4; \ --\blacktriangle-- \ s = 6; \ --\bullet-- \ s = 8;$—theory.

item, and hence only the first intervening item would have a chance of
knocking the item of interest from the buffer; if $\alpha = 1$ and there were no
long-term decay, then the lag curve for this condition would be flat from
lag 1 onward. In this case, however, α is not equal to one and there is
long-term decay; hence the lag curve will decrease somewhat when the
intervening items all have the same stimulus, but not to the extent
found in Fig. 4. This lag curve, called the "all-same" curve, is shown in
Fig. 5; it plots the probability of a correct response as a function of lag,
when all the intervening trials between study and test involve the same
stimulus. The parameters previously estimated were used to generate
predictions for these curves and they are displayed as solid lines. It
seems clear that the predictions are highly accurate.

A converse result, called the "all-different" lag curve, is shown in
Fig. 6. In this condition, every intervening item has a different stimulus,

and therefore the probability of knocking the item of interest from the buffer is maximized. The lag curves for this condition, therefore, should drop faster than the unconditional lag curves of Fig. 4. Predictions were again generated using the previous parameter values and are represented by the solid lines in Fig. 6. Relatively few observations were available in this condition; considering the instability of the data the predictions seem reasonable.

The procedure used in this experiment is an excellent example of what has been traditionally called a negative transfer paradigm. The problems inherent in such a paradigm were mentioned earlier as contributing to the subjects' heavy reliance upon the short-term store. To the extent that there is any use of LTS, however, we would expect intrusion errors from previously correct responses. The model could be extended in several obvious ways to predict the occurrence of such intrusions. For example, the subject could, upon failing to recover the most recent trace from LTS, continue his search and find the remains of the previous, now incorrect, trace. In order to examine intrusion errors, the proportion of errors which were the correct response for the previous presentation of the stimulus in question were calculated for each lag and each condition. The proportions were quite stable over lags with mean values of .065, .068, and .073 for the 4, 6, and 8 stimulus conditions, respectively. If the previously correct response to an item is generated randomly for any given error, these values should not differ significantly from $1/25 = .04$. In both the $s = 4$ and $s = 6$ conditions seven of the nine subjects had mean values above chance; in the $s = 8$ condition eight of the nine subjects were above chance. Intrusion errors may therefore be considered a reliable phenomenon in this situation; on the other hand, the relatively low frequency with which they occur indicates a rather weak and quickly decaying long-term trace.

A second error category of interest includes those responses that are members of the current set of responses to be remembered but are not the correct responses. This set, of course, includes the set of responses in the buffer at any one time; if the subject tends to give as a guess a response currently in the buffer (and therefore highly available), then the probability of giving as an error a response in the current to-be-remembered set will be higher than chance. Since responses may be assigned to more than one stimulus simultaneously, the number of responses in the to-be-remembered set is bound by, but may be less than, the size of the stimulus set, s. Thus, on the basis of chance the error probabilities would be bounded below .12, .20, and .28 for $s = 4$, 6, and 8, respectively. The actual values found were .23, .28, and .35, respectively. This finding suggests that when the subject cannot retrieve the response from his buffer or LTS and is forced to guess, he has a somewhat greater than chance likelihood of giving a response currently in the rehearsal set but assigned to another stimulus. It is not surprising that a subject will give as a guess one of the responses in his buffer since they are immediately available.

Other analyses have been performed on the data of this experiment, but the results will not be presented until a second experiment has been described. Before considering the second experiment, however, a few words should be said about individual differences. One of the reasons for running a single subject for many sessions was the expectation that the model could be applied to each subject's data separately. Such analyses have been made and are reported elsewhere (Atkinson, Brelsford & Shiffrin, 1967). The results are too complex to go into here, but they establish that individual subjects by and large conform to the predictions of the model quite well. Since our aim in this paper is to present a nontechnical discussion of the model, to simplify matters we will make most of our analyses on group data.

B. The "All-Different" Stimulus Procedure (Experiment 2)

In the preceding experiment, the number of stimuli used in a given experimental session and the size of the to-be-remembered set were identical. These two factors, however, can be made independent. Specifically, a set of all-different stimuli could be used while keeping the size of the to-be-remembered set constant. The name, all-different, for this experiment results from the use of all-different stimuli, i.e., once a given stimulus-response pair is presented for test, that stimulus is not used again. In other respects the experiment is identical to Experiment 1.

One reason for carrying out an experiment of this type is to gain some information about the replacement hypothesis for O items. In Experiment 1 we assumed that a new item with a stimulus the same as an item currently in the buffer automatically replaced that item in the buffer; that is, the response switched from old to new. In the all-different experiment subjects are instructed, as in Experiment 1, to forget each item once it has been tested. If an item currently in the buffer is tested (say, 52-G) and a new item is then presented for study (say, 65-Q), we might ask whether the tested item will be automatically replaced by the new item (whether 65-Q will replace 52-G in the buffer). This replacement strategy is clearly optimal for it does no good to retain an item in the buffer that already has been tested. Nevertheless, if the reorganization of the buffer is difficult and time consuming, then the replacement of a tested item currently in the buffer might not be carried out. One simple assumption along these lines would postulate that every item has an independent probability α of entering the buffer.

The all-different experiment was identical to Experiment 1 in all respects except the following. In Experiment 1 the s stimuli were the same throughout an experimental session, with only the associated responses being changed on each trial, whereas in the all-different experiment 100 stimuli were available for use in each session. In fact, every stimulus was effectively new since the stimulus for each study trial was selected randomly from the set of all 100 stimuli under the restriction that no stimulus could be used if it had been tested or studied in the previous 50 trials. There were still three experimental conditions with s equal to 4, 6, or 8 denoting the number of items that the subject was required to try to remember at any point in time. Thus a session began with either 4, 6, or 8 study trials on different randomly selected stimuli, each of which was paired with a randomly selected response (from the 26 letters). On each trial a stimulus in the current to-be-remembered set was presented for test. After the subject made his response he was instructed to forget the item he had just been tested on, since he would not be tested on it again. Following the test a new stimulus was selected (one that had not appeared for at least 50 trials) and randomly paired with a response for the subject to study. Thus the number of items to be remembered at any one time stays constant throughout the session. However, the procedure is quite different from Experiment 1 where the study stimulus was always the one just tested.

Denote an item presented for study on a trial as an O item (old item) if the item just tested was in the buffer. Denote an item presented for study as an N item (new item) if the item just tested was not in the buffer. This terminology conforms precisely to that used to describe Experiment 1. If an O item is presented there will be at least one spot in the buffer occupied by a useless item (the one just tested). If an N item is presented, the buffer will be filled with information of the same value as that before the test. If we assume that an N item has probability α of entering the buffer, and that an O item will always enter the buffer and knock out the item just made useless, then the model for Experiment 1 will apply here with no change whatsoever. In this case we again expect that the lag curves for $s = 4$, 6, and 8 would be separated. In fact, given the same parameter values, exactly the same curves would be predicted for the all-different experiment as for Experiment 1.

As noted earlier, however, there is some doubt that the assumptions regarding N items and O items will still hold for the all-different experiment. In Experiment 1 the stimulus just tested was re-paired with a new response, virtually forcing the subject to replace the old response with a new one if the item was in the buffer. Put another way, if an item is in the buffer when tested, only a minor change need be made in the buffer to enter the succeeding study item: a single response is replaced by another. In the all-different experiment, however, a greater change needs to be made in order to enter an O item; both a stimulus and a response member have to be replaced. Thus an alternative hypothesis might maintain that every entering item (whether an N item or an O item) has the same probability α of entering the buffer, and will knock out any item currently in the buffer with equal likelihood. In this case we predict no differences among the lag curves for the $s = 4$, 6, and 8 conditions.

1. *Results*

The observed lag curves for Experiment 2 are displayed in Fig. 7. It should be emphasized that, except for the procedural changes described

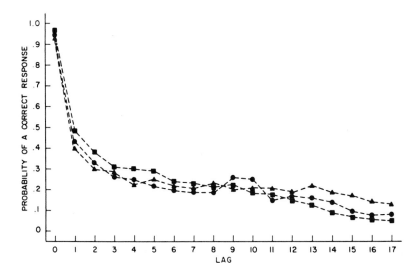

FIG. 7. Observed and theoretical probabilities of a correct response as a function of lag (Experiment 2). $--\blacksquare-- s = 4$; $--\blacktriangle-- s = 6$; $--\bullet-- s = 8$.

above and the fact that a new sample of subjects was used, the experimental conditions and operations were identical in Experiments 1 and 2. The important point about this data is that the lag curves for the three conditions appear to overlap.[13] For this reason we lump the three curves to form the single lag curve displayed in Fig. 8.

Because the three curves overlap, it is apparent that the theory used in Experiment 1 needs modification. The hypothesis suggested above

---

[13] To determine whether the three curves in Fig. 7 differ reliably, the proportions correct for each subject and condition were calculated and then ranked. An analysis of variance for correlated means did not yield significant effects ($F = 2.67$, $df = 2/16$, $p > .05$).

will be used: every item enters the buffer with probability α. If an item enters the buffer it knocks out an item already there on a random basis. This model implies that useless items are being rehearsed on occasion, and subjects reported doing just that despite instructions to forget each item once tested.

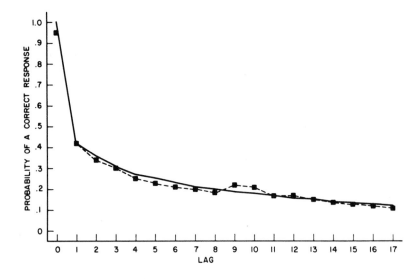

FIG. 8. Observed and theoretical probabilities of a correct response as a function of lag. Data from the $s = 4$, 6, and 8 conditions have been pooled (Experiment 2). --■-- Data;—theory.

The curve in Fig. 8 was fit using a minimum χ^2 procedure; the parameter estimates were $r = 2$, $\alpha = .52$, $\theta = .17$, and $\tau = .90$. It can be seen that the fit is excellent. Except for r, the parameters differ somewhat from those found in Experiment 1, primarily in a slower transfer rate, θ. In Experiment 1 the estimate of θ was .40. This reduction in long-term storage is not too surprising since the subjects were on occasion rehearsing useless information. It could have been argued in advance of the data that the change away from a strong "negative-transfer" paradigm in Experiment 2 would lead to increased use of LTS; that this did not occur is indicated not only by the low θ value, but also by the low probability of a correct response at long lags. One outcome of this result is the possibility that the all-different procedure would give superior long-term memory in situations where subjects could be induced to attempt coding or other long-term storage strategies. It seems apparent that LTS was comparatively usless in the present situation.

2. *Some Statistics Comparing Experiments 1 and 2*

In terms of the model, the only difference between Experiments 1 and 2 lies in the replacement assumption governing the buffer. In Experiment 1, an item in the buffer when tested is automatically replaced by the immediately succeeding study item; if the tested item is not in the buffer, the succeeding study item enters the buffer with probability α, randomly displacing an item already there. In Experiment 2, every study item, independent of the contents of the buffer, enters the buffer with probability α, randomly displacing an item already there. While these assumptions are given credence by the predictions of the various lag curves of Figs. 4 and 8, there are other statistics that can be examined to evaluate their adequacy. These statistics depend upon the fact that items vary in their probability of entering the buffer. Since items which enter the buffer will have a higher probability correct than items which do not, it is relatively easy to check the veracity of the replacement assumptions in the two experiments.

In Experiment 1, the probability that an item will be in the buffer at test is higher the greater the number of consecutive preceding trials that involve the same stimulus. Thus if the study of 42-B is preceded, for example, by six consecutive trials using stimulus 42, there is a very high probability that 42-B will enter the buffer. This occurs because there is a high probability that the stimulus 42 already will be in the buffer when 42-B is presented, and if so, then 42-B will automatically enter the buffer. In any series of consecutive trials all with the same stimulus, once any item in the series enters the buffer, every succeeding item will enter the buffer. Hence, the longer the series of items with the same stimulus, the higher the probability that that stimulus will be in the buffer. Figure 9 graphs the probability of a correct response to the last stimulus-response pair studied in a series of consecutive trials involving the same stimulus; the probability correct is lumped over all possible lags at which that stimulus-response pair is subsequently tested. This probability is graphed as a function of the length of the consecutive run of trials with the same stimulus and is the line labeled Experiment 1. These curves are combined over the three experimental conditions (i.e., $s = 4, 6, 8$). We see that the probability of a correct response to the last item studied in a series of trials all involving the same stimulus increases as the length of that series increases, as predicted by the theory.

In Experiment 2 stimuli are not repeated, so the above statistic cannot be examined. A comparable statistic exists, however, if we consider a sequence of items all of which are tested at zero lag (i.e., tested immediately after presentation). One could hypothesize that the effect displayed in Fig. 9 for Experiment 1 was due to a consecutive sequence of zero-lag tests, or due to factors related to the sequence of correct answers (at zero-lag an item is always correct). These same arguments would apply, however, to the sequence of zero-lag items in Experiment 2. In Fig. 9, the line labeled Experiment 2 represents a probability measure comparable to the one displayed for Experiment 1. Specifically, it is the probability of a correct response on the eventual test of the last S-R pair studied in a consecutive sequence of trials all involving S-R pairs tested at lag zero, as a function of the length of the

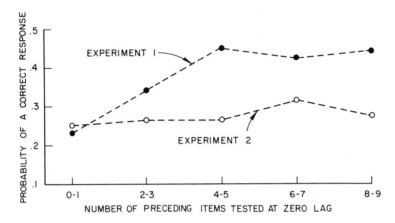

FIG. 9. Probability of a correct response as a function of the number of consecutive preceding items tested at zero lag (Experiment 1 and Experiment 2).

sequence. The model for Experiment 2 with its scheme for entering items in the buffer predicts that this curve should be flat; the data seem to bear out this prediction.

The close correspondence between the predicted and observed results in Experiments 1 and 2 provides strong support for the theory. The assumptions justified most strongly appear to be the fixed-size rehearsal buffer containing number-letter pairs as units, and the replacement assumptions governing O and N items. It is difficult to imagine a consistent system without these assumptions that would give rise to similar effects. Some of the predictions supported by the data are not at all intuitive. For example, the phenomenon displayed in Fig. 9 seems to be contrary to predictions based upon considerations of negative transfer. Negative transfer would seem to predict that a sequence of items having the same stimulus but different responses would lead to large amounts of interference and hence reduce the probability correct of the last item in the sequence; however, just the opposite effect was found. Furthermore, the lack of an effect in Experiment 2 seems to rule out explanations based on successive correct responses or successive zero-lag tests. Intuition notwithstanding, this effect was predicted by the model.

C. A CONTINUOUS PAIRED-ASSOCIATE MEMORY TASK WITH MULTIPLE REINFORCEMENTS (EXPERIMENT 3)

In contrast to a typical short-term memory task, the subjects' strategy in paired-associate learning shifts from a reliance on rehearsal processes to a heavy emphasis on coding schemes and related processes that facilitate long-term storage. There are many factors, however, that contribute to such a shift, and the fact that items are reinforced more than once in a paired-associate learning task is only one of these. In the present experiment, all factors are kept the same as in Experiment 1, except for the number of reinforcements. It is not surprising, then, that subjects use essentially the same rehearsal strategy found in Experiment 1. It is therefore of considerable interest to examine the effects associated with repeated reinforcements of the same item.

In Experiment 3 only one stimulus set size, $s = 8$, was used. Each session began with eight study trials on which the eight stimuli were each randomly paired with a response. The stimuli and responses were two-digit numbers and letters, respectively. After the initial study trials, the session involved a series of consecutive trials each consisting of a test phase followed by a study phase. On each trial a stimulus was randomly selected for testing and the same stimulus was then presented for study on the latter portion of the trial. Whereas in Experiment 1, during the study phase of a trial, the stimulus was always re-paired with a new response, in the present experiment the stimulus was sometimes left paired with the old response. To be precise, when a particular S-R pair was presented for study the first time, a decision was made as to how many reinforcements (study periods) it would be given; it was given either 1, 2, 3, or 4 reinforcements with probabilities .30, .20, .40, and .10 respectively. When a particular S-R pair had received its assigned number of reinforcements, its stimulus was then re-paired with a new response on the next study trial, and this new item was assigned a number of reinforcements using the probability distribution specified above. In order to clarify the procedure, a sample sequence from trials n to $n + 19$ is shown in Fig. 10. On trial $n + 2$ stimulus 22 is given a new response, L, and assigned three reinforcements, the first occurring on trial $n + 2$. The second reinforcement occurs on trial $n + 3$ after a lag of zero. After a lag of 6, the third reinforcement is presented on trial $n + 10$. After a lag of 8, stimulus 22 is re-paired with a new response on trial $n + 19$. Stimulus 33 is sampled for test on trial $n + 6$ and during the study phase is assigned the new response, B, which is to receive two reinforcements, the second on trial $n + 9$. Stimulus 44 is tested on trial $n + 4$, assigned the new response X which is to receive only one reinforcement; thus when 44 is presented again on trial $n + 16$ it is assigned another response which by chance also is to receive only one reinforcement, for on the next trial 44 is studied with response Q. The subject is instructed, as in Experiments 1 and 2, to respond on the test phase of each trial with the letter that was *last* studied with the stimulus being tested.

The same display devices, control equipment, and timing relations used in Experiment 1 were used in this study. There were 20 subjects, each run for 10 or more sessions; a session consisted of 220 trials. Details of the experimental procedure, and a more extensive account of the data

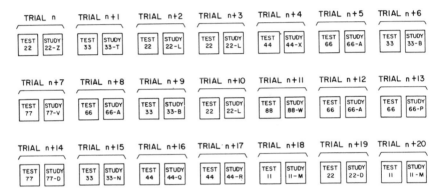

Fig. 10. A sample sequence of trials for Experiment 3.

analysis, including a fit of the model to response protocols of individual subjects, can be found in Brelsford, Shiffrin, and Atkinson (1968).

The model for Experiment 1 may be used without change in the present situation. There is some question, however, whether it is reasonable to do so. The assumptions concerning LTS storage and decay may be applied to items which are given multiple reinforcements: information is transferred to LTS at a rate θ whenever the item resides in the buffer, and decays from LTS by the proportion τ on each trial that the item is not present in the buffer. The assumption regarding O items also may be applied: since the stimulus already is in the buffer, the new response replaces the old one, thereby entering the item in the buffer (if, as is the case in this experiment, the old response is given yet another study, then nothing changes in the buffer). N items, however, are not so easily dealt with. N items, remember, are items whose stimuli are not currently represented in the buffer. In Experiment 1, the stimulus of every N item also was being paired with a new response. In the current experiment this is not always the case; some N items, although not in the buffer, will be receiving their second, third, or fourth reinforcement when presented for study. That is, some N items in this experiment will already have a substantial amount of information stored on them in LTS. It seems reasonable that subjects may not rehearse an item which has just been retrieved correctly from LTS. The assumption regarding N items is therefore modified for purposes of the present experiment as follows. If a stimulus is tested and is not in the buffer, then a search of LTS is made. If the response is correctly retrieved from LTS, and if that stimulus-response pair is repeated for study, then that item will not be entered into the buffer (since the subject "knows" it already). If a new item is presented for study (i.e., the response to that stimulus is changed), or if the correct response is not retrieved from LTS (even though the subject may have made the correct response by guessing), then the study item enters the buffer with probability α. This slight adjustment of the replacement assumption allows for the fact that some items presented for study may already be known and will not enter the rehearsal buffer. This version of the model is the one used later to generate predictions for the data.

1. *Results*

Figure 11 presents the probability of a correct response as a function of lag for items tested after their first, second, and third reinforcements. The number of observations is weighted not only toward the short lags,

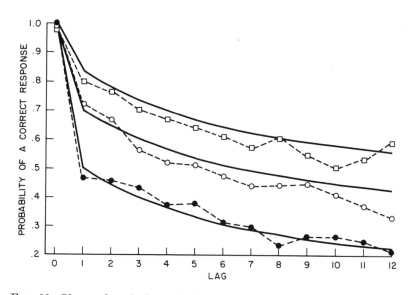

Fig. 11. Observed and theoretical probabilities of a correct response as a function of lag for items tested following their first, second, or third reinforcement (Experiment 3). --□-- Three reinforcements; --○-- two reinforcements; --●-- one reinforcement;— theory.

but also toward the smaller numbers of reinforcements. This occurs because the one-reinforcement lag curve contains not only the data from the items given just one reinforcement, but also the data from the first reinforcement of items given two, three, and four reinforcements. Similarly, the lag curve following two reinforcements contains the data from the second reinforcement of items given two, three, and four reinforcements, and the three-reinforcement curve contains data from the third reinforcement of items given three and four reinforcements. The lag curves in Fig. 11 are comparable to those presented elsewhere in this paper. What is graphed is the probability of a correct response to an item that received its jth reinforcement, and was then tested after a lag of n trials. The graph presents data for n ranging from 0 to 15 and for j equal to 1, 2, and 3. Inspecting the figure, we see that an item which received its first reinforcement and was then tested at a lag of 8 trials gave a correct response about 23 % of the time; an item that received its second reinforcement and was then tested at lag 8 had about 44 % correct responses; and an item that received its third reinforcement and was then tested at lag 8 had about 61 % correct.

The curves in Fig. 11 exhibit a consistent pattern. The probability correct decreases regularly with lag, starting at a higher value on lag 1 the greater the number of prior reinforcements. Although these curves are quite regular, there are a number of dependencies masked by them. For example, the probability of a correct response to an item that received its second reinforcement and was then tested at some later trial will depend on the number of trials that intervened between the first and second reinforcements. To clarify this point consider the following diagram

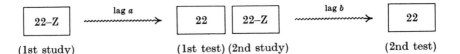

| 22–Z | $\xrightarrow{\text{lag } a}$ | 22 | 22–Z | $\xrightarrow{\text{lag } b}$ | 22 |

(1st study)   (1st test) (2nd study)   (2nd test)

Item 22-Z is given its first reinforcement, tested at lag a and given a second reinforcement, and then given a second test at lag b. For a fixed lag b, the probability of a correct response on the second test will depend on lag a. In terms of the model it is easy to see why this is so. The probability correct for an item on the second test will depend upon the amount of information about it in LTS. If lag a is extremely short, then there will have been very little time for LTS strength to build up. Conversely, a very long lag a will result in any LTS strength decaying and disappearing. Hence the probability of a correct response on the second test will be maximal at some intermediate value of lag a; namely, at a lag which will give time for LTS strength to build up, but not so much time that excessive decay will occur. For this reason a plot of probability correct on the second test as a function of the lag between the first and second reinforcement should exhibit an inverted U-shape. Figure 12 is such a plot. The probability correct on the second test is graphed as a function of lag a. Four curves are shown for different values of lag b. The

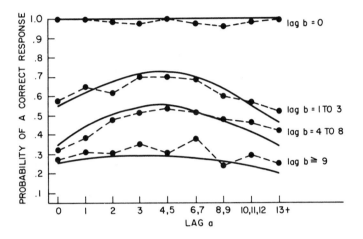

Fig. 12. Observed and theoretical probabilities of a correct response as a function of lag a (the spacing between the first and second reinforcement) (Experiment 3).

four curves have not been lumped over all values of lag b because we wish to indicate how the U-shaped effect changes with changes in lag b. Clearly, when lag b is zero, the probability correct is one and there is no U-shaped effect. Conversely, when lag b is very large, the probability correct will tend toward chance regardless of lag a, and again the U-shaped effect will disappear. The functions shown in Fig. 12 give support to the assumption that information is being transferred to LTS during the entire period an item resides in the buffer. If information is transferred, for example, only when an item first enters the buffer, then our model will not predict the rise in the functions of Fig. 12 for lag a going from zero to about five. The rise is due to the additional information transferred to LTS as lag a increases.

2. Theoretical Analysis

A brief review of the model is in order. O items (whose stimulus is currently in the buffer) always enter the buffer. N items (whose stimulus is not currently in the buffer) enter the buffer with probability α if they are also new items (i.e., receiving their first reinforcement). However, N items do not enter the buffer if they are repeat items and were correctly retrieved from LTS on the immediately preceding test; if they are repeat items and a retrieval was not made, then they enter the buffer with probability α. An O item entering the buffer occupies the position of the item already there with the same stimulus; an entering N item randomly replaces one of the items currently in the buffer. During the period an item resides in the buffer, information is transferred to LTS at a rate θ per trial. This information decays by a proportion τ on each trial after an item has left the buffer.[14] The subject is always correct at a lag of zero, or if the item is currently in the buffer. If the item is not in the buffer a search of LTS is made, and the correct response is retrieved with a probability that is an exponential function of the amount of information currently in LTS (i.e., the same function specified for Experiments 1 and 2). If the subject fails to retrieve from LTS, then he guesses. There are four parameters for this model: r, the buffer size; α, the buffer entry probability; θ, the transfer rate of information to LTS; and τ, the parameter characterizing the LTS decay rate once an item has left the buffer.

Estimates of r, α, θ, and τ were made using the data presented in Figs. 11 and 12. We shall not go into the estimation procedures here, for they are fairly complex; in essence they involve a modified minimum χ^2 procedure where the theoretical values are based on Monte Carlo runs. The parameter estimates that gave the best fit to the data displayed in Figs. 11 and 12 were as follows: $r = 3$; $\alpha = .65$; $\theta = 1.24$; and $\tau = .82$. Once these estimates had been obtained they were then used to generate a large-scale Monte Carlo run of 12,500 trials. The Monte Carlo procedure involved generating pseudo-data following precisely the rules specified by the model and consulting a random number generator whenever an event occurred in the model that was probabilistically determined. Thus the pseudo-data from a Monte Carlo run is an example of how real data would look if the model was correct, and the parameters had the values used in the Monte Carlo computation. In all subsequent discussions of Experiment 3, the predicted values are based on the output of the Monte Carlo run. The run was very long so that in all cases the theoretical curves are quite smooth, and we doubt if they reflect fluctuations due to sampling error. A detailed account of the estimation and prediction procedures for this experiment is given in Brelsford, Shiffrin, and Atkinson (1968).

The predictions from the theory are shown as the smooth curves in

[14] In this experiment an item receiving x reinforcements may enter the buffer as many as x times. When the item is in the buffer the θ-process is activated, and when not in the buffer the τ-process takes over.

Figs. 11 and 12. It should be evident that the predicted values are quite close to the observed ones. Note also that the seven curves in the two figures are fit simultaneously with the same four parameter values; the fact that the spacing of the curves is accurately predicted is particularly interesting.

We now examine a number of statistics that were not used in making parameter estimates. First consider the all-same and all-different curves shown in Fig. 13; these are the same functions displayed in Figs. 5 and 6

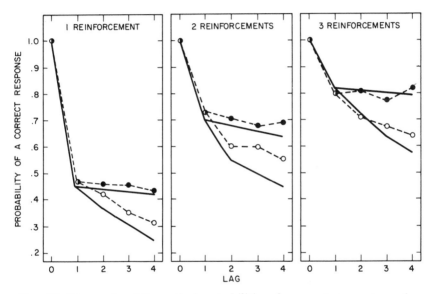

FIG. 13. Observed and theoretical probabilities of a correct response as a function of lag for the "all-same" and "all-different" conditions (Experiment 3). --●-- all-same; --○-- all-different;—theory.

for Experiment 1. For the all-same curve, we compute the probability of a correct response as a function of the lag, when all the intervening items between study and test involve the same stimulus. There are three such curves, depending on whether the study was the first, second, or third reinforcement of the particular S-R pair. The model predicts that once the intervening stimulus enters the buffer, there will be no further chance of any other item being knocked out of the buffer. Hence these curves should drop at a much slower rate than the unconditional lag curves in Fig. 11. The all-different curve plots the probability of a correct response as a function of lag, when the intervening items between study and test all involve different stimuli. Again there are three curves depending on whether the study was the first, second, or third reinforcement of the S-R pair. The all-different sequence maximizes the expected number of intervening N items and therefore the curve should have a much faster drop than the unconditional lag curves in Fig. 11. The predictions are shown in the figure as solid lines. The correspondence between predicted and observed values is reasonably good. It is particularly impressive when it is noted that the parameter values used in making the predictions were estimated from the previous data.

We next examine the data displayed in Fig. 14. Consider a sequence of consecutive trials all involving the same stimulus, but where the

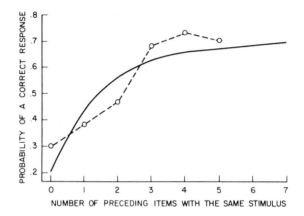

FIG. 14. Observed and theoretical probabilities of a correct response as a function of the number of consecutive preceding items using the same stimulus (Experiment 3).

response paired with the stimulus on the study phase of the last trial in the sequence is different from the response on the immediately preceding trial. Then, the theory predicts that the longer this sequence of consecutive trials, the higher will be the probability of a correct response when the last item studied in the sequence is eventually tested. This is so because the probability of the last item entering the buffer increases as the length of the sequence increases: once any item in the sequence enters the buffer, every succeeding one will. The data is shown in Fig. 14. What is graphed is the length of the sequence of trials all involving the same stimulus versus the probability of a correct response when the last item studied in the sequence is eventually tested. In this graph we have lumped over all lags at which the eventual test of the last item is made. The predictions generated from the previously estimated parameter values are shown as the smooth line. The predicted values, though not perfect, are surprisingly close to the observed proportions correct. It is worth reemphasizing that considerations of negative transfer make this result somewhat unexpected (see p. 140).

We next examine another prediction of the theory that ran counter to our initial intuitions. To make matters clear, consider the following diagram:

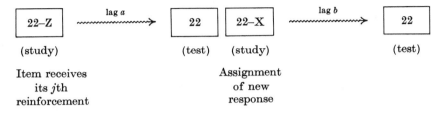

Item 22-Z is studied for the jth time and then tested at lag a; on this trial 22 is paired with a new response X, and tested next at lag b. According to the theory, the shorter lag a, the better performance should be when the item is tested after lag b. This prediction is based on the fact that the more recently a stimulus had appeared, the more likely that it was still in the buffer when the next item using it was presented for study; if the stimulus was in the buffer, then the item using it would automatically enter the buffer. In the present analysis, we examine this effect for three conditions: the preceding item using the stimulus in question could have just received its first, second, or third reinforcement. Figure 15 presents the appropriate data. In terms of the above diagram, what is plotted is the value of lag a on the abscissa versus the probability of a correct response lumped over all values of lag b on the ordinate; there is a separate curve for $j = 1$, 2, and 3.

The predicted curves are based upon the previous parameter estimates. The predictions and observations coincide fairly well, but the effect is not as dramatic as one might hope.[15] One problem is that the predicted decrease is not very large. Considerably stronger effects may be expected if each curve is separated into two components: one where the preceding item was correct at test and the other where the preceding item was not correct. In theory the decrease predicted in Fig. 15 is due to a lessened probability of the relevant stimulus being in the buffer as lag a increases. Since an item in the buffer is always responded to correctly, conditionalizing upon correct responses or errors (the center test in the above diagram) should magnify the effect. To be precise, the decrease will be accentuated for the curve conditional upon correct responses, whereas no decrease at all is predicted for the curve conditional upon errors. If an error is made, the relevant stimulus cannot be in the buffer and hence the new item enters the buffer with probability α

---

[15] A curve comparable to the one displayed in Fig. 15 for the one-reinforcement condition was obtained from the data of Experiment 1. This curve showed a similar but more pronounced drop and was well predicted by the model.

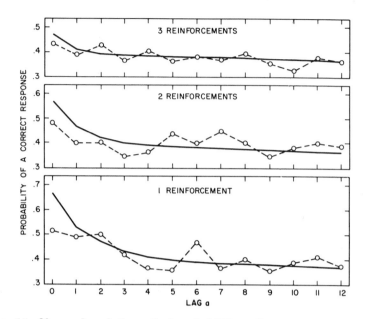

FIG. 15. Observed and theoretical probabilities of a correct response as a function of lag a (the lag of the item preceding the item tested, but using the same stimulus) (Experiment 3). --○-- Data;—theory.

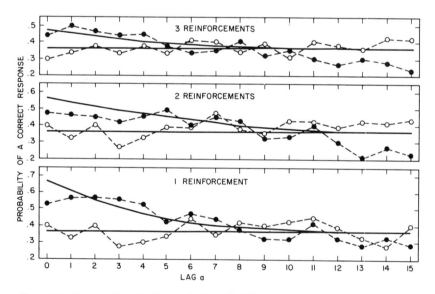

FIG. 16. Observed and theoretical probabilities of a correct response as a function of lag a conditionalized on errors or successes on the test at lag a (Experiment 3). --●-- Correct data; --○-- error data;—theory.

68

independent of lag a. Figure 16 gives the conditional curves and the predictions. The decreasing effect is fairly evident for the "correct" curves; as predicted, the "error" curves are quite flat over lags.[16] Conceivably one might argue that the effects are due to item selection, correct responses indicating easier stimuli and incorrect responses indicating more difficult ones. This objection, however, seems contraindicated in the present case. It is difficult to imagine how item selection could explain the crossing of the correct and error curves found in each of the three diagrams.[17] Indeed, the model does not explain the crossover —the model predicts that the two curves should meet. The model is in error at this point because it has not been extended to include negative transfer effects, an extension which would not be difficult to implement. An item responded to correctly at a long lag probably has a strong LTS trace; this strong trace would then interfere with the LTS trace of the new item which, of course, uses the same stimulus. All in all, these curves and predictions may be considered to provide fairly strong support for the details of the model, even to the extent of illuminating the one aspect omitted, albeit intentionally, from the assumptions.

The aspect left out is, of course, that of LTS response competition, or negative transfer. The model fails to take account of this effect because it fails to keep track of residual LTS strength remaining as a result of the previous items using the same stimulus. This lack is most clearly indicated by the occurrence of intrusion errors, particularly errors which were correct responses on the preceding occurrence of that stimulus. For example, consider the following sequence:

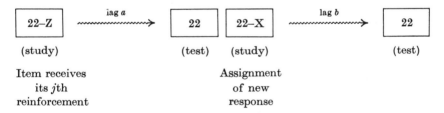

^{16} The astute reader will have noticed that the predicted decrease becomes smaller as the number of reinforcements increases. The fact that the data support this prediction is quite interesting, for it sheds light upon the buffer replacement assumptions used in this model. The decreasing effect as reinforcements increase is predicted because the probability of entering the buffer is reduced for an item receiving its third reinforcement; remember, an item recovered from LTS is not entered into the buffer. Thus as reinforcements increase, the probability of being in the buffer decreases, and the normally increased probability of being in the buffer as a result of a short lag a is partially counterbalanced.

^{17} Undoubtedly there are some selection effects in the data graphed in Fig. 16, but their magnitude is difficult to determine. Thus, these data should be regarded with some wariness.

Item 22-Z is studied for the jth time and then tested at lag a; on this trial 22 is paired with a new response X and next tested at lag b. By an intrusion error we mean the occurrence of response Z when 22 is tested at the far right of the diagram. The model predicts that these intrusion errors will be at chance level (1/25), independent of lag and number of reinforcements. In fact, these predictions fail. Figure 17 presents the

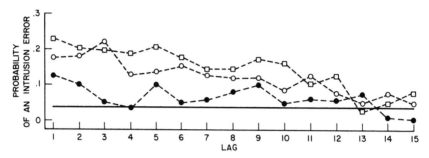

FIG. 17. Probability that the correct response for the preceding item using the same stimulus will be given in error to the present item (Experiment 3). --□-- Three reinforcements; --○-- two reinforcements; --●-- one reinforcement; —chance.

probability of intrusion errors as a function of lag b; where the data have been lumped over all values of lag a, three curves are plotted for $j = 1, 2$, and 3. This failure of the model is not very distressing because it was expected: the model could be extended in a number of obvious ways to take account of competing LTS traces without appreciably changing any of the predictions so far presented. The extension has not been made because our interest in this study is centered upon short-term effects.

Judging by the agreement between theory and data for each of the effects examined, the accuracy of the model is extremely good. It is interesting to note that the multiple-reinforcement procedure is not sufficient by itself to cause the subjects to switch their strategies from rehearsal to coding. The major emphasis still appears to be on rehearsal manipulations in STS, a not entirely surprising result since the situation is identical to that used in Experiment 1 except for the number of reinforcements given. The comments previously made concerning the difficulty associated with LTS storage in Experiment 1 apply here also. Because the emphasis is upon short-term mechanisms, this experiment is not to be considered in any strong sense as a bridge to the usual paired-associate learning situation. Nevertheless, a number of long-term effects, such as intrusion errors and interference caused by previously learned items on new items with the same stimulus, demonstrate that LTS mechanisms cannot be ignored in the theory. In Section V we consider experiments that are designed to provide a sharper picture of the workings of LTS; experimentally this is accomplished by systematically varying the number of items in LTS through which searches must be made. Before considering this problem, however, there are other features of the STS rehearsal strategy to be explored. We turn next to an experiment in which the probability of entering an item into the buffer is manipulated experimentally.

D. OVERT VERSUS COVERT STUDY PROCEDURES (EXPERIMENT 4)

The statistics considered in the previous section leave little doubt about the role of O items, N items, and the buffer entry parameter α. But one question we have not considered is whether α is amenable to experimental manipulation; if the process is really under the control of the subject, such manipulation would be expected. We now turn to a study by Brelsford and Atkinson (1968) which was designed to answer this question.

In Experiment 1, the proportions of O items and N items were varied by changing the size of the stimulus set, and the predicted differences were found. Manipulating α, however, is a somewhat more subtle task since it is the subject's strategy that must be affected. One experimental device which seems likely to increase the probability of an item's entering the buffer is to have the subject recite the item aloud as it is presented for study; this will be referred to as the "overt" study procedure. The "covert" study procedure is simply a replication of the procedure used in Experiment 1 where the subject was not required to recite the item aloud when it was presented for study, but simply told to study it.

1. *Method*

The method was identical to that used in Experiment 1 except for the following changes. The size of the stimulus set was fixed at six for all subjects and sessions. Each session consisted of 200 trials divided into four 50-trial blocks alternating between the overt and covert conditions. The initial 50-trial block was randomly chosen to be either an overt or a covert condition. The covert condition was identical in all respects to Experiment 1; when the word "study" and an S-R pair appeared on the CRT (the display screen) the subjects were told to silently study the item being presented. In the overt blocks, instead of the word "study" appearing on the CRT during the study portion of a trial, the word "rehearse" appeared. This was a signal for the subject to recite aloud twice the item then being presented for study. This was the only difference from the procedure used during the covert trials. It was hoped that the act of repeating the items aloud would raise the subject's probability of entering the item into his rehearsal buffer.

2. *Results*

In order to allow for the subject's acclimation to a change in study conditions, the first 15 trials of each 50-trial block are not included in the data analysis. Figure 18 presents the lag curves for the overt and covert conditions. It is evident that performance is superior in the overt condition. Furthermore, the overt lag curve is S-shaped in form, an

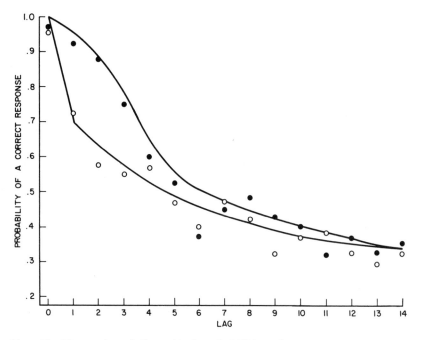

FIG. 18. Observed and theoretical probabilities of a correct response as a function of lag (Experiment 4). ● Overt; ○ covert;—theory.

effect not observed in earlier curves. Since the parameters of the models will be estimated from these curves, the model is presented before considering additional data.

The model for the covert condition is, of course, identical to that used in the analysis of Experiment 1. It has the four parameters r, α, θ, and τ. Since it was hypothesized that α would be raised in the overt condition, we might try estimating α separately for that condition. This version of the model will not fit the overt data, however, because of the pronounced S-shaped form of the lag curve. Although setting α equal to 1.0 will predict better performance in the overt condition, the lag curve will have the form of an exponentially decreasing function, which is clearly not found in the data. In order to account for the S-shaped curve, we need to assume that in the overt condition the subject tends to knock the oldest items out of the buffer first. In the model for the covert case, an entering N item is said to knock out at random any item currently in the buffer. It will be assumed for the overt case that an entering N item tends to replace the oldest item in the buffer; remember O items are items whose stimulus is currently in the buffer and they automatically replace the item with that stimulus. This probability of knocking the oldest items from the buffer first is specified as follows: if there are r items in the buffer and they are numbered so that item 1 is the oldest and item r is the newest, then the probability that an entering N item will knock the jth item from the buffer is

$$\frac{\delta(1-\delta)^{j-1}}{1-(1-\delta)^r}.$$

This equation is derived from the following scheme. The oldest item is knocked out with probability δ. If it is not knocked out, then the next oldest is knocked out with probability δ. The process continues cyclically until an item is finally selected to be knocked out. When δ approaches zero, the knockout probabilities are random, as in the covert case. When δ is greater than zero there will be a tendency for the oldest items to be knocked out of the buffer first; in fact if δ equals one, the oldest item will always be the one knocked out. It should be clear that the higher the value of δ, the greater the S-shaped effect predicted for the lag curve.

The model for the curves in Fig. 18 is therefore structured as follows. The parameters r, θ, and τ will be assumed to be the same for the two conditions; the parameters α and δ will be assumed to be affected by the experimental manipulation. To be precise, in the covert case α will be estimated freely and δ will be set equal to zero, which is precisely the model used in Experiment 1. In the overt case, α will be set equal to 1.0, which means that every item enters the buffer, and δ will be estimated freely. The parameter values that provided the best χ^2 fit to the data in Fig. 30 were $r=3$, $\theta=.97$, $\tau=.90$; for the covert condition the estimate of α was .58 (with δ equal to zero) and for the overt condition the estimate of δ was .63 (with α equal to one). The predictions for this set of parameter values are shown in Fig. 18 as smooth curves. The improvement in performance from the covert to overt conditions is well predicted; actually it is not obvious that variations in either α or δ should affect the overall level of performance. The principal reason for the improvement is due to the value of α; placing every item into the buffer means that an item entering the buffer will be expected to stay there for a shorter period than if some items did not enter the buffer. This shorter period in the buffer, however, is outweighed by the advantages resulting from the entry of every item in the first place. It is not easy to find statistics, other than the gross form of the lag curve, which reflect changes in δ; thus the assumption that the oldest items are lost first is not easy to verify in a direct way. Nevertheless, it is quite common to find experiments that yield S-shaped recency curves and these results can be fit by assuming that the oldest items in the buffer tend to be knocked out first. Other examples will be presented in Section V.

A number of additional aspects of the data will now be examined. First we consider the "all-same" and "all-different" lag curves. Figure 19

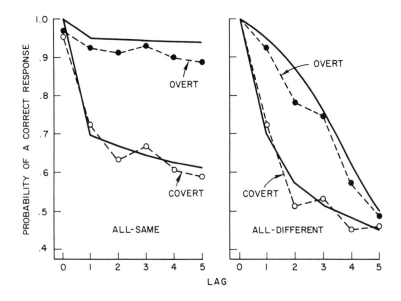

FIG. 19. Observed and theoretical probabilities of a correct response as a function of lag for the "all-same" and "all-different" conditions (Experiment 4).

gives the "all-same" lag curves for the overt and covert conditions. This curve gives the probability of a correct response for an item when all of the intervening items (between its study and test) have the same stimulus. This curve will be quite flat because the items following the first intervening item tend to be O items which will not knock other items from the buffer (for the overt case, *every* item following the first intervening item is an O item, since all items enter the buffer). Figure 19 also presents the "all-different" lag curves. This curve is the probability of making a correct response to a given item when the other items intervening between its study and test all involve different stimuli. The predictions generated by the previous parameter values are given by the smooth curves; they appear to be quite accurate.

We now look for an effect that will be sharply dependent upon the value of α and hence differ for the overt and covert conditions. Such an effect is given in Fig. 20; graphed there is the probability of a correct response as a function of the number of immediately preceding items having the same stimulus as the item in question. This is the same

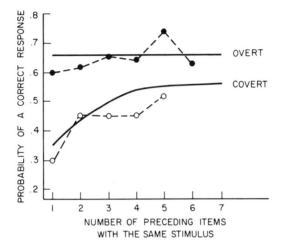

Fig. 20. Observed and theoretical probabilities of a correct response as a function of the number of consecutive preceding items all using the same stimulus (Experiment 4).

statistic that is plotted in Figs. 9 and 14; it is not a lag curve because the probability correct is given as an average over all possible lags at which the item was tested. If α is less than 1, then the length of the preceding sequence of items with the same stimulus will be an important variable; since any item in the sequence which enters the buffer will cause every succeeding item in the sequence to enter the buffer, the probability that the item in question enters the buffer will approach one as the length of the preceding sequence of items all using the same stimulus increases. For α equal to 1 (overt condition), every item enters the buffer and therefore no change would be expected. As indicated in Fig. 20, the data and theory are in good agreement. The slight rise in the data points for the overt condition may indicate that an estimate of α a little below 1.0 would improve the predictions, but the fit as it stands seems adequate.

E. ADDITIONAL VARIABLES RELATED TO THE REHEARSAL BUFFER
(EXPERIMENTS 5, 6, AND 7)

1. *Known Items and the Buffer (Experiment 5)*

In this section we shall consider briefly a number of other variables that relate to the rehearsal buffer. The overt manipulation in the preceding section succeeded in raising to near 1.0 the probability of entering an item in the buffer. As an alternative, one would like an experimental manipulation which would cause the entry probability to drop to near zero for some items. W. Thomson at Stanford University has performed an experiment that satisfies this requirement. The experimental manipulation involves interspersing some extremely well-known items among a series of items never seen before. The assumption is that a well-known item will not enter the rehearsal buffer. The experiment was performed using a modification of the "all-different" stimulus procedure employed in Experiment 2. The stimuli were consonant-vowel-consonant trigrams and the responses were the digits 0–9. For each subject two stimuli were chosen at the start of the first session and assigned responses. These S-R pairs never changed throughout the series of sessions. Except for these two items all other items were presented just once. The size of the to-be-remembered set(s) was six which included the two "known" items. The presentation schedule was as follows: on each trial with probability .5 one of the two known items would be presented for test and then given yet another study period; otherwise one of the four items in the current to-be-remembered set would be tested and a new stimulus-response pair then presented for study. Thus, the task was like that used in Experiment 2, except that on half the trials the subject was tested on, and then permitted to study, an S-R pair which was thoroughly known. The data from the first session in which the known items were being learned will not be considered.

The simplest assumption regarding the two known items is that their probability of entering the buffer is zero. This assumption is the one used in the multiple-reinforcement study (Experiment 3); namely, that an item successfully recovered from LTS is not entered into the buffer.[18] In contrast to Experiment 3, in this study it is easy to identify the items that are known since they are experimentally controlled; for this reason we can look at a number of statistics depending upon the likelihood of entering known items into the buffer. The one of particular interest is presented in Fig. 21. Graphed there is the unconditional lag curve, the

---

[18] Underwood and Ekstrund (1967) have found that insertion of known items from a previously learned list into a succeeding list improves performance on the learning of unknown items on the second list, although list length was a confounded variable.

"all-known-intervening" lag curve and the "all-unknown-intervening" lag curve. By known items we mean the two S-R pairs that repeatedly are being studied and tested; by unknown items we mean those pairs that are studied and tested only once. The unconditional lag curve gives the probability correct for unknown items as a function of lag, independent of the type of items intervening between study and test; of

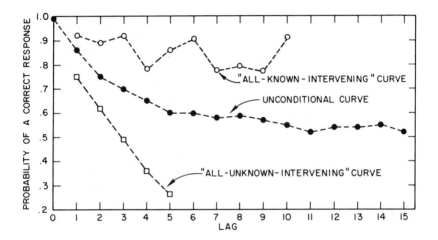

FIG. 21. Observed and theoretical probabilities of a correct response as a function of lag, for the overall condition and for the "all-known-intervening" and "all-unknown-intervening" conditions (Experiment 5).

course, the corresponding curve for known items would be perfect at all lags since subjects never make errors on them. The all-known-intervening curve gives the probability correct as a function of lag, when all of the items intervening between study and test are known items. If none of the known items enter the buffer, this curve should be level from lag 1 on and equal to α, the probability that the item entered the buffer when presented for study. At the opposite extreme is the all-unknown-intervening curve; when all the intervening items are new, the probability of knocking the item of interest from the buffer increases with lag and therefore the curve should decay at a rapid rate. It may be seen that this curve indeed drops at a more rapid rate than the unconditional lag curves. The marked difference between the all-known and all-unknown curves in Fig. 21 leads us to conclude that known and unknown items clearly have different probabilities for entering the rehearsal buffer. If the all-known curve were flat after lag 1, then the probability for entering a known item into the buffer would be zero. Another possibility is that

α is indeed zero for known items, but that the subject occasionally picks an item from LTS for additional rehearsal when a known item is presented.

2. *Response Time Measures (Experiment 6)*

We now turn to a consideration of some latency results. Potentially, latencies offer an avenue of analysis that could be more fruitful than the

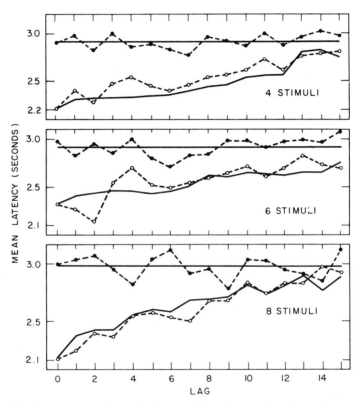

Fig. 22. Observed and theoretical mean latencies as a function of lag for correct and incorrect responses (Experiment 6). --●-- Error latencies; --○-- correct latencies;—predicted latencies.

analysis of choice response data; we say this because the latencies should reflect search and retrieval times from both STS and LTS. A detailed latency analysis is beyond the scope of this paper, but one simple result will be considered. Figure 22 presents the average latencies as a function of lag for correct and incorrect responses in a study by Brelsford *et al.* (1966). This experiment employed the same procedure described earlier in our discussion of Experiment 1 except that only 6 rather than 26 responses were used. As in Experiment 1, this study used three different stimulus-set sizes; i.e., s equalled 4, 6, or 8. For each stimulus set in Fig. 22 it may be seen that the correct and incorrect latency curves converge at long lags. This convergence would be expected since the probability of a correct response is dropping toward chance at long lags. The theoretical curves are based on an extremely simple latency model which assumes that latencies for responses correctly retrieved from either LTS or STS have a fixed mean value λ, whereas a failure to retrieve and a subsequent guess has a fixed mean value of λ'. Thus error responses always have a mean latency λ'; however, a correct response may occur as a result of a retrieval from memory or a correct guess, and consequently its latency is a weighted average of λ and λ'. We can estimate λ' as the average of the points on the latency lag curve for errors, and λ can be set equal to the latency of a correct response at lag zero since all responses are due to retrievals from memory at this lag. In order to predict the remaining latency data, we make use of the observed probability of a correct response as a function of lag; these values are reported in Brelsford *et al.* (1966). If p_i is the observed probability of a correct response at lag i, then

$$p_i = x_i + (1 - x_i)\tfrac{1}{6}$$

where x_i is the probability of retrieving the response from memory and $(1 - x_i)\tfrac{1}{6}$ is the probability of making a correct response by guessing. Estimating x_i in this way, we predict that the mean latency of a correct response at lag i is simply $x_i\lambda + (1 - x_i)\lambda'$. Using this equation and estimating λ and λ' as indicated above, leads to the theoretical curves displayed in Fig. 22. The error latency curve is predicted to be equal to λ' for all lags, whereas the correct latency curve is λ at lag 0 and approaches λ' over lags as the estimate of x_i goes to zero. This latency model is of course oversimplified, and fails to take into account differences in latencies due to retrieval from STS as compared to retrieval from LTS; the results nevertheless indicate that further analyses along these lines may prove fruitful.

3. *Time Estimation (Experiment 7)*

One factor related to our model that has not been discussed is temporal memory. It seems clear that there is some form of long-term temporal memory; in a negative transfer paradigm, for example, there must be some mechanism by which the subject can distinguish between the most recent response paired with a stimulus versus some other response paired with that stimulus at an earlier time. This temporal memory undoubtedly involves the long-term store; somehow when an event is stored in LTS it also must be given a time tag or stored in such a way that the subject can date the event (albeit imperfectly) at the time of retrieval. In addition to long-term temporal storage, there is evidence that a subject's estimate of elapsed time depends upon an item's length of residence in the buffer. An experiment by R. Freund and D. Rundis at Stanford University serves to illustrate the dependence of temporal memory upon the buffer.[19] The study employed essentially

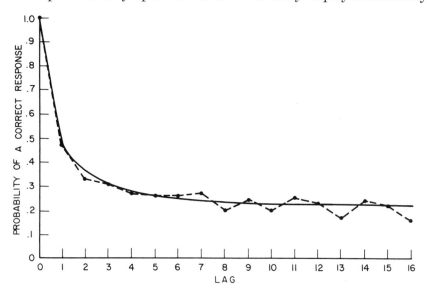

FIG. 23. Observed and theoretical probabilities of a correct response as a function of lag (Experiment 7). – – – Observed;—predicted.

the same procedure used in Experiment 2. There was a continuous sequence of test-plus-study trials and the stimuli kept changing throughout each session; each stimulus appeared only once for study and test. The stimuli were consonant-vowel-consonant trigrams and the responses were the 26 letters of the alphabet; the size of the to-be-remembered set of items was fixed at eight. When a stimulus was tested the subject first gave his best guess of the response that had been previously studied with the stimulus and then gave an estimate of the number of trials that intervened between the item's initial study and final test; this estimate could range from 0 to 13; if the subject felt the lag was greater than 13 he responded by pressing a key labeled 14+.

The unconditional lag curve for the probability of a correct response is presented in Fig. 23. The solid line represents the predictions that were

[19] This study employs a time-estimation procedure similar to one developed by L. R. Peterson (personal communication).

generated by the model used to fit Experiment 2. The parameter values providing the best fit to the lag curve were $r = 2$, $\alpha = .57$, $\theta = .13$, $\tau = 1.0$. The data of interest is presented in Fig. 24. The average lag judgment is plotted as a function of the actual lag. The solid dots are the average lag judgments for those items to which a correct response was given; the open circles are the average lag judgments for those items to which an incorrect response was given. If lag judgments were perfect,

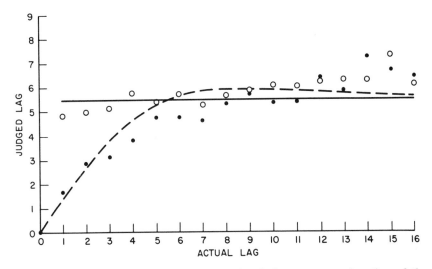

FIG. 24. Observed and theoretical mean lag judgments as a function of the actual lag (Experiment 7). ○ Error data;—error theory; ● correct data; – – correct theory.

they would fall on the 45° diagonal; it may be seen that the correct curve is fairly accurate to about lag 5 and then tails off. The lag judgments associated with incorrect responses seem to be virtually unrelated to the actual lag. This indicates that the retrieval of a correct response and temporal estimation are closely related. An extremely simple model for this data assumes that the mean lag judgment for an item in the buffer is the true lag value; any item not in the buffer is given a lag judgment at random from a distribution that is unrelated to the true lag. The predictions using the above parameter estimates are shown in Fig. 24. Freund and Rundis have developed more elaborate models which include both a long- and short-term temporal memory and have obtained quite accurate predictions; but these models will not be examined here. The point we want to make by introducing these data is that temporal memory may be tied to the short-term system even more strongly than to the long-term system.

V. Experiments Concerned with Long-Term Search and Retrieval

The major purpose of this section is to examine a series of experiments concerned with search and retrieval processes in LTS. These experiments differ from those of the preceding section in that the memory tasks are not continuous; rather, they involve a series of discrete trials which are meant to be relatively independent from one to the next. On each trial a new list of items is presented sequentially to the subject for study; following the presentation a test is made on some aspect of the list. Using this procedure, the size of the list, d, can be systematically manipulated. Variations in list size affect the size of the memory set through which the subject must search when tested, and consequently search and retrieval processes can be examined in more detail than was previously possible. The title of this section is not meant to imply, however, that the short-term processes involved in these experiments are different from those appearing in the continuous-presentation situations; in fact, the models used to describe the experiments of this section will be based upon the same STS rehearsal buffer introduced earlier. The difference is one of emphasis; the long-term processes will be elaborated and explored in greater depth in this section. This exploration of long-term models will by no means be exhaustive, and will be less extensive than that carried out for the short-term processes.

Prior to an examination of particular experiments, a few remarks need to be made about the separability of lists. In any experiment in which a series of different lists is presented, we may ask just what information in LTS the subject is searching through at test. The same problem arises, though less seriously, in experiments where the subject is tested on only one list. Clearly the information relevant to the current list of items being tested must be kept separate from the great mass of other information in LTS. This problem is accentuated when individual lists within a session must be kept separated. How this is managed is somewhat of a mystery. One possible explanation would call for a search along a temporal memory dimension: the individual items could be assumed to be temporally ordered, or to have "time tags." It is not enough to propose that search is made through all items indiscriminately and that items recovered from previous lists are recognized as such and not reported; if this were true, the duration and difficulty of the search would increase dramatically over the session. In fact, the usual result is that there is little change in performance over a session except for effects concentrated at the very start. On the other hand, judging from such factors as intrusion errors from previous lists, the subject is not able to restrict his search solely to the current list. In the experiments to follow, we will make the simplifying assumption, without real justification, that the lists are entirely separated in LTS, and that the subject searches only through information relevant to the list currently being tested.

A. A Serial Display Procedure Involving Single Tests (Experiment 8)

This experiment involved a long series of discrete trials. On each trial a new display of items was presented to the subject. A display consisted of a random sequence of playing cards; the cards varied only in the

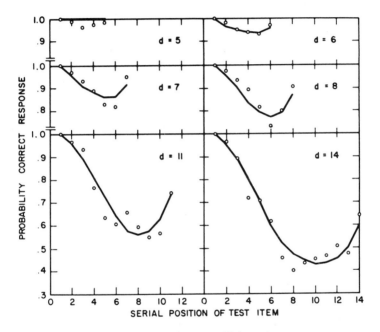

Fig. 25. Observed and theoretical probabilities of a correct response as a function of serial position (Experiment 8).

color of a small patch on one side; four colors (black, white, blue, and green) were used. The cards were presented to the subject at a rate of one card every 2 seconds. The subject named the color of each card as it was presented; once the color of the card had been named it was turned face down on a table so that the color was no longer visible, and the next card was presented. After presentation of the last card in a display, the cards were in a straight row on the table; the card presented first was to the subject's left and the most recently presented card to the right. The trial terminated when the experimenter pointed to one of the cards on the table and the subject attempted to recall the color of that card. The subject was instructed to guess the color if uncertain and to qualify the response with a confidence rating. The confidence ratings were the numerals 1 through 4. The subjects were told to say 1 if they were positive; 2 if they were able to eliminate two of the four possible colors as being incorrect; 3 if one of the four colors could be eliminated as incorrect; and 4 if they had no idea at all as to the correct response.

It is important to note that only one position is tested in a display on each trial. The experiment involved 20 female subjects who participated in five daily sessions, each lasting for approximately 1 hour. Over the course of the five sessions, a subject was given approximately 400 trials. The display size, d, was varied from trial to trial and took on the following values: $d = 3, 4, 5, 6, 7, 8, 11$, and 14. Details of the experimental procedure are presented in Phillips, Shiffrin, and Atkinson (1967).

Figure 25 presents the probability of a correct response at each serial position for displays of size 5, 6, 7, 8, 11, and 14. For displays of sizes 3 and 4, the probability correct was 1.0 at all positions. The circles in the figure are the observed points; the solid lines are predicted curves which will be explained shortly. The serial positions are numbered so that item 1 designates the last item presented (the newest item), and item d designates the first item presented (the oldest item). The most apparent features of the curves are a fairly marked S-shaped recency portion and a smaller, quite steep primacy portion. For all display sizes, the probability of a correct response is 1.0 at serial position 1.

1. *Theory*

We must first decide whether a subject will set up and use a rehearsal buffer in this situation. Despite the fact that the continuous procedure has been dropped, it is still unlikely that the subject will engage in a significant amount of long-term coding. This is true because the task is still one of high "negative transfer"; the stimuli, which are the positions in the display, are constantly being re-paired with new responses as a session continues. Too much LTS encoding would undoubtedly lead to a high degree of interference among lists. It is only for a relatively weak and decaying LTS trace that a temporal search of long-term memory may be expected to keep the various lists separate. This difficulty in LTS transfer leads to the adoption of short-term strategies. Another reason for using a rehearsal buffer in this task depends upon the small list lengths employed; for small list lengths, there is a high probability that the item will be in the buffer at the moment of test. Thus the adoption of a rehearsal buffer is an efficient strategy. There is some question concerning just what the unit of rehearsal is in this situation. For example, the subject could assign numbers to positions in the display and then rehearse the number-color pairs. Most likely, however, the subject uses the fact that the stimuli always remain before her to combine STS rehearsal with some form of visual mnemonic. That is, the unit of rehearsal is the response alone; as the subject rehearses the responses, she "mentally" places each response upon the appropriate card before her. This might therefore be a situation where the a-v-l and visual short-term stores are used in conjunction with each other. In any case, it seems reasonable that the units of rehearsal are the names (or perhaps the abbreviations) of the colors.

We might ask how the buffer will act in this situation. As noted earlier, in reference to the "overt-covert" experiment, the fact that items are read aloud as they are presented will tend to cause the subject to enter each item into the buffer. Furthermore, an S-shaped recency effect would not be unexpected. Indeed, if the units of rehearsal are the responses themselves, then the subject might tend to keep them in consecutive order to ease the visual memory task; if all items enter the buffer and are kept in consecutive order, then the oldest items will tend to be deleted first. That is, when a new item enters the buffer there will be a tendency to eliminate the oldest item from the buffer to make room for it. One other question that should be considered is the size of the buffer the subject would be expected to use in this task. There are a number of reasons why the buffer size should be larger here than in the continuous tasks of Section IV. First, the subject is not continually being interrupted for tests as in the previous studies; more of the subject's attention may therefore be allotted to rehearsal. Second, rehearsal of color names (or their abbreviations) is considerably easier than number-letter combinations. Equivalent to rehearsing "32-G, 45-Q" might be "Black, White, Black, Green" (or even a larger set if abbreviations are used). The magnitude of the difference may not be quite as large as this argument would lead us to expect because undoubtedly some time must be allotted to keeping track of which response goes on which position, but the estimate of the buffer size nevertheless should be larger in this situation than in the continuous tasks.

The STS part of the model for this experiment is similar to that used in the "overt" experiment in Section IV,D in that every item is entered in the buffer when it is presented. There is one new factor, however, that must be considered. Since each trial starts with the buffer empty, it will be assumed that the first items presented enter the buffer in succession, without knocking any item out, until the buffer is filled. Once the buffer is filled, each item enters the buffer and knocks out one of the items currently there. If the most recently presented item is in slot r of the buffer, and the oldest item is in slot 1, then the probability that the item in slot i of the buffer will be the one eliminated is

$$\frac{\delta(1-\delta)^{i-1}}{1-(1-\delta)^r}.$$

This is the same equation that was used to describe the knock-out process for the overt-covert study (Experiment 4). The larger δ, the greater the tendency to delete the oldest item in the buffer when making room for a new one.

The first set of long-term storage and retrieval assumptions that will be considered are essentially identical to those used in the previous sections. Information will be assumed to enter LTS during the entire period an item resides in the buffer at a rate θ per inter-item interval. This process must be qualified with regard to the first few items presented on each trial before the buffer is filled; it is assumed that the subjects divide their attention equally among the items in the buffer. Thus, if the rate of transfer is θ when there is only one item in the buffer, and the buffer size is r, then the rate of transfer will be θ/r when the buffer is filled. That is, since attention must be divided among r items when the buffer is full, each item receives only $1/r$th as much transfer as when the buffer only holds a single item. In general, information on each item will be transferred to LTS at rate θ/j during the interval in which there are j items in the buffer. The effect of this assumption is that more information is transferred to LTS about the items first presented in a list than about later items that are presented once the buffer is full.

The LTS decay and retrieval processes must now be examined. In earlier experiments we assumed that information decayed solely as a result of the number of items intervening between study and test; in other words, only the retroactive interference effect was considered. Because the previous tasks were continuous, the number of items preceding an item's presentation was effectively infinite in all cases. For this reason the proactive effects were assumed to be constant over conditions and did not need explicit inclusion in the model. In the present experiment the variation in list size makes it clear that pro-active interference effects within a trial will be an important variable. The assumption that will be used is perhaps the simplest version of interference theory possible: each preceding and each succeeding item has an equal interfering effect. To be precise, if an amount of information I has been transferred to LTS for a given item, then every other item in the list will interfere with this information to the extent of reducing it by a proportion τ. Thus, if there were d items in the list, the item of interest would have an amount of information in LTS at the time of test equal to $I(\tau^{d-1})$. Clearly, the longer the list the greater the interference effect.

The model can now be completed by specifying the response process which works as follows. An item in the buffer at the time of test is responded to correctly. If the item is not in the buffer, then a search is made in LTS. The probability of retrieving the appropriate response is, as in our other models, an exponential function of this information and equals $1 - \exp[-I(\tau^{d-1})]$; if a retrieval is not made, then the subject guesses.

2. Data Analysis

The parameter values that gave the best fit to the data of Fig. 25 using a minimum χ^2 criterion were as follows: $r = 5$, $\delta = .38$, $\theta = 2.0$, and $\tau = .85$.[20] Remember that r is the buffer size, δ determines the probability of deleting the oldest item in the buffer, θ is the transfer rate to LTS, and τ is the proportional loss of information caused by other items in the list. The theoretical curves generated by these parameter estimates are shown in Fig. 30 as solid lines. The predictions are quite accurate as indicated by a χ^2 value of 44.3 based on 42 degrees of freedom. It should be emphasized that the curves in the figure were all fit simultaneously with the same parameter values.

The primacy effect in the curves of Fig. 25 is predicted because more information is transferred to LTS for the first items presented on each trial. There are two reasons for this. First, the transfer rate on any given item is higher the fewer items there are in the buffer; thus the initial items, which enter the buffer before it is filled, accumulate more information in LTS. Second, the initial items cannot be knocked out of the buffer until the buffer is filled; thus the time period that initial items reside in the buffer is longer on the average than the time for later items. The recency effect is predicted because the last items presented in a list tend to be still in the buffer at the time of test; the S-shape arises because the estimate of δ indicates a fairly strong tendency for the oldest items in the rehearsal buffer to be eliminated first when making room for a new item.

Having estimated a set of parameter values that characterizes the data in Fig. 25, we now use these estimates to predict the confidence rating data. Actually, it is beyond the scope of this paper to analyze the confidence ratings in detail, but some of these data will be considered in order to illustrate the generality of the model and the stability of the parameter estimates. The data that will be considered are presented in Fig. 26; graphed is the probability of giving confidence rating R_1 (most confident) for each list size and each serial position. The observed data is represented by the open circles. It is clear that these results are similar in form to the probability correct curves of Fig. 25. The model used to fit these data is quite simple. Any item in the buffer is given an R_1. If the item is not in the buffer, then a search is made of LTS. If the amount of information in LTS on the item is $I(\tau^{d-1})$ then the probability of giving R_1 is an exponential function of that information: namely the

[20] For details on the method of parameter estimation see Phillips, Shiffrin, and Atkinson (1967).

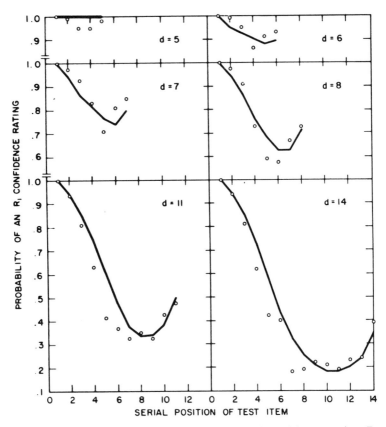

Fig. 26. Observed and predicted probabilities of confidence rating R_1 as a function of serial position (Experiment 8).

function $1 - \exp[-c_1 I(\tau^{d-1})]$, where c_1 is a parameter determining the subject's tendency to give confidence rating R_1. This assumption is consistent with a number of different viewpoints concerning the subject's generation of confidence ratings. It could be interpreted equally well as an assignment of ratings to the actually perceived amount of information in LTS, or as a proportion of the items that are recovered in an all-or-none fashion.[21] In any event, the predictions were generated using the previous parameter values plus an estimate of c_1. The predicted curves, with c_1 equal to .66, are shown in Fig. 26. The predictions are not as accurate as those in Fig. 25; but, considering that only one new parameter was estimated, they are quite good.

[21] The various possibilities may be differentiated through an analysis of conditional probabilities of the ratings given correct and incorrect responses, and through ROC curve (Type II) analyses (Bernbach, 1967, Murdock, 1966) but this will not be done here.

3. *Discussion*

In developing this model a number of decisions were made somewhat arbitrarily. The choice points involved will now be considered in greater detail. The assumption that the amount of transfer to LTS is dependent upon the number of items currently in the buffer needs elaboration. Certainly if the subject is engaged in coding or other active transfer strategies, the time spent in attending to an item should be directly related to the amount of transfer to LTS. On the other hand, the passive type of transfer which we assume can occur in situations where the subject makes use of a rehearsal buffer may not be related to the time spent in rehearsing an item per se, but rather to the total period the item resides in the buffer. That is, direct attention to an item in STS may not be necessary for some transfer to take place; rather a passive form of transfer may occur as long as the item remains in STS. Thus in situations where the rehearsal buffer is used and active transfer strategies such as coding do not occur, it could reasonably be expected that the amount of information transferred to LTS would be related solely to the total time spent in the buffer, and not to the number of items in the buffer at the time. In practice, of course, the actual transfer process may lie some-where between these two extremes. Note that even if the transfer rate for an item is assumed to be a constant (unrelated to the number of items currently in the buffer) the first items presented for study still would have more information transferred to LTS than later items; this occurs because the items at the start of a list will not be knocked out of the buffer until it is filled and hence will reside in the buffer for a longer time on the average than later items. For this reason, the primacy effect could still be explained. On the other hand, the primacy effect will be reduced by the constant transfer assumption; in order to fit the data from the current experiment with this assumption, for example, it would be necessary to adjust the retrieval scheme accordingly. In modeling the free verbal-recall data that follows, a constant transfer assumption is used and accordingly a retrieval scheme is adopted which amplifies more strongly than the present one small differences in LTS strength.

We now consider the decay assumption in greater detail. The assumption is that the information transferred to LTS for a particular item is reduced by a proportion τ for every other item in the list. There are a number of possibilities for the form of this reduction. It could be actual physical interference with the trace, or it could be a reduction in the value of the current information as a result of subsequent incoming information. An example of this latter kind of interference will be helpful. Suppose, in a memory experiment the first item is GEX-5, and the subject stores "G__-5" in LTS. If tested now on GEX, the subject would give the correct response 5. Suppose a second item GOZ-3 is presented and the subject stores "G_-3" in LTS. If he is now tested on either GEX or GOZ his probability of a correct response will drop to .5. Thus the actual information stored is not affected, but its value is markedly changed.

The assumption that every other item in a list interferes equally is open to question on two counts. First of all, it would be expected that an item about which a large amount of information is transferred would interfere more strongly with other items in LTS than an item about which little information is transferred. Certainly when no transfer occurs for an item, that item cannot interfere with other LTS traces. However, the equal interference assumption used in our analysis may not be a bad approximation. The second failing of the equal interference assumption has to do with separation of items. If the list lengths were very long, it might be expected that the number of items separating any two items would affect their mutual interference; the greater the separation, the less the interference. The list lengths are short enough in the present experiment, however, that the separation is probably not an important factor.

4. *Some Alternative Models*

It is worth considering some alternatives to the interference process of the model just presented, henceforth referred to as Model I in this subsection. In particular it is important to demonstrate that the effects of the interference-decay assumption, which could be viewed as a structural feature of memory, can be duplicated by simple search processes. For example, any limited search through the information in LTS will give poorer performance as the amount of that information increases. In order to make the concept of the search process clear, Model II will adopt an all-or-none transfer scheme. That is, a single copy of each item may be transferred to LTS on a probabilistic basis. If a copy is transferred, it is a perfect copy to the extent that it always produces a correct response if it is retrieved from LTS. The short-term features of the model are identical to those of Model I: each item enters the buffer; when the buffer is filled each succeeding item enters the buffer and knocks out an item already there according to the δ-process described earlier.

The transfer assumption for Model II is as follows. If an item is one of the j items in the buffer, then the probability that a copy of that item will be placed in LTS between one item's presentation and the next is θ/j. Therefore, the transfer depends, as in Model I, upon the number of other items currently in the buffer. No more than one copy may be placed in LTS for any one item. The retrieval assumptions are the following. A correct response is given if the item is in the buffer when tested. If it is not in the buffer, then a search is made in LTS. If a copy of the item exists in LTS and is found, then a correct response is given; otherwise a random guess is made. As before, we assume that the information pertinent to the current list is distinguishable from that of earlier lists; thus, the search is made only among those copies of items in the current list. The central assumption of Model II is that exactly R selections are made (with replacement) from the copies in LTS; if the tested item has not been found by then, the search ends. The restriction to a fixed number of searches, R, is perhaps too strong, but can be justified if there is a fixed time period allotted to the subject for responding. It should be clear that for R fixed, the probability of retrieval decreases as the list length increases; the longer the list the more copies in LTS, and the more copies the less the probability of finding a particular copy in R selections. Model II was fit to the data in the same fashion as Model I. The parameter values that gave the best predictions were $r = 5$, $\delta = .39$, $\theta = .72$, and $R = 3.15$. The theoretical curves generated by these parameters are so similar to those for Model I that Fig. 25 adequately represents them, and they will not be presented separately. Whereas the χ^2 was 44.3 for Model I, the χ^2 value for Model II was 46.2, both based on 42 degrees of freedom. The similarity of the predictions serves to illustrate the primary point of introducing Model II: effects predicted by search processes and by interference processes are quite similar and consequently are difficult to separate experimentally.

The search process described above is just one of a variety of such mechanisms. In general there will be a group of possible search mechanisms associated with each transfer and storage assumption; a few of these processes will be examined in the next section on free-verbal-recall. Before moving on to these experiments, however, we should like to present briefly a decay and retrieval process combining some of the features of interference and search mechanisms. In this process the interference does not occur until the search begins and is then caused by the search process itself. The model (designated as Model III) is identical in all respects to Model II until the point where the subject begins the search of LTS for the correct copy. The assumption is that the subject samples copies with replacement, as before, but each unsuccessful search may disrupt the sought-after copy with probability R'. The search does not end until the appropriate copy is found or until all copies in LTS have been examined. If the copy does exist in LTS, but is disrupted at any time during the search process, then when the item is finally retrieved, the stored information will be such that the subject will not be able to recall at better than the chance level. The parameter values giving the best fit for this model were $r = 5$, $\delta = .38$, $\theta = .80$, and

$R' = .25$. The predicted curves are again quite similar to those in Fig. 25 and will not be presented. The predictions are not quite as accurate, however, as those of Models I and II, the χ^2 value being 55.0.[22]

B. Free-Verbal-Recall Experiments

The free-verbal-recall situation offers an excellent opportunity for examining retrieval processes, because the nature of the task forces the subject to engage in a lengthy search of LTS. The typical free-verbal-recall experiment involves reading a list of high-frequency English words to the subject (Deese & Kaufman, 1957; Murdock, 1962). Following the reading, the subject is asked to recall as many of the words as possible. Quite often list length has been a variable, and occasionally the presentation time per item has been varied. Deese and Kaufman, for example, used lists of 10 and 32 items at 1 second per item. Murdock ran groups of 10, 15, and 20 items at 2 seconds per item, and groups of 20, 30, and 40 items at 1 second per item. The results are typically presented in the form of serial position curves: the probability of recall is plotted against the item's position in the list. The Murdock (1962) results are representative and are shown in Fig. 27. It should be made clear that the numbering of serial positions for these curves is opposite from the scheme used in the previous section; that is, the first item presented (the oldest item at the time of test) is labeled serial position 1. This numbering procedure will be used throughout this section to conform with the literature on free-verbal-recall; the reader should keep this in mind when comparing results here with those presented elsewhere in the paper. The primacy effect in Fig. 27 is the rise on the left-hand portions of the curves and the recency effect is the larger rise on the right-hand portions of the curves. The curves are labeled with the list length and the presentation rate per item. Note that the curves are quite similar to those found in Experiment 8 of the previous section; an effect not seen in Experiment 8 (because of the short list lengths used) is the level asymptotic portions of the curves which appear between the primacy and recency effects for the longer lists.

The form of the curves suggests that a buffer process could explain the results, with the words themselves being the units of rehearsal. The recency effect would be due to the probability that an item is still in the buffer at test; this probability goes to near zero after 15 items or so and the recency effect accordingly extends no further than this. The primacy effect would arise because more information accrued in LTS for the first few items presented in the list. Whether a buffer strategy is reasonable in the free-recall situation, however, is worth further discussion. It can hardly be maintained that high-frequency English words are difficult to

[22] For a more detailed account of Models I, II, and III, and a comparison among models, see Atkinson and Shiffrin (1965).

code; on the other hand, the task is not a paired-associate one and cues must be found with which to connect the words. One possibility is that upon seeing each word the subject generates a number of associates (from LTS) and tries to store the group of words; later during testing a search which retrieves any of the associates might in turn retrieve the desired word. We tend to doubt that this strategy, used by itself, will greatly improve performance.[23] To the extent that coding occurs, it

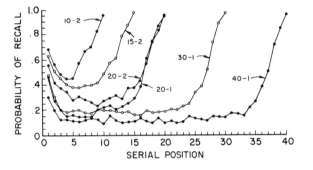

Fig. 27. Probability of correct recall as a function of serial position for free verbal recall. After Murdock (1962).

probably involves connecting words within the presented list to each other. This technique would of course require the consideration of a number of words simultaneously in STS and therefore might be characterized reasonably well by a buffer process. Whether or not coding occurs in the free-recall situation, there are other reasons for expecting the subjects to adopt a buffer strategy. The most important reason is undoubtedly the improvement in performance that a rehearsal buffer will engender. If the capacity of the buffer is, say, 4 or 5 words, then the use of a buffer will assure the subjects of a minimum of four or five items correct on each list (assuming that all of the items may be read out of the buffer correctly). Considering that subjects report on the average only about 8 or 9 items, even for long lists, the items stored in the buffer are an important component of performance.

It will be assumed, then, that the subjects do adopt a rehearsal strategy. The comparability of the curves in Fig. 25 to those in Fig. 27

[23] B. H. Cohen (1963) has presented free-recall lists containing closely related categories of words, e.g., north, east, south, west. Indeed, the recovery of one member of a category usually led to the recovery of other members, but the total number of categories recalled did not exceed the number of separate words recalled from noncategorized lists.

might indicate that a model similar to any of the models presented in the previous section could be applied to the current data. There are, however, important differences between the two experimental paradigms which must be considered: the free-recall situation does not involve pairing a response with a stimulus for each list position, and has the requirement of multiple recall at the time of test. The fact that explicit stimulus cues are not provided for each of the responses desired would be expected to affect the form of the search process. The multiple-response requirement raises more serious problems. In particular, it is possible that each response that is output may interfere with other items not yet recalled. The problem may be most acute for the case of items still in the buffer; Waugh and Norman (1965) have proposed that each response output at the time of test has the same disrupting effect upon other items in the buffer as the arrival of a new item during study. On the other hand, it is not clear whether a response emitted during test disrupts items in LTS. It might be expected that the act of recalling an item from LTS would raise that item's strength in LTS; this increase in strength is probably not associated, however, with the transfer of any new information to LTS. For this reason, other traces will most likely not be interfered with, and it shall be assumed that retrieval of an item from LTS has no effect upon other items in LTS.

Because there is some question concerning the effects of multiple recall upon the contents of the buffer, and because this section is primarily aimed at LTS processes, the part of the free-recall curves that arise from the buffer will not be considered in further analyses. This means that the models in this section will not be concerned with the part of the curve making up the recency effect; since the data in Fig. 27 indicate that the recency effect is contained in the last 15 items (to the right in the figure) of each list, these points will be eliminated from the analyses. Unfortunately, the elimination of the last 15 items means that the short list lengths are eliminated entirely. The problem of obtaining data for short list lengths not contaminated by items in the buffer at the time of test has been circumvented experimentally by a variation of the counting-backward technique. That is, the contents of the buffer can be eliminated experimentally by using an interfering task inserted between the end of the list and the start of recall. We now turn to a consideration of these experiments.

A representative experiment is that by Postman and Phillips (1965). Words were presented at a rate of one per second in all conditions. In one set of conditions three list lengths (10, 20, and 30) were used and recall was tested immediately following presentation. This, of course, is the usual free recall procedure. The serial position curves are shown in the top panel of Fig. 28 in the box labeled "0 second." The same list lengths were used for those conditions employing an intervening task; immediately following presentation of the list the subjects were required to count backwards by three's and four's for 30 seconds. Following this intervening task, they were asked to recall the list. The results are shown in the lower panel in Fig. 28. If the intervening task did not affect the contents of LTS but did wipe out all items in the buffer, then the recency

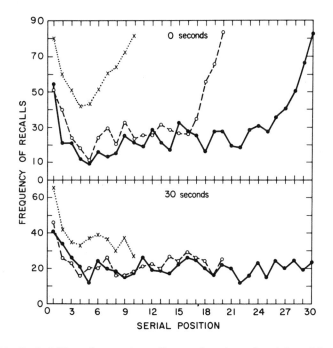

FIG. 28. Probability of correct recall as a function of serial position for free verbal recall with test following 0 seconds and 30 seconds of intervening arithmetic. After Postman & Phillips (1965).

effects would be expected to disappear with the curves otherwise unchanged. This is exactly what was found. The primacy effects and asymptotic levels remain unchanged while the recency effect disappears. It is clear, then, that normal free-recall curves (without intervening arithmetic) from which the last 15 points have been deleted should be identical to curves from experiments using intervening arithmetic. The following data have therefore been accumulated: Murdock's data with the last 15 points of each list deleted; data reported by Deese and Kaufman (1957) using a free-recall paradigm, but again with the last 15 points of each list deleted; the data reported by Postman and Phillips (1965); and some data collected by Shiffrin in which an intervening task was used to eliminate the contents of the buffer.[24] All of these serial position curves have the same form; they show a primacy effect followed by a level asymptote. For this reason the results have been presented in Table I. The first three points of each curve, which make up the primacy

TABLE I
OBSERVED AND PREDICTED SERIAL POSITION CURVES FOR VARIOUS FREE-VERBAL-RECALL EXPERIMENTS

List	Point 1 Obs.	Point 1 Pred.	Point 2 Obs.	Point 2 Pred.	Point 3 Obs.	Point 3 Pred.	Asymptote Obs.	Asymptote Pred.	Number of points
M-20-1	.46	.45	.27	.37	.20	.29	.16	.22	2
M-30-1	.38	.35	.30	.28	.21	.22	.19	.17	12
M-20-2	.55	.61	.42	.51	.37	.41	.31	.32	2
M-40-1	.30	.29	.20	.23	.13	.18	.12	.14	22
M-25-1	.38	.39	.23	.32	.21	.25	.15	.19	7
M-20-2.5	.72	.66	.61	.56	.45	.46	.37	.35	2
D-32-1	.46	.33	.34	.27	.27	.21	.16	.16	14
P-10-1	.66	.62	.42	.52	.35	.42	.34	.32	7
P-20-1	.47	.45	.27	.37	.23	.29	.22	.22	17
P-30-1	.41	.35	.34	.28	.27	.22	.20	.17	27
S-6-1	.71	.74	.50	.64	.57	.52	.42	.40	3
S-6-2	.82	.88	.82	.79	.65	.66	.66	.52	3
S-11-1	.48	.60	.43	.50	.27	.40	.31	.31	8
S-11-2	.72	.76	.55	.66	.52	.54	.47	.42	8
S-17-1	.55	.49	.33	.40	.26	.32	.22	.24	14
S-17-2	.68	.66	.65	.56	.67	.45	.43	.35	14

effect, are given in the table. The level portions of the curves are then averaged and the average shown in the column labeled "asymptote." The column labeled "number of points" is the number of points which have been averaged to arrive at the asymptotic level.[25] The column labeled "list" gives the abbreviation of the experimenter, the list length, and the presentation rate for each of the serial position curves. (M = Murdock, 1962; D = Deese and Kaufman, 1957; P = Postman and Phillips, 1965; S = Shiffrin.)

[24] The Shiffrin data are reported in more detail in Atkinson and Shiffrin (1965).

[25] For the Postman-Phillips and Shiffrin lists the number of points at asymptote are simply list length, d, minus 3. For the Murdock and the Deese-Kaufman lists the number of points is $d - 15 - 3$ because the last 15 points in these lists have been eliminated.

1. *Theoretical Analysis*

Having accumulated a fair amount of parametric data in Table I, we should now like to predict the results. The first model to be considered is extremely simple. Every item presented enters the subject's rehearsal buffer. One by one the initial items fill up the buffer, and thereafter each succeeding item knocks out of the buffer a randomly chosen item. In conditions where arithmetic is used following presentation, it is assumed that the arithmetic operations knock items from the buffer at the same rate as new incoming items. This is only an approximation, but probably not too inaccurate. Information is assumed to be transferred to LTS as long as an item remains in the buffer, in fact as a linear function of the total time spent in the buffer (regardless of the number of other items concurrently in the buffer). If an item remains in the buffer for j seconds, an amount of information equal to θ times j is transferred to LTS. Call the amount of information transferred to LTS for an item its *strength*. When the subject engages in a search of LTS during recall it is assumed that he makes exactly R searches into LTS and then stops his search (the number of searches made might, for example, be determined by the time allowed for recall). On each search into LTS the probability that information concerning a particular item will be found is just the ratio of that item's strength to the sum of the strengths of all items in the list. Thus, items which have a greater LTS strength will be more likely to be found on any one search. The probability that the information in LTS will produce a correct recall, once that information has been found in a search, is assumed to be an exponential function of the strength for that item.

There are just three parameters for this model: r, the buffer size; θ, the parameter determining the rate per second at which information on a given item is transferred to LTS while the item resides in the rehearsal buffer; and R the number of searches made.[26] The probability of a correct response from the buffer is zero for the results in Table I because the contents of the buffer have been emptied experimentally by intervening arithmetic, or because the recency data (which represents recovery from the buffer) has been omitted. The parameters giving the best fit to the data were as follows: $r = 4$, $\theta = .04$, and $R = 34$. The predictions also are presented in Table I. The predictions are rather remarkable considering that just three parameters have been used to predict the results from

[26] It is important to remember that θ for this model is defined as the *rate per second* of information transfer, and thus the time measures listed in Table I need to be taken into account when applying the model. For example, an item that resides in the buffer for three item presentations will have 3θ amount of information in LTS if the presentation rate is one item per second, and 7.5θ if the presentation rate is 2.5 seconds per item.

four different experiments employing different list lengths and different presentation rates. Some of the points are not predicted exactly but this is largely due to the fact that the data tends to be somewhat erratic; the predictions of the asymptotic values (where a larger amount of data is averaged) are especially accurate.

2. *Some Alternative Models*

A number of decisions were made in formulating the free-recall model that need to be examined in greater detail. First consider the effect of an arithmetic task upon items undergoing rehearsal. If the arithmetic caused all rehearsal and long-term storage operations to cease immediately, then the probability of recalling the last item presented should decrease toward chance (since its LTS strength will be negligible, having had no opportunity to accumulate). The serial position curve, however, remains level and does not drop toward the end of the list. One possible explanation is that all transfer to LTS takes place when the item first enters the buffer, rather than over the period the item remains in the buffer; in this case the onset of arithmetic would not affect the formation of traces in LTS. While this assumption could handle the phenomenon under discussion, we prefer to consider the LTS trace as building up during the period the item remains in the buffer. Recall that this latter assumption is borne out by the accuracy of the earlier models and, in particular, the U-shaped functions presented in Fig. 12 for the multiple-reinforcement experiment. The explanation of the level serial position curve implied by our model is that the arithmetic operations remove items from the buffer in a manner similar to that of new entering items. Two sources give this assumption credibility. First, Postman and Phillips (1965) found that short periods of arithmetic (15 seconds) would leave some of the recency effect in the serial position curve, suggesting that some items remained in the buffer after brief periods of arithmetic. Second, the data of Waugh and Norman (1965) suggest that output operations during tasks such as arithmetic act upon the short-term store in the same manner as new incoming items.

Another choice point in formulating the model occurred with regard to the amount of LTS transfer for the first items in the list. The assumption used in an earlier model let the amount of transfer depend upon the number of other items concurrently undergoing rehearsal, as if the attention allotted to any given item determines the amount of transfer. An alternative possibility is that the amount of transfer is determined solely by the length of stay in the buffer and is therefore independent of the number of items currently in the buffer. Another assumption resulting in this same independence effect is that the subject allots to items in the buffer only enough attention to keep them "alive"; when the number of items in the buffer is small, the subject presumably uses his spare time for other matters. A free-verbal-recall experiment by Murdock (1965) seems to support a variant of this latter assumption. He had subjects perform a rather easy card-sorting task during the presentation of the list. The serial position curve seemed unaffected except for a slight drop in the primacy effect. This would be understandable if the card-sorting task was easy enough that the buffer was unaffected, but distracting enough that extra attention normally allotted to the first few items in the list (before the buffer is filled) is instead allotted to the card-sorting task. In any case, it is not clear whether the transfer rate should or should not be tied to the number of items concurrently in the buffer. The model that we have proposed for free-recall (henceforth referred to as Model I in this subsection) assumed a constant transfer process; a model using a variable transfer assumption will be considered in a moment.

The search process used in Model I is only one of many possibilities. Suppose, for example, that the strength value for an item represents the number of bits of information stored about that item (where the term "bits" is used in a nontechnical sense). A search might then be construed as a random choice of one bit from all those bits stored for all the items in the list. The bits of information stored for each item, however, are associated to some degree, so that the choice of one bit results in the uncovering of a proportion of the rest of the information stored for that item. If this proportion is small, then different searches finding bits associated with a particular item will result in essentially independent probabilities of retrieval. This independent retrieval assumption was used in the construction of Model I. On the other hand, finding one bit in a search might result in all the bits stored for that item becoming available at once; a reasonable assumption would be that this information is either sufficient to allow retrieval or not, and a particular item is retrieved the first time it is picked in a search or is never retrieved. This will be called the dependent retrieval assumption.

It is interesting to see how well the alternate assumptions regarding transfer and search discussed in the preceding paragraphs are able to fit the data. For this reason, the following four models are compared:[27]

Model I: Transfer to LTS is at a constant rate θ regardless of the number of other items concurrently in the buffer, and independent retrieval.

Model II: Transfer to LTS is at a variable rate θ/j where j is the number of other items currently in the buffer, and independent retrieval.

Model III: Constant LTS transfer rate, and dependent retrieval.

---

[27] These models and the related mathematics are developed in Atkinson and Shiffrin (1965).

Model IV: Variable LTS transfer rate, and dependent retrieval. Model I, of course, is the model already presented for free-verbal-recall. The four models were all fit to the free-verbal-recall data presented in Table I, and the best fits, in terms of the sums of the squared deviations, were as follows: Model I: .814; Model II: 2.000; Model III: .925; Model IV: 1.602 (the lowest sum meaning the best predictions). These results are of interest because they demonstrate once again the close inter-dependence of the search and transfer processes. Neither model employing a variable transfer assumption is a good predictor of the data and it seems clear that a model employing this assumption would require a retrieval process quite different from those already considered in order to fit the data reasonably well.

Perhaps the most interesting facet of Model I is its ability to predict performance as the presentation rate varies. A very simple assumption, that transfer to LTS is a linear function of time spent in the buffer, seems to work quite well. Waugh (1967) has reported a series of studies which casts some light on this assumption; in these studies items were repeated a variable number of times within a single free-recall list. The probability of recall was approximately a linear function of the number of repetitions; this effect is roughly consonant with an assumption of LTS transfer which is linear with time. It should be noted that the presentation rates in the experiments we analyzed to not vary too widely: from 1 to 2.5 second per item. The assumption that the subject will adopt a buffer strategy undoubtedly breaks down if a wide enough range in presentation rates is considered. In particular, it can be expected that the subject will make increasing use of coding strategies as the presentation rate decreases. M. Clark and G. Bower (personal communication) for example, have shown that subjects proceeding at their own pace (about 6–12 seconds a word) can learn a list of 10 words almost perfectly. This memorization is accomplished by having the subject make up and visualize a story including the words that are presented. It would be expected that very slow presentation rates in free-recall experiments would lead to coding strategies similar to the one above.

One last feature of the models in this section needs further examination. Contrary to our assumption, it is not true that successive lists can be kept completely isolated from each other at the time of test. The demonstration of this fact is the common finding of intrusion errors: items reported during recall which had been presented on a list previous to the one being tested. Occasionally an intrusion error is even reported which had not been reported correctly during the test of its own list. Over a session using many lists, it might be expected that the inter-ference from previous lists would stay at a more or less constant level after the presentation of the first few lists of the session. Nevertheless, the primacy and asymptotic levels of the free-recall serial position curves should drop somewhat over the first few lists. An effect of this sort is reported by Wing and Thomson (1965) who examined serial position curves for the first, second, and third presented lists of a session. This effect is undoubtedly similar to the one reported by Keppel and Underwood (1962); namely, that performance on the task used by Peterson and Peterson (1959) drops over the first few trials of a session. The effects in both of these experiments may be caused by the increasing difficulty of the search process during test.

C. Further Considerations Involving LTS

The models presented in the last section, while concerned with search and retrieval processes, were nevertheless based primarily upon the concept of a rehearsal buffer. This should not be taken as an indication that rehearsal processes are universally encountered in all memory experiments; to the contrary, a number of conditions must exist before they will be brought into play. It would be desirable at this point then to examine some of the factors that cause a subject to use a rehearsal buffer. In addition, we want to consider a number of points of theoretical interest that arise naturally from the framework developed here. These points include possible extensions of the search mechanisms, relationships between search and interference processes, the usefulness of mnemonics, the relationships between recognition and recall, and coding processes that the subject can use as alternatives to rehearsal schemes.

Consider first the possible forms of search mechanisms and the factors affecting them. Before beginning the discussion two components of the search process should be emphasized: the first component involves locating information about an item in LTS, called the "hit" probability; the second component is the retrieval of a correct response once information has been located. The factor determining the form of the search is the nature of the trace in long-term store. The models considered thus far have postulated two different types of traces. One is an all-or-none trace which allows perfect recall following a hit; the other is an unspecified trace which varies in strength. The strength notion has been used most often because it is amenable to a number of possible interpretations: the strength could represent the "force" with which a particular bond has been formed, the number of bits of information which have been stored, or the number of copies of an item placed in memory. It should be emphasized that these different possibilities imply search processes with different properties. For example, if the strength represents the force of a connection, then it might be assumed that there is an equal chance of hitting any particular item in a search, but the probability of giving a correct answer following a hit would depend upon the strength. On the other hand, the strength might represent the number of all-or-none copies stored in LTS for an item, each copy resulting in a correct response if hit. In this case, the probability of a hit would depend upon the strength (the number of copies) but any hit would automatically result in a correct answer. A possibility intermediate to these two extremes is that partial copies of information are stored for each item, any one partial copy allowing a correct response with an intermediate probability. In this case, the probability of a hit will depend on the number of partial copies, and the probability of a correct response following a hit will depend on the particular copy that has been found. A different version of this model would assume that all the partial copies for an item become available whenever any one copy is hit; in this version the probability of a correct answer after a hit would depend on the full array of copies stored for that item. In all the search processes where the retrieval probability following a hit is at an intermediate level, one must decide whether successive hits of that item will result in independent retrieval probabilities. It could be assumed, for example, that failure to uncover a correct response the first time an item is hit in the search would mean that the correct response could not be recovered on subsequent hits of that item.[28] This outline of some selected search processes indicates the variety of possibilities; a variety which makes it extremely difficult to isolate effects due to search processes from those attributable to interference mechanisms.

Other factors affecting the form of the search are at least partially controlled by the subject; a possible example concerns whether or not the searches are made with replacement. Questions of this sort are based upon the fact that all searches are made in a more or less ordered fashion; memory is much too large for a completely random search to be feasible. One ordering which is commonly used involves associations: each item recovered leads to an associate which in turn leads to another associate. The subject presumably exercises control over which associates are chosen at each stage of the search and also injects a new starting item whenever a particular sequence is not proving successful.[29] An alternative to the associate method is a search along some partially ordered dimension. Examples are easy to find; the subject could generate letters of the

[28] For a discussion of partial and multiple copy models, see Atkinson and Shiffrin (1965).

[29] Associative search schemes have been examined rather extensively using free-recall methods. Clustering has been examined by Deese (1959), Bousfield (1953), Cofer (1966), Tulving (1962), and others; the usual technique is to determine whether or not closely associated words tend to be reported together. The effect certainly exists, but a lack of parametric data makes it difficult to specify the actual search process involved.

alphabet, considering each in turn as a possible first letter of the desired response. A more general ordered search is one that is made along a temporal dimension; items may be time-tagged or otherwise temporally ordered, and the subject searches only among those items that fall within a particular time span. This hypothesis would explain the fact that performance does not markedly deteriorate even at the end of memory experiments employing many different lists, such as in the free-verbal-recall paradigm. In these cases, the subject is required to respond only with members of the most recent list; if performance is not to degenerate as successive lists are presented, the memory search must be restricted along the temporal dimension to those items recently stored in LTS. Yntema and Trask (1963) have demonstrated that temporal information is available over relatively long time periods (in the form of "time-tags" in their formulation) but the storage of such information is not well understood.

We now turn to a brief discussion of some issues related to interference effects. It is difficult to determine whether time alone can result in long-term interference. Nevertheless, to the extent that subjects engage in a search based upon the temporal order of items, interference due to the passage of time should be expected. Interference due to intervening material may take several forms. First, there may be a reduction in the value of certain information already in LTS as a result of the entry of new information; the loss in this case does not depend on making any previous information less accessible. An example would be if a subject first stores "the simulus beginning with D has response 3" and later when another stimulus beginning with D is presented, he stores "the stimulus beginning with D has response 1." The probability of a correct response will clearly drop following storage of the second trace even though access to both traces may occur at test. Alternatively, interference effects may involve destruction of particular information through interaction with succeeding input. This possibility is often examined experimentally using a paired-associate paradigm where the same stimulus is assigned different responses at different times. DaPolito (1966) has analyzed performance in such a situation. A stimulus was presented with two different responses at different times, and at test the subject was asked to recall both responses. The results indicated that the probability of recalling the first response, multiplied by the probability of recalling the second response, equals the joint probability that both responses will be given correctly. This result would be expected if there was no interaction of the two traces; it indicates that high strengths of one trace will not automatically result in low strengths on the other. The lack of an interaction in DaPolito's experiment may be due to the fact that subjects knew they would be tested on both responses. It is interesting to note that there are search mechanisms that can explain this independence effect and at the same time interference effects. For example, storage for the two items might be completely independent as suggested by DaPolito's data; however, in the typical recall task the subject may occasionally terminate his search for information about the second response prematurely as a result of finding information on the first response.

Within the context of interference and search processes, it is interesting to speculate about the efficacy of mnemonics and special coding techniques. It was reported, for example, that forming a visual image of the two words in a paired-associate item is a highly effective memory device; that is, one envisages a situation involving the two words. Such a mnemonic gains an immediate advantage through the use of two long-term systems, visual and auditory, rather than one. However, this cannot be the whole explanation. Another possibility is that the image performs the function of a mediator, thereby reducing the set of items to be searched; that is, the stimulus word when presented for test leads naturally to the image which in turn leads to the response. This explanation is probably not relevant in the case of the visual-image mnemonic for the following reason: the technique usually works best if the image is a very strange one. For example, "dog-concrete" could be imaged as a dog buried to the neck in concrete; when "dog" is tested, there is no previously well-learned association that would lead to this image. Another explanation involves the protection of the stored information over time; as opposed to the original word pairs, each image may be stored in LTS as a highly distinct entity. A last possibility is that the amount of information stored is greatly increased through the use of imagery—many more details exist in the image than in the word pair. Since the image is highly cohesive, the recovery of any information relevant to it would lead to the recovery of the whole image. These hypotheses are of course only speculations. At the present time the relation of the various search schemes and interference processes to mnemonic devices is not well understood. This state of affairs hopefully will change in the near future since more research is being directed toward these areas; mediation, in particular, has been receiving extensive consideration (e.g., Bugelski, 1962; Runquist & Farley, 1964).

Search processes seem at first glance to offer an easy means for the analysis of differences between recognition and recall. One could assume, for example, that in recall the search component which attempts to locate information on a given item in LTS is not part of the recognition process; that is, one might assume that in recognition the relevant information in LTS is always found and retrieval depends solely on matching the stored information against the item presented for test.

Our analysis of free-verbal recall depended in part upon the search component to explain the drop in performance as list length increased. Thus if the free recall task were modified so that recognition tests were used, the decrement in performance with list length might not occur. That this will not be the case is indicated by the position-to-color memory study (Experiment 8) in which the number of responses was small enough that the task was essentially one of recognition; despite this fact, the performance dropped as list length increased. One possible explanation would be that search is necessary even for recognition tasks; i.e., if the word "clown" is presented, all previous times that that word had been stored in LTS do not immediately spring to mind. To put this another way, one may be asked if a clown was a character in a particular book and it is necessary to search for the appropriate information, even though the question is one of recognition. On the other hand, we cannot rule out the possibility that part of the decrement in performance in free recall with the increase of list length may be due to search changes, and part to other interference mechanisms. Obviously a great deal of extra information is given to the subject in a recognition test, but the effect of this information upon search and interference mechanisms is not yet clear.

We now turn to a consideration of LTS as it is affected by short-term processes other than the rehearsal buffer. It has been pointed out that the extent and structure of rehearsal depends upon a large number of factors such as the immediacy of test and difficulty of long-term storage. When rehearsal schemes are not used in certain tasks, often it is because long-term coding operations are more efficacious. These coding processes are presumably found in most paired-associate learning paradigms; depending upon conditions, however, the subject will probably divide his attention between coding and rehearsal. Atkinson and Shiffrin (1965) have presented a paired-associate learning model based upon a rehearsal-buffer. Whether a rehearsal strategy would be adopted by the subject in a given paired-associate learning experiment needs to be determined in each case. The answer is probably no for the typical fixed-list learning experiment, because the items are usually amenable to coding, because the test procedure emphasizes the importance of LTS storage, and because short study-test intervals are so infrequent that mainten-ance of an item in STS is not a particularly effective device. If these con-ditions are changed, however, then a paired-associate model based upon a rehearsal buffer might prove applicable.

It is important to note the distinction between coding models and rehearsal models. Rehearsal models actually encompass, in a rough sense, virtually all short-term processes. Coding, for example, may be considered as a type of rehearsal involving a single item. The buffer process is a special type of rehearsal in which a fixed number of items are rehearsed for the primary purpose of maintaining them in STS. A pure coding process is one in which only a single item is considered at a time and in which the primary purpose is the generation of a strong LTS trace; almost incidentally, the item being coded will be maintained in STS through the duration of the coding period, but this is not a primary purpose of the process. These various processes, it should be emphasized, are under subject control and are brought into play as he sees fit; consequently there are many variations that the subject can employ under appropriate conditions. One could have a coding model, for example, in which more than one item is being coded at a time, or a combination model in which several items are maintained via rehearsal while one of the items is selected for special coding.

At the other extreme from the buffer strategy, it might be instructive to consider a coding process that acts upon one item at a time. Although such a process can be viewed as a buffer model with a buffer containing only one item, the emphasis will be upon LTS storage rather than upon the maintenance of the item in STS. The simplest case occurs when the presentation rate is fairly slow and the subject attempts to code each item as it is presented for study. However, the case that seems most likely for the typical paired-associate experiment, is that in which not every item is coded, or in which it takes several presentation periods to code a single item. The first case above could be conceptualized as follows: each item is given a coding attempt during its presentation interval, but the probability of finding a code is ξ. The second case is a bit more complex. One version would have a single item maintained in STS over trials until a code is found. It could be supposed that the probability of a code being found during a single presentation interval is ξ; having once coded an item, coding attempts are focused on the next presented item. This model has something in common with the buffer models in that some items will remain in STS over a period of several trials. This will produce a short-term decay effect as the interval between presentation and test is increased.

It is worth considering the form of the usual short-term effects that are found in a paired-associate learning. Figure 29 presents data from a paired-associate experiment by Bjork (1966). Graphed is the probability of a correct response for an item prior to its last error, as a function of the number of other items intervening between its study and subsequent test. The number of intervening items that must occur before this curve reaches the chance level can be taken as a measure of the extent of the short-term effect. It can be seen that the curve does not reach chance level until after about 20 items have been presented. If the coding model mentioned above were applied to this data, a short-term effect would be

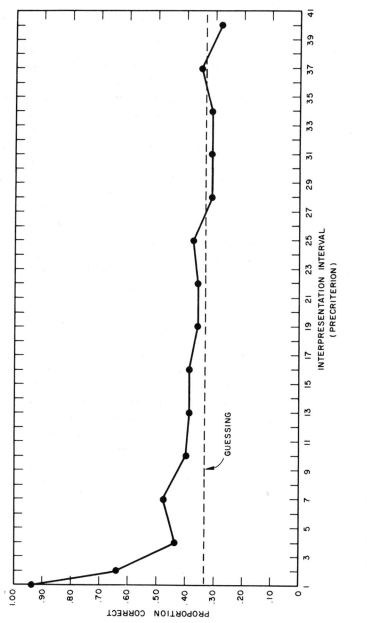

FIG. 29. Probability of a correct response prior to the last error as a function of lag. After Bjork (1966).

predicted due to the fact that some items are kept in STS for more than one trial for coding. It hardly seems likely, however, that any item will be kept in STS for 20 trials in an attempt to code it. Considerations of this sort have led a number of workers to consider other sources for the "short-term" effect. One possibility would be that the effect is based in LTS and is due to retroactive interference. A model in which this notion has been formalized was set forth by Restle (1964) and subsequently developed by Greeno (1967). For our purposes Greeno's presentation is more appropriate. He proposes that a particular code may be categorized as "good" or "bad." A good code is permanent and will not be interfered with by the other materials presented in the experiment. A bad code will be retrievable from LTS for a time, but will be subject to interference from succeeding items and will eventually be useless. Employing this model, the short-term effects displayed in Fig. 29 are due to those items that were assigned bad codes (i.e., codes that were effective for only a short period of time). The interesting feature of this model is its inclusion of a short-term memory effect based not upon features of STS, but upon processes in LTS.[30] One other useful way in which this LTS interference process has been viewed employs Estes' stimulus fluctuation theory (Estes, 1955a, 1955b). In this view, elements of information in LTS sometimes become unavailable; it differs from the above models in that an unavailable element may become available again at a later time. In this sense, fluctuation theory parallels a number of the processes that are expected from search considerations. In any case, the theory has been successfully applied in a variety of situations (Izawa, 1966). There is a great deal more that can be said about paired-associate learning and long-term processes in general, but it is beyond the scope of this paper to enter into these matters. We should like to reemphasize, however, the point that has just been made; namely, that short-term decay effects may arise from processes based in LTS as well as mechanisms in STS; considerable care must be taken in the analysis of each experimental situation in order to make a correct identification of the processes at play.

VI. Concluding Remarks

The first three sections of this paper outlined a fairly comprehensive theoretical framework for memory which emphasized the role of control processes—processes under the voluntary control of the subject such as

[30] It is this short-term effect that is probably captured by the intermediate state in various Markov models for paired-associate learning (Atkinson & Crothers, 1964; Bernbach, 1965; Bjork, 1966; Calfee & Atkinson, 1965; Kintsch, 1965, 1967; Young, 1966). Theorists using these models have been somewhat non-commital regarding the psychological rationale for this intermediate state, but the estimated transition probabilities to and from the state suggest to us that it represents effects taking place in LTS.

rehearsal, coding, and search strategies. It was argued that these control processes are such a pervasive and integral component of human memory that a theory which hopes to achieve any degree of generality must take them into account. Our theoretical system has proved productive of experimental idea. In Sections IV and V a particular realization of the general system involving a rehearsal buffer was applied to data from a variety of experiments. The theoretical predictions were, for the most part, quite accurate, proving satisfactory even when based upon previously estimated parameter values. It was possible to predict data over a range of experimental tasks and a wide variety of independent variables such as stimulus-set size, number of reinforcements, rehearsal procedures, list length, and presentation rate. Perhaps even more impressive are the number of predictions generated by the theory which ran counter to our initial intuitions but were subsequently verified.

It should be emphasized that the specific experimental models we have considered do not represent a general theory of the memory system but rather a subclass of possible models that can be generated by the framework proposed in the first half of the paper. Paired-associate learning, for example, might best be described by models emphasizing control processes other than rehearsal. These models could be formulated in directions suggested by stimulus sampling theory (Estes, 1955a, 1955b, 1968), models stressing cue selection and coding (Greeno, 1967; Restle, 1964), or queuing models (Bower, 1967b).

Finally, it should be noted that most of the ideas in this paper date back many years to an array of investigators: Broadbent (1957, 1958) and Estes (1955a, 1968) in particular have influenced the development of our models. The major contribution of this paper probably lies in the organization of results and the analysis of data; in fact, theoretical research could not have been carried out in the manner reported here as little as 12 years ago. Although conceptually the theory is not very difficult to understand, many of our analyses would have proved too complex to investigate without the use of modern, high-speed computers.

REFERENCES

Atkinson, R. C., Brelsford, J. W., Jr., & Shiffrin, R. M. Multi-process models for memory with applications to a continuous presentation task. *Journal of Mathematical Psychology*, 1967, **4**, 277–300.

Atkinson, R. C., & Crothers, E. J. A comparison of paired-associate learning models having different acquisition and retention axioms. *Journal of Mathematical Psychology*, 1964, **1**, 285–315.

Atkinson, R. C., & Shiffrin, R. M. Mathematical models for memory and learning. Technical Report No. 79, Institute for Mathematical Studies in the Social Sciences, Stanford University, 1965. (To be published in D. P. Kimble (Ed.), *Proceedings of the third conference on learning, remembering and forgetting.* New York: New York Academy of Sciences.)

Averbach, E., & Coriell, A. S. Short-term memory in vision. *Bell System Technical Journal*, 1961, **40**, 309–328.

Averbach, E., & Sperling, G. Short-term storage of information in vision. In C. Cherry (Ed.), *Information theory*. London and Washington, D.C.: Butterworth, 1961. Pp. 196–211.

Barbizet, J. Defect of memorizing of hippocampal-mammillary origin: A review. *Journal of Neurology, Neurosurgery, and Psychiatry*, 1963, **26**, 127–135.

Battig, W. F. Evidence for coding processes in "rote" paired-associate learning. *Journal of Verbal Learning and Verbal Behavior*, 1966, **5**, 171–181.

Bernbach, H. A. A forgetting model for paired-associate learning. *Journal of Mathematical Psychology*, 1965, **2**, 128–144.

Bernbach, H. A. Decision processes in memory. *Psychological Review*, 1967, **74**, 462–480.

Binford, J. R., & Gettys, C. Nonstationarity in paired-associate learning as indicated by a second guess procedure. *Journal of Mathematical Psychology*, 1965, **2**, 190–195.

Bjork, R. A. Learning and short-term retention of paired-associates in relation to specific sequences of interpresentation intervals. Technical Report No. 106, Institute for Mathematical Studies in the Social Sciences, Stanford University, 1966.

Bousfield, W. A. The occurrence of clustering in the recall of randomly arranged associates. *Journal of General Psychology*, 1953, **49**, 229–240.

Bower, G. H. Application of a model to paired-associate learning. *Psychometrika*, 1961, **26**, 255–280.

Bower, G. H. A multicomponent theory of the memory trace. In K. W. Spence and J. T. Spence (Eds.), *The psychology of learning and motivation: Advances in research and theory*, Vol. I. New York: Academic Press, 1967. Pp. 229–325. (a)

Bower, G. H. A descriptive theory of memory. In D. P. Kimble (Ed.), *Proceedings of the second conference on learning, remembering and forgetting*. New York: New York Academy of Sciences, 1967. Pp. 112–185. (b)

Brelsford, J. W., Jr., Shiffrin, R. M., & Atkinson, R. C. Multiple reinforcement effects in short-term memory. *British Journal of Mathematical and Statistical Psychology*, 1968, in press.

Brelsford, J. W., Jr., & Atkinson, R. C. Short-term memory as a function of rehearsal procedures. *Journal of Verbal Learning and Verbal Behavior*, 1968, in press.

Brelsford, J. W., Jr., Keller, L., Shiffrin, R. M., & Atkinson, R. C. Short-term recall of paired-associates as a function of the number of interpolated pairs. *Psychonomic Science*, 1966, **4**, 73–74.

Broadbent, D. E. The role of auditory localization in attention and memory span. *Journal of Experimental Psychology*, 1954, **47**, 191–196.

Broadbent, D. E. Successive responses to simultaneous stimuli. *Quarterly Journal of Experimental Psychology*, 1956, **8**, 145–152.

Broadbent, D. E. A mechanical model for human attention and immediate memory. *Psychological Review*, 1957, **64**, 205–215.

Broadbent, D. E. *Perception and communication*. Oxford: Pergamon Press, 1958.

Broadbent, D. E. Flow of information within the organism. *Journal of Verbal Learning and Verbal Behavior*, 1963, **4**, 34–39.

Brown, J. Some tests of decay theory of immediate memory. *Quarterly Journal of Experimental Psychology*, 1958, **10**, 12–21.

Brown, R., & McNeill, D. The "tip of the tongue" phenomenon. *Journal of Verbal Learning and Verbal Behavior*, 1966, **5**, 325–337.

Bugelski, B. R. Presentation time, total time, and mediation in paired-associate learning. *Journal of Experimental Psychology*, 1962, **63**, 409–412.

Buschke, H. Retention in immediate memory estimated without retrieval. *Science*, 1963, **140**, 56–57.

Buschke, H., & Lim, H. Temporal and interactional effects in short-term storage. *Perception and Psychophysics*, 1967, **2**, 107–114.

Calfee, R. C., & Atkinson, R. C. Paired-associate models and the effects of list length. *Journal of Mathematical Psychology*, 1965, **2**, 254–265.

Cofer, C. N. Some evidence for coding processes derived from clustering in free recall. *Journal of Verbal Learning and Verbal Behavior*, 1966, **5**, 188–192.

Cohen, B.·H. Recall of categorized word lists. *Journal of Experimental Psychology*, 1963, **66**, 227–234.

Cohen, R. L., & Johansson, B. S. The activity trace in immediate memory; a reevaluation. *Journal of Verbal Learning and Verbal Behavior*, 1967, **6**, 139–143.

Conrad, R. Acoustic confusions in immediate memory. *British Journal of Psychology*, 1964, **55**, 1, 75–84.

Conrad, R., & Hille, B. A. The decay theory of immediate memory and paced recall. *Canadian Journal of Psychology*, 1958, **12**, 1–6.

DaPolito, F. J. Proactive effects with independent retrieval of competing responses. Unpublished doctoral dissertation, Indiana University, 1966.

Deese, J. Influence of inter-item associative strength upon immediate free recall. *Psychological Reports*, 1959, **5**, 305–312.

Deese, J., & Kaufman, R. A. Serial effects in recall of unorganized and sequentially organized verbal material. *Journal of Experimental Psychology*, 1957, **54**, 180–187.

Estes, W. K. Statistical theory of distributional phenomena in learning. *Psychological Review*, 1955, **62**, 369–377. (a)

Estes, W. K. Statistical theory of spontaneous recovery and regression. *Psychological Review*, 1955, **62**, 145–154. (b)

Estes, W. K. A technique for assessing variability of perceptual span. *Proceedings of the National Academy of Sciences of the U.S.*, 1965, **4**, 403–407.

Estes, W. K. Reinforcement in human learning. In J. Tapp (Ed.), *Current problems in reinforcement*. New York: Academic Press, 1968, in press.

Estes, W. K., & Taylor, H. A. A detection method and probabilistic models for assessing information processing from brief visual displays. *Proceedings of the National Academy of Sciences of the U.S.*, 1964, **52**, No. 2, 446–454.

Estes, W. K., & Taylor, H. A. Visual detection in relation to display size and redundancy of critical elements. *Perception and Psychophysics*, 1966, **1**, 9–16.

Estes, W. K., & Wessel, D. L. Reaction time in relation to display size and correctness of response in forced-choice visual signal detection. *Perception and Psychophysics*, 1966, **1**, 369–373.

Freedman, J. L., & Landauer, T. K. Retrieval of long-term memory: "Tip-of-the-tongue" phenomenon. *Psychonomic Science*, 1966, **4**, 309–310.

Greeno, J. G. Paired-associate learning with short-term retention: Mathematical analysis and data regarding identification of parameters. *Journal of Mathematical Psychology*, 1967, **4**, 430–472.

Harley, W. F., Jr. The effect of monetary incentive in paired-associate learning using a differential method. *Psychonomic Science*, 1965, **2**, 377–378. (a)

Harley, W. F., Jr. The effect of monetary incentive in paired-associate learning using an absolute method. *Psychonomic Science*, 1965, **3**, 141–142. (b)

Hart, J. T., Jr. Recall, recognition, and the memory-monitoring process. Unpublished doctoral dissertation, Stanford University, 1965.

Hebb, D. O. Distinctive features of learning in the higher animal. In J. F. Delafresnaye (Ed.), *Brain mechanisms and learning.* London and New York: Oxford University Press, 1961. Pp. 37–46.

Hellyer, S. Supplementary report: Frequency of stimulus presentation and short-term decrement in recall. *Journal of Experimental Psychology,* 1962, **64**, 650–651.

Hintzman, D. L. Classification and aural coding in short-term memory. *Psychonomic Science,* 1965, **3**, 161–162.

Hintzman, D. L. Articulatory coding in short-term memory. *Journal of Verbal Learning and Verbal Behavior,* 1967, **6**, 312–316.

Izawa, C. Reinforcement-test sequences in paired-associate learning. *Psychological Reports,* Monograph Supplement, 3-V18, 1966, 879–919.

Katz, L. A technique for the study of steady-state short-term memory. *Psychonomic Science,* 1966, **4**, 361–362.

Keppel, G., & Underwood, B. J. Proactive inhibition in short-term retention of single items. *Journal of Verbal Learning and Verbal Behavior,* 1962, **1**, 153–161.

Kintsch, W. Habituation of the GSR component of the orienting reflex during paired-associate learning before and after learning has taken place. *Journal of Mathematical Psychology,* 1965, **2**, 330–341.

Kintsch, W. Memory and decision aspects of recognition learning. *Psychological Review,* 1967, **74**, 496–504.

Lambert, W. E., & Jakobovitz, L. A. Verbal satiation and changes in the intensity of meaning. *Journal of Experimental Psychology,* 1960, **60**, 376–383.

Landauer, T. K. Rate of implicit speech. *Perceptual and Motor Skills,* 1962, **15**, 646–647.

Madsen, M. E., & Drucker, J. M. Immediate memory by missing scan and modified digit span. *Psychonomic Science,* 1966, **6**, 283–284.

Melton, A. W. Implications of short-term memory for a general theory of memory. *Journal of Verbal Learning and Verbal Behavior,* 1963, **2**, 1–21.

Miller, G. A. The magical number seven, plus or minus two: Some limits on our capacity for processing information. *Psychological Review,* 1956, **63**, 81–97.

Milner, B. The memory defect in bilateral hippocampal lesions. *Psychiatric Research Reports,* 1959, **11**, 43–58.

Milner, B. Neuropsychological evidence for differing memory processes. Abstract for the symposium on short-term and long-term memory. *Proceedings of the 18th international congress of psychology, Moscow,* 1966. Amsterdam: North-Holland Publ., 1968, in press.

Milner, B. Amnesia following operation on the temporal lobes. In O. L. Zangwill and C. W. M. Whitty (Eds.), *Amnesia.* London and Washington, D.C.: Butterworth, 1967. Pp. 109–133.

Montague, W. E., Adams, J. A., & Kiess, H. O. Forgetting and natural language mediation. *Journal of Experimental Psychology,* 1966, **72**, 829–833.

Murdock, B. B., Jr. The serial position effect of free recall. *Journal of Experimental Psychology,* 1962, **64**, 482–488.

Murdock, B. B., Jr. Effects of a subsidiary task on short-term memory. *British Journal of Psychology,* 1965, **56**, 413–419.

Murdock, B. B., Jr. The criterion problem in short-term memory. *Journal of Experimental Psychology,* 1966, **72**, 317–324.

Peterson, L. R. Short-term verbal memory and learning. *Psychological Review,* 1966, **73**, 193–207. (a)

Peterson, L. R. Short-term memory. *Scientific American,* 1966, **215**, 90–95. (b)

Peterson, L. R., & Peterson, M. Short-term retention of individual verbal items. *Journal of Experimental Psychology,* 1959, **58**, 193–198.

Peterson, L. R., Wampler, R., Kirkpatrick, M., & Saltzman, D. Effect of spacing presentations on retention of a paired-associate over short intervals. *Journal of Experimental Psychology*, 1963, **66**, 206–209.

Phillips, J. L., Shiffrin, R. M., & Atkinson, R. C. The effects of list length on short-term memory. *Journal of Verbal Learning and Verbal Behavior*, 1967, **6**, 303–311.

Posner, M. I. Components of skilled performance. *Science*, 1966, **152**, 1712–1718.

Postman, L. The present status of interference theory. In C. N. Cofer (Ed.), *Verbal learning and verbal behavior*. New York: McGraw-Hill, 1961. Pp. 152–179.

Postman, L. Does interference theory predict too much forgetting? *Journal of Verbal Learning and Verbal Behavior*, 1963, **2**, 40–48.

Postman, L. Short-term memory and incidental learning. In A. W. Melton (Ed.), *Categories of human learning*. New York: Academic Press, 1964. Pp. 145–201.

Postman, L., & Phillips, L. W. Short-term temporal changes in free recall. *Quarterly Journal of Experimental Psychology*, 1965, **17**, 132–138.

Restle, F. Sources of difficulty in learning paired associates. In R. C. Atkinson (Ed.), *Studies in mathematical psychology*. Stanford, Calif.: Stanford University Press, 1964. Pp. 116–172.

Runquist, W. N., & Farley, F. H. The use of mediators in the learning of verbal paired associates. *Journal of Verbal Learning and Verbal Behavior*, 1964, **3**, 280–285.

Sperling, G. The information available in brief visual presentations. *Psychology Monographs*, 1960, **74** (Whole No. 498).

Sperling, G. A model for visual memory tasks. *Human Factors*, 1963, **5**, 19–31.

Sperling, G. Successive approximations to a model for short-term memory. *Acta Psychologica*, 1967, **27**, 285–292.

Sternberg, S. High speed scanning in human memory. *Science*, 1966, **153**, 652–654.

Tulving, E. Subjective organization in free recall of "unrelated" words. *Psychological Review*, 1962, **69**, 344–354.

Underwood, B. J., & Ekstrund, B. R. Studies of distributed practice: XXIV. Differentiation and proactive inhibition. *Journal of Experimental Psychology*, 1967, **74**, 574–580.

Waugh, N. C. Presentation time and free recall. *Journal of Experimental Psychology*, 1967, **73**, 39–44.

Waugh, N. C., & Norman, D. A. Primary memory. *Psychological Review*, 1965, **72**, 89–104.

Wickelgren, W. A. Size of rehearsal group and short-term memory. *Journal of Experimental Psychology*, 1965, **68**, 413–419.

Wickelgren, W. A., & Norman, D. A. Strength models and serial position in short-term recognition memory. *Journal of Mathematical Psychology*, 1966, **3**, 316–347.

Wing, J. F., & Thomson, B. P. Primacy-recency effects in free recall. *Proceedings of the 1965 annual convention of the American Psychological Association.* Pp. 57–58.

Yntema, D. B., & Mueser, G. E. Remembering the present state of a number of variables. *Journal of Experimental Psychology*, 1960, **60**, 18–22.

Yntema, D. B., & Mueser, G. E. Keeping track of variables that have few or many states. *Journal of Experimental Psychology*, 1962, **63**, 391–395.

Yntema, D. B., & Trask, F. P. Recall as a search process. *Journal of Verbal Learning and Verbal Behavior*, 1963, **2**, 65–74.

Young, J. L. Effects of intervals between reinforcements and test trials in paired-associate learning. Technical Report No. 101, Institute for Mathematical Studies in the Social Sciences, Stanford University, 1966.

2

COMMENTARY ON
"STORAGE MECHANISMS IN RECALL"

Murray Glanzer

DEPARTMENT OF PSYCHOLOGY, NEW YORK UNIVERSITY

The chapter "Storage Mechanisms in Recall" outlines a number of experimental findings that support a multiple-store model of memory. It focuses on free recall with extensions made to other recall tasks—probe recall, fixed order recall, distractor tasks. Since the publication of the chapter, the study of memory has grown considerably. New techniques have been introduced, such as the use of imposed encoding tasks; new approaches have been taken to key problems, such as the relationship between recognition and recall. In order to bring the chapter up to date I will briefly review some further work from our laboratory, related work by other investigators, and some criticisms of multiple-store models and proposed alternative models.

Further Work from Our Laboratory

EFFECT OF SEMANTIC AND PHONEMIC RELATIONS ON
LONG-TERM AND SHORT-TERM STORE

Work briefly referred to in the chapter was completed (Glanzer, Koppenaal, & Nelson, 1972). It showed that phonemically related words included in free recall lists have no effect on the amount held or retrieved from long-term store. Moreover, as with semantically related words (Glanzer, 1969), phonemically related words are recalled better when they are closer to each other in the list. This distance effect is interpreted as resulting from the conjoint processing of items that are in short-term store at the same time.

The experiments also showed that items in a delay task that are either phonemically or semantically similar to words in the free recall list again have no effect on short-term store but facilitate retrieval from long-term store. This finding establishes another operation that has a clear differential effect on short-term and long-term store.

DETAILS CONCERNING PROCESSING IN SHORT-TERM STORE

A series of studies by Schwartz (1973) further analyzed the role of short-term store in the processing of groups of semantically related words and their transfer to long-term store. She demonstrated that a sequence of semantically related words in a list increases both the storage and retrieval of related words that are presented later. The sequence also increases the retrieval of related words that are presented earlier. The effects were discussed in terms of encoding.

EFFECT OF GROUPING ON LONG-TERM AND SHORT-TERM STORE

Gianutsos (1972) established a strong effect of grouping on the amount recalled from short-term store. She also showed that there was no facilitative effect of grouping on the amount recalled from long-term store. Grouping is of interest in that it also has a differential effect on the long-term and short-term store. It is of particular interest in that there are only two other operations that increase the number of words normally in short-term store: auditory presentation and the incorporation of the words in grammatical sequences (this is discussed later).

The grouping effect may reflect a special function of short-term store, namely, to accumulate sequences of words for efficient encoding. When grouping is imposed on a list, the sequences formed show an initial unitization that results in an increase in recall. If this initial unit can be processed further as a unit, then the facilitation will carry over into long-term store. If, however, this initial unit cannot be processed further as a unit, then no effect will be seen in long-term store. To test this idea, another set of experiments was carried out (Glanzer, 1976). Subjects were presented with word lists containing semantically related word pairs, such as doctor—lawyer. These lists were read with intonation grouping. Some of the word pairs fell within an intonation group; some were split by the intonation, falling into adjacent groups. The results are in line with the idea outlined earlier. When the pair was within a single intonation grouping, recall from long-term store was facilitated; when it was split by the intonation grouping, recall was lowered.

THE UNITS IN SHORT-TERM STORE

A series of studies explored the question of the number and size of units in short-term store (Glanzer & Razel, 1974). We first established the number of words held in short-term store, for free recall, as slightly more than two. We then showed, in a succession of experiments, that this number of units does not change if the number of syllables or the number of morphemes in the words is changed. Moreover, if the list presented to the subject consists of familiar sentences, the number of sentences held in short-term store remains at two. When, however, novel sentences are presented, there is a drop of half a sentence in the mean number of sentences held.

The picture developed is that the short-term store is capable of holding relatively long, complex sequences. This view is further expanded to include a relation of the stages of memory to language processing. Specifically, the argument is that the short-term store serves to accumulate linguistic sequences that are converted into sentence or clause units. The findings of the sensitivity of short-term store to auditory presentation, to grouping, and to linguistic organization all accord with this view.

RELATION OF MULTIPLE STORES TO THE DEPTH OF PROCESSING PROPOSAL

During the past 5 years, there has been an increased concern with encoding processes and their effect on storage and retrieval. An influential paper by Craik and Lockhart (1972) that centered on encoding proposed an alternative to a multiple store. Memory is viewed as a continuous process of repeated coding and recoding of presented information. The successive codings give "deeper" processing that results in better recall and recognition. It is not clear, however, that this proposal is a real alternative to a multiple–store model. We carried out a study (Glanzer & Koppenaal, in press) in which we used both the operation that characterizes levels of processing study—the imposition of an encoding task such classification of words as they are presented—and the analysis that characterizes a multiple-store study—examination of the serial position curve. This combination gave us data that are equally well suited to the vocabulary of multiple-store models and the vocabulary of levels of processing. Except for this matter of vocabulary, the discussions, are, in fact, indistinguishable. Even some assertions that seem unique to the levels approach are not so.

For example, there is an assertion that repetition works only if it gives rise to a change in or "deepening" of encoding. This point is not particularly tied to a "continuous" or levels of processing approach (this is discussed later). If true, it could be made equally well in the context of a multiple-store model. In fact, a closely related point had been made early (Glanzer & Meinzer, 1967) in the course of demonstrating that at least one type of repetition results in a decrease of recall from long-term store.

Work by Other Investigators

This summary is, of course, not exhaustive. I have limited it severely to work that has a close relation to the chapter. The summary is also not detailed. Work from different memory tasks—free recall, distractor tasks—have been lumped together without the appropriate distinctions being made.

DIFFERENTIAL EFFECTS ON SHORT-TERM AND LONG-TERM STORE

There has been further study of variables that affect short-term and long-term store differentially. The variables include imageability of words (Richardson, 1974), spacing of practice or rehearsal (Pollatsek & Bettencourt, 1976), articulatory suppression (Richardson & Baddeley, 1975), and practice in free recall (Goodwin, 1976).[1] Gardiner and Klee (1976) have also shown that subjects remember better whether or not they have recalled a word when it is from the beginning rather than the end of the list.

CHARACTERISTICS OF SHORT-TERM STORE

Work has continued on the factors that determined loss of information from short-term store and the modality effect. Reitman (1971) and Shiffrin (1973) presented evidence that short-term store lost items solely by interference and not decay. Subsequent experiments have questioned those findings (Watkins, Watkins, Craik, & Mazuryk, 1973; Reitman, 1974) and have led to two-factor theories of loss from short-term store. Work on the modality effect centered on whether it could be explained as a result of supplementary information from a precategorical acoustic store. Investigators have rejected this explanation because the modality effect is not reduced by increasing word lengths (Watkins, 1972; Watkins & Watkins, 1973) or by introducing a suffix (Engle, 1974). Both operations should have an effect on a precategorical acoustic store component. The modality

---

[1] Goodwin does not make use of the distinction between long-term and short-term store.

effect continues to be under study (Watkins, Watkins, & Crowder, 1974; Elliot & Strawhorn, 1976).

TRANSFER FROM SHORT-TERM STORE TO LONG-TERM STORE

Multiple-store models have included a distinction between maintenance rehearsal and operations, such as coding, that are important in transferring information to long-term store[2] (see Atkinson & Shiffrin, pp. 26–34, Section III B). The distinction has been emphasized in studies of the negative recency effect in final free recall (Craik, 1970). Explanation of the effect as a result of fewer rehearsals of items from the end of the list has been dropped in favor of explanation of it as a result of type of processing. A series of studies has shown that, with standard free recall procedures, the subject switches from a concentration on transfer of items to long-term store to a concentration on maintenance rehearsal as he approaches the end of the list. This strategy is efficient for immediate free recall. The strategy can be altered by changing the initial recall task—by instruction (Mazuryk, 1974), by imposing delay tasks after the initial free recall list presentation (Craik & Watkins, 1973; Jacoby & Bartz, 1972), or by making the length of the list uncertain (Watkins & Watkins, 1974). With these changes in procedure, the negative recency effect is altered. Gardiner, Thompson, and Maskarinec (1974) have also cleared up another mystery concerning the recency effect. They show that it is possible to obtain a negative recency effect in the initial free recall with appropriately constructed delay tasks.

These results indicate that maintenance rehearsal is less efficient than other operations in transferring information to long-term store. They do not demonstrate that maintenance rehearsal or simple repetition has no effect. Nelson (in press), in an extensive critique of the depth of processing proposal, presents evidence that simple repetition does have an effect in transferring information to long-term store.

Two studies examined the role of spacing of related items in free recall lists. One was concerned with the spacing of repetitions (Foos & Smith, 1974). The other was concerned with the spacing between phonemically related words (Horton, 1976). The findings in both accord with assertions made in the chapter.

---

[2] Some of the recent literature makes it appear as if this distinction were new.

CHARACTERISTICS OF LONG-TERM STORE[3]

Some of the early multiple-store models assigned semantic information wholly to long-term store and acoustic or phonemic information wholly to short-term store. This position has been abandoned. An experimental demonstration of acoustic information storage is long-term store was made by Nelson and Rothbart (1972), using a classical savings method.

MULTIPLE-STORE MODEL IN RECOGNITION MEMORY[4]

The discussion here will be restricted to the Sternberg paradigm. Initial work with this paradigm centered on search and retrieval in short-term store. In the first full presentation of findings with the paradigm, however, Sternberg (1969) compared retrieval from long-term as opposed to short-term store (pp. 441–443). Further work on search and retrieval in long-term store has been carried out by Atkinson and Juola (1974). Work on the comparison of recognition in short-term and long-term store is presented by Mohs and Atkinson (1974). Sternberg (1975) gives a recent general summary of work in the area.

EFFECTS OF BRAIN DAMAGE ON MEMORY[5]

There are several classes of brain damage that isolate memory functions in a way that corresponds to the theoretical separation of short-term and long-term store. One of these is bilateral hippocampectomy, documented fully in a classic series of studies by Milner and her associates (Milner, 1970). The other is found in the Korsakoff syndrome, which involves damage to the mamillary bodies. Extensive work on this disorder has been carried out by Cermak and Butters and their associates (Cermak & Butters, 1973). In both classes of brain damage, the short-term store is unimpaired, but the transfer of new information to long-term store is blocked on a wide range of verbal and apisodic memory tasks. This inability to store new information is called anterograde amnesia. There is also some retrograde amnesia—inability to recall information registered in long-

---

[3] As noted earlier, this summary has been greatly restricted.

[4] As noted earlier, this summary has been greatly restricted.

[5] One critic of multiple-store models has recently dismissed the data on brain-damaged subjects because "extrapolations from pathological deficits to the structure of normal memory are of uncertain validity" (Postman, 1975, p. 308).

term store before the brain damage. The classic picture of retrograde amnesia was that it showed decreasing severity for earlier memories. This regularity has been questioned recently (Saunders & Warrington, 1971), and evidence has been presented that retrograde amnesia occurs equally for remote and recent events. These new data suggest the interesting possibility that there is a common function involved in both anterograde and retrograde amnesia; this function is the retrieval process. A survey of some of the recent empirical and theoretical work on amnesia has been summarized by Warrington and Weiskrantz (1973) and Baddeley (1975).

Criticism of Multiple-Store Models and Proposed Alternatives

Objections to multiple-store models range from the general to the specific. General objections reflect a preference for a single process system. I will not go into the argument about single versus multiple stores or processes here. The best, short statement on this issue is found in Atkinson and Shiffrin (1968, Section II B, pp. 14–21). I will note, however, that, when explicit theories have been presented as general single-store theories, they have always turned out to have two elements: two rehearsal processes, two decay processes. Their difference from multiple-store theories becomes difficult to determine.

The specific objections to multiple-store models concern specific assertions that can be altered within the framework of those models. Examples of such assertions concern the characteristics of rehearsal and transfer to long-term store and the characteristics of loss of items from short-term store. Both were discussed earlier. A recent summary of both general and specific objections is found in the review chapter by Postman (1975).

Among the alternative approaches to memory the most popular, recent approach has been the depth of processing idea which I discussed earlier. Two modified multiple-store models have also been proposed—a working-store model (Baddeley & Hitch, 1974) and a parallel model (Shallice & Warrington, 1970).

WORKING-STORE MODEL

Baddeley and Hitch analyze short-term store as discussed earlier into three components—a working memory, a phonemic rehearsal buffer, which is part of it, and a recency effect, which is independent of it. The analysis is based on their findings that there are variables, such as phonemic similarity, that affect reasoning and comprehension (assumed to tag the working memory) and that also affect immediate memory (assumed to tag the phonemic rehearsal buffer) but do not affect the end peak in free recall (recency). To complete the argument along the same lines, one should demonstrate that variables that do affect the recency peak also do not affect reasoning and comprehension. This has not been done. The proposal will also have to deal with the fact that grouping has a strong effect on both immediate recall and the end peak in free recall.

PARALLEL STORE MODEL

Data on a conduction aphasic patient have been interpreted as indicating an impaired short-term store and an unimpaired long-term store (Shallice & Warrington, 1970; Warrington & Shallice, 1969). This led to the proposal that one view the two stores as set in parallel rather than in series.[6] Further data are needed, however, to support the claim that short-term store is impaired and long-term store unimpaired. The patient can, for example, do successive matching of sequences of four words at a high level of efficiency (Warrington & Shallice, 1969, p. 889). This indicates a functioning short-term store. Only limited information, moreover, is available on his ability to learn, that is to get information into long-term store. A possible interpretation of the problem of the conduction aphasic is that it involves an inability to read information out of short-term store. A recent study of conduction aphasia by Strub and Gardner (1974) accords with this interpretation. Strub and Gardner (1974) also present a detailed critique of the parallel store proposal.

REFERENCES

Atkinson, R. C., & Juola, J. F. Search and decision processes in recognition memory. In D. H. Krantz, R. C. Atkinson, R. D. Luce, & P. Suppes (Eds.), *Contemporary developments in mathematical psychology.* Vol. 1. San Francisco: Freeman, 1974. Pp. 243–293.
Atkinson, R. C., & Shiffrin, R. M. Human memory: A proposed system and its control processes. In K. W. Spence & J. T. Spence (Eds.), *The psychology of learning and*

[6] This distinction is made between terms for simplicity of presentation here. Any fully detailed multiple-store model will not describe a simple arrangement in series. Short-term and long-term store must interact during the course of processing information.

motivation: Advances in research and theory. Vol. 2. New York: Academic Press, 1968. Pp. 89–195.

Baddeley, A. D. Theories of amnesia. In A. Kennedy & A. Wilkes (Eds.), *Studies in long-term memory.* New York: Wiley, 1975. Pp. 327–343.

Baddeley, A. D., & Hitch, G. Working memory. In G. H. Bower (Ed.), *The psychology of learning and motivation: Advances in research and theory.* Vol. 8. New York: Academic Press, 1974. Pp. 47–89.

Cermak, L. S., & Butters, N. Information processing deficits of alcoholic Korsakoff patients. *Quarterly Journal of Studies on Alcohol,* 1973, **34,** 1110–1132.

Craik, F. I. M. The fate of primary memory items in free recall. *Journal of Verbal Learning and Verbal Behavior,* 1970, **9,** 143–148.

Craik, F. I. M., & Lockhart, R. S. Levels of processing: A framework for memory research. *Journal of Verbal Learning and Verbal Behavior,* 1972, **11,** 671–684.

Craik, F. I. M., & Watkins, M. J. The role of rehearsal in short-term memory. *Journal of Verbal Learning and Verbal Behavior,* 1973, **12,** 599–607.

Elliott, L. A., & Strawhorn, R. J. Interference in short-term memory from vocalization: Aural versus visual modality differences. *Journal of Experimental Psychology: Human Learning and Memory,* 1976, **2,** 705–711.

Engle, R. W. The modality effect: Is precategorical acoustic storage responsible? *Journal of Experimental Psychology,* 1974, **102,** 824–829.

Foos, P. W., & Smith, K. H. Effects of spacing and spacing patterns in free recall. *Journal of Experimental Psychology,* 1974, **103,** 112–116.

Gardiner, J. M., Thompson, C. P., & Maskarinec, A. S. Negative recency in initial free recall. *Journal of Experimental Psychology,* 1974, **103,** 71–78.

Gardiner, J. M., & Klee, H. Memory for remembered events: An assessment of output monitoring in free recall. *Journal of Verbal Learning and Verbal Behavior,* 1976, **15,** 227–233.

Gianutsos, R. Free recall of grouped words. *Journal of Experimental Psychology,* 1972, **95,** 419–128.

Glanzer, M. Distance between related words in free recall: Trace of the STS. *Journal of Verbal Learning and Verbal Behavior,* 1969, **8,** 105–111.

Glanzer, M. Intonation grouping and related words in free recall. *Journal of Verbal Learning and Verbal Behavior,* 1976, **15,** 85–92.

Glanzer, M., & Koppenaal, L. The effect of encoding tasks on free recall: Stages and levels. *Journal of Verbal Learning and Verbal Behavior,* 1977, **16,** 21–28.

Glanzer, M., Koppenaal, L., & Nelson, R. Effects of relations between words in short-term storage and long-term storage. *Journal of Verbal Learning and Verbal Behavior,* 1972, **11,** 403–416.

Glanzer, M., & Razel, M. The size of the unit in short-term storage. *Journal of Verbal Learning and Verbal Behavior,* 1974, **13,** 114–131.

Goodwin, C. J. Changes in primacy and recency with practice in single-trial free recall. *Journal of Verbal Learning and Verbal Behavior,* 1976, **15,** 119–132.

Horton, K. D. Phonemic similarity, overt rehearsal and short-term store. *Journal of Experimental Psychology: Human Learning and Memory,* 1976, **2,** 244–251.

Jacoby, L. L., & Bartz, W. H. Rehearsal and transfer in LTM. *Journal of Verbal Learning and Verbal Behavior,* 1972, **11,** 561–565.

Mazuryk, G. F. Positive recency in final free recall. *Journal of Experimental Psychology,* 1974, **103,** 812–814.

Milner, B. Memory and the medial temporal regions of the brain. In K. B. Pribram & D. E. Broadbent (Eds.), *Biology of memory.* New York: Academic Press, 1970. Pp. 29–50.

Mohs, R. C., & Atkinson, R. C. Recognition time for words in short-term, long-term, or both memory stores. *Journal of Experimental Psychology,* 1974, **102,** 830–835.

Nelson, T. O. Repetition and depth of processing. *Journal of Verbal Learning and Verbal Behavior* (in press).

Nelson, T. O., & Rothbart, R. Acoustic savings for items forgotten from long-term memory. *Journal of Experimental Psychology,* 1972, **93,** 357–360.

Pollatsek, A., & Bettencourt, H. O. The space-practice effect in the distractor paradigm is related to proactive interference but not to short-term store. *Journal of Experimental Psychology: Human Learning and Memory,* 1976, **2,** 128–141.

Postman, L. Verbal learning and memory. *Annual Review of Psychology,* 1975, **26,** 291–335.

Reitman, J. S. Mechanisms of forgetting in short-term memory. *Cognitive Psychology,* 1971, **2,** 185–195.

Reitman, J. S. Without surreptitious rehearsal, information in short-term memory decays. *Journal of Verbal Learning and Verbal Behavior,* 1974, **13,** 365–377.

Richardson, J. T. E. Imagery and free recall. *Journal of Verbal Learning and Verbal Behavior,* 1974, **13,** 709–713.

Richardson, J. T. E., & Baddeley, A. D. The effect of articulatory suppression in free recall. *Journal of Verbal Learning and Verbal Behavior,* 1975, **14,** 623–629.

Sanders, H. I., & Warrington, E. K. Memory for remote events in amnesic patients. *Brain,* 1971, **94,** 661–668.

Schwartz, A. K. An analysis of the recall of sequences of related words. *Journal of Verbal Learning and Verbal Behavior,* 1973, 32–43.

Strub, R. L., & Gardner, H. The repetition defect in conduction aphasia: Mnestic or linguistic? *Brain and Language,* 1974, **1,** 241–256.

Watkins, M. J., Watkins, O. C., & Crowder, R. The modality effect in free and serial recall as a function of phonological similarity. *Journal of Verbal Learning and Verbal Behavior,* 1974, **13,** 430–447.

Reprinted from *The Psychology of Learning and Motivation*, 1972, 5, 129–193.

STORAGE MECHANISMS IN RECALL[1]

Murray Glanzer

NEW YORK UNIVERSITY, NEW YORK, NEW YORK

I. Introduction

Information on the recall of words has been organized according to several theoretical views. My own view, and that of a number of other workers, is that recall is a process involving two or more distinct storage mechanisms. This view has been developed recently

[1] This paper was written at The Hebrew University in Jerusalem during the author's holding of a Guggenheim Fellowship. Experimental work by the author was carried out under Contract No. DA 49 193 MD 2496 with the Office of The Surgeon General and RO1 HD 04213 with the National Institute of Child Health and Human Development. The author thanks Doris Aaronson and Micha Razel for their critical comments on an earlier draft of this paper.

in the work of several investigators (Atkinson & Shiffrin, 1968; Glanzer & Cunitz, 1966; Waugh & Norman, 1965). I will show here how this view of multiple storage mechanisms relates to available data, and what its implications are.

I will start by considering free recall of words and then show that the ideas used in the analysis of free recall can be used to understand recall in general. I will then turn to some of the detailed considerations of recall. Following this, more general characteristics of recall mechanisms will be considered. Through most of the paper I will keep the discussion fairly close to the data and fairly simple. The assumed processing of the items that are presented to Ss in a free recall task is shown in Fig. 1. Variant forms of this flow chart have

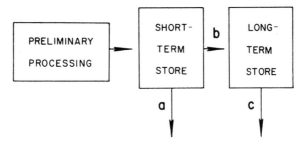

Fig. 1. Flow chart of the processing of items in free recall.

been presented by Atkinson and Shiffrin (1968), Murdock (1967), and Waugh and Norman (1965). An item is viewed here as first going through some preliminary processing at a "sensory" level. This involves some storage of information over very short periods of time (Sperling, 1960). I will not go into this part of the larger system here. The item, that is, information about the item,[2] then appears in short-term store (STS). It resides there for varying periods of time depending on the experimental conditions. Originally it was thought that items were lost from STS because of passage of time — a simple decay notion. It is fairly clear now that displacement by subsequent items is the important factor. Data on this point will be discussed subsequently.

When an item has entered STS it can either stay in or drop out of the system. The loss of the item is indicated by the arrow labeled "a." During its stay in STS a representation of some or all of the information about the item may be registered in long-term store

[2] For the sake of brevity I will write "the item" in all cases in which I mean "the information related to the item."

(LTS). This transfer of information to LTS is indicated by the arrow labeled "b" in the figure.

The arrows labeled a and b represent very different functions. Arrow a represents STS information being lost or becoming unavailable. Arrow b represents transmission of information but does not imply removal of that information from STS. The registration of information from STS in LTS is not viewed here as involving the removal or destruction of the item in STS. An item can be represented in both stores at the same time. Arrow "c" represents LTS information being lost or becoming inaccessible. This function will be discussed only briefly in this paper.

I have used above, as equivalent, the terms registration of information in LTS, transmission of information to LTS, and transfer of information to LTS. The process involved will not be examined in detail here. It is likely that it involves not only the storage of information but also the construction of a retrieval procedure. A factor that affects the recall of items from LTS may have its effect on the information that is stored or the retrieval procedure. I will only note here that the possibility for further analysis exists.

Access to information in STS is relatively direct. Access to information in LTS is relatively indirect. This is seen in the temporal characteristics of responses in recall. Items from STS appear early in the recall, in a burst. Items from LTS appear at a slower, steadier rate.

The STS is seen as very limited in its capacity. Most of the experiments reported here indicate that its capacity is from two to three items. The LTS is not limited in this way. Considered in its fullest sense, LTS can contain an unlimited number of items. It is, however, limited in how much it can accept within a given period of time. Each item that is transmitted to LTS requires some processing time. Therefore, if the amount of time is limited, a limited number of items will be registered in LTS.

There are a number of details that can be added to this picture. I will not go into these additions at length here but will indicate some of them briefly.

1. Various types of store may be distinguished in STS according to the sensory mode through which the items are presented. The role of sensory modality will be considered again later.

2. The LTS that is outlined in the figure is a very extensive system. I will consider only part of that system in analyzing recall situations. The role that it plays in different memory tasks,

moreover, varies considerably in ways that cannot be reflected in the figure. In the free recall situation, for example, the S ordinarily faces a number of items which he knows quite well. He is registering in LTS some additional information about these well-known items, namely, that they have just been presented and should be held ready for a recall task. This is probably not the same as what the S does in a paired associates task. It certainly is very different than his learning a new word. The complexity of the LTS and its probable subdivision or layering, although important, are, however, not of immediate interest here.

3. The relations between STS and LTS are a two-way affair. The items that the S deals with in the free recall experiment are usually words. Long-term information of some type has to be called on to carry out this processing. The nature of this interaction has, however, barely been touched on in the literature. The figure omits the arrows that this interaction would require.

4. There are a variety of activities carried out by the S either to maintain an item in STS or to facilitate its transfer to LTS. The term "rehearsal" has been used as a blanket term to refer to both of these possibly very distinct activities. A recursive arrow on the STS box of Fig. 1 would represent the maintenance function.

II. Interactions with the Serial Position Curve

In the case of free recall, the first reason for assuming such a flow and two separate storage mechanisms may be found in a very prominent and reliable characteristic of free recall — the serial position function. Examples of such curves are shown in Figs. 2 and 3 below.

In the free recall of lists, Ss are more likely to recall the early and late items than the middle items. There are, moreover, a variety of systematic experimental effects that can be worked on this curve. In most cases, the curve is raised or lowered in all positions except the last few. For example, if the rate of presentation is changed, the family of curves seen in Fig. 2 is obtained. There is an interaction between the experimental variable, rate, and serial position. An interaction effect of this type is produced by a number of variables: (1) rate of presentation (Glanzer & Cunitz, 1966; Murdock, 1962; Raymond, 1969); (2) word frequency (Raymond, 1969; Sumby, 1963) (see Fig. 3); (3) list length (Murdock, 1962; Postman &

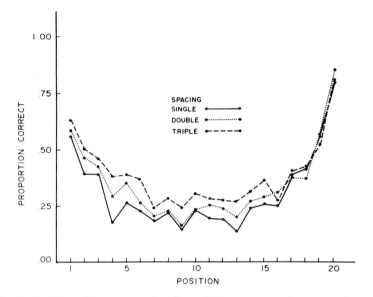

Fig. 2. Serial position curves for three different rates of presentation: single (three seconds); double (six seconds); triple (nine seconds). (After Glanzer & Cunitz, 1966, by permission of Academic Press, Inc., New York.)

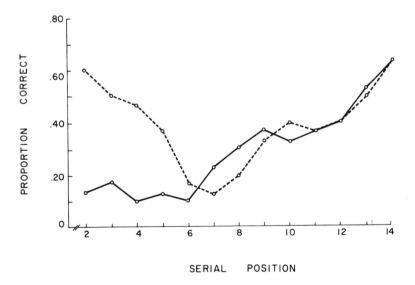

Fig. 3. Serial position curves for high-frequency words (broken line) and low-frequency words (solid line). (After Sumby, 1963, by permission of Academic Press, Inc., New York.)

129

Phillips, 1965) (see Fig. 4); (4) mnemonic or associative structure (Glanzer & Schwartz, 1971) (see Fig. 5).

The effects of lengthening the list are particularly striking. One effect is that the early parts of the list descend as the list increases in length. Another effect, first noted by Murdock, is that as the list becomes longer, and the beginning and end peaks are well separated, it is clear that the middle area of the serial position curve forms a flat, horizontal line.

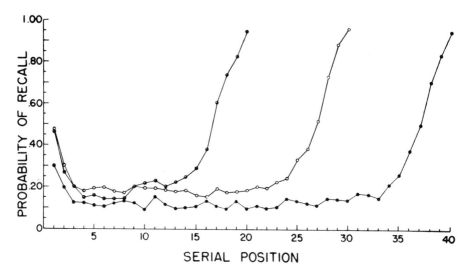

Fig. 4. Serial position curves for three different list lengths. (After Murdock, 1962, by permission of the American Psychological Association, Washington, D.C.)

These interaction effects, differential effects on the two ends of the curve, suggest that the serial position curve reflects output from two different mechanisms. Relating these mechanisms to the elements in Fig. 1, I will assume that all of the serial position curve except the last few positions reflect output primarily or wholly from LTS.[3] The evidence above and further evidence cited below show that the last few positions reflect output from both STS and LTS with the STS dominant.

[3] Craik (1970) has recently carried the separation of STS and LTS effects a step farther. He has demonstrated that the final list items are recalled best with immediate recall but are recalled most poorly when S recalls several preceding lists.

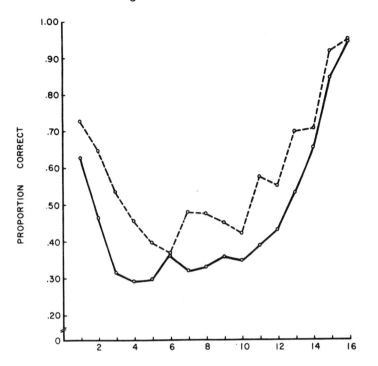

Fig. 5. Serial position curves for high- (broken line) and low- (solid line) mnemonic or associative structure. (After Glanzer & Schwartz, 1971, by permission of Academic Press, Inc., New York.)

I have made two identifications in the statements above. The first identification is that of the early part of the serial position curve with LTS. Assuming that there is a separate store, and assuming that STS is short-term, the identification seems reasonable. Early items in a list would not be expected to be held over in STS. The second identification is that of the experimental variables previously listed with factors affecting LTS. This identification has an interesting characteristic. A few words should be devoted to this.

The list of variables above contains very familiar names. They are the names of the classic variables that are effective in rote learning situations. But it is, of course, LTS that is addressed in a rote learning experiment. This leads to the following generalization. *Any variable that is effective in rote learning will affect all but the last few positions of the free recall serial position curve.* This statement is not completely satisfactory for two reasons. First, it is based on a crude method of separating LTS and STS effects. This method will, however, be replaced by a more refined method. Second, there is at

least one exception to the statement. I will touch on this exception
later in the discussion of grouping effects.

Although the identification of the early portion of the serial
position curve with output from the LTS could be argued on the
basis of the interactions above, a much stronger case is made if an
operation can be applied that would affect only the end peak of the
serial position curve. This is the section that I have assumed to be
overlaid by output from STS. There is such an operation, one that is
suggested by the literature on short-term memory (Brown, 1958;
Peterson & Peterson, 1959). It is delayed recall with some task
carried out during the delay. When such a delay is introduced, a
dramatic effect appears. In one experiment (Glanzer & Cunitz,
1966), the Ss were given free recall lists and after each list had to
wait 0, 10, or 30 seconds before being permitted to recall. During the
10- and 30-second delays they carried out a simple counting task.
The results are shown in Fig. 6. With a 30-second delay task the serial
position curve flattens out completely. All of the postulated STS
seems to be wiped out. The same effect was found by Postman and
Phillips (1965) using a very different theoretical approach.

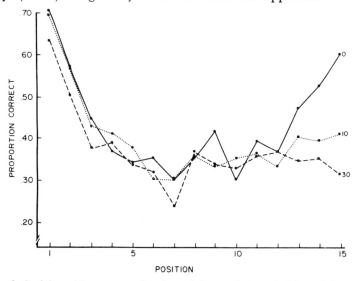

Fig. 6. Serial position curves for three delay periods — 0, 10, and 30 seconds.
(After Glanzer & Cunitz, 1966, by permission of Academic Press, Inc., New York.)

III. Estimation of STS

The use of a delay has been developed as the basis of a standard
technique for estimating the amount of output from STS and the

amount of output from LTS. I noted earlier that changes in the rate of presentation give curves that show an interaction of serial position with rate. Increased rate lowers all but the last few serial positions. Raymond gave lists with fast and slow presentation rates, one and three seconds between successive words, and replicated the findings displayed in Fig. 2. She also used the same presentation rates with a delay task following the lists. The serial position curves obtained are shown in the top panel of Fig. 7. It is clear then that rate continues

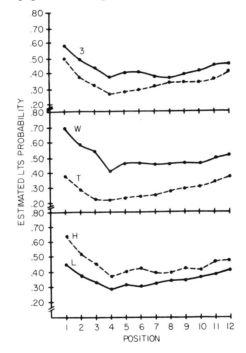

Fig. 7. Serial position curves for three pairs of conditions under delay. Top: fast (one second) *versus* slow (three seconds) presentation rate. Middle: words (W) *versus* trigrams (T). Bottom: high-frequency (H) *versus* low-frequency (L) items. (After Raymond, 1969, by permission of Academic Press, Inc., New York.)

to have its effect through the final list positions, although this steady-state effect is ordinarily concealed by output from STS under no-delay conditions (see Fig. 2).

The experiment by Raymond included two other variables both of which produced the same effect as rate under standard, no-delay conditions. These variables, words *versus* nonsense syllables, and high- *versus* low-frequency words, produce serial position curves that are separate across all but the last few positions. Again, the imposition of delay produces curves that are separate across all positions. These curves are shown in the remaining panels of Fig. 7.

The combined information from the delay and no-delay conditions can be used to get further information about the STS. This is done in the following way. Output from LTS is identified with the output obtained after a delay task. Thus; the delay curves in Fig. 7 are identified as output from LTS, and the probability that an item in list position i is recalled after delay, D, is equated with the probability that the item is in LTS.

$$P_i(\text{LTS}) = P_i(\text{D}) \tag{1}$$

The probability that an item is in STS cannot be estimated quite so directly. It is assumed that an item can be in either STS or LTS or both until the delay imposed by either subsequent list items or the postlist task removes it from STS.

This gives the following for recall in the no-delay (ND) condition:

$$P_i(\text{ND}) = P_i(\text{STS}) + P_i(\text{LTS}) - P_i(\text{STS} \cap \text{LTS}). \tag{2}$$

This equation may be made usable by assuming that the probability of an item being in STS is independent of its being in LTS or that

$$P_i(\text{STS} \cap \text{LTS}) = P_i(\text{STS}) \cdot P_i(\text{LTS}).$$

This gives the following equation for the estimation of the probability that an item is in STS.

$$P_i(\text{STS}) = \frac{P_i(\text{ND}) - P_i(\text{D})}{1 - P_i(\text{D})} \tag{3}$$

The basic form of this equation was first presented and applied by Waugh and Norman (1965) who use the central section of the serial position curve to estimate P_i (LTS). The use of information from both delay and no-delay conditions, as above, was introduced by Raymond (1969). Applying Eq. (3) to the curves in the three panels of Fig. 7, and to their corresponding no-delay curves, the three curves in Fig. 8 were derived by Raymond (1969), for the effect of presentation rate, of words *versus* nonsense syllables, and high-frequency *versus* low-frequency items.

Now that the effects of STS and LTS are separated, a very striking fact becomes clear. All three variables produce a strong effect across all serial positions in LTS (Fig. 7). All three variables produce no effect on STS (Fig. 8).

In this study and others cited below, the estimation of LTS and STS was carried out for each individual S, and the results were

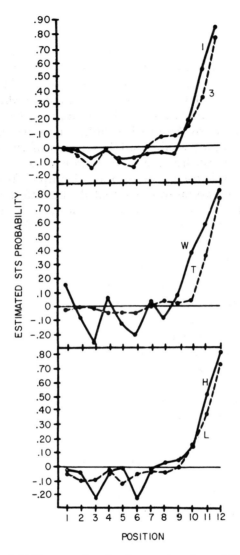

Fig. 8. Derived STS curves for the three pairs of conditions in Fig. 7. Top: fast (one second) *versus* slow (three seconds) presentation rate. Middle: words (W) *versus* trigrams (T). Bottom: high-frequency (H) *versus* low-frequency (L) items. (After Raymond, 1969, by permission of Academic Press, Inc., New York.)

averaged across Ss. The no-delay curves which show the interaction with serial position seen in Figs. 3 - 6 are not shown here. The reader can, however, construct a close approximation to the no-delay curves for each set of data by adding the corresponding p's in the paired curves according to Eq. (2) with $P_i(\text{STS} \cap \text{LTS})$ set equal to $P_i(\text{STS}) \cdot P_i(\text{LTS})$.

At this point, a large amount of information about both STS and LTS has been developed. I will review this information.

1. As successive list items are presented the probability of registering an item in LTS goes into a steady state which persists for the course of the presentation. The asymptote (see Fig. 4) that develops was noted by Murdock (1962). It shows up clearly as a horizontal function across the middle sections of the serial position curve when long recall lists are used. It shows up even more clearly when a delay task is used. The overlay of output from STS is then eliminated and the asymptote is revealed as continuing through the final list positions. This asymptote indicates that transfer of information from STS to LTS settles down to a fixed rate after the first few list items.

2. Increasing the length of the list lowers the LTS component of the serial position curve. The lowering can be seen very clearly in comparing Postman and Phillips' (1965) serial position curves for 10- and 30-word lists under delay. This indicates a retroactive effect of subsequent LTS registrations on earlier registrations. This effect is a very different one than that obtained in STS with a delay task. In the case of LTS, a large number of items produces a relatively small, evenly distributed effect across all list positions. In the case of a delay task acting on STS, a small number of items produces a large effect that is restricted to the last few list positions.

3. The effect of rate on LTS suggests that the transfer of information to LTS requires a certain amount of time. Restriction in time reduces the possibility of transfer. I will not distinguish here the transfer of item information from the setting up of retrieval routines.

4. The STS is unaffected by a wide variety of factors that affect LTS. This was particularly fortunate for the initial stages of work concerned with the separation of these two mechanisms. If there had been many cases in which the two had been similarly affected, the analysis would have been much more difficult to make.

IV. Details of the Storage Process

I will examine in detail some of the points touched on above. In particular, three questions will be considered.

1. How are items removed from STS?

2. What occurs during an item's stay in STS?

The STS functions as an input buffer, holding the items temporarily. While the item is in STS, it is available for further processing, e.g., recoding, computation, transmission of its information to LTS. There are several reasons why it is advantageous to have a temporary store in the system. One is that since processing of the items takes some time, it is useful to be able to hold them until the processing is completed. Second, if there is some inherent relation between successive items, sequences of items may be encoded more efficiently. Third, the operations required for a task may involve several items. It is useful, therefore, to accumulate sets of items. Work will be presented that shows that the STS plays an important role in the processing of sequences of items.

A. How Items Are Removed From STS

It seems most likely at the present time that STS is cleared by subsequent events. The nature of this clearing mechanism will be discussed now because decisions about it will simplify the further discussion of the functions of the STS.

In a series of studies the following factors were examined with respect to their role in the clearing of STS (Glanzer, Gianutsos, & Dubin, 1969): (1) information load or difficulty of subsequent activity, i.e., the delay task; (2) similarity of items involved in subsequent activity; (3) simple number of items processed during subsequent activity; (4) passage of time.

The second and third factors are used in retroactive inhibition (RI) explanations of forgetting. The third factor might be labeled displacement. The fourth factor is used in both trace decay and proactive inhibition explanations.

The first pair of experiments was on the role of information load or difficulty. In both experiments, Ss were given 12 common English words and then delayed in their recall for 1, 5, or 10 seconds. During the delay, the Ss were shown a number to which they added by 1's, 4's, or 7's. These three addition tasks are measurably different in their difficulty for Ss. Their use can, moreover, be rationalized as producing varying degrees of information reduction, along lines suggested by Posner and Rossman (1965). If items in STS are affected by amounts of subsequent information processed, then the elimination of items from STS should be fastest for the adding of 7's and slowest for the adding of 1's.

The experiment was performed twice, once with the Ss pacing their additions during the delay intervals, a second time with the Ss paced by a metronome through the delay interval at one addition per second. The results are virtually identical in the two experiments. They indicate that there is no overall effect of information load or difficulty of subsequent activity on the STS. The curves for the second experiment, with paced addition, are shown in Fig. 9. If the

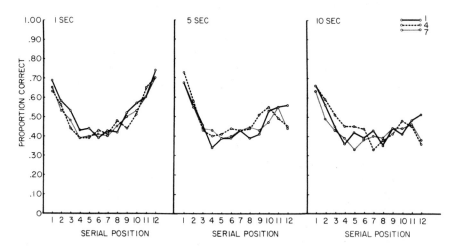

Fig. 9. Serial position curves for 1-, 5-, and 10-second delay at three levels of delay task difficulty — adding 1's, 4's, or 7's. (After Glanzer *et al.*, 1969, by permission of Academic Press, Inc., New York.)

information load had had an effect, then the curves for additions by 1, 4, and 7, should have fanned out at the end positions sometime between the 1- and the 10-second delay. There is little evidence of such an effect in either the figures or the statistical analysis. The results were surprising because Posner and Rossman (1965) have presented evidence that information load plays a major role in short-term memory. The relation of these findings to theirs will be considered below.

The second possible factor in the clearing of STS is similarity of the delay task to the list items. There are two forms of RI explanation that might be entertained. One is a strong RI explanation. It asserts that any postlist item that is similar to a list item has an adverse effect on that list item. Therefore, if a block of postlist items could be constructed with the items similar to the items in positions 1 - 4, the probability of recall of items 1 - 4 would be depressed. If delay task items similar to the items in positions 5 – 8 would be constructed, the probability of recall of those items would be lowered. The reason why the delay task ordinarily affects only the last few positions might be that delay task items are not ordinarily designed to be closely similar to any specific list items. They are, therefore, similar only to the items at the end of the list, on the basis of their temporal position.

A weak RI explanation restricts the RI effect to a limited set of items near the end of the recall list. According to this explanation, when the end of the list is reached, the probability of recall of early list items is already driven down by RI from later list items. The only items that have not already suffered the effects of RI are the end items. They are more likely, therefore, to show the effects of delay items. It would be expected, however, that similarity would have a differential effect on the end items.

To test both of these explanations, Ss were given 12-word lists of common English nouns followed by either a delay task or no delay. The delay task consisted simply of reading aloud four words. The four words were constructed by rearranging the consonants and vowels of either the first, second, or third series of four words in the list. Thus, for example, the following list – soil, life, news, pair, crowd, night, shape, snow, week, car, moon, hill – could be followed by either no delay or a 5-second delay period in which the S read one of the three following delay tetrads:

poise	crate	mere
safe	showed	cool
lure	snipe	win
kneel	now	hawk

The first delay set – poise, safe, lure, kneel – is obtained by reordering the phonemes of the first four list items – soil, life, news, pair. The second and third delay sets are obtained in the same way from the subsequent list items. The experiment was carried out twice – once with the Ss reading the delay list three times during the delay period, the other time with them reading it just once. The results of both experiments were the same. There was no differential effect of the composition of the delay list on either early or late positions. All three delay tasks, whatever their construction, cleared the items held in the STS in the same way (see Fig. 10).

It may be that some other form of similarity should be used to get an effect. The general type of similarity used here, sometimes called "formal similarity," has been used effectively in older work on rote learning with interpolated tasks (Melton & von Lackum, 1941). It

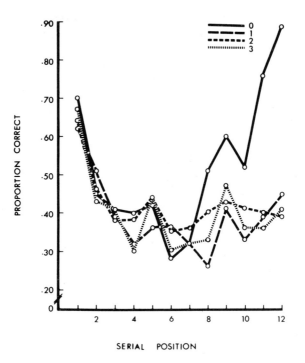

Fig. 10. Serial position curves for four delay conditions: 0, no delay; 1, delay task words similar to first four words; 2, delay task words similar to second four words; 3, delay task similar to third four words. (After Glanzer *et al.*, 1969, by permission of Academic Press, Inc., New York.)

has also been used effectively in more recent work on short-term memory (Wickelgren, 1965). This type of similarity is one that is based on the reordering of elements that make up either the list or units in the list. In the present case, the phonemes making up list words were reordered.

The effectiveness of a particular type of similarity is likely to be determined by the characteristics of the task involved. The free recall task is different from those in which formal similarity has been shown to play a role. It is possible, however, that other types of similarity might be shown to have an effect on STS. Some additional experiments have, however, been completed in which similarity manipulations were based on the distinctive features of phonemes. These experiments display marked similarity effects on LTS but none on STS (Glanzer, Koppenaal, & Nelson, in preparation).

At this point, neither information load nor similarity look

effective as factors in the clearing of STS. The two remaining factors are number of items and time.

There are two sources that indicate that time per se does not play an important role in the clearing of STS. Waugh and Norman (1965) have analyzed a free recall experiment by Murdock that indicates the same amount in STS after slow and fast list presentation. Raymond (1969) has shown by comparison of delay and no-delay conditions that the amount in STS is the same with variations in the rate of list presentation (see Fig. 8).

The effect of time was tested in a different way in the following experiment. Both the duration of the delay task and the number of items in it were varied. Each S was presented with 12-word lists. After each list there was either a 2-second or a 6-second delay. During the delay period, the S read either two or six words. This 2 by 2 factorial arrangement permits the separation of the effects of sheer passage of time and number of items. The results are shown in Fig. 11. The number of items has a clear effect. The length of the delay period has none.

This experiment does not eliminate another interpretation of decay effects. Items might be lost from STS by decay only during the time in which rehearsal is totally blocked, e.g., while the delay task words are being read. On this basis, both a decay and a displacement explanation lead to the same prediction here. It is possible to examine the loss of items from STS so as to separate this view of decay from displacement. The length of the words read during the delay task could be varied. Under this last interpretation of decay, six long words should produce a greater loss from STS than six short words. This experiment has not been carried out. A related experiment has, however, been carried out. Craik (1968) estimated the amount held in STS for lists consisting of short words and lists consisting of long words. He found that STS holds the same number of words whether the words are long or short. This would fit in with a simple displacement view. I will therefore hold to this view.

At this point, the following factors have been demonstrated to have an effect on LTS but not STS — word frequency, rate of presentation, and length of list. I will now turn to check another variable that has an effect on the serial position curve — associative or mnemonic structure. An early attempt had been made to show, by examining the interaction of associative structure with serial position, that the presence of associative relations in the list had no effect on STS (Glanzer & Meinzer, 1967). The attempt did not succeed primarily, I believe, because the structuring of the lists led Ss

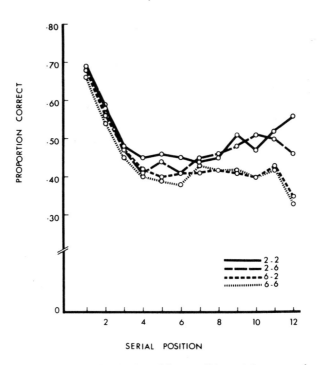

Fig. 11. Serial position curves for the four delay conditions: 2-2, two words read in two seconds; 2-6, two words read in six seconds; 6-2, six words read in two seconds; 6-6, six words read in six seconds. (After Glanzer *et al.*, 1969, by permission of Academic Press, Inc., New York.)

to adopt a special grouping strategy. The experiment has recently been repeated with the lists structured to prevent the development of special strategies (Glanzer & Schwartz, 1971). The amount held in STS was estimated by the technique of subtracting delay from no-delay data. In this experiment, Ss were given lists in which low-frequency associates were placed next to each other. These low-frequency associates have a strong effect on overall recall. They consist of word pairs that have an obvious semantic relation to each other, e.g., house–shack, mutton–veal, sleep–slumber, fruit–cherry. Low-frequency rather than high-frequency associates were used to make sure that the Ss could not develop a strategy of recalling what they could and then giving a very likely associate to each recalled word.

The associated pairs were scattered at random through the lists, occupying half the list positions. The mixed lists formed in this manner were followed either by a delay condition or no delay. The delay and no-delay curves are shown in Fig. 12. The derived STS curves are shown in Fig. 13. The results for the associated and unassociated items in the mixed lists have been separated and plotted separately.

It is clear that there is a large, consistent effect of mnemonic structure on the LTS component as seen in the delay curves of Fig. 12. There is, however, no effect on the STS component. Associated

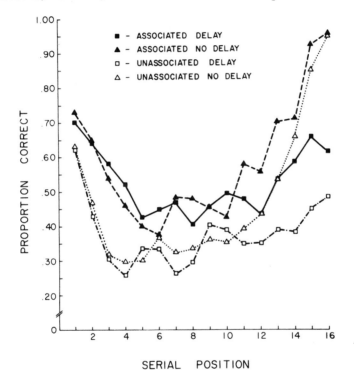

Fig. 12. Serial position curves for the delay, and no-delay conditions with associated and unassociated items. (After Glanzer & Schwartz, 1971, by permission of Academic Press, Inc., New York.)

items take up the same space in STS as do unassociated items. This is borne out by the statistical analysis of the data in Fig. 13.

There is one point that should be noted here. The LTS or delay condition curves in Fig. 12 show an end peak. End peaks also appear in other data on delay conditions, e.g., Fig. 7. They mean either that the delay task was not completely effective in clearing STS or that it was less effective than successive list items in preventing transfer of information to LTS before items were cleared from STS. The second alternative seems more likely on the basis of available evidence. It is possible, however, to make sure that the estimate of STS is not distorted whatever the cause of the rise at the end of the delay curve. Following Waugh and Norman's (1965) procedure, it is possible to use the middle section of the curve to estimate the amount in LTS. With this estimate in place of P_i (ND) in Eq. (3), an estimate of STS can be obtained for the last six serial positions. When this is done, a closely overlapping pair of STS curves is again obtained. The curves do not differ significantly.

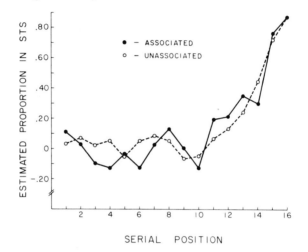
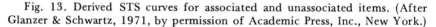

Fig. 13. Derived STS curves for associated and unassociated items. (After Glanzer & Schwartz, 1971, by permission of Academic Press, Inc., New York.)

The results of the studies summarized above can be taken to support a very simple displacement model of STS. All verbal items entering the system remove items from STS. The specific characteristics of the items play no role — their difficulty, length, and similarity to list items. No other factor seems to play a major role. Further work may demonstrate certain limited kinds of similarity effects, but they are not established at present.

Now that the roles of various factors on STS and LTS have been separated and evaluated, I can offer a generalization on STS to match the one given earlier for LTS.

STS is a very robust, insensitive mechanism that responds to nothing except the passage of items through it. There are at least two exceptions to this generalization. I will consider both of these later.

B. WHAT OCCURS IN STS

I will turn now to the actions carried out on items while they are in STS and examine the relations of STS to LTS. In general, the picture of STS is that of an input buffer that can hold a limited number of items. As new items enter, old ones are lost. One function of the STS is to allow time for whatever mnemonic work needs to be done to assure that an item's information is transmitted to LTS. The item, it will be assumed here, can be held in a relatively passive way. It can also have various actions carried out on it either to maintain it in STS or to move it to LTS. Crowder and Morton (1969) and Rundus and Atkinson (1970) have considered some of these activities.

The item can be rehearsed silently either as part of a string of items or by itself. It can be repeated aloud, thus placing it back at the initial input stage, and recycled through the system. It can be put through various types of mnemonic organization at various levels of complexity. The relative frequency and effectiveness of these activities depend on the material and the structure of the task. All three activities have been shown effective. The first two have an effect on maintaining items in STS. Anything that prolongs the stay of an item in STS increases the chance that that item will be transmitted to LTS. If the stay of one item is prolonged without thereby reducing the probability that other items stay in STS, then overall performance on the list will increase. Whether silent rehearsal or repetition aloud do anything beyond increasing the availability of an item in STS for transfer to LTS has not been established.

The setting up of mnemonic structures or the setting up of retrieval routines have an effect on the transfer, registration, and retrieval of items in LTS. The setting up of mnemonic structures may result in a reorganization that helps maintain items in STS. This is relatively unknown territory at this time.

I will now outline one study of free recall that sheds some light on the processing that occurs during an item's stay in STS. My discussion here will not reproduce the logic of the paper as set forth in the original, since a number of factors relevant to the interpretation of the results have come clear through later work.

The study concerned the effect of imposed rehearsal procedures on the S. An S will frequently repeat an item or a string of items during list presentations. The repetition may be silent or overt. The main effect of the repetition is presumably to keep the item in STS. The S, however, has two jobs to carry out. One is to maintain the item in STS, the other is to transfer information to LTS. If the S were pushed to devote all the time between successive items to the repetition of the list items, he might have less time to devote to the transfer of items to LTS. The last statement assumes that the S, in registering an item in LTS or in setting up its retrieval, does something other than mere repetition of the item.

The experiment (Glanzer & Meinzer, 1967) was simple in form. Fifteen-word lists were presented to Ss with approximately 3 seconds between words. During the 3-second interval a metronome clicked six times. For half the lists, the S repeated aloud the word just presented, six times in time with the clicks. For the other half of the lists he did not do this. It was expected that the repetitions would block the activities that permit items to enter LTS. It was also expected, however, that the repetitions would not disturb the items in STS since these would be maintained by such a rehearsal procedure.

The results shown in Fig. 14 are in line with these expectations. The repetition of the items results in a depression of recall at all positions except the last few. The interaction between the experimental variable and serial position effect is all that is directly

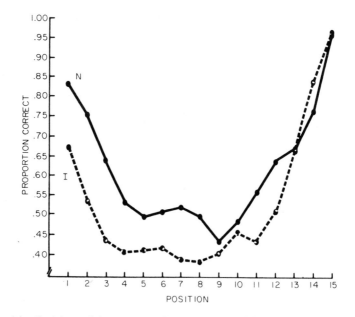

Fig. 14. Serial position curves for repetition (I) and no-repetition (N) condition. (After Glanzer & Meinzer, 1967, by permission of Academic Press, Inc., New York.)

available here. It is possible, however, to obtain an estimate of what is in STS using, as before, the middle items of the list to estimate the amount held in LTS in the final positions. This can be done since the LTS content remains fairly stable after the beginning peak. With this as the basis of estimating LTS, estimates of STS can be obtained. The curves derived on this basis, although rather irregular, show complete overlap. The total of the estimated points is almost the same: 2.26 words for the no-repetition condition, 2.31 for the repetition condition.[4]

There are two points that should be underlined here. One is that the forced repetition has an adverse effect here on overall performance. There are, of course, many situations in which some form of repetition has a positive effect. Indeed, repetition can have a positive, negative, or no effect at all on recall depending on its function in the system. I will try to point out later how repetition varies in its effect depending on how it is applied.

The second point that I will underline is that immediate repetition of individual words has no effect on the total number of different items in STS. This means that repetitions of a word while the word is in STS are not counted by the store as new items. If they were, then multiple repetition of one of the words, as done here, would wipe out all preceding words in STS. This characteristic of not counting repetitions might, on second thought, be a necessary characteristic of a store such as the one I have been describing. If each repetition had the effect of a new separate event, then rehearsal would have in general an adverse rather than beneficial effect. It would not only block transfer to LTS as in this experiment but also clear the STS before much work would be done on any other items.

This characteristic of the STS will appear again as I go over further aspects of the process of transmitting information from STS to LTS. Whether the ignoring of repetitions is a general characteristic of STS or due to a strategy adopted because of the nature of the free recall task cannot be decided now. Those two possibilities remain open.

Several characteristics of STS have been considered thus far. One is its method of entering new items and losing old. Another is its function as an operating register that permits prolonged work on any one item, and work on related sequences of items. The third is its tendency to treat repeated items as single items. The first two characteristics are important in the discussion of the next topic.

---

[4] These figures are obtained by summing the estimate of P_i (STS) over the last five serial positions.

V. Mnemonically Related Words

If two words are presented successively to the S and these words bear an associative or mnemonic relation to each other, the S may make use of this relation in registering the pair in LTS. I will assume that the STS is the operating register and that it is limited to about three items. The probability that a mnemonic relation can be used depends then on how closely the items follow each other in the sequence of inputs. If the items come one after the other then the probability that they will both be in STS together and available for mnemonic work will be very high.

The total amount of time that they will be in STS together can be obtained from the derived STS curve. As other items enter after the two related items, then the probability that both will remain in STS will decline steeply. If the related items do not enter in immediate succession but are separated by other items, then the probability that both will be in STS together is low from the start. That probability then undergoes further decline as other items enter. The larger the number of intervening items, the lower the initial probability.

It follows then that probability of recall of related items should be a declining function of the number of items between the related items. The asymptote of this function should be near three or four intervening items, since STS curves seem to drop to zero after four or five items (see Fig. 8). The following experiment (Glanzer, 1969) was set up to test this idea. Lists were constructed with mnemonically related, i.e., associated, pairs of words as list members. The distance, that is, the number of items that intervened between these pairs, was systematically varied so that there were either zero, one, three, or seven intervening items. Mnemonic relation was obtained here as indicated earlier by selecting low-frequency associates. The experiment was run at two presentation rates — one second per word and three seconds per word. The results are shown in Fig. 15. These are not serial position curves. They are plots of the overall means for the eight experimental conditions.

As expected, a probability of recall declined as the distance between related words increased. The slower presentation rate increases the time to transfer an item to LTS as an individual item or as a pair of related items. This raises the overall function for the slower rate. To explain the details of the two curves requires working out a much more exact and complex statement about the functions involved than will be attempted here. I will only note that the

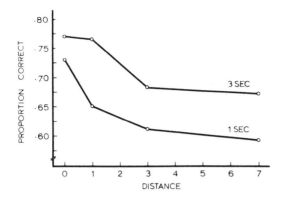

Fig. 15. Proportion of associated words recalled at one- and three-second presentation rates as a function of distance (the number of intervening words). (After Glanzer, 1969, by permission of Academic Press, Inc., New York.)

general shapes of the two curves are what might be expected from the form of the STS serial position curves seen in Figs. 8 and 13.

There have been several studies on the effect of blocking of semantically related words in free recall lists (Dallett, 1964; Puff, 1966; Weingartner, 1964). The results of these studies all show that when semantically related words are close together in a word list, the overall probability of recall increases. These findings would follow from the results and analyses presented above.

VI. Repeated Words

The general approach used above in the analysis of the processing of mnemonically related words can be used in the analysis of the processing of repeated words. In the case of related words, the subject had an advantage when members of the pair appeared together in STS. In the case of repeated words, however, the *S* suffers a disadvantage when the word and its repetitions appear together in STS.

I indicated earlier that repetitions are given a single representation in STS. The simplest way of phrasing what happens with repetition of an item is to say that it resets the probability that an item is in STS to its initial value. From that point on, the item's career in STS is the same as if it had not been entered previously. For the sake of clarification, I will assume here that an item's probability of being in STS upon presentation is 1.00. And again, as an example, I will assume that this probability is halved as each successive item is presented to the S. The function would then be

$$P_j(\text{STS}) = f(j) = (.50)^j$$

where j goes from zero to the total number of items, n, following the item. The area under this function is

$$\sum_{j=0}^{n} P(\text{STS}) = \sum_{j=0}^{n} (.50)^j \approx 2.$$

The total amount of time available for the transfer of the item to LTS is $t \approx 2d$, where d is the amount of time given to each item including the interitem interval. The probability that the first representation of the item is in STS declines to a very small value as j, the number of succeeding items, increases. If then the second representation enters after a large number of intervening items, the item receives the benefit of a full stay in STS of the first representation and a full stay of the second representation. The total time that the item is available for transfer to LTS is $t \approx 4d$. If, however, the second representation enters before the $P_i(\text{STS})$ of the first representation is near zero, a different condition results. The second representation replaces the first and sets the loss function back to its value when $j = 0$. From that point on, the same rate of loss obtains. For example, if the first representation is immediately followed by the second representation, then

$$\sum_{j=0}^{n} P(\text{STS}) = 1.00 + \sum_{j=0}^{n} (.50)^j \approx 3.$$

The first term on the left 1.00 or $(.50)^0$ is the contribution of the first representation. The second term is the contribution of the second representation. The total time available for transfer to LTS is $3d$ rather than $4d$, as above. There is then a disadvantage, not an advantage in having an item appear again in STS before its first representation has cleared STS. From this it follows that the S would get the least benefit out of a repetition if it occurred immediately after the first presentation. As the number of intervening items increases, the chances decrease that the second representation will appear in STS before the first clears STS. The chances therefore increase that the S will have double the period of time to transmit the item to LTS.

An experiment with repeated words was run to test these expectations about the effect of spacing of repetitions. Ss were given word lists at either a fast (one second) or slow (three second) rate.

Each list consisted of 16 words, including four repeated words. The number of words intervening between a word and its repetition was either zero, one, two, or five. It was expected that effect of repetition would be greater as the number of intervening items increased. The results of the experiment are shown in Fig. 16. They agree with the expectations.

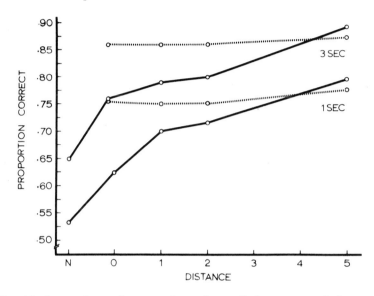

Fig. 16. Proportions of repeated words recalled at one- and three-second presentation rates as a function of distance (the number of intervening words). Also shown are the proportions for unrepeated words (N). The estimated proportions for two independent trials are on the broken lines. (After Glanzer, 1969, by permission of Academic Press, Inc., New York.)

In addition to the plots of recall of repeated items, estimated proportions for two independent transmissions to LTS are shown in the figure. These estimates indicate the probability that an S would transmit information based on the first representation or the second representation or both when the two have appeared at different times in STS. The estimates are based on the proportions of correct unrepeated items in corresponding list positions. These items yield two proportions which are combined according to the equation

$$\text{Estimated } p = p_1 + p_2 - p_1 p_2.$$

It can be seen that the proportion correct of repeated items increases as the number of intervening items increases. The proportions rise to the theoretical asymptotes indicated by the dotted lines. All differences between the observed and corresponding theoretical points are statistically significant except those at distance 5. The fact, however, that both sets of data — those for the fast rate and those for the slow rate — overshoot the theoretical values, may indicate that additional factors are important in the registration of items in LTS. This indication is also found in data of Melton's (1967).

Before turning to other related data, I will draw one implication from what I have summarized above. This implication is analogous to the one drawn concerning the effect of associative relations and tested in the experiment by Glanzer and Schwartz above. It is that the positive effects of repetition are found solely in LTS. To test this it is necessary to carry out an experiment in which repeated items are presented at various list positions. Delay and no-delay conditions would be applied to separate effects on STS from those on LTS. I expect that the positive effect of repetition should be solely in LTS.

The data on spacing of repetitions reported above agree in the main with expectations based on characteristics of STS. There are, however, in the literature three other sets of free recall data, each of which gives a different picture of the effects of spacing of repetitions. Melton (1967) found results similar to those outlined above: increasing distance increases the effect of repetition. The study has been replicated by Madigan (1969). One aspect of the Melton and Madigan data does not fit the picture I have set up. They obtain a continued effect of spacing at distances of 20 and 40 intervening items. The factors that I have considered will cover changes only over much shorter distances. These long-range effects, if supported by further work, would require some special handling. They cannot be handled by available approaches, including the context explanation offered by Melton. This explanation involves, as does the one that I have offered, the assumption that a block of items is held in a limited processor of some type.

Experiments on distance effects in free recall are, however, not univocal. Waugh (1963, 1967) does not find any distance effects. Underwood (1969) finds an increase when the distance between the repeated items is greater than 0, i.e., a gross difference between massed and distributed presentation, but no clear or simple change as the distance increases from 2 to 20 intervening items. The procedures of the experiments above differ in a number of ways. For example, the Melton and the Glanzer experiments use visual presentation. Underwood and Waugh use auditory presentation. The resolution of the differences, however, awaits further exploration. There is sufficient evidence from other sources, e.g., from related paired-associates experiments (Peterson, Wampler, Kirkpatrick, & Saltzman, 1963), that I will hold to the statements above concerning the processing of repeated words.

VII. Relation of Free Recall and the Model to Other Memory Tasks

In this section I will consider the generality of the information that has been developed up to this point. I will first consider several experimental situations and try to establish the correspondences between them. The relations between the several recall tasks have been pointed out by others. I will try to develop the correspondences further here. In addition to the free recall task, the following types of tasks are used in memory experiments:

1. Distractor task. A single item or string of items is followed by a delay task. The length and the characteristics of the delay task may be varied. This is the Peterson and Peterson (1959) design. The main task is often an arbitrary sequence of three consonants. The Ss' job is ordered recall of the trigram. The delay task may be anything from reading numbers or letters to carrying out complex mental operations.

2. Probe task. A series of items is followed by probes for specific items. This takes three popular forms: sequential probe, position probe, and paired associates. In a sequential probe task the S is given a sequence of items, 1 through n, is presented with item i and is asked to recall the following item, $i + 1$. In some cases the preceding item, $i - 1$, is asked for. In a position probe task the item to be recalled is designated by its ordinal position in the sequence, for example, "the third," or by its spatial position (for example, experimenter points to a window or reversed card which displayed the item.) In paired associates, the S is given a sequence of paired items, is then given the first element of the pair, and then asked to recall the second. There are two ways in which the sequential, positional, or paired-associates probes are given to the S. One of the ways has been described above, the main task followed by the series of test items. Another way is to mix the items to be recalled with the test items in a running memory task. In this general class of experimental situations, the later items in the sequence may be viewed as delay tasks for the earlier items.

3. Fixed-order recall task. A series of items is presented, all of which are to be recalled in order. The sequence is usually longer than that used in a distractor task. This task is also called a serial recall task or memory span task. This type of task will be considered separately below.

The simplest situation is perhaps 1, the distractor task. The curve derived for this task has been presented by Peterson and Peterson (see Fig. 17). The curve is very clear. It is important to emphasize the following point. The curve has two parts: a descending slope and an

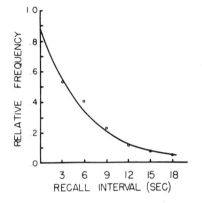

Fig. 17. Proportion of trigrams recalled after varying delay periods. (After Peterson & Peterson, 1959, by permission of the American Psychological Association, Washington, D.C.)

asymptote. The asymptote looks here as if it might be close to zero. According to a formula that Peterson and Peterson derive on the basis of a stimulus sampling model, the asymptote is .0089. This does not, however, tell the full story. The curve in Fig. 17 reflects correct responses made with a latency below 2.83 seconds. If a similar plot is made of correct responses within 14 seconds, a somewhat elevated curve appears that goes to a considerably higher asymptote, approximately .10.

These two parts of the curve, the descending slope and the asymptote, are, I believe, of great importance in the consideration of functions such as that in Fig. 17, and also in the consideration of serial position functions. The asymptote defines what is held in LTS. The peaked part of the curve is a joint function of STS and LTS. The rate at which it descends to an asymptote is an indication of the rate at which STS is cleared.

In some of the cases that I consider below I will discuss an asymptote on the basis of rather incomplete data. I do this with the awareness that more extensive testing would lead to a different definition of the asymptote.

The distractor task bears a double resemblance to the free recall situation. As free recall is ordinarily given, the middle section of the serial position curve corresponds to the asymptote in Fig. 17. The end peak of the serial position curve corresponds to the peak of the curve here. This is the first resemblance. To emphasize the correspondence, the curve in Fig. 17 should be plotted backwards. The second resemblance becomes evident when a delay is imposed after a free recall list. If the probability of recall of the last list item in Fig. 6 is plotted as a function of time, then a curve like Fig. 17 appears. The corresponding descent to an asymptote occurs. This is, of course, the closer correspondence. The drop of probability of the last list item in free recall with delay corresponds most closely to the drop of probability of a trigram with delay in the distractor task.

I will now go over some of the variables that have been shown to affect free recall: rate of presentation, list length, delay. I will bring in data on the effect of these variables in the other classes of memory task listed above. My purpose will be to show that the statements that I have made about free recall can be extended to these other situations. I wish to underline the similarity of the main results. I also wish to stress that the separation of STS and LTS is called for in these other experimental situations. To establish these points, I will try to show that the curves generated with variations of such factors as presentation rate give curves that correspond to those shown in Figs. 2, 3, 4, and 5.

A. Rate of Presentation

Murdock (1963) carried out a series of experiments in which he used paired associates to determine the effect of presentation position. In one of the experiments, he varied the rate of presentation of the five pairs given. The results show some evidence of interaction, of merging of the peaks, and clear separation of the asymptotes. This interaction shows up most clearly in the curves for the 3-second and 2-second rate (see Fig. 18). The interaction of rate and serial position (here, subsequent pairs) is statistically significant. This figure should be compared with the results displayed in Fig. 2. Both types of task indicate an effect restricted to LTS.

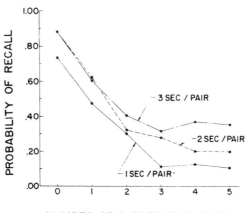

Fig. 18. Proportion of paired associates recalled as a function of position in sequence and presentation rate. (After Murdock, 1963, by permission of Academic Press, Inc., New York.)

B. LENGTH OF LIST

In the same paper, Murdock reports an experiment with a similar paired-associates procedure, in which the variables are number of items in the series and position in the series. The results are displayed in Fig. 19. These results are to be compared with those in Fig. 4 for free recall. A similar pattern of results is found in a spatial probe

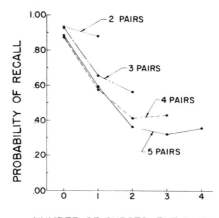

Fig. 19. Proportion of paired associates recalled as a function in sequence and list length. (After Murdock, 1963, by permission of Academic Press, Inc., New York.)

technique experiment reported by Phillips, Shiffrin, and Atkinson (1967). All three techniques give similar results. The results indicate that length affects only LTS.

C. Number of Repetitions

There is a third experiment by Murdock (1963) in which the same interactive pattern is displayed. The experimental variable here is the number of repetitions of the item. Again it is clear that the probability of recalling an item repeated one, two, or three times is much the same after a short delay. With an increase in delay, the probability of recall goes to different asymptotes as a function of number of repetitions. The results above are based on repetition of lists of paired associates. They are paralleled by results of increased recall over trials in free recall learning.

Similar results are found with immediate successive repetitions of items in a distractor task (Hellyer, 1962; Peterson & Peterson, 1959). There is then evidence from both the probe and distractor tasks that repetition affects LTS primarily. A similar demonstration is not available for free recall, although it should be easy to carry out.

The role of repetition in recall is complicated. In an earlier section of this paper, I cited findings (Glanzer & Meinzer, 1967) showing that repetition lowered the probability of recall. I subsequently noted that immediate repetition of a free recall item raised its probability of recall, but that this increase was greater if the repetition was spaced (Glanzer, 1969). In the distractor and probe tasks, the effects of repetitions are, in general, to increase probability of recall. There are important differences between the experimental situations that I will point out now.

In the first case (Glanzer & Meinzer, 1967), the S repeated a word during a fixed interitem interval. There was no increase in the total presentation time for the item. The repetition only encroached on the time needed to register the word in LTS. In the second case (Glanzer, 1969), as in most cases in the literature, a repetition meant a doubling of the total presentation time.

There is, however, another important difference between the probe and distractor experiments as opposed to the free recall experiment. This difference will become critical in the further examination of the effects of immediate repetition. In the probe and distractor experiments, the S repeats not a single item but a sequence of units — a pair as in paired-associates probe procedure or a trigram in the distractor tasks. Before he says the first letters of a trigram a second time he has to say two other letters. This means that the appropriate comparison of repetition effects in free recall and other tasks should make use of repeated sequences of items.

D. Spacing of Repetitions

There are a number of studies using paired-associate probes (Greeno, 1964; Peterson, 1963; Peterson, Wampler, Kirkpatrick, & Saltzman, 1963; Pollatsek, 1969) that show an effect of distribution of repetitions similar to those shown in Fig. 15 for free recall. The Peterson et al. data show in their Experiment I a steady increase in recall as the number of intervening items between repetitions goes from 0 to 1, 2, 4, and 8. Although there is a drop in recall with 16 intervening items in this experiment, the drop is probably not significant. In their Experiment II they use 0, 4, and 30 intervening items. They find an increase in recall from 0 to 4, but no further change beyond that.

E. Delay

The effect of delay is apparent in all three classes of the recall task. The effect, of course, was shown for the distractor task by Peterson and Peterson (1959). It can be found in data for probe recall tasks that involve more than one test in each series of items. In those cases, the first probe corresponds to a no-delay condition, and the later probes correspond to delay conditions. An experiment by Tulving and Arbuckle (1963) gave data on such recall probabilities for paired associates. By using a counterbalanced design, they were able to separate the effect of the serial position of the pair within the list from the effect of delay of the probe. The results are shown in Fig. 20. The early probes gave a serial position function with a high end peak. Later probes gave a serial position function identical in the early positions but with the end peak eliminated. Comparison of Fig. 20 with Fig. 6 shows the similarity of the probe task results to the free recall results. Similar effects of delay on fixed-order recall tasks are cited below.

VIII. Fixed-Order Recall

In the light of the results on the effects of delay, it is possible to understand the special case of the fixed-order or serial recall task.

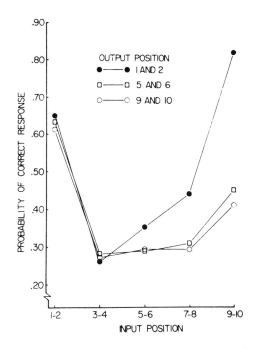

Fig. 20. Proportion of paired associates recalled as a function of serial position and delay. (After Tulving & Arbuckle, 1963, by permission of Academic Press, Inc., New York.)

The information developed so far gives all that is needed to understand that task. In fixed-order recall tasks, the *S* is required to recall the items in the order in which they are presented. Thus, the *S*'s own responses act as a delay task with respect to the items in STS, the items from the end of the list. On the assumption that order information does not play any further role, it would be expected that serial position curves like the delay curves seen before would be produced by serial recall. These are curves without an end peak. Jahnke (1965) has compared the serial position curves obtained with free and fixed-order or serial recall. The curves obtained for 5, 10, and 15 word lists under these two conditions are shown in Fig. 21. Similar results have been found by Deese (1957). Fixed-order recall gives a lower end peak than free recall.

There is, however, one discrepancy. An end peak still remains in the fixed-order serial position curve. This occurs, I believe, because the experimenter, in this situation, does not have strong control over the time at which the *S* starts his response. If the *S* delays without

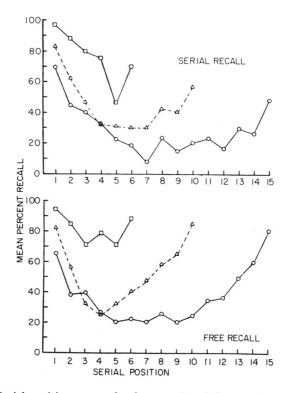

Fig. 21. Serial position curves for free recall and fixed-order, or serial recall, at three list lengths. (After Jahnke, 1965, by permission of the American Psychological Association, Washington, D.C.)

making any overt response, then he can use that empty delay period to register items from the end of the list in LTS.

Two implications about fixed-order recall can be drawn from the last statement.

1. If the experimenter forces the start of recall so that it must be made immediately after the last item, the end peak will disappear. As the S is given more time before the start of recall, the end peak will increase in magnitude. I should underline the fact that the end peak here is all in LTS. It is a conversion of what is held in STS at the end of the presentation. It has to be in LTS because it can only be reported after a number of other items have been reported.

2. A second implication is that the imposition of a delay task immediately after the presentation of the list will also eliminate the end peak. With a delay task, the experimenter would ordinarily make sure that the S responds quickly on the delay task. This operation

has been carried out in an experiment by Jahnke (1968a). The results for a 0-, 3-, 9-, and 18-second delay with a counting task are shown in Fig. 22. The results are very similar to those in Fig. 6 for free recall. Now that the relation of fixed-order recall to free recall has been considered, it is clear why the findings with the two procedures are similar.

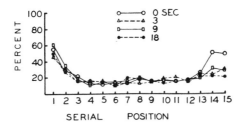

Fig. 22. Serial position curves for fixed-order recall with four delay periods. (After Jahnke, 1968a, by permission of the American Psychological Association, Washington, D.C.)

The following relations have been established by Jahnke. They parallel relations found in free recall and the other memory tasks listed above.

1. Rate of presentation — as in free recall, increase in rate results in a decrease in all serial positions except those at the end of the list (Jahnke, 1968b).

2. List length — as list length increases, the probability of recall decreases in those positions usually associated with LTS, the early and middle list sections (Jahnke, 1963, 1965, 1968a, 1968b). In the case of fixed-order recall, however, the end peak also declines (see Fig. 21). This does not occur to any marked degree in free recall. The reason for this is that in fixed-order recall, the end peak represents items transferred from STS to LTS after the list ends. The factors that lower the probability of registration in LTS with longer lists will also therefore affect end peak items. In free recall, the end peak is obtained in good part from STS which is not affected by list length.

The material presented so far in this section exaggerates the similarities between the several classes of a recall task. There is one extremely important and obvious characteristic in which the free recall task differs from all the rest. It does not require order information. All the rest, including the distractor task, require order information of varying degrees — from the simple order involved in paired associates, to the intermediate order involved in the distractor task to the complex order information required in serial recall.

IX. Evaluation of Other Findings

It is now possible to review a number of problems in recall and to clarify some points on the basis of a multiple store approach. Before doing this, I should distinguish between two terms — the term STS used here as a construct, a theoretical term, and the term short-term memory. Short-term memory is used in the literature to refer to any one of a number of experimental situations in which the S's final test on an item takes place within a minute or two. The term is neutral with respect to theory. Sometimes, however, this term is used as if it has theoretical significance. That is unfortunate because it leads to confusion. The process that I have been considering involves two storage mechanisms. Alternatives to this should certainly and will certainly be proposed. But the proposal should come with a clear differentiation of experimental task and theoretical construct.

I would recommend further that an explicit analysis be made of the role of STS and LTS in any discussion of a short-term memory experiment. A distinction should be made between effects that result in asymptote (LTS) differences and effects that result in differences in the rate of decline (STS).

With these distinctions in mind, I will review some experiments and arguments that appear in the literature. In the light of the distinctions, I believe that the work has a different meaning than first appears.

First, I will go over the proactive interference interpretation of the Peterson and Peterson (1959) findings (e.g., Keppel & Underwood, 1962). According to this interpretation, nothing new is involved in short-term memory. The constructs used for rote learning should, therefore, apply equally well to short-term memory.

There is an element of truth in this claim. Since the short-term memory situation will ordinarily give rise to output both from LTS and STS, factors that affect LTS will play a role. Therefore, factors involved in rote learning will have an effect. This does not mean, as stated above, that nothing new is involved in short-term memory. All that it means is that something old, i.e., familiar, is also involved.

This point and other related points become clear in considering the proactive interference interpretation of the Peterson and Peterson data in Fig. 16. According to this interpretation, proactive interference is what is demonstrated in that figure. Proactive interference increases as a function of two factors: the amount of material learned previously and the amount of time that elapses between study of an item and its test. Therefore, the Peterson and

Peterson curves should appear only after some number of items have already been learned.

This argument and data in support have been presented by Keppel and Underwood (1962) and Loess (1964). The results of Keppel and Underwood's Experiment 2 are shown in Fig. 23. The three curves represent the proportion correct over three delay periods when data for a first, second, and third test are separated.

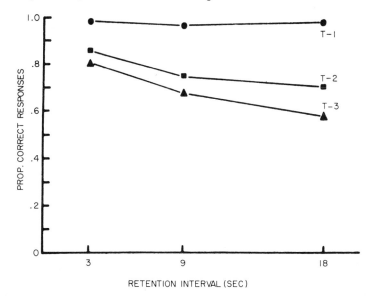

Fig. 23. Proportion of trigrams recalled as a function of delay periods and the number of the trial on which testing occurred: trial 1 (T-1), trial 2 (T-2); or trial 3 (T-3). (After Keppel & Underwood, 1962, by permission of Academic Press, Inc., New York.)

It is clear that the usual distractor task curves start to appear after the first test. The curves form a family, each curve going to a different asymptote. The total number of items affects the asymptote. The effect of number of items on the asymptotes, on the LTS component, is, however, clear in the case of free recall, in the relation between list length and asymptote (Murdock, 1962) discussed earlier. If the asymptote differs, then the appearance of the forgetting curve will differ. It is, for example, impossible to demonstrate a loss when the asymptote is at or near 1.00 as in the case of the top curve in Fig. 23.

The data do not, however, settle any issue. In terms of the multiple-store approach, the Keppel and Underwood experiments show an effect on LTS similar to the effect shown with other experimental arrangements. Indeed, there are not one but two relevant LTS effects that have been demonstrated in free recall, probed recall, and ordered recall. One is the length of list effect. The other is the beginning peak — the so-called primacy effect. Either or both of these could play a role in the decline of information registered in LTS with succeeding trials in the distractor task.

The results of the Keppel and Underwood experiments do not change the picture of two storage mechanisms. In fact they fit in rather nicely with the pattern of results discussed to this point. Figure 23 is parallel to Fig. 4 above. The results lead to the next weak generalization.

Most effects on short-term memory, upon examination, will be found to be effects on LTS. This is simply a result of the large number of variables that affect LTS.

Most of the literature on short-term memory does not separate LTS and STS output. The reports either do not contain or do not present information on the effects of delay. Ordinarily, the amount recalled under various conditions with either a fixed delay or no delay is reported. These studies confound LTS and STS effects. There is no way to separate one from the other.

Even in cases in which delay information is available, the data are often not interpreted properly. There are, for example, data that demonstrate that information load, or task difficulty, affect LTS solely. The point is, however, not made in the report of the study.

Two series of experiments (Posner & Konick, 1966; Posner & Rossman, 1965) have demonstrated such effects with a variant form of distractor task. The curves for the Posner and Rossman data that involve variation of time of delay are shown in Fig. 24. The curves have been replotted in terms of proportion correct instead of proportion incorrect in order to make them comparable to the other distractor task curves shown here. One major effect of the variation of information load is on the asymptote, the LTS component. The difference between the record and backward counting conditions supports this statement. Whether there is also an effect on STS beyond the effect on LTS is not demonstrated. There are not sufficient data. There is nothing in the paper that would lend support to the idea that lesser amounts are held in STS with increased difficulty of delay task.

The results here do give insight, however, into the details of the processing involved in transfer from STS to LTS and how this transfer occurs in various memory tasks. I noted earlier in the

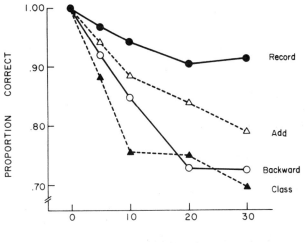

Fig. 24. Proportion of digits recalled as a function of delay task difficulty and length of delay period. (After Posner & Rossman, 1965, by permission of the American Psychological Association, Washington, D.C.)

discussion of the experiments by Glanzer *et al.* (1969) that changes in information load or difficulty of the delay task have no effect on the amount held in either STS or LTS. The results of that experiment on free recall have to be brought in line with those of Posner and Rossman. First it is important to note that there are three ways in which an additional task may affect storage of information: (*a*) it may change the rate of removal of items from STS; (*b*) it may block transfer of items from STS to LTS; (*c*) it may remove items already in LTS.

The data from free recall experiments show that (*a*) is not correct. The end peaks do not decline at different rates with different types of delay task (see Fig. 9). The same data show that alternative (*c*) is not correct. The overall asymptote of the serial position curve does not change with the several types of the delay task.

The one remaining possibility is that variation of the load of the delay task affects the probability of transfer of items from STS to LTS. If that were so then there should be a limited effect on free recall and a strong effect on distractor tasks. There would be a limited effect in free recall, because only the last few items would be affected. Specifically, these would be items that are still in STS and not yet transferred to LTS when the load is imposed. Early list items will already have cleared STS, being either forgotten or registered in

LTS. In this respect free recall differs from the distractor tasks. In distractor tasks, every item is followed closely by the delay task, and there is effective blocking of transfer to LTS for every item. It is possible even within the distractor task to show that the difficulty of the delay task has its greatest effect on that part of the item that most closely precedes the delay task. Posner and Rossman (1965) showed this in their Experiment IV.

From this it follows that in the distractor task every item should be affected. It also follows that in the free recall task with a relatively long series of items, the blocking of transfer would show only at the very end of the list. The specific way in which it would show in both tasks would be in the lowering of the LTS asymptote. Figure 9 does not indicate any strong basis for assuming that anything other than the asymptote has been affected.

The effect of the blocking can be looked at in the free recall curves such as those in Fig. 9. The last position in each curve can be plotted as in Fig. 25. The probability of recall at the last position is plotted for each delay task at each delay duration. Here I have taken

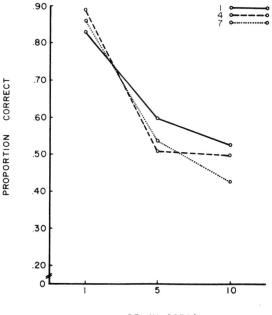

DELAY (SEC)

Fig. 25. The effect of delay with different load upon the proportion of recall of the last list item in free recall. (After Glanzer *et al.*, 1969, by permission of Academic Press, Inc., New York.)

the data from the first experiment mentioned earlier that made use of the variables of delay and information load (Glanzer *et al.,* 1969). The pattern of results in Fig. 25 is very much like that of Posner and Rossman's in Fig. 24. The curve for the adding 1 task goes to a higher asymptote than the other two tasks. Similar although less clear plots are obtained for the next to last and second from the last positions. This would follow from the effect of distance discussed above and verified in Posner and Rossman's Experiment IV.

Difficulty of the delay task then, according to the argument here, has no effect on the removal of items from STS. Its effect is to block the transfer of information from STS to LTS.

To support this analysis it would be good to have some further data. Fortunately, there are such relevant data in experiments by Baddeley, Scott, Drynan, and Smith (1969), Bartz and Salehi (1970), Murdock (1965), and Silverstein and Glanzer (1971). Murdock varied the load on Ss during free recall with a secondary card sorting task. Baddeley *et al.* and Bartz *et al.* used the Murdock arrangement with both postlist delay and no-delay conditions. Silverstein and Glanzer ran an experiment similar to the Baddeley *et al.* and Bartz *et al.* experiments. Since I have the full serial position functions for that experiment I will present them here. I will only note that all the experiments indicate essentially the same results — that imposed load during the list presentation affects the amount held in LTS not STS. In Murdock's experiment, this can be seen in the fact that load interacts with the serial position function. The early part of the serial position curves are separate one from the other. The later sections merge. In the Baddeley *et al.* experiment, this interaction results in a slight separation of the recall averages with no delay but a much more pronounced separation in the delay condition. In the Bartz and Salehi experiments, load affects the early part of the list only, while delay affects the end of the list. Bartz and Salehi also note that their data show no effect of load on the final list positions in the delay conditions. They state that this does not fit a simple dual storage model. Since this discrepancy does not appear in the Silverstein and Glanzer experiment, I will not consider it further here.

The experiment by Silverstein and Glanzer used a delay and no-delay condition. Instead of sorting cards during the list presentations, the Ss added a pair of numbers, e.g., 23 + 4, during the interval between words. The addends were varied, being either 1's, 4's, or 7's, with the larger addend giving the more difficult task. It was expected that the load would have an effect only on LTS and not on STS. Since the load had been applied while every item was present in STS, the blocking effect would be spread over the entire list, not just in the final positions. Both no-delay and delay conditions were used to permit the separation of the LTS and STS. During the delay condition, which was 4 seconds long, the S read six words. The results are shown in Figs. 26, 27, and 28.

Figure 26 displays the serial position curve for free recall without delay under three levels of concurrent task difficulty. The results replicate Murdock's. There is an interaction of task difficulty with serial position. All but the last few positions are lowered as difficulty

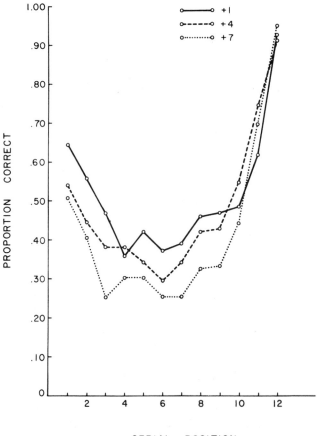

Fig. 26. Serial position curves for three levels of concurrent task difficulty. (After Silverstein & Glanzer, 1971, by permission.)

increases. Figure 27 displays the serial position curve for the delay conditions. Although the separation of the curves is not as clean as that in the curves of Fig. 26, it is clear that the overall effect of the delay task is in line with expectations. There is no evidence of interaction between serial position and task difficulty under

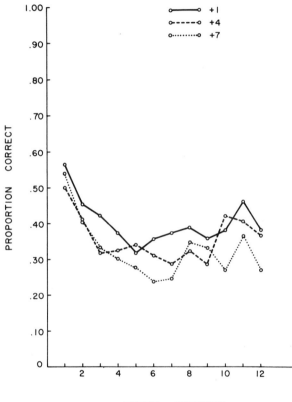

SERIAL   POSITION

Fig. 27. Serial position curves for three levels of concurrent task difficulty, with a postlist delay. (After Silverstein & Glanzer, 1971, by permission.)

statistical test. Figure 28 displays the estimate of STS based on Eq. (3) given earlier. Statistical tests of these data indicate that only serial position is a significant factor. The curves for the three levels of task difficulty do not differ.

Most of the points that I have made above have already been made by Baddeley *et al.* (1969). Murdock notes, moreover, that the task load effects could also be attributed to effects of total presentation

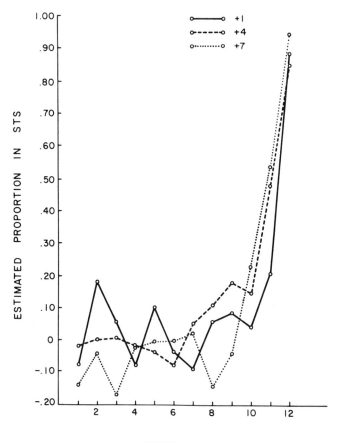

Fig. 28. Derived STS curves for three levels of concurrent task difficulty. (After Silverstein & Glanzer, 1971, by permission.)

time. It can be argued that difficult tasks take more time. In this sense, the results here all follow from the results on rate of presentation. The less available time the S has between successive words the lower the LTS level. The STS remains unaffected (Raymond, 1969).

The experiment above rules out, however, a number of possible theoretical alternatives with respect to information load. It shows that task difficulty or information has the same effect on LTS as rate of presentation. It also has the same effect on STS as rate of presentation — none. If there is something special that information load does beyond rate of presentation or amount of available time, it does not appear here.

A few remarks should be added on this matter of rate of the delay task. Fast rates in a secondary task or a delay task block registration in LTS. If a level asymptote in the serial position curve for a delay condition is desired, it is necessary to set the rate of the delay task processing close to the presentation rate of the main list items. If the rate is too slow, then that part of the asymptote that has not yet been fixed will end up at a higher level giving a slight end peak. If the rate is too fast, then there will be a dip in the end positions. This can be seen in some of the figures presented earlier. The effects of rate of the delay task can be seen in two studies using distractor tasks. The experimenters (Conrad & Hull, 1966; Kulp, 1967) varied the rate of the processing of items in a distractor task. The effect of rate of the delay task is clearly displayed in Fig. 2 of the paper by Kulp. The figure shows that the delay curves for the two rates of delay task go to different asymptotes.

It follows from the arguments above that a delay period filled with several difficult and several easy tasks would have a different effect depending on the order of the tasks. If the difficult tasks came first, then it would have its effect while a large amount of the list information remains in STS. The difficult task would not only remove the items in STS, it would also block their transfer to LTS more completely until they were removed. If the easy delay tasks came first, they would remove the items from STS. They would not, however, be as effective in blocking the transfer of the items to LTS before the items were removed. By the time that the difficult delay task is imposed, the list items have all cleared STS. There is no transfer for the task to block. This deduction is supported in three experiments by Dillon and Reid (1969) using a distractor task.

Now that the differentiation between effects on LTS or asymptote and effects on STS or rate of decline has been gone over, I can turn to some other cases in the literature. In these cases my interpretation is different than the author's because of the differentiation.

There is the general issue of the role of acoustic confusion on STM. Here the reference is to the recall of strings of items that bear some phonetic relation to each other. The most popular form of this task is one in which letter names that share a vowel in pronunciation are presented. This material was first used by Conrad (1964) in an important experiment establishing the role of acoustic factors in memory. In this material a highly similar string would be drawn from the set BCDGPTVZ or from the set FLMNSX. An example of a highly similar string is BGDV. An example of a dissimilar string is FBJQ.

Although there are a large number of studies that show that this type of similarity has an effect on recall, there is little evidence that its effect is on STS. The data are collected in situations with no variation of delay or with no determination of serial position effects. When there is no delay, overall recall scores are a composite of output from STS and LTS. When there is a delay but it is fixed, the recall scores reflect LTS components primarily.

An example of a study using a fixed delay is one by Wickens, Born, and Allen (1963). In this study, the investigators showed that changing the material to be recalled from letters to numbers or numbers to letters in a sequence of distractor trials resulted in a rise in performance. Since the data were obtained with a fixed-delay task the effects are most likely assignable solely to LTS. Whether STS is also involved cannot be determined.

Although the literature on the effects of acoustic similarity on short-term memory is massive, it settles nothing with respect to a key issue: the effect of similarity on STS, and whether that effect is different from the effect on LTS. The relatively few published studies that contain information that separates LTS and STS effects give results that disagree. In particular, the results do not agree with popular generalization that acoustic similarity affects STS, and semantic similarity affects LTS. This generalization is incorrect or at best oversimplified.

Bruce and Crowley (1970) gave free recall lists to Ss with sequences of acoustically similar (gain, cane, vain, reign) or semantically similar words (bean, carrot, corn, potato) embedded in the list. They imposed a delay after each list to remove items in STS. Both types of similarity had an effect on LTS, increasing the total amount held. Craik and Levy (1970) carried out a similar free recall study but used only no-delay conditions and estimated STS for acoustically and semantically similar words. Their findings on LTS agree with those of Bruce and Crowley (1970) — both forms of similarity increase the total amount held in LTS. Their estimates of the amount held in STS showed that acoustic similarity did not have a significant effect on the amount. Semantic similarity did, however, decrease the amount held in STS.

Results in line with the acoustic–STS, semantic–LTS generalization are, however, found in two studies using the probe technique. Levy and Murdock (1968) in their Experiment II, gave 10 word lists to Ss. The lists consisted of either acoustically similar (nest, vest, pest, rest, etc.) or acoustically dissimilar words. They found an interaction of similarity with serial position, with the end peak lower for similar words. Acoustic similarity reduces the amount held in STS.

Kintsch and Buschke (1969) carried out a similar study in which they compared probe recall of lists made up of homophone pairs with lists made up of unrelated words. The results agree with Levy and Murdock's (1968). Recall was poorer at the end of the list for the homophones. They use the serial position curves to isolate the STS and LTS components.

In a parallel experiment, Kintsch and Buschke show an effect of synonym pairs on the recall of items from the early serial positions. They identify this as an effect of semantic similarity specific to LTS. They show that STS is unaffected. This study is a complete demonstration of the acoustic-STS, semantic-LTS pairing that has been argued for by Baddeley and Dale (1966). All that seems necessary at this point is to iron out the differences with the free recall data cited above. Since there are obvious differences between free recall and probe procedure, it might seem easy to reconcile the two sets of results.

Unfortunately, this is not so. There are also results from distractor studies that do not agree.

Posner and Konick (1966) in their Experiments III and IV gave a distractor task, varying the confusability of the letters making up the trigrams to be recalled. The delay task, adding or classifying numbers, was continued by the S for 0, 5, 10, or 20 seconds. The results lend clear support to the idea that there is an effect of similarity on the LTS component. The delay curves go to different asymptotes for high and low similarity conditions. The results do not, however, indicate any clear effect on STS. This would have to appear here as an effect on the rate of approach to the different asymptotes. These results may, of course, merely indicate a difference between free recall and distractor results on the one hand and probe results on the other. Unfortunately, this distinction is not likely to be useful. The probe studies themselves do not agree.

Bruce and Murdock (1968) used a paired-associates probe technique with both acoustically similar and dissimilar words. The serial position curves show a clear effect of similarity on the LTS component and no effect on the STS component (see their Fig. 2). Their data further indicate that the similarity effect on LTS is proactive rather than retroactive, but that point is not important here.

In summary, the effects of similarity on LTS and STS are not established. Most of the work cited on this effect does not differentiate LTS and STS effects. The few studies that do permit the differentiation give conflicting results.

Many of the results on short-term memory are interpreted differently in light of the STS-LTS distinction. One example is found in a study of free recall by Tulving and Patterson (1968). In that study sequences of related words, e.g., father-mother-son-daughter, were embedded in lists. In two of the experimental conditions, the block of successive related words was placed either in the four final list positions, Condition E, or in four middle list positions, Condition M. Tulving and Patterson note a striking pattern of results (see Fig. 29). They claim that these results do not fit a two-storage model (p. 246). An examination of the results in the light of LTS and STS shows, however, a very good fit. The argument that I will make here has also been made by Craik and Levy (1970).

It is clear that the grouping of related words gives them an advantage in their registration in LTS. This has been discussed earlier in relation to distance effects. The LTS asymptote will be different for the blocked related words. The study therefore involves two

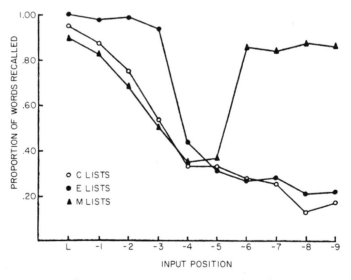

Fig. 29. Serial position curves for control lists condition (C) and for the lists with blocks of four semantically related words in either the middle (M) or end (E) list positions. The curves are plotted backward with the last list position first. Only the last ten positions are given. (After Tulving & Patterson, 1968, by permission of the American Psychological Association, Washington, D.C.)

levels of LTS. LTS_1 is the storage level for the unblocked, unrelated words; LTS_2 is the storage level for the grouped, related words. LTS_1 can be estimated from the middle sections of the curve for the control condition, C, since the STS should not be present there. Similarly, LTS_2 can be estimated from the middle section of the M curve. The last few positions are, as usual, a composite of STS and LTS. In the case of curve M

$$P_i(R) = P(LTS_1) + P_i(STS) - P(LTS_1) \cdot P_i(STS)$$

In the case of curve E

$$P_i(R) = P(LTS_2) + P_i(STS) - P(LTS_2) \cdot P_i(STS)$$

It is possible therefore to use any two of the curves in Fig. 29 to reconstruct the third. By making use of the equations above and the data given on the C and M curves, the following values are obtained: $P(LTS_1) = .21$, from positions 6 through 9 of the C curve; $P(LTS_2) = .86$, from the same positions in the M curve.

$P(LTS_1)$ is used to estimate $P_i(STS)$ for the last four list positions in the C curve. Starting with the last position, $P_i(STS)$ is estimated, according to Eq. (3), as .934, .836, .689, and .415. Combining these estimates with $P(LTS_2)$ the following values are computed for the last four positions of the E curve: .991, .978, .957, and .920. These may be compared with the empirical values read from Fig. 29 — 1.000, .986, .990, and .943. The estimate can be improved by taking account of the fact that the C curve does not actually give the best estimate for $P(LTS_1)$. It is, however, good enough to show that the curves in Fig. 29 can be interpreted in terms of LTS and STS.

X. General Characteristics of STS

Up to this point, I have shown that the STS is a highly buffered system in a limited sense. It is buffered in the sense that very few experimental variables affect it. In the considerable number of variables that I have considered, only two seem to have any strong effect on STS — the number of items entered and the appearance of an exact repetition. It is not clear at this point whether similarity of items has any effect on STS. And the effect of repetition may also be specific to some characteristic of the experimental situation.

There are two ways to rationalize this considerable robustness of the STS. One way is in terms of the system qua memory system. If the STS is one of a set of processors arranged in series, then it would be desirable to have it responsive to as few disturbances as possible.

Its main job is to hold a block of recent items available for further processing. If it does anything other than hold the items, then information is lost to the rest of the system. This is an oversimplified statement. It also may not be the most fruitful way to view the STS. I will present one that I think has certain advantages over this one.

Before I do this I want to emphasize the generality of the LTS-STS distinction and the robustness of STS. In particular, I want to argue that STS is independent of: (a) age; (b) intelligence; (c) mnemonic skill.

A. INDEPENDENCE OF AGE

Craik (1968) has compared adult Ss ages 22 and 65 on free recall tasks. He has separated the STS and LTS components by the method used above and by another analytic formula. He finds that the amount registered in LTS decreases with age, but that the amount in STS is constant.

There also have been several probe-recall studies comparing children of different ages. The results of these studies are, however, unclear. I will turn to a study carried out by Thurm and Glanzer (1971) comparing the performance of 5- and 6-year-old children in free recall. The items used in presentation were pictures of objects whose names were familiar to the children, e.g., apple, clock, lion, star. The children called out the names of these as they were shown at a 3-second rate. They were shown series of items that were systematically varied in length from two to seven items. After each list they were asked to recall as many names as they could. The results are shown in Fig. 30. The curves show two systematic effects. One is the effect of list length that had been noted earlier in the Murdock (1962) data. The other was the effect of age. The five-year-olds clearly do worse than the six-year-olds on list lengths 4, 5, 6, and 7. They do not do worse, however, in the last few positions. The STS holds up across the age levels.

A full examination of the assertion that STS is independent of age must, of course, include a much broader range of ages than I have mustered up here. What has been presented, however, is in line with the assertion.

B. INDEPENDENCE OF INTELLIGENCE

Ellis (1970) has compared the recall performance of retardates with college students of approximately the same age. The Ss were

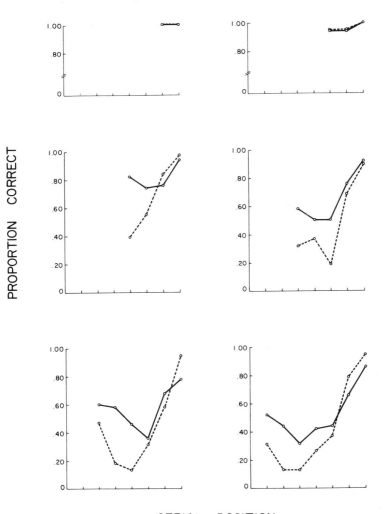

PROPORTION CORRECT

SERIAL POSITION

Fig. 30. Serial position curves for five-year-old (broken line) and six-year-old (solid line) children with lists of length 2, 3, 4, 5, 6, and 7 words. (After Thurm & Glanzer, 1971, by permission.)

given a nine-item position probe task with both fast and slow presentation rates. The serial position curves obtained (see their Fig. 3) show the expected interaction of mental age with serial position. The curves are widely separated across all serial positions except the last few where they merge.

There is another interesting aspect of the results. The data for the normal *Ss* show the interaction between presentation rate and serial position discussed earlier (see Fig. 2). The data for the retardates, however, do not show this interaction. The serial position curves for both fast and slow presentation are almost identical. The retardates evidently do not make use of the additional time available in slow presentation to improve the registration of information in LTS.

C. Independence of Mnemonic Skill

Raymond (1968) separated the data of *Ss* who scored high and those who scored low in free recall. The serial position curves for these two groups of *Ss* are shown in Fig. 31. The standard interaction

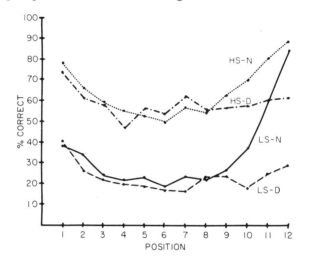

Fig. 31. Serial position curves for high scoring (HS) and low scoring (LS) *Ss* on delay (D) and no-delay (N) free recall. (After Raymond, 1968, by permission of the author.)

effect of the no-delay curves for the two groups is clear. Raymond applied Eq. (3) to derive two serial position curves for STS — one for the high scoring and one for the low scoring *Ss*. When this was done, she obtained two nearly identical curves (see Fig. 32).

I wish to emphasize the generality of the LTS-STS distinction and the robustness of STS to prepare for its further identification. In line with this emphasis, a recent study by Baddeley and Warrington (1970) is of interest. Following up earlier clinical observations of effects of brain damage that are specific to LTS, they demonstrate that, in free recall, their amnesic *Ss* have normal STS but defective LTS.

XI. Relation of STS to Language Processing

I will consider here the idea that the system I have been discussing is intimately involved in the processing of language. A more extreme statement would identify the STS and LTS components with stages in the processing of speech. If this idea is correct, then full understanding of the mechanisms and processes considered would depend on viewing their relation to language processing. Furthermore, this idea would suggest the examination of special aspects of the functioning of STS and LTS.

The close relation of memory to language has been pointed out previously. Usually this is done in discussions of the distinctions

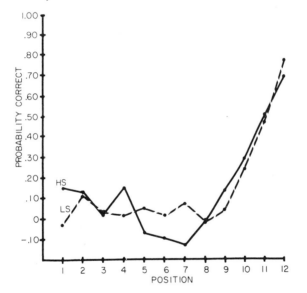

Fig. 32. Derived STS curves for high scoring (HS) and low scoring (LS) Ss. (After Raymond, 1968, by permission of the author.)

between linguistic competence and performance. In those discussions, the role of memory is simply mentioned in a vague and general fashion. Yngve (1960) was the first to examine constructively and in some detail the role of STS in language processing. He identifies STS with the first stage of language processing.[5] It is interesting that he assumed, in his examination, that STS was governed by simple displacement. Yngve went into the details of the computation necessary to process a sentence. On the basis of the

[5] Yngve separates an operating register from the STS in his outline of language processing. I have not done this.

capacity limitations of STS he tried to derive or rationalize some of the special structural characteristics found in natural language, e.g., discontinuous constituents.

Another investigator to consider the relation of memory to language processing is Neisser (1967). He notes the importance of rhythmic pattern in memory and argues that the synthesis of these patterns involves the same mechanisms as the synthesis of speech (p. 235). The role of grouping factors is, I agree, of great importance in the understanding of both language processing and memory. I will expand on this point below.

There are two types of evidence that I will draw on to support the relation or identification of speech processors and memory mechanisms. One is evidence on the special role of auditory as opposed to visual presentation. The other is the role of grouping factors in recall. Both of these types of evidence lend at best indirect support.

A. AUDITORY *VERSUS* VISUAL PRESENTATION

The initial stage of the memory system handles auditory information most efficiently. This can be seen in the fact that when the same list is given with auditory and visual presentation, there is better recall of the auditory list. Examination of the serial position function shows that this advantage is, under ordinary conditions, limited to the last few positions, the positions associated with STS. Murdock and Walker (1969) have presented such curves. Murdock and others have carried out a number of investigations of this effect. A number of proposals have been offered as to the specific characteristics of storage as indicated by various findings. I will not go into these proposals here. It is sufficient that I underline the advantage of auditory material. The system is set up to handle auditory input.

The term auditory might be understood as implying that STS is primitive in the sense that it is restricted to processing of input at a phonemic level. This implication, I believe, is incorrect. I will present some evidence that indicates a rather complex function for STS.

B. GROUPING EFFECTS

The grouping effects noted by Neisser (1967) play a pervasive role in both the production and understanding of speech. They are even strong in the restricted verbal performance permitted in the laboratory. Ebbinghaus (1885) noted that he could not avoid grouping syllables in the reading of his lists. He coped with the effect by imposing a standard intonation pattern on his reading.

When Ss read a list of words out loud, they will produce a recognizable intonation pattern for any regular characteristic of the list that permits grouping. The ubiquity of grouping intonation effects has also been noted by investigators of speech. Lieberman (1967) has, for example, argued for "breath group" as a physiologically based universal of human speech that plays an important role in the segmenting of speech.

At this point there is no basis for distinguishing the effects of intonation pattern from the effects of other types of grouping. As I indicated above, the Ss' intonation patterns are omnipresent and will reflect whatever grouping cues are available. I will handle the two terms, for the present, as roughly equivalent.

A recent study by Gianutsos (1970) sheds light on the differential effect of grouping in LTS and STS. She presented 18-word lists to Ss in which the successive words were temporally grouped by threes or ungrouped, i.e., presented at a steady rate. A number of factors were varied including the presentation rate. One of the striking findings, demonstrated in several of the experiments, is that, in free recall, grouping has a beneficial effect solely on STS. Figure 33 demonstrates this effect.

This pattern is characteristic of several sets of data reported by Gianutsos. They all indicate that grouping facilitates the recall of the last one or two groups.[6] The grouped items were not only recalled better, they were recalled in different order. In the grouped conditions, the final two groups tended to be recalled first and in forward order. In ungrouped lists, although S tends to recall items from the end of the list first, he tends to recall those items in reversed order (Deese & Kaufman, 1957).

There is another clear finding that should be mentioned. The grouping effect is heightened as the overall presentation rate increases. The pattern seen in Fig. 33 is more marked if the 18-word list is given in 18 seconds than if it is given in 36 seconds. Gianutsos notes that this effect may hold the explanation of some of the conflicting results on the effect of rate on short-term memory. An increase in rate, as pointed out earlier, decreases the amount registered in LTS. An increase in rate, however, also facilitates

---

[6] Gianutsos also demonstrated an effect of grouping on LTS. The effect, restricted to the beginning peak, is not relevant to the present discussion.

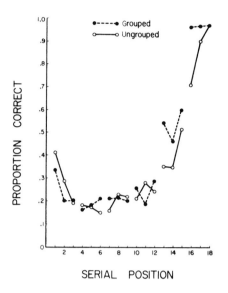

SERIAL POSITION

Fig. 33. Serial position curves for grouped and ungrouped presentation. (After Gianutsos, 1970, by permission of the author.)

grouping and thus increases the amount held in STS. The relative size of these opposed effects will determine the overall effect of rate.

The grouping effect found here is a striking one. One aspect of the effect that requires further examination is the role that grouping plays in registration in LTS over repeated trials. It is clear that grouping is, in that case, advantageous (Müller & Schumann, 1894).[7] The way in which an STS advantage is converted to an LTS advantage has, however, not been analyzed.

In the early sections of the paper, a number of variables were considered, all of which had an effect on LTS but not on STS. It might have seemed that nothing other than other items could affect STS. Indeed, I offered a generalization based on that thought. It now appears that there are two other factors with an effect specific to STS: the modality of the presentation and grouping. Both factors are likely to be important if the STS plays a key role in language processing, like that outlined for it by Yngve.

I will now fit the processing of speech into the flow chart presented in Fig. 1. I will consider only the reception of speech.

[7] Müller and Schumann (1894) also point out that the specific intonation pattern, i.e., trochee *versus* iamb, is important in determining the amount their Ss learned. This implies the role of a factor beyond simple grouping. They also mention the role of breath groups during learning.

Yngve's (1960) analysis was concerned only with the production of speech.

An input sequence goes through initial sensory processing and then appears in STS. The temporal length of the sequence is variable. While the sequence is in STS, a computation is carried out that determines the interpretation of the sequence. The results of the computation are then registered in LTS. The results of the computation are an interpretation of the sequence. An initial determination of the sequence to be analyzed is probably obtained from grouping cues.

Two processes are involved in the computation. One is the checking of tentatively defined units with the Ss' lexicon, a listing of possible units with related information. The other process is the application of the grammar to the sequence. Both these processes, the lexical and the grammatical, probably take place repeatedly and cyclically until a solution that is acceptable on both bases is reached. The processing in STS involves, therefore, repeated exchanges with LTS for both the lexical and grammatical processing.

A question of importance is the size of the unit that is held in STS. The evidence at hand indicates that the unit is at least a word or a morpheme. This is implied by Craik's (1968) finding that the length of the list words did not affect the total number of words held in STS. The evidence at hand also implies that the unit may be less than a newly generated sentence. This inference may be drawn from the fact that even when the S can put a pair of words into mnemonic combination, he still holds individual words in STS (Glanzer & Schwartz, 1971). The answer might be then that the unit in STS is a word or morpheme. I would like, however, to consider another possibility. This is that the unit that STS holds is any item that is in the S's lexicon. This would include units smaller than a word but also, possibly, units larger than a word − phrases, sentences. The phrases and sentences would be set units, not sequences that the S has to construct *de novo* solely on the basis of the input and the stored lexicon and grammar. Computations of sentences that are not already in the S's lexicon will, according to this, be handled as multiple unit sequences in STS.

The possibility that STS holds long sequences as units is particularly interesting for two reasons. One is for the insight it gives into the processing in the system. The other is for the corrective value it has. I noted earlier that the tendency has been to look at STS as a primitive processor handling relatively simple units. I am now considering the possibility that it may handle very large units, if those units are already set in the S's lexicon.

In order to test this idea an experiment was set up,[8] using proverbs as the material for free recall lists. Proverbs are sentences or phrases that are part of S's lexicon. If what I have said above is correct, these should be held in STS much the same way that individual words are held. In particular, it should be possible to generate a serial position curve of the standard form with an end peak. It should also be possible to lower that end peak with a delay task.

To test these assertions, lists of familiar proverbs were assembled, and set up in 15-proverb lists. Each list was read to Ss at the rate of one proverb every four seconds. The Ss then gave immediate recall at the end of half of the lists and delayed recall after the other half. Delayed recall consisted of having the S repeat a sequence of four words before recalling the list proverbs. The experiment was run in two languages with Hebrew speaking Ss given Hebrew proverbs and English speaking Ss given English proverbs. Since the results were the same in both groups, I will present the overall data for the combined groups (see Fig. 34).

There are two important characteristics of the curves. One is that the no-delay condition shows an end peak comparable to the end peaks seen in preceding figures. There is little reason to doubt that the end peak would shift to later positions if the list were lengthened. The material in STS, however, consists not of several words but of several sentences with a mean length of 4 to 4.5 words each.

If there is any doubt about identifying the end peak with STS, the delay curve is of interest. It is clear there that the STS component is vulnerable here to subsequent items as in the case of words. It is also clear that sequences involving a number of morphemes may function as a single unit in STS.

XII. Closing Statement

I have started from a simple free recall task and some simple results. On the basis of the results I have built a detailed picture of some aspects of the recall process. I have, of course, omitted many important aspects of the process. There are many investigators who are actively working on these aspects.

[8] This experiment was carried out with the assistance of Micha Razel and Tova Meryn Zaltz.

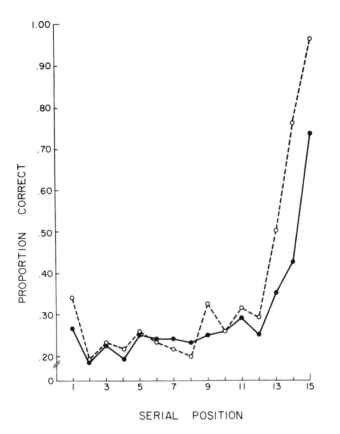

Fig. 34. Serial position curves for free recall of proverbs under delay (solid line) and no-delay (broken line) conditions.

In the course of the examination of recall, I have drawn a picture of the STS as a limited store that holds input for processing. I have claimed that it responds solely to the number of items that enter the overall system, with three exceptions. It handles repetitions of an item currently in STS as if the two representations were one. It responds to intonation grouping. It is particularly responsive to auditory material. I have argued further that the STS is an important part of the system for the processing of language and that a full understanding of either the language processing system or memory system involves an understanding of the overlap or identity of the two systems.

REFERENCES

Atkinson, R. C., & Shiffrin, R. M. Human memory: A proposed system and its control processes. In K. W. Spence & J. T. Spence (Eds.), *The psychology of learning and motivation: Advances in research and theory.* Vol. 2. New York: Academic Press, 1968. Pp. 89–195.

Baddeley, A. D., & Dale, H. C. A. The effect of semantic similarity on retroactive interference in long- and short-term memory. *Journal of Verbal Learning and Verbal Behavior*, 1966, 5, 417–420.

Baddeley, A. D., Scott, D., Drynan, R., & Smith, J. C. Short-term memory and the limited capacity hypothesis. *British Journal of Psychology*, 1969, 60, 51–55.

Baddeley, A. D., & Warrington, E. K. Amnesia and the distinction between long- and short-term memory. *Journal of Verbal Learning and Verbal Behavior*, 1970, 9, 176–189.

Bartz, W. H., & Salehi, M. Interference in short- and long-term memory. *Journal of Experimental Psychology*, 1970, 84, 380–382.

Brown, J. Some tests of the decay theory of immediate memory. *Quarterly Journal of Experimental Psychology*, 1958, 10, 12–21.

Bruce, D., & Crowley, J. J. Acoustic similarity effects on retrieval from secondary memory. *Journal of Verbal Learning and Verbal Behavior*, 1970, 9, 190–196.

Bruce, D., & Murdock, B. B., Jr. Acoustic similarity effects on memory for paired associates. *Journal of Verbal Learning and Verbal Behavior*, 1968, 7, 627–631.

Conrad, R. Acoustic confusions in immediate memory. *British Journal of Psychology*, 1964, 55, 75–84.

Conrad, R., & Hull, A. J. The role of the interpolated task in short-term retention. *Quarterly Journal of Experimental Psychology*, 1966, 18, 266–269.

Craik, F. I. M. Two components in free recall. *Journal of Verbal Learning and Verbal Behavior*, 1968, 7, 996–1004.

Craik, F. I. M. The fate of primary memory items in free recall. *Journal of Verbal Learning and Verbal Behavior*, 1970, 9, 143–148.

Craik, F. I. M., & Levy, B. A. Semantic and acoustic information in primary memory. *Journal of Experimental Psychology*, 1970, 86, 77–82.

Crowder, R. G., & Morton, J. Precategorical acoustic storage (PAS). *Perception & Psychophysics*, 1969, 5, 365–373.

Dallett, K. M. Number of categories and category information in free recall. *Journal of Experimental Psychology*, 1964, 68, 1–12.

Deese, J. Serial organization in the recall of disconnected items. *Psychological Reports*, 1957, 3, 577–582.

Deese, J., & Kaufman, R. A. Serial effects in recall of unorganized and sequentially organized verbal material. *Journal of Experimental Psychology*, 1957, 54, 180–187.

Dillon, R. F., & Reid, L. S. Short-term memory as a function of information processing during the retention interval. *Journal of Experimental Psychology*, 1969, 81, 261–269.

Ebbinghaus, H. *Uber das Gedächtnis: Untersuchungen zur experimentellen Psychologie.* Leipzig: Duncker & Humbolt, 1885. Translation by H. A. Ruger

& C. E. Bussenius, *Memory: A contribution to experimental psychology.* New York: Teachers College, Columbia University, Bureau of Publications, 1913.

Ellis, N. R. Memory processes in retardates and normals: Theoretical and empirical considerations. In N. Ellis (Ed.), *International review of research in mental retardation.* Vol. 4. New York: Academic Press, 1970. Pp. 1–32.

Gianutsos, R. Free recall of grouped words. Unpublished doctoral dissertation, New York University, 1970.

Glanzer, M. Distance between related words in free recall: Trace of the STS. *Journal of Verbal Learning and Verbal Behavior,* 1969, 8, 105–111.

Glanzer, M., & Cunitz, A. R. Two storage mechanisms in free recall. *Journal of Verbal Learning and Verbal Behavior,* 1966, 5, 351–360.

Glanzer, M., Gianutsos, R., & Dubin, S. The removal of items from short-term storage. *Journal of Verbal Learning and Verbal Behavior,* 1969, 8, 435–447.

Glanzer, M., Koppenaal, L., & Nelson, R. Effects of relations between words on short-term storage and long-term storage. In preparation.

Glanzer, M., & Meinzer, A. The effects of intralist activity on free recall. *Journal of Verbal Learning and Verbal Behavior,* 1967, 6, 928–935.

Glanzer, M., & Schwartz, A. Mnemonic structure in free recall: Differential effects on STS and LTS. *Journal of Verbal Learning and Verbal Behavior,* 1971, 10, 194–198.

Greeno, J. G. Paired-associate learning with massed and distributed repetitions of items. *Journal of Experimental Psychology,* 1964, 67, 286–295.

Hellyer, S. Supplementary report: Frequency of stimulus presentation and short-term decrement in recall. *Journal of Experimental Psychology,* 1962, 64, 650.

Jahnke, J. C. Serial position effects in immediate serial recall. *Journal of Verbal Learning and Verbal Behavior,* 1963, 2, 284–287.

Jahnke, J. C. Supplementary report: Primacy and recency effects in serial-position curves of immediate recall. *Journal of Experimental Psychology,* 1965, 70, 130–132.

Jahnke, J. C. Delayed recall and the serial-position effect of short-term memory. *Journal of Experimental Psychology,* 1968, 76, 618–622. (a)

Jahnke, J. C. Presentation rate and the serial-position effect of immediate serial recall. *Journal of Verbal Learning and Verbal Behavior,* 1968, 7, 608–612. (b)

Keppel, G., & Underwood, B. J. Proactive inhibition in short-term retention of single items. *Journal of Verbal Learning and Verbal Behavior,* 1962, 1, 153–161.

Kintsch, W., & Buschke, H. Homophones and synonyms in short-term memory. *Journal of Experimental Psychology,* 1969, 80, 403–407.

Kulp, R. A. Effects of amount of interpolated activity in short-term memory. *Psychological Reports,* 1967, 21, 393–399.

Levy, B. A., & Murdock, B. B., Jr. The effects of delayed auditory feedback and intralist similarity in short-term memory. *Journal of Verbal Learning and Verbal Behavior,* 1968, 7, 887–894.

Lieberman, P. *Intonation, perception, and language.* Cambridge, Mass.: MIT Press, 1967.

Loess, H. Proactive inhibition in short-term memory. *Journal of Verbal Learning and Verbal Behavior,* 1964, 3, 362–368.

Madigan, S. W. Intraserial repetition and coding processes in free recall. *Journal of Verbal Learning and Verbal Behavior,* 1969, 8, 828–835.

Melton, A. W. Repetition and retrieval from memory. *Science*, 1967, 158, 532.

Melton, A. W., & von Lackum, W. J. Retroactive and proactive inhibition in retention: Evidence for a two-factor theory of retroactive inhibition. *American Journal of Psychology*, 1941, 54, 157-173.

Müller, G., & Schumann, F. Experimentelle Beiträge zur Untersuchung des Gedächtnisses. *Zeitschrift für Psychologie und Physiologie der Sinnesorgane*, 1894, 6, 81-190, 257-339.

Murdock, B. B., Jr. The serial position effect of free recall. *Journal of Experimental Psychology*, 1962, 64, 482-488.

Murdock, B. B., Jr. Short-term memory and paired-associate learning. *Journal of Verbal Learning and Verbal Behavior*, 1963, 2, 320-328.

Murdock, B. B., Jr. Effects of a subsidiary task on short-term memory. *British Journal of Psychology*, 1965, 56, 413-419.

Murdock, B. B., Jr. Recent developments in short-term memory. *British Journal of Psychology*, 1967, 58, 421-433.

Murdock, B. B., Jr., & Walker, K. D. Modality effects in free recall. *Journal of Verbal Learning and Verbal Behavior*, 1969, 8, 665-676.

Neisser, U. *Cognitive psychology*. New York: Appleton-Century-Crofts, 1967.

Peterson, L. R. Immediate memory: Data and theory. In C. N. Cofer and B. S. Musgrave (Eds.), *Verbal behavior and learning: Problems and processes*. New York: McGraw-Hill, 1963. Pp. 336-353.

Peterson, L. R. Short-term verbal memory and learning. *Psychological Review*, 1966, 73, 193-207.

Peterson, L. R., & Peterson, M. Short-term retention of individual verbal items. *Journal of Experimental Psychology*, 1959, 58, 193-198.

Peterson, L. R., Wampler, R., Kirkpatrick, M., & Saltzman, D. Effect of spacing presentations on retention of a paired associate over short intervals. *Journal of Experimental Psychology*, 1963, 66, 206-209.

Phillips, J. L., Shiffrin, R. M., & Atkinson, R. C. Effects of list length on short-term memory. *Journal of Verbal Learning and Verbal Behavior*, 1967, 6, 303-311.

Pollatsek, A. Rehearsal, interference, and spacing of practice in short-term memory. Technical Report No. 16. Human Performance Center, University of Michigan, 1969.

Posner, M. I., & Konick, A. F. On the role of interference in short-term retention. *Journal of Experimental Psychology*, 1966, 72, 221-231.

Posner, M. I., & Rossman, E. Effect of size and location of informational transforms upon short-term retention. *Journal of Experimental Psychology*, 1965, 70, 496-505.

Postman, L., & Phillips, L. W. Short-term temporal changes in free recall. *Quarterly Journal of Experimental Psychology*, 1965, 17, 132-138.

Puff, C. R. Clustering as a function of the sequential organization of stimulus word lists. *Journal of Verbal Learning and Verbal Behavior*, 1966, 5, 503-506.

Raymond, B. Factors affecting long-term and short-term storage in free recall. Unpublished doctoral dissertation, New York University, 1968.

Raymond, B. Short-term and long-term storage in free recall. *Journal of Verbal Learning and Verbal Behavior*, 1969, 8, 567-574.

Rundus, D., & Atkinson, R. C. Rehearsal processes in free recall; A procedure for direct observation. *Journal of Verbal Learning and Verbal Behavior*, 1970, 9, 99-105.

Silverstein, C., & Glanzer, M. Difficulty of a concurrent task in free recall: Differential effects on STS and LTS. *Psychonomic Science,* 1971, **22,** 367–368.

Sperling, G. The information available in brief visual presentations. *Psychological Monographs,* 1960, 74 (Whole No. 498).

Sumby, W. H. Word frequency and serial position effects. *Journal of Verbal Learning and Verbal Behavior,* 1963, 1, 443–450.

Thurm, A. T., & Glanzer, M. Free recall in children: Long-term store versus short-term store. *Psychonomic Science,* 1971, **23,** 175–176.

Tulving, E., & Arbuckle, J. Y. Sources of intratrial interference in immediate recall of paired associates. *Journal of Verbal Learning and Verbal Behavior,* 1963, 1, 321–334.

Tulving, E., & Patterson, R. D. Functional units and retrieval process in free recall. *Journal of Experimental Psychology,* 1968, 77, 239–248.

Underwood, B. Some correlates of item repetition in free-recall learning. *Journal of Verbal Learning and Verbal Behavior,* 1969, 8, 83–94.

Waugh, N. C. Immediate memory as a function of repetition. *Journal of Verbal Learning and Verbal Behavior,* 1963, 2, 107–112.

Waugh, N. C. Presentation time and free recall. *Journal of Experimental Psychology,* 1967, 73, 39–44.

Waugh, N. C., & Norman, D. A. Primary memory. *Psychological Review,* 1965, 72, 89–104.

Weingartner, H. The free recall of sets of associatively related words. *Journal of Verbal Learning and Verbal Behavior,* 1964, 3, 6–10.

Wickelgren, W. A. Acoustic similarity and retroactive interference in short-term memory. *Journal of Verbal Learning and Verbal Behavior.* 1965, 4, 53–61.

Wickens, D. D., Born, D. G., & Allen, C. K. Proactive inhibition and item similarity in short-term memory. *Journal of Verbal Learning and Verbal Behavior,* 1963, 2, 440–445.

Yngve, V. A model and an hypothesis for language structure. *Proceedings of the American Philosophical Society,* 1960, 104, 444–466.

3

COMMENTARY ON "WORKING MEMORY"

Alan D. Baddeley and Graham Hitch

MRC APPLIED PSYCHOLOGY UNIT
CAMBRIDGE, ENGLAND

Our concept of working memory sprang from a concern for the role of memory in other information processing tasks. It suggested a framework that was in many ways similar to the modal model of Atkinson and Shiffrin, but that differed in a number of respects. In the 3 years since our chapter was published, the framework has continued to be used in explaining existing data, in generating testable hypotheses, and in providing a tool for investigating other tasks, such as mental arithmetic and reading. Our subsequent work can be divided into three categories: consolidation of work originally described in the chapter; extension of the model to other aspects of memory; and, finally, its use as a conceptual framework for investigating "real life" tasks, such as arithmetic and reading. These will be considered in turn.

Consolidation

THE WORD LENGTH EFFECT

As we pointed out, subjects have a considerably better span for short words than for long words, a phenomenon we attributed to the articulatory loop in our model. This interpretation has been explored in greater detail (Baddeley, Thomson, & Buchanan, 1975) in a series of studies that showed that the effect holds across a wide range of materials and is time based; subjects appear to be able to remember as much material as they can read in about 1.50 seconds. When material is presented visually and rehearsal is prevented by a concurrent articulatory task, such as counting from one to six, the word length effect disappears. This is consistent with the assumption that it depends on an articulatory loop that can be pre-empted by the suppression procedure. When presentation is auditory, however, even suppression does not prevent the word length effect, suggesting that the loop should not be literally identified with activity of the articulatory muscles. It seems likely that the motor programs involved in the articulatory loop may be primed either articulatorily or through audition.

EFFECTS OF MEMORY LOAD ON FREE RECALL

One of the most unexpected results of our earlier work was the observation that a concurrent digit span task impaired the long-term component of free recall of a word list but had no effect on recency. The experiments on which this conclusion was based, however, involved auditory presentation of the words, together with visually presented digits. A study by Anderson and Craik (1974) using a rather different paradigm indicated that auditorily presented material may be much more resistant to a concurrent visual task than the reverse. Therefore, we replicated our study with the exception that the words to be remembered for free recall were presented visually, and the digit span was presented auditorily. Results were substantially the same as before; there was still no evidence for the massive disruption of recency that would be expected on the assumption that the recency effect and digit span were both based upon the same limited capacity STS (Baddeley & Hitch, 1977).

RECENCY IN LONG-TERM MEMORY

We suggested that the recency effect was probably dependent on an ordinal retrieval strategy that could be applied to any clearly classified class of events "for example, football games, parties, or meals at restaurants, all of which introspectively appear to exhibit their own recency effect [Baddeley & Hitch, 1974, p. 85] ." We have subsequently tested this by requiring rugby football players to recall the teams they had played against earlier in the season (Baddeley & Hitch, 1977). We tested members of two separate teams, and both showed the same marked recency effect, with performance being dependent on the number of interpolated games rather than elapsed time.

THE CONCEPT OF "WORK SPACE"

In our earlier discussion, we hypothesized that part of the working memory system consisted of a general purpose work space. We interpreted our data as suggesting that the limited capacity of the work space could be flexibly distributed between the two functions of processing and storing information, according to task demands. Therefore, one would expect a trade-off in any particular situation between the amount of work space devoted to these two uses; this accords with our observation that a concurrent retention task slows down the rate of information processing on a second task. It is not easily demonstrable, however, that it is information storage that is directly responsible for the interference. It could just as well be the information-processing operations associated with retention that underlie the effect. We have recently discussed in some detail our results from the verbal reasoning task (Hitch & Baddeley, 1976) and have not been able to verify our original suggestion. Indeed, it seems that a "passive" retention task (that is, storage without much associated information processing) does not influence the rate of concurrent information processing on a second task. Our present bias is, therefore, away from our earlier view and toward the central component as an executive processor. As such, it interacts with different cognitive subsystems, such as the articulatory loop, long-term storage, and the sensory stores. We are still interested, however, in the distinction between storage and processing and are still searching for empirical techniques that will allow us to separate them. It has turned out to be a much more difficult enterprise than we thought at first.

Extension to Other Problems

RETRIEVAL

Several experiments have been carried out, but not yet published, on the role of working memory in retrieval. The first of these used a free recall paradigm in which lists of 15 words were presented and then recalled after a filled delay. During the recall phase, subjects were either unencumbered by a secondary task, were required to suppress articulation by a counting task, or were required to retain sequences of six random digits. No reliable effects of any of the secondary tasks were obtained. Two further studies used concurrent card sorting as a secondary task and contrasted sorting during learning with sorting during retrieval. Both showed the clear effort of sorting load on learning that was first shown by Murdock (1965) but showed no evidence for an impairment of retrieval. A fourth experiment used paired-associate learning and again found that a concurrent task, in this case digit span, impaired performance during input but had no effect during retrieval. Therefore, the evidence seems to suggest that working memory is not essential for retrieval. It seems likely, however, that we will find cases in which working memory is important, particularly in situations in which retrieval closely resembles a problem solving task. An example might be Norman's (1970) illustration of a subject attempting to answer a question of the sort "Where were you living 5 years ago?"

We were encouraged by the apparent success of the model in drawing attention to a new phenomenon. In particular, it emphasizes the distinction between the working memory approach and a rather general concept, such as limited channel capacity, which might lead one to predict that a supplementary task would have a comparable effect on all cognitive tasks.

VISUAL WORKING MEMORY

Subsequent unpublished work on visual imagery (described in Baddeley, 1976, pp. 222–234) has further explored the concept of a visual working memory. The evidence suggests that it is, in fact, spatial rather than visual. It was disrupted by a concurrent task that involved a blindfold subject in tracking a moving sound source, while it was unaffected by a nonspatial visual task, namely judging the brightness of a field. The system appears to be used in visual imagery mnemonics, particularly when these involve spatial manipulation, but it is not affected by whether verbal material is concrete or abstract in nature. The relationship between this system and the central executive component of working memory has yet to be explored. At present, however, we have no reason for rejecting the assumption that the spatial system functions in an analagous way to the articulatory loop, forming a peripheral slave system that supplements the central executive.

Applications of the Working Memory Concept

MENTAL ARITHMETIC

Mental arithmetic is a fairly common activity despite the advent of pocket calculators. People appear to utilize well-learned strategies, which seem to involve the temporary storage of information. The concept of working memory has been used in investigating the task in some detail. A series of studies explored errors in the addition of pairs of numbers; each number of a pair contained two or three digits. Results show that different people use a variety of information processing strategies, but nonetheless, nearly all the strategies appear to consist of sequences of more elementary arithmetical steps. A typical step can be decomposed into the retrieval of starting information (from working storage), its arithmetical transformation (using long-term knowledge), and, finally, either direct output of the result of "holding" it pending some later operation (again in working storage). This view of the task emphasizes the close interplay between information processing and temporary storage, in line with working memory concept. Analysis of performance in several versions of the addition task tends to confirm the hypothesis and suggests that rapid forgetting of any information held in working storage is a major source of error (Hitch, in preparation). Thus, we can already say with some confidence that the concept of working memory has provided a useful framework for investigating arithmetic, although there is admittedly a great deal of work still to do.

READING

We have been exploring the possible role of the articulatory loop in reading (Hitch & Baddeley, 1977). Conrad (1972) noticed that children begin to show a phonemic similarity effect when remembering sequences of pictures at about the age that they begin to learn to read. Furthermore, Liberman, Shankweiler, Liberman, Fowler, and Fisher (1976) have shown that children who are poor at reading do not show a phonemic similarity effect when remembering sequences of visually presented consonants. There is also evidence (Naidoo, 1970) that dyslexic children show poorer memory spans than one might expect on the basis of other aspects of their general intelligence. All of these effects can be explained plausibly by assuming that the articulatory loop serves a function in the process of learning to read and that inadequate use of the loop will impair the development of reading. One way in which this might occur is in the process of translating the individual letters of a word into sounds and then blending them to produce something sounding more like the normal word, for example, blending the sound of the letters *m, a,* and *d* into the word *mad.* Such blending, if it does occur, must logically require storage of the sounds of the individual letters. The articulatory loop seems to be very appropriate for this task.

In the case of experienced readers, the articulatory loop may also play an important role—though, of course, in a rather different way.

A series of experiments reported by Kleiman (1975) studied the effects of articulatory suppression on the ability to make various types of decisions about visually presented material. He found that suppression interfered with judgments about the sounds of individual words but did so less with judgments about their letter patterns or meanings. Judgments about the meanings of whole sentences, however, were affected by suppression. In the latter case, Kleiman argues that a whole sequence of words has to be stored before the judgment can be made. Arguably, such storage involves the articulatory loop. For individual words of course, use of the loop is probably not necessary. A similar conclusion is hinted at in a study by Hardyck and Petrinovich (1970) who show that very often people do subvocalize during reading, especially if the material is difficult. Presumably, with harder material, more of it must be temporarily stored before it can be successfully interpreted.

We believe that there is strong evidence suggesting that a task as complex as reading may involve the working memory system and that it may be profitable to use the working memory framework to study reading.

In conclusion, we are continuing to find the concept of working memory extremely useful in providing a framework that has sufficient flexibility to allow development, while at the same time suggesting specific testable hypotheses.

REFERENCES

Anderson, C. M. B., & Craik, F. I. M. The effect of a concurrent task on recall from primary memory. *Journal of Verbal Learning and Verbal Behavior*, 1974, **13**, 107–113.

Baddeley, A. D. *The psychology of memory*. New York: Harper & Row, 1976.

Baddeley, A. D., & Hitch, G. J. Working memory. In G. H. Bower (Ed.), *The psychology of learning and motivation: Advances in research and theory*. Vol. 8. New York: Academic Press. Pp. 47–89.

Baddeley, A. D., & Hitch, G. J. Recency re-examined. In S. Dornic (Ed.), *Attention and performance VI*. London: Academic Press, 1977.

Baddeley, A. D., Thomson, N., & Buchanan, M. Word length and the structure of short-term memory. *Journal of Verbal Learning and Verbal Behavior*, 1975, **14**, 575–589.

Conrad, R. The developmental role of vocalizing in short-term memory. *Journal of Verbal Learning and Verbal Behavior*, 1972, **11**, 521–533.

Hardyck, C. D., & Petrinovich, L. F. Sub-vocal speech and comprehension level as a function of the difficulty level of reading material. *Journal of Verbal Learning and Verbal Behavior*, 1970, **9**, 647–652.

Hitch, G. J., & Baddeley, A. D. Verbal reasoning and working memory. *Quarterly Journal of Experimental Psychology*, 1976, **28**, 603–621.

Hitch, G. J., & Baddeley, A. D. Working memory and information processing. [In *Cognitive psychology, course no. D303.* Milton Keynes: Open University Press, 1977.

Hitch, G. J. The role of short–term working storage in mental arithmetic (in preparation).

Kleiman, G. M. Speech recoding in reading. *Journal of Verbal Learning and Verbal Behavior,* 1975, **14**, 323–339.

Liberman, I. Y., Shankweiler, D., Liberman, A. M., Fowler, C., & Fisher, F. W. Phonetic segmentation and recoding in the beginning reader. In A. S. Reber & D. Scarborough (Eds.), *Reading: The C.U.N.Y. conference.* New York: Erlbaum, 1976.

Murdock, B. B., Jr. Effects of a subsidiary task on short-term memory. *British Journal of Psychology,* 1965, **56**, 413–419.

Naidoo, S. The assessment of dyslexic children. In A. W. Franklin & S. Naidoo (Eds.), *Assessment and teaching of dyslexic children.* London: Invalid Children's Aid Association, 1970.

Norman, D. A. Comments on the information structure of memory. In A. F. Sanders (Ed.), *Attention and performance III,* Amsterdam: North Holland, 1970.

Reprinted from *The Psychology of Learning and Motivation*, 1974, 8, 47–89.

WORKING MEMORY

Alan D. Baddeley[1] *and Graham Hitch*[1]

UNIVERSITY OF STIRLING, STIRLING, SCOTLAND

I. Introduction

Despite more than a decade of intensive research on the topic of short-term memory (STM), we still know virtually nothing about its role in normal human information processing. That is not, of course, to say that the issue has completely been neglected. The short-term store (STS)—the hypothetical memory system which is assumed to be responsible for performance in tasks involving short-term memory paradigms (Atkinson & Shiffrin, 1968)—has been assigned a crucial role in the performance of a wide range of tasks including problem solving (Hunter, 1964), language comprehension (Rumelhart, Lindsay, & Norman, 1972) and most notably, long-term learning (Atkinson & Shiffrin, 1968; Waugh & Norman, 1965). Perhaps the most cogent case for the central importance of STS in general information processing is that of Atkinson and Shiffrin (1971) who attribute to STS the role of a controlling executive system responsible for coordinating and monitoring the many and complex subroutines that are responsible for both acquiring new material and retrieving old. However, despite the frequency with which STS

---

[1] *Present address:* Medical Research Council, Applied Psychology Unit, 15 Chaucer Road, Cambridge, England.

has been assigned this role as an operational or working memory, the empirical evidence for such a view is remarkably sparse.

A number of studies have shown that the process of learning and recall does make demands on the subject's general processing capacity, as reflected by his performance on some simultaneous subsidiary task, such as card sorting (Murdock, 1965), tracking performance (Martin, 1970), or reaction time (Johnston, Griffith & Wagstaff, 1972). However, attempts to show that the limitation stems from the characteristics of the working memory system have proved less successful. Coltheart (1972) attempted to study the role of STS in concept formation by means of the acoustic similarity effect, the tendency for STM to be disrupted when the material to be remembered comprises items that are phonemically similar to each other (Baddeley, 1966b; Conrad, 1962). She contrasted the effect of acoustic similarity on concept formation with that of semantic similarity, which typically effects LTM rather than STM (Baddeley, 1966a). Unfortunately for the working memory hypothesis, her results showed clear evidence of semantic rather than acoustic coding, suggesting that the long-term store (LTS) rather than STS was playing a major role in her concept formation task.

Patterson (1971) tested the hypothesis that STS plays the important role in retrieval of holding the retrieval plan, which is then used to access the material to be recalled (Rumelhart *et al.*, 1972). She attempted to disrupt such retrieval plans by requiring her experimental group to count backwards for 20 seconds following each item recalled. On the basis of the results of Peterson and Peterson (1959), it was assumed that this would effectively erase information from STS after each recall. Despite this rather drastic interference with the normal functioning of STS however, there was no reliable decrement in the number of words recalled.

The most devastating evidence against the hypothesis that STS serves as a crucially important working memory comes from the neuropsychological work of Shallice and Warrington (Shallice & Warrington, 1970; Warrington & Shallice, 1969; Warrington & Weiskrantz, 1972). They have extensively studied a patient who by all normal standards, has a grossly defective STS. He has a digit span of only two items, and shows grossly impaired performance on the Peterson short-term forgetting task. If STS does indeed function as a central working memory, then one would expect this patient to exhibit grossly defective learning, memory, and comprehension. No such evidence of general impairment is found either in this case or in subsequent cases of a similar type (Warrington, Logue, & Pratt, 1971).

It appears then, that STS constitutes a system for which great claims have been made by many workers (including the present authors), for which there is little good evidence.

The experiments which follow attempt to answer two basic questions: first, is there any evidence that the tasks of reasoning, comprehension, and learning share a common working memory system?; and secondly, if such a system exists, how is it related to our current conception of STM? We do not claim to be presenting a novel view of STM in this chapter. Rather, our aim is to present a body of new experimental evidence which provides a firm basis for the working memory hypothesis. The account which follows should therefore be regarded essentially as a progress report on an on-going project. The reader will notice obvious gaps where further experiments clearly need to be performed, and it is more than probable that such experiments will modify to a greater or lesser degree our current tentative theoretical position. We hope, however, that the reader will agree that we do have enough information to draw some reasonably firm conclusions, and will feel that a report of work in progress is not too out of place in a volume of this kind.

II. The Search for a Common Working Memory System

The section which follows describes a series of experiments on the role of memory in reasoning, language comprehension, and learning. An attempt is made to apply comparable techniques in all three cases in the hope that this will allow a common pattern to emerge, if the same working memory system is operative in all three instances.

In attempting to assess the role of memory in any task, one is faced with a fundamental problem. What is meant by STS? Despite, or perhaps because of, the vast amount of research on the characteristics of STS there is still little general agreement. If our subsequent work were to depend on a generally acceptable definition of STS as a prerequisite for further research, such research would never begin. We suspect that this absence of unanimity stems from the fact that evidence for STS comes from two basically dissimilar paradigms. The first is based on the traditional memory span task. It suggests that STS is limited in capacity, is concerned with the retention of order information, and is closely associated with the processing of speech. The second cluster of evidence derives from the recency effect in free recall. It also suggests that STS is limited in capacity; however, its other dominant feature is its apparent resistence to the effects of other variables, whether semantic or speech-based (Glanzer, 1972). Rather than try to resolve these apparent discrepancies, we decided to begin by studying the one characteristic that both approaches to STS agreed on, namely its limited capacity. The technique adopted was to require S to retain one or more items while performing the task of reasoning, language comprehension, or learning. Such a concurrent memory load might reasonably be expected to absorb some of the storage capacity of a limited capacity working memory system, should such a system exist. The first set of experiments describes the application of this technique to the study of a reasoning task. To anticipate our results, we find a consistent pattern of additional memory load effects on all three tasks that we have studied: reasoning, language comprehension, and free recall. Additionally, all three tasks show evidence of phonemic coding. From this evidence we infer that each of the tasks involves a spanlike component, which we refer to as working memory. Further evidence from the free recall paradigm shows that the recency effect is neither disrupted by an additional memory span task nor particularly associated with phonemic coding. We therefore suggest a dichotomy between working memory and the recency effect, in contrast to the more usual view that both recency and the memory span reflect a single limited capacity short-term buffer store (STS).

A. The Role of Working Memory in Reasoning

The reasoning task selected was that devised by Baddeley (1968) in which S is presented with a sentence purporting to describe the order of occurrence of two letters. The sentence is followed by the letters in question, and S's task is to decide as quickly as possible whether the sentence correctly describes the order in which the letters are presented. For example, he may be given the sentence *A is not preceded by B-AB*, in which case he should respond *True*. A range of different sentences can be produced varying as to whether they are active or passive, positive or negative, and whether the word *precedes* or *follows* is used. This task is typical of a wide range of sentence verification tasks studied in recent years (Wason & Johnson-Laird, 1972). Its claim to be a reasoning task of some general validity is supported by the correlation between performance and intelligence (Baddeley, 1968) and its sensitivity to both environmental and speed-load stress (Baddeley, De Figuredo, Hawkswell-Curtis, & Williams, 1968; Brown, Tickner, & Simmonds, 1969). The first experiment requires S to perform this simple reasoning task while holding zero, one, or two items in memory. If the task relies on a limited capacity system, then one might expect the additional load to impair performance.

1. Experiment I: Effects of a One- or Two-Item Preload

Subjects were required to process 32 sentences based on all possible combinations of sentence voice (active or passive), affirmation (affirmative or negative), truth value (true or false), verb type (precedes or follows), and letter order (AB or BA). The experiment used a version of the memory preload technique in which S is given one or two items to remember. He is then required to process the sentence and having responded "True" or "False," he is then required to recall the letters. A slide projector was used to present the sentences, each of which remained visible until S pressed the "True" or "False" response key. Twenty-four undergraduate Ss were tested. The order in which the three conditions were presented were determined by a Latin square. For half the Ss the preload was presented visually, while the other half was given an auditory preload. In the zero load condition, S was always presented with a single letter before the presentation of the sentence. However, the letter was the same on all trials, and S was not required to recall it subsequently. With the one- and two-letter loads, the letters differed from trial to trial but were never the same as those used in the reasoning problem. All Ss were informed of this.

TABLE I

MEAN TIME (SEC) TO COMPLETE VERBAL REASONING PROBLEMS AS A FUNCTION OF SIZE OF ADDITIONAL MEMORY LOAD AND METHOD OF READING MEMORY ITEMS

Method of reading	Memory load		
	Zero	1-letter	2-letters
Silent	3.07	3.35	3.21
Aloud	3.33	3.26	3.41
Means	3.20	3.31	3.31

The results are shown in Table I. There was no reliable effect of memory load on solution time regardless of whether the load was one or two letters, and was presented visually or auditorily ($F < 1$ in each case). Since letter recall was almost always perfect, it appears to be the case that Ss can hold up to two additional items with no impairment in their reasoning speed. This result suggests one of two conclusions; either that the type of memory system involved in retaining the letters is not relevant to the reasoning task, or else that a load of two items is not sufficient to overtax the system. Experiment II attempts to decide between these two hypotheses by increasing the preload from two to six letters, a load which approaches the memory span for many Ss.

2. Experiment II: Effects of a Six-Digit Preload

Performance on the 32 sentences was studied with and without a six-letter memory preload. In the preload condition each trial began with a verbal "ready" signal followed by a random sequence of six letters spoken at a rate of one per second. The reasoning problem followed immediately afterwards, details of presentation and method of responding being the same as in Experiment I. After solving the problem, S attempted to recall verbally as many letters as possible in the correct order. In the control condition, the reasoning problem followed immediately after the "ready" signal. After completing the problem, and before being presented· with the next problem, S listened to a six-letter sequence and recalled it immediately. This procedure varies the storage load during reasoning, but roughly equates the two conditions for total memorization required during the session.

Separate blocks of 32 trials were used for presenting the two conditions, each block containing the 32 sentences in random order. Half the Ss began with the control condition and half with the preload condition. Two groups of 12 undergraduate Ss were tested. The two groups differed in the instructions they were given. The first group (equal stress) was told to carry out the reasoning task as rapidly as possible, consistent with high accuracy, and to attempt to recall all six letters correctly. The second group (memory stress) was told that only if their recall was completely correct could their reasoning time be scored; subject to this proviso, they were told to reason as rapidly as they could, consistent with high accuracy. All Ss were given a preliminary three-minute practice session on a sheet of reasoning problems, and were tested individually.

TABLE II

MEAN REASONING TIMES AND RECALL SCORES FOR THE "EQUAL STRESS"
AND "MEMORY STRESS" INSTRUCTIONAL GROUPS

Instructional emphasis	Mean reasoning time (sec)		Mean no. items recalled (max = 6)	
	Control	Memory preload	Control	Memory preload
"Equal stress"	3.27	3.46	5.5	3.7
"Memory stress"	2.73	4.73	5.8	5.0

Mean reasoning times (for correct solutions) and recall scores for
both groups of subjects are shown in Table II. For the "equal stress"
Ss memory load produced a slight but nonsignificant slowing down
in reasoning time (on a Wilcoxon test, $T = 31, N = 12, P > .05$),
while for the "memory stress" Ss memory load slowed down reasoning considerably ($T = 4, N = 12, P < .01$). There appears to have
been a trade-off between reasoning and recall in the memory load
condition. The equal stress Ss achieved their unimpaired reasoning
at the expense of very poor recall compared with that of the memory
stress Ss.

The results show then, that there is an interaction between additional short-term storage load and reasoning performance. In comparison with the results of Experiment I these suggest that the interaction depends on the storage load since, up to two items can be
recalled accurately with no detectable effect. Thus the reasoning task
does not seem to require all the available short-term storage space.
The results show additionally that the form of the interaction depends on the instructional emphasis given to S. It seems likely therefore that interference was the result of the active strategy that Ss
employed. One possibility is that the "memory stress" Ss dealt with
the memory preload by quickly rehearsing the items, to "consoli-
date" them in memory before starting the reasoning problem. If this
were the case, then reasoning times ought to be slowed by a constant
amount (the time spent rehearsing the letters), regardless of problem
complexity. Figure 1 shows mean reasoning time for the memory
stress group for different types of sentence. Control reaction times
(RTs) show that problems expressed as passives were more difficult
than those expressed as actives, and that negative forms were more
difficult than affirmatives. However, the slowing down in reasoning
produced by the memory preload was roughly constant regardless
of problem difficulty. Analysis of variance showed significant effects

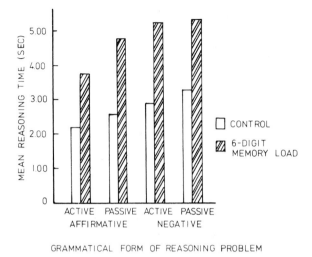

Fig. 1. Mean reasoning time for different forms of the problem for the "memory stress" group of subjects.

of memory load [$F(1,10) = 8.51, P < .025$], sentence voice [$F(1,10 = 7.34, P < .025$], and negation [$F(1,10 = 34.9, P < .001$]. None of the interaction terms involving the load factor approached significance.

The results of this experiment do not adequately demonstrate that the verbal reasoning task involves a short-term storage component. Subjects seem to have adopted a strategy of time-sharing between rehearsal of the memory letters and reasoning. While the time-sharing may have been forced by competition between the tasks for a limited storage capacity, this is not necessarily the case. The tasks may, for example, have competed for use of the articulatory system, without having overlapping storage demands.

Experiment III attempts to prevent the strategy of completely switching attention from the memory task to the reasoning test by changing from a preload to a concurrent load procedure. In the concurrent load procedure, S is required to continue to rehearse the memory load items aloud while completing the reasoning task. Since the process of articulation has itself been shown to impair performance in both memory (Levy, 1971; Murray, 1967, 1968) and reasoning (Hammerton, 1969; Peterson, 1969), two additional conditions were included to allow a separation of the effects of memory load and of articulation.

3. Experiment III: Effects of a Concurrent Memory Load

All Ss performed the 32 reasoning problems under each of four conditions, the order in which the conditions were tested being determined by a Latin square. In the control condition, a trial began with a verbal warning signal and the instruction "say nothing." The problem was then presented and solved as quickly and accurately as possible. The second condition used the articulatory suppression procedure devised by Murray (1967). Subjects were instructed to say the word "the" repeatedly, at a rate of between four and five utterances per second. After S had begun to articulate, the problem was presented, whereupon he continued the articulation task at the same high rate until he had pressed the "True" or "False" response button. The third condition followed a procedure adopted by Peterson (1969) in which the articulation task consisted of the cyclic repetition of a familiar sequence of responses, namely the counting sequence "one-two-three-four-five-six." Again, a rate of four to five words per second was required. In the fourth condition, S was given a random six-digit sequence to repeat cyclically at a four- to five-digit per second rate. In this condition alone, the message to be articulated was changed from trial to trial. The three articulation conditions therefore range from the simple repetition of a single utterance, through the rather more complex articulation involved in counting, up to the digit span repetition task, which presumably make considerably greater short-term storage demands. Degree of prior practice and method of presentation were as in Experiment II.

Table III shows the performance of the 12 undergraduate Ss tested in this study. Concurrent articulation of "the" and counting up to six produced a slight slowing of reasoning time, but by far the greatest slowing occurred with concurrent articulation of random digit sequences. Analysis of variance showed a significant main effect of

TABLE III

MEAN REASONING TIMES AND ERROR RATES AS A FUNCTION OF CONCURRENT ARTICULATORY ACTIVITY

Concurrent articulation	Mean reasoning RT (sec)	Percent reasoning errors
Control	2.79	8.1
"The-The-The . . ."	3.13	10.6
"One-Two-Three . . ."	3.22	5.6
Random 6-digit No.	4.27	10.3

conditions $[F(3,33) = 14.2, P < .01]$. Newman-Keuls tests showed that the effect was mainly due to the difference between the random digit condition and the other three. The slight slowing down in the suppression-only and counting conditions just failed to reach significance.

These results suggest that interference with verbal reasoning is not entirely to be explained in terms of competition for the articulatory system, which may be committed to the rapid production of a well-learned sequence of responses with relatively little impairment of reasoning. A much more important factor appears to be the short-term memory load, with the availability of spare short-term storage capacity determining the rate at which the reasoning processes are carried out. Since difficult problems presumably make greater demands on these processes, one might expect that more difficult problems would show a greater effect of concurrent storage load. Figure 2 shows the mean reasoning times for problems of various kinds. As is typically the case with such tasks (Wason & Johnson-Laird, 1972), passive sentences proved more difficult than active sentences $[F(1,11) = 55.2, P < .01]$, and negatives were more difficult than affirmatives $[F(1,11) = 38.5, P < .01]$. In addition to the main effect of con-

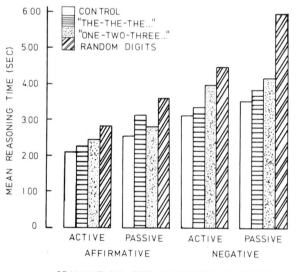

Fig. 2. Effects of concurrent articulatory activity on mean reasoning time for different types of problem.

current activity, activity interacted with sentence voice [$F(3,33) =$ 5.59, $P < .01$] and with negativity [$F(3,33) = 5.29, P < .01$]. Figure 2 shows that these interactions were due largely to performance in the random digit condition. Additional storage load seems to have slowed down solution times to passives more than actives and to negatives more than affirmatives. Thus the greater the problem difficulty, the greater the effect of an additional short-term storage load.

In summary, it has been shown that additional STM loads of more than two items can impair the rate at which reasoning is carried out. Loads of six items can produce sizable interference, but the effect may depend on the instructional emphasis given to Ss (Experiment II). The interference effects may be partly due to the articulatory activity associated with rehearsal of the memory items, but there is a substantial amount of interference over and above this which is presumably due to storage load (Experiment III). The trade-off between reasoning speed and additional storage load suggests that the interference occurs within a limited capacity "workspace," which can be flexibly allocated either to storage or to processing.

The effect of articulatory suppression in Experiment III was small and did not reach statistical significance. However, Hammerton (1969) has reported evidence that suppression can produce reliable interference in this task. His Ss repeated the familiar sentence "Mary had a little lamb" while carrying out the Baddeley reasoning task. Performance was impaired when contrasted with a control group who said nothing when reasoning. This result together with those of Peterson (1969) suggests that reasoning may resemble the memory span task in having an articulatory component. Experiment IV explores the relation between the memory span and working memory further by taking a major feature of the verbal memory span, namely its susceptibility to the effects of phonemic similarity, and testing for similar effects in the verbal reasoning task.

4.   Experiment IV: Phonemic Similarity and Verbal Reasoning

One of the more striking features of the memory span for verbal materials is its apparent reliance on phonemic (either acoustic or articulatory) coding. This is revealed both by the nature of intrusion errors (Conrad, 1962; Sperling, 1963) and by the impairment in performance shown when sequences of phonemically similar items are recalled (Baddeley, 1966b; Conrad & Hull, 1964). As Wickelgren (1965) has shown, phonemic similarity has its disruptive effect principally on the retention of order information, and since the reasoning task employed depends on the order of the letters concerned, it seems reasonable to suppose that the manipulation of phonemic similarity might prove a suitable way of disrupting any STS component of the task. Experiment IV, therefore, studied the effect of phonemic similarity on the reasoning task and compared this with the effect of visual similarity, a factor which is typically found to have little or no influence on memory span for letters.

A group testing procedure was used in which Ss were given test sheets containing 64 reasoning problems printed in random order and were allowed three minutes to complete as many as possible. A 2 × 2 factorial design was used with phonemic and visual similarity as factors. There were two replications of the experiment, each using different letter pairs in each of the four conditions. The sets of letter pairs used were as follows: *MC, VS* (low phonemic similarity, low visual similarity); *FS, TD* (high phonemic, low visual similarity); *OQ, XY* (low phonemic, high visual similarity); and *BP, MN* (high phonemic, high visual similarity). Thirty-two undergraduate Ss were tested, half with one letter set and half with the other. All Ss were first given a preliminary practice session using the letter-pair *AB*. Each S then completed a three-minute session on each of the four types of problems. Problems were printed on sheets, and Ss responded in writing. The order of presenting the four conditions was determined using a Latin square.

Table IV shows the mean number of correctly answered questions in the various conditions. Since there were no important differences between results from the two replications, data from the two sets of letter pairs have been pooled. Only the effect of phonemic similarity was significant ($N = 32$, $Z = 2.91$, $P < .002$), while visual similarity appeared to have no effect ($N = 32$, $Z < 1$). It appears then that the verbal reasoning task does require the utilization of phonemically

TABLE IV

Mean Number of Reasoning Problems Correctly Solved in Three Minutes as a Function of Phonemic and Visual Similarity of the Letters Used in the Problems

		Phonemic similarity of letters	
		Low	High
Visual similarity of letters	Low	43.2	40.9
	High	42.9	39.8

coded information, and, although the effect is small, it is highly consistent across Ss.

In summary then, verbal reasoning shows effects of concurrent storage load, of articulatory suppression, and of phonemic similarity. This pattern of results is just what would be expected if the task depended on the use of a short-term store having the characteristics typically shown in the memory span paradigm. However, the magnitude of the effects suggest that the system responsible for the memory span is only part of working memory. We shall return to this point after considering the evidence for the role of working memory in prose comprehension and learning.

B. Comprehension and Working Memory

While it has frequently been asserted that STS plays a crucial role in the comprehension of spoken language (e.g., Baddeley & Patterson, 1971; Norman, 1972), the evidence for such a claim is sparse. There is, of course, abundant evidence that language material may be held in STM (Jarvella, 1971; Sachs, 1967) but we know of no evidence to suggest that such storage is an essential function of comprehension under normal circumstances, and in view of the lack of any obvious defect in comprehension shown by patients with grossly defective STS (Shallice & Warrington, 1970), the importance of STS in comprehension remains to be demonstrated. Experiments V and VI attempt to do so using the memory preload and the concurrent memory load techniques.

1. Experiment V: Effects of a Memory Preload on Comprehension

In this experiment, S listened to spoken prose passages under each of two memory load conditions and was subsequently tested for retention of the passages. In the experimental condition, each sentence of the passage was preceded by a sequence of six digits spoken at a rate of one item per second. After listening to the sentence, S attempted to write down the digit sequence in the correct order in time to a metronome beating at a one-second rate. Hence S was required to retain the digit sequence while listening to the sentence. In the control condition the digit sequence followed the sentence and was recalled immediately afterward. Thus both conditions involved the same amount of overt activity, but only in the experimental condition was there a temporal overlap between the retention of the digits and sentence presentation. In both conditions the importance of recalling the digits accurately was emphasized. After each passage, S was allowed three minutes to complete a recall test based on the Cloze technique (Taylor, 1953). Test sheets comprised a typed script of each of the passages, from which every fifth word had been deleted. The passages contained approximately 170 words each, and hence there were about 33 blanks which S was instructed to try to fill with the deleted word. This technique has been shown by Rubenstein and Aborn (1958) to be a reasonably sensitive measure of prose retention. Three different types of passage were included in the experiment: descriptions, narratives, and arguments. Two examples of each type were constructed giving six passages in all, each of which contained ten sentences. Each of 30 Ss was tested on all six passages, comprising one experimental and one control condition for each of the three passage types. Subjects were tested in two separate groups, each receiving a different ordering of the six passages.

Table V shows the mean number of correctly completed blanks for the control and experimental conditions together with the mean number of digit sequences correctly reported in the two conditions. The digit preload impaired performance on the comprehension test for all three types of passage. Differences were significant for the descriptions ($Z = 2.81$, $P < .01$, Wilcoxon test) and the narratives ($Z = 2.91$, $P < .01$), but not for the arguments ($Z = 1.14$, $P > .05$). Thus, test performance is impaired when digits have to be held in store during presentation of the passage. Digit recall scores were

TABLE V

COMPREHENSION AND DIGIT RECALL SCORES WITH AND WITHOUT ADDITIONAL MEMORY LOAD FOR THREE TYPES OF PASSAGE

Type of passage	Memory load condition	Comprehension score[a]	Digit recall score[b]
Description	No load	16.8	11.8
	Load	13.3	7.7
Narrative	No load	20.1	11.4
	Load	18.0	7.8
Argument	No load	14.5	11.4
	Load	13.6	8.1

[a] Mean no. of blanks correctly filled in—max = 33
[b] Mean no. of digit strings correctly reported—max = 14

also poorest in the experimental condition, but this was, of course, to be expected in view of the long filled retention interval in this condition.

While the results can be interpreted as showing that comprehension is impaired by an additional short-term storage load, this conclusion is not unchallengeable. Firstly, the Cloze procedure is probably a test of prompted verbatim recall and may not measure comprehension. Secondly, the control condition of the experiment may not have been entirely satisfactory. If the time *between* sentences is important for comprehension of the meaning of the passage as a whole, the control group itself may have suffered from an appreciable amount of interference. The next experiment goes some way to overcoming both these objections, using the concurrent memory load procedure instead of the preload technique.

2. *Experiment VI: Effects of a Concurrent Memory Load on Comprehension*

This experiment compared the effects of three levels of concurrent storage load on prose comprehension. In all three conditions, the memory items were presented visually at a rate of one per second using a TV monitor. The concurrent memory load tasks were as follows. In the three-digit load condition, S was always presented with sequences of three digits, each sequence being followed by a 2-second blank interval during which S attempted to recall and write down the three digits he had just seen. In the six-digit condition, the sequences all comprised six items and were followed by a 4-second blank interval. Again S was instructed not to recall the digits until the sequence had been removed. Time intervals were chosen so as to keep S busy with the digit memory task, and were also such that all conditions would require input and output of the same total number of digits. In the control condition, S was presented with sequences of three and six digits in alternation. After each three-digit list there was a 2-second blank interval, and after each six-digit list the blank interval was 4 seconds. In this case, however, S was simply required to copy down the digits while they were being presented. It was hoped that this task would require the minimal memory load consistent with the demand of keeping the amount of digit writing constant across conditions. The main difference between the three conditions was, therefore, the number of digits which S was required to store simultaneously. Instructions emphasized the im-

portance of accuracy on all three digit tasks, and an invigilator
checked that Ss were obeying the instructions.

Comprehension was tested using six passages taken from the Neale
Analysis of Reading Ability (Neale, 1958). Two passages (those
suited for 12- and 13-year-old children) were selected from each of
the three parallel test forms. Each passage comprised approximately
120 words and was tested by eight standardized questions. These
have the advantage of testing comprehension of the passage without
using the specific words used in the original presentation. They can,
therefore, be regarded as testing retention of the gist of the passage
rather than verbatim recall. Answers were given a score of one if
correct, half if judged almost correct, and zero otherwise. At the
start of each trial, the experimenter announced which version of the
digit task was to be presented before testing began. After a few
seconds of the digit processing task, the experimenter began to read
out the prose passage at a normal reading rate and with normal
intonation. At the end of the passage, the digit task was abandoned
and the experimenter read out the comprehension questions. A
total of 15 undergraduates were tested in three equal-sized groups,
in a design which allowed each passage to be tested once under each
of the three memory load conditions.

The mean comprehension scores for the three conditions are
shown in Table VI. The Friedman test showed significant overall
effects of memory load ($\chi_r^2 = 7.3$, $P < .05$). Wilcoxon tests showed
that the six-digit memory load produced lower comprehension scores
than either the control condition ($T = 19$, $N = 14$, $P < .05$), or the
three-digit condition ($T = 19.5$, $N = 15$, $P < .05$). There was no
reliable difference between the three-digit load and control conditions ($T = 44.5$, $N = 14$, $P > .05$). Thus, comprehension is not reliably affected by a three-item memory load, but is depressed by a
six-item load, a pattern of results which is very similar to that observed with the verbal reasoning task.

TABLE VI

Mean Comprehension Scores as a Function of Size of Concurrent
Memory Load

	Memory load		
	Control (1-digit)	3-digit	6-digit
Mean comprehension score (max = 8)	5.9	5.6	4.8

While Experiments IV and V present *prima facie* evidence for the role of working memory in comprehension, it could be argued that we have tested retention rather than comprehension. From what little we know of the process of comprehension, it seems likely that understanding and remembering are very closely related. It is, however, clearly desirable that this work should be extended and an attempt made to separate the factors of comprehension and retention before any final conclusions are drawn.

If comprehension makes use of STM, it should be possible to impair performance on comprehension tasks by introducing phonemic similarity into the test material. To test this hypothesis using the prose comprehension task of the previous experiment would have involved the difficult task of producing passages of phonemically similar words. We chose instead to study the comprehension of single sentences, since the generation of sentences containing a high proportion of phonemically similar words seemed likely to prove less demanding than that of producing a whole passage of such material.

3. Experiment VII: Phonemic Similarity and Sentence Comprehension

The task used in this experiment required *S* to judge whether a single sentence was impossible or possible. Possible sentences were both grammatical and meaningful, while impossible sentences were both ungrammatical and relatively meaningless. Impossible sentences were derived from their possible counterparts by reversing the order of two adjacent words near the middle of the possible sentence. Two sets of possible sentences were constructed, one comprising phonemically dissimilar words and the other one containing a high proportion of phonemically similar words. An example of each type of possible sentence together with its derived impossible sentence is shown in Table VII. In order to equate the materials as closely as

TABLE VII

Examples of the Sentences Used in Experiment VIII

	Possible version	Impossible version
Phonemically dissimilar	Dark skinned Ian thought Harry ate in bed	Dark skinned Ian Harry thought ate in bed
Phonemically similar	Red headed Ned said Ted fed in bed	Red headed Ned Ted said fed in bed

possible, each phonemically similar sentence was matched with a phonemically dissimilar sentence for number of words, grammatical form, and general semantic content. There were nine examples of each of the four conditions (phonemically similar possible; phonemically similar impossible; phonemically dissimilar possible, and phonemically dissimilar impossible), giving 36 sentences in all.

Each sentence was typed on a white index card and was exposed to S by the opening of a shutter approximately half a second after a verbal warning signal. The sentence remained visible until S had responded by pressing one of two response keys. Instructions stressed both speed and accuracy. Twenty students served as Ss and were given ten practice sentences before proceeding to the 36 test sentences which were presented in random order.

Since reading speed was a potentially important source of variance, 13 of the 20 Ss were asked to read the sentences aloud at the end of the experiment and their reading times were recorded. The 36 sentences were grouped into four sets of nine, each set corresponding to one of the four experimental conditions and were typed onto four separate sheets of paper. The order of presenting the sheets was randomized across Ss, and the time to read each was measured by a stopwatch.

Table VIII shows mean reaction times for each of the four types of sentence, together with reading rate for each condition. It is clear that phonemic similarity increased the judgment times for both possible and impossible sentences $[F(1,9) = 8.77, P < .01]$, there being no interaction between the effects of similarity and grammaticality $[F(1,9) < 1]$. An interaction between the effects of phonemic similarity and sentence type $[F(8,152) = 4,38, P < .001]$ suggests that the effect does not characterize all the sentences presented. Inspec-

TABLE VIII

RESULTS OF EXPERIMENT VIII

Sentence type	Mean RT for judgment of "possibility" (sec)			Mean reading time (sec)		
	Possible version	Impossible version	Average	Possible version	Impossible version	Average
Phonemically dissimilar	2.84	2.62	2.73	2.93	3.18	3.06
Phonemically similar	3.03	2.83	2.93	2.96	3.19	3.08

tion of the three sentence sets out of nine which show no similarity effect suggests that this is probably because the dissimilar sentences in these sets contained either longer or less frequent words than their phonemically similar counterparts. Clearly, future experiments should control word length and frequency.

Reading times did not vary appreciably with phonemic similarity [$F(1,12) < 1$]. It is, therefore, clear that phonemic similarity interfered with the additional processing over and above that involved in reading, required to make the possible/impossible judgment. As Table VIII suggests, although impossible sentences took longer to read than possible sentences [$F(1,12) = 41.6$, $P < .001$], they were judged more rapidly [$F(1,19) = 17.3$, $P < .001$]. This contrast suggests that when judging impossible sentences, S was able to make his judgment as soon as an unlikely word was encountered and did not have to read the entire sentence.

To summarize the results of this section: first, comprehension of verbal material is apparently impaired by a concurrent memory load of six items but is relatively unimpaired by a load of three or less. Second, it appears that verbal comprehension is susceptible to disruption by phonemic similarity. It should be noted, however, that use of the term comprehension has necessarily been somewhat loose; it has been used to refer to the retention of the meaning of prose passages on the one hand and to the detection of syntactic or semantic "impossibility" on the other. Even with single-sentence material, Ss can process the information in a number of different ways depending on the task demands (Green, 1973). It should, therefore, be clear that the use of the single term "comprehension" is not meant to imply a single underlying process. Nevertheless, it does seem reasonable to use the term "comprehension" to refer to the class of activities concerned with the understanding of sentence material. Tasks studied under this heading do at least appear to be linked by the common factor of making use of a short-term or working memory system. As in the case of the verbal reasoning studies this system appears to be somewhat disrupted by the demands of a near-span additional memory load and by the presence of phonemic similarity.

It might reasonably be argued that the reasoning task we studied is essentially a measure of sentence comprehension and that we have, therefore, explored the role of working memory in only one class of activity. The next section, therefore, moves away from sentence material and studies the retention and free recall of lists of unrelated words. The free recall technique has the additional advantage of allowing us to study the effects that the variables which appear to have influenced the operation of working memory in the previous experiments have on the recency effect, a phenomenon which has in the past been regarded as giving a particularly clear indication of the operation of STS.

C. Working Memory and Free Recall

1. Experiment VIII: Memory Preload and Free Recall

This experiment studied the free recall of lists of 16 unrelated words under conditions of a zero-, three-, or six-digit preload. The preload was presented before the list of words and had to be retained throughout input and recall, since S was only told at the end of the recall period whether to write the preload digit sequence on the right- or left-hand side of his response sheet. The experiment had two major aims. The first aim was to study the effect of a preload on the LTM component of the free recall task, hence giving some indication of the possible role of working memory in long-term learning. The second aim was to study the effect of a preload on the recency effect. Since most current views of STS regard the digit span and the recency effect as both making demands on a common short-term store, one might expect a dramatic reduction of recency when a preload is imposed. However, as was pointed out in the introduction, there does appear to be a good deal of difference between the characteristics of STS revealed by the digit span procedure (suggesting that it is a serially ordered speech-based store) and the characteristics suggested by the recency effect in free recall (which appears to be neither serially ordered nor speech-based).

All lists comprised 16 high-frequency words equated for word length and presented auditorily at a rate of two seconds per word. Subjects were given a preload of zero, three, or six digits and were required to recall the words either immediately or after a delay of 30 seconds during which subjects copied down letters spoken at a one-second rate. In both cases, they had one minute in which to write down as many words as they could remember, after which they were instructed to write down the preload digits at the left- or right-hand side of their response sheets. Instructions emphasized the importance of retaining the preload digits.

The design varied memory load as a within S factor, and delay of recall between Ss. The same set of 15 lists were presented to both immediate and delayed recall groups. Within each group there were three subgroups across which the assignment of particular lists to particular levels of preload was balanced. For each group the 15

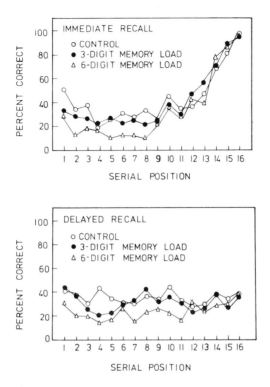

Fig. 3. Effects of additional short-term memory load on immediate and delayed free recall.

trials of the experiment were divided into blocks of three, in which each load condition occurred once. Subject to this constraint, the ordering of conditions was random. Twenty-one undergraduates served in each of the two subgroups. Figure 3 shows the serial position curves for recall as a function of size of preload for the immediate and delayed recall conditions. Analysis of variance showed significant effects due to delay [$F(1,40) = 9.85$, $P < .01$], serial position [$F(15,600) = 49.4$, $P < .001$], and the delay $\times$ serial position interaction [$F(15,600) = 33.4$, $P < .001$]. These correspond to the standard finding that delaying free recall abolishes the recency effect. There were also significant effects due to memory load [$F(2,80) = 35.8$, $P < .001$], to the memory load $\times$ serial position interaction, [$F(30,1200) = 1.46$, $P < .05$], and to the load $\times$ serial position $\times$ delay interaction [$F(30,1200) = 1.80$, $P < .01$].

The overall percentage of words recalled declined with increased

TABLE IX

PERCENTAGES OF WORDS RECALLED IN THE VARIOUS
CONDITIONS OF EXPERIMENT X

	Memory load		
	Zero	3-digits	6-digits
Immediate recall	43.9	41.6	35.2
Delayed recall	35.5	32.3	24.5

preload (see Table IX). Comparison between means using the New-man-Keuls procedure showed that the impairment due to a three-digit preload was just significant ($P < .05$) while the six-digit preload condition was significantly worse than both the control and the three-digit preload conditions at well beyond the .01 significance level.

It is clear from Fig. 3 that the load effect was restricted to the long-term component of recall and did not substantially influence the recency effect.

The first conclusion from this study is that performance on the secondary memory component of free recall is adversely effected by a digit preload, with the size of the decrement being a function of the size of the preload. A somewhat more dramatic finding is the apparent absence of a preload effect on the recency component. There are, however, at least two classes of interpretations of this result. The first is to conclude that an STM preload does not interfere with the mechanism of the recency effect. This would be a striking conclusion, since the "standard" account of recency assumes that the last few items are retrieved from the same store that would be used to hold the preload items. To accept this hypothesis would require a radical change of view concerning the nature of the recency effect. An alternative hypothesis is to assume that S begins to rehearse the preload items at the beginning of the list, and by the end of the list has succeeded in transferring them into LTS, freeing his STS for other tasks. Two lines of evidence support this suggestion: firstly, there was only a marginal effect of preload on recall of the last few items when recall was delayed (see Fig. 3). This suggests that the preload effect diminished as the list progressed. Secondly, when questioned after the experiment, 37 out of 39 Ss stated that they carried out some rehearsal of the digits, and 26 of these said that they rehearsed the digits mostly at the beginning of the word list. Clearly, our failure to control Ss, rehearsal strategies prevents our drawing any firm conclusions about the influence of preload on the recency effect. The next experiment, therefore, attempts to replicate the present results under better controlled conditions.

Before passing on to the next experiment, however, it is perhaps worth noting that the delayed recall technique for separating the long- and short-term components in free recall is the only one of the range of current techniques which would have revealed this potential artifact. Techniques which base their estimates of the two components entirely on immediate recall data assume that the LTS component for later items in the list can be estimated from performance on the middle items. In our situation, and possibly in many others, this assumption is clearly not valid.

2. Experiment IX: Concurrent Memory Load and Free Recall

This experiment again studied the effects of three levels of memory load on immediate and delayed free recall. In general, procedures were identical with Experiment VIII, except that the concurrent load rather than the preload technique was used. This involved the continuous presentation and test of digit sequences throughout the presentation of the memory list. In this way, it was hoped to keep the memory load relatively constant throughout the list and so avoid the difficulties of interpretation encountered in the previous study.

The concurrent load procedure was similar to that described for Experiment VI and involved the visual presentation of digit sequences. In the six-digit concurrent load condition, sequences of six digits were visible for four seconds, followed by a four-second blank interval during which S was required to recall and write down the six digits. The three-digit concurrent load condition was similar except that the three-digit sequences were presented for only two seconds and followed by a two-second blank interval, while in the control condition, S saw alternate sequences of three and six digits, followed, respectively, by gaps of two and four seconds. In this condition, however, he was instructed to copy down the digits as they appeared. The three conditions were thus equal in amount of writing required, but differed in the number of digits that had to be held in memory simultaneously.

The procedure involved switching on the digit display and requiring S to process digits for a few seconds before starting the auditory presentation of the word list. The point at which the word list began was varied randomly from trial to trial. This minimized the chance that a particular component of the digit task (e.g., input or recall) would be always associated with particular serial positions in the word list. After the last word of each list, the visual display was switched off and Ss immediately abandoned the digit task. In the immediate recall condition, they were allowed one minute for written recall of the words, while in the delayed condition they copied a list of 30 letters read out at a one-second rate before beginning the one-minute recall period.

The design exactly paralleled that used in the previous experiment, with 17 undergraduates being tested in the immediate recall condition and 17 in the delayed condition. High accuracy on the digit task was emphasized; each of the three-digit processing procedures was practiced before beginning the experiment, and behavior was closely monitored during the experiment to ensure that instructions were obeyed.

The immediate and delayed recall serial position curves are shown in Fig. 4. Because of the scatter in the raw data, scores for adjacent serial positions have been pooled, except for the last four serial positions. Analysis of variance indicated a significant overall effect of memory load [$F(2,64) = 45.2$, $P < .01$], with mean percentage correct scores being 31.8, 31.2, and 24.8 for the zero-, three- and six-item load conditions, respectively. The Newman-Keuls test indicated a significant difference between the six-digit load condition and both other conditions ($P < .01$), which did not differ significantly between themselves.

As Fig. 4 suggests, there were highly significant effects of serial position [$F(15,480) = 70.7$, $P < .01$], of delay [$F(1,32) = 26.6$, $P < .01$], and of their interaction [$F(15,480) = 29.1$, $P < .001$], indicating the standard effect of delay on the recency component. The analysis showed no evidence of a two-way interaction between memory load and serial position ($F < 1$) and very weak evidence for a three-way interaction among memory load, serial position, and delay [$F(30,960) = 1.32$, $P > .10$]. The general conclusion, therefore, is that an additional concurrent memory load, even of six items, does not significantly alter the standard recency effect.

This conclusion confirms the result of the previous experiment, but rules out one of the possible interpretations of the earlier data. With the preload technique, the absence of an effect of load on recency might have been due to a progressive decline in the "effort" or "difficulty" associated with the digit task during input of the word list. Such an explanation is not appropriate for the present results since the concurrent load procedure ensured that the digit memory task was carried out right through input of the word lists, a conclusion which is supported by the continued separation of the

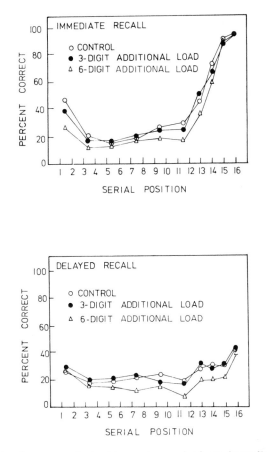

Fig. 4. Effects of concurrent short-term storage load on immediate and delayed free recall.

three- and six-digit load conditions over the last few serial positions in the delayed recall condition (see Fig. 3). Thus, even though six digits are concurrently being stored during the input of the final words of the list, the recency effect is unimpaired. To account for this, it must be assumed that the recency mechanism is independent from that involved in the memory span task. According to most dual-store theories, the digit span task ought to keep STS virtually fully occupied. Since the recency effect is commonly supposed to depend on output from this store, the digit span task should seriously reduce the amount of recency observed. It seems, therefore, that the buffer-storage account of recency is faced with a major difficulty.

Our data suggest then that a concurrent load of six items does impair the long-term component of free recall. Furthermore, as in the case of our reasoning task and prose comprehension studies, a load of three items has only a marginal effect. These results are consistent with the hypothesis of a working memory, which has some features in common with the memory span task. Since the memory load was present only during input of the words and not during recall, it is reasonable to conclude that working memory is concerned with the processes of transferring information to LTM. The absence of an effect of concurrent storage load on the recency effect suggests that working memory may have little or nothing to do with the recency effect. This hypothesis is discussed more fully in the concluding section of the chapter, when extra evidence against a buffer-storage account of recency is presented and an alternative interpretation suggested.

3. Experiment X: Speech Coding and Free Recall

In the case of both verbal reasoning and comprehension, we observed a similar effect of preload to that shown in the last two experiments, together with clear evidence of phonemic coding. This was revealed by effects of both acoustic similarity and articulatory suppression in the reasoning task, and by acoustic similarity effects in comprehension. There already exists evidence that phonemic similarity may be utilized in free recall (Baddeley & Warrington, 1973; Bruce & Crowley, 1970), provided at least that the phonemically similar items are grouped during presentation. The effects observed were positive, but since acoustic similarity is known to impair recall of order while enhancing item recall (Wickelgren, 1965), this would be expected in a free recall task. It is perhaps worth noting in connection with the dichotomy between span-based indicators of STS and evidence based on the recency effect suggested by the results of the last two experiments that attempts to show that the recency effect is particularly susceptible to the effects of phonemic similarity have proved uniformly unsuccessful (Craik & Levy, 1970; Glanzer, Koppenaal, & Nelson, 1972). Although there is abundant evidence that Ss may utilize phonemic similarity in long-term learning, this does not present particularly strong evidence in favor of a phonemically based working memory, since Ss are clearly able to utilize a very wide range of characteristics of the material to be learnt, possibly using processes which lie completely outside the working memory system. The next experiment, therefore, attempts to examine the role of articulatory coding in long-term learning more directly using the articulatory suppression technique. It comprises one of a series of unpublished studies by Richardson and Baddeley and examines the effect of concurrently articulating an irrelevant utterance on free recall for visually and auditorily presented word sequences.

Lists of ten unrelated high-frequency words were presented at a rate of two seconds per word either visually, by memory drum, or auditorily, which involved the experimenter reading out the words from the memory drum, which was screened from S. A total of 40 lists were used, and during half of these S was required to remain silent during presentation, while for the other half he was instructed to whisper "hiya" [an utterance which Levy (1971) found to produce effective suppression] at a rate of two utterances per second throughout the presentation of the word list. Half the Ss articulated for the first 20 lists and were silent for the last 20, while the other half performed in the reverse order. Manipulation of modality was carried out according to an *APBA* design, with half the Ss receiving visual as the first and last conditions, and half receiving auditory first and last. Each block of ten lists was preceded by a practice list in the appropriate modality and with the same vocalization and recall conditions. Following each list, S was instructed to recall immediately unless the experimenter read out a three-digit number, in which case he was to count backwards from that number by three's. Half the lists in each block of ten were tested immediately and half after the 20-second delay; in each case S was allowed 40 seconds for recall. Sixteen undergraduates served as Ss. The major results of interest are shown in Fig. 5, from which it is clear that articulatory suppression impaired retention [$F(1,1185) = 19.6$, $P < .001$]. The effect is shown particularly clearly with visual presentation and appears to be at least as marked for the earlier serial positions which are generally regarded as dependent on LTS, as for the recency component. This result is consistent with the suggestion of a working memory operating on phonemically coded information and transferring it to LTS. It further supports Glanzer's (1972) conclusion that the recency effect in free recall does not reflect articulatory coding and lends further weight to the suggestion that working memory is probably not responsible for the recency effect.

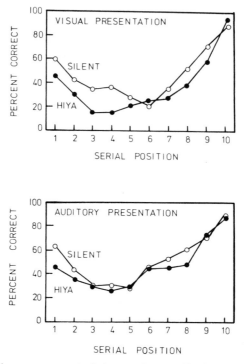

Fig. 5. Effect of concurrent articulation on free recall of visually and aurally presented word lists. (Data from Richardson and Baddeley, unpublished.)

III.   A Proposed Working Memory System

We have now studied the effect of factors which might be supposed to influence a working memory system, should it exist, across a range of cognitive tasks. The present section attempts to summarize the results obtained and looks for the type of common pattern which might suggest the same system was involved across the range of tasks.

Table X summarizes our results so far. We have studied three types of task: the verbal reasoning test, language comprehension, and the free recall of unrelated words. As Table X shows, these have in all three cases shown a substantial impairment in performance when an additional memory load of six items was imposed. In contrast to this, a load of three items appears to have little or no decremental effect, an unexpected finding which is common to all three situations. In the case of phonemic similarity, we have found the type of

TABLE X

SUMMARY OF EXPERIMENTAL RESULTS (PARADIGM)

| | | Verbal reasoning | Comprehension | Free recall | |
				LTS	Recency
Memory load				Small	
	1–3 items	No effect	No effect	decrement	No effect
	6 items	Decrement	Decrement	Decrement	No effect
Phonemic similarity		Decrement	Decrement	Enhancement	No effect
Articulatory suppression		Decrement	Not studied	Decrement	No effect

effect that would be expected on the assumption of a working memory system having characteristics in common with the digit span. Such effects are reflected in a performance decrement in those tasks where the retention of order is important (the reasoning and sentence judging tasks), coupled with a positive effect in the free recall situation for which the recall order is not required. Finally we have found that articulatory suppression, a technique which is known to impair digit span (Baddeley & Thomson, unpublished), has a deleterious effect in the two situations in which we have so far studied it, namely reasoning and free recall learning.

There appears then to be a consistent pattern of effects across the three types of task studied, strongly suggesting the operation of a common system such as the working memory initially proposed. This system appears to have something in common with the mechanism responsible for the digit span, being susceptible to disruption by a concurrent digit span task, and like the digit span showing signs of being based at least in part upon phonemic coding. It should be noted, however, that the degree of disruption observed, even with a near-span concurrent memory load, was far from massive. This suggests that although the digit span and working memory overlap, there appears to be a considerable component of working memory which is not taken up by the digit span task. The relatively small effects of phonemic coding and articulatory suppression reinforce this view and suggest that the articulatory component may comprise only one feature of working memory. Coltheart's (1972) failure to find an effect of phonemic similarity on a concept formation task is, therefore, not particularly surprising.

We would like to suggest that the core of the working memory system consists of a limited capacity "work space" which can be divided between storage and control processing demands. The next three sections comprise a tentative attempt to elaborate our view of the working memory system by considering three basic questions: how work space is allocated, how the central processing system and the more peripheral phonemic rehearsal system interact in the memory span task, and, finally, whether different modalities each have their own separate working memory system.

A. ALLOCATION OF WORK SPACE

Our data suggest that a trade-off exists between the amount of storage required and the rate at which other processes can be carried out. In Experiment III, for example, Ss solved verbal reasoning problems while either reciting a digit sequence, repeating the word *the,* or saying nothing. It is assumed that reciting a digit sequence requires more short-term storage than either of the other two conditions. Reasoning times, which presumably reflect the rate at which logical operations are carried out, were substantially increased in this condition. Furthermore, problems containing passive and negative sentences were slowed down more than problems posed as active and affirmative sentences. Since grammatically complex sentences presumably require a greater number of processing operations than simple sentences, this result is consistent with the assumed trade-off between storage-load and processing-rate.

The effect of additional memory load on free recall may be used to make a similar point. Experiments on presentation rate and free recall suggest that "transfer" to LTS proceeds at a limited rate. Since increasing memory load reduced transfer to LTS, it is arguable that this may result from a decrease in the rate at which the control processes necessary for transfer could be executed.

However, although our evidence suggests some degree of trade-off between storage-load and processing-rate, it would probably be unwise to regard working memory as an entirely flexible system of which any part may be allocated either to storage or processing. There are two reasons for this. In the first place, there may ultimately be no clear theoretical grounds for distinguishing processing and storage: they may always go together. Secondly, at the empirical level, a number of results show that it is difficult to produce appreciable interference with additional memory loads below the size of the span. This may mean that a part of the system that may be used for storage is not available for general processing. When the capacity of this component is exceeded, then some of the general-purpose work space must be devoted to storage, with the result that less space is available for processing. We shall discuss this possibility in more detail in the next section.

The final point concerns the factors which control the trade-off between the amount of work space allocated to two competing tasks. Results show that instructional emphasis is at least one determinant. In Experiment II, for example, *Ss* for whom the memory task was emphasized showed a very much greater effect of a six-digit preload on reasoning time than was shown by a second group who were instructed that both tasks were equally important. Evidence for a similar effect in free recall learning has been presented by Murdock (1965). He showed that a concurrent card-sorting task interfered with the long-term component of free recall and that the trade-off between performance on the two tasks was determined by the particular payoff specified in the instructions.

B. The Role of Working Memory in the Memory Span

We have suggested that the working memory system may contain both flexible work space and also a component that is dedicated to storage. This view is illustrated by the following suggested interpretation of the role of working memory in the memory span task. It is suggested that the memory span depends on both a phonemic response buffer which is able to store a limited amount of speechlike material in the appropriate serial order and the flexible component of working memory. The phonemic component is relatively passive and makes few demands on the central processing space, provided its capacity is not exceeded. The more flexible and executive component of the system is responsible for setting up the appropriate phonemic "rehearsal" routines, i.e., of loading up the phonemic buffer and of retrieving information from the buffer when necessary. Provided the memory load does not exceed the capacity of the phonemic buffer, little demand is placed upon the central executive, other than the routine recycling of the presumably familiar subroutines necessary for rehearsing digits. When the capacity of the phonemic buffer is exceeded, then the executive component of working memory must devote more of its time to the problem of storage. This probably involves both recoding in such a way as to reduce the length or complexity of the phonemic subroutine involved in rehearsal and also devoting more attention to the problem of retrieval. It is, for example, probably at this stage that retrieval rules

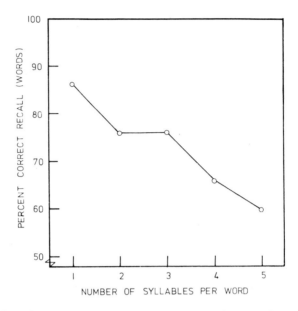

Fig. 6. Effect of word length on short-term serial recall. (Data from Baddeley and Thomson, unpublished.)

become useful in allowing S to utilize his knowledge of the experimental situation in order to interpret the deteriorated traces emerging from an overloaded phonemic buffer (Baddeley, 1972).

According to this account, the span of immediate memory is set by two major factors: the capacity of the phonemic loop, which is presumably relatively invariant, and the ability of the central executive component to supplement this, both by recoding at input and reconstruction at the recall stage. We have begun to study the first of these factors by varying word length in the memory span situation. Figure 6 shows the results of an experiment in which eight Ss were presented with sequences of five words from each of five sets. Each set comprised ten words of equal frequency of occurrence, but sets varied in word length, ranging in number of syllables from one through five. There is a clear tendency for performance to decline as word length increases. A similar result was independently obtained by Standing (personal communication) who observed a negative correlation between the memory span for a given type of material and the speed at which that material can be articulated. It is perhaps worth noting at this point that Craik (1968) reports that the recency effect in free recall is unaffected by the word length, suggesting once again a clear distinction between factors influencing the recency effect in free recall and those affecting the memory span. Watkins (1972) has further observed that word length does not influence the modality effect, but does impair the long-term component of verbal free recall. The former result would tend to suggest that the precategorical acoustic store on which the modality effect is generally assumed to rely (Crowder & Morton, 1969) lies outside the working memory system.

We, therefore, appear to have at least tentative evidence for the existence of a phonemic buffer, together with techniques such as articulatory suppression and the manipulation of word length which hopefully will provide tools for investigating this component in greater depth. It is possible that this component plays a major role in determining the occurrence of both acoustic similarity effects in memory and perhaps also of such speech errors as tongue twisters and spoonerisms. It seems likely that although it does not form the central core of working memory the phonemic component will probably justify considerably more investigation.

The operation of the central component of working memory seems likely to prove considerably more complex. It seems probable that it is this component that is responsible for the "chunking" of material which was first pointed out by Miller (1956) and has subsequently been studied in greater detail by Slak (1970), who taught subjects to recode digit sequences into a letter code which ensured an alternation between consonants and vowels. This allowed a dramatic reduction in the number of phonemes required to encode the sequence and resulted not only in a marked increase in the digit span, but also in a clear improvement in the performance of a range of tasks involving the long-term learning of digit sequences. A similar recoding procedure, this time based on prior language habits, is probably responsible for the observed increase in span for letter sequences as they approximate more closely to the structure of English words. This, together with the decreased importance of phonemic similarity, suggests that S is chunking several letters into one speech sound rather than simply rehearsing the name of the letter (Baddeley, 1971).

During retrieval, the executive component of the working memory system is probably responsible for interpreting the phonemic trace; it is probably at this level that retrieval rules (Baddeley, 1972) are applied. These ensure that a trace is interpreted within the constraints of the experiment, with the result that Ss virtually never produce completely inappropriate responses such as letters in an experiment using digits. We have unfortunately, however, so far done little to investigate this crucial central executive component; techniques aimed at blocking this central processor while leaving the peripheral components free should clearly be developed if possible.

C. One or Many Working Memories?

Our work so far has concentrated exclusively on verbal tasks, and the question obviously arises as to how general are our conclusions. It seems probable that a comparable system exists for visual memory which is different at least in part from the system we have been discussing.

Brooks (1967, 1968) studied a number of tasks in which S is induced to form a visual image and use this in an immediate memory situation. He has shown that performance in such a situation is impaired by concurrent visual processing, in contrast to equivalent phonemically based tasks, which are much more susceptible to concurrent verbal activity. We have confirmed and extended Brooks' results using visual pursuit tracking (Baddeley, Grant, Wight, & Thomson, 1974) which was found to cause a dramatic impairment in performance on a span task based on visual imagery, while producing no decrement in performance on an equivalent phonemically based task. Further evidence for the existence of a visual memory system which may be unaffected by heavy phonemic processing demands comes from the study by Kroll, Parks, Parkinson, Bieber, and Johnson (1970), who showed that Ss could retain a visually presented letter over a period of many seconds of shadowing auditory material.

From these and many other studies, it is clear that visual and auditory short-term storage do employ different subsystems. What is less clear is whether we need to assume completely separate parallel systems for different modalities, or whether the different modalities may share a common central processor. Preliminary evidence for the latter view comes from an unpublished study by R. Lee at the University of St. Andrews. He studied memory for pictures in a situation where Ss were first familiarized with sets of pictures of a number of local scenes, for which they were taught an appropriate name. Several slightly different views of each scene were used although only half of the variants of each scene were presented during the pretraining stage. Subjects were then tested on the full set of pictures and were required in each case to name the scene, saying whether the particular version shown was an "old" view which they had seen before or a "new" one. Subjects' performance was compared both while doing this task alone and while doing a concurrent mental arithmetic task (e.g., multiplying 27 and 42). Subjects were able to name the scenes without error in both conditions, but made a number of errors in deciding whether or not they had seen any given specific view of that scene; these errors were markedly more frequent in the mental arithmetic condition, suggesting that the visual recognition process was competing for limited processing capacity with the arithmetic task. One obvious interpretation of this result is to suggest that the central processor which we have assumed forms the core of working memory in our verbal situations plays a similar role in visual memory, although this time with a separate peripheral memory component, based on the visual system. What little evidence there exists, therefore, suggests that the possibility of a single common central processor should be investigated further, before assuming completely separate working memories for different modalities.

D. WORKING MEMORY AND THE RECENCY EFFECT IN FREE RECALL

A major distinction between the working memory system we propose and STS (Atkinson & Shiffrin, 1968) centers on the recency effect in free recall. Most theories of STM assume that retrieval from a temporary buffer store accounts for the recency effect, whereas our own results argue against this view. It is suggested that working memory, which in other respects can be regarded as a modified STS, does not provide the basis for recency.

Experiment IX studied the effect of a concurrent digit memory task on the retention of lists of unrelated words. The results showed that when Ss were concurrently retaining six digits, the LTS component of recall was low, but recency was virtually unaffected. Since six digits is very near the memory span, the STS model would have to assume that STS is full almost to capacity for an appreciable part of the time during the learning of the words for free recall. On this model, both recency and LTS transfer should be lowered by the additional short-term storage load. As there was no loss of recency, it seems that an STS account of recency is inappropriate. Instead, it seems that recency reflects retrieval from a store which is different from that used for the digit span task. Perhaps the most important aspect of this interpretation is that the limited memory span and limited rate of transfer of information to LTS must be regarded as having a common origin which is different from that of the recency effect. It would be useful to consider briefly what further evidence there is for this point of view.

E. The Memory Span, Transfer to LTS, and Recency

There is a wide range of variables which appear to affect the memory span (or short-term serial recall) and the LTS component of free recall in the same way, but which do not affect the recency component of free recall. In addition to the effects of word length and articulatory suppression which we have already discussed, which probably reflect the limited storage capacity of the working memory system or of one of its components, there are a number of variables which have been shown to affect the second limitation of the STS system, namely the rate at which it is able to transfer information to LTS. Several sets of experimental results show that the recency effect is not influenced by factors which interfere with LTS transfer. Murdock (1965), Baddeley, Scott, Drynan, and Smith (1969), and Bartz and Salehi (1970) have all shown that the LTS component of free recall is reduced when Ss are required to perform a subsidiary card-sorting task during presentation of the items for free recall. The effect is roughly proportional to the difficulty of the subsidiary task. However, there is no effect on the recency component of recall. Similar results have been reported by Silverstein and Glanzer (1971) using arithmetic varying in level of difficulty as the subsidiary task. As most of these authors concluded, the results suggest that there is a limited capacity system mediating LTS registration which is not responsible for the recency effect. On the present hypothesis, the subsidiary task is viewed as interfering with working memory and does not necessarily, therefore, interfere with recency as well. Hence the crucial difference in emphasis between the two theories (working memory-LTS, and STS-LTS) is that working memory is supposed to have both buffer-storage and control-processing functions, with recency explained by a separate mechanism.

IV. The Nature of the Recency Effect

So far, the most compelling argument for rejecting the buffer-storage hypothesis for recency has been the data from Experiment XI, in which a concurrent memory span task did not abolish recency in free recall. Clearly the argument needs strengthening.

Tzeng (1973) presented words for free recall in such a way that before and after each word, S was engaged in a 20-second period of counting backwards by three's. Under these conditions the serial position curve showed a strong recency effect. After learning four such lists, S was asked to recall as many words as possible from all four lists. Even on this final recall, the last items from each of the lists were recalled markedly better than items from earlier positions. Neither of these two recency effects is easily attributable to retrieval from a short-term buffer store. With the initial recall, the counting task ought to have displaced words from the buffer. In the case of the final recall the amount of interpolated activity was even greater. Tzeng's results, therefore, suggest at the very least that the recency effect is not always attributable to output from buffer storage. Tzeng cites further evidence (unpublished at the time of writing) from Dalezman and from Bjork and Whitten, in both cases suggesting that recency may occur under conditions which preclude the operation of STS.

Baddeley (1963) carried out an experiment in which Ss were given a list of 12 anagrams to solve. Anagrams were presented one at a time for as long as it took for a solution to be found, up to a limit of one minute, at which time the experimenter presented the solution. After the final anagram, S was questioned about his strategy and was then asked to freely recall as many of the solution words as possible. The results of the recall test are shown in Fig. 7 since they were not reported in the original paper. They show that despite the unexpected nature of the recall request and the delay while S discussed his strategy, a pronounced recency effect occurs. Since each item except the last was followed by up to a minute of problem-

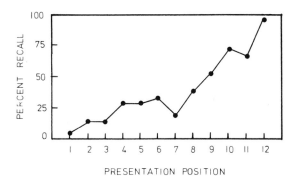

Fig. 7. Recall of anagram solutions as a function of order of presentation of the problems. (Data from Baddeley, 1963.)

solving activity and the last item was followed by a period of ques-
tion-answering, it is difficult to explain this recency effect in terms
of a temporary buffer store.

An experiment by Glanzer (1972) which we have successfully
replicated (Baddeley & Thomson, unpublished) presents further
problems for a simple buffer-store interpretation of the recency
effect. Instead of unrelated words, Glanzer used proverbs as the
material to be recalled. His results showed two striking phenomena:
first, the recency effect extended over the last few proverbs rather
than the last few words; and second, a filled delay reduced, but by
no means eliminated, the marked recency effect observed. The extent of recency, therefore, seems to be defined in terms of "semantic
units" rather than words. This is not, of course, incompatible with
a buffer-storage account, although in this experiment, a good deal
of semantic processing would presumably have to occur before entry
of a proverb into this buffer. The assumption of a more central store
does have the additional advantage of "explaining" the durable recency effect observed in this study, in terms of the suggestion by
Craik and Lockhart (1972) that greater depth of processing is associated with greater durability. However, it is clearly the case that
such a depth of processing is by no means essential to the recency
effect. Indeed, the effect appears to be completely unaffected by
factors such as presentation rate (Glanzer & Cunitz, 1966), concurrent
processing load (Murdock, 1965), and type of material (Glanzer,
1972), all of which would be expected to have a pronounced influence on depth of processing.

A more promising alternative explanation of recency might be to
elaborate the proposal made by Tulving (1968) that recency reflects
the operation of a retrieval strategy, rather than the output of a
specific store. Provided one assumes that ordinal recency may be one
accessible feature of a memory trace, then it is plausible to assume
that Ss may frequently access items on the basis of this cue. The
limited size of the recency effect, suggesting that recency is only an
effective cue for the last few items, might reasonably be attributed
to limitations on the discriminability of recency cues. One might assume, following Weber's Law, that with the newest item as a reference point, discriminability of ordinal position ought to decrease
with increasing "oldness." The advantage of assuming an ordinal
retrieval strategy of this kind is that it can presumably be applied
to any available store and possibly also to any subset of items within
that store, provided the subset can be adequately categorized. Thus,
when an interpolated activity is classed in the same category as the

learned items, the interpolated events will be stored in the same dimension as the to-be-remembered items and will hence supersede them as the most recent events. When the interpolated activity is classed in a different category from the learned items, recency will be unaffected. This presumably occurred in the case of proverbs and the anagram solutions. It also seems intuitively plausible to assume that a similar type of recency is reflected in one's own memory for clearly specified classes of events, for example, football games, parties, or meals at restaurants, all of which introspectively at least appear to exhibit their own recency effect. It is clearly necessary to attempt to collect more objective information on this point, however.

The preceding account of recency is highly tentative, and although it does possess the advantage of being able to deal with evidence which presents considerable difficulties for the buffer-store interpretation, it does leave two very basic questions unanswered. The first of these concerns the question of what factors influence the categorization of different types of events; it seems intuitively unlikely that backward-counting activity should be categorized in the same way for example as visually presented words, and yet counting effectively destroys the recency effect in this situation. This is, of course, a difficult problem, but it is no less a problem for the buffer-store interpretation which must also account for the discrepancy between Tzeng's results and the standard effect of a filled delay on recency.

The second basic question is that of how ordinal recency is stored, whether in terms of trace-strength, in terms of ordinal "tags" of some kind, or in some as yet unspecified way. Once again, this problem is not peculiar to the retrieval cue interpretation of recency; it is clearly the case that we are able to access ordinal information in some way. How we do this, and whether ordinal cues can be used to retrieve other information, is an empirical question which remains unanswered.

V. Concluding Remarks

We would like to suggest that we have presented *prima facie* evidence for the existence of a working memory system which plays a central role in human information processing. The system we propose is very much in the spirit of similar proposals by such authors as Posner and Rossman (1965) and Atkinson and Shiffrin (1971). However, whereas earlier work concentrated principally on the memory system *per se,* with the result that the implications of the system for nonmemory tasks were largely speculative, our own work has been focused on the information processing tasks rather than the system itself. As a consequence of this, we have had to change our views of both working memory and of the explanation of certain STM phenomena.

To sum up, we have tried to make a case for postulating the working memory-LTS system as a modification of the current STS-LTS view. We would like to suggest that working memory represents a control system with limits on both its storage and processing capabilities. We suggest that it has access to phonemically coded information (possibly by controlling a rehearsal buffer), that it is responsible for the limited memory span, but does not underly the recency effect in free recall. Perhaps the most specific function which has so far been identified with working memory is the transfer of information to LTS. We have not yet explored its role in retrieval, so that the implications of Patterson's (1971) results for the nature of working memory are still unclear. Our experiments suggest that the phonemic rehearsal buffer plays a limited role in this process, but is by no means essential. The patient K.F., whom Shallice and Warrington (1970) showed to have grossly impaired digit span together with normal long-term learning ability, presents great difficulty for the current LTS-STS view, since despite his defective STS, his long-term learning ability is unimpaired. His case can, however, be handled quite easily by the view of working memory proposed, if it is assumed that only the phonemic rehearsal-buffer component of his working memory is impaired, while the central executive component is intact. Our experiments also suggest that working memory plays a part in verbal reasoning and in prose comprehension. Understanding the detailed role of working memory in these tasks, however, must proceed hand-in-hand with an understanding of the tasks themselves.

We began with a very simple question: *what is short-term memory for?* We hope that our preliminary attempts to begin answering the question will convince the reader, not necessarily that our views are correct, but that the question was and is well worth asking.

ACKNOWLEDGMENTS

Part of the experimental work described in this chapter was carried out at the University of Sussex. We are grateful to colleagues at both Sussex and Stirling for valuable discussion and in particular to Neil Thomson whose contribution was both practical and theoretical. The financial support of both the British Medical Research Council and the Social Sciences Research Council is gratefully acknowledged.

REFERENCES

Atkinson, R. C., & Shiffrin, R. M. Human memory: A proposed system and its control processes. In K. W. Spence & J. T. Spence (Eds.), *The psychology of learning and motivation: Advances in research and theory*. Vol. 2. New York: Academic Press, 1968. Pp. 89–195.

Atkinson, R. C., & Shiffrin, R. M. The control of short-term memory. *Scientific American*, 1971, **225**, 82–90.

Baddeley, A. D. A Zeigarnik-like effect in the recall of anagram solutions. *Quarterly Journal of Experimental Psychology*, 1963, **15**, 63–64.

Baddeley, A. D. The influence of acoustic and semantic similarity on long-term memory for word sequences. *Quarterly Journal of Experimental Psychology*, 1966, **18**, 302–309. (a)

Baddeley, A. D. Short-term memory for word sequences as a function of acoustic, semantic and formal similarity. *Quarterly Journal of Experimental Psychology*, 1966, **18**, 362–366. (b)

Baddeley, A. D. A three-minute reasoning test based on grammatical transformation. *Psychonomic Science*, 1968, **10**, 341–342.

Baddeley, A. D. Language habits, acoustic confusability and immediate memory for redundant letter sequences. *Psychonomic Science*, 1971, **22**, 120–121.

Baddeley, A. D. Retrieval rules and semantic coding in short-term memory. *Psychological Bulletin*, 1972, **78**, 379–385.

Baddeley, A. D., De Figuredo, J. W., Hawkswell-Curtis, J. W., & Williams, A. N. Nitrogen narcosis and performance under water. *Ergonomics*, 1968, **11**, 157–164.

Baddeley, A. D., Grant, S., Wight, E., & Thomson, N. Imagery and visual working memory. In P. M. Rabbitt & S. Dornic (Eds.), *Attention and performance*. Vol. 5. New York: Academic Press, 1974, in press.

Baddeley, A. D., & Patterson, K. The relationship between long-term and short-term memory. *British Medical Bulletin*, 1971, **27**, 237–242.

Baddeley, A. D., Scott, D., Drynan, R., & Smith, J. C. Short-term memory and the limited capacity hypothesis. *British Journal of Psychology*, 1969, **60**, 51–55.

Baddeley, A. D., & Warrington, E. K. Memory coding and amnesia. *Neuropsychologia*, 1973, **11**, 159–165.

Bartz, W. H., & Salehi, M. Interference in short- and long-term memory. *Journal of Experimental Psychology*, 1970, **84**, 380–382.

Brooks, L. R. The suppression of visualization in reading. *Quarterly Journal of Experimental Psychology*, 1967, **19**, 289–299.

Brooks, L. R. Spatial and verbal components in the act of recall. *Canadian Journal of Psychology*, 1968, **22**, 349–368.

Brown, I. D., Tickner, A. H., & Simmonds, D. C. V. Interference between concurrent tasks of driving and telephoning. *Journal of Applied Psychology*, 1969, **53**, 419–424.

Bruce, D., & Crowley, J. J. Acoustic similarity effects on retrieval from secondary memory. *Journal of Verbal Learning and Verbal Behavior*, 1970, **9**, 190–196.

Coltheart, V. The effects of acoustic and semantic similarity on concept identification. *Quarterly Journal of Experimental Psychology*, 1972, **24**, 55–65.

Conrad, R. An association between memory errors and errors due to acoustic masking of speech. *Nature* (London), 1962, **193**, 1314–1315.

Conrad, R., & Hull, A. J. Information, acoustic confusion and memory span. *British Journal of Psychology*, 1964, **55**, 429–432.

Craik, F. I. M. Two components in free recall. *Journal of Verbal Learning and Verbal Behavior*, 1968, **7**, 996–1004.

Craik, F. I. M., & Levy, B. A. Semantic and acoustic information in primary memory. *Journal of Experimental Psychology*, 1970, **86**, 77–82.

Craik, F. I. M., & Lockhart, R. S. Levels of processing: A framework for memory research. *Journal of Verbal Learning and Verbal Behavior*, 1972, **11**, 671–684.

Crowder, R. G., & Morton, J. Precategorical acoustic storage (PAS). *Perception & Psychophysics*, 1969, **5**, 365–373.

Glanzer, M. Storage mechanisms in free recall. In G. H. Bower (Ed.), *The psychology of learning and motivation: Advances in research and theory*. Vol. 5. New York: Academic Press, 1972. Pp. 129–193.

Glanzer, M., & Cunitz, A. R. Two storage mechanisms in free recall. *Journal of Verbal Learning and Verbal Behavior*, 1966, **5**, 351–360.

Glanzer, M., Koppenaal, L., & Nelson, R. Effects of relations between words on short-term storage and long-term storage. *Journal of Verbal Learning and Verbal Behavior*, 1972, **11**, 403–416.

Green, D. W. A psychological investigation into the memory and comprehension of sentences. Unpublished doctoral dissertation, University of London, 1973.

Hammerton, M. Interference between low information verbal output and a cognitive task. *Nature (London)*, 1969, **222**, 196.

Hunter, I. M. L. *Memory*. London: Penguin Books, 1964.

Jarvella, R. J. Syntactic processing of connected speech. *Journal of Verbal Learning and Verbal Behavior*, 1971, **10**, 409–416.

Johnston, W. A., Griffith, D., & Wagstaff, R. R. Information processing analysis of verbal learning. *Journal of Experimental Psychology*, 1972, **96**, 307–314.

Kroll, N. E. A., Parks, T., Parkinson, S. R., Bieber, S. L., & Johnson, A. L. Short-term memory while shadowing: Recall of visually and aurally presented letters. *Journal of Experimental Psychology*, 1970, **85**, 220–224.

Levy, B. A. Role of articulation in auditory and visual short-term memory. *Journal of Verbal Learning and Verbal Behavior*, 1971, **10**, 123–132.

Martin, D. W. Residual processing capacity during verbal organization in memory. *Journal of Verbal Learning and Verbal Behavior*, 1970, **9**, 391–397.

Miller, G. A. The magical number seven plus or minus two: some limits on our capacity for processing information. *Psychological Review*, 1956, **63**, 81–97.

Murdock, B. B., Jr. Effects of a subsidiary task on short-term memory. *British Journal of Psychology*, 1965, **56**, 413–419.

Murray, D. J. The role of speech responses in short-term memory. *Canadian Journal of Psychology*, 1967, **21**, 263–276.

Murray, D. J. Articulation and acoustic confusability in short-term memory. *Journal of Experimental Psychology*, 1968, **78**, 679–684.

Neale, M. D. *Neale Analysis of Reading Ability*. London: Macmillan, 1958.

Norman, D. A. The role of memory in the understanding of language. In J. F. Kavanagh & I. G. Mattingly (Eds.), Cambridge, Mass.: MIT Press, 1972.

Patterson, K. A. Limitations on retrieval from long-term memory. Unpublished doctoral dissertation, University of California, San Diego, 1971.

Peterson, L. R. Concurrent verbal activity. *Psychological Review*, 1969, **76**, 376–386.

Peterson, L. R., & Peterson, M. J. Short-term retention of individual verbal items. *Journal of Experimental Psychology*, 1959, **58**, 193–198.

Posner, M. I., & Rossman, E. Effect of size and location of informational transforms upon short-term retention. *Journal of Experimental Psychology*, 1965, **70**, 496–505.

Rubenstein, H., & Aborn, M. Learning, prediction and readability. *Journal of Applied Psychology*, 1958, **42**, 28–32.

Rumelhart, D. E., Lindsay, P. H., & Norman, D. A. A process model for long-term memory. In E. Tulving & W. Donaldson (Eds.), *Organisation and memory*. New York: Academic Press, 1972.

Sachs, J. D. S. Recognition memory for syntactic and semantic aspects of connected discourse. *Perception & Psychophysics*, 1967, **2**, 437–442.

Shallice, T., & Warrington, E. K. Independent functioning of verbal memory stores: a neuropsychological study. *Quarterly Journal of Experimental Psychology*, 1970, **22**, 261–273.

Silverstein, C., & Glanzer, M. Difficulty of a concurrent task in free recall: differential effects of LTS and STS. *Psychonomic Science*, 1971, **22**, 367–368.

Slak, S. Phonemic recoding of digital information. *Journal of Experimental Psychology*, 1970, **86**, 398–406.

Sperling, G. A model for visual memory tasks. *Human Factors*, 1963, **5**, 19–31.

Taylor, W. L. "Cloze procedure": A new tool for measuring readability. *Journalism Quarterly*, 1953, **30**, 415–433.

Tulving, E. Theoretical issues in free recall. In T. R. Dixon & D. L. Horton (Eds.), *Verbal behaviour and general behaviour theory*. Englewood Cliffs, N.J.: Prentice-Hall, 1968.

Tzeng, O. J. L. Positive recency effect in delayed free recall. *Journal of Verbal Learning and Verbal Behavior*, 1973, **12**, 436–439.

Warrington, E. K., Logue, V., & Pratt, R. T. C. The anatomical localization of selective impairment of auditory verbal short-term memory. *Neuropsychologia*, 1971, **9**, 377–387.

Warrington, E. K., & Shallice, T. The selective impairment of auditory verbal short-term memory. *Brain*, 1969, **92**, 885–896.

Warrington, E. K., & Weiskrantz, L. An analysis of short-term and long-term memory defects in man. In J. A. Deutsch (Ed.), *The physiological basis of memory*. New York: Academic Press, 1973.

Wason, P. C., & Johnson-Laird, P. N. *Psychology of reasoning: Structure and content*. London: Batsford, 1972.

Watkins, M. J. Locus of the modality effect in free recall. *Journal of Verbal Learning and Verbal Behavior*, 1972, **11**, 644–648.

Waugh, N. C., & Norman, D. A. Primary memory. *Psychological Review*, 1965, **72**, 89–104.

Wickelgren, W. A. Short-term memory for phonemically similar lists. *American Journal of Psychology*, 1965, **78**, 567–574.

4

COMMENTARY ON
"REACTION TIME MEASUREMENTS
IN THE STUDY OF MEMORY PROCESSES:
THEORY AND DATA"

John Theios

DEPARTMENT OF PSYCHOLOGY, UNIVERSITY OF WISCONSIN, MADISON

Reaction Time Measurements in the Study of Memory Processes: Theory and Data" (RTM) demonstrates a method for investigating human memory by considering the time taken by humans to process stimulus information in relation to predictions made by highly specific mathematical models of the temporal properties of memory mechanisms. Since the initial publication of RTM, hundreds of experimental and theoretical articles using reaction time to study human memory processes have appeared. Far and away, the bulk of these studies have used the dubious additive factor method and have tended to "test" vague, fairly global aspects of reaction time data, rather than specific hypotheses derived from well-formulated mathematical models of memory. A few notable exceptions are the very careful theoretical works of Atkinson and Juola (1973, 1974), Green and Luce (1974), Link (1975), Townsend (1974, 1976), and Taylor (1976). The theoretical systems suggested by each of these theorists can be characterized as basically parallel processing (or continuous information processing) systems, as opposed to the strictly serial stage processing models that seem to be the current favorite interpretation among most experimental psychologists.

The "Introduction" of RTM contains an overview of both the class of speeded information processing tasks to be considered and the theoretical system to be proposed. In addition, a brief summary is given of Donders' classic subtractive method and Sternberg's additive factor method. The section ends with some cautionary remarks regarding use of the additive factor method. Recently, other authors have also made the same cautionary remarks. Pachella (1974, p. 57) says that "the manipulation of factor levels may cause a fundamental change in the processing sequence as may happen with the deletion of an entire stage within the Subtractive Method." He goes on to further caution that "a model of processing in which the stages are defined by an Additive Factor analysis may not be identifiably different from an alternative model *based on a different definition of stage....*" Townsend (1974, 1976) and Taylor (1976) have demonstrated just this point by constructing parallel processing models of memory that are mathematically isomorphic to standard serial stage processing models that seem to have been "dictated" by noninteracting, additive factors at the level of reaction time data. Taylor (1976, p. 171) points out that it is traditionally assumed that the following properties characterize a reaction process:

> (a) stages—Reaction process consists of a fixed and finite set of stages; (b) seriality—Execution of stages is strictly serial, with each stage being initiated when the preceding stage is completed; (c) stage independence—The distributions which describe the stage times are independent of one another, in the sense that a change in the distribution for one stage does not affect the distributions for the other stages; and (d) stochastic independence—The times required by various stages on a given observation (reaction) are independent of one another.

By relaxing some of these restrictive assumptions, Townsend (1974) and Taylor (1976) open up new classes of reaction time theories, the mathematical properties of only a few of which have begun to be investigated. Taylor (1976, pp. 189—190) ends his analysis by stating that

> It is shown that given such a process, if two or more factors produce a significant interaction effect on mean reaction time, then these factors influence one or more stages in common, and this joint influence is not additive. It is also shown that the inverse of this statement is not generally true; that is, a failure to obtain an interaction does not imply that the factors influence disjoint sets of stages. Hence, while interactive effects can be interpreted with confidence, the interpretation of additive effects is hazardous.

Section II of RTM presents a mathematical model for memory scanning. The model represents memory scanning as a largely serial, self-terminating process. In order for the model to account for data from memory scanning experiments, however, the model had to have a parallel component. Thus, strictly speaking, the proposed process is a hybrid serial—parallel model. At this point in time, given the work of Townsend (1974) and Taylor (1976), one could substitute an isomorphic (or at least a very similar acting) parallel model for the one I chose. In fact, in two subsequent chapters (Theios, 1975, 1977) I have outlined parallel processing models that are consistent with a larger segment of the general human information processing reaction time data than is the serial model explicated here. Specifically, in the cases of the naming of alphanumeric characters (Theios, 1975) and the reading of words (Theios, 1977), the response determination process and the response selection process do not exhibit the limited capacity, serial properties that are required by the serial, self-terminating model.

In RTM, I implied that the naming of alphanumeric characters and the reading of words was a "special" linguistic process that was so highly developed, so automatic, and so fast that it by-passed the serial response determination and response program selection stages characteristic of tasks requiring manual responses. In my 1975 and 1977 papers, however, I do not consider articulation to be a special process, but rather an example of an asymptotic, minimum variance, parallel (or direct access) memory retrieval process that achieved its speed and efficiency through a lifetime of use with a consistent one-to-one stimulus–response mapping. As such, reading and articulation only act "specially" when compared to the tasks involving arbitrary stimulus–response mappings and limited practice that are typically investigated by experimental psychologists.

Although a specific mathematical model is presented in Section IIE of RTM, the important assumptions for any adequate theory of the temporal properties of human memory may be simply stated as follows:

1. *Recency:* If an observer effectively processed a stimulus at time t_0, then the expected time to process that same stimulus at time t_1 is less than or equal to the expected time to process the stimulus at time t_2, for $t_0 < t_1 < t_2$.

2. *Frequency:* Given two equivalent stimulus–response processing tasks, if one stimulus–response sequence has been executed N times and the other has been executed M times, then if N is greater than M, the expected time to process the first stimulus–response sequence is less than or equal to the expected time to process the second sequence.

3. *Uncertainty:* The processing of stimuli is a stochastic process such that measurements of processing time will have an inherent variability.

In my opinion, any model that incorporated these three assumptions would reflect, to some degree, the data considered in RTM as well as much of the reaction time data in the field in general. How well a model reflects the data will depend upon its specific assumptions, and it is the job of theoretical psychologists to discover just what are the most general and most accurate assumptions that cover a wide variety of human information processing tasks.

Second III of RTM considers predictions from the theoretical model in relation to experimental data. Section IIIA considers stimulus naming and choice reaction times with equally likely stimuli. The time taken to name numerals is short and independent of stimulus ensemble size. By contrast, the time taken to react to the numerals with a manual response is typically slower, and it increases as a negatively accelerated function of stimulus ensemble size. Two follow-up chapters (Theios, 1975, 1977) document this difference between naming and manual responding as a characteristic and strong finding. The time taken to name or read alphanumeric characters and short words is independent of experimental ensemble size. These results have very important implications for the way in which we construct human information processing models: (1) Stimulus encoding is independent of experimental ensemble size; and (2) the transformation of a linguistic stimulus from a visual code to an articulatory code (i.e., the access and retrieval of an articulatory response) is independent of experimental ensemble size. This may mean that the identification of visually presented linguistic stimuli is a content addressable, direct access memory retrieval process.

Section IIIC considers two-choice naming times as a function of stimulus presentation probability. I found that naming times did not vary as the presentation probability of individual stimuli was varied from .2 to .8. Miller and Pachella (1973) performed a similar naming experiment using eight digits as stimuli and presentation probability from .025 to .275. They also had a stimulus contrast manipulation, and, unfortunately, in both their degraded and "intact" condition, the presented digit evolved out of a fading white square, slightly larger than the digit. With the higher contrast stimuli, they found a small but systematic effect of probability of about 15 msec on naming times. The probability effect was somewhat larger for the low contrast condition. Using the additive factor logic, Miller and Pachella (1973) suggested that stimulus probability affected stimulus encoding since, in their study, stimulus degradation and stimulus probability interacted to a small degree. I would suggest an alternative interpretation: Stimulus probability has little or no effect on stimulus encoding when the stimuli are superclear with very high contrast, as in the studies reviewed by Theios (1973, 1975, 1977). On the other hand, top-down processing (Norman & Rumelhart, 1975) takes place if there is any delay in encoding due to stimulus degradation or low contrast. With noisy stimuli or limited viewing time, the top-down processing will speed up the encoding of highly probable stimuli due to sophisticated guessing and expectancy strategies on the part of the observer.

Section IIID and IIIE of RTM consists of a very careful consideration of multichoice reaction times with varying stimulus probabilities. Further work on this topic has been done by Lupker and Theios (1975, 1977) who conducted four-choice and six-choice reaction time experiments and varied stimulus presentation probability in each. They tested two-state, three-state, and four-state versions of the probabilistic push-down stack model presented in RTM. After extensive statistical tests of the fine-grained sequential properties of the data, Lupker and Theios concluded that the two-state model gave the best representation of the data. This included satisfying Falmagne's (1968) very strong fixed-point property for reaction time distributions from two-state models.

Section IIIF of RTM considers memory-scanning character-classification tasks using a many-to-one stimulus response mapping. It is pointed out that the data exhibit independent stimulus probability and sequence effects and response probability and sequence effects. The probabilistic push-down stack model presented in RTM easily accounts for this dynamic pattern of results. Using the additive factor logic, it has recently become popular for other authors to attribute the stimulus probability and sequential effects in memory scanning to the encoding stage of processing (e.g., Juola, 1973; Miller & Pachella, 1973; Shiffrin & Schneider, 1974; Sternberg, 1975). This assertion that stimulus probability and repetition effects in the memory-scanning character-classification tasks can be accounted for by the stimulus encoding stage is completely untenable, given the naming results of Miller and Pachella (1973) and Theios (1975, 1977). Using identical stimuli as those used in memory-scanning tasks, naming times vary only slightly or not at all with stimulus probability and repetition. Since stimulus encoding is the same in both the naming task and the memory-scanning task, encoding cannot be causing the relatively large probability effect that one finds in the memory-scanning situation. Biederman and Stacy (1974) have come to a similar conclusion based on the results of a carefully designed experiment dealing with the very limited effects of probability on naming times.

Section IV ends RTM with an overall summary and conclusion of the chapter. The six empirical results to be accounted for by an adequate human information processing memory access and retrieval model remain unchanged after several years of additional experimental research. In fact, they are reinforced by the newer results reviewed by Theios (1975, 1977).

RTM ended with the statement that "Clearly, the next important theoretical task is to develop a theory of errors which is consistent with reaction times, so that both response measures may be predicted by the same theory and set of parameter values." Several advances have been made on this problem. Falmagne, Cohen, and Dwivedi (1975) have presented a formal theory of errors for the two-state version of the probabilistic push-down stack memory model for reaction times. They jointly account for error probabilities and sequential reaction times from several observers who were tested extensively.

Clearly, the expanded model allowing for errors now needs to be extended to a general probabilistically ordered memory-scanning process. Link (1975) can jointly account for reaction times and errors in a two-choice task, but, as yet, his static relative judgment theory does not have a dynamic mechanism for generating trial-by-trial sequential reaction times and errors.

Atkinson and Juola (1973, 1974) can jointly account for errors and reaction times in multistimuli tasks. Their model, however, also suffers from being static without any dynamic mechanism to generate sequential reaction times and conditioned error probabilities.

Despite its drawbacks, the probabilistic push-down stack model presented in RTM is almost unique in the field in that it does provide for an explicit stochastic process that tracks stimulus and response frequency and recency. In my opinion, this is a critically necessary component for any serious theory of human information processing. A weak attempt at making the exhaustive scanning model account for stimulus presentation probability effects has been made by Shiffrin and Schneider (1974). They proposed a two-state binary mixture of a fast processing expectancy state and a slower exhaustive scanning process. There are a number of problems with this model. First, for reaction times, it predicts no interaction between stimulus probability and target set size. Theios and Walters (1974) have found significant stimulus probability and set size interactions, and similar data have been reported by Biederman and Stacy (1974). Second, since the distribution of reaction times in Shiffrin and Schneider's (1974) model is predicted to be the result of a two-state process, the burden of proof is on the authors to show that their empirical reaction time distributions satisfy the fixed-point property for binary mixtures (Falmagne, 1968; Lupker & Theios, 1975, 1977). Third, upon close mathematical inspection, it becomes clear that the two-state model suggested by Shiffrin and Schneider (1974) is isomorphic to the limiting, special case of the probabilistic push-down stack model presented in Section III of RTM. Their slower processing state only needs to be interpretated as a parallel process rather than a serial exhaustive process (cf. Townsend, 1974, 1976).

There have been several criticisms of the processing theory presented in RTM. The first is that Sternberg (1975), considering memory scanning, claimed that "the model, tailored as it is to the fixed-set procedure cannot readily account for results from the varied set procedure, without adding special assumptions about how associations involving items in the negative set on each trial are stored and ordered." Reed (1976), however, conducted a varied set memory-scanning experiment and tested the data against predictions from 14 different models. The best fit to the varied set data was obtained by the probabilistic push-down stack model presented in RTM.

Sternberg (1975) has rightly pointed out that, in the serial self-terminating memory-scanning models presented in RTM, the *minimum* of several samples of reaction times from different target set size conditions should be (roughly) a constant, since no matter how thinly spread the presentation probability becomes, some stimulus is always going to be in the first serial memory position on each trial, and, on some of the trials, a match will be obtained on the first comparison, stopping the scanning process. On the other hand, the serial exhaustive scanning process strongly predicts that the minimum reaction time should systematically (and linearly) increase with target set size. Sternberg (1975) cites preliminary data that suggests that the empirical minimum reaction times of the samples do increase with set size. He is well aware, however, that estimating a population minimum from the minimum of a sample is a risky statistical procedure. To overcome the problem, Sternberg (1973) has considered a more robust statistic based upon cumulative reaction time distributions.

He tested this "short reaction time" distribution property on sets of his own choice reaction time and memory-scanning data. The tests consistently indicated that a *serial* self-terminating memory search process would have difficulty in accounting for the increase in short reaction times as set size increases. I have not tested these short reaction time properties in my own data, and, to my knowledge, nor has any other investigator. In view of Sternberg's (1973) results, however, indicating that serial self-terminating models have difficulty accounting for the distributional properties and the fact that the serial exhaustive scanning model has difficulty in accounting for trial sequence, stimulus probability, and serial position effects, an entirely new alternative model seems to be needed. I think the most promising alternative is the class of limited capacity, self-terminating parallel processing models of the type described by Townsend (1974, 1976), which do not require Sternberg's (1973) short reaction time distribution property to hold.

REFERENCES

Anderson, J. A. A theory for the recognition of items from short memorized lists. *Psychological Review,* 1973, **80**, 417–438.

Atkinson, R. C., & Juola, J. F. Factors influencing speed and accuracy of word recognition. In S. Kornblum (Ed.), *Attention and performance, IV.* New York: Academic Press, 1973. Pp. 583–612.

Atkinson, R. C., & Juola, J. F. Search and decision processes in recognition memory. In D. Krantz, R. C. Atkinson, R. D. Luce, & P. Suppes (Eds.), *Contemporary developments in mathematical psychology.* San Francisco: Freeman, 1974.

Biederman, I., & Stacy, E. W., Jr. Stimulus probability and stimulus set size in memory scanning. *Journal of Experimental Psychology,* 1974, **102**, 1100–1107.

Falmagne, J. C., Note on a simple property of binary mixtures. *British Journal of Statistical and Mathematical Psychology,* 1968, **21**, 131–132.

Falmagne, J. C., Cohen, S. P., & Swivedi, A. Two-choice reactions as an ordered memory scanning process. In P. M. A. Rabbitt & S. Dornic (Eds.), *Attention and Performance V.* London: Academic Press, 1975. Pp. 296–344.

Green, D. M., & Luce, R. D. Counting and timing mechanisms in auditory discrimination and reaction time. In D. W. Krantz, R. C. Atkinson, R. D. Luce, & P. Suppes (Eds.), *Contemporary developments in mathematical psychology.* Vol. II. San Francisco: Freeman, 1974. Pp. 372–416.

Juola, J. F. Repetition and laterality effects on recognition memory for words and pictures. *Memory and Cognition,* 1973, **1**, 183–192.

Link, S. W. The relative judgment theory of two choice response times. *Journal of Mathematical Psychology,* 1975, **12**, 114–135.

Lupker, S. J., & Theios, J. Tests of two classes of models for choice reaction times. *Journal of Experimental Psychology: Human Perception and Performance,* 1975, **104**, 137–146.

Lupker, S. J., & Theios, J. Further tests of a two-state model for choice reaction times. *Journal of Experimental Psychology: Human Perception and Performance* (in press).

Miller, J. O., & Pachella, R. G. Locus of the stimulus probability effect. *Journal of Experimental Psychology,* 1973, **101**, 227–231.

Norman, D. A., & Rumelhart, D. E. *Explorations in cognition.* San Francisco: Freeman, 1975.

Pachella, R. G. The interpretation of reaction time in information-processing research. In B. H. Kantowitz (Ed.), *Human information processing: Tutorials in performance and cognition.* Hillsdale, New Jersey: Erlbaum, 1974. Pp. 133–185.

Reed, A. V. List length and the time course of recognition in immediate memory. *Memory and Cognition,* 1976, **4**, 16–30.

Sternberg, S. Evidence against self-terminating memory search from properties of RT distributions. Paper presented at the meeting of the Psychonomic Society, St. Louis, November, 1973.

Sternberg, S. Memory scanning: New findings and current controversies. *Quarterly Journal of Experimental Psychology,* 1975, **27,** 1–32.

Shiffrin, R. M., & Schneider, W. An expectancy model for memory search. *Memory and Cognition,* 1974, **2,** 616–628.

Taylor, D. A. Stage analysis of reaction time. *Psychological Bulletin,* 1976, **83,** 161–191.

Theios, J. Reaction time measurements in the study of memory processes: Theory and data. In G. H. Bower (Ed.), *The Psychology of Learning and Motivation: Advances in Research and Theory.* Vol. 7. New York: Academic Press, 1973. Pp. 43–85.

Theios, J. The components of response latency in simple human information processing tasks. In P. M. A. Rabbitt & S. Dornic (Eds.), *Attention and performance, V.* London: Academic Press, 1975. Pp. 418–440.

Theios, J., & Muise, J. G. The word identification process in reading. In N. J. Castellan, Jr., D. Pisoni, & G. R. Potts (Eds.), *Cognitive Theory II.* Hillsdale, N.J.: Erlbaum, 1977. Pp. 289–327.

Theios, J., & Walter, D. G. Stimulus and response frequency and sequential effects in memory scanning reaction times. *Journal of Experimental Psychology,* 1974, **102,** 1092–1099.

Townsend, J. T. A stochastic theory of matching processes. *Journal of Mathematical Psychology,* 1976, **14,** 1–52.

Townsend, J. T. Issues and models concerning the processing of a finite number of inputs. In B. H. Kantowitz (Ed.), *Human information processing: Tutorials in performance and cognition.* Hillsdale, New Jersey: Erlbaum, 1974. Pp. 133–185.

Reprinted from *The Psychology of Learning and Motivation*, 1973, 7, 43–85.

REACTION TIME MEASUREMENTS IN THE STUDY OF MEMORY PROCESSES: THEORY AND DATA[1]

John Theios

DEPARTMENT OF PSYCHOLOGY, UNIVERSITY OF WISCONSIN, MADISON, WISCONSIN

[1] This article is dedicated to the memory of Robert R. Bush who not only provided me with encouragement, direction, and reinforcement during a critical time in my career, but whose life as a scientist and scholar has had a lasting influence on me and many others.

Many of the theoretical ideas presented in this article grew out of long conversations and collaborative theoretical work with Jean-Claude Falmagne. His influence on this article is so great that he should be considered a precursor if not a coauthor. Acknowledgment is also due to Dominic W. Massaro who influenced the sections on the stimulus identification and naming processes. Finally, much appreciation is due to my research staff, Diane Flakas, Melvyn C. Moy, Peter G. Smith, Jane Traupmann, and Dennis Walter, who worked very hard on this research over a number of years.

The research reported in this article was conducted in part during the author's tenure as a John Simon Guggenheim Memorial Fellow and was supported by Public Health Service Research Grant MH 19006 from the National Institute of Mental Health. Computing time and other support was made available from the Wisconsin Alumni Research Foundation in part through funds from the National Science Foundation.

I. Introduction

The research reported in this article investigates the human memory process through the use of reaction time measurements. Traditional human information processing tasks such as stimulus naming, choice reaction, and stimulus classification are related to current conceptions of short-term and long-term memory and subsumed under a single information processing theory. The guiding principles in this endeavor are the following assumptions:

1. To respond discriminatively to a stimulus, an observer must first identify (or classify) the stimulus and then determine the particular response which is appropriate. For very familiar stimuli such as alpha-numeric characters, stimulus identification is a relatively automatic process which is independent of the probability and number of stimuli in the experimental ensemble.

2. Human memory can be partitioned into a very large capacity long-term store and a number of very limited capacity short-term (working) stores. Representations of all stimulus-response codes are stored in long-term memory, and these are always potentially retrievable. Retrieval of information from long-term memory is assumed to be relatively slow and take a constant amount of time. As such retrieval from long-term memory can be thought of as a *content addressable* (essentially parallel) search process.

3. In many situations (especially in artifically contrived learning, memory, and information processing tasks), a small set of stimuli and responses recur at a fairly high frequency. In these situations, it is convenient to assume that "copies" of the memory representations of the recurring stimuli and responses may be held and organized into serially scanned, short-term stores or memory buffers. Retrieval from the short-term memory buffers is relatively fast since the serial scanning is assumed to be fast.

A basic thesis of this article will be that in serial human information processing tasks, the short-term stores become completely filled up with representations of the occurring stimuli and responses, and that to the extent that there is any structure in the sequence of physical stimuli and required responses, that structure will be mirrored in (or at least affect) the structure and organization of the serially searched, short-term stores. In particular, it will be postulated that the organization of the short-term stores will be greatly influenced by the sequential (recency) properties of the recurring stimuli and responses.

A. Continuous Information Processing Tasks

Given the assumption of serial short-term stores in human memory, it is our conjecture that there are tasks which can completely tie up one's short-term stores. If this is true, then these tasks can give the experimenter a great deal of control in studying the short-term memory systems of humans. We will call these tasks *continuous information processing tasks*. One example of this type of task is the classic serial, choice reaction time situation (e.g., Falmagne, 1965). In this type of experiment, the subject monitors a serial sequence of two or more different stimuli, differentially reacting to each stimulus as quickly as possible after it is presented. The next stimulus is usually presented very quickly after the subject's response. From the subject's point of view, the task is essentially continuous if the response-stimulus interval is about .5 seconds or less.

Another group of continuous information processing tasks are the stimulus identification experiments in which the subject is asked to identify, name, or read each of a sequence of stimuli. Character naming experiments (e.g., Davis, Moray, & Treisman, 1961; Morin & Forrin, 1965) are good examples of stimulus identification. If the response-stimulus interval is made short enough, the task can be made to appear continuous for the subject, and the experimenter can "drive" or completely engage the subject's short-term memory system.

A final example of an "attention-locking" continuous information processing task is a speeded version (Theios, Smith, Haviland, Traupmann, & Moy, 1973) of Sternberg's (1967) character classification experiment. Here the subject is required to keep a constant set of stimuli in memory, and to classify each of a sequence of stimuli as being a member or not a member of the memory set. Nickerson (1972) has recently reviewed the experimental studies of this type of binary classification. Again, if the response-stimulus interval is kept short enough, the experimenter can "lock up" all of the subject's attention or short-term memory capabilities. We use the terms "tie up," "drive," or "lock up" the subject's attention or short-term memory because if a subject is distracted or thinks about something else in these speeded types of identification-reaction time tasks, he will be unable to perform the task quickly, and reaction times become long. Presumably, the reaction times become long because the subject's short-term memory is being filled by information extraneous to the task, so that in order to respond differentially to the incoming experimental stimuli, the necessary internal stimulus-response representations now have to be retrieved from long-term memory. This will take much longer than if they had been temporarily stored in short-term memory. Of course, the more traditional way of saying this is that the subject's "attention" is being diverted away from the experimental task. Thus, in this article we will occasionally equate "attention" and "short-term memory."

B. Use of Reaction Time to Measure Cognitive Processing

1. *History: Donders' Subtractive Method*

Over a hundred years ago, Franciscus Cornelis Donders introduced the use of reaction time to measure the speed of unobservable, internal human events. Given the current revival of the use of reaction time measures in psychological research, Donders' (1868–1869) theoretical analysis and his experimental conceptualization seem incredibly advanced. In a typical experiment, Donders used plosive consonant-vowel clusters (ka, ke, ki, ko, ku) as stimuli, either presented auditorially (spoken) or visually (rapid illumination), and the subject's task was to repeat the stimulus as quickly as he could. He tested the subjects under three experimental conditions:

a. Simple Reaction Time. Using a tone as a warning signal, the stimulus ka, for example, would be presented for many trials, and an estimate of the subject's mean and minimum reaction time to the stimulus ka would be obtained. This simple reaction time estimate, t_a, would be the time to respond with a known response to an expected stimulus. Presumably, t_a would simply be a measure of stimulus input and response output time, and would not contain decision time components for stimulus identification or response selection. Thus,

$$t_a = t_i + t_o \tag{1}$$

where t_i represents stimulus *input* time and t_o represents response *output* time.

b. Choice Reaction Time. Using the same subjects and the same stimuli, Donders would also measure reaction time to an uncertain stimulus. For example, on any trial, one of the five consonant-vowel sounds would be selected more or less at random, and the subject had to repeat it as soon as he determined what sound it was. Choice reaction time, t_b, thus had four additive components; stimulus input time t_i, stimulus identification time t_s, response selection time t_r, and response output time, t_o. Thus,

$$t_b = t_i + t_s + t_r + t_o. \tag{2}$$

From the assumption that the times of the various psychological events are additive, Donders argued that they would also be subtractive. Thus,

$$t_b - t_a = t_s + t_r \tag{3}$$

which is a measure of the decision time for both stimulus identification and response selection.

   c. *Selective Reaction Time.* In a third testing condition, Donders had his subjects monitor an uncertain, random sequence of stimuli and respond only when a particular (memory or target) stimulus occurred. Donders theorized that reaction time in the selective task, t_c, would be composed of three additive components (stimulus input time t_i, stimulus identification time t_s, and response output time t_o), but would not include response selection time. Thus,

$$t_c = t_i + t_s + t_o. \tag{4}$$

It follows by subtraction that an estimate of response selection time can be obtained as

$$t_r = t_b - t_c \tag{5}$$

and an estimate of stimulus selection time can be obtained as

$$t_s = t_c - t_a. \tag{6}$$

In a typical experiment on himself, Donders (1868–1869) estimated stimulus identification time to be about 47 msec, response selection time to be about 36 msec, and combined stimulus-input and response-output time to be about 201 msec.

There are problems with Donders' subtractive method. The conjecture that the times are additive (subtractive) is based upon the assumption that all the component times are constant from task to task. This is not likely to hold across the three methods, but rather, the means for a given time component will probably vary from method to method. For example, in all probability the t_a estimates will be too short because in the simple reaction time task the subject can anticipate the signal. Effectively, the main objection is that using Donder's subtractive method, one has no or little control over the subject's response criteria (in the signal detectability sense).

2. Sternberg's Additive Factor Method

The reasoning behind Sternberg's (1969, 1971) *additive-factor* or *serial-stage* method is very similar to that of Donders. However,

Sternberg's analysis of variance approach enables one to evaluate the independence or covariation among various experimental variables affecting reaction time. If two variables are *independent* they are assumed to affect separate processing stages, and their effects on reaction time means and variances are *additive*. If two variables *interact* they are assumed to affect at least one stage in common, and their effects on reaction time are not additive. Sternberg (1969, 1971) has postulated four serial stages which seem necessary for many information processing tasks:

a. Stimulus Encoding. Presumably, this stage involves sensory input time and the time to transform the sensory information into a form which can be operated on in memory. Encoding time is affected by such variables as stimulus detectability, intensity, and quality. Sternberg has not been clear on whether or not this stage involves stimulus identification (cognition).

b. Memory Search and Comparison. In this stage, properly encoded stimulus representations are evaluated as to class membership. This stage could involve the identification or cognitive interpretation of the stimulus. The memory search and comparison time is affected by the size of the stimulus ensemble, nature of the task, and instructions to the subject.

c. Response Decision. Depending upon the task, the subject is required to differentially respond to different stimuli. The results of the prior memory search and comparison operations are evaluated, and a decision to make a particular response is made. The response decision stage may be affected by speed-accuracy instructions and the types of permissible responses.

d. Response Selection and Evocation. Once a decision as to the appropriate response has been made, a response evocation "program" is selected and executed. Sternberg (1971) has called this the *translation and response organization* stage. Its duration is affected by such variables as response relative frequency, number of response alternatives, and stimulus-response compatibility.

e. Cautionary Remarks. A number of excellent presentations of the additive factor method have been made (Sternberg, 1969, 1971), and we will not further explicate it here. We do, however, wish to make the following cautionary remarks. The linear analysis of variance model has often been used in conjunction with the additive factor method. In these cases it suffers from all the restrictive assumptions of the analysis of variance, namely, the requirement of identically distributed (equal variance) normal distributions. In point of fact, empirical reaction times are not normally distributed but are skewed with a high positive tail. Further, and more importantly, the means and variances of empirical reaction time distributions are most often positively correlated, a direct violation of the equal variance assumption. Much of the research using the additive factor method (Sternberg, 1969, 1971) has centered around demonstrating additivity (the independence of variables affecting different processing stages), and this has been done by showing *lack* of significant interactions in analysis of variance tests. With the large variances of reaction time measurements and the typically small number of subjects used in information processing experiments contributing to low power of the analysis of variance, failure to find significant interactions has been interpreted as indicating additive (independent) effects of experimental variables where the noninteracting variables affect separate processing stages. Thus, any Type II decision errors (accepting the null hypothesis when it is in fact false) in the interaction tests favor an independent stage–additive factor interpretation. One does not know how often it is the case that two variables really interact to *a small degree,* but the power of the analysis of variance is too low to detect the interaction. To avoid this "acceptance of the null hypothesis" problem, we propose that investigators construct precise, well formulated mathematical models to describe the processes which they are investigating, and that they continually modify the models as new data are made available. One primary purpose of this article will be to show that specific descriptive models with strong assumptions about processing operations can provide much more information about human information processing and memory than can the additive factor method used alone. The main point of this theoretical difference is that one asks different questions about the data and does different experiments if one is looking for additive factors than if one is looking for specific processes. The additive factor (functionalist) approach essentially asks "What variables have effects, and how do they interact?" The specific descriptive model (process) approach essentially asks "What are the processes involved, and how do the variables affect the process?" In the remainder of the article we will introduce and test a very robust descriptive process model of human memory and information processing.

II. Self-Terminating Memory Scanning Model

A. Stimulus Encoding

Stimulus encoding time (t_e) is assumed to be composed of two components. The first component (t_i) is the time it takes for the physical stimulus energy to be input and transformed in the brain to information which can be used to identify or classify the stimulus. The second component (t_s) is the time it takes to identify the stimulus given the coded information from the physical stimulus. It is assumed that to identify the stimulus, contact must be made with long-term memory by matching the stimulus to a stored representation or by uniquely specifying the stimulus as a member of some class following an analysis operating on the features of the coded stimulus. The identification process is assumed to be a content addressable or a net discrimination process so that for sets of well-defined stimuli such as numbers or letters, encoding time averaged over the experimental ensemble of stimuli should be essentially a constant, independent of size of the experimental ensemble. Encoding time, of course, may vary from stimulus to stimulus, due to unique features.

B.   RESPONSE DETERMINATION

The response determination stage of processing follows stimulus encoding. If the task involves reading or naming the stimulus (a highly compatible response), then a simple transformation is made on the stimulus information which will enable a relatively direct output of the response. The stimulus-to-name transformation will take a constant amount of time. Essentially, it is assumed that names (and perhaps other highly compatible responses) are stored in long-term memory in or near the location of the stimulus code, and that little or no additional memory searching (for a response) is necessary for reading, naming, and other highly compatible responses.

With responses that are not naturally related to the stimulus, a *response determination search* must take place before the appropriate response can be selected. For button pushing or other types of indicator responses, it is assumed that the set of stimulus-response codes are stored in a list or "dictionary" in some other location in long-term memory. Further, in speeded tasks, the set of stimulus-response codes may be organized into a short-term, serially scanned, limited capacity buffer. In fact, elements of the long-term "dictionary" may be sequentially loaded into the short-term buffer for processing. To the extent that the fast-access, serial, short-term buffer is used, response determination time (t_r) will be an increasing function of the number of stimulus-response pairs. The short-term buffer is conceived of as a dynamic stack or hierarchy in which representations of the stimulus-response pairs are changing positions from trial to trial and are probabistically ordered on the basis of recency and frequency of stimulus occurrence according to a process similar to that proposed by Falmagne and Theios (1969) and Theios *et al.* (1973). The scan of the stimulus-response buffer is assumed to be serial and self-terminating. Thus, representations of recent and more frequent stimuli are more likely to be located faster, since they are more likely to have favored buffer positions (be higher in the stack). Infrequent and nonrecent stimuli are more likely to have their representations stored further down in the buffer. In that the buffer is of limited capacity, infrequent and nonrecent stimuli may not be represented in the buffer at all, and thus, retrieval of their responses must be made from the slower, long-term memory dictionary. The size of the serial buffer may be variable (in part under the control of the observer) and may be influenced by instructions and the demands of the specific task at hand. With a one-to-one assignment of stimuli to responses, response determination may be a simple transformation taking a small, relatively constant amount of time.

C.   Response Evocation

After the stimulus has been identified and the appropriate response determined, the response must be output by the observer. Response output time can be decomposed into two components. The first is the time to select the appropriate response output program. The response output programs may be organized into a dynamic, serial, self-terminating response output buffer which is probabilistically reorganized from trial to trial on the basis of frequency and recency of response occurrence. Output programs for most recent and more frequent responses are located faster than programs for infrequent and nonrecent responses. The second component of response evocation time is simply the motor time involved in making the response.

D.   Flow Chart of the System

Figure 1 presents a flow diagram of the self-terminating memory system. Information in the physical stimulus S is input to the sensory receptors and transformed and coded by the nervous system into a form usable by the memory process. This takes time t_i, and the result is coded information about the stimulus which we represent as s. The coded information is then processed by the long-term memory identification system which either finds a coded representation of the name of the stimulus (n) as a result of a content addressable memory retrievable process or a sequential feature testing, net discrimina-

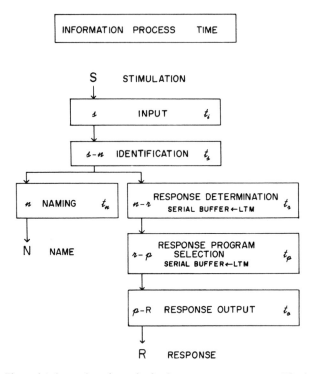

Fig. 1. Flow of information through the human memory system. Physical stimulation S is input to the memory taking time t_i to be converted to a sensory code s. The sensory code s is fed into the identification process, taking time t_s to determine the name code n of the stimulus. (s-n denotes the link from s to n). If the task requires naming the stimulus, the name code is fed into a naming process which outputs the name of the stimulus, taking time t_n. The total time it takes to name a stimulus is $t_i + t_s + t_n$. If the task requires making some other response to the stimulus, the name code n is fed into the response dictionary which determines the appropriate response code assigned to the stimulus, taking time t_r. For tasks with a compatible one-to-one stimulus response mapping, t_r is effectively a constant near zero. In tasks with a many-to-one stimulus-response mapping, a serially searched, self-terminating buffer may be set up which is fed response codes by a long-term store. The response code r is fed into a system which selects a response program taking time t_p and outputs a response taking time t_o, yielding an overt response R. The total time it takes to respond to a stimulus is $t_i + t_s + t_r + t_p + t_o$.

tion process. The stimulus identification process takes time t_s. If the task at hand requires a simple name response, a transformation is performed on the coded name information n to produce an overt name response N. If some other indicator response is required by the task, the coded name information n is fed into the response determination system which has two components which operate in parallel. One component is a content addressable (or sequential feature testing) long-term memory system which can produce the required response for any stimulus. The other component is a limited capacity, short-term buffer which determines the response by a serial, self-terminating scan of the buffer. The coded name information n is compared sequentially to each of a small set of name-to-response (n-r) pairs stored in the buffer until a match is obtained. If a buffer match is obtained, coded information about the response (r) is fed into the response output buffer where a response is selected and executed. There are two ways to think about the operation of the long-term memory response determination process.

1. Parallel Operation

As soon as the long-term response determination system "computes" the response, the response code r is fed directly into the response output system for response selection and execution. This may happen before the serial scan of the short-term buffer has located the response. Thus, the time to retrieve a response from long-term memory may determine the effective capacity of the short-term buffer. If the time it takes to retrieve a response from long-term memory is t_L and the scan rate of the short-term buffer is t_S, then the effective short-term buffer capacity is $K = t_L/t_S$.

2. Yoked Operation

This process was suggested by Jean-Claude Falmagne. Assume that the long-term memory system loads the short-term buffer with the representations of potential n-r pairs, and that the actual response decision is made by the self-terminating, serial buffer scan process. At the beginning of a trial the buffer is already loaded with the (locally) most likely n-r pairs in sequential order. During the buffer scan, the long-term memory system continues to load likely n-r pairs into the buffer. The effective capacity of the short-term buffer is determined by the average time it takes for the long-term memory to feed the correct n-r pair to the buffer. If the estimated capacity of the buffer were K, this would mean that the average time for the long-term memory to retrieve and feed the correct n-r pair to the buffer would be $(K - 1)t_S$, where t_S is the buffer scan time for a single pair.

After the appropriate response code r has been determined, it is fed into the response output system. The response output system may work very similarly to the response determination system, having both a long-term and a short-term memory component. The response output programs may be selected by a fast, serial, self-terminating scan of a dynamic, response buffer or by a slower long-term memory retrieval process. The time to select the response program can be designated as t_p. The time to output an overt response can be designated as t_o.

E. Specific Representation of the Model

This section may be skipped by readers who understand the model as conceptually presented in the previous sections. The following presentation is given to resolve ambiguities that may result from the inexactness of the English language, and to help investigators who wish to obtain quantitative predictions from the model or to do further mathematical and computer research with the model.

Suppose a set S containing I ($I \geqslant 2$) stimuli $\{S_1, S_2, S_3, \ldots, S_i, \ldots, S_I\}$, a set R containing M ($2 \leqslant M \leqslant I$) responses $\{R_1, R_2, R_3, \ldots, R_m, \ldots, R_M\}$ and a binary function of the form $\{(S_i, R_m)\}$ which is a subset of the cross product of the sets S and R which maps the set S onto the set R.

Definition 1: Stimulus Input

The time to input a stimulus S_i to the system and convert it to a usable representation s_i is t_i which is a random sample from a distribution $f_i(t)$ having mean μ_i and variance σ_i^2. This distribution may vary somewhat from stimulus to stimulus.

Definition 2: Stimulus Identification

The time taken by the system to determine the name code n_i of representation s_i is t_s which is a random sample from a distribution $f_s(t)$ having mean μ_s and variance σ_s^2. This distribution may vary somewhat from name to name.

Definition 3: Naming

The time to convert the name code n_i to an overt name response N_i is t_n, which is a random sample from a distribution $f_n(t)$ having mean μ_n and variance σ_n^2. This distribution may vary somewhat from name to name.

Axiom 1: Naming Time

The time to overtly name a stimulus S_i is

$$NT_i = t_i + t_s + t_n \tag{7}$$

where t_i, t_s, and t_n are random variables defined in Definitions 1–3.

Definition 4: Memory Stack Response Dictionary

If the stimulus-response mapping is not one-to-one, then at each trial there is an ordering of appropriate name-response pairs (n_i-r_m) in memory such that every pair can be given a position k, where $1 \leqslant k \leqslant Z$, and $Z \leqslant I$.

Axiom 2: Response Determination

If the stimulus-response mapping is not one-to-one, and if stimulus S_i is presented, and if K is the dictionary position in which the matching memory pair n_i-r_m is stored, then the time to determine the appropriate response code r_m is

$$t_r = \sum_{k=1}^{K} t_k \tag{8}$$

where t_k is a random sample from a distribution $f_k(t)$ having mean μ_k and variance σ_k^2. With a one-to-one stimulus-response mapping, the dictionary position may equal one for all name-response codes.

Definition 5: Response Output Buffer

At any time there is an ordering of the response output programs such that every response program can be given a position j, $1 \leqslant j \leqslant W$, in memory, with $W \leqslant M$.

Axiom 3: Response Output Program Selection

If the execution program for response R_m is stored in position J of the output buffer, then the time to select the program is

$$t_p = \sum_{j=1}^{J} t_j \tag{9}$$

where t_j is a random sample from a distribution $f_j(t)$ having mean μ_j and variance σ_j^2.

Definition 6: Response Output Time

Given that the response output program has been selected, the time to output the overt response R_i is t_o, a random sample from a distribution $f_o(t)$ having mean μ_o and variance σ_o^2. This distribution may vary somewhat from response to response.

Axiom 4: Reaction Time

The reaction time to stimulus S_i is the sum of the times to input and identify the stimulus and the times to determine the appropriate response and select and output the response

$$RT_i = t_i + t_s + t_r + t_p + t_o. \tag{10}$$

For a one-to-one stimulus-response mapping, t_r may equal a nonnegative constant.

Axiom 5: Memory Differentiation

Positions 1 through $Z - 1$ of the serial response dictionary each contain only one name-response code pair $(n\text{-}r)$ whereas the long-term response dictionary may be considered as position Z which contains all the relevant $n\text{-}r$ codes.

Likewise, positions 1 through $W - 1$ of the serial output buffer each contain only one response output program, whereas the long-term response output memory may be considered as position W which contains all the relevant response output programs.

Axiom 6: Dictionary Position Changes

Let $X_{i,N}$ be a random variable indicating the dictionary position of name-response pair $n_i\text{-}r_m$ on trial N. If $n_i\text{-}r_m$ is represented at memory position K and if stimulus S_i is presented on trial N, then the probability that pair $n_i\text{-}r_m$ moves up to position K' $(K' < K)$ before trial $N + 1$ is

$$\Pr(X_{i,N+1} = K' | X_{i,N} = K) = (1 - a_i)^{K'-1} a_i. \tag{11}$$

The probability that pair $n_i\text{-}r_m$ remains in the Kth memory position is

$$\Pr(X_{i,N+1} = K | X_{i,N} = K) = 1 - \left[\sum_{k=1}^{K-1} (1 - a_i)^{k-1} a_i \right]. \tag{12}$$

The parameter a_i represents the conditional probability that pair n_i-r_m will replace pair n_j-r_o in the kth position of the dictionary stack given it did not replace any pair higher in the stack. If memory pair n_i-r_m moves up to memory position K' from position K following the presentation of stimulus S_i on trial N, then all the intervening pairs in positions K' through $K - 1$ move down one, to positions $K' + 1$ through K, with their order preserved.

Axiom 7: Output Position Changes

Let $Y_{m,N}$ be a random variable indicating the buffer position of the response output program for response R_m on trial N. If response R_m was made on trial N and its output program was located at buffer position J on trial N, then the probability that the program moves up to position J' ($J' < J$) before the next trial is

$$\Pr(Y_{m,N+1} = J' | Y_{m,N} = J) = (1 - b_m)^{J'-1} b_m. \tag{13}$$

The probability that the program remains in the Jth position is

$$\Pr(Y_{m,N+1} = J | Y_{m,N} = J) = 1 - \left[\sum_{j=1}^{J-1} (1 - b_m)^{J-1} b_m \right]. \tag{14}$$

The parameter b_m represents the conditioned probability that the response output program for response R_m will replace some other program in the jth position of the buffer given that it did not replace any program located higher in the buffer. Following a response R_m, if the response program moves up to position J' from position J, then all the intervening programs in positions J' through $J - 1$ move down one to positions $J' + 1$ through J with their order preserved.

Axioms 6 and 7 are not fundamental to the system. They could be replaced by other axioms which determine memory positions for the name-response pairs and the output programs. What is crucial is that the time to locate a name-response code and an output program be directly related to the number of intervening stimuli and responses since the last occurrence of the stimulus and response in question.

A number of testable hypotheses follow directly from the definitions and axioms, assuming standard statistical theory and reasonable simplifying assumptions. The simplifying assumptions which will be made in this treatment are:

1. All the component time distributions [$f_i(t)$, $f_s(t)$, $f_j(t)$, $f_k(t)$, and $f_o(t)$] are statistically independent of each other.
2. Mean stimulus input time (μ_i), mean stimulus identification

time (μ_s), mean naming time (μ_n), and mean response output time (μ_o) are independent of stimulus presentation probability and the size of the experimental set of stimuli.

3. Dictionary comparison time t_k and output buffer comparison time t_j are independent of memory positions k and j.

4. Dictionary position change probabilities a_i are equal for all stimulus names assigned to the same response.

5. With a one-to-one stimulus-response mapping, the dictionary process cannot be differentiated (mathematically) from the response buffer process. Thus, in situations with a one-to-one S-R mapping, it will be assumed that the response determination time t_r will equal a nonnegative constant.

III.   Experimental Tests of the Model

A.   Stimulus Naming and Choice Reaction Time with Equally Likely Stimuli

Prediction 1: Mean Stimulus Name Time. Given the above definitions, axioms, and assumptions, the mean time to name a stimulus S_i is independent of the number of other equally likely stimulus alternatives and is equal to a constant

$$\overline{NT}_i = \mu_i + \mu_s + \mu_n. \tag{15}$$

This result follows directly from Axiom 1.

Our next prediction requires a preliminary result. The derivation of this result is straightforward and will not be given here.

Expected Response Buffer Position.   Given I equally likely stimuli with a one-to-one stimulus-response mapping, and a response output buffer capacity of W, the asymptotic expected buffer position for any response program is

$$E(Y_I) = \left(\frac{I - W + 1}{I}\right) W + \frac{1}{I} \sum_{j=1}^{W-1} j. \tag{16}$$

In the present model, the serial buffer capacity $(W - 1)$ is a parameter that must be estimated from the data.

Prediction 2: Mean Reaction Time.   Given the above definitions, axioms, and assumptions, the mean time to differentially react to a stimulus with a uniquely assigned response is a linear function of the expected buffer position of the response output program.

$$\overline{RT}_i = (\mu_i + \mu_s + \mu_r) + (EY_i)\mu_j + \mu_o \qquad (17)$$
$$= \mu E(Y_i) + B$$

where B, the reaction time intercept, is equal to $\mu_i + \mu_s + \mu_r + \mu_o$ (the mean stimulus input, identification, response determination, and output time) and $\mu = \mu_j$ is the mean response selection buffer scan time. This result follows directly from Axioms 4, 5, and 7 and Eq. (16).

1. Stimulus Naming Experiment

This experiment was conducted with the aid of Diane Flakas and Peter G. Smith. The subjects were 12 University of Wisconsin undergraduate student volunteers who received $2.00 for participation in the experiment. The apparatus was the same as that described in detail in Theios et al. (1973). Each subject was tested individually on two successive days during a session which lasted less than 50 minutes. On one day the subject was required to name the stimuli (the numerals 0–9). On the other day the subject was required to indicate the stimulus by pushing a response button uniquely assigned to each stimulus. Half of the subjects received the naming task on their first day and half the subjects received the button-pushing task on their first day. In the naming task each subject received six experimental conditions of 300 trials each. The variable was the number of equally likely stimuli (2, 4, 6, 8, or 10). The first condition each subject received was practice with 10 stimuli. Each subject then received the conditions of 2, 4, 6, 8, and 10 stimuli in a random order which was different for each subject.

In the button-pushing task each subject received five experimental conditions of 300 trials each. The variable was the number of equally likely stimuli (2, 4, 6, and 8). The first condition each subject received was practice with eight stimuli. In the next four conditions, the order of the conditions of 2, 4, 6, and 8 stimuli were distributed among the 12 subjects according to three Latin squares which balanced the order of presentation. The eight response buttons were located under the subject's eight fingers, and the stimulus-response mapping was 2–9 with the fingers from left to right. The stimulus sets were (5, 6), (4, 5, 6, 7), (3, 4, 5, 6, 7, 8), and (2, 3, 4, 5, 6, 7, 8, 9).

In both tasks, the response-stimulus interval was .5 second, and the stimuli were presented by an Industrial Electronics Engineers Inc., Series 10 rear-projection visual readout unit. The stimuli were selected and presented by a PDP-8 computer which also recorded the stimulus, response, and response time on magnetic tape. The subjects' verbal naming responses were recorded on audio tape, and a Lafayette voice sensitive relay was used to trigger the naming times. The subject sat in a sound-attenuated booth and wore earphones which delivered a wide-band white noise mask.

Figure 2 presents mean response time as a function of number of stimulus-response alternatives for name responses as well as button-push responses. As can be seen, the mean name response times are effectively a constant, approximately 450 msec, independent of number of stimulus-name alternatives. On the other hand, the mean button-pushing reaction times increase with the number of stimulus-response alternatives. This pattern of results was true for each of the twelve subjects individually, and it is consistent with the results of many other experiments (e.g., Brainard, Irby, Fitts, & Alluisi, 1962; Davis *et al.*, 1961; Morin & Forrin, 1965).

The results have three important implications for information processing models. The first is that of the *locus of cognition*. After a stimulus has been encoded and before it is used in any serial memory scan, the stimulus has been identified. The subject "knows" what the stimulus is since he can report the name of the stimulus fast without any serial scanning dependent upon the size of the experimental set of stimuli.

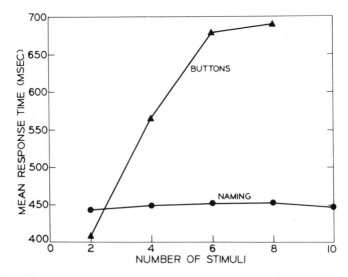

Fig. 2. Mean response time (msec) as a function of number of equally likely stimulus alternatives for the verbal naming and button-pushing response conditions.

The second implication is that the typical serial component of reaction time is a *response* process such as response determination or
response selection. Presumably, in the Sternberg (1967) character
classification task, the subject should be able to identify (name) the
stimulus before he can determine whether it is or is not a member
of the target set.

The third implication is that, in the context of the present model,
the response output buffer must be of limited capacity. If the response output buffer was large enough to hold all the output programs, then mean reaction time in the button-pushing condition
should be a *linear* function of the number of stimulus-response alternatives. Obviously, the obtained function is not linear. This implies
that the response output buffer is of limited capacity. The capacity
of the buffer may be estimated by selecting the capacity $W - 1$ which
makes mean reaction time a linear function of expected buffer position. In Figure 3 it can be seen that a buffer capacity $W - 1$ equal
to three gives a linear relationship between mean reaction time and
expected buffer position. The theoretical interpretation of this is that

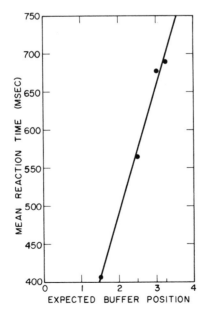

Fig. 3. Mean reaction time (msec) to equally likely stimuli in the button-
pushing condition as a function of theoretically expected position in the response output buffer. The four ordered buffer positions indicated by the points correspond to
two, four, six, and eight stimulus alternatives.

the buffer can serially scan three positions, before long-term memory will supply the correct response program. The slope of the linear function is approximately 168 msec, which is to be interpreted as the time needed to go from the coded name of the test stimulus to a determination of its response output program.[2] According to the theory, it took long-term memory approximately four times 168 msec or 672 msec after stimulus identification to find the response output program. However, with I equally likely stimulus alternatives, the serial buffer came up with the response program in 336 ± 168 msec on a proportion $3/I$ of the trials when I was equal to or greater than 3. When there was only two stimulus alternatives, the buffer produced the appropriate response program in 252 ± 84 msec on every trial.

Table I presents the mean and standard deviation of the proportion of errors. For the naming condition, the probability of an error was virtually nonexistent, and for the button-pushing condition it was low (.045) and did not vary much as a function of the number of stimulus-response alternatives.

TABLE I

MEAN PROPORTION OF ERRORS

	Number of equally likely stimuli				
	2	4	6	8	10
Naming	.007	.011	.006	.004	.005
Buttons	.032	.042	.057	.054	

B. TWO-CHOICE REACTION TIMES

If indeed the capacity of the serial, short-term output buffer is three response programs, then for a traditional two-choice reaction time task, both response output programs should fit into the response buffer. The theorem that mean reaction time is a linear function of expected buffer position can then be tested by varying stimulus presentation probability, since according to the model, expected buffer position is a function of stimulus presentation probability.

Theios and Smith (1972) have worked out the mathematics for the

---

[2] This estimate of the slope seems unusually high, but it may be understandable in that the stimulus-response compatibility was not high in this task. The stimulus 2 was paired with the first finger, the stimulus 3 was paired with the second finger, and so on. A more compatible S-R mapping would have been to pair the stimulus 1 with the first finger, the stimulus 2 with the second finger, and so on.

two-stimuli case of the model being considered in this article. The asymptotic probability of the response output program for stimulus S_i being in the first position of the buffer is

$$\Pr(Y_i = 1) = (\pi_i b_i)/[\pi_i b_i + (1 - \pi_i) b_j] \tag{18}$$

where π_i is the presentation probability for stimulus S_i, b_i is the buffer position exchange probability for stimulus S_i, and b_j is the buffer position exchange probability for the other stimulus, S_j. The expected buffer position for the response output program of stimulus S_i is then just

$$E(Y_i) = (1)[\Pr(Y_i = 1)] + (2)[1 - \Pr(Y_i = 1)]. \tag{19}$$

According to Prediction 2, the expected mean reaction time to a stimulus S_i presented with probability π_i is simply a linear function of its expected buffer position [Eq. (17)].

1. Remington's Experiment

Remington (1969) varied stimulus presentation probability in a two-choice reaction time task, using probabilities of (.3, .7) and (.5, .5). The stimuli consisted of left and right lights and the corresponding responses were a left- and a right-hand index finger button push. Each trial began with a red warning light followed by a 1-second foreperiod before the presentation of a stimulus light. The inter-stimulus interval averaged about 4 seconds. Each of five human subjects were given 1200 trials on each problem in alternating blocks of 200 trials, and the data considered here represents the last 800 trials for the (.5, .5) problem and the last 1000 trials for the (.3, .7) problem.

For this experiment, the best estimate of the buffer exchange probability (b_m of Axiom 7) was .18 for the .3 stimulus, .22 for the .5 stimuli, and .38 for the .7 stimulus. Thus, according to Eq. (19), the expected buffer positions are 1.17 for $\pi = .7$, 1.50 for $\pi = .5$, and 1.83 for $\pi = .3$. Figure 4 shows mean reaction time in Remington's experiment as a function of expected buffer position. As can be seen, the relationship is linear. The intercept (B) is 209 msec and the slope (scan rate) is 54 msec.

2. Stimulus-Response Sequential Effects

Predictions can be made about stimulus-response sequential effects using the same parameter estimates used to predict the mean reaction

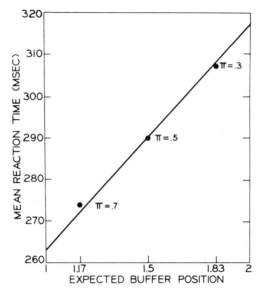

Fig. 4. Remington's (1969) mean two-choice reaction time data as a function of theoretically expected response output buffer position.

times. Equation 17 is again used to predict the reaction times, but instead of $E(Y_i)$ representing the unconditional asymptotic expected buffer position, it represents the asymptotic buffer position *conditional* on a specific sequence of preceding stimuli. For example, during a run of presentations of stimulus S_1, the expected buffer position of response program r_1 approaches 1.0. Likewise, during a run of stimulus S_2 the expected buffer position of response program r_1 approaches 2. Thus, depending upon the previous sequence of S_1 and S_2 stimuli, the asymptotic expected buffer position will be somewhere between 1 and 2, and an entire space of sequential effects is possible. The first four orders of sequential effects are represented in Fig. 5 as a tree. A sequence *ijkl* should be interpreted to mean that we are considering the average reaction time to stimulus S_i on all occasions on which it was preceded by stimulus S_j on the previous trial, preceded by stimulus S_k two trials before, and by stimulus S_l three trials before. Predictions were made for each stimulus probability (.3, .5, .7) separately, and then pooled together, as were the observed conditional mean reaction times. As can be seen, the predictions of the model are closely approximating the data. The square root of the weighted mean squared error between ob-

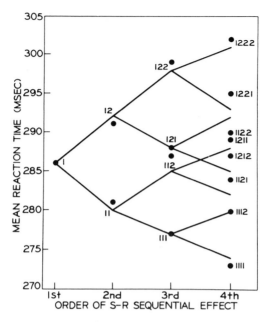

Fig. 5. Sequential effects in Remington's (1969) two-choice reaction time experiment. Observed (points) and predicted (lines) mean reaction times conditional on the sequence of preceding stimuli, averaged over the three stimulus probability values. For example, the point 1212 represents the mean reaction time to a stimulus (call it S_1) given that the other stimulus (call it S_2) occurred on the previous trial, S_1 occurred two trials before, and S_2 occurred three trials before.

served and predicted conditional reaction times is less than 3 msec. Thus, the model can account for sequential effects in two-choice reaction times.

C.   Two-Choice Naming Times and Stimulus Probability

We have just seen that two-choice (button pushing) reaction times decrease markedly as stimulus probability is increased. According to the model presented in Section II, the time to name a stimulus in a two-choice task should not be a function of stimulus presentation probability. This prediction follows since naming is assumed to be a content-addressable process or a feature testing process.[3] To test this

[3] The feature-testing process envisioned here is one in which, for sets of basic verbal-linguistic stimuli such as numerals or letters, the identification process is automatic with respect to all the elements of the set, irrespective of how many elements the

prediction, ten human subjects were tested in a two-choice naming experiment in which stimulus presentation probabilities were varied as (.2,.8), (.3,.7), (.4,.6), and (.5,.5). After a practice session with probabilities of (.5,.5), each subject was given 300 trials at each of the four pairs of presentation probabilities, in a different random order. The stimuli were the digits 4 and 5, and the experimental method was similar to that of the naming experiment described in Section III, A. For stimulus probability increasing from .2 to .8 in steps of .1, the obtained mean naming times were 356, 356, 351, 357, 348, 347, and 346 msec. The obtained naming times did not differ significantly from their overall mean of 351 msec [$F(6,54) = .27$]. Thus, there is no evidence for a stimulus or response probability effect in two-choice naming of stimuli such as exists for two-choice button-pushing reaction times. The results of this experiment constitute further evidence in support of the hypothesis that stimulus identification is a process that occurs early, before any serial, self-terminating memory scanning.[4]

D. THREE-CHOICE REACTION TIMES

Consider an experiment with a one-to-one stimulus-response mapping in which there are three uncertain stimulus events, S_1, S_2, S_3 which recur with constant probabilities of $\pi_1 = \pi$, and $\pi_2 = \pi_3 = (1 - \pi)/2$. For this special case, the following result follows from Axiom 7 if it is assumed that $b_m = b$ for all responses.

Asymptotic buffer position probabilities for special case of three stimuli and responses: As N becomes large, the probabilities that

---

experimenter is presenting in the task. Thus, identification time will be effectively a constant irrespective of the size of the *experimental* ensemble of alpha-numeric characters. For less basic sets of stimuli such as colors, pictures, and words, the identification process is less automatic, and identification time may depend upon the size of the experimental ensemble of stimuli. This analysis is supported by the results of experiments by Morin, Konick, Troxell, and McPherson (1965).

[4] In the present two-alternative experiment, the naming times were approximately 100 msec faster than in the two-alternative condition of the previous experiment. This difference is due to differences in the level of accuracy used by the subjects. In the first naming experiment, the error percentage was less than 1% for the two-alternative equally likely condition. In the corresponding condition of the second experiment, the error percentage was 2.3%. This is in the neighborhood of the error percentage of the two-alternative button-pushing condition of the first experiment (3.2%). Holding error probability roughly constant, two-choice naming times are faster (357 msec) than two-choice button-push reaction times (408 msec).

response output code $<n_1, r_1>$ is stored in the first, second, or third buffer position approaches, respectively

$$\lim_{N \to \infty} \Pr(Y_{1,N} = 1) = \pi , \tag{20}$$

$$\lim_{N \to \infty} \Pr(Y_{1,N} = 2) = \frac{\pi(1 - \pi)}{.5(1 + \pi)} , \tag{21}$$

$$\lim_{N \to \infty} \Pr(Y_{1,N} = 3) = \frac{(1 - \pi)^2}{(1 + \pi)} . \tag{22}$$

Since the other two stimuli S_2 and S_3 are equally likely, it directly follows that

$$\lim_{N \to \infty} \Pr(Y_{2,N} = 1) = \lim_{N \to \infty} \Pr(Y_{3,N} = 1) = \frac{1}{2} [1 - \lim_{N \to \infty} \Pr(Y_{1,N} = 1)], \tag{23}$$

$$\lim_{N \to \infty} \Pr(Y_{2,N} = 2) = \lim_{N \to \infty} \Pr(Y_{3,N} = 2) = \frac{1}{2} [1 - \lim_{N \to \infty} \Pr(Y_{1,N} = 2)], \tag{24}$$

$$\lim_{N \to \infty} \Pr(Y_{2,N} = 3) = \lim_{N \to \infty} \Pr(Y_{3,N} = 3) = \frac{1}{2} [1 - \lim_{N \to \infty} \Pr(Y_{1,N} = 3)]. \tag{25}$$

Given the asymptotic buffer position probabilities, the expected buffer position for any response code $<n_i, r_i>$ will be equal to

$$E(Y_i) = (1) \lim_{N \to \infty} \Pr(Y_{i,N} = 1) + (2) \lim_{N \to \infty} \Pr(Y_{i,N} = 2)$$
$$+ (3) \lim_{N \to \infty} \Pr(Y_{i,N} = 3). \tag{26}$$

Given the expected buffer positions, Eq. (17) can be used to generate predictions for mean reaction time.

1. Three Stimuli Experiments

In order to test the predictions from the model, two choice reaction experiments each involving three stimuli and responses were conducted. The experiments were conducted with the aid of Jane Traupmann and Peter G. Smith. The general experimental method was similar to that used in the button-pushing reaction time experiment described in Section III A. The stimuli were the numerals 1, 2, and 3 which were mapped, respectively to the index, middle, and ring finger of the subject's right hand. The subjects were 48 right-handed

University students, 24 in each experiment. There were four experimental conditions in each experiment, each involving 300 trials. Experiment 1 used stimulus presentation probability schedules (π_1, π_2, π_3) of (1/3, 1/3, 1/3), (1/2, 1/4, 1/4), (1/4, 1/2, 1/4), and (1/4, 1/4, 1/2). Experiment 2 used stimulus presentation probability schedules of (1/3, 1/3, 1/3), (5/12, 5/12, 1/6), (1/4, 1/4, 1/2), and (1/3, 1/6, 1/2). Within an experiment, each subject received his four experimental conditions in a different order.

Obtained mean reaction times as a function of stimulus-response pair and stimulus probability are presented in Table II, along with predictions from the self-terminating memory stack model. The values of the parameters of the model were estimated by having Chandler's (1969) subroutine STEPIT select values for the parameters which minimized the weighted squared error between observed and predicted mean reaction times. For experiment 1, the best fitting parameters were μ (scan rate) = 69 msec, B_1 = 336 msec, B_2 = 346 msec, and B_3' = 353 msec, where B_i is the reaction time intercept ($\mu_i + \mu_s + \mu_r + \mu_o$) for stimulus S_i and response R_i, $i = 1$, 2, 3. For Experiment 2, the best fitting parameters were μ = 78 msec, B_1 = 322 msec, B_2 = 348 msec, B_3 = 332 msec. Condition IV of Experiment 2 does not fall within the special case considered in this section; however, the predictions for this condition were obtained by computer simulation of the process using the same parameter values. In Table II, all 24 predicted means are well within plus and minus one standard error of the obtained mean reaction times. The strong stimulus probability effect should be noted in the data of Table II. For every stimulus-response pair, in each experiment, mean reaction time increases as stimulus presentation probability is decreased. Thus, the serial, self-terminating push-down stack model is able to account for three-choice reaction times with unequal stimulus-response probabilities.

E. N-Choice Reaction Times with Varying Stimulus Probabilities

Consider the class of choice reaction time experiments with an arbitrary number N of stimuli and an unequal distribution of presentation probabilities among the N stimuli. Restrict the consideration here to one-to-one stimulus-response mappings. For this class of experiments, the self-terminating model presented in Section II, E does not yield explicit solutions, in general. This is largely due to Axiom 7 in which the expected buffer positions will be functions

TABLE II

THREE STIMULI EXPERIMENTS: OBTAINED (Obt.) AND PREDICTED (Pre.) MEAN REACTION TIMES (msec) AS A FUNCTION OF STIMULUS PRESENTATION PROBABILITY (π) AND STIMULUS-RESPONSE (S-R) PAIR

Experiment 1 conditions

S-R	I π	Obt.	Pre.	II π	Obt.	Pre.	III π	Obt.	Pre.	IV π	Obt.	Pre.	Mean Obt.	Pre.
1	1/3	471	474	1/2	452	451	1/4	489	485	1/4	484	485	470	469
2	1/3	482	484	1/4	488	495	1/2	463	462	1/4	500	495	480	480
3	1/3	492	491	1/4	507	502	1/4	502	502	1/2	466	469	487	487
Mean		482	483		475	475		479	478		479	479	479	479

Experiment 2 conditions

S-R	I π	Obt.	Pre.	II π	Obt.	Pre.	III π	Obt.	Pre.	IV π	Obt.	Pre.	Mean Obt.	Pre.
1	1/3	471	477	5/12	455	458	1/4	494	492	1/3	463	471	468	472
2	1/3	499	503	5/12	484	484	1/4	512	518	1/6	532	538	501	504
3	1/3	489	487	1/6	524	525	1/2	478	479	1/2	466	459	482	479
Mean		486	489		479	480		491	493		476	476	483	484

of the exact sequence of stimuli experienced. However, predictions can be obtained from the model using Monte Carlo simulation methods. Preliminary investigation has indicated that if the b_m parameters of Axiom 7 are all set equal to each other ($b_m = b$), then the asymptotic buffer positions are independent of b, as long as b is not equal to zero.

1. Falmagne's Six-Choice Reaction Time Experiment

Falmagne (1972) conducted a six-choice reaction time experiment in which the stimulus presentation probabilities were .32, .25, .18, .13, .08, and .04. A compatible, left to right, one-to-one stimulus-response mapping was used with the stimuli being the numerals 1–6, and the responses being the ring, middle, and index fingers of each hand. The experiment had a Latin square design such that each of six subjects received a different distribution of probabilities over the six stimuli. The subjects were tested on 10 different days, receiving 1000 trials per day. The data reported here are from three asymptotic days of testing. The obtained mean reaction times are presented in Table III where it can be seen that mean reaction time increased

TABLE III

Obtained Mean Reaction Time (msec) for Falmagne's Experiment as a Function of Stimulus Presentation Probability (π) and Corresponding Means Simulated from the Push-Down Stack Model

π	Obtained	Predicted
.32	397	407
.25	438	427
.18	452	454
.13	484	483
.08	529	525
.04	571	575

systematically as stimulus probability decreased. Table III also presents predictions for the Falmagne experiment obtained from 20 simulations of the push-down stack model. The capacity of the output buffer ($W - 1$) was set equal to six. The estimated buffer scan rate was 65 msec with a reaction time intercept of 252 msec. The predicted mean reaction times given in Table III are close to the obtained mean reaction times. The linear correlation between obtained and simulated mean reaction times is .994, with the model accounting for .99% of the variance between means. In any case, the model is accounting for the overall stimulus-response probability effect. Thus far we have seen that the self-terminating push-down stack model can account for the data from two-choice, three-choice, and N-choice reaction times.

F. CHARACTER CLASSIFICATION

Sternberg (1966, 1967, 1969) has introduced a binary-choice, character classification task which is particularly relevant to the information processing theory proposed in this article. A subject memorizes a small target set of stimuli, and then either one or a sequence of stimuli are presented. After the presentation of a stimulus the subject must indicate as quickly as he can whether the presented stimulus is or is not a member of the target set. In studies of this type, it is typically found that mean reaction time to both target and nontarget stimuli is an approximately linear function of the size of the target set. Further, the slopes of the functions relating mean reaction time to target set size are typically about equal for both target and nontarget stimuli. This pattern of results led Sternberg (1966, 1967) to propose a serial, exhaustive memory scanning process to account for the data in these binary classification experiments. In order to respond correctly, a subject presumably had to compare a representation of the test (or probe) stimulus to those of the target set already stored in memory. The fact that the mean reaction times increased as a linear function of target set size led Sternberg (1966, 1967) to propose that the memory comparison (scanning) process is serial in nature. That is, each stimulus added to the target set added a constant increment of time to the mean reaction time. Secondly, the fact that the slopes of the reaction time functions were equal for target and nontarget stimuli led Sternberg to propose that the search of the memorized target set was exhaustive. Sternberg reasoned that if the subjects were using a self-terminating memory search, the slope of the reaction time function for nontarget stimuli should be twice that of the target stimuli. Assuming that the subject scans only representations of the target set and that the memory scan is self-terminating, the average number of memory comparisons made would be one half the number of target stimuli if a target probe was presented, but would be equal to the number of target stimuli if a nontarget probe was presented. This line of reasoning led Sternberg (1966, 1967) to reject serial, self-terminating memory

processes as reasonable for these types of tasks. The key to this rejection is the assumption that the subject scans only the set of target
stimuli. In this paper, a serial, self-terminating memory scanning
process is proposed in which elements of both the target and nontarget set of stimuli may be represented in the scanning process.
This expanded serial, self-terminating scanning process can account
for data of the type published by Sternberg (1966, 1967) as well as
for stimulus probability and sequential effects which are not easily
accounted for by an exhaustive scanning process.

1. Sternberg's Design

Using a constant target set procedure, Sternberg (1967) performed
a binary classification experiment in which target set size was varied
as 1, 2, and 4. In that experiment, all 10 digits were used as stimuli.
The design was such that stimulus presentation probability was
confounded with set size, but within a given target set size condition
the individual target stimuli were equally likely. The individual
target presentation probabilities were $4/15, 2/15$, and $1/15$ for target
set sizes of 1, 2, and 4, respectively. Within the set of nontarget
stimuli, the individual stimuli differed in their presentation probabilities. Sternberg (1967) did not report the results of analyses of
stimulus probability or of stimulus or response sequential effects.
The self-terminating memory stack model predicts stimulus probability and sequential effects for this type of experiment. In order
to gain information about the effect of stimulus probability and
sequential effects, we essentially replicated the Sternberg (1967) design in our laboratory. Since it is commonly assumed that sequential
effects in reaction time occur only with a short response-stimulus
interval, the length of the response-stimulus interval was also varied
in our experiment.

The experiment was run by Dennis Walter as his masters thesis
research. The subjects were 48 university students. The apparatus
and general procedure was that described in Theios et al. (1973),
but the design of the experiment closely followed that of Sternberg
(1967). Using a within-subjects design and blocks of 108 trials, subjects were tested with both a short response-stimulus interval (.5
second) and a long response-stimulus interval (2.0 seconds). Figure 6
presents mean reaction time for target and nontarget stimuli as a
function of target set size (the points on the graph). The data are in
essential agreement with Sternberg (1967); 97% of the variance is
accounted for by the hypothesis of parallel linear functions. The data

do, however, differ *significantly* from the best fitting parallel lines and also from their individual best fitting lines (F's > 6.04, $df = 1$, 94). This difference between our replication and Sternberg's (1967) data is most likely due to the fact that the power of the analysis of variance is much greater in our experiment where four times as many subjects were given twice as many trials. In Fig. 6 the lines represent

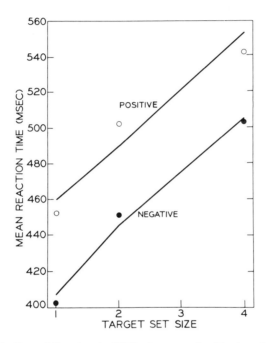

Fig. 6. Replication of Sternberg's (1967) character classification design. Mean reaction time (circles) as a function of target set size. The lines are predictions obtained from a simulation of the self-terminating memory stack model.

predicted means generated from a computer simulation of the self-terminating memory stack model. The simulation procedure followed that described in Theios *et al.* (1973). Table IV presents obtained and simulated mean reaction times for all the conditions in the experiment. The obtained means do not differ significantly from the simulated means $F(10, 912) = 1.06$, $p \gg .05$. The values of the parameter used in the simulation were obtained with Chandler's (1969) subroutine STEPIT and were, for the short and long response-stimulus intervals respectively: mean stimulus input, identification and positive response time (which is $B = \mu_i + \mu_s + \mu_{p,+} + \mu_{o,+}$)

TABLE IV

Observed Mean Reaction Times (Obs.) (msec), Standard
Errors (SE), Simulated Means from the Self-Terminating
Memory Stack Model (Sim.) and Parameter Values
Used in the Simulation

	Short RSI[a]			Long RSI		
	Sim.	Obs.	SE	Sim.	Obs.	SE
Target set size 1						
Positive 4/15	435	434	8	485	471	10
Negative 2/15	384	376	8	429	426	12
Negative 1/15	386	380	8	431	429	11
Target set size 2						
Positive 2/15	468	480	12	512	524	14
Negative 4/15	415	414	10	459	470	12
Negative 1/15	427	430	10	470	482	13
Target set size 4						
Positive 1/15	533	529	10	573	560	11
Negative 4/15	464	472	11	508	510	11
Negative 2/15	489	488	12	530	516	11
Negative 1/15	504	505	12	544	544	13
Parameter values						
Positive response time intercept (mseconds)		379			428	
Negative response time intercept (mseconds)		300			349	
Comparison time		43			41	
Positive stack prob. a_+		.34			.43	
Negative stack prob. a_-		.06			.08	

[a] RSI, response-stimulus intervals.

equals 379 and 428 msec, mean dictionary scan time (μ_r) equals 43
and 41 msec, mean difference between positive and negative responses
in response selection and output time $[(\mu_{p,+} + \mu_{o,+}) - (\mu_{p,-} + \mu_{o,-})]$ equals 79 and 79 msec, positive dictionary stack replacement
probability (a_+) equals .34 and .43, and negative dictionary replace-
ment probability (a_-) equals .06 and .08. Finally, the capacity of the
serial response dictionary ($Z - 1$) was set to equal the target set size.[5]

[5] The rationale for this assumption has been given in Theios et al. (1973). We
assume that the subject attempts to perform the classification task as instructed, focusing
only on target stimuli and programming only $Z - 1$ dictionary buffer positions for
the $Z - 1$ target stimuli. However, as a result of the dynamic nature of the buffer
and the occurrence of nontarget stimuli, representations of the nontarget name-response
codes replace representations of target name-response codes in the buffer.

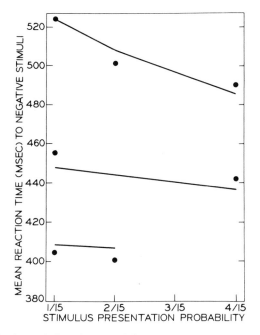

Fig. 7. Replication of Sternberg's (1967) character classification design. Mean reaction time (dots) to nontarget stimuli as a function of stimulus presentation probability and target set size. The lower two points are for a target size of one, the middle two points are for a target size of two, and the upper three points are for a target set size of four. The lines represent predictions obtained from a simulation of the self-terminating memory stack model. Note the significant interaction between stimulus probability and memory set size.

As is clearly seen in Fig. 6, the self-terminating model predicts mean reaction time functions which are close, but not necessarily equal to parallel straight lines.

a. Stimulus Presentation Probability Effects. Figure 7 shows mean reaction time to negative stimuli as a function of target set size (M) and stimulus presentation probability. Analyses of variance indicated that there are significant effects due to both stimulus probability, target set size, and their interaction. The stimulus probability effect is especially difficult for an exhaustive scanning model to account for. If scanning is exhaustive over only the target set, then why should there be a stimulus probability effect for the nontarget stimuli? If it is argued that stimulus probability affects encoding time, then the significant stimulus probability by target set size interaction is difficult to handle with an exhaustive scanning process. Set size is assumed to affect the scanning stage, but not the encoding stage (Sternberg,

1969). Thus, stimulus probability effects should be independent of set size. The nontarget stimulus probability by target-set-size interaction indicates that these two variables are affecting a common processing stage, presumably memory scanning. This strongly suggests that nontarget stimuli are on or can get on the list of scanned elements (as postulated in the present self-terminating model). The nontarget stimulus probability effect strongly suggests that the scan is self-terminating on a memory ordered more or less on the basis of presentation probability.

The lines in Fig. 7 represent means simulated from the self-terminating model. Inspection of Table IV and Figs. 6 and 7 indicate that the self-terminating model is giving a reasonable account of the data and easily accounts for the stimulus probability and stimulus probability by set size interaction, the two effects for which the exhaustive model has difficulty accounting.

   b.   *Sequential Effects.*   According to the self-terminating memory model (especially the Axioms 2, 3, 4, 6, and 7), in tasks like binary character classification which utilize a many-to-one stimulus-response mapping, both stimulus and response sequential effects should be observed. Presentation and repetition of a stimulus should move its name-response code higher in the response dictionary, leading to faster reaction times to that stimulus. Likewise, the occurrence and repetition of a response should move its response output program higher in the output buffer, also leading to faster mean reaction times to stimuli having that response. The converse will be true for a stimulus not presented or a response not made. Figure 8 presents conditional mean reaction times as a function of sequence of preceding stimuli. For example, the upper point DDS represents the mean reaction time over all stimuli to a stimulus S given that a different stimulus was presented on the preceding two trials. The lower point SSS represents the mean reaction time to a stimulus S given that stimulus S was also presented on the preceding two trials. As can be seen in Fig. 8, there are systematic stimulus sequential effects in both the long and short response-stimulus interval conditions. The effects are *slightly* larger for the short response-stimulus interval, but they certainly are large and significant in the long response-stimulus interval condition. The same pattern of sequential effects occurs regardless of stimulus probability, set size, or whether the stimulus is a target or nontarget item.

Figure 9 presents conditional mean reaction times as a function of sequence of preceding responses. The upper point DDS represents the mean reaction time over all stimuli to a stimulus S given that the other (different) response was made on the preceding two trials. The

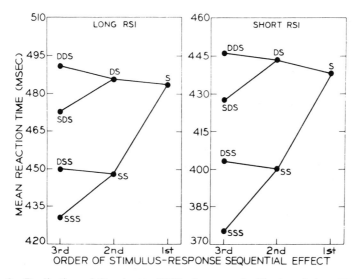

Fig. 8. Replication of Sternberg's (1967) character classification design. Mean reaction time (msec) as a function of sequence of preceding stimuli for both long
(2.0 seconds) and short (.5 second) response-stimulus intervals (RSI). For example, the
point DDS represents the mean reaction time to a stimulus S given that a different
stimulus was presented on the preceding two trials.

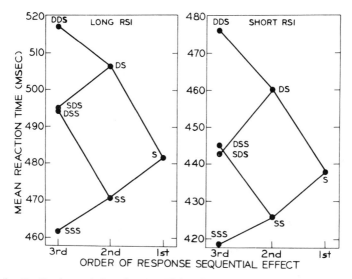

Fig. 9. Replication of Sternberg's (1967) character classification design. Mean
reaction time (msec) as a function of preceding sequence of responses for both
long (2.0 seconds) and short (.5 second) response-stimulus intervals (RSI). For example,
the point DSS represents the mean reaction time to a stimulus S given that the same
response was made on the previous trial but a different response was made two trials
previously.

287

lower point SSS represents the mean reaction time to stimulus *S* given that the same response was made on the preceding two trials. Again, there are systematic response sequential effects in reaction time for both the long and the short response-stimulus interval conditions.

While the stimulus-response mapping is not one-to-one in this classification task, it is true, of course, that stimuli and responses are not completely independent. It is possible that the stimulus sequential effects merely reflect the embedded response sequential effects. To check on this possibility, a further sequential analysis was performed. Figure 10 shows mean reaction time over all stimuli to a stimulus *S* as a function of sequence of preceding stimuli given that the response is the same during the entire sequence. In this analysis, since the response is held constant, we can see the pure stimulus sequential effect, uncontaminated by the response sequential effect.

In Fig. 10 the difference in time between points S and DS is the reduction in response time due to a single response repetition, uncontaminated by a stimulus repetition. The difference between points DS and SS is the reduction in response time due to a single stimulus repetition with the effect due to the necessary response repetition taken

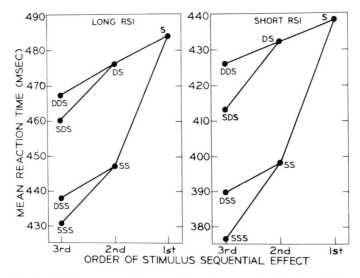

Fig. 10. Replication of Sternberg's (1967) character classification design. Mean reaction time (msec) as a function of sequence of stimuli during runs of the same response. For example, the point DDS is the mean reaction time to a stimulus *s* given that different stimuli requiring the same response were presented on the two previous trials.

out. As can be seen, the "pure" stimulus repetition effect is larger than the "pure" response repetition effect. These data demonstrating both "pure" stimulus repetition and "pure" response repetition effects are consistent with results published by Bertelson (1965) and Rabbitt (1968) for choice reaction times with a many-to-one stimulus-response mapping. The two types of sequential effects illustrated in Fig. 10 are entirely consistent with the self-terminating memory stack model and are the basis of the assumption of both a probabilistically ordered response dictionary process and a probabilistically ordered response output buffer in choice tasks involving a many-to-one stimulus-response mapping.

As published by Sternberg (1966, 1967), the exhaustive memory scanning model has no mechanisms to account for stimulus sequential effects. If, in the exhaustive scanning model, it were assumed that stimulus repetition lowered encoding time, then in Sternberg's (1967) design (which we replicated) differential frequencies of repetitions for the various stimuli would differentially affect mean reaction time, and the prediction of parallel linear reaction times for positive and negative stimuli as a function of target set size would be lost.

Inspection of Figs. 8, 9, and 10, and Table IV indicate that in the present experiment, response-stimulus interval had little effect on reaction time other than that of generally increasing mean reaction time in the long response-stimulus interval condition. As indicated by the estimated parameters of the computer simulation of the memory stack model, only the reaction time intercept (B) is greatly affected (elevated 49 msec) by the long response-stimulus interval. The values of the other parameters are probably within chance limits for the short and long response stimulus intervals.

2. Stimulus Probability Effects in Target and Nontarget Sets of Equal Size

Using the constant target set procedure and a response-stimulus interval of .5 second, Theios et al. (1973) conducted a character classification experiment in which the size of the target and nontarget sets were equal as target set size was increased. Their experimental design which is given in Table V also varied stimulus presentation probability symmetrically within each stimulus set. In two replications, a total of 40 subjects were given 200 trials at each target set size. The error rate was less than 2.5% and all errors were excluded from the analyses.

Table VI shows that, for both target and nontarget stimuli, mean

TABLE V

Design of the Experiment

	Stimuli	Positive target set					Negative nontarget set				
		s_0	s_1	s_2	s_3	s_4	s_5	s_6	s_7	s_8	s_9
Target Set Size	2	.35	.15				.35	.15			
	3	.30	.15	.05			.30	.15	.05		
	4	.20	.15	.10	.05		.20	.15	.10	.05	
	5	.20	.15	.05	.05	.05	.20	.15	.05	.05	.05

reaction time is a decreasing function of stimulus presentation probability. Using Monte Carlo computer simulation procedures, quantitative predictions were obtained from the self-terminating memory stack model presented in this article. A statistical response protocol corresponding to the self-terminating process was obtained for every response protocol given by a real subject in both replications of the experiment. After specific, restrictive assumptions were made about

TABLE VI

Mean RT (msec) Observed and Simulated from the Self-Terminating Model as a Function of Set Size, Stimulus Probability, and Type of Response ($+$, $-$) and Observed Standard Errors of the Means

Set size	Probability	Positive target set			Negative nontarget set		
		Simulated	Observed	SE	Simulated	Observed	SE
2	.35	507	498	10	529	519	10
	.15	533	543	15	548	550	13
	Mean	515	512	11	535	528	11
3	.30	519	522	9	550	546	14
	.15	553	549	16	578	570	18
	.05	590	604	20	597	634	22
	Mean	536	538	13	563	562	14
4	.20	551	546	14	590	589	19
	.15	570	576	18	606	612	21
	.10	594	597	16	616	628	20
	.05	622	609	20	634	626	20
	Mean	572	572	15	604	607	18
5	.20	560	578	16	599	611	20
	.15	581	587	18	614	624	18
	.05	650	630	18	670	658	24
	Mean	593	596	16	625	629	18

the values of some of the parameters of the model, Chandler's (1969) subroutine STEPIT was used to find values of the remaining free parameters which minimized the weighted squared error between the means of the pooled data and the means obtained from the simulation of the self-terminating process. In the simulation, the capacity of the serial response dictionary $(Z - 1)$ was set to equal the size of the target set. The best estimates of the remaining parameters were: mean stimulus input, identification, and response output time $(B = \mu_i + \mu_s + \mu_p + \mu_o)$ equals 429 msec, mean dictionary scan time (μ_r) equals 45 msec, target dictionary replacement probability (a_+) equals .62, and nontarget dictionary replacement probability (a_-) equals .28. The obtained and predicted (simulated) mean reaction times for the various conditions are given in Table VI, along with the obtained standard errors of the means. A goodness-of-fit analysis of variance indicated no significant difference between the simulated and obtained means $[F(19, 936) = .90, p > .50]$.

Figure 11 shows mean reaction time as a function of target set size

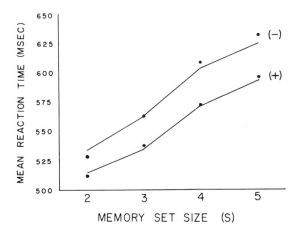

Fig. 11. Obtained mean reaction time (msec) (dots) as a function of target set size for positive target and negative nontarget stimuli, and predictions obtained from a simulation of the self-terminating memory stack model.

for both target and nontarget stimuli. In Fig. 11, neither the obtained means nor the means simulated from the self-terminating scanning model differ significantly from two parallel straight lines predicted by the exhaustive scanning model (F's < 1.00). Again, the self-terminating model is predicting and accounting for the essentially linear, parallel mean reaction time functions, the set size effect, and for stimulus presentation probability effects in both the target and non-target sets. Stimulus presentation probability effects have been reported in this type of task by Hawkins and Hosking (1969) and Krueger (1970).

IV. Summary and Conclusions

In this article, the case has been made that the study of choice reaction times in continuous (serial) information processing tasks can be very useful in investigating human short-term memory. The subtractive method of Donders (1868–1869) and the additive factors method of Sternberg (1969) have been briefly reviewed. A third method which is suggested and illustrated in this article is the construction and testing of specific process models which make clear-cut quantitative predictions for carefully designed experiments which fall within the boundary conditions of the process models.

In this article a serial, self-terminating memory scanning model is proposed to account for human behavior in stimulus identification, naming, choice-reaction, and (memory scanning) character classification tasks. The model assumes that after stimulus information is input, it makes contact very soon with long-term memory, where the information is interrogated and the stimulus is identified. The identification process operates in parallel (or is a net-discrimination, feature-testing process with the property that for well-defined stimulus ensembles, such as letters or numerals, identification time is effectively a constant, independent of size of *experimental* ensemble). The evidence in support of this is that the time to name a character is independent of stimulus ensemble size and stimulus probability (cf. Forrin, Kumler, & Morin, 1966). The serial component of memory scanning which many investigators have found (cf. Sternberg, 1966, 1967), is due to the response determination and selection processes. Evidence has been given here suggesting the existence of a response dictionary process which determines the appropriate response code associated with a stimulus in a specific task. The response dictionary process is especially needed in tasks such as character classification which involve a many-to-one assignment of stimuli to response. Presumably, the response dictionary is also important in tasks involving a one-to-one stimulus-response mapping in which a response transformation is necessary, such as the use of an incompatible as compared to a compatible assignment of stimuli to responses. The response dictionary process has been shown to have a serial component as evidenced by an effect due to stimulus ensemble size. The presence of stimulus probability effects and stimulus sequential effects strongly suggests that the serial component of the response dictionary is a self-terminating process. Evidence from character classification experiments varying the number of stimulus alternatives suggests that the serial component of the response dictionary is of limited (and varied) capacity which may be determined in part by the instructions to the subject and by the nature of the task. After the appropriate response has been determined, the response must be selected and executed. The response output process seems to have a limited capacity serial component as evidenced by response probability effects and response sequential effects.

All in all, the theoretical model, which can be conceived of as a sequence of processing stages with two, limited capacity, serial, self-terminating scanning buffers, makes the following general predictions about performance in human information processing tasks:

1. Stimulus naming times and other highly overlearned compatible responses may be fast and independent of stimulus presentation probability and number of stimulus-response alternatives.

2. With equally likely stimuli (responses), mean reaction time will not, in general, be an increasing linear function of number of stimuli (responses), but will be a negatively accelerated increasing function of the number of alternatives. The function may be effectively linear up to four alternatives.

3. As stimulus (response) probability is increased, mean reaction time will decrease.

4. Mean reaction time in tasks with compatible stimulus-response mappings will be faster than in tasks with incompatible stimulus-response mappings.

5. In character classification (memory scanning) tasks, mean reaction time to target and nontarget stimuli will be essentially linear, parallel functions of target set size.

6. There will be both stimulus and response sequential effects in reaction time data.

The above qualitative predictions from the self-terminating memory stack model cover a number of the major, well-known empirical relationships in the choice-reaction time and character classification research literature. It is felt that the model provides a useful and potentially fruitful theoretical framework within which human memory and information processing can be investigated. As such, the model is viewed as a heuristic which summarizes many known empirical relationships. As it now stands, many details of the model have yet to be worked out, and modifications and elaborations will surely have to be made. In addition, much of the human information processing research literature needs to be reevaluated from the standpoint of the present model.

The weakest point of the theoretical model is that (like most other reaction time models) it has completely ignored response errors. The model is assumed to hold in situations in which the subject is giving errorless or essentially errorless performance. In the reaction time tasks that we have considered, error rates are low (under 2.5%). However, there is an increasing body of literature which suggests that errors can exert a surprising effect on reaction times, and that they cannot be ignored. Clearly, the next important theoretical task is to develop a theory of errors which is consistent with reaction times, so that both response measures may be predicted by the same theory and set of parameter values.

REFERENCES

Bertelson, P. Serial choice reaction-time as a function of response versus signal-and-response repetition. *Nature (London)*, 1965, **206,** 217–218.

Brainard, R. W., Irby, T. S., Fitts, P. M., & Alluisi, E. A. Some variables influencing the rate of gain of information. *Journal of Experimental Psychology,* 1962, **63,** 105–110.

Chandler, J. P. STEPIT: Finds local minima of a smooth function of several parameters (CPA 312). *Behavioral Science,* 1969, **14,** 81–82.

Davis, R., Moray, N., & Treisman, A. Imitative responses and the rate of gain of information. *Quarterly Journal of Experimental Psychology,* 1961, **13,** 78–89.

Donders, F. C. Over de snelheid van psychische processen. Onderzoekingen gedaan in het Physiologisch Laboratorium der Utrechtsche Hoogeschool, 1868–1869, Tweede reeks, II, 92–120. (Translated by W. G. Koster, In W. G. Koster (Ed.), *Attention and performance II. Acta Psychologica,* 1969, **30,** 412–431.)

Falmagne, J.-C. Stochastic models for choice reaction time with applications to experimental results. *Journal of Mathematical Psychology,* 1965, **12,** 77–124.

Falmagne, J.-C. Biscalability of error matrices and all-or-none reaction time theories. *Journal of Mathematical Psychology,* 1972, **9,** 206–224.

Falmagne, J.-C., & Theios, J. On attention and memory in reaction time experiments. In W. G. Koster (Ed.), *Attention and performance II. Acta Psychologica,* 1969, **30,** 316–323.

Forrin, B., Kumler, M., & Morin, R. E. The effects of response code and signal probability in a numeral-naming task. *Canadian Journal of Psychology,* 1966, **20,** 115–142.

Hawkins, H. L., & Hosking, K. Stimulus probability as a determinant of discrete choice reaction time. *Journal of Experimental Psychology,* 1969, **82,** 435–440.

Krueger, L. E. Effect of stimulus probability on two-choice reaction time. *Journal of Experimental Psychology,* 1970, **84,** 377–379.

Morin, R. E., & Forrin, B. Information-processing: Choice reaction times of first- and third-grade students for two types of associations. *Child Development,* 1965, **36,** 713–720.

Morin, R. E., Konick, A., Troxell, N., & McPherson, S. Information and reaction time for "naming" responses. *Journal of Experimental Psychology,* 1965, **70,** 309–314.

Nickerson, R. S. Binary classification reaction time: A review of some studies of human information-processing capabilities. *Psychonomic Monograph Supplements,* 1972, **4** (Whole No. 65), 275–318.

Rabbitt, P. M. A. Repetition effects and signal classification strategies in serial choice-response tasks. *Quarterly Journal of Experimental Psychology,* 1968, **20,** 232–240.

Remington, R. J. Analysis of sequential effects in choice reaction times. *Journal of Experimental Psychology,* 1969, **82,** 250–257.

Sternberg, S. High-speed scanning in human memory. *Science,* 1966, **153,** 652–654.

Sternberg, S. Two operations in character recognition: Some evidence from reaction-time measurements. *Perception & Psychophysics,* 1967, **2,** 45–53.

Sternberg, S. The discovery of processing stages: Extensions of Donder's method. *Attention and Performance II. Acta Psychologica,* 1969, **30,** 276–315.

Sternberg, S. Decomposing mental processes with reaction-time data. Invited address, presented at the annual meeting of the Midwestern Psychological Association, Detroit, Michigan, May 1971.

Theios, J., & Smith, P. G. Can a two-state model account for two-choice reaction time data? *Psychological Review,* 1972, **79,** 172–177.

Theios, J., Smith, P. G., Haviland, S. E., Traupmann, J., & Moy, M. C. Memory scanning as a serial self-terminating process. *Journal of Experimental Psychology,* 1973, **97,** 323–336.

5

COMMENTARY ON

"ORGANIZATION AND MEMORY"[1]

George Mandler

UNIVERSITY OF CALIFORNIA, SAN DIEGO

It has been 10 years since "Organization and Memory" was published, and over 12 years since the data were collected. Like much research, this line of enquiry had an unclear parentage and unexpected offsprings. The program started off with a chapter originally designed to explore freed and constrained concept acquisition (Mandler & Pearlstone, 1966). It eventually led us to a hierarchical model of semantic memory and a quite unexpected interest in recognition processes. In the course of these developments, the notion of organization has become respectable, and the assertion, made in the opening sentence of my chapter concerning the "tattered reputation" of the concept of organization has been rectified. Even the most consistent critics (e.g., Postman, 1972) take organizational concepts seriously. One of the most gratifying consequences of my chapter has been the fact that it is frequently used as a general reference for demonstrating the importance of organizational factors in human memory.

It is best to read what follows after one has read or reread the original chapter. I am using "Organization and Memory" as a jumping off point to show where our own research has gone, what surprises lay in store for us, and how we choose to reply to the few criticisms that our research has engendered. I shall be concerned

[1] Preparation of this paper was supported in part by National Science Foundation Grant BNS 76-15154. I am most grateful both to the National Science Foundation and to the National Institute of Mental Health, through a grant to the Center for Human Information Processing, for making this line of research both possible and unburdened by major financial stringencies. Whereas I have written this paper in the first person, I frequently use the collective "we." In that collective, I am joined by the many students and assistants who have been members of our laboratory and have contributed more significantly to the research than their occasional appearance as authors of articles might indicate. In particular, I want to thank the following for friendship and colleaguial research: R.E. Anderson, W. Boeck, M. Borges, P. Dean, A. Graesser II, T. Jackson, H. Koopmans, R.H. Meltzer, K.E. Patterson, Z. Pearlstone, J. Rabinowitz, and P. Worden.

primarily with extensions and developments rather than replications. The latter can be found throughout the literature; in our own research, we have replicated the category—recall relationship many times over (e.g., Mandler, Pearlstone, & Koopmans, 1969; Mandler, 1970; Mandler & Boeck, 1974).

The Major Findings Are Consolidated and Extended

I was able to dismiss two possible artifacts in the original chapter. First, I examined and rejected the possibility that subjects spend more trials in sorting larger number of categories than in sorting smaller numbers. Worden and Ritchey (1977) obtained actual exposure time and found no diminution in the category—recall relationship when exposure time to the items was partialled out.

The second question that we were able to dismiss concerned subject selection. The possibility was raised that subjects who used large numbers of categories might be better able to recall or might be somehow more effective and that, therefore, the category—recall relationship reflected subject selection.

The most interesting refutation of this conjecture involved an intrasubject design. The same subjects were tested repeatedly on equivalent sets of items, but the number of categories that they were instructed to use was systematically varied. Under these conditions, individual performance varies directly with numbers of categories used (Mandler, 1968, 1970). In the 1968 chapter, we obtained individual category—recall functions for 5 subjects who were tested for 12 sessions, 2 for each number of category value from 2 to 7. Not only did we obtain individual category—recall slopes with values of about 4, but the data also generated independent evidence on the relationship between numbers of categories used and trials used in sorting. Using a 95% criterion of consistency, the 5 subjects reached criterion in 2 trials for 47% of the 60 sessions and needed 3 trials in another 47% of the sessions. For the last 30 sessions, 63% of the time, subjects reached criterion in 2 trials and in 33% of the sessions in 3 trials. One should note that to reach criterion in 2 trials means that subjects were 95% consistent on the *first and second* sorting trial. The use of two or three trials was randomly distributed among the six levels of numbers of categories (two to seven). In other words, the sorting task is relatively easy for practiced subjects, unaffected by the number of categories used, and effective in producing consistent intraindividual variations in recall.

CATEGORIES BEHAVE LIKE INSTANCES

In "Organization and Memory", I hypothesized that a hierarchical system should show retrieval effects for categories similar to those that we have shown for items within categories. In Figure 7 of the original chapter, I included some data from Tulving and Pearlstone (1966) that supported this notion. The general problem was pursued by Sawyers (1975). In a series of experiments, she combined variations in items per categories (IPC) and number of categories (NC) presented. Figure 5.1, which shows a typical result of her experiments, summarizes the data from four subjects, all of whom showed the same individual functions. Each subject was presented with all possible combinations of 6, 12, and 24 IPC and NC, for a total of 9 lists each. The data are unambiguous. Number of categories recalled (CR) is a linear function of NC, and number of words recalled (WPC) is a linear (and parallel) function of IPC. Conversely, number of categories recalled (CR) is independent of items per category (IPC), and the number of words per category recalled (WPC) is independent

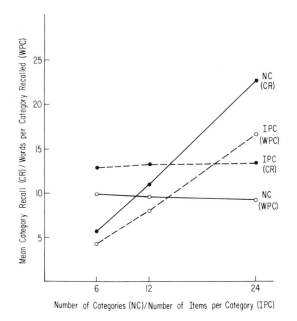

Fig. 5.1. Recall of categories (CR) and of words within categories (WPC) as a function of number of categories (NC) and items per category (IPC). Thus, "IPC(CR)" shows the number of categories recalled as a function of number of instances per category presented. Data from Sawyers (1975).

of the number of categories (NC) in the list. The function for category recall is at a higher level because subjects saw those categories labeled more frequently than any single instance, but the recall functions are highly similar and support the general hierarchical model.

RETRIEVAL FROM SEMANTIC STORAGE IS CATEGORICAL

In 1967, Peter Dean and I started a series of experiments to show that retrieval from long-term semantic storage was very similar to what we have found in the experimental laboratory situation. For example, Patterson, Meltzer, and Mandler (1971) had shown that category retrieval from experimentally presented lists followed predicted temporal patterns, with increasing interresponse times between clusters of words retrieved from categories and relatively flat interresponse times for items within the clusters.

Moving to long-term storage and a more natural situation, we used a task apparently originally introduced by Bousfield and Sedgwick (1944). Subjects were asked to name all the members of a particular category (e.g., animals) that they could think of. These emissions were tape-recorded, and interitem latencies were determined. Based on the distribution of these latencies, we identified "fast" clusters of words. Subsequent to the emission experiment, and independent of it, subjects were asked to sort the words that they had emitted into categories or groups that belonged together. Two findings are of immediate relevance: First, whereas intracluster times did not increase, intercluster intervals did increase over the course of the experiment. These data suggested that subjects found it increasingly difficult to access new subcategories but that, after they had entered a particular category, retrieval within that category was relatively constant. Second, Dean determined the probability of two words being sorted together in the sorting task, given that they occurred together in a fast sequence during the emission task, and these values were around .80 (Mandler, 1970; Dean, 1971).

We have replicated Dean's free emission studies in a more detailed investigation of the phenomenon and also extended his findings to show that retrieval from long-term semantic memory is, in fact, hierarchical (Graesser, Mandler & Vining, 1975).

ORGANIZATION DEVELOPS WITH AGE

The question of a developmental trend in organizational strategies was explored in a series of experiments by Worden (1974, 1975;

Worden & Ritchey 1976; see also Mandler & Stephens, 1967). Worden (1974) demonstrated the category—recall effect and showed that the sorting procedure provided first, third, and fifth graders with strong categorical organizations for retrieval. Worden and Ritchey (1976) found that the slope of the category—recall functions increased with increasing age from grade four through grade six to adults. In addition, the category—recall function was also more reliable for older than for younger subjects.

Some Critics Are Confounded

In a series of experiments, Higgins and Basden (1968) reversed the experimental procedure that we used in our original presentation. Subjects were first required to recall 52 words presented on a memory drum; then they were given a sorting task. No significant relationship was found between number of items recalled and number of categories used in *subsequent* sorting. Higgins and Basden concluded that "when categorization precedes recall, a strong relationship is obtained between number of categories in recall; however, when recall precedes categorization, such a relationship is not apparent."

There is, of course, no reason at all why one would expect such a symmetrical finding. When subjects are first asked to recall the items and are subsequently required to categorize the items, there is no reason why the subsequent sorting should reflect the organization used during recall. Since Higgins and Basden were good enough to share their data with our laboratory, we suggested that one might obtain the relationship if, *after* recall, subjects were requested to sort words so as to reflect any organization or clustering that they might have used during recall.

Such a procedure was followed in Basden and Higgins (1972), and their second experiment is of particular interest. Following the procedure of asking subjects to "reveal any groupings . . . employed as an aid to learning" and letting subjects use as many categories as they wished during sorting, Basden and Higgins found a significant correlation between numbers of categories and recall. It is apparent from their Figure 1 (p. 159) that the relationship between number of categories and words recalled is essentially flat above seven categories, and the relationship below that, while positive, has a slope value that is not as high as one would find in the traditional experiment. When (in their Experiment 1) Basden and Higgins restricted subjects to seven categories or less, they failed to find any relationship between categories and words recalled. There is, of course, no reason why subjects should restrict themselves to seven categories in free recall; the major purpose in using that limit is to make sure that there is no significant category loss during recall. In summary, one can conclude that there is at least some awareness by subjects of the categories used during a free recall experiment and that this is reflected in subsequent sorting.

In a third experiment, Basden and Higgins (1972) present a partial replication of our Experiment G. Their sorting procedure, however, was somewhat different; all 52 items were available to the subjects at one time for the purpose of sorting, and only two sorting trials were conducted. They note that the correlation between number of categories and items recalled is essentially equal for subjects using up to 7 categories and for subjects using 8 to 20 categories. The crucial question, however, is not the magnitude of the correlation, which describes the reliability of the data, but rather the magnitude of the slope relating the two variables. An examination of their Figure 2, which presents the scattergram for the full range of data, suggests that the slope for categories 2 through 7 is at least as large as 3, and that the slope from categories 8 through 20 is probably near 1, and certainly below 1.5.

The only known failure to replicate some of our results is an experiment by Schwartz and Humphreys (1972). These authors used the method reported in our Experiment H in which subjects categorized words on study sheets. The main discrepancy between their results and our Experiment H was a nonsignificant slope of .6 in one experiment and a significant slope of 1.7 in another. Schwartz and Humphreys themselves note that the intercept in both of their experiments was very high and higher than that found in any of our experiments, which suggests some differences in procedure that generated extraexperimental organization. Their sample of words was different from ours, and, apparently, their subjects were simply instructed to "categorize" the words. We have always been fairly careful to say explicitly that by categorization we mean the sorting of words that "go together" according to some semantic criterion or dimension. A simple instruction to "categorize" may have generated relatively shallow processing of the items and, therefore, low recall. This theory is further substantiated by the fact that their overall level of recall is about 20% lower than that found in our parallel experiments. Given a low level of recall and a high intercept due to external or extraexperimental organization of the items, one would have to preduct a relatively shallow slope.

A 1976 paper by Schwartz and Humphreys is most puzzling. In

this study, 4 groups were used—subjects were sorted into 3 or 6 "categories" for 5 or 10 trials. At the end of a rather involved, if not convoluted, argument, using highly derivative measures of clustering and sorting consistency that tend to hide the basic data, these authors conclude that "(1) Subjects who choose to sort into six categories are better recallers than are subjects who sort into three categories. (2) Sorting into six categories is a more difficult task than sorting into three categories, so subjects take longer to do the former task and presumably learn more (pp. 659–660)." This conclusion is strange since their data (1) show no significant differences in recall as a function of *either* number of categories *or* number of trials used and (2) are not based in any way on subjects who "choose" one or the other number of categories. It is difficult to prove or disprove a point with such evidence. Schwartz and Humphreys also chose to ignore all our data subsequent to 1967, particularly the highly relevant demonstrations of intrasubject variations in recall as a function of categories (Mandler, 1968, 1970).

We Are Surprised and
Find Retrieval Processes in Recognition

After we had established the category–recall relationship in free recall, the first order of priority was what seemed to us as a rather simple experiment. Conventional wisdom at the time, and still in some parts of the psychological community today, held that, whereas recall was determined by retrieval (e.g., organizational) factors, recognition provided direct access to the target items and was based on a simple decision process using strength or familiarity. The simple experiment consisted of repeating our sorting and recall experiment but substituting a recognition test for the recall test. That simple experiment resulted in a great many more experiments because we found that recognition performance was, in fact, a function of number of categories, that is, of organizational factors. Mandler, Pearlstone and Koopmans (1969) reported the correlation between organization and recognition (both hit rate and d') and found that these correlations were significant, but substantially lower than those found for the category–recall relationship. In order to accommodate this initially surprising, but now familiar, finding, we proposed a theoretical framework, originally called the "retrieval check hypothesis," which has become a most useful instrument since then, and the rather cumbersome name has been dropped.

The hypothesis postulates two separate and successive processes in recognition: an immediate judgment in terms of occurrence of familiarity or perceptual information and a subsequent search or retrieval process. A very similar hypothesis was presented by Atkinson and Juola (1974) in a somewhat more elegant form.

These two processes involve the use of two different codes. The first, which we call the *presentation code,* is retrieved fairly quickly and probably automatically upon presentation of the recognition probe. Under the presentation code, we subsume such variables as familiarity, occurrence information, perceptual (visual and auditory) information, and similar events. In a yes—no test, two criteria are established along the presentation dimension. If the value of the presentation information is higher than the "yes" criterion, the item is automatically called "old"; if it is below the "no" criterion, it is automatically called "new." For items that fall between these two criteria, when presentation information is uncertain or the subject is not confident of his response, the second kind of code is used. We call the second code the *conceptual code,* which represents all the conceptual, organizational, and structural information available about the item—in short, all possible contextual and conceptual information. Depending on the nature of the original encoding and the retrieval processes available as a function of task and instructions, the subject then goes through a search process using the conceptual code. If that conceptual code successfully identifies an item as retrievable, then it is called "old."[2]

Our initial experiments concerned the general utility of this distinction between these two processes. For example, Mandler, Pearlstone, and Koopmans (1969) showed that the correlation between numbers of categories and recognition increased as time since presentation increased. Since we assume that the presentation code decays over time, we would expect contextual or organizational variables to become more powerful as significant time passes since presentation. Mandler and Boeck (1974) used the implication of the double access recognition hypothesis to predict that organizational effects should be different for fast and slow recognition responses. For fast responses, access is presumably achieved through the presentation code, but, for slow responses, the organizational structure is invoked, and organizational effects should appear—as they did. In Mandler (1972), I reviewed the general literature on the relationship between

[2] The distinction between the two codes is similar to the one made by Atkinson and Wescourt (1975) between perceptual and conceptual codes, although we subsume more than the usual perceptual features under the presentation code.

organization and recognition and also presented some further data and extensions of our general position on the influence of organizational processes on recognition.

A recent discussion of the relationship between recognition and recall has questioned whether the phenomena illustrating the effect of organization on recognition should be attributed to organizational variables or whether they might not more properly be attributed to "depth of processing" variables. Lockhart, Craik, and Jacoby (1976) note that "it could be argued with equal plausibility that the task of sorting items into categories involves processing of a kind that establishes a more durable, more distinctive trace, and that the more categories employed, the deeper and more discriminating that processing will be (p. 76)." In elaboration of this point, they note:

> That there can be no general answer to the question of whether or not organization facilitates recognition; it may facilitate, hinder, or have no effect at all, depending on the relationship between such organization and the conditions at the time of the test. Insofar as organization represents increased depth and distinctiveness of processing, and test conditions are such as to encourage identical processing of the probe, recognition should be enhanced [p. 90].

One set of data that argue against the Lockhart, Craik, and Jacoby position was presented in Mandler, Pearlstone, and Koopmans (1969). After sorting 100 words to criterion, subjects were retested later and given all the words plus the category names that they had used. The probability of correctly placing an item in its original category was higher for words coming from lists using two, three, or four categories, than for those coming from lists using five, six, or seven categories.

One difficulty with Lockhart et al.'s position is that it assumes that the effects of organization are very different for a retrieval and for a recognition test. It is difficult to see how increased depth and distinctiveness of processing would be responsible for the specific nature of the category—recall relationship or for clustering effects. Thus, one would have to assume that, for recall, an organizational schema is used, while for recognition another schema—of distinctiveness and depth of processing—applies. Another issue has to do with the definition of recognition and recall. I have recently noted that such a distinction is not made easily, either for empirical or theoretical purposes (Mandler, 1976; see also Tulving, 1976). For example, in everyday life, we are often required not only to specify whether something is old or new, but also what it is. My point of view on organizational variables in recognition has been that the same kind of experimental variable that produces organizational effects in retrieval is also effective in recognition. I have noted, however, that, for different kinds of tasks, the retrieval used in the recall tasks may be different from the retrieval in the recognition task, and we must ask whether or not the requisite organizational structures were built up during the original presentation (cf. Rabinowitz, Mandler, & Barsalou, 1976).

The notion that recognition involves only a "yes–no" judgment is typically restricted to the experimental, laboratory situation. Clearly, particularly in contemporary research, items that are used are always "old" in a general sense, the judgment required is merely whether they occurred in a particular context. This preoccupation with building theories about laboratory experiments has also led to the distinction between episodic and semantic memory. Theories of this order fail to address important problems of everyday memory, such as, for example, the realization that one can recognize a face (it is "old"), but one does not know where one has seen it before or what the person's name is. It is in this context that the two-step recognition theory is most useful; it consists of the retrieval of a presentation code followed by the use of a conceptual code. Presumably, it is the value of the presentation code that provides the initial "old" judgment, while a subsequent conceptual search, using organizational structures, provides the more specific conceptual–contextual information.

This last point is also important in terms of the preoccupation with the concrete "conditions at the time of test," which Lockhart, Craik, and Jacoby invoke. The availability of organizational structures and the search through them at some time after the presentation or original experience with a particular event may, to a very large extent, be independent of the "conditions at the time of test." The problem of recognition and naming of the face is a case in point. It is quite true that we do not recognize our barber's face in the subway, although we easily recognize it in the barbershop. Once having made the "old" judgment in the subway, however, we then search for a possible context and organizations into which that face fits—we may find it (or we may not) relatively independently of the "conditions at the time of test." Lockhart, Craik, and Jacoby agree that the presentation codes (or the physical or sensory characteristics to which they refer) are prior and that organizational characteristics may be invoked after these codes have failed, but they fail to take the next step and realize that the use of the conceptual organizational schema is not necessarily situationally bound.

Looking Backwards and Ahead

The psychological world in North America has changed in the past 10 years. Notions about organizational processes that were becoming respectable then have become commonplace now. If one listens carefully, one can already hear the first murmerings of an anticognitive trend as the cycle swings back. If it does, however, it will create a new synthesis based on a cognitive psychology firmly established in the structure of psychological science. In the meantime, I hope to be surprised again—10 years ago we did not expect to be preoccupied with recognition today; who knows what will intrigue us 10 years hence. In the meantime, organizational concepts are alive and well.

REFERENCES

Atkinson, R. C., & Juola, J. F. Search and decision processes in recognition memory. In D. H. Krantz, R. C. Atkinson, & P. Suppes (Eds.), *Contemporary developments in mathematical psychology.* New York: Freeman, 1974.

Atkinson, R. C., & Wescourt, K. T. Some remarks on long-term memory. In P. M. A. Rabbitt & S. Dornic (Eds.), *Attention and performance V.* London: Academic Press, 1975.

Basden, D. R., & Higgins, J. Memory and organization: Category recall and retrieval capacity. *Journal of Verbal Learning and Verbal Behavior,* 1972, **11,** 157–163.

Bousfield, W. A., & Sedgwick, C. H. W. An analysis of sequences of restricted associative responses. *Journal of General Psychology,* 1944, **30,** 149–165.

Dean, P. J. Organizational structure and retrieval processes in long-term memory. Unpublished doctoral dissertation, University of California, San Diego, 1971.

Graesser, A., Mandler, G., & Vining, S. Limited processing capacity affects semantic encoding and retrieval from semantic memory. Paper presented at 1975 meetings of the Psychonomic Society, Denver.

Higgins, J., & Basden, J. R. Memory and organization. *Proceedings of the 76th Annual Convention of the American Psychological Association,* 1968, *3,* 75–76.

Lockhart, R. S., Craik, F. I. M., & Jacoby, L. Depth of processing, recognition and recall. In J. Brown (Ed.), *Recall and recognition.* London: Wiley, 1976.

Mandler, G. Organized recall: Individual functions. *Psychonomic Science,* 1968, **13,** 235–236.

Mandler, G. Words, lists, and categories: An experimental view of organized memory. In J. L. Cowan (Ed.), *Studies in thought and language.* Tuscon: University of Arizona Press, 1970.

Mandler, G. Organization and recognition. In E. Tulving & W. Donaldson (Eds.), *Organization of memory*. New York: Academic Press, 1972.

Mandler, G. Memory research reconsidered: A critical view of some traditional methods and distinctions. Paper presented at the 21st International Congress of Psychology, Paris, 1976. Technical Report 64, Center for Human Information Processing, University of California, San Diego, September, 1976.

Mandler, G., & Broeck, W. Retrieval processes in recognition. *Memory and Cognition*, 1974, **2**, 613–615.

Mandler, G., & Pearlstone, Z. Free and constrained concept learning and subsequent recall. *Journal of Verbal Learning and Verbal Behavior*, 1966, **5**, 126–131.

Mandler, G., Pearlstone, Z., & Koopmans, H. J. Effects of organization and semantic similarity on recall and recognition. *Journal of Verbal Learning and Verbal Behavior*, 1969, **8**, 410–423.

Mandler, G., & Stephens, D. The development of free and constrained conceptualization and subsequent verbal memory. *Journal of Experimental Child Psychology*, 1967, **5**, 86–93.

Patterson, K. E., Meltzer, R. H., & Mandler, G. Interresponse times in categorized free recall. *Journal of Verbal Learning and Verbal Behavior*, 1971, **10**, 417–426.

Postman, L. A pragmatic view of organization theory. In E. Tulving & W. Donaldson (Eds.), *Organization of memory*. New York: Academic Press, 1972.

Rabinowitz, J. C., Mandler, G., & Barsalou, L. Recognition failure: A case of retrieval failure. Paper presented at 1976 meetings of the Psychonomic Society, St. Louis.

Sawyers, B. K. Category and item retrieval from memory. Unpublished doctoral dissertation, University of California, San Diego, 1975.

Schwartz, R. M., & Humphreys, M. S. Examinations of the category-recall function. *American Journal of Psychology*, 1972, **85**, 189–200.

Schwartz, R. M., & Humphreys, M. S. Further examinations of the category-recall function. *Memory and Cognition*, 1976, 4, 655–660.

Tulving, E. Ecphoric processes in recall and recognition. In J. Brown (Ed.), *Recall and recognition*. London: Wiley, 1976.

Tulving, E., & Pearlstone, Z. Availability versus accessibility of information in memory for words. *Journal of Verbal Learning and Verbal Behavior*, 1966, **5**, 381–391.

Worden, P. E. The development of the category-recall function under three retrieval conditions. *Child Development*, 1974, 45, 1054–1059.

Worden, P. E. Effects of sorting on subsequent recall of unrelated items: A developmental study. *Child Development*, 1975, **46**, 687–695.

Worden, P. E., & Ritchey, G. H. The development of the category-recall relationship in the sorting-recall task. Paper presented at Society for Research in Child Development, New Orleans, 1977.

Reprinted from *The Psychology of Learning and Motivation*, 1967, **1**, 327–372.

ORGANIZATION AND MEMORY[1]

George Mandler

UNIVERSITY OF CALIFORNIA, SAN DIEGO

LA JOLLA, CALIFORNIA

Organization has had a somewhat tattered reputation in the history of modern psychology. Many theorists have talked about it and others have viewed it from a distance—with either affection or alarm—but

[1] The initial experiment on free categorization was presented at the meetings of the Psychonomic Society at Niagara Falls, Ontario, in October, 1964, where the hypothesis of the category–recall relation was outlined. The general model and some preliminary data were discussed at a Conference on the Quantification of Meaning in January, 1965, at La Jolla, California, and at a colloquium at the Center for Cognitive Studies, Harvard University, in February, 1965. The major experimental data were presented at the meeting of the Psychonomic Society in Chicago, Illinois, in October, 1965.

The preparation of this chapter and the research reported in it were supported by Grant GB 810 from the National Science Foundation, Grant APA 64 from the National Research Council, Canada, and a travel grant from the University of California, San Diego.

most of the efforts either to develop a generally acceptable class of variables that might be called organizational or to find a single acceptable measure of organization have tended to be short-lived. This has been particularly true in the area of memory and learning. Perception has fared somewhat better, although the efforts of the Gestalt psychologists to translate perceptual concepts into other areas of psychology have often produced a feeling of failure and ennui. Too often the concept of organization has become the rallying cry for theoretical battles; as a result, its connotation frequently has become emotional rather than scientific. There is no doubt that less strictly drawn battle lines in the 1920's, 1930's, and 1940's might have produced more fruitful attention to organizational concepts on either side of the fence.

Organizational variables have assumed a new importance in human psychology, particularly in the area of human memory. The present paper will be devoted to the illustration of three general principles: First, memory and organization are not only correlated, but organization is a necessary condition for memory. Second, the organization of, and hence memory for, verbal material is hierarchical, with words organized in successively higher-order categories. Third, the storage capacity within any one category or within any level of categories is limited.

Memory as used here comprises memory for specified verbal units—the memory for lists of words; long-term memory—memory extending over periods longer than a few seconds; and memory in free recall—memory for lists of words where no restrictions are placed on the order or time in which a person recalls these words. This chapter will not deal with unintegrated verbal material (such as nonsense syllables), memory for connected passages, short-term memory, nor serial or paired-associate learning. The paradigm to be explored is the free recall experiment in which the subject is presented with a list of words and then asked to recall as many of those words as possible in any order he wishes.

I. The Concept of Organization

In 1940 George Katona wrote a book called *Organizing and Memorizing* in which he elaborated a Gestalt position as it applied to human memory; it is in a sense an unfortunate book, for Katona's preoccupation with grand theoretical points hides many of the book's empirical contributions, and some of his specific theoretical insights were inconsistent with the temper of a period that called for the development of grand general schemes. Hidden among vague generalities—about undefined wholes, inner necessities, and "real" understanding—and general denigrations of the role of prior experience is the assertion that organization is a requirement for successful memorization. He avoids any specific definition of organization, but he does suggest that organization involves the formation and perception of groupings and of their relations. Organization is a process that establishes or discovers such relations. Throughout the book Katona emphasizes the grouping of verbal stimuli as an important variable in memorizing; for example, in one series of experiments he shows how an otherwise "unrelated" sequence of digits is better retained in memory when the digits are regrouped according to categories or principles supplied by the E or S. The notion that memory is limited when grouping is not used and that grouping overcomes such limitations was plainly stated for anyone who cared to pay attention. But for the next decade or two, few psychologists did.

Like his associationist brethren, Katona had little use for mnemonic devices. He neither cared to investigate them nor felt that they really aided memory; they excluded "real understanding." Katona failed to see that all organizations are mnemonic devices; the "real" ones are those chosen by the experimenter or generally agreed to be more "relevant" to the problem. There was not then nor is there now any evidence that the use of socially learned organizations is better than or different from the use of unusual or idiosyncratic ones. Katona also maintained a distinction between rote or senseless memory on one hand and organized or meaningful memory on the other. The former he attacked as "pure" memorization, partly because associationists wanted to make "pure" memorization the basis of all learning or memory. Except possibly in the sense of immediate or primary memory (cf. Waugh & Norman, 1965), it is questionable whether the distinction between rote memory and other kinds can be maintained today (cf. Underwood, 1964).

Following Wertheimer (1921), Katona considered a set of stimuli to be meaningful when the existence and quality of the parts are determined by the structure of the whole. The notion that meaning, and hence organization, can be defined by the relations among the units of the set has persisted and has found its way into modern and more serviceable formulations.

Garner (1962), for example, prefers the term "structure" to "organization," but is obviously talking about the same problem. His very attractive definition of structure is worthy of quotation.

By structure I mean the totality of the relations between events. When we say that a picture composed of randomly located dots is meaningless, we imply that we see no relations between the dots and that, therefore, the picture has no structure. If the same total number of dots is rearranged, however, we can perceive structure and the picture becomes meaningful. . . . Meaning . . . refers to the entire set of relations, not just to the significations of each individual word. A particular word may be meaningful in the sense of signification, but the entire language becomes meaningful only if some structure is perceived in the total set of symbols. I am definitely not implying that meaning as structure is simply the sum of the significations of the individual words, but rather that the structure is itself meaningful (Garner, 1962, p. 141).

Organization and structure are clearly related to the general problem of grouping. G. E. Müller had been concerned with grouping at the turn of the century, as had Selz early in this century; and in 1932 Thorndike had wrestled with the concept of "belongingness"; two events "belong" when it is apparent to the S that "this goes with that." Belongingness defined the boundaries of groupings.

We can propose a general use for the term organization at this point: A set of objects or events are said to be organized when a consistent relation among the members of the set can be specified and, specifically, when membership of the objects or events in subsets (groups, concepts, categories, chunks) is stable and identifiable.

II. The Limits of Memory and the Unitization Hypothesis

The importance of organization and grouping was made obvious to psychologists interested in information processing in two papers by Miller (1956a; 1956b). Miller started with a puzzle. Evidence from a large number of sources had suggested that there were limitations on the capacity of the human organism for processing information; limitations that were observed over a range of tasks from the absolute judgment of unidimensional variables to immediate memory. In all these cases, Miller suggested, the limiting value—the "magical" number—was 7 ± 2. Subjects usually can not distinguish more than about seven alternatives of a unidimensional variable, nor remember more than about seven items from an input list in immediate memory. Given these limitations, some mechanism must be responsible for extending human judgment and memory, since we obviously do remember more than seven items and can judge across a wider range. Miller's solution to this puzzle was, in the case of human memory, the unitization hypothesis.

The unitization hypothesis (Miller, 1956b) states, first, that the memory limit cannot be extended by simply adding more sets of seven items. The second set of seven apparently makes us forget the first and human memory can deal only with seven items at a time. The only way to extend the amount of information is to enrich each item, that is, to increase the amount of information each item conveys. Miller refers to informationally rich units in memory storage as chunks. The input items must be recoded or reorganized into new units or chunks. Miller talks about "grouping or organizing the input sequence into units or chunks" (1956a, p. 93), specifically suggesting that "by organizing the stimulus input simultaneously into several dimensions and successively into a sequence of chunks, we manage to break . . . [the] informational bottleneck" (1956a, p. 95). In summary, organization is absolutely necessary if memory is to exceed the limit of individual items that the system can deal with at any one time. This process of organization involves recoding the input material into new and larger chunks. Memory consists of the recall of a limited number of chunks (that is, about seven) and retrieval of the contents of these chunks.

The influence of this formulation on the area of human learning and memory has been both fruitful and decisive (cf. Mandler, 1967). However, relatively few extensions of the unitization hypothesis in the specific area of human verbal memory are available. Some of these extensions, by Tulving, Cohen, and others, will be discussed later, but first some further elaborations and extensions of Miller's model are necessary.

Miller's 1956 papers suggested that if the number of chunks is limited to about seven, the chunks themselves may contain apparently unlimited informational riches. The following excerpts illustrate Miller's suggestions:

The span of immediate memory seems to be almost independent of the number of bits per chunk, at least over the range examined to date (1956a, p. 93) . . . . The process if memorization may be simply the formation of chunks, or groups of items that go together, until there are few enough chunks so that we can recall all the items (1956a, p. 95). Since the memory span is a fixed number of chunks, we can increase the number of bits of information that it contains by building larger and larger chunks containing more information than before (1956a, p. 93).

The general import is that there is no limit to the amount of information a chunk may contain. Miller's major suggestion for enriching the information in a chunk was to increase the size of the set of alternatives from which an item is chosen. A second possibility involves a hierarchical arrangement in which the number of items in a chunk is limited to 7 ± 2, just as the number of chunks is initially limited to that number. This does not imply that memory is limited to 49 items—seven items with seven items per chunk. Rather, the seven items in a chunk may in turn be informationally rich—containing again about 7 ± 2 items. This extension of Miller's unitization hypothesis will form the major theoretical argument of this paper. A hierarchical system recodes the input into chunks with a limited set of items per chunk and then goes on to the next level of organization, where the first-order chunks are recoded into "superchunks," with the same limit applying to this level, and so forth. The only limit, then, appears to be the number of levels the system can handle, a problem to be discussed later. It might be noted that whereas Miller's early formulation advances the general notion of informationally rich chunks, later formulations discuss hierarchical systems similar to the one advocated here (Miller, 1962, p. 49; Miller, Galanter, & Pribram, 1960).

In the organization of words as items, chunking proceeds primarily by way of conceptualization or categorization of sets of words. A further assumption, therefore, is that a category is equivalent to Miller's chunk.

Given that a limit constrains the number of words that can be recalled from a category and that a similar limit constrains the number of subcategories, categories, and superordinate categories that can be recalled, what is the numerical value of that limit? Miller suggested "the magical number seven, plus or minus two." As he points out however, the span for monosyllabic English words is only about five (cf. also Tulving & Patkau, 1962) and, in fact, the immediate memory experiment may hide an artifact that spuriously inflates the limiting value. Since Miller's work there has been a recurrent interest in immediate or short-term memory, dealing with memory effects within 30–60 seconds following input (cf. Melton, 1963). When a S is required to memorize relatively large sets of words, the mechanism apparently involves two separate processes: Short-term, or primary, memory (Waugh & Norman, 1965), which produces recall of the words immediately preceding the output; and organized memory, which typically includes earlier words from the list (cf. Waugh, 1961). Thus the number of 7 ± 2 may be made up of two components: 4 ± 1 plus 3 ± 1. Since the present concern is not with short-term or immediate memory in the sense of recovering items from some temporary or buffer storage, it seems likely that the value of items to be recalled per chunk is below seven; for working purposes, and in light of some of our subsequent data, a value of 5 ± 2 seems more appropriate.

To recapitulate: Given a set of words, a human organism categorizes them and, if the length of the list requires an extended organization, arranges the categories in turn into superordinate categories. When a category contains more than about five words it may, if necessary and possible, again be subdivided into two or more subordinate categories. Thus it is assumed that if recall from a list contains more than five items, then the S has used more than one category and some of his categories contain more than one item. Conversely, if a list of words is categorized into several categories such that each category contains one or more words, then recall should be a direct function of the number of categories used during organization of the list. The experimental data presented in the following discussion pertain directly to the relation between the number of categories used in organization and the number of words recalled.

In the sense of the unitization hypothesis and its elaborations presented in this section, the process of memorization is a process of organization. Katona's formulation thus is correct; memorization or learning depends on organization and the organizational variables (rather than the number of trials, for example) determine memory.

If organization determines recall, then the categories available to a S should also determine the form of his output. Members of categories should be recalled together if the S remembers categories and then their content. Extensive work has been done on this effect of organization and we will briefly review some of the experimental studies on clustering in free recall.

III. Clustering: The Organization of Recall

A large number of studies has been concerned with the tendency for categorized items to cluster during recall. This particular line of research was initiated with an experiment by Bousfield and Sedgewick (1944), who found that Ss instructed to produce all the items in a particular language category (such as birds) would cluster subcategories during recall. In 1953 Bousfield initiated a program of research to investigate further the tendency of members of a category to appear contiguously during recall. In the first experiment (Bousfield, 1953) Ss were given a randomized list of 60 items consisting of four categories (animals, names, professions, and vegetables) with 15 items per category. Following a single presentation Ss listed the items they could recall and Bousfield's data showed conclusively that such recall contained clusters of the categories built into the lists.

It should be noted that in this and almost all subsequent experiments on clustering the categories investigated were only the categories pre-established by the experimenter. Such a procedure presents two serious problems of analysis: first, the problem of the distinction between the discovery and use of these categories, and second, the necessary tendency to ignore any clustering or organization used by the S but different from the organization expected by the E.

Concerning the distinction between discovery and use, consider the following problem. Assume that I make up a list of names of all the people in my acquaintance and then categorize this list into those people who are blood relations, those who are professional acquaintances, and those who are social acquaintances. In my recall of such a list, I would probably cluster these categories according to these three characteristics. If the same list were presented to a total stranger, it is unlikely that his recall would show any significant clustering in terms of my categories. If I were to present the list to a professional colleague, however, we would find some clustering in terms of one of the categories, and if I gave the list to my wife, there would probably be significant clustering for all three categories. Similarly, any pre-categorized list will show clustering to the extent that the S has available the categories that the E has put into the list. On the other hand, the S might know of these categories but may not discover that the list in fact contains them.

Closely related to this difficulty is the possibility that a S may in fact discover the categories but choose not to use them, or he may use some combination of these categories and some of his own construction. In either case the analysis of clustering in terms of the preestablished categories will usually underestimate the actual degree of clustering imposed by the subject.

When, as is usual, the data from a group of Ss are averaged in a typical clustering experiment, the idiosyncratic clusters are never examined. Subjects will be included in the analysis who use their own rather than the experimenter's organization, because of some idiosyncratic preference or because they never discovered the experimenter's categories. In general, then, both final performance and clustering data will contain an inordinate amount of noise and variance.

There is one aspect of these studies that is of general interest and is the point of major emphasis of workers in this field; it concerns those variables that affect discovery and clustering. For example, Bousfield, Cohen, and Whitmarsh (1958) have shown that if the categories contain items with high taxonomic frequency, the recall and clustering values will be significantly greater than for categories with items of low taxonomic frequency. Taxonomic frequency thus is one variable that affects the likelihood that a category will be discovered and used. Similarly it is reasonable to suppose that the discovery and use of highly overlearned categories will produce a more stable organization and therefore better recall than the *ad hoc* categories a *S* may impose on the material. In a summary of a large program of research on factors that affect the organizational characteristics of free recall, Cofer (1965) arrived at a similar conclusion.

Cofer and his associates have also compared the occurrence of *E*- and *S*-defined clusters. Their data suggest that the more "obvious" the *E*-defined categories or pairs, the less likely it is that idiosyncratic *S*-defined clusters or pairs will occur in recall; that is, the more likely it is that the *E*'s and *S*s' categories coincide. Similarly, Marshall and Cofer (1961) have shown that if word relations have "some prominence," telling the *S*s to look for such relations increases the degree of clustering of these pairs in recall.

In summary, the various studies on clustering show that clustering of *E*-defined categories will occur and that such clustering is a function of the ease with which the *S* can discover these categories. In addition, important advances have been made to define the variables that will influence the ease of such discovery and, finally, the variety of different conceptual schemes that *S*s may use to categorize lists of words is illustrated by the large variety of *E*-defined schemes that affect clustering. These include categorical, associative, syntactic, and semantic factors, and probably extend to a variety of idiosyncratic schemas that are a function of the individual *S*'s past experience and past word usage.

More immediately relevant to our present interests are those studies that have investigated the relation between the number of categories in a list and free recall from that list. The earliest of these was a study by Mathews (1954); two more recent ones were those of Dallett (1964) and Tulving and Pearlstone (1966). The results obtained in these studies will be discussed after some of our data have been presented and the category–recall relationship has been discussed in greater detail. What should be noted now is that these studies also have used *E*-defined categories. In addition, they have held list length constant while varying number of categories, and have thereby confounded list length with items per category. Although such confounding is inevitable when list length, number of categories, and number of items per category are varied, it presents some difficulty in interpretation. This point will be discussed later, but as far as *E*-defined categories are concerned, the same criticism applies to these studies as to the clustering studies. Although in the clustering studies the relation between the discovery and use of categories is a minor problem if the main point of interest is the specification of the variables that will produce organization and clustering, any attempt to specify the relation between recall and number of categories becomes dubious when it is not known whether the S did in fact discover and use the categories built into the list. Only Tulving and Pearlstone paid detailed attention to this problem and demonstrated the occurrence of subjective clustering of objective categories.

It will be the major import of the studies presented here to show just such a relation. The difficulty of some of the prior studies on this topic will be better illuminated in that context, but it seems that one of two conditions must be met in order to be able to demonstrate the relation between categories and recall. The first possibility is to provide the S with the names or labels of the categories and to show him the actual categorical structure of the list. If that is done during input only, one might be fairly certain that an input organization has taken place that is at least similar to that desired by the E. The S may, of course, still impose some of his own category system on the list. If the S is also provided with category labels during the output, we can further be sure that he will remember all the categories speci-fied by the E. Tulving and Pearlstone (1966), for example, have ful-filled these conditions.

Another possibility, the one used here, is to permit the S to impose his own organization on the input. Such a method not only avoids the problems mentioned earlier but also permits us to see how organi-zation proceeds and what the preferred or optimal organizational schemas might be.

IV. Subjective Organization

There have been several recent attempts to investigate the organiza-tion that Ss impose on input materials. Tulving (1962) and Seibel (1964) have been most directly concerned with subjective organization in free recall. Tulving's paper raises the question—derived from some of Miller's (1956a) notions—whether or not the improvement in per-formance in multitrial free recall is a direct function of the increase in organization. In his demonstration study Ss were given a list of "un-related" words, that is, words not organized by the E. The order within input lists was changed in a random fashion from trial to trial.

Tulving developed a measure of the sequential dependencies in the output of successive trials. This measure, called SO for "subjective organization," evaluated the Ss tendency "to recall items in the same order on different trials in the absence of any experimentally manipulated sequential organization among items in the stimulus list." Tulving concluded "that the Ss do impose a sequential structure on their recall, that this subjective organization increases with repeated exposures and recall of the material, and that there is a positive correlation between organization and performance" (1962, p. 352). A similar conclusion was reached by Bousfield, Puff, and Cowan (1964). Both their measure and the SO measure only evaluate pairwise dependencies and can only tell us that organizational activity is in fact revealed in the output. It is not designed to evaluate the categorical organization by the S, nor can it evaluate the occurrence of organized units larger than pairs.

The last deficiency is a major argument against using either a clustering or SO measure in evaluating the organization imposed by the S. A cluster of two items that occurs in repeated trials does not imply that the category to which the cluster belongs is not in fact larger than two, and this argument applies to an output cluster of any size. A S may in fact produce one or two members of a category, use his written output as a reminder while recalling other items, and then return to the category that he had previously started. For example, a list may contain a "furniture" cluster; the S recalls "table" and "chair," then recalls some other items, checks the list, and on seeing "table" and "chair" may then give additional items from the furniture category.

Finally, the SO and clustering approaches do not tell us what the organization at the time of input was, nor how output and input organization are related to each other or to performance. Tulving (1962) has suggested the need for studying both the input and output phases of free recall. Our experiments are more directly addressed to the relation between organization during input and performance. For the reasons just listed, less emphasis will be placed on the dependent measures of organization developed by Bousfield, Tulving, and others.

Seibel (1964) has reported some initial work in which the subjective organization of the input lists was related to performance and clustering. His Ss were presented with 40 words at a constant rate and were required to write these words on a study sheet containing an array of blank cells. On this sheet Ss could—though they were not instructed to do so—organize the input according to categories of their own choosing. After the presentation of the list, Ss were required to recall at a constant rate. Seibel found that Ss' recall contained clusters that corresponded to the clusters on the study sheet and that performance of the experimental group was superior to the performance of a group that had been instructed to write down the words from the input list in the order in which they were given. The performance of the latter group was indistinguishable from that of another control group whose members did not write down the input list at all. In other words, subjective organization significantly improved recall and affected subsequent clustering in recall.

With this background on prior work on organization and memory, some of our experimental studies can be considered, starting with a recapitulation of a study on free and constrained conceptualization and the relevance of free conceptualization or organization to the problem at hand. This will be followed by a series of six studies on the category–recall relationship. Finally, a brief experiment on organizing and memorizing instructions will be discussed.

V. Free and Constrained Conceptualization

In our discussion of experiments on clustering we have suggested that E-imposed categories may frequently hide the Ss' system of organization. In addition, a procedure that focuses on such categories gives us little information about how the average human organism might go about organizing an input list. Similar arguments can be addressed to the typical experiment in concept learning where Ss are required to attain some concepts specified by the E. Since categories and concepts are, in the present sense, interchangeable notions, an examination of an experiment by Mandler and Pearlstone (1966) on this topic provides the first step in the program of research reported here.

Mandler and Pearlstone argued that the typical concept-learning experiments not only hide important aspects of conceptual behavior but also present the S with an interference paradigm. It is assumed that any set of stimuli will invoke some categorization or conceptualization on the part of the S. The initial categories imposed by the S and those imposed by the E are not likely to be identical. To the extent, then, that the S must suppress, extinguish, or ignore his own system of conceptualization, such activity will interfere with the acquisition of the E-defined conceptual categories.

Subjects were given either free or constrained concept-learning tasks with four different kinds of materials, of which the high frequency words are of particular interest. Subjects in the "free" groups were given a deck of 52 cards, each of which had a word printed on it. They were asked to sort these cards into anywhere from two to seven categories according to any system they wished to use. They were also told that following their first sorting trial they would be given another deck with the same words in a different order and would be asked to sort the words again and to continue in this manner until they had achieved identical categorizations in two successive trials. The Ss in the "constrained" group learned the same category systems as the free Ss by yoking one constrained S with one free S. The constrained S thus was in a typical concept-learning or attainment situation, with the target concepts being those of the yoked free Ss. Following attainment of the concept-sorting criterion, Ss in both groups were asked to recall as many words as possible from the set they had just sorted.

The major relevant findings were that constrained groups needed twice as many trials as free groups to reach criterion in sorting, but that both groups recalled the same number of words, about 20 out of 52. In addition, the various free groups used a fairly stable mean number of categories in sorting, that is, from 4.0 to 4.6, regardless of the materials they were asked to sort.

Thus the assumption that constrained concept learning represented an interference paradigm was supported by the data. Furthermore, numbers of sorting trials did not affect recall; if a stable categorization had been achieved by the two groups, recall was identical.

These findings supported our notion that the free or subjective organization of verbal materials could be fruitfully investigated and that the method used in this experiment provided one approach to the investigation of the organizing behavior of human Ss. We have already mentioned Tulving's (1962) approach to a similar problem; Imai and Garner (1965) have also made the distinction between free and constrained classificatory behavior.

The major finding of the Mandler and Pearlstone study that is relevant here, and the starting point for subsequent experiments, concerned the relation between recall (R) and number of categories (NC) used during sorting. Since Ss in the free group could use any number of categories from two to seven, it was possible to relate these values to free recall performance. Figure 1 shows the observed relation between NC and R for the 10 free Ss. The correlation between these two variables is .95 and the equation for a straight line fitted by the method of least squares has a slope of 5.59 and a y-intercept of —6.0. In other words, Ss remembered on the average 5.6 words for each category and their recall was a direct function of the number of categories used. It was this reassuring suggestion that the category–

recall relation could be directly investigated that launched the following set of experiments.

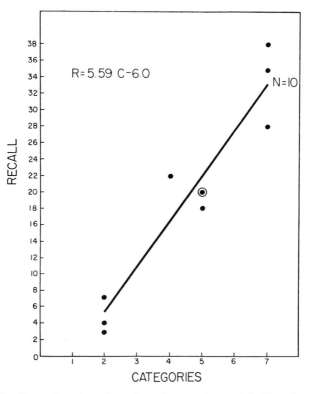

Fig. 1. Recall as a function of number of categories used in Experiment A. Data points are for individual Ss. The equation shown is for the line of best fit.

VI. The Category–Recall Function

The following six experiments are all variations on the theme developed in the Mandler and Pearlstone study, which will be referred to as Experiment A. Free categorization was used to investigate the categorization behavior of the Ss and to establish stable and reliable category systems. Following such free categorization, free recall of the words used in sorting was tested in order to investigate further the category–recall relationship. The general method used in all six experiments will be described first, followed by the specification of the variations incorporated in each of Experiments B to G and the description of the relevant data from these experiments.

A. General Method and Procedure

All Ss received identical basic instructions. They were given decks of cards that they had to sort in successive trials until they had achieved two identical sorts. Subjects were not allowed to put one card into one category and all others in another; apart from this restriction, any method of sorting or categorization was permitted. Following their last criterion sort they were asked to write on a sheet of paper all the words they could recall. They were given enough time to write down all the words immediately available to them. Recall terminated after a pause of about 1 minute with no recall had occurred. During sorting Ss were allowed to proceed at their own speed. However, if a S was not able to reach criterion within about $1\frac{1}{4}$ hours the session was discontinued. Column 4 of Table I shows the number of Ss in each group who

TABLE I

Summary of Design of Experiments A–G

Exp.	Initial N	Noncontent Ss^a	Noncri- terion Ss^b	Ss with more than 7 categories	Final N	Criterion (%)
A	10	2	0	—	10	100
B	70	17	10	—	43	100
C	32	7	12	6	7	100
D	40	8	17	—	15	100
E	39	11	3	5	20	100
F	49	16	8	—	25	95
G	64	19	14	3	28	95

[a] Over-all percentage of Ss who did not use content categories was 26%.
[b] Over-all percentage of Ss who failed to reach criterion was 21%.

failed to reach criterion. This number also contains some Ss who continuously changed numbers of categories and for whom no stable NC (number of categories) value could be determined.

Subjects were seated at a table with a sorting hamper with seven slots slightly larger than the 3- by 5-inch cards on which the words were printed. They were always able to inspect the top card of any category, but they were not allowed to inspect any other card during the sorting task. In some experiments Ss were allowed to use more than seven categories. In these cases the table top was subdivided with chalk lines into an array of 20 compartments. Otherwise the procedure was identical.

The Ss were first-year psychology students of both sexes at the University of Toronto who had not previously participated in any free recall experiments.

B. MATERIALS

Three sets of words were used. The first set, identical with that used in the Mandler and Pearlstone study, consisted of 52 words from a fairly wide range of Thorndike-Lorge values—the *52-range* set. Frequencies ranged from 14 per million to AA. There were 50 nouns, 1 adjective, and 1 adverb, though 20 of the nouns also had verb functions and 3 also had adjective functions. Six different decks were prepared in random order, and Ss who used more than six trials were given the same decks over again.

The second set of words consisted of *52 AA* nouns, 33 of which also had verb functions and 1 of which also an adjective function. The third set of words consisted of *100 AA* words, the 52 from the previous set plus another 48. Of these 100 nouns, 59 also had verb functions and 1 had an adjective function. They were arranged in six decks just as the first one.

C. DATA ANALYSIS AND RATIONALE

It has already been noted that Ss who did not reach criterion were excluded from our analysis. For Experiments B, C, D, and E, the criterion was the same as that for Experiment A, namely, two identical sorts in succession. The high degree of attrition suggested an attempt to use a less stringent criterion, which was applied in Experiments F and G, where the 100-word vocabulary was used. Criterion was reached when sorting on two successive trials differed for no more than 5 words out of the 100. In other words, a 95% sorting consistency criterion was used instead of 100%.

One other source of S loss must be discussed. Since Ss were told that they could use any sorting or categorization criterion they wished, some Ss used organizations based on systems other than word content. However, such organizations of words in terms of alphabetizing the initial letters or using word length or counting number of vowels is potentially or actually useless for purposes of recall. When words are sorted according to the alphabet, the S need only look at the first letter of the word. Since Ss were not told that they would be asked to recall the words following the categorization task, such noncontent sorting was fairly frequent. Column 3 of Table I shows the number of Ss in each experiment (except for Experiment A) who were discarded because they did not use content categories. The over-all percentage of such Ss was 26%. Since a subsequent experiment showed that additional *recall* instructions prior to categorization did not affect recall, future studies can avoid this source of attrition. If Ss are instructed to recall, the use of alphabetical and other noncontent categories declines markedly.

Finally, for purposes of initial analysis only those Ss were used who restricted themselves to seven categories or less in those Experiments (C, E, and G) where Ss were permitted to use more than seven categories. The restriction to seven categories in most of our experiments and in all of our analyses arose out of the consideration of the major purpose of the studies. We are concerned with (a) the relation of number of categories to number of words recalled and (b) the number of words that are recalled per category. For present purposes it would have obscured some of our major findings if the task had been complicated by also including category recall. It was felt that with a maximum of seven categories and with several trials during which the S could become thoroughly familiar with his categories, the likelihood that a S would forget a category would be relatively small and that the results would not be a function of both category recall and recall within categories. This reasoning was fully borne out by our data. Using Cohen's (1963) criterion for category recall (that is, counting a category as recalled if at least one member of the category set is recalled), the incidence of failure to recall categories was extremely low. Out of a total of 680 categories appearing in our final protocols, only 13 categories, or less than 2%, did not appear in the recall data. Thus restricting both the Ss and the analysis to seven categories or less assures us that the data presented will present a picture of items recalled per category and will, except in rare cases, not be confounded by problems of category recall. Data on Ss who used more than seven categories will be presented separately.

The "Final N" column in Table I shows, for each of the experiments, the number of Ss included in the analysis in Table II. These Ns include only Ss who reached the criterion, used content criteria in their categories, and used seven categories or less—where that restriction is applicable.

Table II shows, in successive columns: (1) the final number of Ss (N); (2) the mean number of categories used (NC); (3) the mean number of trials needed to reach criterion (T); (4) the mean total recall (R); (5) the correlation between NC and R; (6) the correlation between T and R; (7) the partial correlation between NC and R, holding T constant; (8) the slope of the line of best fit for the NC-R function; (9) the intercept of that line; (10) the mean ratio of repetition (RR) developed by Bousfield to measure clustering (Cohen, Sakoda, and Bousfield, 1954). It is defined as $R/(N-1)$ where R is the number of times a word from a category follows another word

TABLE II
Summary Data for Experiments A–G

Exp.	N	Mean cat. (NC)	Mean trials (T)	Mean recall (R)	Correlations NC–R	T–R	NC–R (T constant)	Slope	Intercept	RR[a]	Vocabulary
A	10	4.6	4.6	19.5	.95[b]	.45	.94[b]	5.6	−6.0	.63	52 Range
B	43	4.4	6.9	23.4	.74[b]	.16	.75[b]	2.9	10.6	.56	52 Range
C	7	4.6	5.4	23.6	.39	.30	.30	1.7	15.7	.56	52 AA
D	15	5.5	6.1	35.3	.70[b]	.24	.73[b]	2.5	21.2	.72	52 AA
E	20	5.0	6.2	28.2	.60[b]	−.22	.61[b]	3.9	8.7	.70	52 Range
F	25	4.2	6.2	38.8	.84[b]	−.02	.86[b]	7.5	7.5	.68	100 AA
G	28	3.7	6.3	40.7	.64[b]	.10	.64[b]	7.2	14.4	.68	100 AA
Median		4.6	6.2		.70+	.16	.73+	3.9	10.6	.68	

[a] Mean ratio of repetition.
[b] $p < .01$.

from that category and N is the total number of words recalled; (11) the vocabulary used in the experiment.

It should be noted that the line of best fit for the NC–R function was obtained from the raw data of all final Ss, even though Figs. 2–4 only show the mean recall for each NC value.

D. Experimental Data

1. *Experiment B*

In order to assure adequate sampling for all values of NC, it was decided to impose one additional constraint on the Ss, namely, to instruct them on the number of categories they were to use. The additional instructions for each of the six NC groups who were told to use from 2 to 7 categories informed Ss that they must use a certain number of categories but that they were free to use any category system within that limitation. Data were collected for 10 Ss in each NC group who reached the sorting criterion. The NC–R relation is shown in Fig. 2

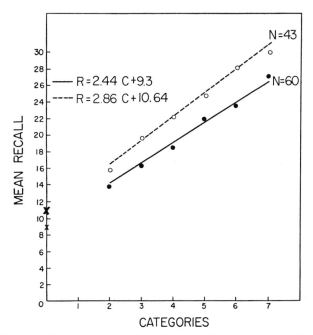

FIG. 2. Mean recall as a function of number of categories used in Experiment B. Filled circles and solid line are for original 60 Ss; open circles and dashed line, for the 43 Ss using content categories only. The equations shown are for the line of best fit.

for these 60 Ss as well as for 43 Ss who only used content categories. The data in Table II are for the latter group. The 17 Ss who used noncontent categories were rectangularly distributed across the NC groups; two came from the 2-NC group and three from each of the others.

The slope of the function is reduced from that obtained in Experiment A. But the straight line fit is obviously excellent. Subjects recall about 2.9 words per category and the y-intercept is positive. It might be noted that comparisons with Experiment A are probably spurious. The N in that experiment is small, the data include points from Ss who alphabetized, and the negative y-intercept is difficult to interpret. The general significance of the y-intercept will be discussed at the conclusion of the experimental discussion.

Table II shows that the Ss used a mean of 4.5 trials to reach criterion. The mean number of categories used is, of course, fixed in this experiment. There is highly significant correlation of .74 between NC and R and the T and R correlation is nonsignificant. The RR is .56.

2. *Experiments C and D*

It was thought that the constraint imposed on the Ss in Experiment B might have depressed the slope value of the NC–R function and Experiments C and D were conducted with a new, high frequency vocabulary. In Experiment C, Ss were allowed up to 20 categories; in Experiment D the conditions were similar to Experiment A. Unfortunately the attrition due to noncriterion Ss was heaviest in these two experiments, reaching a value of 40%.

In Experiment C, Ss chose more than seven categories more frequently than in the similar unlimited-category Experiments E and G. As a result the final N for Experiment C was only 7. In Experiment D a large number of Ss continued to switch numbers of categories and the final N was only 15.

For Experiment C the slope was 1.7 and the intercept 15.7. The correlation between NC and R was .39 and between T and R, .30.

Experiment D produced another low slope value of 2.5 with a very high intercept of 21.2. The NC–R correlation was .70; the T–R correlation was .24.

In general these two experiments produced the most disappointing results of the series. In trying to remove the constraint imposed in Experiment B, we not only reduced the NC requirement but also provided Ss with a combination of the shortest list of the series (52 words) and the most familiar vocabulary (AA). The possibility exists that these lists were so easily organized that *S*s might have used the sorting task to impose organization over and above the obvious associations and clusters apparent in the list. In such a case, the organization produced by the categorization task is not in fact the organization that determines recall, and recall might have been a function of both the overt and other covert organizing schemes.

It should be noted that Experiment D was essentially a replication of Experiment A but produced a less stable, though still highly significant, relationship between NC and R.

3. *Experiment E*

On the assumption that the 52 AA list was too easy for the task in Experiment C, the original 52-range list was used in Experiment E in which *S*s were allowed unlimited number of categories. Table I shows that only 5 *S*s out of 36 criterion *S*s used more than seven categories. The slope of 3.9 for the criterion content *S*s is within the expected limits and the intercept is 8.7. The NC and R correlation is .60, and the recall and trials correlation is negative and low at −.22.

Figure 3 shows the NC–R relation for Experiment E. The fitted line

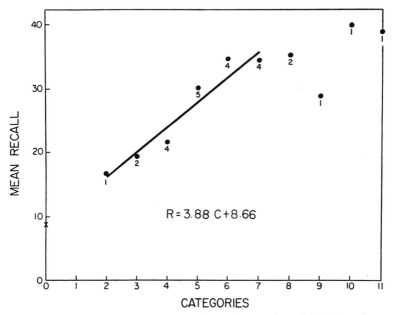

$$R = 3.88\,C + 8.66$$

Fig. 3. Mean recall as a function of number of categories used in Experiment E. Numbers next to data points indicate number of *S*s contributing to the mean value shown. The equation is for line of best fit for all *S*s using seven categories or less.

is for the Ss with seven categories or less only. The data for the other five Ss are also shown. It is quite clear from inspection of this figure that the category–recall function does not hold beyond seven categories. In fact, the line of best fit for the five Ss who used more than seven NC has a slope of 1.65 with a high intercept of 20.6. In the previous unlimited category experiment (C), the slope for the comparable six Ss was 0.88, the intercept was 29.7.

4. *Experiments F and G*

If the 52 AA vocabulary was too easy, in the sense that the list was relatively short considering the high familiarity of the items, another way to avoid parallel organizations, that is, those that the sorting task might not detect, is to increase the length of the list. Experiments F and G therefore used the 100 AA list, with F restricting Ss to seven categories, while G again permitted Ss to use unlimited NC. At the same time, the new criterion of two successive trials with only 95% overlap was introduced. The results are shown in Fig. 4 for the NC–R relation.

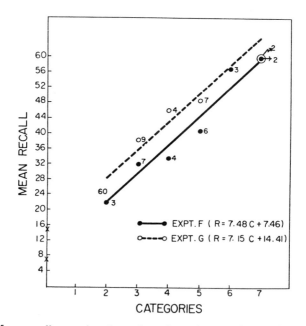

FIG. 4. Mean recall as a function of number of categories used in Experiments F and G. Number next to data points indicate number of Ss contributing to the mean value shown. Equations shown are for the lines of best fit.

The data for Experiment F in Table II are in the expected direction. The slope of the NC–R relation is 7.5 with an intercept of 7.5 and all other values are within the ranges that by now had become fairly stable.

Experiment G produced only 3 Ss who used more than seven categories; the remaining 28 content criterion Ss produced results very similar to Experiment F, with a slope of 7.2, an intercept of 14.4, and other comparable values.

In order to check on the acceptability of the new criterion, 10 of the 25 Ss in Experiment F who had reached the old 100% criterion provided data for a separate analysis. These Ss used a mean of 4.1 categories, 5.8 trials, and recalled 38.7 words. Their slope value was 8.0, the intercept was 6.3. Thus, the data can be said to be quite comparable whether the 100% or 95% criterion is used.

E. SUMMARY OF THE CATEGORY–RECALL RELATION

With Experiments F and G the present program of research terminated, since the relation between NC and R seems to have been fairly stably established under a variety of different conditions.

The consistency of some of the dependent variables is quite remarkable. The last row of Table II shows the median of the major variables of interest. The value of 4.6 categories for median NC is consistent with the Mandler and Pearlstone (1966) data that Ss will, on the average, select about 4–5 categories out of 7. While the range for all Ss is determined at 2–7, the preference for about 5 ± 2 categories during conceptualization seems to be fairly well established. In all the unlimited-category experiments only 20% of the Ss used more than seven categories. The same general level applies if Ss are examined regardless of content or criterion restrictions.

A surprising finding was the general stability of the mean number of trials (T) needed to reach criterion. The median was 6.2, with a range of 4.6–6.3. While the materials used were, of course, quite homogeneous, the stability of this value is still somewhat unusual.

More important for understanding the trials variable is the relation among NC, T, and R. Table II shows that the median value for the correlation between NC and R is .70. This coefficient expresses the major thesis of this paper, that is, that there is in fact a highly significant positive relation between number of categories and recall. The significance level of the individual correlation coefficients also permits an evaluation of the stability of the straight line fit.

It might be argued that the NC–R relation hides a more basic relation between trials and recall. Thus it would have been possible that Ss take more trials the more categories they use and that the more trials they had during which they were exposed to the input list, the better would be their recall. In that case we would expect a high NC–R correlation, mediated by the trials variable.

The column of correlation coefficients for the T–R relation suggests that such an argument is inadmissible. Not only is there a generally nonsignificant, if not negative, relation between trials and recall (median $= .16$), but the NC–R relation remains essentially stable when it is corrected for the mediating effects of trials. The median partial correlation between NC and R with T held constant is .73. Thus trials are an unimportant variable in the particular relations investigated here. (When total time expended during sorting is used instead of number of trials, the relation with both NC and recall is very similar to that obtained with trials.) Subjects need a certain number of trials to reach a criterion of organization, but it is the nature of that organization, not the number of trials needed to produce its stability, that determines recall. In other situations, the apparent effects of trials would, of course, be greater. Thus in a multitrial free recall experiment, organization would develop more slowly with trials, and there would be a much larger correlation between trials and recall, though we would argue that such a relation hides the basic category–recall function. Multitrial free recall will be discussed later in more detail.

The median slope value for the various experiments is 3.9, which is within the range of our hypothesized value of 5 ± 2. On the average, Ss in these experiments add about 4 words to recall for every additional category used, with a range of 1.7–7.5.

The median y-intercept value is 10.6. The theoretical meaning of the y-intercept is somewhat complicated. The straight line function suggests that when Ss use no category they would recall about ten words from the list. This is theoretically meaningless for our purposes, since we assume that categorization is essential for memory and, by definition, words cannot be classified in zero categories. If anything, the value of the intercept might be applicable to the situation where all items in the list are categorized into a single set or category, but the function does not, of course, make that prediction.

It seems reasonable to suggest that the function is in effect discontinuous between 0 and 1, primarily because of the theoretical and empirical lack of interpretation of a zero-category sort. The y-intercept can be used as an estimate of the amount of material recalled on the basis of organizations other than those assessed by the NC variable. It is of course possible, as we have already discussed in relation to the 52 AA vocabulary, for Ss to use two or more concurrent organizational schemas. In that case we would expect the y-intercept to be fairly large and the effect of the NC variable should be interfered with. In fact, such a relation between the slope and the intercept does exist in our data. For the seven experiments there is a rank order correlation of $-.68$ ($p = .05$) between slope and intercept values. This is not artifactual since the intercept could, of course, change with the slope staying constant, and vice versa. It is therefore defensible to use the y-intercept value as an index of concurrent but unevaluated organizational schemas.

One other possible explanation that could be advanced for the category–recall relation needs to be discussed briefly. In all experiments except Experiment B the number of categories used was selected by individual Ss. It could be argued that the category–recall correlation is mediated by some individual capacity such as general intelligence, with the more intelligent Ss selecting more categories and also recalling more words. Such an explanation cannot be advanced for the data on Experiment B, however, where the number of categories to be used was randomly assigned to Ss. The correlation between NC and R in that experiment was .74, above the median for all the studies, and the slope was at 2.9, below the over-all median. We have argued that the latter low figure was due to the additional constraint on the Ss. These data make an explanation based on self-selection less tenable.

F. CLUSTERING AND CATEGORIZATION

The clustering scores (RR) in Table II show a median of .68 and a range of values, as one would expect, generally greater than that found in the clustering of E-defined categories.

Another way to evaluate the clustering behavior of Ss in this situation is to consider clustering scores as a function of NC. In order to be able to obtain relatively stable values, N per NC must be fairly large, and only Experiments B and G provided enough data for such an analysis. Figure 5 shows, for Experiment B ($N = 43$), three values at each NC level: first, the obtained mean ratio of repetition (RR); second, the random RR value determined by randomizing each S's recall protocol; and finally, the maximum value that would be obtained if each S had recalled the words from each category in a single cluster.

Both the limiting values (random and maximum) are affected by NC; both decline, with the random value dropping much more steeply

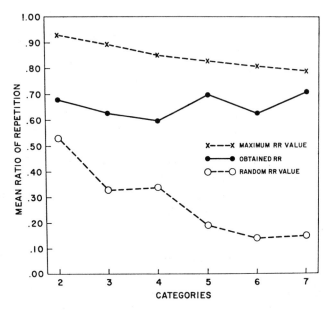

Fig. 5. Mean ratio of repetition (RR) as a function of number of categories used in Experiment B ($N = 43$). Solid line shows observed data; dashed line with crosses shows maximum possible if perfect clustering had occurred; dashed line with open circles shows RR values for a random rearrangement of output.

as a function of NC. The empirical values, however, remain remarkably stable and are essentially unaffected by NC. In other words, as NC increases, Ss diverge more from the random model and approach the maximum or perfect clustering score. The same relationship was found when the clustering data for Experiment G were analyzed.

The clustering data show that the free organization of material produces a very strong tendency for members of the same category to be recalled in a cluster. This tendency apparently increases as the number of categories increases and, of course, as the total number of words recalled increases. With small NC values Ss apparently have more of a tendency (a) to switch from category to category during recall than with large NC values, where categories are recalled in more consistent clusters, or (b) to use categories not evaluated by the categorizing task.

G. Long-Term Memory of Organized Material

Although no plans had been made to retest the Ss in the various experiments, it was discovered during the course of conducting Experiment G that most of the *S*s in Experiments C–G had been recruited from two lecture classes. One half week after conclusion of Experiment G, the available *S*s in these two classes were retested for long-term recall. It should be noted that these *S*s had no information at the time of the first recall that they would be retested, nor, as a matter of fact, had the *E*. The same *E* who had conducted the original session addressed the students in the two classes, reminded them of the experiment by describing the categorizing task and the recall, and then asked them to write on a sheet of paper all the words they could recall from that experiment.

Figure 6 shows the recall data for those *S*s whose data were used in the final analyses of the original experiments and who were avail-

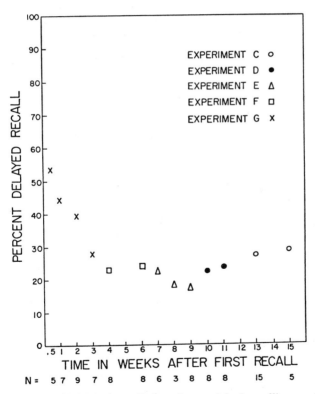

Fig. 6. Percentage of delayed recall (based on original recall) as a function of time since original recall for Experiments C–G. Bottom line on abscissa shows number of *S*s contributing to each data point.

able at the retest. The figure shows the delayed recall as a percentage of the number of words the Ss were able to recall during the original experimental session. This percentage of delayed recall is plotted as a function of time since the original recall session. Delayed recall drops very sharply within the first 3–4 days to a little over 50% and reaches a relatively stable level of 20%–30% after about three weeks. While few data are available in the literature (cf. McGeoch and Irion, 1952) on memory decay over long periods of time, these data do seem to be more similar to long-term memory for connected, meaningful passages, rather than to the memory for lists. It appears that memory for organized material shows a sharp initial decay, but no further loss, even after three or four months. The nature of this long-term storage is further illustrated by category recall. Using a single word recalled from a category as an index of category recall, percentage of category recall is much more variable than percentage of word recall. However, category recall generally drops from about 90% to about 75% during the first six weeks, then drops to about 60% in the seventh week, whereupon it stabilizes at approximately 50%–60%. These figures should be compared with a category recall of 98% during immediate recall. It can be argued that the persisting memory of the list over 15 weeks is to some extent due to the high percentage of recall for the coding categories.

The importance of the category system for long-term recall is also supported by the clustering analysis for long-term recall. Even after 14 weeks recall is still clustered relative to a random measure. The RR for 10 Ss from Experiment C was .24 as against .16 for the random measure. However, the clustering score declines generally over time from .56 at $\frac{1}{2}$ weeks to .24 after 14 weeks.

An important additional set of data on the relation between recall and category size will be discussed after the next section, which will present a final experiment on the category–recall function.

H. Organization and Recall as a Function of Instructions

The following experiment was conducted for two reasons. First, having argued that organization is a necessary condition for recall and having shown that organization was directly related to recall, it was decided to explore the further step that organization is a sufficient condition for recall and that asking Ss to remember something implies that they are instructed to organize. Do instructions to organize have the same effect on recall as instructions to remember? Second, the previous series of experiments had shown that recall was apparently unrelated to number of trials of exposure, that the recall–category relation was independent of number of trials. That demonstration, however, has been only statistical. The next experiment was designed to produce an experimental demonstration of the recall–trials–category relation.

1. *Method*

In the main study four groups of Ss were run, comprising the four cells of a 2 × 2 design involving the presence or absence of instructions (a) to categorize or (b) to recall material. An additional group was tested for incidental memory. The five groups and the N in each group follow, with "Category" and "Recall" indicating the instructions given: (1) Category-Recall, $N = 21$; (2) Category-No Recall, $N = 21$; (3) No Category-Recall, $N = 19$; (4) No Category-No Recall, $N = 19$; (5) Incidental; No Category-No Recall, $N = 15$. All data were collected in five group sessions, one for each of the experimental groups; Ss were assigned to groups at random. Word lists were presented aurally at a 4-sec rate and had been pretaped for five presentation trials, each of which consisted of a random rearrangement of a 52-word list. The lists were the 52-range lists with five words changed because of their auditory confusability. Subjects in all groups were given booklets consisting of five sheets with seven columns and a final blank sheet. The instructions varied as follows.

(1) Category: Ss were told that this was an experiment in categorizing words and that they were to divide the words into any number of categories from two to seven. After hearing a word, they were to write it in a column and then add to that column any other word that went with it. They were asked to try to use the same organization on successive trials, and were not allowed to look at the category sheet of a previous trial. With a fixed number of trials, aural presentation, and written sorting, this procedure was similar to that used in the previous experiments.

(2) No Category: Ss were instructed to write the first word they heard in the first column, the second word in the second, and so forth, followed by the eighth word in the first column, and so on; and to continue this until the end of the trial.

(3) Recall: Ss were told at the beginning of the experiment that they would have to recall all the words at the end of the experiment.

(4) No Recall: Ss were given no additional instructions.

(5) Incidental: Ss were given the same words, but on a different tape on which each word was followed by a randomly selected digit from one to nine. They were asked to write the words down just as the

No Category group and were told that their task was to remember how often each of the digits appeared. At the end of each trial, they were required to write down their estimate of the number of times that each digit was heard.

At the end of the five trials, all groups were asked to write down all the words from the lists that they could remember.

2. Results

Table III shows the mean number of words recalled by each of the five groups. The only significant result for the four main groups was

TABLE III
Mean Number of Words Recalled in Five Experimental Groups

Categorization instructions	Recall instructions	
	Present	Absent
Present	31.4	32.9
Absent	32.8	23.5
Incidental condition		10.9

the difference between the No Category-No Recall group and the other three main groups ($p < .01$). The Incidental group performance was significantly below the lowest of the other four groups ($p < .01$). Either organization or recall instruction produce the same level of recall, significantly better than that produced in the absence of instructions. It could be assumed that the No Category-No Recall group was self-instructed and therefore organized to some extent, either because they expected to be asked to recall or more generally because Ss tend to organize material to some extent, even in the absence of instructions. It might be noted that half of the Ss in the No Category-No Recall group reported after the experiment that they expected to have to recall the words. It should be noted, however, that recall instructions produce the same results as organizing instructions, thus supporting our initial hypothesis. When organization is inhibited by directing Ss attention to another task, as in the Incidental group, recall drops to a level about one-third that of the organizing groups. Even in that last group, however, 4 of the 15 Ss reported that they expected to be asked to recall the words.

As far as the category–recall relationship is concerned, it should be noted that all Ss received five trials and identical amounts of time during the input presentation. Any relation between NC and R, therefore, is and must be independent of number of trials.

The change in procedure retarded speed of categorization. Only 3 of the 42 *S*s in the categorizing groups reached the criterion of two identical successive trials and two of those *S*s used alphabetic organization. But even with these relatively unstable organizational schemas, the same NC–R relationship is discernible as in the previous studies. The correlation between NC and R was .64 ($p < .01$) for the Category-No Recall group and .53 ($p < .02$) for the Category-Recall group. The respective equations for the line of best fit were 3.7 Cat. + 11.2 and 3.0 Cat. + 13.9, respectively. Thus, despite a low level of organization and constant number of trials, we obtained a stable NC–R relation with three or more words added to recall per category.

This last experiment has shown that recall is a function of the number of categories used and that this relation cannot be derived from some mediating effects of number of trials; moreover, the data support the notion that both recall or organizing instructions produce equivalent organization and equivalent recall. Thus, with some of our assumptions more firmly anchored, we can return to the more general problems of the Category-Recall function. In particular, we shall now consider how category size affects recall from that category. Following this discussion we will also be able to evaluate some prior studies on the category–recall relationship.

I. CATEGORY SIZE AND RECALL

How many items can a *S* recall from a category of a given size? We have already suggested the importance of this problem when we assumed that recall from sets of a given size follows the same general function whether the set is a category made up of word items or whether it is a set of categories from which categories must be recalled prior to word recall. At present we can evaluate only word recall from categories of given sizes, since our experiments were deliberately designed to maximize recall of all the categories. Data of category recall from other investigators will be compared with our data to demonstrate the generality of the relationship.

The basic data for the category size–recall function was obtained from all useable protocols in Experiments B–G. Category size varied from 1, which was permissible if *S*s used more than two categories, to 96, which is, of course, only possible for 100-word lists. For each category size, all *S*s who used that category size in any experiment were combined into a single group. The data from all available categories are shown in Fig. 7. For purposes of presentation a log scale is used for category size and the number of categories contributing to each value is shown on the abscissa. For large category sizes (beyond

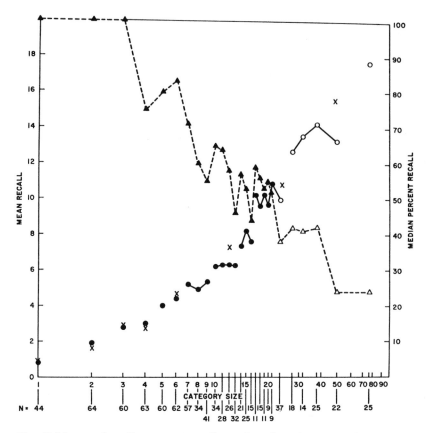

F<small>IG</small>. 7. Mean and median percent recall as a function of category size. Solid line, circles, and left-hand ordinate show mean recall. Triangles, dashed line, and right-hand ordinate show median percent of category size recalled. Open circles and triangles indicate that several category sizes have been combined. For the mean recall function, adjacent points that differ at the .01 level of statistical significance (*t* tests) have not been joined. The abscissa shows category size on a logarithmic scale. The bottom line on the abscissa shows the number of categories observed at each size. Single crosses show data from Tulving and Pearlstone (1966) see text for explanation.

21), data were combined for several sizes and are shown as empty circles. Figure 7 also shows recall as a percentage of category size.

The means shown in Fig. 7 form a fairly stable function of recall as a function of category size. It should be noted that the means of the low values of category size somewhat underestimate actual recall. The medians for category sizes 1, 2, 3, 4, 5, and 6 were 1, 2, 3, 3, 4, and 5, respectively. For the larger values the means and medians agree more closely.

For small category sizes Ss recall close to 100% up to about size three, then drop to about 75% at sizes up to about seven items per category (IPC), after which the percentage function drops rapidly to the 50% level and reaches 25% for very large categories. In other words, the relative recall from categories decays rapidly after the 5 ± 2 level has been passed. For the time being it can be assumed that up to an IPC size of seven, recall is fairly stable. But what of categories that contain more than seven items, and what of category recall as a function of the size of the set of categories? Before dealing with that problem directly, some data from several other studies must be considered.

J. RELATED STUDIES

Tulving and Pearlstone (1966) presented Ss with preorganized lists of varying lengths and varying numbers of items per category (IPC). Category size varied from 1 to 2 to 4 IPC, while list length varied from 12 to 24 to 48 words. Thus different lists contained from 3 to 48 categories—from list length 12 with 4 IPC to list length 48 with 1 IPC. During input, Ss were given category names and after one presentation, they were tested either with (cued) or without (noncued) presentation of the category name. Rather than investigating the relation between recall and number of categories, as Mathews (1954), for example, had done, Tulving and Pearlstone chose to investigate the relation between list length and IPC. They concluded that list length affected the number of categories recalled but not the number of words recalled within a recalled category. Their criterion of category recall was the same as Cohen's (1963), that is, recall of any one member of the category was taken as a criterion of category recall. It must be noted, however, that as list length increased, so did the number of categories within any value of IPC. Thus, category recall increased as a function of list length but also as a function of number of categories to be recalled. Tulving and Pearlstone suggest, in accord with the present orientation, that category recall and recall within a category are independent. So far so good; but they do not raise the question whether or not the mechanism of category recall is the same as the mechanism of word recall within categories. In other words, the number of items recalled from a particular category and the number of categories recalled from a set of categories should—and do—follow the same general function.

Their data permit a reanalysis that tests this proposal.[2] Word recall from categories was obtained from their cued condition in which Ss were given category names, thus assuring category recall, which is necessary to assess recall within a category. Recall per category was obtained from all categories of a given IPC value. This procedure provides values for recall from categories of sizes 1, 2, and 4. If, at the same time, the sets of categories are considered with 3, 6, 12, 24, and 48 categories per list, then the number of categories recalled, as defined earlier, provides data for recall of sets of sizes 3–48. These later values were taken from their Table 2, which shows number of categories recalled for different list lengths and different IPCs under noncued conditions. It is, of course, only in the noncued condition that category recall can be investigated. These values also were averaged for all sets with identical numbers of categories. The resulting data from both analyses for sets of sizes 1, 2, 3, 4, 6, 12, 24, and 48 are shown as crosses in Fig. 7. Despite the different Ss, materials, and procedures used, Tulving and Pearlstone's data fit nicely into the general relation between set size and mean recall shown for our various experiments. This concordance suggests that mechanisms for the recall of categories and of words within categories follow the same general function. Subjects recall a fixed number of words from any category of a particular size, and they recall the same proportion of categories from a set of categories of that size. Thus, although it is reasonable to argue that category recall and recall within categories are independent processes, they do follow the same size–recall function.

Since we are dealing with Tulving and Pearlstone's data, their major finding should be noted. When Ss were given category names during recall, their performance dramatically improved, suggesting that these additional words had been available but were accessible only when the category was also recalled. Interestingly enough, their data failed to show any superiority of cued recall when only three categories were used (list length 12 with 4 IPC). Considering the present argument this is not surprising since cuing for three categories cannot provide much if any advantage over the already high—if not perfect—recall of the three categories. Subjects should be able to recall three categories and cuing does not help. As soon as the number of categories becomes 6 or larger, cuing—the addition of category names—does and should produce significant advantages.

In a summary of an extended program of research on coding behavior dealing primarily with the recall of categorized word lists, Cohen (1966) has discussed the "some-or-none" characteristics of

---

[2] I want to thank the authors for making these data available to me.

coding behavior. He has shown that under a variety of different conditions Ss will recall a fairly constant proportion of the members of a particular category. His research has dealt primarily with category sizes 3 and 4, and therefore contributes relatively little to the generality of the present data, but some of his data on category sizes 2–5 suggest the same general function as the one shown in Fig. 7. His values are somewhat lower than those in Fig. 7, primarily because his procedure includes data from Ss who recall words from some categories that they have in fact not used in a categorical fashion. Thus, although Cohen points out that Ss recall a constant proportion from a category of a given size if they recall any word from that category, the means for category recall include data from Ss who may have recalled a word or two from a category without having discovered the complete categorical structure of the list. As was pointed out earlier, if Ss do not discover a category, then recall from that category will not follow the general mechanism apparent in category recall. The free conceptualization method insures that Ss not only discover these categories but, in fact, develop them in the first place.

Just as Tulving and Pearlstone did, Cohen distinguishes between category recall and recall within categories. Once a category has been recalled, "performance on these recalled categories appears to be invariant." He notes in passing that Ss recall about 10–14 categories from an 18- or 20-category list. These values are consistent with the function in Fig. 7. Recall within the category of categories is the same process as recall within a category.

In another study Cohen (1963) was concerned with the contrast between the recall of unrelated words and the recall of categories. He found that when presentation time was held constant, the recall of categories—scored as the recall of one or more words from a category—was similar to the recall of unrelated words. He concludes that these data support Miller's (1956a) notion that the recall of chunks should be constant, whether these chunks are single words or categorized groups of words. This general finding supports the assumption that category recall and IPC recall are limited by the same general mechanism, though they may not be influenced by the same variables.

Both Cohen, and Tulving and Pearlstone thus support the general notion that, given a particular category size, recall from that category will be constant if it occurs at all. In general, then, the recall of organized material depends (a) on the number of categories used, which determines the number of categories that will be recalled, and (b) on the size of the recalled categories, which determines the amount to be recalled from each category. When category size is constant, the function is a simple multiplicative one of recalled categories times items recalled within categories, a relationship proposed by Tulving and Pearlstone in their paper.

This position suggests a simple trading relationship between size of the set of categories and the number of items within the categories. When the set of categories is small (6 or less), a large proportion of the categories will be recalled and, if the category is large, a relatively large amount per category will be recalled because of subcategorizing, and the total amount of recall will be large. But if the number of categories is large, the percentage of categories recalled will be relatively small and recall, particularly if the category size is small, will be relatively low. This relationship explains some data on the recall of categorized material.

Dallett, in one of his experiments (1964, Exp. IV), demonstrated a decreasing amount of recall with increasing number of categories. However, by keeping list length constant at 24 and keeping IPC constant within any one list, his lists varied from 2 categories with 12 IPC to 12 categories with 2 IPC. Given the multiplicative function suggested earlier, these two sets of values should produce identical recall. Dallett's Ss were not, however, given the category names nor told that the list contained, in the extreme case, 12 categories. In the absence of discovery of the category structure by the Ss, the set of categories from which category recall occurs is frequently smaller than 12. In that case we would expect a decreasing function as the number of categories increases. It should be noted that Tulving and Pearlstone's Ss were given the category names during input and some of their data suggest that their Ss had the category structure available at time of noncued output.

Mathew, in a pioneering experiment on categorization and recall, also used a constant-length list with varying numbers of categories and varying IPC. In her experiment, however, Ss had category names available to them at the time of recall. With 2, 3, and 6 categories per list and 12, 8, and 4 IPC, respectively, she found increasing recall as a function of number of categories. With no problem of category recall, the large drop in the proportion of items recalled between 4 and 12 IPC would predict such a function on the basis of the values shown in Fig. 7 and the simple multiplicative function discussed earlier.

The discussion of these various studies makes it apparent that experimenter-defined categories, varying numbers of categories, and varying IPC make possible any one of several functions between the number of categories used and the resultant recall. The values obtained from Fig. 7 permit the construction of ascending or descending functions, just as these various experiments have shown.

The data from our experiments permit the evaluation of the more general relationship between numbers of categories and recall. In the first instance, the categories are subject-selected and therefore not dependent on discovery during input. We can assume that all Ss have their categories available and accessible. Second, the extensive conceptualization training overtrains Ss on these categories so that there should be no loss due to forgetting of the categories up to about seven categories, and our data have shown this to be the case. Finally, by permitting Ss to vary category size freely there is no general interaction between category size and number of categories. It is true, of course, that Ss who use a large number of categories will also tend to use fewer items per category—on the average. But with any given choice of number of categories, the size of any one category may, and does, vary widely.

K. CATEGORY SIZE AND ORGANIZATION

The discussion of the generality of the relation between mean recall and category size should not obscure or confuse some of our earlier findings. It was concluded previously that in the recall of organized lists, Ss will, depending on conditions, recall about 3–7 words per category. In the first instance, that statement was limited to those cases where Ss use seven categories or less, and use categories that are immediately available (that is, not subject to forgetting). In the light of Fig. 7 and the subsequent discussion, what is the relevance of the number 5 ± 2? Obviously Ss recall less when IPC is very small and as much as three times the implied limit when category size is large. For the lower values of IPC an obvious ceiling is operating and it has already been shown that up to an IPC value of about 4 the median value of recall is equal to the items in the category. For the larger values it seems reasonable to argue that whenever recall goes above 7–9 items, Ss are using subcategories within the categories. Some evidence on this point will be discussed later. For the time being all that needs to be said is that the number of items gained per category is, of course, an average value, made up of recall from different categories with varying values of IPC. The generality of the category–recall relation is not disturbed by the subsequent, more detailed, analysis that showed that there is a highly stable and general function between IPC and recall. Given a well-organized list of items, it may still be said that Ss will add about 5 ± 2 items per category to their recall.

It has been noted that in situations where category recall occurs under conditions similar to IPC recall, the same function applies. Up till now we have dealt only with two levels of organization, categories and items within categories. Is it reasonable to expect more extended organization, and what does such an assumption imply for the organization of human memory?

It is appropriate to consider evidence from some of the categories—necessarily large ones—where recall was well above the assumed limit of five to seven words per category. We will first examine such instances and then proceed to a more general discussion of higher level organization.

Even cursory inspection shows that whenever a S did use a very large category, the category name or label was vague and the concept used to determine category membership tended to be highly inclusive. Three Ss from Experiment F will be discussed here for illustrative purposes: S F1 used three categories to sort the 100 words and obtained a recall score of 31. His first category, labeled "senses," contained 6 items and produced a recall of 5 items; his second category, containing 9 items, was labeled "spirit, mind, character," and produced a recall of 5 items, while the third category, of interest here, contained 85 items, was labeled "everything else," and produced a recall of 21 words. Looking at the recall protocol, it is quite obvious that "everything else" was subdivided by the S and the following list of the third-category items, in the order in which they were produced in recall, makes this quite obvious. Ellipses indicate intervening recall of items from the other categories.

GRASS	END	UNCLE
PAINT	MOUTH	GENTLEMAN
. . .	. . .	QUEEN
TABLE	MUSIC	. . .
KITCHEN	CLASS	WALK
DINNER	MEMBER	SUPPORT
. . .	. . .	. . .
SKIP	FEAR	SALT
. . .	FACT	. . .
FINGER	. . .	FLOWER

The list contains such obvious categories as "kitchen items" and "people" and other clusters that have been organized by being fitted into mnemonic devices such as images, syntactic clusters, and others.

Similar sequential clustering can be found for S F2, who used four categories: "verbs," with 20 items and a recall of 5; "art," with 17 items and a recall of 11; "abstract ideas," with 10 items and a recall of 3; "ordinary words," with 53 items and a recall of 19. The last category distributed its recall in the protocol as follows.

WIND	PAPER	. . .	TASTE
. . .	. . .	HOUR	. . .
CENTURY	UNCLE	YEAR	SENSE
. . .	. . .	. . .	SILVER
OFFICE	GENTLEMAN	COAT	FARMER
BUILDING	DINNER	. . .	. . .
NEWS	FOOD	SHOULDER	HAIR

And finally, the recall by S F3 of a category called "objects" with 64 items and a recall of 17 words was as follows.

LIFE	GENTLEMAN	BOAT
. . .	QUEEN	TABLE
SOUND	FINGER	. . .
. . .	FARMER	COMPANY
BUILDING	. . .	CROSS
MATERIAL	CENTURY	END
. . .	DAY	. . .
OIL	PERIOD	
. . .	. . .	

Some of these clusters are obvious, others are obscure, and some "intrusions" within clusters (for example, finger) are highly idiosyncratic.

These quite typical protocols suggest that whenever very large categories are used by the Ss, they tend to be superordinate categories that include several subordinate categories. Few categories could be more superordinate than "everything else." It should also be noted that the recall from these large categories occurs in clusters of from one to five words. While Ss frequently recall all the words from a small category in one sequential cluster, the recall from the large clusters is broken up into smaller sequential units.

In other words, when categories with large membership are formed, they tend to be superordinate categories with recall from these categories being determined by the number of subordinate categories they contain. We can now refer back to Fig. 7 and consider the general function represented there. It seems likely that up to about 10–15 IPC we may be dealing with a single function with recall being directly determined by category size. Above these values, both theoretical consideration and the foregoing suggestive evidence support the notion that these categories produce recall as a function of the categories they themselves contain. In Fig. 7, the adjacent points of the mean recall graph that are significantly different at the .01 level have not been joined. The data suggest that the function contains several discrete recall levels. Figure 7 shows particularly distinct plateaus at 8, 10, 14, and 18 words of mean recall. Pending further investigation this suggests that categories of large sizes may contain, on the average, 2–5 subcategories with recall of about 3–5 words from each of these categories. The number of categories will depend on the size of the larger category, producing about 2 when category size is around 20 and rising to about 5 subcategories when category size is as large as 75.

The abscissa of Fig. 7 also shows the number of categories of each size. Although these values suggest that the preferred category sizes are 1–7, containing 44% of all categories, another 32% of the categories fall in the size range 8–15, with a respectable 24% in the 16–96 range.

VII. The Organization of Memory

It is now possible to suggest the general outline of the organizational system. We assume first the basic limit of the organizing system at 5 ± 2 per set of items. For any single chunk the organism can handle only that many units. Given that limitation, categories will be formed and 3–7 items assigned to them. We might note in passing that some categories will be smaller than that simply because the list may contain only one or two relevant items. Once these initial categories are filled up, new categories will be created to accommodate additional items. But in turn, there will be a limit of about 5 ± 2 categories at this first level of categorization. When all slots are taken up with first-level categories, a second level of categories will be formed, each of which may contain up to about seven first-level categories, and so forth. In this manner, a hierarchical system of categories can be built up with an increasing level of complexity and an exponential growth in the size of the system. We will return shortly to some speculations about the size of these organized systems. First, two additional items of evidence for this general scheme are relevant.

Applying these notions to multitrial experiments of free recall suggests the following mechanism to explain the increase in free recall as a function of repeated exposure to a particular list of items. We agree with Tulving (1964) and others that the free recall experiment using words is not a learning but a retention situation; that is, the S must retain the items presented on any one trial. In the sense of response learning, the items have been "learned" prior to the experiment and in terms of retention, any single word could be retained if it were presented alone. Thus, an item is "learned" at the time of presentation.

The present analysis assumes that at the time of the first trial, when S is given information as to list length and the words contained in the list, the processing system establishes the requisite number of categories, probably and preferably about five, to which the words are to be assigned. If list length is about 25 or less (that is, 5 categories with 5 items per category), this should present no particular problem. If it is longer, it is likely that superordinate categories are established in order to accommodate eventually all the words in the list. Recall after the first trial probably reflects category recall, that is, approximately one word from a large proportion of the categories. On subsequent trials these categories are then "filled up" with items up to the capacity of 5 ± 2. Given a constant number of categories, the optimal strategy might be to add one item to each category on each trial. There are serious limitations to such a process, since it is highly likely that the initial categorization might undergo changes in order to accommodate the items in the list, and it also might prove difficult to assign every word to a particular category as fewer items remain to be organized.

However, support for some such process can be found in the arguments and data presented by Tulving (1964). Tulving showed that, except for artifactual effects, intratrial retention (the number of items recalled on a trial that were not recalled on the previous trial) is constant across trials, whereas intertrial retention (items recalled on trial n that were also recalled on trial $n - 1$) increases as a function of trials. The constant intratrial effect is consistent with the reasoning presented earlier. Tulving also presents some data that suggest that the value for the intratrial retention component increases with list length. With a list length of 22 words, both initial recall on Trial 1 and the intratrial retention value for early trials were about five. With a list length of 52, the intratrial retention value is close to nine. Furthermore, the SO (subjective organization) values increase as a function of trials and covary with intertrial retention. In terms of the present model, with increasing trials, more and more words from the category are recalled in clusters.

These suggestions also offer a possible explanation why single-trial recall varies as a function of list length. The longer the list, the more initial categories will be established after a single exposure. Finally, the model predicts that multitrial free recall experiments should produce relatively inefficient learning in the sense that performance cannot reach the asymptote of 100% recall for relatively long lists. The inefficiency and subsequent rigidity of the initial category system prevents the organization of all the items and eventually prevents some items from being recalled. Contrast such a system to one that permits the S to organize the list prior to recall, as in our studies.

For example, the three Ss in Experiment G who used 8 or more categories recalled an average of 76.7 items out of 100 with an average of only 4.6 categorization trials.

The rigidity of established categorical organizations has recently been illustrated by Ozier (1965). Her Ss were given varying numbers of trials of free recall followed by instructions to recall according to alphabetic categories. The data unequivocally show a drop in recall on the trial immediately following the instructions, with the size of the decrease being a direct function of the number of previous recall trials. In other words, the organization imposed by the S becomes increasingly fixed and more difficult to exchange for a new organizational schema. Similarly, it is unlikely that the organizational schema can be changed in the late trial of a free recall experiment in order to accommodate items that do not "fit" the previously established categories.

In the experiments presented here, no attempt was made specifically to investigate the power of superordinate categories. Cohen and Bousfield (1956), however, have studied the effect of single and double level of categorization on recall. Using forty word lists, they present data for three kinds of lists: (1) four-category single-level lists with 10 IPC; (2) eight-category single-level lists with 5 IPC; and (3) eight-category dual-level lists, that is, lists with four categories, each of which had two subcategories, and with 5 IPC. In terms of the present analysis, recall should improve in ascending order for these groups. In the first group, Ss must recall 4 categories and 10 IPC; in the second, 8 categories and 5 IPC, and in the last, 4 superordinate categories times 2 subordinate categories with 5 IPC. Taking approximate values for these groups from Fig. 7, the three recall means should be 19.2, 20.1, and 24.1 for lists 1, 2, and 3, respectively. Cohen and Bousfield's data show values of 15.6, 17.6, and 18.1. Since their lists were E-constructed categories, the lower levels of recall can be expected.

Another question that our analysis raises concerns the way in which words in general may be recalled when, for example, somebody is asked to say all the words he can think of, or all the animals or countries. The prediction must be that such recall from general storage should proceed in the same way as the special categorization imposed in the laboratory. Superordinate categories must be followed by subordinate, and so forth until the search system comes to a first-level category, recalls about five words from it, proceeds to another category, and so forth. Bousfield and Sedgewick (1944) have shown that when Ss are asked, for example, to list all the birds they can think of, they will in fact produce these in clusters of subcategories with some evidence that these clusters occur in temporally discriminable sets, that is, with short pauses separating the clusters. In other words, recall from permanent vocabulary storage follows the same general organizational schema as the assignment of specific words in a memory experiment. We can also assume that the categories Ss use in the conceptualization and memory experiments are very similar to those that are represented in free emission. In that sense, the experimental situation simply utilizes the existing organization of the Ss' vocabulary. Some new organization may at times be imposed to accommodate unusual words or clusters, but generally the memory experiment is an experiment on the utilization of existing organizational schemas.

What are the limits of this kind of organization? Taking a value of five per set, we have suggested that the total content of an organizational schema rises exponentially with about five new units per level. It seems possible that the system also needs some limits on the number of levels that can be contained in a single organizational schema. One reason for this is the need to identify the level at which a particular search starts, since the level may influence a decision whether to go down the hierarchy, or up, or across. Similarly, the ease with which one can identify superordinate and subordinate concepts suggests that level identification is both useful and necessary. If levels are identified, we can assume that the limit on this task is also five, which then limits the content, in terms of final units, of an organizational schema to the value of approximately 5^5 or about 11–12 bits. Is this the limit of human memory? By no means; these speculations have only touched on a single schema. Obviously a particular unit may be contained in more than one schema, and some units or words may be in one schema and not in another. It is difficult to determine whether the number of such parallel schemas is in turn limited in light of the vast overlap of different organizations and the very specialized organizations that we construct. However, if such limits do in fact exist, they provide some interesting basis for further investigation into limits on the size of natural language vocabularies. On a highly speculative note, two suggestions might be entertained. First, the organization of any single coherent natural vocabulary may be limited to the value of 5^5 items. It is enticing to note that such divergent vocabularies as the basic sign language of the deaf, the ideographic vocabulary taught to the Japanese school child, and the basic vocabulary taught in foreign language schools all tend to fall at about 1500–2000 items, a value nicely between 5^4 and 5^5.

Second, it is possible that separate, though overlapping, organizational schemas may be organized at a still higher level of schemas of schemas.

Again assuming that the identification of schema membership is necessary for storage and retrieval, such a superorganization would contain another five levels and would produce an estimate of 5^{55} units that could be stored. Such a figure, in contrast to 5^5, is reassuringly large. It involves about 10^{17} units, certainly adequate for storing any reasonable set of human memory units.

A problem that this paper and most psychologists have avoided concerns the functional unit of memory. At the verbal level, a psychologist is tempted to say that the unit of behavior is the word, even though groups of words may, of course, make up larger units. The recent rapprochement between linguistics and psychology, on the other hand, has tempted some to speculate that verbal units may be phonemes or morphemes.

At the theoretical level it is necessary to speak of units as constructs. Such units have the main characteristics of being activated in an all-or-none manner and of being emitted in the same fashion; that is, it is not possible either to activate or emit part of a unit. If such partial activation or emission is possible, this would be prima facie evidence that the unit has constituents. None of these suggestions solve the problem of the psychological unit; they postpone the important issues. Eventually we must come to terms with the theoretical unit, which may be an image, an idea, a word, or a category (cf. Morton and Broadbent, 1964).

For the present we have confined ourselves to nouns, though the organization of other verbal units, such as adjectives or verbs, should follow similar laws. The restriction to nouns has also avoided the problem of the role of syntax in verbal memory, though grammatical considerations obviously play an important role in the organization of memory (cf. Cofer, 1965).

Within these rather restricting limitations, this chapter has talked about the organization of memory. But as we have seen previously, memory—the sheer recovery of a set of units—is just one outcome of organization. Given an organized set of units, we can recall some or all of these units according to rather simple rules. Given knowledge of the organization, we can predict with a fair degree of accuracy the amount of recall that is possible when the system is instructed to emit the constituents of the organized set. In our speculation about the organization of the available vocabulary, we have suggested that any memory experiment with words (that is, with units that are in the vocabulary), is just one way of tapping already existing organizations. In that sense, then, this chapter was not really about organization *and* memory, it was about the organization of parts of the human verbal repertory and it used memory as a way of evaluating what that organization might be. Granted that the conditions of presentation or input present certain limiting conditions for what can or will be recalled, it seems quite certain that the major limit on the memory for words is the organization of verbal units. Such organization is fully developed in adult *S*s and probably changes little over time. If we are to investigate how organization develops, we must go to the developmental study of language, semantics, and verbal behavior. That is probably the only source that will tell us about the development of organizational schemas.

ACKNOWLEDGMENTS

I am extremely grateful to Dr. Donald E. Broadbent of the Applied Psychology Research Unit, Cambridge, England, for making available the congenial facilities of his laboratory, where this chapter was written in July, 1965.

Mrs. Shirley Osler contributed faithful and hard work, imaginative suggestions, and endless patience to the execution and analysis of Experiments B–G. Miss Leslie Waghorn collected the data for the experiment on organizing and recall instructions. I am greatly indebted to William Kessen, George A. Miller, Endel Tulving, and Jean M. Mandler for critical comments on a previous draft of this paper. None of them can be blamed for any errors or misinterpretations that it still contains.

REFERENCES

Bousfield, W. A. The occurrence of clustering in the recall of randomly arranged associates. *J. gen. Psychol.*, 1953, **49**, 229–240.

Bousfield, W. A., Cohen, B. H., & Whitmarsh, G. A. Associative clustering in the recall of words of different taxonomic frequencies of occurrence. *Psychol. Rep.*, 1958, **4**, 39–44.

Bousfield, W. A., Puff, C. R., & Cowan, T. M. The development of constancies in sequential organization during repeated free recall. *J. verb. Learn. verb. Behav.*, 1964, **3**, 489–495.

Bousfield, W. A., & Sedgewick, C. H. W. An analysis of sequences of restricted associative responses. *J. gen. Psychol.*, 1944, **30**, 149–165.

Cofer, C. N. On some factors in the organizational characteristics of free recall. *Amer. Psychologist*, 1965, **20**, 261–272.

Cohen, B. H. Recall of categorized word lists. *J. exp. Psychol.*, 1963, **66**, 227–234.

Cohen, B. H. Some-or-none characteristics of coding behavior. *J. verb. Learn. verb. Behav.*, 1966, 182–187.

Cohen, B. H., and Bousfield, W. A. The effects of a dual-level stimulus-word list on the occurrence of clustering in recall. *J. gen. Psychol.*, 1956, **55**, 51–58.

Cohen, B. H., Sakoda, J. M., & Bousfield, W. A., The statistical analysis of the incidence of clustering in the recall of randomly arranged associates. Tech. Rep. No. 10, ONR Contract Nonr-631(00), Univer. of Connecticut, 1954.

Dallett, K. M. Number of categories and category information in free recall. *J. exp. Psychol.*, 1964, **68**, 1–12.

Garner, W. R. *Uncertainty and structure as psychological concepts.* New York: Wiley, 1962.

Imai, S., & Garner, W. R. Discriminability and preference for attributes in free and constrained classification. *J. exp. Psychol.*, 1965, **69**, 596–608.

Katona, G. *Organizing and memorizing.* New York: Columbia Univer. Press, 1940.

Mandler, G. Verbal learning. In *New Directions in Psychology III.* New York: Holt, 1967.

Mandler, G., & Pearlstone, Zena. Free and constrained concept learning and subsequent recall. *J. verb Learn. verb Behav.*, 1966, **5**, 126–131.

Marshall, G. R., & Cofer, C. N. Associative, category and set factors in clustering among word pairs and triads. Tech. Rep. No. 4, Contract Nonr 285 (47), Office of Naval Research, New York Univer., 1961.

Mathews, Ravenna. Recall as a function of number of classificatory categories. *J. exp. Psychol.*, 1954, **47**, 241–247.

McGeoch, J. A., & Irion, A. L. *The psychology of human learning.* New York: Longmans, Green, 1952.

Melton, A. W. Implications of short-term memory for a general theory of memory. *J. verb. Learn. verb. Behav.*, 1963, **2**, 1–21.

Miller, G. A. The magical number seven, plus or minus two: Some limits on our capacity for processing information. *Psychol. Rev.*, 1956, **63**, 81–97. (a)

Miller, G. A. Human memory and the storage of information. *IRE, Trans. Inf. Theor.*, 1956, **2**, 129–137. (b)

Miller, G. A. *Psychology: The science of mental life.* New York: Harper, 1962.

Miller, G. A., Galanter, E., & Pribram. K. H. *Plans and the structure of behavior.* New York: Holt, 1960.

Morton, J., & Broadbent, D. E. Passive vs. active recognition models or Is your homunculus really necessary. Paper read at the AFCRL Sympos. on models for the perception of speech and visual forms, Boston, November, 1964.

Ozier, Marcia. Alphabetic organization in memory. Unpublished doctoral dissertation, Univer. of Toronto, 1965.

Seibel, R. An experimental paradigm for studying the organization and strategies utilized by individual Ss in human learning and an experimental evaluation of it. Paper presented at meetings of The Psychonomic Soc., Niagara Falls, Ontario, October, 1964.

Tulving, E. Subjective organization in free recall of "unrelated" words. *Psychol., Rev.*, 1962, **69**, 344–354.

Tulving, E. Intratrial and intertrial retention: Notes towards a theory of free recall verbal learning. *Psychol. Rev.*, 1964, **71**, 219–237.

Tulving, E., & Patkau, Jeannette E. Concurrent effects of contextual constraint and word frequency on immediate recall and learning of verbal material. *Canad. J. Psychol.*, 1962, **16**, 83–95.

Tulving, E., & Pearlstone, Zena. Availability versus accessibility of information in memory for words. *J. verb. Learn. verb. Behav.*, 1966, **5**, 381–391.

Underwood, B. J. The representativeness of rote verbal learning. In A. W. Melton (Ed.), *Categories of human learning.* New York: Academic Press, 1964. Pp. 47–78.

Waugh, Nancy C. Free versus serial recall. *J. exp. Psychol.*, 1961, **62**, 496–502.

Waugh, Nancy C., & Norman, D. A. Primary memory. *Psychol. Rev.*, 1965, **72**, 89–104.

Wertheimer, M. Untersuchungen zur Lehre von der Gestalt. I. *Psychol. Forsch.*, 1921, **1**, 47–58.

6

COMMENTARY ON
"ELABORATIVE STRATEGIES
IN VERBAL LEARNING AND MEMORY"

William E. Montague

DEVELOPMENT OF TRAINING TECHNOLOGY PROGRAM
NAVY PERSONNEL RESEARCH & DEVELOPMENT CENTER
SAN DIEGO, CALIFORNIA

Five years after preparing this chapter, it is apparent that the trends of which our research form a part have grown stronger and have created considerable interest. During this period, an overwhelming number of research reports and theoretical discussions have focused on the importance of subjects' use of elaborative strategies, the variables controlling these strategies, and the way in which they affect learning and memory. The chapter was an attempt to describe and to put into the perspective of what was then current theorizing several years of our research efforts at the University of Illinois.

The work began in the early 1960s in paired associate experiments that examined the effect of mediational chaining (Jenkins, 1963) on transfer and resistance to forgetting. Puzzled by the lack of predicted effects in the early experiments, we adopted a procedure that was unusual for that time. We asked subjects to report on their associations to the experimental material in order to see whether or not the expected associations would be reported. We were dismayed to find few reports of the trained mediational chain so laboriously built into the material. At the same time, subjects reported rich and varied sets of "idiosyncratic" associations to the task, which they claimed assisted them in remembering the materials. We dubbed them "natural language mediators" and suggested that they might interfere with experimental manipulations. From that time on, our efforts concentrated on attempts to document and control these normally covert processes in a variety of memory tasks: paired-associates learning, short-term memory, serial learning, incidental learning, and so on. These studies were part of the growing concern for subjects' covert cognitive processing in response to specific and nonspecific task demands.

Using the perspective of information processing models, the chapter attempts to document how processes that are under subjects' conscious control can confound experiments (and experimenters) and produce systematic, but sometimes unwanted, effects on performance. The work represents a small part of of what was a significant shift in the Zeitgeist[1] in the field in reaction to the seeming sterility of simple stimulus–response conditioning conceptions of the learner. The learner is now characterized as more dynamic: He constructs and reconstructs his experiences, consciously interacts with his past memories, and interprets the current situation in order to actively guide or control his performance. Postman (1975), in describing this emphasis, indicates that the language changed from talking about habits, to talking about information processing, storage, and retrieval. Most importantly, perhaps, he noted that research interest was revived in old concepts, such as imagery, attention, consciousness, organization, and mnemonics.[2] This viewpoint has been widely accepted as more representative of the complexity of the processes and stimulus relationships that influence learning and memory.

In order to bring the chapter up to date, no substantial changes in orientation seem warranted by more recent events. To be sure, concern for semantic processing in the paper has blossomed in the field to a concern for levels or depth of processing (e.g., Craik & Lockhart, 1972). The numerous additional studies published, however, simply reinforce the idea that covert cognitive processes in response to task conditions, requirements, or demands have decided effects on recalling the nominal information presented (e.g., see Postman, 1975; Jenkins, 1974; Craik & Tulving, 1975 for summaries). Whether or not these effects are beneficial seems dependent upon the relationship between the task requirements and the way in which retention is measured. There has not been adequate development of a means of specifying depth of processing independently of outcomes on performance (Postman, 1975). One might observe that this trend in research, although it has not produced an adequate theory, has forced experimenters to consider that a large number of contextual variables need to be considered routinely in memory experiments. This may turn out to be the major benefit of the change in outlook.

---

[1] The term Zeitgeist means the spirit or intellectual climate of the time; it is suggested that ideas and theories are accepted or promoted by the dominant thought patterns current in the field of interest (Boring, 1950).

[2] It is interesting to note that these topics had been decreed unworthy of scientific attention by behaviorists who introduced the stimulus–response viewpoint in the first place.

Perhaps this preface is a good place in which to re-emphasize the point made in the chapter that the empirical findings and the general theoretical conception are relevant to instructional practice. They provide a framework for interpreting unexpected results and developing instructional techniques. For example, feedback to students about the correctness of their answers to test questions has been found to be more effective after a delay than when given immediately (e.g., Kulhavy & Anderson, 1972; Sturges, 1969). (Since we had assumed, on the basis of research on rewards and punishments, that feedback must be immediate, this result was disconcerting.) Although no completely satisfying explanation exists, recent studies have demonstrated a complex relatiionship between students' confidence in their responses and differences in cognitive activities produced at the time of feedback (e.g., Sturges, 1972). Other work has focused on "asking people questions about what they are reading," a procedure that improves retention, presumably because it promotes better semantic processing of the instructional content (e.g., see Anderson & Biddle, 1975). The bulk of this work was done in the laboratory. However, in a recent set of experiments testing the effects of adjunct questions on learning from a text in a semester long college course, facilitation of final test performance was obtained (T. Anderson *et al.,* 1974, 1975). Frase (1975) has also discussed how the structure of textual materials is presumed to influence a student's cognitive activities, and, thereby, produce differences in the aspects of the material retained. In addition, development of optimal instructional strategies based on models of student performance has been proposed by Atkinson and Paulson (1972).

Not only can one structure the instructional situation and material in order to promote semantic processing, but one can also train the student to utilize empirically proven techniques. The research in elaborative strategies has reawakened interest in the practical utilization of mnemonic devices (e.g., Atkinson, 1975) and in teaching students to study effectively (e.g., Frase, 1975). These are only a few of the possibilities of practical applications that have been stimulated by research on cognitive strategies. We can expect a considerable increase in such work in the near future.

REFERENCES

Anderson, T. H., Anderson, R. C., Dalgaard, B. R., Paden, D. W., Biddle, W. B., Surber, J. R., & Alessi, S. M. An experimental evaluation of a computer-based study management system. *Educational Psychologist,* 1975, 11, 184–190.

Anderson, T. H., Anderson, R. C., Dalgaard, B. R., Weitecha, E. J., Biddle, W. B., Paden, D. W., Smock, H. R., Alessi, S. M., Surber, J. R., & Klemt, L. L. A computer-based study management system. *Educational Psychologist,* 1974, **11**, 36–45.

Anderson, R. C., & Biddle, W. B. On asking people questions about what they are reading. In G. H. Bower (Ed.), *The psychology of learning and motivation.* Vol. 9. New York: Academic Press, 1975.

Atkinson, R. C. Mnemotechnics in second-language learning. *American Psychologist,* 1975, **30**, 821–828.

Atkinson, R. C., & Paulson, J. A. An approach to the psychology of instruction. *Psychological Bulletin,* 1972, **78**, 49–61.

Boring, E. G. *A history of experimental psychology* (2nd ed.) New York: Appleton, 1950.

Craik, F. I. M., & Lockhart, R. S. Levels of processing: A framework for memory research. *Journal of Verbal Learning and Verbal Behavior,* 1972, **11**, 671–684.

Frase, L. T. Prose processing. In G. H. Bower (Ed.), *The psychology of learning and motivation.* Vol. 9. Pp. 1–48. New York: Academic Press, 1975.

Jenkins, J. J. Mediated associations: Paradigms and situations. In C. N. Cofer & B. S. Musgrave (Eds.), *Verbal behavior and learning.* New York: McGraw-Hill, 1963.

Jenkins, J. J. Remember that old theory of memory? Well, forget it! *American Psychologist,* 1974, **29**, 785–795.

Kulhavy, R. W., & Anderson, R. C. The delay-retention effect with multiple-choice tests. *Journal of Educational Psychology,* 1972, **63**, 505–512.

Postman, L. Verbal learning and memory. *Annual Review of Psychology,* 1975, 291–335.

Sturges, P. T. Information delay and retention: Effect of information feedback and tests. *Journal of Educational Psychology,* 1972, **63**, 32–43.

Sturges, P. T. Verbal retention as a function of the informativeness and delay of information feedback. *Journal of Educational Psychology,* 1969, **60**, 174–177.

Reprinted from *The Psychology of Learning and Motivation*, 1972, **6**, 225–302.

ELABORATIVE STRATEGIES
IN VERBAL LEARNING AND MEMORY

William E. Montague

UNIVERSITY OF ILLINOIS AT URBANA-CHAMPAIGN
URBANA-CHAMPAIGN, ILLINOIS

I. Introduction

During the last ten years or so research and theorizing on verbal learning and memory has gone in a new direction. Gradually, it has become apparent that the learner controls much, and in some cases all of what he learns in experiments relatively independently of the *E*. What has happened is that the *S*, with his mind and his knowledge, his imagination and his reminiscences, has crept back into the research spotlight from which he was banished by the behaviorists. There has been a growing recognition that the *S*s' awarenesses of a task given to him, of what and how to memorize or store the new information, or of how to retrieve or remember it at a later time, are most important topics for understanding learning and retention phenomena. In memorizing, *S*s elaborate tasks and materials; they transform, recode, encode, reorganize, give meaning to, or make sense out of seeming nonsense. In remembering they search and hopefully retrieve the product of that earlier labor, decode it into some communicable form, decide upon its accuracy, and about whether or not to say it. Admittedly, this is a gross, oversimplified, and perhaps an inadequate description of what is involved in memorizing and remembering, but it seems to summarize a point of view held with growing communality (e.g., Adams & Bray, 1970; Atkinson & Shiffrin, 1968; Bower, 1970b; Mandler, 1967b; Norman & Rumelhart, 1970; Paivio, 1971; Saltz, 1971). This view contrasts radically with the older view that memorizing-remembering is simply and directly controlled by external, E-controlled stimuli and stimulus feedback from the environment.

This paper will summarize a variety of lines of research which indicate this change in viewpoints. The scope of the summary is not exhaustive and will attempt to show merely the omnipresence of these subjective control processes in learning and memory tasks, justify the thesis that the prevalence of such processes in memorizing and remembering demands concerted theoretical and experimental attention, and indicate some directions theorization should take.

After a statement of the general orientation which will put the problems in perspective, the bulk of the paper will concentrate on the role of elaborative transformations of nominal verbal materials presented to Ss for memorization.

II. General Orientation—A Memory Model

During the first half of this century, theorists of a behavioristic persuasion dominated research and theorizing about verbal learning. This S-R associationism held that verbal learning phenomena could be understood in terms of the strengthening and/or weakening of bonds of associations between stimuli and responses. These bonds were strengthened via (reinforced) practice. In learning to make a response B in the presence of stimulus or cue A, progress was gradual across repeated trials, i.e., responding became quicker and more accurate. Speed and accuracy of response were measures of association (A-B) strength. Furthermore, the A-B strength would transfer to another task and facilitate or interfere with the new association depending on its similarity to A-B. Very gradually, it became apparent that this associationism, which was conceived of as an extension of a basic conditioning model, could not account for many of the observed phenomena. Primarily, the associationistic model did not require any awareness, comprehension, control, or understanding on the part of the S. More and more research indicated that such cognitive factors were of primary importance in determining the level of performance (see Mandler, 1967b).

For example, older theories of paired-associate learning assumed that the stimulus as presented to the S (nominal stimulus) was identical to the stimulus he used in associative learning (functional stimulus). Some research was done which indicated that this assumption was wrong. In several experiments, Underwood and his colleagues obtained evidence that Ss select or attend to only a part of a complex stimulus in learning (Underwood, 1963; Underwood & Keppel, 1963). Other experiments indicated that Ss transform the stimuli in a variety of ways (e.g., Bower, 1970b; Kiess & Montague, 1965). They organize lists of unrelated words in ways that facilitate recall (e.g., Mandler, 1967a; Tulving, 1968). They are aware of contingencies of reward and, when so motivated, can respond in conformity with the E's instructions (e.g., Dulany, 1968). Adams (1967) indicates that Ss are sensitive to inaccuracy in recall, and they can reject or identify their errors.

Such findings led theorists to favor information-processing models, which emphasize the role played by covert processes and Ss' cognitions in determining performance. Such approaches attempt to analyze the flow of information into discrete stages which are inferred from the results of various kinds of studies. For example, in one experimental paradigm, Ss are presented for a very brief time with arrays of numbers, letters, or forms which exceed their immediate memory span. Only part of the array is to be reported, and the E indicates which, either before, during, or sometime after presentation. The Ss' ability to respond accurately allows inferences to be made about the memory processes involved. Similarly, the common finding of a U-shaped serial position curve in free-recall studies is interpreted as being made up of two curves, each representing output from a different compartment of memory (Glanzer & Cunitz, 1966). The high recall of items at the beginning of the list represents items from long-term storage, while the high recall of items at the end of the list represents items in a short-term storage compartment. Evidence of this kind has resulted in the development of a number of *information processing models* which have considerable similarity to that shown in Fig. 1 (e.g., Atkinson & Shiffrin, 1968; Bower, 1967b; Broadbent, 1958; Mandler, 1967b; Neisser, 1967; Norman, 1969; Sperling, 1963, 1967).

Such models have heuristic and mnemonic value since they are designed to summarize a considerable body of research and provide a source of further sensible hypotheses. The form of the model shown in Fig. 1 has certain obvious similarities in form and details to the models presented by those theorists cited above. There are, however, some changes in emphasis. In representing the flow of information through the system (i.e., the S) a response-monitoring process is

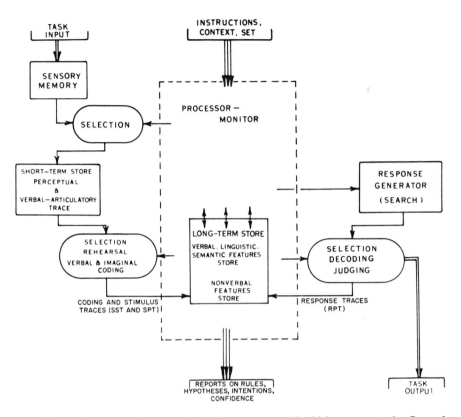

Fig. 1 Schematic of a general verbal memory model which represents the flow of information through the system. Task input is "selected" in terms of task set determined either by instructions or the processor/monitor's own biases which also influence the elaboration of material. Perceptual and coded traces are stored in long-term memory along with traces from responding. In addition to nominal task output, important information is obtained about the functional processes via S reports.

featured together with two types of relatively permanent storage. For the most part, other models have emphasized neither response monitoring nor multiple memory traces. The changes in emphasis are in response to certain research results which will be discussed.

The major parts of the model are the sensory memory (SM), the short-term store (STS), a long-term store (LTS), a response generator, and a processor/monitor. Two kinds of input to this system are shown. The first, which directly affects the way in which the processor reacts to the task, is probably determined by several sources, such as instructions about the task, prior experience with similar tasks, and the demand-characteristics of the task as perceived by the S. All of these factors may influence the "rules of the game" for the processor and, therefore, the behavioral output. The description which follows will refer to the parts and the "flow" of events depicted in Fig. 1.

Incoming information enters the temporary store and resides briefly in SM (Atkinson & Shiffrin, 1968) as an "icon" or "echo" (Neisser, 1967). Briefly occurring arrays of stimuli thus persist for a time and are available for processing when the external input has ceased. Although information in SM rapidly decays, part of it is selected and transferred into a somewhat more permanent STS. Sperling (1963) and Neisser (1967) discuss the effectiveness of the selection process and how it can be controlled. However, the SM is of little importance for most verbal memory tasks, since usually stimulus presentation is of relatively long duration, and one can assume that all relevant information is transferred to the STS.

A most consistent research finding is that the capacity of the STS or the working memory is limited. Miller (1956) in his classic article reviewed a number of diverse lines of research on immediate memory and concluded that the STS can process about 7 ± 2 items. Considerable corroboration of this view has been amassed, and all current theorizing about human memory recognizes this system limitation. The relatively large amount of information in SM is "filtered" or "selected" according to instructions or S biases, and only a limited amount gets transferred into STS.

The form of the representation encoded into STS from or through SM has been the subject of considerable study. Linguistic material presented visually may be encoded into an auditory form. Conrad (1964) found that errors of intrusion for materials presented visually were similar to those found when materials were presented auditorially. Presumably, the encoding from SM is accomplished by implicit speech and resides in STS in an acoustic form. Some evidence for such an encoding process has been provided by Eriksen and his colleagues (e.g., Colegate & Eriksen, 1970; Eriksen, Pollack, & Montague, 1970). In the Colegate and Eriksen study, two groups learned to label nonsense forms with one-or three-syllable responses. A circular array of the forms was then presented tachistoscopically, followed shortly by a bar indicating the position of the figure to be named. The one-syllable labeling group was able to identify more figures correctly than the three-syllable group. Presumably, they were able to encode or label more figures before the information in SM (icon) faded. Thus, there seems to be reasonable agreement that linguistic information (letters, digits, etc.) is often transformed in the selection process into some verbal form (Atkinson & Shiffrin, 1968; Conrad, 1964; Sperling, 1963).

However, there is evidence that nonverbal forms of the information also exist in STS (Posner, 1969). In experiments on short-term motor memory in which Ss were required to remember the location of a hand movement, verbalization plays only a minor role (Posner & Konick, 1966). Yet position information is apparently retained since reliable reduction in error occurs across repeated trials (Adams & Dijkstra, 1966; Montague & Hillix, 1968). Similarly, in studies of tactile memory, where verbal encoding is very unlikely, retention is similar to that for verbal memory, showing a decline with time, repetition, and interference effects, etc. (Bogartz, Helgoe, & Weigel, 1970). Chase and Posner (1965) present evidence for direct visual representation in STS. In a task where an array of four letters was presented either simultaneously with a test letter or where the test letter was shown 1 second after Ss completed a 10-second memorization period, Ss were asked to judge whether or not the test letter was a member of the array. Reaction times to visually confusing arrays of letters were longer than to auditorily or non-confusion arrays. This suggests that the array was present in visual form. Evidence was provided by Kroll, Parks, Parkinson, Breber, and Johnson (1970) that visual aspects of the stored item were retained over periods which exceed that of the SM storage. Therefore, some perceptual trace of the stimulus seems to be present in STS.

In his recently published book, Paivio (1971) presents a convincing argument for the existence of two symbolic representational systems in memory, one a verbal-articulatory system, and the other characterized as nonverbal-imaginal. The major reaction to objects and linguistic stimuli are, therefore, considered to be verbal and/or mental images. The two systems contribute differentially to performance depending on the time, the task, and the material to be learned. For example, in recognition memory and free recall, the concreteness or image-evoking potential of words is of major importance, while in tasks such as immediate memory span where sequence information must be retained, verbalization is most important. The model in Fig. 1, therefore, indicates the two types of storage.

The information in STS may remain there or, under certain conditions, may be stored in a long-term store (LTS). The mechanisms for this transfer are not perfectly clear, but repetition and rehearsal controlled by the processor are probably both primary transfer processes (see Bjork, 1970b). The role of encoding in such transfer has been increasingly recognized in recent publications. Strategies of encoding used by the processor may introduce changes in the information. Presumably, encoding operations relate the information to other material stored already in LTS. Encoding strategies selectively alter or elaborate the information in the STS and may often be very idiosyncratic to a particular S (Adams, 1967; Atkinson & Shiffrin, 1968; Bower, 1967b; Paivio, 1971; Posner, 1969).

Linguistic information which is memorized is stored in LTS in both verbal (Adams, 1967; Baddeley, 1966) and nonverbal forms as indicated by recent evidence concerning imagery (Paivio, 1969, 1971), and in evidence provided by Bahrick and Boucher (1968), Brooks (1968), and Dallett and Wilcox (1968), that visual aspects of a stimulus must be represented in LTS also (Posner, 1969). Therefore, in Fig. 1 the LTS system is represented as having both verbal and nonverbal storage. Adams and Bray (1970) in a closed-loop model for verbal learning and retrieval, theorize that a nonverbal trace is stored and forms the reference for a S's judgment of the correctness of his responses at recall.

Although most current models of memory recognize that responses must be generated to conform to task requirements, they seldom pay close attention to the idea that the S monitors and controls response output. The only detailed examination of response monitoring as an intrinsic part of the storing (learning)-retrieval (recall) sequence of events has been provided by Adams and his colleagues (Adams, 1967; Adams & Bray, 1970; Adams, Marshall, & Bray, 1971; Wearing, 1971b). Their work will be used to describe the sequence of events involved in storing and retrieving information from LTS and will summarize the flow of events in the general memory system in Fig. 1.

In his book *Human Memory,* Adams (1967) recognized that the traditional S-R association model for verbal learning and memory has considerable difficulty in explaining three phenomena. (1) Ss are aware of the correctness of a retrieved covert response and can withhold an overt response when the covert response seems wrong. (2) Sometimes after making an overt response the S recognizes it as incorrect and attempts to retrieve the correct response if it is accessible. He rejects an error. This feature of Ss' behavior is apparent in research reported by R. Brown and McNeil (1966) on "tip-of-the-tongue" behavior. Dictionary definitions of uncommon words were read to Ss who were asked to say the word being defined. In many instances, Ss were unable to recall the word exactly but they were able to write down words which sounded the same, had the same meaning, and could guess the number of syllables or the first letter. When a word was on the "tip-of-the-tongue," they often recalled the first letter or the number of syllables correctly. (3) In similar research, Hart (1965, 1967) had Ss judge their "feeling-of-knowing" for items which they could not recall. Recognition performance on a subsequent test was better for items for which Ss reported a strong feeling-of-knowing than for items with weak reports. These findings suggest that Ss are able to assess the correctness of their overt and covert behavior and they behave appropriately in terms of this knowledge by inhibiting responses or correcting them.

Peterson (1967) also indicates that implicit responses are tested (by the processor/monitor) for correctness before responses are emitted. Those judged incorrect are rejected and another attempt at retrieval is made. Eimas and Zeaman (1963) also infer a response-monitoring system which they use to explain paired-associate learning. They assume that Ss store all information on learning trials and on tests compare their response output with the stored traces. When a match occurs, the association is strengthened (this is called self-reinforcement). A response monitoring process is also implicit in research in which Ss are required to evaluate their confidence in their responses (Adams, 1967; Murdock, 1966; Wearing, 1971b).

A brief review of Adams' account of response-monitoring behavior will provide a summary description of the flow of information and storage in the memory system and will indicate the areas of research to be discussed in more detail. In acquisition, the presentation of an item for learning results in the storage of some kind of perceptual trace (stimulus perceptual trace, SPT_L) and stimulus semantic trace (SST_L) which is the encoded form of the trace from STS. Most learning tasks require Ss to make responses (either covert or overt), and presumably such responses have stimulating effects, i.e., response-produced perceptual trace (RPT_L). Thus, "feedback," generated by making responses as required by most tasks, is stored along with stimulus and semantic (associations, relations) components forming a multicomponent or multidimensional memory trace. At recall, a search process, relying on contextual cues and instructions, retrieves part of the trace and generates a response which itself has perceptual aftereffects (RPT_r). These are compared with other stored components, and if a reasonable match occurs between the response-produced traces stored when learning (SPT_L and RPT_L) and that generated in recall (RPT_r), an overt response will be made. Therefore, in recalling, the semantic components of the memory trace (SST_L) provide the necessary information for response generation, and the feedback from this recall is compared with traces from learning. Subjects are aware of discrepancies between the two sets of traces, and this awareness is the basis for confidence ratings of a response he might make, his feeling of knowing, as well as "tip-of-the-tongue" judgments. The flow diagram of the memory system shows these parts and processes.

Adams' descriptive model provides a rather dynamic characterization of the processes involved in storage and retrieval. The "memory trace" is conceived to be composed of several dimensions, components, or modalities, produced by stimulus input, elaboration of material, and feedback from responding, which is a view held by a number of other theorists also (e.g., Bower, 1967b; Murdock, 1967; Paivio, 1971; Underwood, 1969). Emphasis is placed on remembering as a dynamic process of response generation or reconstruction from some components of the trace, which at completion is judged against other components for adequacy (cf. Bartlett, 1932). Therefore, the model places strong emphasis on Ss' role in memorizing and remembering. Within the frame of reference provided by this model, the remainder of this paper will discuss research concerned with Ss' strategies in verbal learning tasks.

III. Ss' Control of the Transfer of Information into LTS

The purpose of this section is to document in detail the role of the S in determining the storage of information for the long term. There are two primary aspects to this discussion. The first involves the Ss' control over whether or not information is stored. In Fig. 1, this control is represented by the flow of information from STS via a selection processor to LTS. It is not clear at this time how effective this control is, but recent research findings indicate that, at least in some cases, such control determines whether material is retrievable. The second part of this section will document the role of Ss' elaborations of material in LTS.

A. To Store or Not to Store, That Is Selection

There is a considerable amount of evidence that control processes are directly involved in how well verbal materials are retrieved from LTS. Control operations may affect the ways in which material is stored, i.e., whether certain aspects of materials are stored at all.

Traditional theories of acquisition have emphasized the role of external variables and procedures in producing long-lasting effects. Practice or repetition and meaningfulness, for example, are major variables determining recall adequacy. But recent evidence indicates that the effect of such variables is often modified by S biases, intentions, instructions, and encoding strategies.

The recent flurry of research on selective forgetting (e.g., Bjork, 1970a; Bjork, LaBerge, & LeGrand, 1968; Block, 1971; Davis & Okada, 1971; Elmes, Adams, & Roediger, 1970; Weiner & Reed, 1969; Woodward & Bjork, 1971) indicates that the S can somehow differentiate traces, and thereby modify their recallability and ability to interfere with other materials. In selective forgetting experiments, Ss are given a signal that they can forget some of the items presented in the task. The signal might be given with or immediately after an item, or a block of items. The finding of relevance here is that Ss show remarkable ability to "forget" the items as instructed. Bjork *et al.* (1968), for example, had Ss read strings of digits and their color. One or two consonant tetragrams (CCCC) were imbedded among the digits. In one condition, Ss were to recall both consonant strings. In another, colored dots were shown with two digits immediately prior to the second tetragram, informing the Ss to forget the first one. In a control condition only one tetragram was given in a position corresponding to either the first or second position in the other strings. Relative to the control condition, considerable interference in recall was found when Ss had to recall both consonant strings. When instructions to forget were given, the amount of interference was reduced significantly although not completely. Several explanations were postulated for these findings, and subsequent research concentrated on trying to uncover the most plausible one. All of the explanations, however, indicate that the S actively operates on or modifies either the material to be forgotten or what is to be remembered. Bjork *et al.* (1968) and Block (1971) list three hypotheses which could account for the results: (1) *selective erasure,* where the information is erased from STS, thereby reducing proactive interference (PI); (2) *rehearsal,* where the S is able to rehearse the to-be-remembered items more often; and (3) *differentiation,* where Ss can actively code or tag the items to make them different from one another. Block's data along with those of Woodward and Bjork (1971) seem to support the differentiation hypothesis, although a combination of rehearsal and differentiation hypotheses might do as well. As Rundus (1971) indicates, rehearsal may involve repeated attempts to code the material.

The differentiation hypothesis is supported by evidence which shows that the "to-be-forgotten" (F) items remain in memory, although they do not interfere with recall of other items. For example, Block (1971) presented strings of 12 words to Ss sometimes instructing them to forget the first six just prior to presenting the second six. Control sequences contained only the second six words. If all 12 items were to be recalled, reliably poorer performance was observed for the second six words in relation to recall on control sequences (PI). On strings where the first six words were to be forgotten, recall of the second six was about the same level as for controls (release from PI).

After all lists had been presented, Ss were given a recognition test where they were to distinguish words which had been presented from "distractor" words regardless of whether or not they had been cued to forget them. Figure 2 replots Block's data showing that the proportion of the initial six words correctly recognized was the same for items to be forgotten (F) or to be remembered (R). The "C" curve represents the proportion of distractor words identified as having been presented. Woodward and Bjork (1971) and Davis and

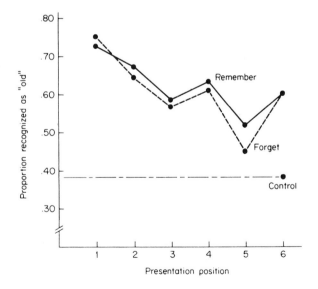

Fig. 2. Mean proportion of to-be-forgotten or to-be-remembered items recognized as "old" compared with the proportion of distractor (control) words recognized. (Redrawn from Block, 1971.)

Okada (1971) also present data indicating that traces of the to-be-forgotten items remain in memory. Therefore, they favor the hypothesis that the release from PI observed in recall is due to differentiation of the to-be-remembered and to-be-forgotten material.

These data also can be taken to substantiate the idea that the basis for recognition is different than that for recall, a hypothesis which has received attention recently (e.g., Adams & Bray, 1970; Kintsch, 1970; Murdock, 1967; Tulving & Thompson, 1971). Recognition depends primarily on perceptual, nonverbal attributes of materials, while recalling may be involved with the storage and retrieval of semantic and response attributes. When Ss perform tasks requiring recall, they rehearse and code materials (e.g., see Rundus, 1971), storing information (attributes) about responding, meaning, and associative relationships. When told to forget some items, this process stops and attention is directed to the other items. On the other hand, as Baddeley and Levy (1971) indicate, perceptual information may be stored more rapidly, and therefore, is affected less or not at all by instructions to forget. In this way, the release from proaction can be interpreted as the result of Ss attempting to memorize the to-be-remembered items for later recall by rehearsing.

It seems reasonable to expect that this rehearsal procedure is not simply repetition (Rundus, 1971), and that it involves differentiation of items in terms of their strength (Battig, 1966) or from coding.

B. INTENTIONAL LEARNING

Other evidence also demonstrates the role of S strategies in memorizing and retrieving. For example, a considerable body of literature exists which investigates the role of Ss' intentions in learning, and intention, as operationalized in experiments, may involve the selective processing or elaboration of materials. The experiments usually involve a comparison between Ss performing on an "orienting task" (that is, where the task requirements do not indicate that recalling at a later time will be important), and those Ss who are told to memorize the material for recall. Superior performance by the latter Ss is interpreted as being due to intention to learn. Perhaps "intention to remember" would be more descriptive.

Results for such experiments show considerable heterogeneity, sometimes finding superiority for intentional (I) over nonintentional (NI) learners, and sometimes not. After reviewing much of these data, Saltz (1971) concludes that only in tasks where the orienting task-set for NI Ss and the learning task-set for the I Ss produces differential processing (and presumably storage), are reliable differences between NI and I groups found. In an experiment by Postman, Adams, and Phillips (1955), for example, NI Ss acted as Es presenting lists of nonsense syllables varying in meaningfulness to I Ss who were told to learn the list. Both NI and I Ss were later asked to recall the lists. Reliable differences in retention were found for lists made up of low-meaningfulness items, while the retention of high-meaningfulness items was about the same for the groups. Since high-meaningfulness syllables are words or near words, they are well integrated or differentiated verbal items. Low-meaningfulness syllables are not. Thus, Ss in both NI and I groups easily attend to, process, and store attributes of well-differentiated items, but for more difficult, unfamiliar items, encoding elaborations of some sort are necessary to differentiate them, and NI Ss may not elaborate material in a way amenable to recalling. If this is the case, then in situations where encodings are provided which act to differentiate the items for NI Ss, or cues for recall are presented, differences between NI and I performance should be reduced or eliminated. Data bearing on this idea were obtained in an experiment in which both NI and I Ss were asked to think of an idiosyncratic, meaningful association to digit pairs (e.g., important dates, addresses, telephone numbers, etc.). No difference in retention between NI and I groups was found (Saltzman, 1956). In a recent extension of Saltzman's study, Montague, Gibbs, and Baechle (1971a) asked Ss, only half of whom were aware that a recall test would be given, to give associations or codings to 50 digit pairs, half of which were high and half low-association value (as rated by Battig & Spera, 1962). A free-recall test was given followed by a recognition test containing all digit pairs from 00-99.

Although high-association value digits were recalled almost twice as well as low-association value pairs ($F = 167.4, p < .01$), the NI-I instruction produced no difference in recall ($F = 1.04$). There was, however, a significant interaction between instructions and association value ($F = 7.62, p < .05$). Fewer low-association value pairs were recalled by NI Ss, a finding which agrees with that of Postman et al. (1955), where poorly differentiated items were more poorly recalled. Fewer associations were given by NI Ss to the low-association value digits, however, but recall proportions for those items were about the same as the corresponding proportions for I Ss. No significant differences were observed in recognition between the groups, although more high- than low-association value items were recognized correctly.

Additional data indicating that associations given to items facilitate recalling have been obtained by Wearing (1971a). He compared three groups of Ss who learned four lists of 20 CVC pairs (which were all words or near words) after giving them different instructions. All the Ss were asked to give some sort of association to each pair, but one group (NI) was not told about an impending recall test. That group generated only about half as many (35 for the 80 pairs) associations as did the other groups (65 and 62), and they recalled reliably fewer items. Wearing considers that the critical factor in recall is whether or not associations were generated for the pairs. Since the NI Ss generated fewer associations, they recalled fewer items.

In another study, Postman et al. (1955) reported no performance advantage for I learners in cued recall, while in free recall, a reliable difference was found. They had NI and I groups rate a list of adjectives in terms of the frequency of use in speech. Recall was either free or cued by strong associatively connected words which should be facilitative or by remotely connected words which should elicit competing words. In free recall, I Ss recalled reliably more than NI Ss, but in both cued-recall tasks, recall was about equal for I and NI groups.

Saltzman's (1956) data and those from the Montague et al. (1971a) and Wearing (1971a) studies suggest that elaboration of material provides a basis for recalling. Saltz (1971) relies on data such as these to theorize that when I learners recall more than NI learners a differentiation process is responsible, which is the same hypothesis preferred by Bjork (1970a) and Block (1971) to explain results found in experiments on selective forgetting. However, even when recall differences exist, material can be made accessible, either by cuing recall (Postman et al., 1955) or by having Ss identify the material they have seen (Montague et al., 1971a; Saltzman, 1956). Sufficient memory storage occurs in the orienting task to provide a basis for recognizing but not recalling, a fact which suggests that different storage dimensions or attributes are responsible for the two kinds of retention tests (Adams, 1967; Bower, 1967b; Estes & DaPolito, 1967; Kintsch, 1970; Underwood, 1969). Intentional learners probably store additional attributes via rehearsal and/or elaboration of material which facilitates recalling. On the other hand, in some orienting tasks, NI Ss store only relatively simple, unelaborated attributes, e.g., perceptual aspects of the material. When such is the case, superiority of I over NI Ss in recall occurs, which can be overcome by insuring that NI Ss elaborate the materials in the orienting tasks, or by providing external cues for recall, or by using a recognition task where the materials are immediately present. Therefore, the differences in recalling sometimes observed between I and NI Ss may be explained by differential strategies used by Ss in response to task requirements, which results in somewhat different sets of attributes being memorized.

The next section discusses the role in memorization of rehearsal and encoding procedures used by Ss in response to task requirements. Once the material is held in the STS, the S directs his attention to certain aspects of the material, rehearsing it or transforming it, which in turn determines various aspects of the features or attributes stored in LTS, and therefore, subsequent retrievability. The next section will briefly review certain aspects of rehearsal strategies wherein transformation of the material is seen to play a minor role, and the following sections will deal with research on encoding strategies where transformations are of primary importance.

C. Rehearsals and Natural Language Mediation

1. Rehearsal Strategies

We recognize that the simplest procedure an S can engage in to attempt to remember materials is to rehearse it. In fact most experimental paradigms used to study memorization attempt to control rehearsal by manipulating trials or exposures to items to be remembered by the amount of time allowed for studying items, by filling intervals with irrelevant tasks, or by instructions to rehearse in a particular manner. The main problem of control, of course, is that an S's overt behavior may conform to the task as set forth by the Es, while his covert behavior may not. On the simplest level we often assume that rehearsal is merely a repetition of the material whether it is overt or covert. There is some question about this idea, since rehearsal may represent the S's repeated attemps to relate the items to be learned to his existing store of linguistic and other knowledge, i.e., encode the material (Bower, 1970b; Neisser, 1967; Rundus, 1971). However, under certain experimental circumstances, we are reasonably confident that simple rehearsal is probable. The immediate concern is for its control by the E or by the S and its effect on recall.

Psychologists have consistently held the belief that the quality (or strength) of a memory depends on practice. More recently, memory models assume that rehearsal effects transfer of information into LTS (e.g., Atkinson & Shiffrin, 1968, 1971). Some evidence which is taken to demonstrate the role of covert rehearsal comes from Es in which Ss are given lists of items to recall in any order. In such studies, the common finding is that the most recently presented items are recalled best (recency effect), and the first several items on the list are recalled next best (primacy effect). If the recall of the list is delayed for a time after the last item is presented by having Ss perform an irrelevant task, the recency effect disappears but the primacy effect is unaffected (e.g., Glanzer & Cunitz, 1966; Postman & Phillips, 1965). The interpretation given these data is that the early items were covertly rehearsed and had been transferred to LTS, while the last items were still in STS. The filler task prevents rehearsal of these items. Other procedures which prevent rehearsal also result in losing the recency effect. If the recall of the last items is prevented by making Ss recall the list in serial order, recency is severely reduced (e.g., Tulving & Arbuckle, 1963). In order to implicate rehearsal more directly, Rundus and Atkinson (1970) asked Ss to rehearse aloud the words from a list as it was presented, and recorded the vocalizations on a tape recorder. The standard U-shaped serial position curve was found showing the primacy and recency effects. The analysis of protocols revealed that the early items on the list were rehearsed more often than other items, and that except for the last few words in the list, recall probability closely paralleled the number of rehearsals. The recency effect presumably depends on retrieval from STS and is not dependent on the number of rehearsals. More recently, Rundus (1971) utilized this procedure to clarify certain phenomena prevalent in free-recall data. For instance, the Von Restorf effect is that distinctive items inserted in a list are recalled with a probability higher than that for other items in the list. Rundus reports an increase in rehearsal frequency for distinctive and adjacent items which is associated with the higher recall for those items. In another experiment, in which words from different categories were included in the list, the recorded rehearsals indicated that Ss rehearsed together items from the same category. Therefore, the "organization" or clustering in recall (Mandler, 1967a; Tulving, 1968) is a manifestation of the S's rehearsal strategies. Examination of trial-by-trial rehearsal protocols for Ss reveals the development of organization.

Since rehearsals play such an important role in producing phenomena in free recall, it should be possible to modify the results by controlling Ss' rehearsals.

Atkinson and Shiffrin (1971) report an experiment comparing Ss given two different rehearsal strategies (see also, Fischler, Rundus, & Atkinson, 1970). One group rehearsed each word three times prior to the presentation of the next word (one-word strategy), the other rehearsed the three most recent items (three-word strategy). Using the second rehearsal strategy thereby produces more rehearsals for the early items than using the first. For example, in a list: house, cow, map, foot, . . . etc., the one-word strategy would result in the following protocol: "house, house, house; cow, cow, cow; map, map, map; foot, foot, foot; etc. . . ." The second strategy produces this sequence of rehearsals: "house, house, house; cow, cow, house; map, cow, house; foot, map, cow; etc. . . ." In the latter case, house receives five rehearsals, cow receives four, and so on. Recall probability for Ss using the second procedure shows a standard primacy effect for the early positions, while no primacy is found for the one-item rehearsal strategy.

Covert rehearsal that is S-controlled is implicated also in experiments using other procedures. In Peterson and Peterson's study (1959) short-term memory paradigm trigrams are presented briefly for memorizing, and the short retention interval which follows is filled with an irrelevant task. The purpose of the irrelevant filler task is to prevent covert rehearsal, but Ss often report being able to rehearse the criterion item while performing the filler task (e.g., Groninger, 1966; Keppel, 1965; Neimark, Greenhouse, Law, & Weinheimer, 1965). When different filler tasks are used, different levels of recall of the criterion items are found. This seems to be a result of both the amount of rehearsal possible with a particular filler task and the filler task's similarity to the criterion material (Loess & McBurney, 1965; Posner, 1966). Posner (1966) and Dillon and Reid (1969) argue that the degree of attention demanded by the filler task is the important factor here. Where the filler task requires a high degree of concentration, rehearsal of the criterion task at the same time should be low. With a simple filler task Ss can "think about" and rehearse criterion items during the retention interval.

Recent data obtained by Hillix and Peeler (1967) document the effect of rehearsal during the retention interval. Using Peterson and Peterson's paradigm, with backward counting as the filler task, they asked Ss to report each time they "practiced the trigram" or if the trigram "came to mind" during a 30-second retention interval by pressing a button. Overall, correct recall was found to be a function of the number of rehearsals. However, Ss differed widely in terms of the frequency with which they reported rehearsals which produced

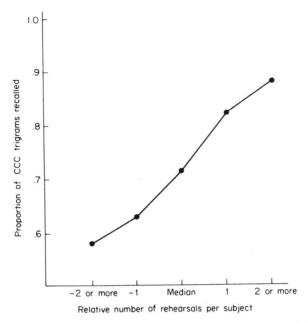

Fig. 3. The mean proportion of consonant trigrams correctly recalled per trial as a function of the number of rehearsals more or less than each *S*'s median number of rehearsals calculated over all trials. (Data taken from Hillix and Peeler, 1967.)

data of considerable variability. Therefore, it was necessary to take this ability factor into account by analyzing and reporting the data in reference to each *S*'s own performance. Figure 3 shows some of their results. To control for individual differences in overall rehearsal frequency, rehearsals are plotted relative to the median number of rehearsals reported by each *S* across all trials. All *S*s are represented at the three middle points, and 19 of 20 *S*s contributed observations to all five points. On any trial, if an *S* reported one rehearsal *fewer* than his median number, the probability of his being wrong is about twice the probability of his being wrong if he reported one *more* rehearsal than his median number. Thus, covert rehearsal is a powerful variable influencing recall even though *S*s must intersperse these rehearsals with performance of the filler task. Hillix and Peeler also reported that the greatest frequency of rehearsal reports occur within a few seconds after the retention interval begins. There is a rapid drop initially and then a gradual decrease in frequency during the remainder of the retention interval. Other studies, too, have found recall to be a function of covert rehearsals (e.g., J. Brown, 1958;

Sanders, 1961), but in those studies no direct reports of rehearsals were made. Rehearsals were presumed to occur during unfilled intervals.

The ability of Ss to rehearse during the retention interval even while performing another task becomes a problem when task requirements identify some items as somehow more important or otherwise different than others. For example, in recent experiments using Peterson and Peterson's paradigm, Weiner and Walker (1966) and Kernoff, Weiner, and Morrison (1966) examined the effects of incentives on short-term memory for items. They found that rewarded items were recalled better than nonrewarded items, and they concluded that incentives directly influenced the quality of the memory trace. Closer examination of the task requirements suggests that the effect of incentives is mediated by differential rehearsal during the filler task (Tarpy & Glucksberg, 1966; Wickens & Simpson, 1968) rather than direct effects upon the memory trace. Recent data from our laboratory will be used to demonstrate the role of rehearsal in mediating the recall differences (Montague, Hillix, Kiess, & Harris, 1970).

We first ran a study examining the effect of rewarding Ss for recalling CVC syllables using the Peterson's paradigm with digit reading as the filler task. Two groups were used, one was rewarded with 5¢ for each CVC recalled, and the other group was not rewarded. No reliable differences in recalling were found between the two groups, a finding at variance with Weiner and Walker (1966) and Kernoff et al. (1966). Our tentative hypothesis was that Ss were more likely to react differently to rewarded and unrewarded items when they are contrasted with one another within the same list. In fact, all previous studies had utilized this "within-Ss" procedure. Therefore, in a second experiment we presented CCC trigrams, half of which were rewarded and half not, and we used digit reading as the filler task. During digit reading, Ss were to report repetition of the CCC by pressing a switch. Since we were concerned with variation in task requirements, on some trials performance on the filler task was rewarded also. Thus, prior to a trial Ss were told that 5¢ was (or was not) offered for correctly recalling the trigram, and 1¢ was (or was not) offered for each row of digits correctly read. Rehearsals of the CCC and digit reading were expected to vary with the various incentive conditions and with the retention intervals (5 and 30 seconds). They did. Figure 4 shows the mean number of rehearsals reported for the four incentive combinations over the two retention intervals. The differences in number of rehearsals at 5 seconds was

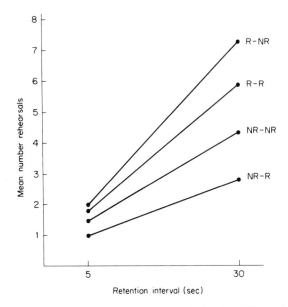

Fig. 4. Mean number of reports of trigram rehearsals for the different incentive conditions over the retention intervals. R indicates reward and NR indicates no reward was given for the trigram or the filler task. (Redrawn from Montague *et al.*, 1970.)

not significant but at 30 seconds was highly so. More rehearsals occurred in the condition where the trigram rather than the digit reading was rewarded (R-NR). Similarly, fewer rehearsals were found over 30 seconds for the condition where digits and not trigram recall were rewarded (NR-R). The other conditions were intermediate. The rehearsal data were reflected in the number of trigrams correctly recalled, i.e., more correct recalls in the R-NR condition than for the NR-R condition after 30 seconds but not after 5 seconds. Therefore, *S*s are able to selectively rehearse them in spite of the filler task if the task requirements "demand" it.

These studies demonstrate that "simple" rehearsal or repetition is an important factor in storing items in LTS. Considerably more complete summaries of the effects of rehearsals can be found in Kintsch (1970) and Norman (1970). However, other aspects of rehearsal may be even more important in determining remembering from LTS. These aspects involve coding or elaborating the material to be learned for more effective retrieval.

2. Natural Language Mediation

Emphasis on an S's capability to modify or elaborate material to be memorized in terms of what he already knows has increased during the last 10 or 15 years. Current memory models recognize that the S controls coding or encoding of materials in many experiments (e.g., Adams, 1967; Atkinson & Shiffrin, 1968, 1971; Norman & Rumelhart, 1970). On the basis of their past knowledge, Ss *choose* to relate selected information from their LTS to the immediate task materials. In this way they transform nominal materials into functionally different materials. These transformations or elaborations constitute what is learned or stored in verbal learning experiments. This section will summarize some evidence regarding such transformations and their role in learning and recalling.

The conception that an S's coding of material presented to him is an important consideration in memory research, began its rise to recent popularity with George Miller's restatement of the nineteenth century philosopher William Hamilton's observation that the span of apprehension is limited to about seven items (Miller, 1956). Although immediate memory can absorb about seven items at once, the items can be information-poor or information-rich. Thus, if an S can organize or code presented materials into "information-richer" units or chunks, more can be recalled immediately. Miller's well-known description of Smith's research on coding digit strings exemplifies this point. Smith found his memory span for strings of zeros and ones (binary digits) to be about 12. He trained himself to code the binary digit strings so that groups of three digits represented single digits in the octal number system. By then, he had increased his ability to recall binary digit strings to over 36 digits. The number of octal digits he remembered was still about 12, but these are decodable into the long string of binary digits.

Miller later argued that all learning of verbal materials (beyond immediate memory span) is a product of coding and recoding of materials, or in his terms, creating a PLAN for retrieval (Miller, Galanter, & Pribram, 1960). The argument goes that the individual codes information into chunks, and these chunks are organized as parts of still larger chunks, which gives a sort of hierarchical structure to memory (Mandler, 1967a) and permits the retrieval of larger amounts of information from LTS. In such storage or memorizing, the role of the learner is important since he must actively code materials for storage in terms of what he already knows. The retrieval

PLAN's that Ss generate for materials are often very idiosyncratic in nature, and an example from Miller *et al.* (1960) demonstrates this well. An *S* was asked to memorize this list of nonsense syllables: BOF, XAJ, MIB, ZYQ. The following description of how he learned the list was given:

> Now, that first nonsense syllable, BOF, was just plain remembered the way it came, but the second one reminded him of 'XAJerate,' the third one turned into 'MIBery,' and the fourth turned from ZYQ to 'not sick.' So he had a kind of sentence, 'BOF exaggerates his misery because he is not sick,' instead of the cryptic BOF, XAJ, MIB, ZYQ, and he could imagine a hypochondriac named BOF who continually complained about his health [Miller *et al.*, 1960, p. 126].

The syllables were transformed into words, and the words were integrated into meaningful phrases and sentences. Since these coding procedures change the nominal nonlanguage items into functional items which are meaningful in the *S*'s natural language system, we refer to the process as "natural language mediation," and refer to the codes for specific nominal items as natural language mediators or NLM's (Adams, 1967; Kiess & Montague, 1965; Montague, Adams, & Kiess, 1966; Prytulak, 1971). Presumably, where materials, time, *S* instructions, and strategies permit, NLM codes are devised and memorized. Recall of the NLM code may present a decoding problem, as is indicated in the continuation of the description of the *S*'s protocol reported above by Miller *et al.*

> That MIBery-misery association wasn't too good, however, because for two or three trials through the list he remembered MIS instead of MIB. But he finally worked it out by thinking of 'mibery' as a new word meaning 'false misery.'

If a coded compound is retrieved at recall, performance accuracy depends on how easily the NLM can be decoded into the form required in the task.

As is apparent from the description of the *S*'s protocol taken from Miller *et al.* above, one way of documenting the use of NLM's comes from *S* reports taken at the time material is presented or after several learning trials. Although procedures of this sort were common early in the century (e.g., see Müller, 1911; Reed, 1918), they fell into disrepute until revived in the early 1960s. In recent research two general types of procedures have been used to examine the effect of coding on learning and remembering. The first to be discussed will be questioning Ss about their idiosyncratic, spontaneous encoding during or after learning materials are presented. For the most part, this research documents the correlation between recall performance and the Ss' reports. Another approach has been to attempt to externalize the coding process either by instructing Ss to form NLM codes in one way or another, training Ss to use certain coding procedures, or by presenting particular codings along with the material. Since these procedures rely on covert aspects of Ss' behavior, the results from experiments are sometimes difficult to interpret. Obviously, when an S reports an NLM for an item, it is difficult to decide whether the encoding report reveals an intrinsic and important part of the process of memorizing and retrieving verbal material. Similarly, there is no way of guaranteeing that Ss follow instructions or employ a coding device given to them by an E. The decision about the relevance of the reports and instructional procedures depends on the consistency of the experimental results across various methodologies. The next sections describe some of the relevant research.

a. *Research Relying on Reports of NLM Use.* Although some mention was made of NLM's in learning research during the period between about 1920 and 1960, nothing much was done about them since they were considered not to be important to the understanding of the learning process. Apparently, they were considered merely to contribute random variation to task performance and not to interact with other variables. In the early part of this century, Reed (1918) reported that "associative devices" were used by Ss to assist their learning and remembering of verbal materials. In form they were quite diverse, often consisting of sentences, words, sound similarities, etc. The presence of such "aids" was recognized by subsequent investigators, such as McGeoch (McGeoch & Irion, 1952; Woodworth & Schlosberg, 1954), but the importance of their relation to performance and other experimental variables was not explored systematically. In a discussion of paired-associate learning, Köhler (1947) in citing evidence from Müller (1911) went so far as to suggest that NLM's were the natural way such learning was effected by Ss. However, no direct research approach was taken.

Study of implicit verbal mediation was undertaken in complex experiments on transfer among lists of paired associates. The general assumption was that connections between verbal items could be established by their common association with a third item. Using this idea as a model, one could imagine successive steps in associative chains so that if item A was associated with B, and B with C, and C with D, a mediated connection between A and D was automatically established. Attempts were made to demonstrate that such chaining occurred and was assumed to be the probable basis for many associative relationships observed in our language. Experiments were done in which Ss learned successive lists arranged to establish mediational chains, e.g., A-B, B-C, A-C. Mediational facilitation is demonstrated if Ss who learn the successive lists learn faster than other Ss for whom the B-C training is omitted. The connection between the A, B, and C items was thought to be automatic, needing no cognitive awareness of the relationships between the lists to produce facilitation. In fact, awareness was often specifically denied (Bugelski & Scharlock, 1952; Horton & Kjeldergaard, 1961). When more complex chains involving several intermediate steps (e.g., A-B-C-D) were investigated, mediational facilitation became more difficult to find. The failures to find mediational facilitation indicated to some researchers that "cognitive understanding" or "awareness" on the part of the S was necessary for facilitation to occur. Jenkins (1963, p. 221) suggested that "The mediating process itself must be elicited and reinforced." Mandler (1963) expressed a preference for viewing mediational processes as conceptual in nature, involving the specific application of rules of a logical nature to such tasks. Horton (1964) found that Ss who reported being aware of the relation between the lists demonstrated greater facilitation. In his experiment, Ss learned lists in chaining paradigms (e.g., A-B, B-C, A-C). He instituted specific questioning after the final list was learned to ascertain whether an S recognized or was aware of the relationship between the lists he learned. From answers to his questions he was able to classify Ss into three classes: unaware, marginally aware but unclear, and completely aware. Unaware Ss' performance showed no mediational facilitation, while increasing amounts of facilitation were found for the two classes of aware Ss. Runquist and Farley (1964) and R. B. Martin and Dean (1964) also indicated that mediational facilitation was found only when Ss reported knowledge of the organization of the lists. Using an A-B, B-C, C-D, A-D paradigm where the B-C and C-D associations were inferred from association norms, Martin and Dean asked Ss how they had learned each A-D pair. Mediational facilitation of performance on A-D was found only when Ss could indicate explicitly the relationships between the B and D items.

Alexander Wearing and I performed an experiment which obtained data from an examination of Ss' NLM reports which clearly shows that Ss attend to the relationships between the lists in a chaining paradigm. Groups of Ss learned two (CVC-word) lists in an A-B, (B-C), A-C paradigm where, for a "mediation" group, the B-C relation was taken from free association norms. An "interference" group learned lists where the B and C items were unrelated, and for a "control" group the first list items were unrelated (D-B A-C). After each list was learned to criterion, Ss were asked to report how they learned each pair, then, after 24 hours, they returned and were tested for recall.

Fewer errors were made by the mediation Ss in learning the A-C list than the control and the interference Ss made. The data of importance here comes from a comparison between the reports given for the two lists by the different groups. The reports obtained for the first list were classified into NLM, Rote, and Forgot categories. The same was done for the second list. Then, another classification was made by comparing the reports made by each S for related items of the two lists. "Related NLM's" were those in which the NLM code generated for the first list item was included in or semantically related to that reported for the second list item. Another category was labeled as "Different" when the two NLM's were unrelated. If items on the second list were learned by "Rote", or if Ss "Forgot" how they learned the item, they were counted in those categories. Figure 5 contains a histogram which shows the proportions of reports falling into the various categories for the different groups. In about 85% of the cases for the mediation group, the NLM's were judged to be related, while only 19% for the interference group were related. There seems little doubt that the Ss in the mediation group recognized and utilized the relationships between the lists in generating NLM's while learning the second list. When less obvious relationships among list items in mediation paradigms are used, this commonality decreases. In other studies done in our laboratory in which the mediational chain was established by the sequence of lists (e.g., A-B, B-C, A-C) rather than via association norms, a direct, obvious, relationship between NLM's in learning the A-B and A-C lists is less apparent. More idiosyncratic NLM's are used, and only about 20% of them were judged to be related.

Another research paradigm added some impetus to the consideration of the S's role in controlling what and how he learns when asked to learn verbal material. The fact that Ss develop consistent recall orders when given lists of words to learn directed attention toward organizational factors in memory (Bower, 1970b; Mandler, 1967a; Tulving, 1968). The S, it developed, was not passive in memorizing materials, and his role in organizing the material determines how much he recalls.

Yet another indication that covert mediational processes influence learning can be taken from the interest shown in the role of the meaningfulness of materials which have been used in verbal learning experiments. The number of associates a syllable or word arouses is recognized to be related to its learnability and retainability. Con-

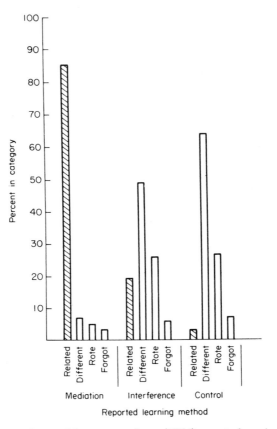

Fig. 5. Percent of natural language mediator (NLM) reports for pairs on the two lists falling into the various categories for the groups receiving the different paradigms.

sequently, we have a number of scalings and ratings of nonsense syllables in which "meaningfulness" is defined as either the number of associations an S gives or thinks he can give to a stimulus item (e.g., Noble, 1952) or the association value, i.e., the number of Ss able to give an association to the item (e.g., Archer, 1960). Theorizing explains the effects of these measures on learning by assuming that the more associates syllables have the more likely it is that already established associations can mediate a connection between two paired associates or provide an easy path to recall for a single item (e.g., see Underwood & Schulz, 1960). Until recently (e.g., Clark, Lansford, & Dallenbach, 1960; Prytulak, 1971), no direct attempt was made to document in detail how such covert procedures might be accomplished. Research concentrated simply on the correlation of scaled meaningfulness and rates of learning or level of recall.

The general reluctance to consider Ss' reports as evidence for covert mediational activity relevant to learning and remembering began to change in the early 1960s. Underwood and Schulz (1960, pp. 296-300) discuss a study by Mattocks in which paired associates composed of low-meaningfulness stimulus terms and high-meaningfulness response terms were learned using the anticipation method. The Ss reported using NLM's as learning aids for 73% of the items. Also, those items with NLM reports had more correct anticipations during learning than those without NLM's. Clark *et al.* (1960) made a similar report, as did Bugelski (1962) who was studying item presentation time effects in learning paired associates. Using 6, 8, 10, 12, or 19 seconds as item presentation times, Bugelski found that total time to learn the list (presentation time × items × trials) was essentially constant. He questioned Ss regarding their use of NLM's and found such reports increased with presentation time, and that out of the 160 possible item-by-subject combinations for each group, the proportion of NLM's reported varied between 59 and 79%.

In a study done in the Illinois laboratory, Kiess and Montague (1965) instituted a change in procedure in an attempt to document further the role of NLM's in paired-associate learning. The earlier studies questioned Ss after learning. In the revised procedure Ss studied each of eight (low-meaningful stimuli, high-meaningful response) pairs for 5 seconds, then attempted to recall the appropriate response for each stimulus presented for 5 seconds. Immediately, on another test trial, they were asked again to recall each response, if possible, and also to report how they learned the pair, whether they merely repeated the items (classed as "No NLM"), employed an NLM, or just tried to guess. Their responses were tape recorded. This study, test, question-test procedure continued for eight trials. Figure 6 shows the basic results. In the top part of the Figure, the use of NLM's is seen to increase consistently over the trials. On the eighth trial, 73 items (of 80) were correct, and of these, NLM's had been reported for 75%. The number of No NLM items increased slightly (and significantly) over the trials, but number of guesses did not. The NLM's are used on all trials for some items, and they increase in frequency with repeated exposure to the list. This frequency is highly correlated with correct recall. The lower portion of the Figure shows results for another group of Ss who received a different list on each trial. Although those curves show slight increases over trials in number of NLM and No NLM reports, they are insignificant. There-

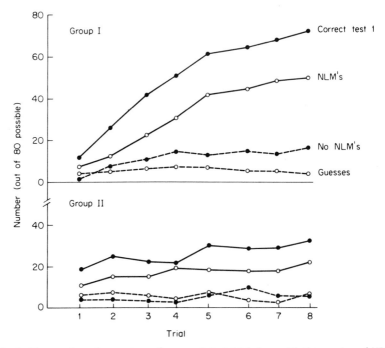

Fig. 6. The number of correct recalls on each test trial along with the number of NLM, No-NLM, and guess reports. Group I learned a list of paired CVC's, and Group II saw different list on each trial. (Data from Kiess and Montague, 1965.)

fore, NLM use is not simply a response to the demands of the task.

Further evidence for the importance of NLM's in learning and recalling paired associates comes from a study by Montague *et al.* (1966). Their results showed that items for which NLM's were reported at learning greatly enhanced recall performance a day later. A list of 96 CVC pairs was presented once. Different groups of *S*s had either 15 or 30 seconds to write down an NLM for a pair if they could. The pair items were both either high or low in meaningfulness. At recall a day later, *S*s were asked to recall the response for each stimulus item *and* the NLM or other mode of learning if they could. These results are summarized in the histogram shown in Fig. 7. The recall proportions for high (H) and low (L) meaningfulness pairings presented for either 15 or 30 seconds is shown in terms of whether the NLM code at recall was the *Same*, had *Changed*, or learning was by *Rote* repetition. The effect of NLM's on recall is immediately apparent. If the same encoding is reported at recall, performance is

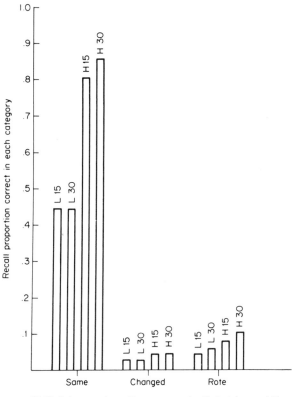

Fig. 7. Proportion of correct recalls of low (L) and high (H) meaningfulness items which had been presented for either 15 or 30 seconds. They were classified as to whether the learning-mode report at recall mentioned the same NLM or one different from that used in acquisition, or was rote in both cases. (Data taken from Montague *et al.*, 1966.)

very good (mean recall proportion .73); if it is changed or forgotten, recall is very poor (proportion of recall about .02). If, in learning and recalling, *S*s reported no NLM coding, recall is also very poor (proportion of correct recalls .06). These results suggested that learning consisted of storing the CVC-NLM-CVC compound, and that when the compound was changed, correct reconstruction of the response was improbable.

In an attempt to determine whether NLM's affect primarily learning or remembering, Thomas Nelson, John Carter, and I recently carried out extensions of the Montague *et al.* experiment. In one study, 16 Ss saw 45 CVC-word pairs, each presented once for 15 seconds while they wrote down any NLM they used for each pair. In order to examine which items had actually been memorized, an immediate recall test was given. The relation between recall level and coding was readily apparent in the data. The probability of recall given that an NLM was reported during the study trial was .48, and that if no NLM was reported was .20. After a week, the Ss returned for another recall test. In this case, our primary concern was for the recall proportion for items in the NLM or No NLM classes which had been correct on the immediate test. These conditional proportions were .53 for items with NLM's correct on the first test and .31 of the items with no NLM, a significant difference, $(t(15) = 2.22, p < .05)$. Thus, items with NLM's which are available on an immediate test are recalled a week later somewhat better than those items immediately available without NLM's. This suggests that such coding devices facilitate remembering. In another experiment, 80 high-association value CVC-Noun pairs were studied for 15 seconds each by 16 Ss, and then 40 pairs were selected for an immediate recall test. Again, while studying each pair and when recalling, Ss wrote any NLM that came to mind. Once again, there was a reliable difference in the proportion of immediate correct recalls for the NLM (.49) and No NLM (.24) classifications. On a retention test given 1 week later, of those items correct on the immediate recall test having generated an NLM 61% were correct, and for those eliciting No NLM 48% were correct, an insignificant difference favoring items with an NLM. For the 40 pairs given no immediate test, the overall recall level was much lower than for those items tested immediately, $F(1,15) = 15.76$, $p < .001$. Only 3% of the rote items and 11% of the items with NLM's were correct after 1 week, a significant difference, $F(1,15)8.48$, $p < .01$. These results generally confirm the results of Montague et al. (1966). More pairs for which Ss generate NLM's in study are recalled on an immediate recall test and when recall is delayed for a week. Data in the second experiment also demonstrated the strong relationship between recall of the NLM and recall of the item. Of the items learned with NLM's, if the NLM is recalled exactly, 86% of the recalls were correct on the immediate test. At 1 week (for items tested immediately), 97% of the items are recalled when their NLM's are correctly recalled. Performance was somewhat lower for items tested after only 1 week (and not immediately); 26 out of 35 instances where NLM's were recalled were correct. This result suggests that an initial recall test provides important learning about decoding the NLM.

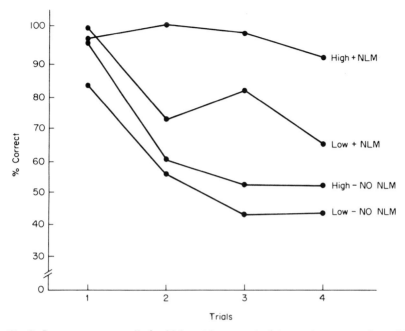

Fig. 8. Percent correct recalls for high and low meaningfulness trigrams over four trials for items with and without reported NLM codings. (Redrawn from Groninger, 1966.)

Recall for single items for which an NLM code was reported has been the subject of several experiments. Groninger (1966) used Peterson and Peterson's paradigm with high- and low-association value consonant trigrams, and questioned Ss after each of four 30-second recall tests about forming an NLM or otherwise rehearsing the trigram. Figure 8 summarizes some of the data. The apparent difference between groups receiving high- and low-association value trigrams with and without NLM's is highly significant. For the high-association value items about 50% were reported with NLM's on the first trial and about 65-70% on succeeding trials. The proportion of NLM-use reports for low-association value trigrams increased over the four trials from about 20% on the first trial to about 40% on the fourth. The usual proaction effect found over a series of trials is modified considerably by the presence of NLM's. With NLM's less proaction occurs. Without NLM's, high- and low-association value items are not appreciably different.

In subsequent, more elaborate studies, Kiess (1968) varied levels of association value, exposure times, and retention intervals, and

TABLE 1

DATA SHOWING FREQUENCY OF OCCURRENCE OF
CORRECT (C) AND INCORRECT (I) CVC RECALLS FOR ITEMS WITH
AND WITHOUT NLM'S FOR DIFFERENT LEVELS OF ASSOCIATION
VALUES OVER VARIOUS RETENTION INTERVALS

| Group | Category | Retention interval (sec) | | | | | |
		0	5	10	15	30	Total
	NLM-C	86	66	64	71	53	340
Low association value	NLM-I	0	13	13	18	22	66
	No NLM-C	130	115	97	81	80	503
	No NLM-I	2	35	51	60	62	210
	NLM-C	148	137	140	138	143	706
Medium association value	NLM-I	2	7	10	18	15	52
	No NLM-C	74	68	60	49	50	301
	No NLM-I	2	9	14	17	21	63
	NLM-C	212	221	203	203	206	1045
High association value	NLM-I	1	4	5	13	15	38
	No NLM-C	27	14	26	21	18	106
	No NLM-I	0	0	1	2	2	5

Data Taken from Kiess (1967).

recorded NLM generation reports and trigram recall using the Petersons' paradigm. In contrast to Groninger's procedure of having Ss report NLM's after recall, he had Ss report any NLM's at the time of CVC presentation and again at recall.[1]

In accord with the previous studies cited, high-association value produced more NLM's and greater recall. Table I shows some of Kiess' (1967) data, where the frequencies of correct and incorrect CVC-recalls are shown for items with and without NLM's and for the different levels of association value. The data are clear: association

[1] Groninger's Ss may have generated some NLM's during the filler task performance. Montague et al. (1970) found that when Ss were asked to report rehearsal/repetitions and NLM codings during the filler task by pressing buttons, some Ss for some items reported rehearsal for a few seconds, then began reporting NLM's. The inference is that some codings, perhaps being more complex, take longer to form and do not occur immediately. However, Kiess found Ss reported generating NLM's during the filler task less than 3% of the time.

value and retention interval have massive effects. The effects on NLM frequency is clear also: more NLM's are used as association value increases. The proportion of items with NLM's show higher recall proportions than items without NLM's. In a second experiment, variation in presentation time (2, 3, or 4 seconds) produced systematic increases in the number of NLM's reported and in the number of CVC's recalled. As in the Montague *et al.* (1966) study, the relation between NLM recall and item recall was strong. Although only about 3% of the NLM's reported at initial presentation of the CVC were forgotten, for those items recall was essentially zero. The CVC-NLM complex is formed quickly at presentation and stored. When it is retrieved, the NLM must be decoded into the CVC response. Without the NLM code, recall is improbable. Thus, the proportion of CVC recalls is highly correlated with recall of the NLM's, as in the present studies. Prytulak (1971) explicitly demonstrates that errors in decoding are a function of the Ss' forgetting how an item was coded, and errors are produced when he uses the wrong rule to decode.

b. *Characteristics of NLM Coding.* NLM's have been shown to be commonly reported by Ss in paired associates and in short-term memory experiments. Such ubiquity in the use of these coding procedures suggests that it is such coding that provides the basis for storing and remembering the criterion items in the tasks. In a recent article, Horowitz and Prytulak (1969) suggest that Ss seem to reduce their memory load by incorporating task materials such as nonsense syllables into words or strings of words and they call this process "redintegration." The generation of the coding is redintegrative, since the given items become part of a larger unit which is what is stored and retrieved. The classification of elaborative or redintegrative strategies into gross categories such as, "Used an NLM" and "Used no NLM" is unsatisfying, since the description is gross and because it gains us little in understanding the procedures used by Ss in coding, and the relative efficiency of different coding strategies. Obviously, codings will differ in their "complexity," and their complexity is probably directly related to performance at recall, since the NLM code must be decoded to produce the criterion items. This section will concentrate on the classification of NLM strategies, their analysis, and the effects on performance.

Mattocks (cited in Underwood & Schulz, 1960) found that a variety of NLM's were used by Ss which could be classified as to how many coding steps or stages were involved in NLM formation. Only about 14% of the NLM's involved two or more steps. Presumably, the more steps the lower the efficiency, but Mattocks provided no analysis of efficiency. A more systematic analysis was accomplished by Bugelski (1962) in an experiment in which Ss learned CVC pairs. He classified NLM's into five general types: those where (1) Ss formed one word from the two syllables, whereby DUP-TEZ becomes "deputize"; (2) two separate words were generated from the syllables and used as a phrase elicited by the stimulus item, as CEZ-MUN becomes "says man" or "send money"; (3) syllables would be transformed into phrases or words that sound like the syllables, e.g., GEY-NUR becomes "a grey nurse"; (4) Ss attempted to form more abstract NLM's, e. g., BIH-XIR is coded as "they both had an I"; (5) Ss reported a vague association to part of one syllable and thus, GAC-QET becomes "tourniquet." Bugelski also reported that with increases in item exposure time, more NLM reports are made. Of the 537 NLM's reported, more than 70% were included in the first three classes. The more complicated NLM codes were considerably less frequently used.

With consonant trigrams, in his study of NLM's in short-term memory, Groninger (1966) reported differences in the type of NLM's as a function of association value. For high-(92%) association value items, mostly (187 out of 250 NLM's) one-word codes (e.g., PND to PoND) were generated with relatively few (43/250) instances of using each consonant to initialize a word (e.g., RFD to Rural Free Delivery). "Other" codes were even more infrequent (20/250). On the other hand, low-(25%) association value trigrams resulted in relatively few single words being generated (33/128), and proportionately more use of the consonants to initialize several words (56/128) and other codings involving several stages (39/128). Thus, for low-association value items, Ss generate fewer mediatiors which are longer and probably more complex. This may account for the poorer recall of low-association value items with NLM's relative to those of high-association value seen in Fig. 8.

Similarly, with CVC's, Schaub and Lindley (1964) and Prytulak (1971) report that single-word NLM's are the rule with high-association value CVC's (more than 90% in both studies). For low-association value items, Schaub and Lindley reported only about 45% one-word NLM's and, therefore, a preponderance of longer, presumably more complicated codings. Prytulak's data are also in general agreement. Although Kiess (1967) did not analyze the length of mediators, he did provide some relevant data on association value and NLM's. Of 70 errors in recall where the error could be directly attributed to the decoding of the NLM (e.g., the CVC to be recalled was DEV, the NLM was "Divide," and the recall "DIV"), 54 of them were made to low-association value items. Perhaps, NLM's to low-association value items are not only longer, but this complexity is revealed in a greater problem in reproducing the criterion item from the remembered NLM code. Schaub and Lindley report that for high-association value items, Ss generate NLM codes containing the same sequence of letters as in the trigram about 66% of the time, while for low-association value trigrams, the sequence is preserved only about 3% of the time. Codes retaining the sequence should be easier to decode at recall.

Other data regarding NLM coding complexity comes from studies by Adams, McIntyre, and Thorsheim (1969). Using the Petersons' paradigm they presented consonant strings of differing lengths (i.e., 2, 3, and 4) for 4 seconds, asking Ss to report any NLM's immediately. They reported a large superiority for items reported as coded over those not so coded, which agrees with results from other studies. Most interesting for our present consideration is that the difficulty of forming an NLM increased with the length of the consonant string. About 70% of the bigrams, 60% of the trigrams, and 49% of the tetragrams generated NLM reports. Of these, after varying intervals up to 30 seconds, recall was nearly perfect for coded bigrams, declined somewhat to average between 80 and 90% for trigrams, and declined to about 60% for tetragrams. Therefore, the longer strings were not only more difficult to code but once coded produced differential recall due perhaps to the more complex decoding required for longer NLM's.

These results suggest that the type of NLM coding generated depends on whether the materials are letter trigrams or words, or combinations of trigrams and words. Considerably more variability in NLM codes would be expected where pairs are made up of nonword letter strings. In the case where both items are of low meaningfulness, coding might involve several steps. For example, both items might be coded into words, and then the words related semantically by insertion of a verb or another connective. Various stimulus selection options are possible, since the stimulus item in paired-associates tasks does not need to be coded completely, since it is presented on each trial as a cue for recalling the response item. When trigram-word pairs are used, selected elements of the stimulus can be coded into a word and then related meaningfully to the response. When word pairs are used, relatively more straightforward and less complex coding rules generate NLM's. In this case, Ss may merely generate a sentence or phrase including the word pair. It is apparent that the frequency of use and the complexity of coding and decoding covers a considerable range in verbal learning tasks.

In several studies, C. J. Martin and his colleagues attempted to make a detailed classification of NLM's reported in paired-associates learning and to examine effectiveness for the various coding strategies (e.g., C. J. Martin, Boersma, & Cox, 1965). The Ss learned eight pairs of low-meaningful paralogs (e.g., RENNET-QUIPSON, taken from Noble, 1952) for 10 trials and then were asked to report how they had attempted to form an association for each pair. Martin et al. identified seven categories of strategies and then ranked them in terms of their assumptions about relative complexity of the encoding ranging from no associations and simple repetition, to the formation of words from the items and relating them syntactically. Table II shows their classification system. They then correlated an S's strategy score with his performance. A strategy score for an S was found by summing the ranks for his NLM reports given to the eight items. A strong positive relationship ($r = .62$) was found between the number of correct responses over the 10 trials and the strategy scores. In addition, in two experiments they computed the mean number of correct responses per category ranking for all Ss. In both cases, there was a monotonically increasing relationship between strategy rank and performance. Their data are shown in Fig. 9.

In an experiment from our laboratory, two groups of Ss learned two lists of 12 CVC-word pairings, and then reported any NLM's. The Martin et al. classification system was applied to the data (Montague & Wearing, 1967a). There was close agreement between our data and theirs. As strategy ranking increases, the corresponding increase in correct performance occurs. However, we obtained a quite different pattern of frequency use for the various NLM strategies than they did. For the seven classifications, Martin et al. found the mean percent of strategy use to be 12, 11, 14, 10, 6, 29, and 18 for strategy categories 1-7, respectively. Our data showed a bimodal distribution in which categories 2, 6, and 7 account for about 90% of the reports: categories 1-7 contain 4, 33, 6, 2, 0, 16, and 40% of the cases, respectively. Boersma, Conklin, and Carlson (1966) obtained a distribution similar to ours. This change in the use of NLM coding strategies most likely was produced by differences in the meaningfulness of items used to form pairs. C. J. Martin et al. (1965) used nonsense dissyllables, and for these, single-letter and multiple-letter cues are often more appropriate for redintegrative coding. In our study and that by Boersma et al. (1966), low-meaningful stimuli

TABLE II

CLASSIFICATION OF ASSOCIATIVE STRATEGIES

Associative strategy	Type of cue S reported using	Example of verbal report
No reported associations	S was not able to state how he managed to make the association	Sagrole-Polef: "Don't know how I learned this pair"
Repetition	S reported rehearsing the pair	Volvap-Nares: "Just kept repeating these words to myself"
Single letter cues	S reported using a single letter in each of the paralogs in making the association	Tarop-Gojey: "Noticed that each word contained an O"
Multiple letter cues	S reported using multiple letters in each of the paralogs	Sagrole-Polef: "Each word contains an OLE"
Word formation	S reported that an actual word was embedded in one or both of the paralogs and made use of these words in making the association	Meardon-Zumap: "The word EAR is contained in Meardon and learned that EAR goes with Zumap"
Superordinate	S reported selecting elements from each of the two paralogs that had some relationship to each other	Sagrole-Polef: "Sagrole begins with S and Polef with P, thought of State Police"
Syntactical	S reported selecting elements from each of the two paralogs and embedding these elements into a sentence, phrase, or clause	Rennet-Quipson: "Changed Rennet to Bennet and saw Quips in Quipson— thought; Bennet Cerf Quips on TV"

From C. J. Martin et al. (1965).

were paired with high-meaningful responses. When learning word pairings in more recent experiments (e.g., Adams & Montague, 1967; Duffy, 1971; Duffy & Montague, 1971), Ss almost exclusively report constructing some sort of syntactic NLM code or nothing at all. Low

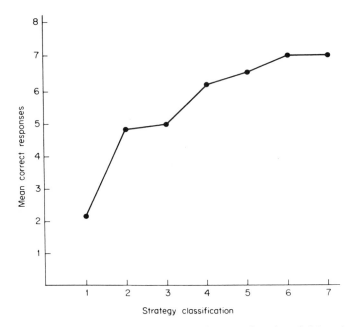

Fig. 9. Mean number of correct responses per item as a function of elaborative strategy classification. (Data from C.J. Martin *et al.*, 1965).

meaningfulness items require considerable transformation before they form words and phrases, and it seems reasonable to expect that Ss use a greater variety of strategies in coding such material.

The most systematic approach for documenting and analyzing the covert procedures Ss use to transform unfamiliar material into more memorable form has been reported recently by Prytulak (1971). He emphasizes that nominal CVC stimuli, not part of natural language, are transformed into functional NLM's which are. Then, at recall, these NLM's are translated back into nominal form. The data previously reviewed demonstrate that a variety of procedures varying in complexity and in effectiveness are used to transform given items into more meaningful form. However, the classifications which have been made have been relatively cursory. Prytulak provides a more complete analysis. He emphasizes that in a very general sense, verbal learning can be characterized as a sequence of stages, i.e., coding of items into NLM's, storing, retrieving, and then decoding.

In order to simplify matters somewhat, he focuses on learning CVC lists. The approach he used was to externalize the normally covert coding and decoding procedures used by Ss in learning lists of CVC's, and then to classify the rules or strategies that were observed. Some strategies were found to be more effective in that they produced more accurate decoding of the NLM's than others, and by using this information Prytulak constructed a model which simulates the natural language mediation process. Then, the model was applied to several experimental tasks with success.

Recognizing that differences in the length of nominal stimulus and in task requirements (as between lists of single items and paired associates) would produce considerable variability in the NLM codings and complicate problems of classification, Prytulak concentrated on NLM's for single CVC's. He showed Ss 130 CVC's varying in meaningfulness and had them write down any meaningful thing that came to mind, i.e., words, phrases, acronyms, or even the CVC if it was already meaningful. The Ss were instructed to try to code every item, and that they would have to reconstruct the CVC from the code after they finished coding all the items. This is called the coding-decoding or "association-reconstruction" phase of the study.

A classification system was devised describing both the CVC's and the NLM transformations, and eight types of operations Ss used were identified. These are shown in Table III along with some examples of NLM codes. Capital letters in the third column designate those in a CVC which were left intact, while those in lower case identify changes made in the syllables. Thus, cVC designates that the first consonant was changed (e.g., FET to "pet") and CVcC indicates that a consonant was added (e.g., BAK to "back"). Every change in a CVC counted as an "operation" and is named in the Table. Notice that the Table contains relatively simple, single-step operations. Earlier classifications of NLM's by Bugelski (1962), C. J. Martin et al. (1965), Groninger (1966), etc., found many of the NLM codes generated were describable only if several steps or operations were involved. In the Ss' NLM codes, Prytulak also found many that could not be characterized as single operations. For example, the item WOD was coded by one S into "wonder," where the NLM-type is CVcCx which requires a combination of two operations, i.e., 2Ab and 4a (listed in Table III). Similarly, an S generating the NLM "train" for LOC was considered to have changed LOC by operation 4A to "locomotive" and that by operation 6 to "train." The sequence of one or more operations on a CVC which yields the NLM code is called a "Transformation." The same classification procedures were used to analyze the decoding of the CVC from the NLM code. The decoding Transformation is a set of operations working

TABLE III
OPERATIONS USED TO FORM NLM's

Type of operation	Operation name	Product of operation[a] (NLM)	Examples CVC NLM
Identity	0	CVC	TEX — tex
Substitution	1A	cVC	CIG — zig
	1B	CvC	YAS — yes
	1C	CVc	SAQ — sag
Internal addition:			
Of consonant	2Aa	CcVC	CIP — clip
	2Ab	CVcC	PAK — pack
Of vowel	2Ba	CvVC	FEL — fuel
	2Bb	CVvC	PEL — peal
	2Bc	$CV_1 v_1 C$	FEL — feel
Permutation	3	$VC_1 C_2$, $CV_2 C_1$, $C_2 VC_1$, $C_1 C_2 V$, or $C_2 C_1 V$	
External addition:			
Suffixing	4A	CVCx	LOC — locomotive
Prefixing	4B	xCVC	VED — moved
Deletion	5A	VC_2	BUP — up
	5B	$C_1 C_2$	TEV — TV
	5C	$C_1 V$	GOH — go
Semantic association	6	x	
Phrasing	7	Cx, Vx, Cx	MEV — million

From Prytulak (1971).

[a] "x" indicates any string of letters. Two additional operations were formed by adding the diacritic "nch" to 1A or 1C to specify that the substitution of consonants had produced *no change* in pronunciation.

backward, so that for an operation which adds a suffix (4A), it is now deleted.

The results of Prytulak's analysis directly confirmed much that had been inferred from previous data. For example, the probability of generating an NLM for an item was correlated with its meaningfulness (e.g., see Groninger, 1966; Kiess, 1968; Montague & Kiess, 1968). Also, as meaningfulness declines, the Transformation for an NLM contains more operations. Remember that in Martin's *et al.* (1965) scaling of NLM's for nonsense dissyllables, the third and fourth classification intervals indicated that several operations were used to code a pair. Similar data from Montague and Wearing (1967a) indicated that with CVC-word pairs, very few NLM-codes took this form. Groninger (1966) reported predominantly one-word NLM's were formed with high-meaningful trigrams and multiple word codings for low-meaningful items. Prytulak found that more operations were used in transforming low-meaningfulness CVC's. In addition, the more operations required to generate an NLM, the more errors were produced in decoding.

The coding-decoding study allowed Prytulak to construct a model simulating the process based on the fact that some Transformations were found to be used more often than others, and some were decoded more accurately. Transformations were ranked in terms of ease of generating NLM's which were easy to decode. This ranking is the "T-stack." Upon receiving a CVC to learn, Ss are assumed to work down through the T-stack applying one Transformation after another untill an NLM is generated. The NLM is assumed to be stored along with the Transformation. At recall, the NLM-Transformation compound is retrieved, and the S attempts to reconstruct the item from the NLM and the remembered Transformation.

Several straightforward inferences may be taken from these ideas. One is that if Ss engage in searching a T-stack for operations which successfully generate an NLM, the search should take time. Other researchers, such as Earhard and Mandler (1965), Bourne (1966), and McManama (1971) have made similar assumptions regarding mediational activity on the part of Ss. Therefore, we should expect that the presentation time for an item in learning should affect how many NLM's are generated. A considerable amount of data exist supporting this contention. In his study of the use of NLM codes in short-term memory, Kiess (1968) found more Ss generated more NLM's with increasing exposure times for the trigram. Also, Montague et al. (1966) found an increase in NLM generation with longer exposure time. In yet another experiment, Montague and Kiess (1968) attempted to manipulate the associability of CVC pairs independently of meaningfulness level. Associability is defined as the proportion of Ss in another independent group able to generate an NLM for a pair of CVC's. Using a 2-second presentation rate, differences in associability had no effect, but when the interval was increased to 5 seconds, a reliable effect was found both on learning and on the number of NLM's reported after learning. Presumably, with longer intervals, Ss have sufficient time to search the T-stack for an appropriate Transformation.

Another implication is that the further down the T-stack an *S* searches, the less likely he is to generate an NLM. Limitations in time for materials which are difficult to code would reduce NLM frequency, as suggested above. Also, variations in meaningfulness should affect the latency of NLM formation. Here again, the implication is supported by empirical evidence. Kiess (1968) found significant increases in NLM latency with decreases in association value of the CVC's. Prytulak (1971) and Schaub and Lindley (1964) also obtained evidence that as meaningfulness decreases so does NLM probability.

In remembering, the *S*s must retrieve the NLM and Transformation, and then, by applying the remembered operations in reverse, decode the NLM for the CVC. Therefore, correct recall of the CVC depends on remembering both the NLM and its Transformation. In much of the research already reviewed (e.g., Adams, 1967; Montague *et al.*, 1966), a strong and consistent relationship was shown between NLM recall and correct response production. When NLM's were changed or forgotten, the criterion item was not retrieved. Prytulak's model indicates further that by forgetting operations in the Transformation, errors would be produced. Among the factors influencing forgetting of operations should be both the number of operations used in a Transformation and the particular type of operation. For example, operations which replace or substitute other vowels or consonants (e.g., Operations 1A, 1B, 1C in Table III) should present problems of decoding.

In data from his coding-decoding study, Prytulak finds that as more operations are used in coding the CVC, the proportion of times the same decoding operations are used in reconstructing the trigram decreases rapidly. The *S*s tend to use fewer operations in remembering than they used in encoding. Also, it is apparent that some Transformations are less memorable than others. Operations which are most obvious in the NLM retrieved are those which added vowels, consonants, prefixes, or suffixes to the CVC, and Prytulak finds that *S*s use these operations in decoding often excluding or forgetting others which were used in coding. Therefore, retrieval of an NLM "castle" suggests that the coding was by addition (4A), but it is not obvious, and it may not be recalled that another operation was also involved (i.e., 1C) to code CAZ to "cas" which then (by 4A) is coded as "castle." Therefore, errors in decoding are produced by *S*s forgetting certain operations and using only the more salient one(s), i.e., those which are cued by the NLM.

Although no experiments have been reported which were specifically intended to explore the relationship between NLM recall and recall of the Transformation, some relevant data exist. Kiess (1968) in his short-term memory experiments, asked Ss to report NLM's at the time of CVC presentation and to recall the NLM later. NLM recall was nearly perfect (97%+), but association value had a reliable effect on recall of the CVC. This finding result suggests that forgetting of certain operations in the Transformation may have produced this effect, especially since lower meaningfulness material requires a greater number of operations, and these items showed greater forgetting. Adams *et al.* (1969) also showed nearly perfect retention of NLM's in short-term memory along with forgetting for criterion items which might be ascribed to interference with decoding.

However, data from experiments involving retention over longer time periods show considerable loss in recall for both criterion items and NLM's as meaningfulness decreases (e.g., Montague *et al.*, 1966; Montague & Kiess, 1968). For high- and low-meaningfulness items, if NLM's were recalled, correct CVC recall was relatively high. Although the overall performance level for low-meaningfulness items was poorer than for high-meaningfulness ones, whether the effect was due to NLM or Transformation retention losses cannot be decided. More recent evidence (Montague, Nelson, & Carter, 1971c), however, suggests a difference in recall of NLM's with different levels of concreteness. Immediately after viewing 80 pairs and giving NLM's for them, Ss attempted to recall the response and the NLM as each stimulus was presented for half of the pairs. The pairs were composed of high-association value (nonword) CVC's and either concrete or abstract nouns (Paivio, Yuille, & Madigan, 1968b). The immediate test revealed the usual superiority of recall for items reported with an NLM code, and that concrete items were recalled reliably better (.43) than more abstract items (.30). Notice that NLM recall differed for the concrete and abstract items. Out of 173 NLM's generated for concrete items, 94 were correctly recalled, and 85 produced the correct response noun. For abstract items, 160 NLM's were generated and 71 were recalled, of which 57 produced correct responses. These data show that NLM's are less well retained for the abstract material, and furthermore, that in retrieving the response item from the NLM code, additional advantage accrues to the concrete items. Although we have no data on the number of operations of the NLM's for these materials, it seems reasonable to assume that more operations are used in forming NLM's for abstract materials. Montague, Klemt, & Carter (1971b) found that when Ss are asked to estimate the ease with which they could form NLM's to concrete and abstract word pairs, the latter received lower estimates. We have already reviewed Prytulak's argument that low-meaningfulness CVC's require Transformations containing more operations and take longer to generate. The same reasoning applied to the effect of concreteness-abstractness seems acceptable.

The data reviewed suggest that the argument for a multistage coding and decoding model describing memorizing-remembering has credibility. The Ss readily report coding or transforming nominal items. Reports of such transformations are highly correlated with accuracy in recall. However, in remembering, what is retrieved from memory is the transformed information which must be decoded if the proper response is to be made. When an S forgets how the coding was done, his experimental performance suffers. Therefore, the detailed analysis of Transformations seems to be imperative.

Prytulak's T-stack model had success in predicting errors in a CVC-coding experiment and in prediking how well CVC's are remembered in short-term memory studies. In the coding study, CVC items were transformed by the application of certain operations into words, e.g., MIS by 4A to "mist," MAL by 2Ba to "meal," GUF by 2Ab to "gulf," etc. Since different Transformations can make different words out of CVC's (e.g., MAL by 4A to "malt," by 2Ba to "meal," by 2Ab to "mail," etc.), and in decoding can derive different CVC's from a word (e.g., "gulf" by 4A to GUL, by 2Ab to GUF) some interference was expected in learning the CVC-coded word pairs. Errors in learning these paris were found to be dependent on the number and saliency of possible Transformations which could apply to a particular pair. If a particular CVC was coded using a Transformation relatively low in the T-stack hierarchy, competition existed from other Transformations which could also be applied to the CVC which were higher in the T-stack. It sems clear that specification of interference in learning must take into account not only similarities among items but competition among Transformations.

In two short-term memory experiments, Prytulak attempted to predict CVC memorability using the T-stack depth data along with more traditional predictors, e.g., trigram frequency, letter frequencies, conditional-emitted letter frequencies, and an additive-interference index (from Underwood & Schulz, 1960). The best predictor was the T-stack depth, which indicates that Transformations producing NLM's which are not efficiently decodable produce errors.

There is little doubt that the processes involved in verbal learning indeed involve a complex sequence of mediational activities on the part of the *S*. Prytulak's model demonstrates that a systematic analysis of these steps can be achieved, and that it provides a powerful tool for describing and understanding learning in such complex tasks. Although Prytulak utilized a restricted set of tasks and materials in order to demonstrate the analysis, it is apparent that the approach has potentially wide generality in describing and explaining a variety of other human verbal learning and memory tasks.

For example, it seems but a relatively small jump to specify the Transformations used and their efficiency in learning paired-associates lists composed of CVC pairs. The operations shown in Table IV may be assumed to apply in a process in which the CVC's are first transformed into words and then associated by additional (syntactic and semantic?) operations.

A brief example will make this point clear. Arranged in Table IV are 12 CVC pairs. They were selected from among high- and low-associability items provided by Montague and Kiess (1968). Associability provides an estimate of NLM probability averaged over large groups of *S*s given 15 seconds to respond to each pair. Associability reliably predicts the rate of paired-associate learning (e.g., Montague & Kiess, 1968; Montague & Wearing, 1967a). These pairs were given to an *S* who was asked to generate NLM's for all pairs which are shown in the Table. Then, these NLM's were analyzed for the operations used to transform each CVC, and these are shown along with the NLM's.

Several things are apparent from the Table. The six highly associable items are transformed into words usually in a single step. The operations used to transform these items were relatively frequently used by Prytulak's *S*s and reside high in the T-stack, i.e., they produced accurate decoding. On the other hand, the codings for the low-associability items include more operations, and those Transformations produced relatively poor decoding for Prytulak's *S*s. Once words were generated, a phrase or a sentence was generated to complete the NLM. It is apparent that at recall, although the phrase or sentence might be remembered, the use of a variety of relatively inefficient operations would reduce the decoding accuracy considerably especially in any time-limited task.

Different materials to be learned require different operations to elaborate or transform the materials. If words were used, no operations are required to code the materials into words, and Transforma-

TABLE IV
NLM Transformations of High and Low Associability CVC Pairs

Pairs		AS	Operations and CVC codes				NLM phrases containing codes
S	R			S		R	
BOK	DET	80	2Bb	"Book"	2Bb	"Debt"	The *book* is overdue at the library and I'm in *debt*
SAF	DUX	80	4A	"Safe"	1C^{nch}	"Ducks"	To be *safe* make sure he *ducks* under the pitch
RIV	SAF	81	4A	"River"	4A	"Safe"	At the bottom of the *river* they found the *safe*
DEY	LAZ	83	1B^{nch}	"Day"	4A	"Lazy"	This is a good *day* for being *lazy*
RIS	MUL	83	4A	"Vise"	4A	"Mule"	He lifted the *vise* with the help of a *mule*
CIV	JUS	87	4A	"Civil"	4A	"Justice"	*Civil* courts dispense *justice*
HAQ	ZIV	25	1C^{nch}, 4A	"Hack"	1A, 2Bb, 4A	"Sieve"	He *hacked* at the bowl to make a *sieve*
WUQ	XIR	25	1A, 1C^{nch}, 4B	"Luck"	1A^{nch}	"Sir"	With *luck* he'll be called "*sir*"
XER	QAJ	25	4B, 4A	"Exercise"	1C^{nch}, 4A, 7	"Quad jump"	In order to *exercise* do the *quad jump*
VUF	XOM	25	1A, 1C^{nch}	"Rough"	1A^{nch}, 4A	"Some"	It is really *rough* not to have *some* food
RAX	YOC	25	2Ba, 2Aa	"Relax"	7, 4A	"Yo carcass"	Sit here and *relax* "*yo carcass*"
FAP	PUW	27	0	"Fap!"	7	"Person"	*Fap!* That *person is under water* Help!
						"Underwater"	

tions would consist of operations relating the words. Adams and Montague (1967) reported that in learning paired adjectives, Ss generated a variety of NLM's including sentences, and word, sound, and letter associations as a basis for the NLM's. Although no data on efficiency of producing the response from the NLM are available at this time, it seems reasonable to expect certain operations to be more efficient in decoding, and therefore a T-stack analysis should prove useful.

There is one aspect of the T-stack model which deserves additional comment. Prytulak assumes that the NLM-code *and* the Transformation are independently stored in memory which would make them independently forgettable. However, the errors Ss make in reconstructing the CVC from the NLM indicate that they "forget" to use certain operations from a Transformation and substitute others which may be more preferred or salient. Since certain of these operations (e.g., suffixing, 4A) are common to many Transformations, it is difficult to decide whether the Transformation is only partially recalled, or whether reconstruction is other than the direct procedure Prytulak postulates. The Transformation for a particular NLM coding may not be stored at all. Rather, the S may use a hierarchy of operations to decode the NLM as he does to code the CVC. As suggested by Adams and Bray (1970) and Wearing (1971b), retrieval may involve generation of CVC's from the NLM which are judged for accuracy against the stored representation of the original item until a "satisfactory" match is found. This kind of process would account for the type of errors made by Ss in Prytulak's CVC-coding experiment where recall errors are produced by Ss using more salient operations.

A similar, parallel problem has received attention in research on sentence retention. Adapting a transformational grammar model from linguistics (Chomsky, 1957), Miller (1962) theorized that Ss memorize sentences by transforming them (if they are complex) into a simple, basic semantic string, called a kernel. The Transformation was assumed to be stored along with the kernel to be used at recall to reconstruct the sentence for verbatim recall. The results of recent research (e.g., Bregman & Strasberg, 1968) suggest that although under certain circumstances Ss transform the sentence when memorizing, it is doubtful that the specific Transformation is stored at the same time. It is more likely that the S attempts to reconstruct the nominal sentence from other cues. Therefore, retrieving the nominal sentences or CVC's may both involve a closed loop process as suggested by Adams.

D. IMAGERY AS AN ELABORATIVE STRATEGY

So far the discussion of Ss' elaborations of verbal materials has concentrated on verbal Transformations or coding of the nominal items. It is apparent that such coding generally facilitates learning and recalling. A notable feature of this research is the predominance of the use of nonsense materials which probably leads Ss to utilize verbal codes. However, there is considerable evidence which suggests that when concrete words are learned, the elaborations of the material may involve nonverbal imagery processes. For example, Paivio, Yuille, and Smythe (1966) questioned Ss about the use of both verbal and imaginal codes after they had learned lists of concrete or abstract noun pairs. The Ss reported using predominantly imaginal codes for concrete pairs, while verbal codes were most common for abstract pairs. Paivio (1971) reviews a massive amount of data which demonstrates convincingly that imaginal elaborations of material consistently facilitate recall. Although the primary emphasis of imagery research has been concerned with "visual" elaboration of the material, it is apparent that other modalities are involved. For example, Luria (1968) described a man who remembered material not only by "picturing" the scene in which he learned it, but by other associations such as sounds, smells, and feels. Blind Ss are sensitive to rated auditory imagery of words but not to visual imagery (Paivio & Okovita, 1971). This section will review briefly some of the experimental evidence and conclusions from experiments concerned with visual or imaginal elaboration of material in memorizing and recalling.

Visual elaborations have long been recommended for memorizing materials (see Richardson, 1969; Yates, 1966) and received research attention during the early years of this century. However, as was true for cognitive processes in general, the biases of Behaviorism made such research unacceptable. As a result, research on the effects of imagery on memory was very limited and done by individuals out of the mainstream of research on learning and memory. Holt (1964) documents the reawakening of general interests in imagery, and Bower (1970a, 1972) and Paivio (1969, 1971) review a considerable amount of recent research and theorizing.

A variety of experimental paradigms have been used which have demonstrated considerable facilitation of learning or recalling which can be ascribed to the generation of images. For example, instructions to generate images for noun pairs are found to facilitate performance when compared to repetition or standard instructions (e.g., Aiken, 1971; Bower, 1972; Gupton & Frincke, 1970; Hulicka & Grossman, 1967; Rimm, Alexander, & Eiles, 1969). Also, with materials rated for imagery-evoking potential (Paivio et al., 1968b), consistently superior learning and recall are found for words rated high over those rated low (Paivio, 1969, 1971). Ss' postlearning reports also reveal learning to be superior for items on which Ss reported using imagery than for items without elaboration (Paivio et al., 1966). The use of imagery-based mnemonic systems by experimental Ss has been shown to produce superior recall performance in comparison to control Ss not using the systems (e.g., Bower, 1970a; Bugelski et al., 1968; Paivio, 1968; Smith & Noble, 1965). Pictures of objects presented along with paired associates for one group and not for another facilitate recalling when the pictures are no longer present even for low-imagery value (abstract) pairs (Wollen, 1968).

Ascribing these results to visual elaboration of material assumes that Ss form images of the objects specified by the words, phrases, and sentences presented for memorization. Since it is difficult to separate "images" from verbal elaborations in many of the experiments involving imagery manipulations, it has been of some concern to demonstrate their "visual" character. There are several converging lines of evidence which allow the conclusion that some kind of visualization process is involved which is functionally distinct from verbalization. Paivio (1971) reviews the research in considerable detail. Perhaps the most convincing is that which indicates that the process of forming an image is susceptible to external interference from visual stimulation; and that blind Ss, lacking the capability to generate images, show an insensitivity to materials varying in visual image-evoking potential not shown by sighted Ss.

Atwood (1969, 1971) assumed visualizing and verbalizing to be distinct processes, and as such, they should be susceptible to selective interference. If this is so, generating an image for concrete materials should be incompatible with performing another visual task, but not with performing an auditory-verbal task. On the other hand, more abstract tasks involve a verbalization process predominantly, and therefore, should be affected by another task requiring verbalization, but not visualization. To test these ideas, Atwood performed an experiment where Ss listened to recordings of phrases, each of which designated a concrete highly imaginable scene and were told to visualize it, e.g., "*nudist* devouring a *bird*," and "*violin* floating in a *river*" were two phrases used. About 1 second after the phrase was read, a simple task was given, presented visually for one group and auditorially for another. For a group of control Ss, no intruding task was given. Either the digit "1" or "2" was presented, and the S was required to say the other digit for whichever one was given. If Ss were forming images of the objects specified in the phrases, the intruding visual task should degrade them while the auditory task should not. A recall test was given after all the phrases had been presented by presenting the first word of each phrase as a cue. For three other groups of Ss, he constructed phrases using abstract words assumed to be difficult to visualize, e.g., "*democracy* is government by a *majority*" and "*obsession* is being possessed by an *idea*." Since these phrases would not involve imagery, but involve implicit verbalization, the intrusion of the auditory task and not the visual one should produce a decrement in recall. The results conformed to the predictions. For the concrete phrases, the auditory task produced only slightly (not significant) poorer recall than that for noninterrupted control Ss. However, the visual task produced significantly less recall by about 24%. Recall for the abstract phrases showed a similar pattern, but now the visual intruding task did not produce a reliable decrement while the auditory task did (about 25%).

Research by Bower (1970a) also shows selective interference with generation of images. He compared groups instructed to learn pairs by generating images or by rote repetition and gave them either a visual or tactile task to perform at the same time. The Ss asked to form images performed much better than those merely repeating the material and, for the latter Ss, the secondary task had no effect. However, the visual task significantly reduced recall performance compared to the tactile task for Ss told to form images. Such results strongly imply that a genuine visual imagery process of some sort is involved in learning concrete materials, and the results using abstract material imply that a verbal-auditory process predominates.

A visual imagery process is also implicated in the results of experiments comparing the learning of sighted Ss with congenitally blind Ss who presumably are deficient in visualization capability. Montague and Cohen (1971) compared a group of congenitally blind college students with a group of sighted Ss in the free recall of nouns, half of which were high and half low in rated imagery value (Paivio *et al.*, 1968b). Although there was a reliable effect of imagery value on recall for sighted Ss, there was none for the blind Ss. Paivio and Okovita (1971) showed conclusively that paired-associate learning for blind Ss was facilitated by rated auditory imagery of the words and not rated visual imagery value of the words. Sighted Ss showed the opposite results.

A considerable amount of other data is cited by Paivio (1971) which indicates that visual and verbal elaboration processes function independently in these tasks. For example, Ss' reports indicate that imagery elaborations are reported more frequently in learning concrete than abstract material. Verbal elaborations are reported about equally often with such material (Paivio, Smythe, & Yuille, 1968a). Also, the time it takes to report an image is longer for abstract than for concrete words, while latencies for generating verbal codes are about the same for all levels of concreteness (Yuille & Paivio, 1967). When control over the use of imaginal and verbal codes is effected, images prove to be superior to sentences for concrete word pairs, while slightly inferior for abstract pairs (Paivio & Foth, 1970).

The data just reviewed demonstrate conclusively that visual elaboration of verbal materials can significantly influence recall performance in memory task somewhat independently of verbal elaboration. As Paivio (1970) indicates, Ss use visual or verbal coding as mediation in tasks as seems appropriate to them for learning the verbal material. With concrete words, using imagery codes seems to be a preferred strategy, while with abstract words, verbal coding is more common. However, the two types of strategies probably interact under some conditions providing more adequate elaboration of material, thereby facilitating performance. Such interaction is indicated in studies where instructions to generate images are given in addition to providing (or instructing for) verbal codings (e.g., sentences) for the materials. Bower (1972), for example, reported that Ss recall more concrete words embedded in sentences if they are told to imagine the scene specified by the sentence. Also, Rimm *et al.* (1969) report superior recall for Ss instructed to use imagery over recall by other Ss told to learn by generating phrases or sentences, or by those given standard paired-associate learning instructions. There is also a little evidence that imagery can facilitate learning abstract word pairs. Paivio (1971) cites a thesis by MacDonald in which recall of abstract pairs was very high when they were reported as learned using a concrete image. Furthermore, Yuille and Paivio (1968) suggest that the effectiveness of verbal elaboration can be enhanced by imagery, and Wollen (1968) reported that pictures accompanying abstract words in learning facilitate recall.

It seems reasonable to hypothesize that imaginal and verbal elaborations can be used alternately by Ss for memorizing verbal materials or can supplement one another. For learning some materials (e.g., concrete words), images provide a preferred and excellent means of recalling items, while for more abstract materials image generation is more difficult, takes longer, and would be less facilitating in rapidly paced tasks. Also, it would seem that images generated for abstract items might be more difficult to decode. Bugelski (1970) exemplified this problem when he described the image reported by an S for the word "communism." The S said, "I saw a red velvet wall with a large yellow hammer and sickle." It seems apparent that if such an image was remembered, other words than communism might be decoded from it. Obviously, this reasoning parallels Prytulak's (1971) discussion of complex verbal coding and decoding generated by Ss for low-meaningful CVC's.

E. Attempts to Externalize Control Over Elaborative Strategies

From the foregoing review, reports of covert, idiosyncratic elaboration of material are easily elicited from Ss, and items reported as coded are learned faster and remembered better than items not coded. One question which has been raised about these observations is concerned with whether the elaborations determine the acquisition and recall of the materials or represent merely correlated behavior. Underwood (1964), for example, asked whether or not the reports obtained from Ss are valid descriptions of what is learned. The NLM code reported may be merely a response to the demands of the questioning procedures (Underwood & Schulz, 1960). A similar argument can be made about imaginal elaborations. As evidence for this contention, data are cited which show a lack of correspondence between reports of elaboration and performance or demonstrate that Ss report using elaborations not because they generate them in learning, but because they are asked to in questioning.

In one experiment, Runquist and Farley (1964) asked Ss to learn a paired-associates list, then give an NLM code for each pair (if they could), and were then asked whether they had used the NLM's in learning. For about 45% of the cases where an item was correct on the last learning trial, and had been reported as having been learned using an NLM, the latency of the NLM report exceeded the time allowed on learning trials to make responses. Because of this, Runquist and Farley suspected that the NLM was not essential to learning. (The Ss may not have been aware that the latency of the NLM reports was being timed, however.) In another experiment using the same procedures, Runquist (1966) gave one group a test rather than having them report NLM's. They later reported using fewer NLM's for learning than Ss who were asked to generate NLM's.

Once again, this implies that task requirements increase the likelihood of obtaining NLM reports. Other *E*s have found that *S*s report using more NLM's when instructed to learn material by using them, but performance is usually improved also (e.g., Garskof, Sandak & Malinowski, 1965; Schwartz, 1969).

In order to circumvent this criticism, a variety of procedures have been used which all obtain results which lend support to the thesis that NLM coding is an intrinsic part of the memorization process. Kiess and Montague (1965) asked *S*s to report NLM's on each learning trial. Kiess (1968) and Adams *et al.* (1969), in short-term memory experiments, had *S*s report any NLM when the item was presented. However, since these procedures rely on reports taken from subjects within the experiments, the thesis remains questionable. More convincing data have been obtained in experiments wherein predictions about learning are made from data about NLM coding obtained from other *S*s.

In one approach, Montague and Kiess (1968) found the NLM coding probability for several hundred pairs of CVC's. The items in a pair were of about equal association value, and pairs ranged from low- to high-association value. The *S*s were given 15 seconds to write down any NLM they could generate which would "link" the pair. The proportion of *S*s generating NLM's for a pair is its associability (AS) value. In experiments in which lists of pairs were chosen varying in AS, the rate of learning and the frequency of postlearning reports of NLM use are directly related to AS value (Masters 1969, 1970; Montague & Kiess, 1968; Walker, Montague, & Wearing, 1970; Wearing & Montague, 1967; Wearing, Walker, & Montague, 1967). In addition, Prytulak's (1971) T-Stack analysis of data taken from the coding-decoding operations of one group of *S*s provided reasonably accurate predictions of errors of decoding made by other *S*s and the memorability of items in a short-term memory experiment.

Additional data demonstrating the effect of AS value in list learning comes from data reported by Montague and Wearing (1967a). In one experiment, they had *S*s learn two CVC-noun pair lists constructed to be of about equivalent difficulty. The CVC items for the two lists were chosen from the same range of association value, and the word frequencies (Thorndike-Lorge) were about the same. However, *S*s made fewer errors in learning one of the lists than they did for the other. On the hypothesis that the AS of the pairs for the two lists might have been different, another group of *S*s was asked to generate NLM's for each pair within 15 seconds. The list on which more errors had been made had a significantly lower mean AS score.

An approach parallel to that of deriving and using the AS measure for verbal coding was undertaken by Paivio and his colleagues for imagery elaborations. Ratings of the potential for eliciting images were obtained for nouns (Paivio *et al.,* 1968b), and these "I" values were used subsequently as a variable in a variety of memory tasks. The results indicate consistent superiority of recall for items rated high in I value compared to those with lower ratings. Paivio (1971) confronts arguments that other dimensions of the words, such as familiarity, associative meaningfulness, and word frequency, are more fundamental to an explanation of the results. He convincingly demonstrates that these other attributes are inconsistently related to recall performance and concludes that ". . . imagery-concreteness is the best predictor of memory performance in tasks such as recognition memory and free recall, which require the retention of item information [p. 242]." Presumably, this is because of an imaginal process aroused automatically by the concrete words and serves as an effective retrieval process also. For other tasks, such as those where item sequence is to be retained, a verbal process predominates, and I value is less predictive.

As Paivio suggests, many verbal learning tasks probably involve verbal *and* imaginal coding, and the response requirements determine which coding is more useful. Similarly, the AS measure may include reports of imaginal codings which have not been identified as such. Perhaps the AS- and I-value measures indicate merely the probability of some sort of elaborative coding for words pairs or words rather than the type of coding. In fact, when ratings of the imagery-evoking potential and AS are compared for the same materials, they correlate highly, and it is difficult to decide which process (if any) is more basic. In a recent study (Montague *et al.,* 1971b) Ss were asked to rate 50 high I and 50 low I noun pairs (from Paivio *et al.,* 1968b) in terms of each pair's potential for generating a verbal coding *and* imaginal coding. The correlations between the two ratings for high I pairs is .78, and for low I pairs is .87. Therefore, without additional information, the measures can only be roughly indicative of the type of encoding used by Ss in memory tasks.

Although Ss "spontaneously" transform nominal materials presented in an experiment, it is possible to modify both the frequency and the type of coding operations using instructions. One method which has had considerable success merely instructs one group to code and omits that instruction for control Ss. Any superiority in performance for the former over the latter group is considered to have been produced by the instructions which presumably elicit more or better coding. In cases where no difference results, the reason for the failure is difficult to ascertain unless some record of the S reports has been made. Although such records are obviously important when the attempt is to modify the covert procedures used by Ss, they are not always made. However, although we cannot often indicate the details of the differences in Ss' coding strategies, they are implicated in many experiments which simply compare instructed with uninstructed (self-instructed?) Ss and find recall differences.

Garskof *et al.* (1965) gave different instructions to Ss who learned paired associates in a study utilizing a retroactive interference paradigm. One group was instructed to generate NLM's, the other was not. Learning was faster for the instructed group, but no assessment was made regarding the effect of the instructions on NLM reports, or how much "spontaneous" mediation occurred for the controls. R. B. Martin and Dean (1966) also instructed Ss to mediate, increasing the frequency with which Ss reported using NLM's, and resulting in reliably faster learning. Working with children, Jensen and Rohwer (1965) presented colored pictures of objects as items in a paired-associate task. Some of the children were asked to make up a sentence which would link the two objects. Their learning rate was reliably faster than that of other children not asked to generate sentences. Bower and Clark (1969) presented 10-noun lists to Ss, half of whom were instructed to learn the list by generating a story which would embed the nouns in their proper order. The other Ss were told merely to learn the list, and each was given the same amount of study time as an "instructed" S. Immediate recall tests were given, and the Ss in both instruction conditions performed alike. After 10 lists had been learned and tested, a delayed recall test was given for all lists by presenting the first word on each list. The Ss who coded the words into stories recalled about 93% of the words, while uninstructed Ss recalled only about 14%. In another study in which lists of 20 pairs of nouns were learned, Bower (1967a) reported superiority for instructed over uninstructed Ss of 85-58% recall. Instructions to form NLM's have been found to interact with concreteness or imagery and paired-associates learning.

Paivio and Yuille (1967, 1969) gave different groups instructions to learn word pairs by forming images, by generating a phrase or sentence, or by repeating them over and over. Pairs varied in their image-evoking capacity and in meaningfulness. Results showed that the Ss, given instructions merely to repeat the item in learning, recalled significantly fewer items than the other groups which did not differ from each other. In a subsequent study (Yuille & Paivio, 1968) manipulating the same factors, once again the repetition-rehearsal Ss were found to perform poorly, and Ss with NLM's or images to perform relatively better. More recently, Paivio and Foth (1970) found instructions to generate image mediators produced superior recall for concrete noun pairs compared with instructions to generate verbal mediators.

Time for studying or remembering items has been varied along with instructions to form NLM's, and the results are consistent with the thesis that coding and decoding take time, and longer presentation facilitates both coding and performance. For example, Schwartz (1969) reported an experiment in which Ss who were instructed to generate NLM's reported doing so more frequently than Ss not so instructed. However, acquisition performance was unaffected. Only two seconds were allowed for recall, which was probably insufficient to allow subjects to decode their NLM's. Therefore, in a second experiment, the recall period was untimed and performance was facilitated for Ss instructed to form NLM's. Similar data come from a report by Wood (1967) in which various types of mediation-coding instructions were given to different groups, and their performance was compared with standard instruction control Ss. Wood found increased recall performance for all groups with increased presentation time but greater increases for Ss instructed to generate elaborations of various kinds.

These studies by no means exhaust the list of those which demonstrate facilitation of performance for Ss instructed to transform nominal material presented for memorization. The effect is apparently reliable and strong. However, there are a few studies in which no difference was found between instructed and uninstructed groups. In such cases, it is possible that instructed and uninstructed Ss have the same task set. For example, Dallett and D'Andrea (1965) found no difference in recall, and *post hoc* questioning revealed that the groups reported coding the items about equally often.

Additional problems with Ss' ignoring or modifying instructions are apparent in research which attempted to evaluate the effectiveness of verbal and imaginal elaboration strategies (Paivio, 1971). The Ss, instructed to use one or the other strategy, may idiosyncratically use the other strategy. In several experiments, Paivio (1971) reports that both strategy "sets" facilitate performance compared with that of uninstructed Ss, and that the instructed Ss used both strategies interchangeably. When Ss were asked to draw a picture of their image for some word pairs or write out a sentence for others, Paivio and Foth (1970) found superiority of imagery over verbal instructions for concrete words. Therefore, it is apparent that task demands may dictate the Ss' choice of strategies rather than instructions, unless special care is taken to guarantee the use of one or the other strategy.

Usually, instructions provide only loose control over the use and characteristics of the elaborative strategies Ss use in verbal learning tasks. Furthermore, although NLM and imagery reports may reveal the complexity of the Transformations used to modify the material, it is difficult and laborious to relate the Transformations to performance. Therefore, in attempts to circumvent idiosyncratic coding, various Es have presented coding operations or NLM's as part of the task materials presented to the Ss. This procedure allows the E to control various aspects of the coding and decoding process, thereby enabling him to systematically vary complexity, number of operations, etc. One difficulty with this attempt at control is apparent in the results from a number of experiments. The coding strategy provided may not be used by the Ss, and its presence may "instruct" the S to generate his own (Keppel, 1968). A brief review of some of the studies and these problems follows.

Direct manipulation of coding has been used to control the characteristics of NLM's. For example, Lindley and his co-workers (Lindley, 1963, 1965; Lindley & Nedler, 1965; Schaub & Lindley, 1964) compared short-term recall for trigrams which were presented embedded in words with others presented alone. In their experiment, Schaub and Lindley (1964) had one group of Ss generate NLM codes for CVC's, and then they selected common and uncommon ones. A common coding for FOJ was "fog," and an uncommon one was "fudge." Then, in a short-term memory experiment using the Petersons' technique, either the common or uncommon coding was presented, followed by the trigram and a retention interval filled by counting. As compared with presenting no NLM, the presence of a NLM code facilitated recall, with the common coding producing the greatest effect. Thorsheim (1970) and Duffy (1971) found also that the presence of a NLM code reliably facilitated performance.

Some experiments have relied upon E- generated NLM codes for materials to be learned, which enables more precise control over the complexity of the Transformation involved. In a series of experiments, Underwood and Erlebacher (1965) examined the effect of various E generated codings of nonsense syllables on free recall and paried-associates learning. The Ss were told that the letters of the syllable could be rearranged to form a word. When the same operation generated words for all the syllables (e.g., interchanging the consonants), Ss learned faster than controls. However, when two or four different coding operations were needed to transform the syllable into a word, no facilitation was found. In similar studies, Mueller, Edmunds, and Evans (1967) and Underwood and Keppel (1963) reported that the number of items recalled by Ss is inversely related to the number of coding operations used. Prytulak (1971), C. J. Martin *et al.* (1965), and Montague and Wearing (1967a) made similar observations in analyzing idiosyncratic, S-generated NLM's.

When word pairs are learned, NLM elaborations take the form of sentences or phrases which syntactically and semantically relate the items. Those Ss who learned two successive lists of adjective pairs reported using some form of NLM for about 66 and 70% of the pairs in the first and second lists, respectively (Adams & Montague, 1967). Of these, more than one third were classified as sentences or phrases on the first list, and about half were on the second list. In another study (Wearing, Walker, & Montague, 1970), Ss learned 15 pairs of (CVC) words after being given instructions either to write out a memory device (NLM) or a sentence for each pair, if possible. The latter Ss generated sentences for about 73% of the pairs, while the former group generated grammatical strings for about 82%. These strings were not always complete sentences. Both groups, therefore, generated high proportions of phrases or sentences which related the words. We were unable to isolate any consistent syntactic structure which facilitated subsequent recall. The considerable heterogeneity of syntactic structure used by S idiosyncratically indicates the necessity for more precise control over the structure of the NLM codes for words if important characteristics are to be isolated. A number of experiments which will be reviewed have used a procedure which embeds word pairs in a phrase or sentence generated by the E to effect this control (Rohwer, 1966; Rohwer & Lynch, 1967; Rohwer, Lynch, Suzuki, & Levin, 1967; Suzuki & Rohwer, 1969).

The procedure results in reliable facilitation of childrens' learning but not adults.' In one experiment, for example (Rohwer, 1966), sixth-grade children learned noun pairs embedded in sentences varying in semantic and syntactic features. High-frequency nouns were connected in verbal strings using either standard English or nonsense words, and using different parts of speech to connect the pairs. For strings of Fnglish words, conjunctions, verbs, and prepositions were used as connectives, and for nonsense word strings analogs of those connectives were used. For example, the pair COW-BALL was embedded in the sentences: "The running COW chases the bouncing BALL," or "The ludding COW chases the spraking BALL," which are the verb-connective forms of the "English" or "nonsense" sentences respectively. Control Ss learned only the pairs. The controls made reliably fewer correct responses in acquisition than those Ss who learned the pairs embedded in English sentences, but about the same number correct as Ss learning the items embedded in pseudo sentences. For the English sentences, the degree of facilitation depended on the type of connective, verbs producing greatest learning, prepositions somewhat less, and conjunctions the least, which was about the level of learning produced by control conditions where pairs were presented alone. Similar results for the effects of manipulation of the part of speech of the connective in phrase or sentence NLM's have been found in other experiments (e.g., Rohwer & Lynch, 1967). On the basis of the results from Rohwer's *et al.* experiments, it is apparent that presenting NLM's with items to be learned can be facilitative, and furthermore, that the sentence form which embeds the words can be a major factor in producing facilitation. This conclusion may need qualification, however, since the results were obtained using fifth and sixth grade children as Ss. Similar experiments using adult Ss have obtained inconsistent results, sometimes finding facilitation, at other times no effect, or even interference attributable to the sentence embedding.

Epstein, Rock, and Zuckerman (1960) reported that Ss who learned word pairs connected by prepositions and in verb phrases learned faster than those learning just the words, or words connected by conjunctions. Bower and Winzenz (1970) and Duffy (1971) also reported facilitation for adult Ss who learned the words in sentences. However, in similar research with adult Ss, my colleagues and I have found poorer performance for adult Ss provided with sentence codings for noun pairs in comparison to control Ss learning the pairs alone (e.g., Duffy & Montague, 1971; Duffy, Walker, & Montague, 1970). Suzuki and Rohwer (1969) found no difference in the effect due to the part of speech of connectives which had produced differences in childrens' learning. Explanation of these divergent results is not perfectly clear, but differential task set is indicated. For example, Duffy and Montague had Ss report whether they had used the sentences provided or had learned each pair by generating their own sentence in preference to the one given. For about 37% of the pairs embedded in sentences, Ss reported generating their own idiosyncratic mediators. Apparently, these NLM codes conflicted with those provided, thereby producing interference. In addition, Ss in the control condition reported generating their own mediators for up to 65% of the pairs.

Additional evidence implicating task set was reported in several recent studies which compared the effectiveness of E-provided and S-generated NLM's for paired associates (Bobrow & Bower, 1969; Bower & Winzenz, 1970; Pelton, 1969; Schwartz, 1971). Their results also indicate that E-provided NLM's produce inferior performance. Since the sentence NLM's provided are likely not to be the same as those generated for a pair by the S, the disadvantage may result from some competition between them (e.g., Bobrow & Bower, 1969; Pelton, 1969). However, Schwartz (1971) demonstrates that even when the NLM provided is identical to that generated, its disadvantage remains.

Based on the results just reviewed, the explanation for the interference found by Duffy and Montague (1971) seems plausible. Those Ss required to learn the pairs alone generate many NLM's, which for noun pairs take the form of sentences. The other Ss, provided with sentences containing the nouns which they did not generate, may be at a disadvantage, because they also generate their own sentence which competes with that given. However, other task demand factors seem to be involved. Kulhavy (1970) found nonsignificant differences in recall between groups learning noun pairs alone, connected by verbs or embedded in sentences. His analysis of postexperiment questionnaires revealed that the Ss often did not "pay attention" to the E-provided connections. Similar observations were made by Paivio and Yuille (1969), where Ss were found not to use the type of mediation as instructed. The experimental control over the characteristics of the NLM, which was a major reason for providing the NLM's in the first place, may be inadequate. Apparently, Ss are more sensitive to task demands than has been recognized by Es. They attend to and process materials only as demanded by the task. Where a task allows Ss considerable latitude in performing it, they may behave in an unexpected manner.

F. Meaningful Processing of Materials

The preceding sections examined research concerned with Ss' control over coding and decoding of material to be memorized and how this can be directed by task requirements. One implication which can be drawn from these data is that the S, to a very large extent, responding to cues, biases, and instructions, determines much about the way in which material is stored in memory and its accessibility at later times. The Ss can process material superficially or more comprehensively in response to perceived or stated task demands. Meaningful processing refers to the fact that Ss can vary the level to which they process material. When they "intend" to be able to recall on a forthcoming recall test, they process the material differently than when they do not "intend" to recall. Perhaps, this involves attempts to differentiate the material by verbal coding (Montague *et al.*, 1966; Prytulak, 1971), generating images (Paivio, 1971), or in practicing retrieving or recalling (e.g., Adams & Bray, 1970). This section will review briefly some evidence in an attempt to indicate the problem as it relates to difficulties in experimental control, and more practically, to educational technology.

In the preceding section, studies in which external control of the characteristics of NLM's and other mnemonics was undertaken with varied success. For example, learning of noun pairs embedded in sentences sometimes was facilitated, sometimes not. It seems likely that this may have been due to the fact that control Ss generated subjectively better sentences than do Es (Schwartz, 1971). However, it was found that Ss given the sentences also generated their own mnemonic devices to aid learning, thereby not attending to or processing the given mediators (Kulhavy, 1970). Therefore, it may not be that the coding given by the E is ineffective per se, but that Ss ignore it, i.e., do not process it meaningfully.

Results reported by Bobrow and Bower (1969) may be interpreted to support this contention. In their study, Ss who generated their own NLM's for pairs outperformed those who were given NLM's. They suggested that recall is facilitated when Ss "comprehended the meaning" of the sentences. The task of generating sentences requires comprehension of a meaningful relation between the words. In the results of their first experiments, they suggest that the recall superiority of those Ss who generate over those who merely read the E's sentences may have been due to the lack of meaningful processing for the latter Ss. In a second series of experiments, they manipulated the task requirements for Ss viewing sentences in an incidental learning task. One experiment required one group to find a word with ambiguous meaning in a sentence (e.g., "The cow chased the rubber ball." Is "ball" a dance or a spherical object?) while another group looked for obvious spelling errors (e.g., "balll" in the sentence above). Another experiment used the same sentences but had one group continue or make up another sentence which was a continuation of the presented one (e.g., "The farmer found a diamond" might elicit from an S: "He sold it and bought a tractor."). Another group merely read the sentence aloud repeatedly. The results were clear-cut. In both experiments, in the task requiring Ss to attend to the meaning of the sentences (disambiguation and continuation), they recalled about twice as many predicate nouns as did control Ss.

Anderson, Royer, Kulhavy, Thornburg, and Klemt (1971) describe an experiment in which another procedure was used to establish task demands to ensure comprehension of material presented in sentences. The Ss were to learn CVC-noun pairs. These pairs were embedded in sentences constructed in such a way that Ss would be able to guess the noun if it was omitted from the sentence. For example, the pair SIG YELLOW was embedded in the sentence: "Before turning red, traffic SIG are_____." It is necessary to comprehend the meaning of the sentence in order to generate the response term. In one experiment, group 1 learned a set of 28 pairs in sentences of that sort, i.e., where the probability of guessing the correct word for the blank was high because of the sentence context. Group 2 learned the pairs in sentences which did not produce accurate guessing and presumably the same comprehension. In learning the sentences, Ss were presented with a blank where the noun was to be for 4 seconds, and then the noun was shown. After all sentences were presented, a recall test showing the CVC's was given. Figure 10 shows that group 1 was consistently superior to the other group over the four trials of the study. Anderson *et al.* (1971) conclude that it is the processing of the meaning of the sentences which provides the advantage for recall. The results of this study and that by Bobrow and Bower (1969) emphasize the role of meaningful elaborations in memorizing material. In tasks which do not demand such processing, what is stored in LTS may be considerably different and is unable to produce very accurate recall. Therefore, if the effects of characteristics of NLM codes are to be ascertained by presenting them to Ss, procedures must be used which guarantee that Ss meaningfully process (comprehend) the E-generated relationships.

Other research also indicates that task requirements influence directly the meaningful processing level utilized by Ss in memorizing verbal materials. Anderson (1970) argues that in educational situations, for example, the way instructors set up learning tasks often determines the degree to which students will meaningfully process the material to be learned. He reminds us that people can read material ". . . without bringing to mind the meaning of the words . . . [p. 364]." Intuitive evidence is readily available to us all. Who, while reading text, has not been brought up short by the recognition that

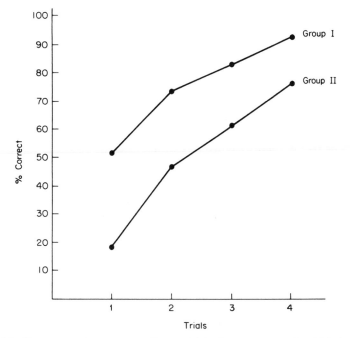

Fig. 10. Mean percent correct recalls per trial of response words which had been embedded in sentences which allowed accurate guessing (Group I), or in sentences which did not produce accurate guessing (Group II). (Data from Anderson *et al.,* 1971.)

what they had read during the last few moments had not been processed? Experimental evidence is available too. For example, Bower (1972) reported experiments in which Ss, asked merely to repeat pairs of words aloud, recalled much less than others told to imagine or visualize a relationship between the objects named by the words. Such elaboration results in considerable qualitative and quantitative advantage. Such evidence argues for a two-stage processing or dual encoding analysis of learning tasks (Anderson, 1970; Bobrow, 1970). One stage would correspond to perceptual selection and the other to semantic coding. Semantic coding is essentially equivalent to what we have referred to as elaborative processes, and presumably such processing results in the storage of an intricately related set of attributes in memory which can provide easier access at recall. Since this processing is often under the S's control, the task requirements to which he responds are not always those desired by the E. In loosely controlled learning tasks (e.g., programmed instructional situations), Ss may attempt to get through the material with a minimum of effort, selecting or attending to only part of the stimulus material (Underwood, 1963), and in so doing circumvent or ignore material provided by the instructor to facilitate learning. In programmed instruction, prompts may aid the student in finding an answer without ever processing the meaning of the material and generating his or her own answer. Anderson and Faust (1967) demonstrated this in a Russian vocabulary task which simulated a self-instructional program. In the program, each instruction frame consisted of five sentences using English words as subject nouns and Russian words as predicate nouns, e.g., "A table is a stohl. A rag is a tryapka. A bridge is a mohst. ..." Following each frame, one sentence was repeated with a blank instead of the Russian word. In one version of the task, the relevant Russian word in the paragraph was underlined; in another version it was not. In the underlined version, Ss could fill in the correct vocabulary word without reading the paragraph or even the English equivalent. The no-underline task required the S to notice the English word that went with the Russian word, at least. Those Ss in the latter version recalled more of the Russian words. Anderson (1970) interprets this result (along with those of Faust, 1967; Royer, 1969) to indicate that in the no-underline conditions, Ss were forced to attend to the material and process the material meaningfully.

The same explanation is offered for the problems found in experiments which provide coding context for learning word pairs. Rohwer's *et al.* (see previous section) finding that children recall more noun pairs when they are embedded in sentences may indicate that they attend to and comprehend the meaningful relationship between the items provided, while adults approach the task with another set (Duffy & Montague, 1971).

IV. Summary and Conclusions

The position taken in this paper is that traditional theories of learning and memory are insufficiently complex to allow adequate description or understanding of the complex network of processes and variables involved in memorizing and remembering. Somewhat more adequate approaches are those which recognize this complexity and attempt to identify the processes and how they function in a variety of tasks. The paper has placed major emphasis on S-controlled processes which directly influence the adequacy of recall performance in certain tasks. This section will summarize the more important empirical findings and will identify certain problem areas which may need more attention.

A. EMPIRICAL SUMMARY

1. The results from various research paradigms strongly implicate S-control processes in determining how well material is stored in memory, and its form. Accuracy in recall is directly related to characteristics of these processes. The pattern of free recall, for example, and its organization is determined by the pattern of Ss' rehearsals (Rundus, 1971). Furthermore, covert rehearsal complicates other experiments in spite of attempts to control it. In short-term memory procedures, the retention interval is filled with an irrelevant task in order to prevent rehearsal. However, rehearsal does occur, and where it is more advantageous for Ss to rehearse under some conditions than others, they do (e.g., Montague *et al.*, 1970). Therefore, in tasks where rehearsal set might interact with experimental variables, more adequate control is necessary.

2. It is clear that "rehearsal" often involves coding or transformation of verbal items. In fact, elaborative coding strategies are almost universally used in verbal learning by the adults who form the S population for most experiments. It is suggested that the codes increase the accessibility of the verbal items at recall. As is the case for rehearsal or repetition, coding strategies interact with E-controlled variables under certain conditions. Such an explanation is offered for the results of some experiments attempting to examine "intention" in learning. That is to say, when a difference in recall performance is found between Ss who anticipate (I) and those who do not anticipate (NI) a recall test, it can be attributed to the difference in the extent to which the different groups elaborate the material. If Ss elaborate the items equally, their recall is about equal regardless of their intention. Under some conditions, intention interacts with such variables as meaningfulness of items, and NI Ss do less elaboration and recall less. However, the proportion of coded items recalled is about equal for both I and NI Ss (Montague *et al.*, 1971a; Wearing, 1971a). Therefore, the elaborative coding of material is implicated as important for retrieval. A similar conclusion is derived from the results of experiments on selective forgetting. The Ss react differently to materials they have been told to forget. Since recall of to-be-forgotten items is poor and recognition is relatively good (Block, 1971), a rehearsal-elaboration (differentiation) process is implicated which makes to-be-remembered items more accessible.

3. A large number of diverse experiments have revealed that Ss use verbal and imaginal elaborations to assist them in learning verbal items.

a. In experiments in which postexperiment questioning has been undertaken, a consistent, positive relation has been found between reports of having used elaborative coding strategies for items and their recall. It is difficult or perhaps impossible for Es to differentiate between verbal and imaginal codes in such reports, although Ss seem to have no difficulty classifying their own coding (Paivio, 1971). The Ss apparently can use whichever coding seems appropriate for the material and the task, sometimes using them independently and at other times to supplement one another. The frequency of use and the characteristics of the codings, therefore, may vary considerably with task conditions, but the relation between the reported use of a coding stragegy and item recall is consistent. However, from such facts alone, it is impossible to conclude that the elaborations actually determine recall, since the reports may be merely given in response to the questioning. A variety of other results, not relying on evidence from questionnaires, also strongly suggests that elaborative coding is crucial for recall.

Recall performance and the use of coding strategies can be predicted from normative data obtained for material in other contexts. For example, association value and image-evoking potential predict learning rates, recall, and report frequency for learning single items, and AS does so for paired associates. Also, results directly implicating coding strategies demonstrate their relationship to other variables. Presentation time, for example, is systematically related to the frequency with which Ss report using both verbal and nonverbal codes. Verbal codes are less frequent as association value or AS is reduced, and imaginal codes are less frequent with abstract words. This effect of item attributes can be attenuated somewhat by increases in presentation time.

b. Other characteristics of the coding strategies change as material and task requirements are varied. For concrete words, for example, imagery codes are a preferred strategy, while for abstract words, verbal codes predominate. Imaginal elaboration can facilitate learning abstract words, however, given time and proper instructions. With CVC's, verbal codes predominate, and their complexity varies inversely with the meaningfulness of the items. The codes generated for low-meaningfulness items or abstract words are more complicated (involve more operations or more extensive transformations) and are thus harder to decode.

c. It is difficult to experimentally control the S's use of elaborative strategies, although a considerable number of attempts have been successful. Instructions to use elaborative strategies can increase both the frequencies of the reported use and correct recalls compared with uninstructed control Ss. This result relies on the instructions to elicit more coding than Ss would do idiosyncratically in the task. The characteristics of elaborative coding are very difficult to manipulate by instructions alone. The Ss tend to ignore an instructional set when another seems more appropriate for the material to be learned (Paivio, 1971).

Direct control of the characteristics of elaborative strategies using E-generated codes has met with limited success. The problem, once again, is that Ss sometimes ignore the codes given to them in favor of their own (Kulhavy, 1970). However, when procedures are adopted which insure that Ss comprehend the meaning of the E-generated materials, recall performance is improved (e.g., Bobrow & Bower, 1969).

B. PROBLEMS FOR FURTHER STUDY

A considerable amount of empirical data has been reviewed indicating that S-controlled elaborative strategies strongly determine performance in memory tasks. Since the strategies are selected and controlled by the Ss, they present various problems for E and theorists who attempt to understand the processes of learning and remembering. Some of these problems will be described briefly in this section.

1. A most important problem arises from the simple fact of idiosyncratic coding by Ss in verbal learning tasks. The coding generated for the items provides a means of storing and retrieving them at recall, and also differentiates them from other nominal items. Therefore, explanations of learning and memory phenomena which rely only on externally specified relations between the nominal items will be inadequate or incomplete. For example, the most widely held explanation of forgetting accounts for the recall loss in terms of interference from similar materials learned in or outside the laboratory. However, as Postman (1963) indicated, the amount of forgetting found in experiments is far less than might be expected, and he proposed that "principles of conservation" systematically reduce the amount of forgetting. Elaborative strategies used idiosyncratically by Ss in verbal tasks exemplify some of these principles. When NLM codes are generated for nominal CVC's, their similarity

to other CVC's is not determined by relationships specified by the E, but by the relationships with other functional codes. The failure of several experiments to demonstrate interference from extraexperimental associations (e.g., Ekstrand & Underwood, 1965) may have been due to Ss' frequent transformations of the nominal material (Montague & Wearing, 1967b). Groninger (1966) and Adams and Montague (1967) also presented data demonstrating that when Ss code items in learning, less interference results from the nominal relationships built into the materials. Therefore, an important problem is to gain more precise control over the functional codings used by Ss.

2. Definitions of complexity of elaborative strategies have been somewhat contradictory. C. J. Martin *et al.* (1965) used a scaling procedure which indicated that multistage codes were less complex than single-step codes, which is in contrast to Prytulak's (1971) definition of complexity. This disagreement seems more apparent than real, and probably because Martin *et al.* were rating reports in terms of how closely the codes resembled syntactic phrases or semantic relations. They found (as did Montague & Wearing, 1967a) that reports given lower rankings were often complex in the sense that they involved several stages or operations. In agreement with Prytulak, they found recall performance to be poorer for multistage Transformations. It seems reasonable to prefer a working definition of complexity specified in terms of the number of coding operations involved. However, since Prytulak reports that some operations are more decodable than others, any attempt to manipulate complexity must also take that fact into account.

3. A problem which runs counter to intuition and conceptions about the limited capacity of immediate memory is that elaborations facilitate recall while increasing the amount to be remembered. Normally we would expect decreases in memory load to be associated with more efficient memorization. This problem has been recognized for centuries. Quintillian (cited in Yates, 1966) was concerned about this problem and, in fact, recommended against widespread use of mnemonic elaborations in favor of rote memorization, since elaborations would ultimately crowd memory and impede remembering. Although we have no really adequate explanation, current theorists have considered the problem. Norman (1969) suggests that mnemonic elaborations actually reduce memory load by providing fewer chunks or units to remember. In his systematic analysis of a mnemonic device, Bower (1970a) explains that elaborations are facilitative because they provide a framework for remem-

bering. When the S is asked to recall, he has a frame of reference for monitoring his performance and judging its accuracy or completeness.

The suggestions that elaborative coding provides a means of retrieving and judging responses is similar to the description of retrieval presented by Adams and Bray (1970), Shiffrin (1970), and Wearing (1971b). The process of remembering has received relatively scant attention. We understand little of the process where Ss search and retrieve salient data and judge the accuracy of their retrieval. How do elaborations facilitate the search and judgment processes?

4. A problem related to concern about the retrieval process derives from observations that reports of using codes to assist learning verbal items increases and then decreases in frequency with trials (Adams & McIntyre, 1967; Prytulak, 1971; Reed, 1918). It becomes difficult to understand how the codes provide a framework for recall if, with practice, they are abandoned. The acquisition process may involve multiple stages in which verbal or imagery codes are facilitative only initially.

5. Finally, there are implications and interpretations of the data which raise problems. There seems little reason to question the empirical role of elaborative strategies in memory tasks. The research overwhelmingly reveals that codings produce increases in recall. However, considerably more information is needed to provide an understanding of the way in which the process operates.

It appears that idiosyncratic use of elaborative codes by Ss are an attempt to increase the meaning of arbitrary verbal items (cf. Bartlett, 1932; Horowitz & Prytulak, 1969). In one sense, elaboration implies that the dimensions or features stored for an item are increased in number. In coding, higher order verbal and nonverbal associations are used by Ss to incorporate the nominal items. Presumably, with more of these associations or dimensions stored for an item, the more probable retrieval will be. There are little data available to support these ideas directly.

When nominal material (e.g., CVCs) is transformed significantly, the decoding process takes on special importance. Although code may be retrieved because of its increased meaning in relation to the item, reconstruction operations must produce a recognizable item. Prytulak's analysis and data demonstrate the importance of decoding, but the process is not clearly understood. How are the decoding operations stored? Also, Paivio (1971) indicates that imaginal codes may be especially useful for remembering certain types of information, in which the spatial character of the image is important. The process by which Ss reconstruct items from imaginal codes is conjectural.

C. FINAL COMMENT

This article has reviewed research which indicates the significance of covert processes used by the S in determining his memory for verbal materials. Rehearsal and verbal and nonverbal coding of verbal materials are procedures by which the memory trace is structured and retrieval facilitated. Although there are substantial gaps in our understanding of the storage and retrieval processes, they can be conceptualized reasonably well within the information-processing model presented initially. Learning or memorizing is conceived to be a process in which a search for meaning provides a basis for retrieval. Retrieval is a search and reconstruction process in which the stored codes are decoded until a recognizable response is generated. At all stages in the model S-controlled processes play vital roles in determining the adequacy of performance. This conception of memorizing and remembering seems accurate as a description and will guide considerable research, hopefully leading us to greater understanding of the phenomena.

REFERENCES

Adams, J. A. *Human memory.* New York: McGraw-Hill, 1967.

Adams, J. A., & Bray, N. A closed-loop theory of paired-associate verbal learning. *Psychological Review,* 1970, 77, 385-405.

Adams, J. A., & Dijkstra, S. Short-term memory for motor responses. *Journal of Experimental Psychology,* 1966, 71, 314-318.

Adams, J. A., Marshall, P. H., & Bray, N. W. Interference and retrieval. *Journal of Verbal Learning and Verbal Behavior,* 1971, 10, 548-555.

Adams, J. A., & McIntyre, J. S. Natural language mediation and all-or-none learning. *Canadian Journal of Psychology,* 1967, 21, 436-449.

Adams, J. A., McIntyre, J. S., & Thorsheim, H. I. Response feedback and verbal retention. *Journal of Experimental Psychology,* 1969, 82, 290-296.

Adams, J. A., & Montague, W. E. Retroactive inhibition and natural language mediation. *Journal of Verbal Learning and Verbal Behavior,* 1967, 6, 528-535.

Aiken, E. G. Linguistic and imaginal mnemonics. *Psychonomic Science,* 1971, 24, 91-92.

Anderson, R. C. Control of student mediating processes during verbal learning and instruction. *Review of Educational Research,* 1970, 40, 349-369.

Anderson, R. C., & Faust, G. W. The effects of strong formal prompts in programmed instruction. *American Educational Research Journal,* 1967, 4, 345-352.

Anderson, R. C., Royer, J. M., Kulhavy, R. W., Thornburg, S. D., & Klemt, L. L. Thematic prompting in paired-associate learning. *Journal of Educational Psychology,* 1971, 62, 315-321.

Archer, E. J. A re-evaluation of the meaningfulness of all possible CVC trigrams. *Psychological Monographs,* 1960, **74** (10, Whole No. 497).

Atkinson, R. C., & Shiffrin, R. M. Human memory: A proposed system and its control processes. In K. W. Spence & J. T. Spence (Eds.), *The psychology of learning and motivation: Advances in research and theory.* Vol. 2. New York: Academic Press, 1968.

Atkinson, R. C., & Shiffrin, R. M. The control of short-term memory. *Scientific American,* 1971, **225,** 82-90.

Atwood, G. E. Experimental studies of mnemonic visualization. Unpublished doctoral dissertation, University of Oregon, 1969.

Atwood, G. E. An experimental study of visual imagination and memory. *Cognitive Psychology,* 1971, **2,** 290-299.

Baddeley, A. D. The influence of acoustic and semantic similarity on long-term memory for word sequences. *Quarterly Journal of Experimental Psychology,* 1966, **18,** 302-309.

Baddeley, A. D., & Levy, B. A. Semantic coding in short-term memory. *Journal of Experimental Psychology,* 1971, **89,** 132-136.

Bahrick, H. P., & Boucher, B. Retention of visual and verbal codes of the same stimuli. *Journal of Experimental Psychology,* 1968, **78,** 417-422.

Bartlett, F. C. *Remembering.* Cambridge, Engl.: Cambridge University Press, 1932.

Battig, W. F. Evidence for coding processes in "rote" paired-associate learning. *Journal of Verbal Learning and Verbal Behavior,* 1966, **5,** 177-181.

Battig, W. F., & Spera, A. J. Rated association values of numbers from 0-100. *Journal of Verbal Learning and Verbal Behavior,* 1962, **1,** 200-202.

Bjork, R. A. Positive forgetting: The non-interference of items intentionally forgotten. *Journal of Verbal Learning and Verbal Behavior,* 1970, **9,** 255-268. (a)

Bjork, R. A. Repetition and rehearsal mechanisms in models for short-term memory. In D. A. Norman (Ed.), *Models of human memory.* New York: Academic Press, 1970. (b)

Bjork, R. A., LaBerge, D., & LeGrand, R. The modification of short-term memory through instructions to forget. *Psychonomic Science,* 1968, **10,** 55-56.

Block, R. A. Effects of instructions to forget in short-term memory. *Journal of Experimental Psychology,* 1971, **89,** 1-9.

Bobrow, S. A. Memory for words in sentences. *Journal of Verbal Learning and Verbal Behavior,* 1970, **9,** 363-372.

Bobrow, S. A., & Bower, G. H. Comprehension and recall of sentences. *Journal of Experimental Psychology,* 1969, **80,** 455-461.

Boersma, F. J., Conklin, R. C., & Carlson, J. E. Effects of reporting associative strategies on the retention of paired-associates. *Psychonomic Science,* 1966, **5,** 463-464.

Bogartz, R., Helgoe, R., & Weigel, A. Short-term tactile memory. Unpublished manuscript, University of Illinois, 1970.

Bourne, L. E. *Human conceptual behavior.* Boston: Allyn & Bacon, 1966.

Bower, G. H. Mental imagery and mnemonics, Unpublished mimeo., Stanford Univ., 1967.(a)

Bower, G. H. A multicomponent theory of the memory trace. In K. W. Spence & J. T. Spence (Eds.), *The psychology of learning and motivation: Advances in research and theory.* Vol. I. New York: Academic Press, 1967. (b)

Bower, G. H. Analysis of a mnemonic device. *American Scientist,* 1970, **58,** 496-510. (a)

Bower, G H. Organizational factors in memory. *Cognitive Psychology,* 1970, **1,** 18-46. (b)

Bower, G. H. Mental imagery and associative learning. In L. Gregg (Ed.), *Cognition in learning and memory.* New York: Wiley, 1972, in press.

Bower, G. H., & Clark, M. C. Narrative stories as mediators for serial learning. *Psychonomic Science,* 1969, **14,** 181-182.

Bower, G. H., & Winzenz, D. Comparison of associative learning strategies. *Psychonomic Science,* 1970, **20,** 119-120.

Bregman, A. S., & Strasberg, R. Memory for the syntactic form of sentences. *Journal of Verbal Learning and Verbal Behavior,* 1968, 7, 396-403.

Broadbent, D. *Perception and communication.* New York: Pergamon, 1958.

Brooks, L. R. Spatial and verbal components of the act of recall. *Canadian Journal of Psychology,* 1968, 22, 349-368.

Brown, J. Some tests of the decay theory of immediate memory. *Quarterly Journal of Experimental Psychology,* 1958, 10, 12-24.

Brown, R., & McNeill, D. The "tip of the tongue" phenomenon. *Journal of Verbal Learning and Verbal Behavior,* 1966, 5, 325-337.

Bugelski, B. R. Presentation time, total time, and mediation in paired-associate learning. *Journal of Experimental Psychology,* 1962, 63, 409-412.

Bugelski, B. R. Words and things and images. *American Psychologist,* 1970, 25, 1002-1012.

Bugelski, B. R., Kidd, E., & Segmen, J. Image as a mediator in one-trial paired-associate learning. *Journal of Experimental Psychology,* 1968, 76, 69-73.

Bugelski, B. R., & Scharlock, D. P. An experimental demonstration of unconscious mediated association. *Journal of Experimental Psychology,* 1952, 44, 334-338.

Chase, W. G., & Posner, M. I. The effect of visual and auditory confusability on visual and memory search tasks. Paper presented at the meeting of the Psychonomics Society, Chicago, October 1965. Cited by Posner, 1969.

Chomsky, N. *Syntactic structures.* The Hague: Mouton, 1957.

Clark, L. L., Lansford, T. G., & Dallenbach, K. M. Repetition and associative learning. *American Journal of Psychology,* 1960, 73, 22-40.

Colegate, R. L., & Eriksen, C. W. Implicit speech as an encoding mechanism in visual perception. *American Journal of Psychology,* 1970, 83, 208-215.

Conrad, R. Acoustic confusions in immediate memory. *British Journal of Psychology,* 1964, 55, 75-84.

Dallett, K., & D'Andrea, L. Mediation instructions versus unlearning instructions in the A-B, A-C paradigm. *Journal of Experimental Psychology,* 1965, 69, 460-466.

Dallett, K., & Wilcox, S. G. Remembering pictures vs. remembering descriptions. *Psychonomic Science,* 1968, 11, 139-410.

Davis, J. C., & Okada, R. Recognition and recall of positively forgotten items. *Journal of Experimental Psychology,* 1971. 89, 181-186.

Dillon, R. F., & Reid, L. S. Short-term memory as a function of information processing during the retention interval. *Journal of Experimental Psychology,* 1969, 81, 261-269.

Duffy, T. M. Mnemonics and intra-list interference in paired-associate learning. *Canadian Journal of Psychology,* 1971, 25, 33-41.

Duffy, T. M., & Montague, W. E. Sentence mnemonics and noun pair learning. *Journal of Verbal Learning and Verbal Behavior,* 1971, 10, 157-162.

Duffy, T. M., Walker, C., & Montague, W. E. Sentence mnemonics and the role of verb class in paired-associate learning. Unpublished manuscript, University of Manitoba, 1970.

Dulany, D. Awareness, rules, and propositional control: A confrontation with S-R behavior theory. In T. R. Dixon & D. L. Horton (Eds.), *Verbal behavior and general behavior theory.* Englewood Cliffs, N.J.: Prentice-Hall, 1968.

Earhard, B., & Mandler, G. Mediated associations: Paradigms, controls, and mechanisms. *Canadian Journal of Psychology,* 1965, 19, 346-372.

Eimas, P. D., & Zeaman, D. Response speed changes in an Estes' paired-associate "miniature" experiment. *Journal of Verbal Learning and Verbal Behavior,* 1963, 1, 384-388.

Ekstrand, B. R., & Underwood, B. J. Free learning and recall as a function of unit-sequence and letter sequence interference. *Journal of Verbal Learning and Verbal Behavior*, 1965, 4, 390-396.

Elmes, D. G., Adams, C., & Roediger, H. L. Cued forgetting in short-term memory: Response selection. *Journal of Experimental Psychology*, 1970, 86, 103-107.

Epstein, W., Rock, I., & Zuckerman, C. B. Meaning and familiarity in associative learning. *Psychological Monographs*, 1960, 74, (4, Whole No. 491).

Eriksen, C. W., Pollack, M. D., & Montague, W. E. Implicit speech: Mechanism in perceptual encoding? *Journal of Experimental Psychology*, 1970, 84, 502-507.

Estes, W. K., & DaPolito, F. Independent variation of information storage and retrieval processes in paired-associate learning. *Journal of Experimental Psychology*, 1967, 75, 18-26.

Faust, G. W., The effects of prompting in programmed instruction as a function of motivation and instructions. Unpublished doctoral dissertation, University of Illinois, 1967.

Fischler, I., Rundus, D., & Atkinson, R. C. Effects of overt rehearsal procedures on free recall. *Psychonomic Science*, 1970, 19, 249-250.

Garskof, B. E., Sandak, J. M., & Malinowski, E. W. A. Controlling the "fate" of first list associates. *Psychonomic Science*, 1965, 2, 315-316.

Glanzer, M., & Cunitz, A. R. Two storage mechanisms in free recall. *Journal of Verbal Learning and Verbal Behavior*, 1966, 5, 351-360.

Groninger, L. D. Natural language mediation and covert rehearsal in short-term memory. *Psychonomic Science*, 1966, 5, 135-136.

Gupton, T., & Frincke, G. Imagery, mediational instructions and noun position in free recall of noun-verb pairs. *Journal of Experimental Psychology*, 1970, 86, 461-462.

Hart, J. T. Memory and the feeling-of-knowing experience. *Journal of Educational Psychology*, 1965, 56, 208-216.

Hart, J. T. Second-try recall, recognition, and the memory-monitoring process. *Journal of Educational Psychology*, 1967, 58, 193-197.

Hillix, W. A., & Peeler, M. H. An effective indicant of covert rehearsal in short-term memory. Unpublished manuscript, University of Missouri, 1967.

Holt, R. R. Imagery: The return of the ostracized. *American Psychologist*, 1964, 19, 254-264.

Horowitz, L. M., & Prytulak, L. Redintegrative memory. *Psychological Review*, 1969, 76, 510-531.

Horton, D. L. The effects of meaningfulness, awareness, and type of design in verbal mediation. *Journal of Verbal Learning and Verbal Behavior*, 1964, 3, 187-194.

Horton, D. L., & Kjeldergaard, P. M. An experimental analysis of associative factors in mediated generalizations. *Psychological Monographs*, 1961, 75, (11, Whole No. 515).

Hulicka, I. M., & Grossman, J. L. Age-group comparisons for the use of mediators in paired-associate learning. *Journal of Gerontology*, 1967, 22, 46-51.

Jenkins, J. J. Mediated associations: Paradigms and situations. In C. N. Cofer & B. S. Musgrave (Eds.), *Verbal behavior and learning*. New York: McGraw-Hill, 1963.

Jensen, A. R., & Rohwer, W. D. Syntactical mediation of serial and paired-associate learning as a function of age. *Child Development*, 1965, 36, 601-608.

Keppel, G. Problems of method in the study of short-term memory. *Psychological Bulletin*, 1965, 63, 1-13.

Keppel, G. Verbal learning and memory. *Annual Review of Psychology*, 1968, 19, 169-202.

Kernoff, P., Weiner, B., & Morrison, M. Affect and short-term rentention. *Psychonomic Science,* 1966, 4, 75-76.

Kiess, H. O. The effects of natural language mediation in short-term memory. Unpublished doctoral dissertation, University of Illinois, 1967.

Kiess, H. O. Effects of natural language mediators on short-term memory. *Journal of Experimental Psychology,* 1968, 77, 7-13.

Kiess, H.O., & Montague, W. E. Natural language mediators in paired-associate learning. *Psychonomic Science,* 1965, 3, 549-550.

Kintsch, W. *Learning, memory and conceptual processes.* New York: Wiley, 1970.

Köhler, W. *Gestalt psychology.* New York: Liveright, 1947.

Kroll, N. E., Parks, T., Parkinson, S. R., Breber, S. L., & Johnson, A. L. Short-term memory while shadowing: Recall of visually and orally presented letters. *Journal of Experimental Psychology,* 1970, 85, 220-224.

Kulhavy, R. W. Natural language mediators and paired-associate learning in college students. *Psychological Reports,* 1970, 26, 658.

Lindley, R. H. Effects of controlled coding cues in short-term memory. *Journal of Experimental Psychology,* 1963, 66, 580-587.

Lindley, R. H. Effects of trigram recoding cue complexity on short-term memory. *Journal of Verbal Learning and Verbal Behavior,* 1965, 4, 274-279.

Lindley, R. H., & Nedler, S. E. Further effects of subject-generated recoding cues on short-term memory. *Journal of Experimental Psychology,* 1965, 69, 324-325.

Loess, H., & McBurney, J. Short-term memory and retention interval activity. *Proceedings of Annual Convention of the American Psychological Association,* 1965, 73, 85-86.

Luria, A. R. *The mind of a mnemonist.* (Transl. by L. Solotaroff) New York: Basic Books, 1968.

Mandler, G. Comments on Professor Jenkins' paper. In C. N. Cofer & B. S. Musgrave (Eds.), *Verbal behavior and learning.* New York: McGraw-Hill, 1963.

Mandler, G. Organization and memory. In K. W. Spence & J. T. Spence (Eds.), *The psychology of learning and motivation: Advances in research and theory.* Vol. I. New York: Academic Press, 1967. (a)

Mandler, G. Verbal learning. In T. M. Newcomb (Ed.), *New directions in psychology.* Vol. III. New York: Holt, 1967. (b)

Martin, C. J., Boersma, F. J., & Cox, D. L. A classification of associative strategies in paired-associate learning. *Psychonomic Science,* 1965, 3, 455-456.

Martin, R. B., & Dean, S. J. Implicit and explicit mediation in paired-associate learning. *Journal of Experimental Psychology,* 1964, 66, 21-27.

Martin, R. B., & Dean, S. J. Reported mediation in paired-associate learning. *Journal of Verbal Learning and Verbal Behavior,* 1966, 5, 23-27.

Masters, L. The effects of percentage of knowledge of results and item associability in paired-associates learning. Unpublished master's thesis, University of Illinois, 1969.

Masters, L. Knowledge of results and item associability in paired-associates learning. *American Journal of Psychology,* 1970, 83, 76-85.

McGeoch, J. A., & Irion, A. L. *The psychology of human learning.* New York: Longmans, Green, 1952.

McManama, C. S. Time factors in verbal mediation. Unpublished master's thesis, University of Illinois, 1971.

Miller, G. A. The magical number seven, plus or minus two: Some limits on our capacity for processing information. *Psychological Review,* 1956, 63, 81-97.

Miller, G. A. Some psychological studies of grammar. *American Psychologist,* 1962, 17, 748-762.

Miller, G. A., Galanter, E., & Pribram, K. *Plans and the structure of behavior.* New York: Holt, 1960.

Montague, W. E., Adams, J. A., & Kiess, H. O. Forgetting and natural language mediation. *Journal of Experimental Psychology,* 1966, 72, 829-833.

Montague, W. E., & Cohen, A. Effect of rated imagery in free recall of blind and sighted subjects. Unpublished manuscript, University of Illinois, 1971.

Montague, W. E., Gibbs, W., & Baechle, D. NLM coding, intention, and recall of high and low association value digits. Unpublished manuscript, University of Illinois, 1971. (a)

Montague, W. E., & Hillix, W. A. Intertrial interval and proactive interference in short-term memory. *Canadian Journal of Psychology,* 1968, 22, 73-78.

Montague, W. E., Hillix, W. A., Kiess, H. O., & Harris, R. Variation in reports of covert rehearsal and in STM produced by differential payoff. *Journal of Experimental Psychology,* 1970, 83, 249-254.

Montague, W. E., & Kiess, H. O. The associability of CVC pairs. *Journal of Experimental Psychology,* 1968, 78, No. 2, Part 2.

Montague, W. E., Klemt, L. L., & Carter, J. A comparison of ratings of associability and interactive imagery for 100 noun pairs. Unpublished manuscript, University of Illinois, 1971. (b)

Montague, W. E., Nelson, T. O., & Carter, J. Effect of a post-criterion test on item and NLM-code recall. Unpublished manuscript, University of Illinois, 1971. (c)

Montague, W. E., & Wearing, A. The complexity of natural language mediators and its relation to paired-associate learning. *Psychonomic Science,* 1967, 7, 135-136. (a)

Montague, W. E., & Wearing, A. Natural language mediation: A source of interference with extra-experimental interference. *Psychonomic Science,* 1967, 9, 317-318 (b)

Müller, G. E. Zur analyse der Gedächtnistäligkeit und des Vorstellungsverlaufes. *Zeitschrift für Psychologie,* Ergänzungsband. 1911, No. 5. Cited by Woodworth & Schlossberg, 1954.

Mueller, M. R., Edmonds, E. M., & Evans, S. H. Amount of uncertainty associated with decoding in free recall. *Journal of Experimental Psychology,* 1967, 75, 437-443.

Murdock, B. B. The criterion problem in short-term memory. *Journal of Experimental Psychology,* 1966, 72, 317-324.

Murdock, B. B. Auditory and visual stores in short-term memory. *Acta Psychologica,* 1967, 27, 316-324.

Neimark, E., Greenhouse, P., Law, S., & Weinheimer, S. The effect of a rehearsal preventing task upon retention of CVC syllables. *Journal of Verbal Learning and Verbal Behavior,* 1965, 4, 280-285.

Neisser, V. *Cognitive psychology.* New York: Appleton, 1967.

Noble, C. E. An analysis of meaning. *Psychological Review,* 1952, 59, 421-430.

Norman, D. A. (Ed.) *Memory and attention.* New York: Wiley, 1969.

Norman, D. A. (Ed.) *Models of human memory.* New York: Academic Press, 1970.

Norman, D. A., & Rumelhart, D. E. A system for perception and memory. In D. A. Norman (Ed.), *Models of human memory.* New York: Academic Press, 1970.

Paivio, A. Effects of imagery instructions and concreteness of memory pegs in a mnemonic system. *Proceedings of the Annual Convention of the American Psychological Association,* 1968, 76, 77-78.

Paivio, A. Mental imagery in associative learning and memory. *Psychological Review,* 1969, 76, 241-263.

Paivio, A. *Imagery and verbal processes.* New York: Holt, 1971.

Paivio, A., & Foth, D. Imaginal and verbal mediators and noun concreteness in paired-associate learning: The elusive interaction. *Journal of Verbal Learning and Verbal Behavior,* 1970, 9, 384-390.

Paivio, A., & Okovita, H. W. Word imagery modalities and associative learning in blind and sighted subjects. *Journal of Verbal Learning and Verbal Behavior*, 1971, 10, 506-510.

Paivio, A., Smythe, P. C., & Yuille, J. C. Imagery versus meaningfulness of nouns in paired-associate learning. *Canadian Journal of Psychology*, 1968, 22, 427-441. (a)

Paivio, A., & Yuille, J. C. Mediation instructions and word attributes in paired-associate learning. *Psychonomic Science*, 1967, 8, 65-66.

Paivio, A., & Yuille, J. C. Changes in associative strategies and paired-associate learning over trials as a function of word imagery and type of learning set. *Journal of Experimental Psychology*, 1969, 79, 458-463.

Paivio, A., Yuille, J. C., & Madigan, S. A. Concreteness, imagery, and meaningfulness values for 925 nouns. *Journal of Experimental Psychology*, 1968, 76, (Monogr. Suppl. 1, Part 2). (b)

Paivio, A., Yuille, J. C., & Smythe, P. C. Stimulus and response abstractness, imagery and meaningfulness, and reported mediators in paired-associate learning. *Canadian Journal of Psychology*, 1966, 20, 362-377.

Pelton, L. H. Mediational construction vs. mediational perception in paired-associate learning. *Psychonomic Science*, 1969, 17, 199-200.

Peterson, L. R. Search and judgment in memory. In B. Kleinmuntz (Ed.), *Concepts and the structure of memory*. New York: Wiley, 1967.

Peterson, L. R., & Peterson, M. J. Short-term retention of individual verbal items. *Journal of Experimental Psychology*, 1959, 58, 193-198.

Posner, M. I. Components of skilled performance. *Science*, 1966, 152, 1712-1718.

Posner, M. I. Abstraction and the process of recognition. In G. Bower & J. T. Spence (Eds.), *The psychology of learning and motivation: Advances in research and theory*. Vol. 3. New York: Academic Press, 1969. Pp. 43-100.

Posner, M. I., & Konick, A. F. Short-term retention of visual and kinesthetic information. *Organizational Behavior and Human Performance*, 1966, 1, 71-86.

Postman, L. Does interference theory predict too much forgetting. *Journal of Verbal Learning and Verbal Behavior*, 1963, 2, 40-48.

Postman, L., Adams, P. A., & Phillips, L. W. Studies in incidental learning: II. The effects of association value and of method of testing. *Journal of Experimental Psychology*, 1955, 49, 1-10.

Postman, L., & Phillips, L. W. Short-term temporal changes in free recall. *Quarterly Journal of Experimental Psychology*, 1965, 17, 132-138.

Prytulak, L. S. Natural language mediation. *Cognitive Psychology*, 1971, 2, 1-56.

Reed, H. B. Associative aids: I. Their relation to learning, retention and other associations. *Psychological Review*, 1918, 25, 128-155.

Richardson, A. *Mental imagery*. New York: Springer Publ., 1969.

Rimm, D. C., Alexander, R. A., & Eiles, R. R. Effects of different mediation instructions and sex of subject on paired-associate learning of concrete nouns. *Psychological Reports*, 1969, 25, 935-940.

Rohwer, W. D. Constraint, syntax and meaning in paired-associate learning. *Journal of Verbal Learning and Verbal Behavior*, 1966, 5, 541-547.

Rohwer, W. D., & Lynch, S. Form class and intralist similarity in paired-associate learning. *Journal of Verbal Learning and Verbal Behavior*, 1967, 6, 551-554.

Rohwer, W. D., & Lynch, S., Suzuki, N., & Levin, J. R. Verbal and pictoral facilitation of paired-associate learning. *Journal of Experimental Child Psychology*, 1967, 5, 294-302.

Royer, J. M. Inspection behavior during verbal learning. Unpublished master's thesis, University of Illinois, 1969.

Rundus, D. Analysis of rehearsal processes in free recall. *Journal of Experimental Psychology*, 1971. 89, 63-77.

Rundus, D., & Atkinson, R. C. Rehearsal processes in free recall: A procedure for direct observation. *Journal of Verbal Learning and Verbal Behavior,* 1970, 9, 99-105.

Runquist, W. N. Intralist interference as a function of list length and interstimulus similarity. *Journal of Verbal Learning and Verbal Behavior,* 1966, 5, 7-13.

Runquist, W. N., & Farley, F. The use of mediators on the learning of verbal paired-associates. *Journal of Verbal Learning and Verbal Behavior,* 1964, 3, 280-285.

Saltz, E. *The cognitive bases of human learning.* Homewood, Ill.: Dorsey, 1971.

Saltzman, I. J. Comparison of incidental and intentional learning with different orienting tasks. *American Journal of Psychology,* 1956, 69, 274-277.

Sanders, A. F. Rehearsal and recall in immediate memory. *Ergonomics,* 1961, 4, 29-34.

Schaub, G. R., & Lindley, R. H. Effects of subject-generated recoding cues on short-term memory. *Journal of Experimental Psychology,* 1964, 68, 171-175.

Schwartz, M. Instructions to use verbal mediators in paired-associate learning. *Journal of Experimental Psychology,* 1969, 79, 1-5.

Schwartz, M. Subject-generated versus experimenter-supplied mediators in paired-associate learning. *Journal of Experimental Psychology,* 1971, 87, 389-395.

Shiffrin, R. M. Memory search. In D. A. Norman (Ed.), *Models of human memory.* New York: Academic Press, 1970.

Smith, R. K., & Noble, C. E. Effects of a mnemonic technique applied to verbal learning and memory. *Perceptual and Motor Skills,* 1965, 21, 123-134.

Sperling, G. A model for visual memory tasks. *Human Factors,* 1963, 5, 19-31.

Sperling, G. Successive approximations to a model for short-term memory. *Acta Psychologica,* 1967, 27, 285-292.

Suzuki, N., & Rohwer, W. D. Verbal facilitation of paired-associate learning: Type of grammatical unit vs. connective form class. *Journal of Verbal Learning and Verbal Behavior,* 1968, 7, 584-588.

Suzuki, N. & Rohwer, W. D. Deep structure in the noun-pair learning of children and adults. *Child Development,* 1969, 40, 911-919.

Tarpy, R. M., & Glucksberg, S. Effect of incentive and incentive-cue position on short-term retention. *Psychonomic Science,* 1966, 5, 313-314.

Thorsheim, H. I. NLM strength and CVC-CVC response-time recall. *Psychonomic Science,* 1970, 20, 101-102.

Tulving, E. Theoretical issues in free recall. In T. R. Dixon & D. L. Horton (Eds.), *Verbal behavior and general behavior theory.* Englewood Cliffs, N.J.: Prentice-Hall, 1968.

Tulving, E., & Arbuckle, T. Y. Sources of intertrial interference in immediate recall of paired-associates. *Journal of Verbal Learning and Verbal Behavior,* 1963, 1, 321-334.

Tulving, E., & Thompson, D. M. Retrieval processes in recognition memory: Effects of associative context. *Journal of Experimental Psychology,* 1971, 87, 116-124.

Underwood, B. J. Stimulus selection in verbal learning. In C. N. Cofer & B. S. Musgrave (Eds.), *Verbal behavior and learning.* New York: McGraw-Hill, 1963. Pp. 33-48.

Underwood, B. J. The representativeness of rote verbal learning. In A. W. Melton (Ed.), *Categories of human learning.* New York: Academic Press, 1964.

Underwood, B. J. Attributes of memory. *Psychological Review,* 1969, 76, 519-531.

Underwood, B. J., & Erlebacher, A. Studies of coding in verbal learning. *Psychological Monographs,* 1965, 79, (13, Whole No. 606).

Underwood, B. J., & Keppel, G. Coding processes in verbal learning. *Journal of Verbal Learning and Verbal Behavior,* 1963, 1, 250-257.

Underwood, B. J., & Schulz, R. W. *Meaningfulness and verbal learning.* Philadelphia: Lippincott, 1960.

Walker, C. B., Montague, W. E., & Wearing, A. J. Natural language associability in paired-associate learning. *Journal of Experimental Psychology,* 1970, 84, 264-267.

Wearing, A. J. Natural language, and word frequency in paired-associate learning. Unpublished mimeo., Yale University, 1971. (a)

Wearing, A. J. On the Adams-Bray retrieval model. *Journal of Experimental Psychology,* 1971, 89, 96-101. (b)

Wearing, A. J., & Montague, W. E. Associability of CVC-word pairs and its relation to list difficulty. *Psychonomic Science,* 1967, 7, 133-134.

Wearing, A. J., Walker, C. B., & Montague, W. E. Recall of paired-associates as a function of their associability. *Psychonomic Science,* 1967, 9, 533-534.

Wearing, A. J., Walker, C. B., & Montague, W. E. Syntactic structure and natural language mediation. *Psychonomic Science,* 1970, 19, 348-349.

Weiner, B., & Reed, H. Effects of the instructional sets to remember and to forget on short term retention: Studies of rehearsal control and retrieval inhibition (repression). *Journal of Experimental Psychology,* 1969, 79, 226-232.

Weiner, B., & Walker, E. L. Motivational factors in short-term retention. *Journal of Experimental Psychology,* 1966, 71 190-193.

Wickens, D. D., & Simpson, C. K. Trace cue position, motivation, and short-term memory. *Journal of Experimental Psychology,* 1968, 76, 282-285.

Wollen, K. A. Effects of relevant or irrelevant pictorial mediators upon forward and backward recall. Paper presented at the meeting of the Psychonomic society, November, 1968.

Wood, G. Mnemonic systems in recall. *Journal of Educational Psychology, Monograph,* 1967, 58 (6, Part 2, Whole No. 645).

Woodward, A. E., Jr., & Bjork, R. A. Forgetting and remembering in free recall: Intentional and unintentional. *Journal of Experimental Psychology,* 1971, 89, 109-116.

Woodworth, R. S., & Schlosberg, H. *Experimental psychology.* New York: Holt, 1954.

Yates, F. A. *The art of memory.* Chicago: University of Chicago Press, 1966.

Yuille, J. C., & Paivio, A. Latency of imaginal and verbal mediators as a function of stimulus and response concreteness-imagery. *Journal of Experimental Psychology,* 1967, 75, 540-544.

Yuille, J. C., & Paivio, A. Imagery and verbal mediation instructions in paired-associate learning. *Journal of Experimental Psychology,* 1968, 78, 436-441.

7

COMMENTARY ON

"THE MULTICOMPONENT THEORY

OF THE MEMORY TRACE"

Gordon Bower

DEPARTMENT OF PSYCHOLOGY,
STANFORD UNIVERSITY

One seldom has the opportunity to evaluate the impact of a piece of one's own writing in retrospect. In the 10 years since the "multi-component theory" chapter was written, several new developments have made use of and elaborated on the ideas of this chapter. When the chapter was written, the state of memory theories was in revolutionary transition—mainly concerning memory dynamics, as espoused, for example, in the Atkinson and Shiffrin chapter (pp. 7–113). The time seemed ripe for a simple idea concerning a possible "formal structure" for the memory trace of an episode. The multicomponent theory simply postulates that the memory trace of a perceptual event consists of a set of descriptors, properties, or attributes, which was to be the internal representation of the event in memory. The theory was written on an abstract level so that any attributes or descriptors might be included—not only perceptual features but also subvocal names, implicit associates, semantic features, or images aroused by the input event. In the chapter, these different levels were labeled as "primary" (perceptual) codes and "secondary" (verbal–semantic) codes.

This general idea is easily reformulated in the modern idioms of semantic-network theories by using the episodic-semantic memory distinction. Figure 7.1 illustrates the way in which the multicomponent conception of an episodic trace might be diagrammed. The memory trace of an episode is conceived as a structure of *associative relations* among *tokens* of known concepts. The concepts pre-exist as *types* in long-term memory. The new event trace is given an internal name, address, or access point in the memory system. In a standard serial memory word-list experiment, for example, the relation–value pairs might be: "serial position = 4"; "list number = 10"; "modality = visual"; "location of presentation = upper left of screen"; "item =

437

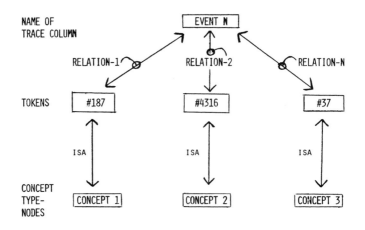

Fig. 7.1. Representation of the memory trace of an event in terms that are compatible with the multicomponent theory.

token of word CUP"; and so on. The form, however, is general enough to encompass verb-based scenarios, either from linguistic or perceptual inputs, of the sort proposed by Schank (1972), and Norman, Rumelhart, and the LNR Research Group (1975). That is, the event of "Jane hitting John on the head with a stick" would be represented in memory in terms of the time and place of the event (or indeed whether it was just an artificial sentence in an experiment) and relation–token pairs, such as act–hit; actor–Jane; recipient–John; instrument–a stick; location of action–head of John. What is missing in this translation, of course, is the interrelationships or connections existing among the concepts or properties fulfilling certain slots in the event frame, such as, for example, that the location is a part of John's body and that the stick is in Jane's hand. These are the types of information supplied in decompositional theories of meaning representation. Of course, as soon as one makes these substantive identifications of features within the multicomponent theory, there are strong inducements to abandon the "homogeneity of features" assumption that made the model in the chapter so tractable, that is, the idea that all features had equal retention and equal guessing parameters.

The multicomponent idea seems to have been used by a number of later theorists. Some theorists have found it to be a useful framework within which to reformulate their experimental results. Thus, Wickens (1970) was led to conceive of a memory trace as a multiattribute entity since his interesting "release from proactive interference" paradigm seems to have identified so many distinct attributes of traces. Underwood (1969) also found this framework congenial for talking about numerous attributes of memory traces, such as their recency, frequency, and contextual features.

Section VIII of the multicomponent chapter applied the theory to perceptual identification and confusions among degraded stimuli, dealing mainly with intelligibility of words articulated in a noisy channel. Rumelhart (1970) greatly extended this approach so as to account for the way in which subjects identified familiar patterns, such as letters or digits from a brief visual exposure. Perception of an alphanumeric character at a given location in the display was seen as resulting from the extraction and accumulation (over millisecond durations) of sufficient visual features so that the person could identify the input character at that location. Rumelhart suggested that the extraction of features at a given location proceeded more slowly as the number of characters in the foveal field requiring analysis increased. Subsequent results (see Schneider and Shiffrin, 1977) suggest this latter assumption is true only for poorly learned or difficult form discriminations. If the alternative stimuli are very familiar and easily discriminated, then detection and identification tasks seem to be performed effortlessly, independently of the display size, within foveal limits. In either case, the multicomponent theory provides a background against which to formulate competing theories.

A problem for any model of pattern recognition (such as word perception) is how to combine the influence of prior semantic context with sensory variables so as to have a tractable model predicting perceptual identification in context. Identification of a word in the multicomponent theory would correspond to activating a sufficient number of criterial features to distinguish it from other, available alternatives. The influence of semantic context (for example, identification of WEST in the prior context "NORTH, SOUTH, EAST?") would be to increase the activation of (or "fill in in advance") some of the features of the target's representation from semantic memory, with the result that fewer sensory features would have to be extracted from the array to identify the pattern. This description leads to a model that is mathematically isomorphic to Morton's logogen model (1969), which was explicitly designed to describe the integration of sensory and contextual information in word identification. Similar reasoning seems to apply to the lexical decision task of Meyer, Schvaneveldt, and Ruddy (1975); that is, subjects are faster to decide that NURSE is a word (rather than a nonword) if they have recently read or been primed with an associate such as DOCTOR.

There have been many other applications of the multicomponent theory to memory phenomena (e.g., Norman & Rumelhart, 1970). To take recent examples, papers by Gregory Jones (1976, in press) have applied a modified version of the multicomponent theory to results on forgetting of multiattribute items in arrays. In one experiment, Jones (1976) had people learning the color, shape, location in space, and position in a temporal series of a set of nine-item series (pictured objects). The memory representation of each object in the study series would be characterized by four variables (see Figure 7.1). After study of a list, Jones' subjects were cued with one, two, or three features (e.g., "the blue thing that was in spatial location four?"). They were required to recall the remaining features. The pattern of recall dependencies was best explained by assuming that, at the time of recall, subjects could remember only some probabilistic "fragments" of the complete four-component vector describing a given event trace. For example, if the fragment of a given event remaining in memory associated only color and shape but not the spatial or temporal location in the series, then the subject would be able to recall that the triangle was blue (or vice versa) but only guess at its spatial location or time order of presentation. If the cue for recall was not in the memory fragment, then only "guessing" of the other components could occur. Jones estimated the likelihood that the several fragments of an event trace were remembered (e.g., fragments consisting of attributes 1 + 2, 1 + 3, 1 + 4, 1 + 2 + 3, etc.) in order to fit best the empirical recall results.

In a later paper, Jones (in press) extended the same analysis to the recall of declarative sentences, using data collected by Anderson and Bower (1973, Chap. 10, Exp. 1). For example, in a list of 40 unrelated sentences, the subject might study "In the kitchen the policeman interviewed the celebrity." In the deep structure, these terms comprise location, subject, verb, and object of an event. In Jones' theory, the possible fragments of a given sentence's memory trace remaining at the time of test are either no elements, any one element, all pairs (e.g., location + verb), all triples, and the complete quartet of content words. By estimating fragment retention probabilities, Jones was able to fit quantitatively the array of fragment recall probabilities to various cues in the experiments on sentence memory by Anderson and Bower (1973, Chap. 10). Moreover, his fit was closer and required fewer parameters than the fit of the HAM theory proposed by the authors. Jones' "fragment memory" theory

is a special case of the multicomponent theory: The retention probabilities of particular component patterns are estimated directly from
the data rather than being predicted by a rational theory.

Further, recent, unpublished experiments by the author and by the
author and Peter Arnold (Arnold, 1976) have supported a version of
the multicomponent theory for cued recall and recognition of pairs,
triples, and quartets of arbitrary words. In one experiment, the
subject studied quartets of concrete nouns and was later cued for
recall by providing one, two, or three words of a quartet. In other experiments, the subject studied triplets of mouns and was later tested
for recall (with one or two cues from the triplet) or for true–false
recognition of a pair from the same triplet or for recognition of a
joint triplet. In all such cases, the model that fit best was a version of
the multicomponent theory wherein each triplet (or quartet) was
represented in memory as a key node (see Figure 7.1) to which each
word was connected probabilistically.

In retrospect, it is easy to see certain extensions of an idea that
could have been pursued and developed more fully than they were in
the original chapter. For example, it is now clear that we should
conceive of many natural-language concepts in terms of fuzzy
boundaries around "prototypes"; the prototypes are like average
values of the component features characterizing "typical" members
of the concept class. For instance, robin is prototypic of birds,
whereas duck or ostrich are not (see Rosch, 1973; Smith, Rips, &
Shoben, 1974). The multicomponent theory is well suited to deal
with prototypes or with classification behavior that appears to be
generated by prototypes. In teaching a concept to someone, the
experimenter presents instances of the class varying in features of
different criteriality. If the subject took a frequency-weighted
average of the exemplars of a given class (i.e., averaged the component descriptors of a given class) and classified new patterns
according to their discrepancy ("distance") from the several average
prototypes he was learning, he would behave like subjects in recent
prototype-learning studies of Reed (1972) and Hayes-Roth and
Hayes-Roth (unpublished). That is, each multiattribute stimulus
creates a perceptual vector that (by an integration strategy) becomes
averaged into a class-average prototype. In this integration, however,
the subject would lose the ability to discriminate between exactly
which stimulus patterns were presented during learning and which
were new, although he could decide which were consistent with the
rules for generation of the set.

Another extension of the multicomponent idea would be the

popular "levels of processing" approach of Craik and Lockhart (1972), which is a topic of current interest. In the standard incidental-learning experiment, the subject performs an orienting task requiring either discrimination of a word's meaning ("Is it a vegetable?") or discrimination of its surface form ("Does it have an E in it?"). Later memory for the word is better with more meaningful semantic processing. The multicomponent theory has two ways in which to explain such effects. One is to postulate that the components of the word event filled into the memory trace contain primarily those attributes involved in the orienting task and that different attributes (graphemic, phonetic, semantic) have inherently different forgetting rates (see, e.g., Wickelgren, 1973). That approach, however, is distressingly ad hoc. An alternative approach suggested by Klein and Saltz (1976) is that semantic processing tasks cause the word event to be encoded along more numerous or distinctive dimensions so that its trace occupies a more unique partition of "cognitive space" (their metaphor). Events encoded along few dimensions are diffusely specified and, hence, are easily interfered with by many other prior or subsequent events in the memory experiment. Semantic orienting tasks for a word do not only activate graphemic features, but also a network of semantic features that lend distinctiveness and uniqueness to the event, protecting it from interference. These ideas are clearly cast within the framework of the multicomponent theory. Evidence from Klein and Saltz (1976) and Moscovitch and Craik (1976) suggest this is a fruitful approach to "levels-of-processing" phenomena.

This survey has touched on some current research topics that could be reformulated in terms of the multicomponent theory. Its viability suggests that its theoretical value has been to provide an orienting framework within which to formulate more specific hypotheses for particular experiments and that, perhaps, should be the fate of most useful abstract ideas in psychology.

REFERENCES

Anderson, J. R., & Bower, G. H. *Human associative memory.* Washington, D.C.: Hemisphere Press, 1973.

Arnold, P. A distinct-associations model for learning and memory. Unpublished doctoral dissertation. Stanford University, 1976.

Craik, F. I. M., & Lockhart, R. S. Levels of processing: A framework for memory research. *Journal of Verbal Learning and Verbal Behavior,* 1972, **11,** 671–684.

Hayes-Roth, B., & Hayes-Roth, F. Concept learning and the recognition and classification of exemplars. Unpublished manuscript, Santa Monica, RAND Corporation, 1976.

Jones, G. V. A fragmentation hypothesis of memory: Cued recall of pictures and of sequential position. *Journal of Experimental Psychology: General,* 1976, **105**, 277–293.

Jones, G. V. Isomorphic recall of pictures, sentences, and visual images. *British Journal of Psychology* (in press).

Klein, K., & Saltz, E. Specifying the mechanisms in a levels-of-processing approach to memory. *Journal of Experimental Psychology: Human Learning and Memory,* 1976, **2**, 671–680.

Meyer, D. E., Schvaneveldt, R. W., & Ruddy, M. G. Loci of contextual effects on visual word-recognition. In P. M. A. Rabbitt & S. Dornic (Eds.), *Attention and performance V.* London: Academic Press, 1975.

Morton, J. Interaction of information in word recognition. *Psychological Review,* 1969, **76**, 165–178.

Moscovitch, M., & Craik, F. I. M. Depth of processing, retrieval cues, and uniqueness of encoding as factors in recall. *Journal of Verbal Learning and Verbal Behavior,* 1976, **15**, 447–458.

Norman, D. A., & Rumelhart, D. E. A system for perception and memory. In D. A. Norman (Ed.), *Models of human memory.* New York: Academic Press, 1970. Pp. 21–66.

Norman, D. A., Rumelhart, D. E., & the LNR Research Group. *Explorations in cognition.* San Francisco: Freeman, 1975.

Reed, S. K. Pattern recognition and categorization. *Cognitive Psychology,* 1972, **3**, 382–407.

Rosch, E. On the internal structure of perceptual and semantic categories. In T. E. Moore (Ed.), *Cognitive development and the acquisition of language.* New York: Academic Press, 1973.

Rumelhart, D. E. A multicomponent theory of the perception of briefly exposed visual displays. *Journal of Mathematical Psychology,* 1970, **7**, 191–218.

Schank, R. C. Conceptual dependency: A theory of natural language understanding. *Cognitive Psychology,* 1972, 3, 552–631.

Smith, E. E., Rips, L. J., & Shoben, E. J. Semantic memory and psychological semantics. In G. H. Bower (Ed.), *The psychology of learning and motivation.* Vol. 8. New York: Academic Press, 1974.

Schneider, W., & Shiffrin, R. M. Controlled and automatic human information processing: I. Detection, search and attention. *Psychological Review,* 1977, **84**, 1–66.

Underwood, B. J. Attributes of memory. *Psychological Review,* 1969, **76**, 559–573.

Wickelgren, W. A. The long and short of memory. *Psychological Bulletin,* 1973, **80**, 425–438.

Wickens, D. D. Encoding categories of words: An empirical approach to meaning. *Psychological Review,* 1970, **77**, 1–15.

Reprinted from *The Psychology of Learning and Motivation*, 1967, **1**, 229–325.

A MULTICOMPONENT THEORY OF THE MEMORY TRACE

Gordon Bower[1]

STANFORD UNIVERSITY
STANFORD, CALIFORNIA

[1] Research supported by a grant (HD-00954) from the National Institute of Child Health and Human Development. The paper was written during the author's tenure on an NIH special fellowship (F3-MH-8585) as a visitor in the Department of Psychology, University College, London.

445

I. Introduction

Recent years have witnessed a tremendous surge of research on human memory, particularly as regards short-term or immediate memory. For reviews of this research, the reader is referred to papers by Keppel (1965), Melton (1963), Peterson (1963), Posner (1963), and Postman (1964). Despite the rapid accumulation of factual knowledge about short-term memory, there has not been a corresponding increase in formal theoretical efforts to understand or explain the facts. In this paper a modest attempt is made to begin redressing some of this imbalance of facts over theories.

A particular hypothesis concerning the formal structure of a memory trace will be proposed. The basic idea appears reasonable, probably commonly agreeable, and does not go much beyond conceptions regularly used in discussions of memory by many investigators. However, the chief concern here will be with developing the implications of this idea for a variety of memory experiments. It turns out to have an unexpectedly wide range of implications and, in consequence, provides a common basis for understanding a diversity of memory phenomena. And neither of these virtues of the idea is apparent before its implications are systematically developed. Although some new evidence will be presented in congruence with this hypothesis, it must be admitted at the outset that the marshaling of evidential support on each topic discussed is not our purpose. The purpose, rather, is to demonstrate a common theme running throughout diverse branches of the research tree on human memory. Such a discussion serves its function if all it does is to focus attention on relationships existing among diverse phenomena connected with memory.

Perhaps it is wise to first expose our theoretical bias so that the reader is fairly warned. We take it that the job for a theory of memory is to specify the structures, organization, and rules of operation of a machine (a model) that will behave in a manner that resembles or simulates memory phenomena in important respects. The machine, of course, need not actually be built if its behavior can be forecast by arguments, either verbal, mathematical, or in computer programs.

Advocates of this bias include Miller, Galanter, and Pribram (1960), the computer-simulation theorists, and several British psychologists, notably Broadbent (1958), Craik (1943), Crossman (1964), Deutsch (1960), and MacKay (1956). In general, this approach represents the model organism in terms of an array of information-processing mechanisms, each of which carries out certain elementary operations upon information provided to it. These mechanisms, moreover, are assumed to be organized and sequenced in a way designed to achieve certain results. The job of constructing a completely adequate model of human memory is vast and well beyond available capabilities for quite some time. However, it is possible to artificially segment the over-all problem into subproblems and then try to attack these separately. The basic flaw guaranteed by such a separatist strategy is that the theories so developed will of necessity be incomplete or even vague regarding those aspects of the system not under immediate consideration. Nonetheless, such failings may be acceptable so long as the theory better elucidates the operation of at least a part of the over-all system. It was with this strategy in mind that the present paper was written.

There are many such subproblems; included among them would be such issues as the operation of the short-term store, the transfer of items into long-term storage, the format in which information is represented in storage, retrieval of stored material, and so on. The first two subproblems have been discussed in papers by Atkinson and Shiffrin (1965), Bower (1964), Broadbent (1957), and Waugh and Norman (1965). In those theories, items of information input for storage by the system are treated as unitary elements that queue up in a short-term store for processing by some central program. These theorists then derive the consequences of assuming that the queueing system is governed by certain reasonable principles.

The subproblem to be discussed here is that regarding the format in which information is encoded and stored in the machine. In other words, this paper is concerned with the possible formal structure of a memory trace. To delimit matters further, it will be concerned with the way a memory trace might be functionally characterized by a logician or mathematician, rather than by a neurochemist or neurophysiologist. In our opinion, the past history of theories about the memory trace (see Gomulicki, 1953) contains many hypotheses that have been unprofitably tied to further guesses about the neurological mechanisms involved; and the functional hypothesis is discredited when the postulated neurology is proven incorrect, inadequate, or naive. To limit matters further, the paper will not be concerned with the causes of forgetting. The contending views on this—interference versus autonomous decay—are discussed elsewhere (Bower, 1964; Melton, 1963; Postman, 1964). For what follows here, either view may be adopted without materially affecting the discussion. To repeat, the emphasis here is upon the formal structure of a memory trace—what it "looks like" when it is initially established and during the subsequent course of its disintegration.

A. Perception, Encoding, and the Memory Trace

It seems reasonable to tie the memory trace of an event to the variables operating in the perception of that event. Within this context, the major assumption seems innocuous: it is supposed that the person does not store the literal input stimulus, but rather some encoded representation of it. The representation stored is either the primary code by which the event is recognized or a secondary code that labels the primary code. In either event, the representation stored is sufficient to the degree that when it is fed into a motor-output system, salient features of the original input event can be reconstructed and output. The general block diagram of the system is shown in Fig. 1.

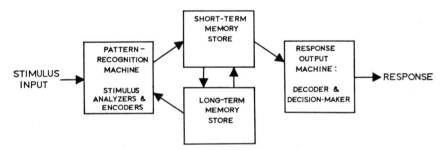

Fig. 1. Block diagram representing the flow of information through the theoretical system. See text for explanation.

It is supposed that the stimulus is first fed into a stimulus-analyzing mechanism, or a pattern-recognition machine. There is no need to give a detailed account of the output from this pattern recognizer, except to assume that it has a particular form. The development of a successful model for pattern recognition is, of course, one of the major enterprises currently in computer-simulation work. Practically all of the more successful programs in current operation (see Nilsson, 1965; Uhr, 1963; Uhr, 1965) employ some variety of "attribute-value" listing to characterize the stimulus. Many submechanisms are designed which measure or identify the value of different properties, attributes, whole–part relationships, or features of the stimulus. In general, the term feature counter will be used to refer to any one of these attribute-analyzing mechanisms. The attributes examined, how many there are, and their possible values all depend, of course, on the program and the population from which the input stimulus is selected and from which it is to be differentiated. However, for present purposes, the important point is that the stimulus is represented in coded form as an ordered *list* of attributes with their corresponding values. This listing will be called the *primary code*. From this point on, the various recognition programs diverge in how this list is used to decide what to call the stimulus; here various principles may enter, such as template matching, discriminant-function analysis, parallel processing with differential weighting of the several features, and the like.

Let us suppose that the primary code may elicit an identifying label and, if so, that this label is fed into the short-term store. If it is subvocalized, the subvocalization constitutes a feedback stimulus that is itself represented in coded form as a list of vocal features (that is, as a list of auditory or phonetic sound features, or as the movements of the speech musculature involved in vocalizing the label). This will be called the *secondary code* of the input stimulus. It consists of a small "program" which, when fed to the motor-output machine, suffices for the speech apparatus to output a verbal label for the stimulus.

It is supposed that what is stored in memory is either the primary code, the secondary code, or both. That is, a memory trace will be represented as an ordered list of attributes with their corresponding values. It will also be referred to as a *vector* of N ordered components.

Perhaps a word of explanation is required for the primary–secondary code distinction and the equivocation about which of the two is stored. The primary–secondary distinction parallels roughly that between filtered sense data and meaning. The property list stored may not be the stimulus as analyzed by the feature counters, but as described or labeled by the vocal subject. Various experimental results, including those on semantic and synonymic confusion in recall of visually presented information, incline one to this view. Perhaps the strongest evidence comes from the experiments of Conrad (1964) and others suggesting that the human short-term memory system operates in terms of either auditory- or phonetic-feature coding of visually presented verbal materials.

Because of the importance of Conrad's results, they will be described in more detail. Two experiments, one on perceptual recognition and one on memory, were done by Conrad. In the recognition experiment, single letters of the English alphabet were spoken over a noisy channel and the listener indicated the letter he thought he heard. The results were arrayed in a confusion matrix with entries indicating how frequently a given letter sent was misidentified as some other letter. In the memory experiment, Ss were presented with strings of six letters presented *visually* at a rate slow enough to be read distinctly. They then attempted immediate recall of the letters in the order presented. Analyzing those cases in which only one error occurred, Conrad derived a recall confusion matrix, indicating how frequently each letter was misrecalled as some other letter. The important point was that the confusion matrices of the two experiments were in substantial agreement. The pattern of confusion errors in recall were substantially like those occurring when the letter sounds were being identified from a noisy auditory channel. The fact that recall confusions of visually presented letters tended to follow the similarities of their auditory (rather than visual) representations suggests that Ss were subvocalizing the letters and storing this auditory code. In terms of the earlier distinction, the auditory or phonetic pattern is the secondary code, whereas the output of analyzing the graphemic (visual) letters is the primary code. In this case, the secondary code is clearly what is stored and it controls the recall. For other stimulus populations, however, the primary code may be stored and control recall. For our purposes here, which are admittedly abstract, it makes little difference which code is stored, so long as the items in a particular experiment are encoded and stored in roughly the same way. For particular conditions it will be supposed simply that each item for storage is represented as a vector of N components, where the same attributes or features are used to encode each item. We will let X_i denote the vector for item i and x_{ji} denote the value of the jth component of X_i. For purposes of simplicity in what follows, it will be assumed that the number of possible values of each component is v, the same for each attribute.

B. RETRIEVAL IN RECALL

Since we are interested in what this representation implies about recall, we must first specify something about how a given memory trace is retrieved to then guide recall. Generally speaking, recall tests can be classified as either "cued" or "free" recall. In the former case, an explicit cue is either provided (e.g., the stimulus member of a paired-associate item) or is inherent in the serial nature of the task (e.g., ordinal position in a digit-span test); in the latter case, a cue is neither explicitly provided nor can one be easily imagined (e.g., free verbal recall). Presumably in the latter case retrieval is controlled by searching along some temporal dimension of the memory traces and effectively pulling out those items that have occurred "recently" in the past (see Yntema & Trask, 1963).

Since we do not wish to be sidetracked here in specifying an elaborate model for retrieval, we will accordingly restrict ourselves to cued recall experiments where the different cues are distinct. Paired-associates learning with well-differentiated stimuli is the obvious prototype. It is assumed that when a pair A–B is shown for study, S stores a compound vector, denoted (CA, CB), consisting of encoded information about A and about B. It is further assumed that upon the later test with A alone, this input, encoded as CA, is matched successively to the various traces, obtaining the maximum match to the trace (CA, CB). Thus the trace (CA, CB) is retrieved, and the response output will be guided by the vector CB. The main concern is with the forgetting of CB, the response information; retrieval difficulties caused by such factors as loss of stimulus information will be ignored in what follows. In a strict sense, the model presented here applies only to experiments in which such retrieval difficulties are minimized. Since it will be assumed that the stimulus retention and retrieval operate perfectly, the state of the system will be characterized in terms of the state of CB, the vector of response information retrieved on a test trial. At the end of the paper some more complicated retrieval schemes will be considered.

II. Forgetting of Component Information

A. General Effects of Forgetting

Assuming that CB is stored as a vector of information components, then forgetting (from whatever cause) would consist in the blurring, erasure, or change in value of some of the components of the initial vector. As forgetting proceeds and the trace is further degraded, it conveys less and less information about the initiating event B. For simplicity, it is assumed that the loss of the original information in any one component of the vector is an all-or-nothing event. However, since the vector will usually consist of many components, the loss of information in the over-all trace of CB will appear more or less gradual.

In recall, the degraded trace of CB is retrieved and given to the motor-output unit. This unit uses the information in the degraded trace either to construct or to "locate" and generate a response. If the value of a given component of the trace has been erased (for example, replaced effectively by a question mark), then the output unit lacks a command concerning the value to use there. Assume that it randomly assigns one of the possible values for that component, thus showing complete equivocation regarding responses that differ only in that feature.

One outcome of such a model is that it will show a restricted range of confusion errors in recall. Events that are encoded similarly, with few distinguishing features, will be readily confused in recall. The range or "bandwidth" of the confusion errors in recall will increase directly with the number of components forgotten from the original trace. A few seconds after some input event S's response will convey nearly all the information about the event that has been extracted by his stimulus analyzers; but as the trace is degraded over time, less and less information about the original event is transmitted by the response. In everyday terms, it would be said that S retains the general gist of the event for some time but that he becomes more and more vague or in-accurate about the exact details of it. The trace system is functioning here in the same way that Bartlett (1932) suggested in his "schemata" concepts.

B. THE ORDER IN WHICH COMPONENTS ARE FORGOTTEN

There are two theoretical decisions that must be made about the forgetting of components, and depending on these decisions one of four different variants of the model is obtained. One decision concerns whether the components are forgotten in a strict hierarchial order, from most detailed to most general information, or whether they are forgotten independently regardless of their possible location in a hier-archy of importance. The other decision concerns whether a forgotten value of a component is replaced by a null (guessing) state or is re-placed by some other value selected at random.

1. *Hierarchial Loss of Components*

The hierarchial-loss idea presupposes that the N components of the vector can be strictly ordered in "importance" or specificity of the in-formation conveyed. It roughly corresponds to the information structure utilized by a sorting tree or serial processing system. Figure 2 il-lustrates a sorting tree for vectors consisting of three binary compo-nents. It will correctly partition only 2^3 patterns. A tree of N nodes each with V branches could correctly partition V^N patterns. If S were to partition the response ensemble in this manner, with the first (top) node conveying the most important information and the last (bottom) node the least important, then it is further reasonable to assume that retention of a component would vary directly with its importance to him. Thus, the last component would be forgotten first, then the next to last would be forgotten, and so on.

For purposes of calculating response probabilities at recall, knowledge of the probability distribution of the number of components retained at any time t after input of the N-component vector is needed. Let

$R_i(t)$ denote the probability that exactly i components of the original N are still retained at time t. To derive $R_i(t)$ for this system requires an assumption about forgetting. The simplest assumption is that the components are arrayed in a linear chain, and that after $i - 1$ components have been forgotten, the probability of forgetting the ith

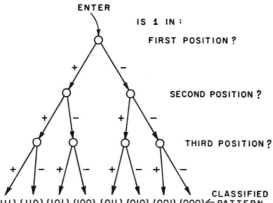

FIG. 2. A binary sorting tree with three nodes that classifies eight patterns. The stimulus vector enters the tree at the top node and is then shunted by the left or right branch, depending on how it answers the questions at successive nodes.

component is a constant f in each small time unit Δt. This assumption implies the following differential-difference equation

$$R_i(t + \Delta t) = [R_i(t)(1 - f) + R_{i+1}(t)f]\,\Delta t.$$

Converting to differentials in dt and adding in the boundary condition $R_N(0) = 1$, the following system is obtained

$$\frac{dR_i(t)}{dt} = \begin{cases} -fR_i(t), & \text{for } i = N \\ f[R_{i+1}(t) - R_i(t)], & \text{for } 1 \leq i \leq N - 1 \\ fR_{i+1}(t), & \text{for } i = 0. \end{cases} \tag{1}$$

This is simple "death process" of constant intensity f. The time between successive "deaths" is exponentially distributed, and the time until the kth death has the Erlang (gamma) distribution. By taking successive differences between the cumulatives of the gamma for i and $i + 1$, the number of components retained at time t is found to be distributed as

$$R_i(t) = \frac{(ft)^{N-i}e^{-ft}}{(N - i)!}, \qquad \text{for } i > 0. \tag{2a}$$

The absorbing state is $i = 0$, when all components have been forgotten. Its probability is given by

$$R_0(t) = 1 - e^{-ft} \sum_{i=0}^{N-1} \frac{(ft)^i}{i!} = e^{-ft} \sum_{i}^{\infty} {}_{N} \frac{(ft)^i}{i!} \qquad (2b)$$

There are several features of this hierarchial-loss idea that are unattractive. First, the distinction between important and unimportant information components is inexact and fuzzy, and we do not know how to sharpen the distinction. If N bits are required to uniquely specify a member of some ensemble, then all components are needed and are, in this sense, equally important. In Fig. 2, for example, whichever bit is forgotten (erased), the probability of correctly locating the pattern is reduced by a multiplicative factor of $\frac{1}{2}$. So the probability of correct recall is a function only of the number of bits forgotten, and is independent of their location in the hierarchial sorting tree. Second, to use this scheme at all, one is forced to assume a particular forgetting process (such as the Poisson process described earlier) and the entire scheme may mispredict data because the particular forgetting process assumed is incorrect. The alternate scheme, considered in the following section, separates the model of the trace and the law describing forgetting, and thus has the advantage of allocating separate responsibility for mispredictions. Finally, the equations for $R_i(t)$ derived from even the simplest forgetting assumptions (Eqs. 2a,b) are relatively intractable. And since the aim is to apply the general trace model to a variety of situations, the intractability of the hierarchial-loss scheme thwarts that aim. These difficulties do not appear in the alternate scheme, which will now be discussed.

2. Independent Loss of Components

According to the independence scheme, all N information components are equally important and show equal resistance to forgetting. Roughly speaking, this is the information structure appropriate for a classifying system that operates by parallel (rather than serial) processing of information. For immediate purposes, the important point is that component bits of information are forgotten independently and at the same rate. For any particular amount of interpolated material or length of retention interval of time t, $r(t)$ is defined as the probability that the value of any single component of the trace has been retained, and $1 - r(t)$ as the probability that it has been forgotten. Since the total number correctly retained, R, is the sum of N independent component-retention variables, it has the binomial distribution given by

$$P(R = i) = \binom{N}{i} r(t)^i (1 - r(t))^{N-i}, \tag{3}$$

with mean $Nr(t)$ and variance $Nr(t)(1 - r(t))$. One advantage of this scheme is that no particular assumptions about $r(t)$ need be adopted. Also, Eq. 3 is particularly simple to work with in later derivations.

C. INTERPRETATIONS OF COMPONENT FORGETTING

The other theoretical decision regards the interpretation of a component's value after the initial value has been forgotten. According to one view, when the original value of a trace component is forgotten, it reverts to a null state (effectively a blank or question mark). According to the alternate view, forgetting consists in the replacement of the original value of the component by some incorrect, nonnull value. The first assumption can lead to "fuzzy" memories regarded by S with low confidence as to their accuracy; the second assumption will lead to clear but inaccurate memories. On recall, when a null state is encountered, the motor-output unit chooses at random (guesses) among the v possible values at that position in constructing or locating a response. According to the random-replacement view, however, the motor unit never has to guess; it has been tricked by its memory into believing that all components are known.

It is not clear that one of these interpretations will always be more appropriate than the other; on some occasions the first interpretation would seem warranted, and on other occasions, the second. The null-state interpretation corresponds roughly to the decay notion of forgetting and the replacement interpretation to the interference notion; but these are intuitive, not exact, identifications. In what follows, the null-state interpretation of forgetting will be primarily used. This is preferred because it provides a more natural interpretation of confidence ratings of remembered material, and of a possible threshold for recall.

It may be noted that for some purposes, the two interpretations lead to isomorphic prediction equations (for example, for probability of correct recall). However, their implications for performance on recognition tests of memory are different, and it is not yet clear which equations would be more accurate in describing the data. For this reason, in the

discussion of recognition memory, predictive equations for both interpretations will be developed.

D. The Recall Function

Consider the probability of a correct recall in situations in which response omissions are prohibited. This condition is easily satisfied if S
knows the response ensemble and is penalized for failing to respond.
The probability of a correct recall will be a function of the number of
components forgotten and the probability of a correct recall given that
so many components have been forgotten. For the null-state interpretation, let $g = 1/v$ denote the probability of a correct guess on a forgotten component. If i of N bits are retained (and $N - i$ lost), the
probability that all the individual component guesses are correct is
g^{N-i}. For the replacement notion, if any component is changed, the
probability of a correct recall is zero.

The distribution of the number of components retained, according to
the independent-loss scheme, is the binomial given in Eq. 3. Letting
$C(t)$ denote the probability of a correct recall when a test is given at
time t, the recall function is

$$
\begin{aligned}
C(t) &= \sum_{i=0}^{N} P(R(t) = i) P(C \mid R = i), \\
&= \sum_{i=0}^{N} \binom{N}{i} r(t)^i (1 - r(t))^{N-i} g^{N-i}, \\
&= [r(t) + g(1 - r(t))]^N.
\end{aligned}
\tag{4}
$$

The term $r + g(1 - r)$ is the probability that any given component is
given correctly, either because it is retained or is correctly guessed. The
probability of a totally correct recall is the likelihood that all N components are correct, which is just the factor $r + g(1 - r)$ raised to the
Nth power. If the null-state interpretation of forgetting is used, then
$g = 1/v$. If the random replacement interpretation is used, then $g = 0$
in Eq. 4.

E. The Component-Retention Function

Although Eq. 4 may be tested independently of assumptions about
$r(t)$, it is nonetheless of interest to examine the implications for recall
of particular $r(t)$ functions. Two approaches are available. On the one
hand, one can derive "rational" $r(t)$ functions from more elementary
assumptions; on the other, $r(t)$ may be assumed to have some empirical
shape and its implications for $C(t)$ in Eq. 4 may be determined.

Since short-term memory for elementary units of experimental materials (e.g., a letter or a digit) is being considered, the $r(t)$ function should start at unity when $t = 0$, decrease monotonically with time, and end at some asymptote (possibly zero). Although the discussion here will refer to time elapsed as the effective variable for forgetting, it is a simple matter to interpret the equations in terms that suppose that the effective variable is the amount of interfering material (n) presented between a study and test trial. For most experimental paradigms, t and n are proportional. Thus, writing retention functions in terms of elapsed time involves no commitment to either an autonomous decay or interference view of the causes of forgetting.

A simple theory of $r(t)$ for the null-state interpretation would assume that transitions between the original correct value (state C) and the null-value (state G) form a continuous-time Markov process. Suppose the transition probabilities are as given in the matrix of Eq. 5.

		State at $t + \Delta t$		
		C	G	
State at	C	$1 - f$	f	(5)
time t:	G	c	$1 - c$	

The structure holding the value of this component shows hysteresis with a bias toward the value originally set by the storage operation. In other words, the probability that the structure reverts to the null state in Δt is f; if it has reverted to its null state, then it may return to its original (correct) state with probability c in each Δt. Starting in state C at time 0 the probability that it is in state C (retained) at time t is

$$r(t) = \frac{c}{c + f} + \left(1 - \frac{c}{c + f}\right)(1 - f - c)^t,$$

$$= J + (1 - J)a^t. \tag{6}$$

This gives $r(t)$ as an exponential decay function of time and is the same as the forgetting equation derived by Estes (1955) from his stimulus fluctuation theory. According to Eq. 6, $r(t)$ is concave upward; $C(t)$ is also concave upward with greater concavity for larger N and smaller a values. Figures 3a and 3b show some hypothetical curves of $C(t)$. Those in Fig. 3a have $J = .20$, $g = .25$, $a = .9$, while N is varied from 1 to 4. The curves in Fig. 3b have $N = 4$, $g = .25$, $a = .9$, and the asymptote J is varied from 0 to .9. The asymptotes of the curves decrease as N and $(1 - J)$ increase.

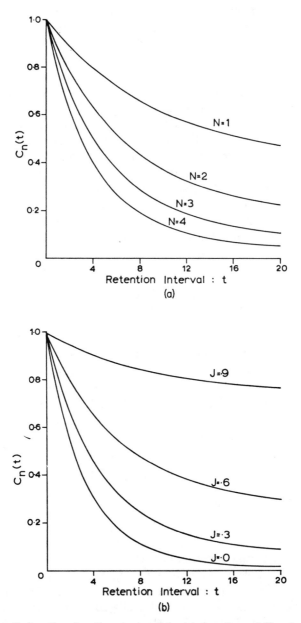

Fig. 3. Recall function for the exponential $r(t)$ function of Eq. 6. In (a), the number of components N is varied. In (b), the asymptote J of the component-retention function is varied.

458

The $r(t)$ function in Eq. 6 was based on the null-state interpretation of forgetting. However, a similar equation can be derived for the random-replacement interpretation. In the matrix of Eq. 5, replace the guessing state G by an error state E, and replace c by $c/v - 1$. That is, the correct value is changed with probability f in each Δt; if some incorrect value has been substituted, then it changes with probability c to one of the other $v - 1$ values selected at random. Starting in state C the probability that the structure will be in state C declines exponentially to an asymptote of

$$J' = \frac{(c/v - 1)}{f + (c/v - 1)}$$

If there is no bias toward holding the original value, then $f = c$ and $J' = 1/v$; that is, at asymptote the value of the component is random relative to its initial value. For $c \neq f$, suitable choice of parameters of this replacement scheme will lead to curves identical to those in Figs. 3a and 3b.

The recall curves derived from exponential $r(t)$ functions may be compared to those from linear $r(t)$ functions to note their similarities. A linear $r(t)$ function descending from 1 at rate a to an asymptote of b would have the corresponding recall function

$$C(t) = \begin{cases} [1 - (1 - g)at]^N, & \text{for } t \leq \dfrac{1 - b}{a} \\[2ex] [b + g(1 - b)]^N, & \text{for } t \geq \dfrac{1 - b}{a}. \end{cases}$$

For $N > 1$, successive derivatives of this $C(t)$ function alternate in sign, so the curves have the same concave-upward shape as does the exponential function. For visual comparison to Fig. 3, some hypothetical curves based on the linear $r(t)$ function are shown in Fig. 4 for the parameters $N = 4$ and $g = .25$. For one set of curves, the asymptote b is zero and the decay rate a is varied; for the other set with $a = .04$, the asymptote b is varied. When b is large, the recall function is two-limbed—describing the descent and the plateau. When b is small, the curves look similar to those in Fig. 3 for the exponential $r(t)$ function with small J. Thus, when $C(t)$ has a low asymptote and N is unknown, it would be difficult to discriminate between a linear and an exponential $r(t)$ function. If N is known, then $r(t)$ can be estimated directly from $C(t)$ and its descriptive law thus determined.

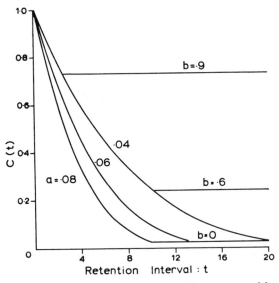

FIG. 4. Recall functions for the linear function $r(t) = 1 - at$, with asymptote at b. For the curves to the left, $b = 0$ and the rate of decay a varies. The plateaus give the asymptotes when $a = .04$ and the parameter b is varied.

III. New Experiments on Recall

A. EXPERIMENT I

The experiments to be reported attempt to test the recall function in Eq. 4. They were carried out at Stanford University with the able and generous assistance of Mr. James Hinrichs. The three experiments are very similar, differing in only minor details. We wished to test Eq. 4 without making assumptions about $r(t)$, the component retention function. This required an experimental situation for which the parameter N, the number of components in the response member of a paired-associate item, could be determined in advance. Given recall functions for several known and different N values, Eq. 4 permits predictions of one N function from any other N function.

1. Method

The method tried to induce a particular encoding and N value by presenting the response ensemble to S in terms of a binary sorting tree. The perceptual layout of the response ensemble for S is shown in Fig. 5. This shows eight push buttons, each with a small jewel light above it. The spatial separations between terminals emphasized their organization in groups of two and then of four on either side. This organization was pointed out to S (with no further comments to use it) and was perceptually emphasized by red tape lines on the board, as indicated in Fig. 5. If S organized and encoded this response ensemble in the way we hoped he would, then the vector description of the memory trace (of the response term) is simple and direct. The eight-alternative ensemble in Fig. 5 consists of $N = 3$ components, each component having two possible values (left or right). Thus for this setup, we would hope that $N = 3$ and $g = 1/v = .50$. The experiment is as much a test of whether this encoding assumption is correct as it is a test of Eq. 4.

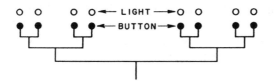

Fig. 5. Spatial arrangement of the eight-response ensemble, with eight push buttons and corresponding jewel lamps. The grouping of the responses into binary clusters was emphasized by red tape lines corresponding to the lines in the figure.

The experimental procedure involved a continuous stream of presentations and tests on single paired-associate items. S first studied a given S-R pair for 2 seconds, and was then tested several seconds later for recall of the response to the stimulus member of the pair. During the retention interval, other pairs were presented for study or for test. Each pair received one presentation, one test, and then was discarded. This procedure is similar to that introduced by Peterson and Peterson (1962).

The stimuli were high-frequency common nouns presented auditorily by a tape recorder at the rate of one every 2.5 seconds. The response was depressing one of the push buttons on the panel before S (see Fig. 5). For an item's first presentation (a study trial), the stimulus word was heard simultaneously with the onset of the light above the correct button. S was instructed to push this button immediately and to associate it with the word heard. After either 1, 3, 5, 7, or 9 interpolated items (some studied, some tested), the target word recurred alone, this time preceded by a brief beep of a tone indicating a recall test. On the test trials, S was allowed 2.5 seconds in which to push the button he recalled as being associated with the test word, being told to guess if necessary.

Each S was run with four different sizes of the response ensemble, with one "list" run for each ensemble condition. The number of response alternatives was either 2, 4, 8, or 16 buttons, representing N values of 1, 2, 3, or 4 binary components of information. Before each list (ensemble condition) began, the appropriate subset of the buttons was indicated to S. For example, an S might have the extreme right-hand pair of buttons in Fig. 5 for his $N = 1$ condition, the right-hand four buttons for his $N = 2$ condition, and so on. When 16 responses were used, a complementary set of 8 was provided below the 8 shown in Fig. 5.

The four ensemble conditions occurred in an order counterbalanced over Ss, and this order will be ignored in data analyses. Each ensemble condition comprised a list containing 10 occurrences of items tested at each of the lags of 1, 3, 5, 7, and 9 intervening items. The particular word lists used with the ensembles were also interchanged among Ss. The Ss were 25 undergraduates fulfilling a service requirement for their Introductory Psychology course.

2. Results and Predictions

The results of interest concern the recall curves, shown in Fig. 6. These show the average percentage of items correctly recalled as a function of the number of items (test or study, or both) interpolated between study and the recall test. Each point is based on 250 observations. The curves decline in an irregular manner with increasing amounts of interpolated material, which is confounded here with retention inter-

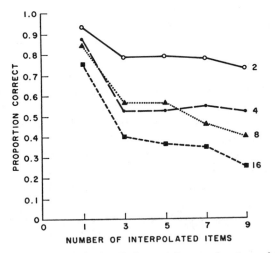

Fig. 6. Percentage of test pairs recalled correctly as a function of the number of items intervening between study and test of the pair. The number of response alternatives is the parameter of the four curves.

val. In general, the curves are ordered from top to bottom in terms of the number of response alternatives. The inversion in two points of the 4- versus 8-alternative curves suggests some misfortunes of sampling variability (not replicated in later experiments), so any reasonable theory may be expected to be somewhat inaccurate in predicting one or another of these curves.

These curves are to be fitted with Eq. 4, where $r(t)$ is to be estimated as a parameter for lags of $t = 1, 3, 5, 7,$ and 9. Since g is constant throughout at $\frac{1}{2}$, set $u(t) = r(t) + g(1 - r(t))$ and write Eq. 4 as

$$C_N(t) = (u(t))^N, \tag{7}$$

where $C_N(t)$ is the recall probability at lag t for ensembles specified by N bits of information. The $u(t)$ parameter is to be estimated to best fit the four observed $C_N(t)$ values at each lag t. Because of the nature of Eq. 7, straightforward least-squares or minimum chi-square procedures lead to seventh-degree polynomials to solve for the $u(t)$ estimate. A more tractable procedure is to minimize the sum of squared deviations about log $C_N(t)$. This leads to the following estimation equation.

$$\hat{u}(t) = \exp\left[\frac{\sum\limits_{N=1}^{4} N \log C_N(t)}{\sum\limits_{N=1}^{4} N^2}\right]$$

The properties of such rule-of-thumb estimates are unknown, but they surely are not the best possible. Their sole advantage is their ease of computation.

The estimates of $u(t)$ obtained in this manner were .940, .798, .791, .772, and .725 for lags of 1, 3, 5, 7, and 9 items, respectively. These $u(t)$ values correspond to $r(t)$ values of .880, .596, .582, .544, and .450, respectively. The irregularity of these $r(t)$ values will be discussed later.

These $u(t)$ estimates were substituted into Eq. 7 for $N = 1, 2, 3, 4$, leading to the predictions displayed in the four panels of Fig. 7. The predictions are generally quite accurate, especially so for $N = 1$ and $N = 4$. The poorest predictions occur at the two inverted points (lags 3 and 5) on the $N = 2$ and $N = 3$ curves, the aberrant points noted before. A chi-square goodness-of-fit test was applied. There are 20 points and 5 parameters, the $u(t)$'s, were estimated, yielding 15 degrees of freedom. The chi-square was 15.11, a value far from significant. It is noteworthy that 84% of this total chi-square was contributed

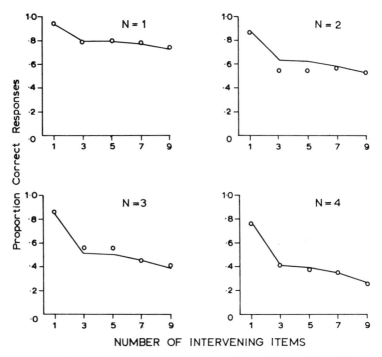

Fɪɢ. 7. Proportion of correct responses as a function of the number of intervening items and N. The line connects the predicted values; the open dots are the observed proportions.

by the two aberrant points on the $N = 2$ and 3 curves. Thus, we may accept the fit of Eq. 7 as satisfactory.

3. *Measures and Predictions of Information Retained*

Let us consider some further predictions of these data. The theory will in principle tell us the probability that S's recalled response will fall within various sectors of the ensemble relative to the location of the correct response. A problem is to find a convenient way to summarize these "error profiles." The method illustrated here scores the recalled response in terms of information retained, which scores will be denoted as I. A decision was made to calculate I scores according to a hierarchial view of component forgetting. This is an arbitrary scheme, but no better one came to mind for scoring the single response. The customary measure, contingent uncertainty or transmitted information (cf. Garner, 1962), uses the entire input-output matrix and can assign no score to single instances of recalled responses. To illustrate this scoring procedure, consider the eight-response ensemble with the bit clusters being (1, 2), (3, 4) versus (5, 6), (7, 8), and suppose the correct response is 1. Recall of 1 is assigned an I score of 3 bits; recall of 2 is assigned a score of 2; recall of 3 or 4 is assigned a score of 1; and recall of 5, 6, 7, or 8 is assigned an I score of 0 bits. Note that the responses are scored in terms of the number of hierarchial bits retained that would lead to that response. The I scores were so obtained and then averaged over Ss and observations for each N and each lag.

Consider now the derivation of predictions for the information retained scores so obtained. Equation 3 gives the probability that i of N bits are retained and, on the assumption of independent loss, each combination of $N-i$ losses out of N is equally likely. Using this assumption, the expected I score is calculated for retention of i of N bits, and then these are summed, being weighted by the probability that i bits are retained. The procedure will be illustrated with the eight-alternative $N = 3$ case, where the three bits are denoted as a, b, c, going from most detailed to most general (that is, moving from the top of the tree to the bottom in Fig. 5). If the number of bits retained R is 3, then a correct response ensues and the I score is 3 bits. If $R = 0$, then all eight responses are equally likely, and the expected value of I in this case is

$$E(I \mid R = 0) = \tfrac{1}{8}(3 + 2 + 1 + 1 + 0 + 0 + 0 + 0) = \tfrac{7}{8} \text{ bits.}$$

Suppose $R = 2$; then three equiprobable combinations of bits retained are $(a\ b)$, $(a\ c)$, and $(b\ c)$. If $(a\ b)$ is the pair retained, then response 1 and response 5 are equally likely, so the average value of I in this case is $\tfrac{1}{2}(3 + 0) = 1.5$. If $(a\ c)$ are retained, then responses 1 and 3 are equiprobable, so the average I will be 2. If $(b\ c)$ are retained, responses 1 and 2 are equiprobable, so the average I will be 2.5 bits. Since these three possibilities of two bits retained are equiprobable, the average I score when $R = 2$ is

$$E(I \mid R = 2) = \tfrac{1}{3}(1.5 + 2 + 2.5) = 2 \text{ bits.}$$

By a similar line of reasoning from the independent-loss assumption, the average information retained when $R = 1$ may be found to be 1.33 bits for a three-bit ensemble.

Finally, these theoretical expectations of I are used to calculate the expected I score at each N and t value, according to the formula

$$E(I_N(t)) = \sum_{i=0}^{N} E(I_N \mid R_N = i)\, P(R_N(t) = i).$$

Estimates of the distribution of $R_N(t)$ are made by using Eq. 3 along with the previous estimates of $r(t)$ from the mean recall curves.

These curves for $N = 2$, 3, and 4 are shown in the panels of Fig. 8. The curve for $N = 1$ is not shown since it is identical to the percentage-correct recall curve in Fig. 7. The fit of predicted to observed values is fairly good except that the values of the $N = 2$ and $N = 4$ data are often overpredicted, indicating slightly more scattered responding in these cases than even the independence model will allow for. This overprediction could occur if Ss were choosing the "mirror-image" alternative somewhat more than the model predicts. The fit of the model is generally satisfactory, although there is some room for improvement.

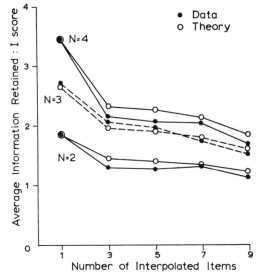

Fig. 8. Average score of information retained in recall as a function of N and the number of intervening items. The solid dots are the observed averages; the open dots are the predicted values. See text for explanation.

4. Comparison to Simple All-or-None Model

The simple all-or-none model (Bower, 1961a; Estes, 1961) assumes that a memory trace is either completely retained or not at all. It corresponds to the assumption that all N components are tied together so that when one goes, they all go together. When all components are forgotten, it is assumed that S guesses at random among the 2^N alternatives. If $r(t)$ is the retention probability, then the probability of a correct recall of an N-bit response is

$$C_N(t) = r(t) + (1 - r(t)) \cdot 2^{-N}. \tag{8}$$

This equation, in fact, is implicit in the common practice of "correcting" response proportions for guessing.

To compare this model with the multicomponent model, least-squares estimates of $r(t)$ in Eq. 8 were obtained and the recall probabilities in Fig. 6 were predicted by Eq. 8. The fit of these predictions was poor relative to the fit of the multicomponent predictions. The chi-square for goodness of fit was significant ($\chi^2(15) = 28.02$, $p < .01$). The average absolute discrepancy between observed and predicted proportions of this model was .054, about twice as large as the discrepancies for the multicomponent model. Also as would be expected from this outcome, the predictions of information retained, or I scores (cf. Fig. 8), were consistently poorer than the predictions based on the multicomponent model. From these comparisons it may be concluded that the results are inconsistent with the idea that forgetting of the entire vector of information is all or none. However, they are consistent with the idea that individual components of the stored vector are forgotten in all all-or-none manner.

5. The Empirical $r(t)$ Function

The recall curves in Fig. 6 are quite irregular and this shows up, of course, in the $r(t)$ estimates for lags of 1, 3, 5, 7, and 9 interpolated items. Because the list was constructed with interleaved tests and study trials on new items, the intervening events for a particular lag varied in the number of tests versus new-item presentations. A reanalysis of the recall data showed that test trials caused relatively little retention loss, whereas new-item presentations (requiring storage) caused relatively greater retention losses. The differential forgetting due to retrieval versus storage operations is shown in Figs. 9a and 9b. Figure 9a is a plot of recall probabilities against the number of intervening storage operations (new-item study trials) between storage of the target item and its later test. The number of intervening test trials is ignored in these calculations. Figure 9b shows a similar recall function plotted against the number of intervening tests (retrieval operations), with the number of intervening study trials ignored (in fact, permitted random variation). Recall probability declines monotonically with intervening study of new pairs but not monotonically with tests of old pairs; in fact, the latter curves are quite irregular. Since test and study trials occupied the same length of time, these results favor an interference rather than an autonomous decay principle of forgetting. Worded in terms of the model, the main event promoting erasure of component bits of a memory already in storage is the act of storing similar memories (vectors) regarding the same ensemble.

New estimates of $r(n)$ were obtained from Fig. 9a, where n is understood to be the number of intervening first presentations. The estimates

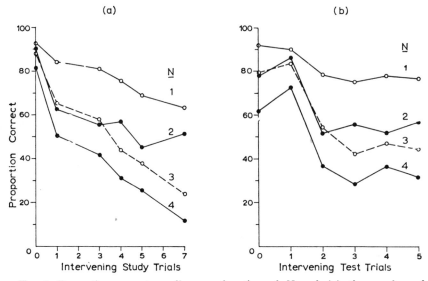

FIG. 9. Proportion correct recalls as a function of N and (a) the number of intervening study trials, and (b) the number of intervening test trials. For each graph, the variable not specified on the abscissa varies randomly over the points plotted.

for $N = 1, 3, 4$ are plotted in Fig. 10. The estimates are similar at each n value; their decline is well described by the straight line $r(n) = .856 - .088n$. Using this fitted $r(n)$ function, the $C_N(n)$ data in Fig. 9a can be fairly well predicted via Eq. 4.

B. EXPERIMENTS II AND III

1. Method

These experiments used the same button-light board and differed from Experiment I in only one major respect. Experiment I had interleaved study trials and test trials in a continuous task; in Experiments II and III the study trials occurred in large blocks followed by a block of test trials measuring recall of several pairs selected from the preceding study block.

In Experiment II a study block consisted in presentation of 12 new pairs (aural words associated to button presses as before) presented at a 3.5-second rate. The test block, preceded by a buzzer, consisted of 5 recall tests; the pairs tested were those presented in positions 3, 5, 7, 9, and 11 in the 12-item list, corresponding to 9, 7, 5, 3, and 1 intervening items before the test block began. The order in which these 5 items were tested was counterbalanced over test blocks. For each re-

sponse ensemble condition (2, 4, 8, or 16 alternatives), each of 24 *Ss*
had a list consisting of 10 study-test blocks. This then yields recall
curves for each N value and each $n = 1, 3, 5, 7, 9$, with 240 observations
per point.

Experiment III was similar except the study block consisted of 8
pairs presented at a 2.5-second rate, and 4 of these items were tested for
recall in the following test block. The 4 items tested were selected
equally often from each presentation position of the preceding 8-item

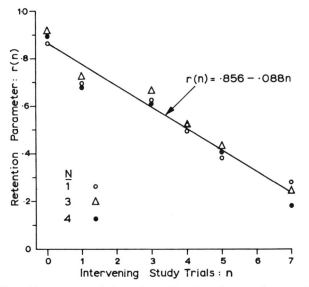

Fig. 10. The $r(t)$ estimates derived from Fig. 9a, where n denotes the number
of intervening study trials. The points for the $N = 2$ condition are not plotted. In
theory, the three estimates at each n value should be identical.

study block. The order in which items were tested was counterbalanced
over test blocks. For each response ensemble condition, each of 24 *Ss*
had a list consisting of 16 such study-test blocks. The recall curves
are based on 192 observations per point. As in Experiments I and II, the
particular word lists used with the different response ensembles were counterbalanced over *Ss*.

2. Results and Predictions

The order in which items were tested had practically no effect upon
their recall probability. The main exception to this statement is that
recall probability of the eighth (last) item in Experiment III was
higher when it was tested first rather than later. Except for this point,

test order had almost no effect on recall. Consequently, results are pooled over various test orders in what follows.

The average recall probabilities for the two experiments are shown in Fig. 11a and 11b. For each graph, the abscissa is the number of

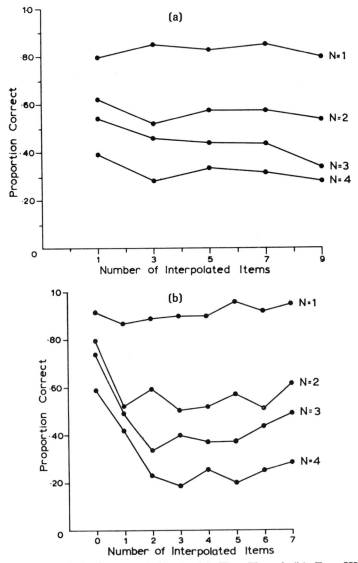

Fig. 11. Proportion of correct recalls in (a) Exp. II, and (b) Exp. III, as a function of the number of interpolated study trials before the test block began. The order of testing was counterbalanced and is ignored in these calculations.

items studied between presentation and the start of the test block. The information in the response ensemble is the parameter in each set of curves.

The recall curves of Experiment II in Fig. 11a are essentially flat, but are well separated according to the information in the response. On the other hand, recall in Experiment III (Fig. 11b) shows definite serial position curves (except for $N = 1$) with a marked recency effect and a slight primacy effect. We have no explanation for the difference in recall functions obtained in these two experiments; they differed in several respects, including the number of items per study block, the number of items tested, and the trial rate. Judging from other experiments using a similar procedure (e.g., Murdock, 1963a), the bowed curves in Fig. 11b are the usual result, whereas the flat curves in Fig. 11a are atypical.

The average recall with the two-response ensemble in both experiments is unusually high relative to what would be expected on the basis of the curves for N's of 2, 3, and 4. This, we feel, was probably due to the block, or "short-list," study procedure employed here. Subjects frequently volunteered the information that a simple strategy sufficed to learn the two-response blocks. Since each block (of 12 or 8 study items) contained only half of each response, they could rehearse or concentrate on only those words going with response 1 and ignore the rest. On test trials, any word they did not remember as a 1 would be responded to as a 2. However, they reported that this strategy was of no help for the larger response ensembles and so was not used for them.

To the extent that this strategy is used, the retention parameter for the $N = 1$ data will be higher than for the $N > 1$ data—as indeed it is. This would follow, for example, if it is held that the effective event promoting forgetting is the act of storing other material. By the halving strategy, the number of interfering events for $N = 1$ would be about half of those encountered when $N > 1$. For this reason, Eq. 7 will be tested with only the $N > 1$ data since it can be reasonably presumed that $u(t)$ will be similar in these cases. The surprising fact is that this halving strategy was not used by Ss in Experiment I (none reported it); apparently, the continuous interleaving of study and test trials in that experiment lowered the saliency of such strategies.

In testing Eq. 4 with the $N > 1$ data, recall results are pooled over all lags t because of their essential constancy, and an average retention parameter r is estimated by the same procedure as before. The results of this procedure are shown in Table I. The fit is quite good in both experiments; neither chi-square value is significant, despite the power

TABLE I

AVERAGE RECALL PROBABILITIES

Experiment II			Experiment III		
N	Observed	Predicted	N	Observed	Predicted
2	.569	.572	2	.575	.572
3	.444	.435	3	.455	.434
4	.323	.325	4	.303	.323
	$\hat{r}$ = .514			$\hat{r}$ = .512	
	n = 1200[a]			n = 1536[a]	
	$\chi^2(2)$ = .33			$\chi^2(2)$ = 3.48	
	p > .50			p > .10	

[a] Total observations in each proportion.

of the test afforded by the large number of observations. It may be noted that the average recall scores are approximately the same in the two experiments. Attempts to fit the recall curves in Fig. 11b by estimating separate r's at each serial position proved only moderately successful. The general irregularity of the empirical curves prevented a really good fit. Even so, the average discrepancy between observed and predicted proportions was only .03.

3. Comparison to All-or-None Model

The fit of the multicomponent predictions in Table I may be again compared to those of the simple all-or-none model. The fit of the latter's predictions are considerably poorer in each experiment, yielding chi-squares (with 2 df) for goodness of fit of 22 and 43, respectively, for Experiments II and III. These chi-squares are 66 and 12 times larger, respectively, than those for goodness of fit of the multicomponent model. Thus, these data again contradict the idea that the total information in the memory trace is lost in an all-or-none fashion; however, the data are consistent with the idea that individual components of the memory vector are lost in an all-or-none manner.

These recall experiments do not, of course, prove that the multi-component model of memory traces is the only one possible, since few alternatives have been tested against it. The experiments do, however, yield evidence consistent with the vector model and suggest that it is not altogether an idle practice to examine further implications of the model. This is done in the remaining sections of the paper, where we turn to examination of various tests of recognition memory to see what light the model may shed on problems of interrelating performance on a variety of such tests.

IV. Recognition Memory

A. CLASSIFICATION OF RECOGNITION TASKS

Some implications of the theory will now be derived for measures of recognition memory. Tests of recognition memory fall naturally into two types. First are *single-stimulus* tests, in which a single unit of learning (e.g., an S-R pair) is shown and S rates this in some way according to its familiarity to him. Often the rating is dichotomous ("Yes, I've seen it before" or "No, I've not seen it before"), but it can be done with as many rating categories as S can handle (for example, the S may be instructed to "Rate on a 7-point scale your adjudged likelihood of having seen this unit before"). The dichotomous judgment may be supplemented by a confidence rating ("Rate on a 5-point scale your confidence that your Yes or No answer is correct"). In data analysis, the yes-no response plus its confidence rating is unfolded and treated in practice as a straightforward rating scale regarding the familiarity of the test unit.

Second are *multiple-choice* tests in which several learning units are shown. These tests take a variety of forms depending on how S is instructed to partition the set of n alternatives. Examples of instructed partitions would be (a) pick the most familiar item; (b) pick the k most familiar of the n; (c) pick the k least familiar of the n; (d) rank order all n on the basis of their judged familiarity; and so on.

Presumably, an S's performance on all these tasks should be interrelated since, in some sense, they are simply different kinds of output from one and the same memory structure. However, development of quantitative models to describe these interrelationships have hitherto proved difficult. In the following, the vector model of the memory trace will be applied to this problem.

B. THE DECISION THEORY VIEWPOINT

Before proceeding to the main discussion, however, the general viewpoint to be employed will first be presented. The viewpoint is that of statistical decision theory, which has been widely used in dealing with psychophysical experiments on detection and recognition. The best-known model employing decision theory concepts in psychophysics is the theory of signal detectability, or TSD (see Swets, Tanner, & Birdsall, 1961). Egan (1958) was the first to propose the relevance of decision theory concepts to interpretation of performance on recognition tests of memory, and this point of view is now widely accepted (e.g., Bernbach, 1964; Bower, 1964; Murdock, 1965; Norman & Wickelgren, 1965;

Parks, 1966; Pollack, Norman, & Galanter, 1965). The decision-theoretic concepts are used to describe S's judgment "criterion" and how this is manipulated by situational variables.

To illustrate the main concepts, let us consider a yes-no recognition test with single stimuli in which S is to decide whether or not a test item is one he has seen before in a list of items he has just studied. This decision presumably is made on the basis of some "feeling of familiarity" that S experiences when the test item is compared to what he has stored in memory. Let us admit that this feeling of familiarity may vary over a range of values for both previously studied (old) items as well as for novel items not previously seen (new, or distractor, items). Admitting this structure, S's problem is this: given a particular feeling of familiarity produced by a test item, decide from which population of items (old or new) it comes. It is presumed that S resolves this decision problem by choosing a cutpoint or criterion on the familiarity continuum that partitions the range into a region of acceptance and a region of rejection. Test items whose familiarity exceeds the criterion are accepted as old (Respond "Old" or "Yes, I've seen it before"); otherwise the test item is rejected (Respond "New" or "No, I've not seen it before").

If S were to act in a manner approaching that of an optimal decision-maker, several factors would have to be taken into account in selecting the criterion of acceptance. We will discuss later the optimal criterion, but the factors entering into it can be briefly mentioned at once. They are the payoffs and penalties involved for accepting versus rejecting new and old items, and the relative likelihood that a given feeling of familiarity results from an old, as opposed to a new, item. The main components of the latter likelihood are the probability that any test item is old instead of new, and the probability distribution of familiarity ratings given old and given new items. For convenience in the immediate discussion, let x denote the feeling of familiarity, with large numbers representing high familiarity; and let $f_o(x)$ and $f_n(x)$ denote the probability densities of x for old and new items, respectively; TSD assumes that x is a continuous variable and that f_o and f_n are normal density functions. Figure 12a shows possible distributions of $f_o(x)$ and $f_n(x)$, with a particular criterion indicated.

The choice of a criterion determines the "hit rate," that is, the probability that an old item is accepted, $P(A \mid o)$; and a corresponding "false alarm rate," the probability that a new item is accepted as old, $P(A \mid n)$. These represent, respectively, the probability areas of $f_o(x)$ and $f_n(x)$ above the criterion in Fig. 12a. Since the criterion is under S's control and it may vary from one experimental condition to another, a simple measure of hit rate is not by itself an adequate description of recognition memory since it varies greatly according to the criterion involved. An adequate measure can be obtained, however, by noting that as the criterion in Fig. 12a is varied, the hit rate and false alarm rate will covary, constrained in a manner determined by the two underlying density functions. For the particular distributions of Fig. 12a, the covariation of $P(A \mid o)$ and $P(A \mid n)$ is depicted in Fig. 12b. For example, if the criterion were set very low, far to the left in Fig. 12a, then all area under both distributions exceeds the criterion and the point at (1, 1) on Fig. 12b is obtained. If the criterion were set very

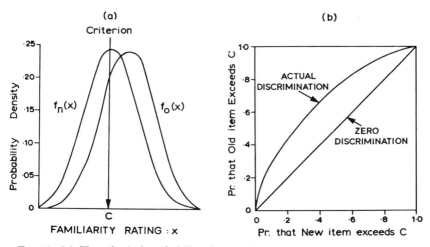

FIG. 12. (a) Hypothetical probability density functions for old (f_o) and for new (f_n) items on the familiarity axis x. A criterion is indicated at C. (b) The covariation of the probability that an old versus a new item exceeds a criterion C as C is varied. The line marked "zero discrimination" would result in case $f_o(x)$ and $f_n(x)$ were identical, so S could not distinguish old from new items.

high, far to the right in Fig. 12a, the point at (0, 0) is obtained. Intermediate criteria lead to intermediate points on the curve in Fig. 12b. The straight line in Fig. 12b labeled "zero discrimination" shows the result obtained when $f_o(x)$ and $f_n(x)$ are identical.

Curves of this kind in psychophysical detection situations are called either receiver-operating-characteristic (ROC) curves or isosensitivity curves. For recognition memory, the terms that have been proposed are memory-operating-characteristic (MOC) curves or isomemory curves. Why *iso*memory? Because all points falling along this curve represent the same ability to discriminate between old versus new items. If some variable simply moves S's performance from one point to another on the same curve, then that manipulation has affected his criterion (or "response bias") but not his memory or whatever produces discriminability of items along the familiarity axis. Increasing memory, or discriminability, would, on the other hand, have the effect of shifting the entire MOC curve of Fig. 12b toward the upper left-hand corner at (0, 1). From such considerations it follows that a more adequate (that is, criterion-invariant) description of recognition memory is provided either by the entire MOC curve or its parameters.

C. MULTICOMPONENT MODELS FOR RECOGNITION MEMORY

In applying the multicomponent model to recognition tasks, it will be supposed generally that S compares the test stimulus (or stimuli) to the degraded memory trace of the item he holds in store, and depending on the outcome of this comparison (or of several comparisons, if there are several test stimuli), he decides how to respond to the test stimulus (or stimuli). Different models result, depending on (a) the assumptions about the memory trace (for example, whether a null-return or random-replacement interpretation of component forgetting is used), (b) the performance required of S (for example, pick one, rank k, or rate one), and (c) the different decision rules assumed. As in the earlier discussion, the discussion here applies strictly only to tasks that minimize retrieval difficulties, so that, metaphorically, the model-subject knows which memory trace to pull out of its store for comparison to the test stimulus. A convenient prototype would be a modification of the light-board experiments reported earlier: a target pair S_1-R_1 is shown for study, and later S is shown a single test pair S_1-R_x to judge, or is shown several test pairs with different responses paired with S_1, S_1-R_1, S_1-R_2, S_1-R_3, and so on, and is required to choose the correct pairing he has seen before. It is presumed that on the test S retrieves the memory vector (CS_1, CR_1) and compares CR_1 (or its degraded form) to the encoding of the test item, or CR_x. It is assumed that all items are encoded into homogeneous vectors N components in length and that some mechanism compares the values of the N corresponding components of the two vectors.

The outcome to be expected from this comparison process depends on whether forgetting is interpreted as consisting in null-state return or random replacement of a component's value in the original memory trace. If the random-replacement idea is used, then the output of the comparator will be a two-level score, described as M matches (same value in corresponding components) and $N - M$ mismatches (different values in corresponding components). Alternatively, if the null-state idea is used to interpret forgetting, then the output of comparing the test item to the degraded memory trace can be a three-level score, consisting of M matches, $R - M$ mismatches, and $N - R$ question marks. In the latter cases, the original value of the component has been erased and the comparator has nothing (or only a null value) in that position to compare to the value of the test item on that component. Note that in all cases the comparator is deciding simply "same," "different," or "do not know" and is not grading component value-pairs according to how close they are in any metric sense of distance. To apply these ideas to recognition tests, we must first derive from the model the probability distributions of the various scores resulting from the comparator.

1. Distribution of Comparison Scores for Old Items

Consider first the distribution of scores given that the test item is, in fact, old or correct. Thus a degraded memory trace is being compared to what, in effect, it looked like when it was first stored. Recall that the distribution of the number of components correctly retained R is binomial with parameters N and r.

Consider first the null-state interpretation of forgetting. According to this view, the number of matches for an old test item will be exactly R (since all components retained match the test item), there will be no mismatches, and the number of question marks will be $N - R$. Letting M_o denote the matches for an old item, its distribution is the same as R, namely

$$P(M_o = x) = P(R = x) = \binom{N}{x} r^x (1 - r)^{N-x}. \tag{9}$$

The match score suffices to characterize the two-level score in this case.

Consider next the random-replacement interpretation of forgetting. According to this view, the number of matches will be R and the number of mismatches will be $N - R$. Since r denotes the probability that a given component retains its original correct value, the distribution of match scores is given by Eq. 9, and $N - M_o$ is the number of mismatches. But again, M_o completely characterizes the comparison score for the case of an old item.

2. Distribution of Comparison Scores for New Items

a. Representation of Item Dissimilarity. The match scores when new (distractor) items are compared to a memory trace will depend primarily on how different the distractors are from the correct (old) item in question. To get on with the task here, it must be decided how to represent in formal terms this notion of the similarity of a set of distractors to a particular old item.

The most convenient representation found so far is the following: beginning with a known, old target item consisting of N bits, a population of distractors to this target is generated by changing each bit in the original vector to some different value with independent probability d, and leaving the original value of the component the same with probability $1 - d$. The change parameter d then gives a convenient index of the average difference between an old item and a population of distractors generated for comparison with it. In principle, d is under the control of the experimenter (according to how similar he makes the distractors), but it cannot be preset numerically unless S's precise encoding system is known. Thus, experimentally, distractor populations can usually only be rank ordered in similarity, hence in the parameter d. For this reason, with most experimental materials d will serve as a parameter to be estimated from performance curves.

As a consequence of the foregoing independent-change representation, the probability that a given distractor in the population has exactly x changes is given by the binomial law with parameters N and d. The probability distribution of matching scores is to be derived for the case where a degraded memory trace is compared to a distractor selected at random from a population of such distractors. Again the answer differs depending on whether forgetting is interpreted as null state or random replacement of the original value of a component.

b. *The Null-State Interpretation.* Suppose that the trace has degraded to the extent that R components are retained, whereas $N - R$ components are forgotten (have null values). When an N-component distractor is compared bit by bit to this degraded trace, the outcome may be generally described by the following three-level score: there are M matches, $R - M$ mismatches, and $N - R$ question marks. The probability of M_n matches out of R retained components is binomial with parameters R and $1 - d$. From these considerations, it follows that the unconditional probability of x matches and y mismatches is

$$P(M_n = x \quad \text{and} \quad R - M_n = y) = P(R = x + y) \cdot P(M_n = x \mid R = x + y),$$

$$= \binom{N}{x + y} r^{x+y}(1 - r)^{N-x-y} \binom{x + y}{x} (1 - d)^x d^y, \tag{10}$$

for $x, y = 0, 1, \ldots, N$, and $x + y \leq N$. This is a joint probability distribution of two random variables, the number of matches and the number of mismatches.

For some purposes, it may be assumed that the decision-maker takes account only of the number of matches, thus ignoring the number of mismatches. The marginal distribution of M_n may be obtained from Eq. 10 by summing out y from 0 to $N - x$, namely

$$P(M_n = x) = \sum_{y=0}^{N-x} \binom{N}{x+y} r^{x+y}(1 - r)^{N-x-y} \binom{x+y}{x}(1 - d)^x \, d^y.$$

The summing is simplified by using the factorial identity

$$\binom{N}{x+y}\binom{x+y}{x} = \binom{N}{x}\binom{N-x}{y}.$$

After summing over y, the marginal probability distribution of M_n is found to be

$$P(M_n = x) = \binom{N}{x}[r(1 - d)]^x[1 - r(1 - d)]^{N-x}. \tag{11}$$

This is a binomial distribution of match scores with parameters N and $r(1 - d)$. The parameter $r(1 - d)$ is the probability that an individual component is both retained in the trace and not changed in the distractor. In fact, the intuitive derivation of Eq. 11 could have proceeded from just this observation without the intervention of Eq. 10 and the summation. As might be expected from the foregoing, the distribution of the number of mismatches is also binomial with parameters N and rd. If the difference parameter d is zero, then the distribution in Eq. 11 reduces to that of Eq. 9 for old items, as it should.

c. The Random-Replacement Interpretation. Consider next the distribution of M_n implied by the random-replacement interpretation of component forgetting. If there are no null values, then comparisons yield only two-level scores, the number of matches M_n and of mismatches $N - M_n$; thus only the distribution of M_n is of concern.

To begin the derivation, suppose that R of the trace components retain their correct (original) values, whereas $N - R$ have been changed to some other value selected at random from the remaining $v - 1$ possibilities at each component. Of the R retained components, each has probability $1 - d$ of matching the corresponding component of the distractor. Hence the number of matches from this source will be binomially distributed with parameters R and $1 - d$. If a trace component has been forgotten (replaced in value), then the corresponding component of the distractor may match it with probability $d/v - 1$; that is, with probability d that component was changed in generating the distractor, and with probability $1/v - 1$ the value assigned there will accidentally coincide with the random value replacing the original value of that trace component. Hence, the number of matches contributed by this source is binomially distributed with parameters $N - R$ and $d/1 - v$.

A rigorous derivation can be produced from the foregoing considerations, but an intuitive rationale for the end result is easily provided and is given here. The probability that a given component of the trace will be matched by the corresponding component in the distractor is

$$m = r(1 - d) + \frac{(1 - r)d}{v - 1}.$$

Since the N components are independent, the distribution of the number of matches is binomial, namely,

$$P(M_n = x) = \binom{N}{x} m^x (1 - m)^{n-x},$$

where
$$m = r(1 - d) + \frac{(1 - r)d}{v - 1}, \tag{12}$$

$$= r - d\left(\frac{r - g}{1 - g}\right).$$

In the last line, g has been substituted for v^{-1}.

The average match score for old items (Nr) exceeds that for new items (Nm) whenever retention exceeds the chance level g. Since for most reasonable forgetting schemes, $r(t) \geq 1/v$ (e.g., Eq. 6 ff.), the average match score will usually be higher for old than for new items.

Having derived the distributions of comparison scores for old and new items, we turn now to their implications for various tasks involving recognition memory.

D. MULTIPLE-CHOICE TESTS

Multiple-choice tests are considered first because the decision rule is simple and obvious in these cases. The rule is to choose that alternative which yields the higher matching score to the memory trace; in case several alternatives are tied for the maximal matching score, then S is presumed to choose among these, possibly with some response bias. This rule is equivalent to the "cross-out" rule that Murdock (1963b) found accurately described Ss' operating strategy on multiple-choice tests, namely, cross out those alternatives known to be wrong and choose at random among the remaining candidates. Viewing the memory trace and the K-encoded answers as points in an N-dimensional vector space, the aforementioned decision rule is the same as one which prescribes choice of that answer-vector having the minimal distance from the memory-vector. Furthermore the rule is equivalent to one based on maximum likelihood wherein the elements are the K Bayesian probabilities that the degraded memory-vector could have arisen given that answer i ($i = 1, 2, \ldots, K$) were the initial input or correct answer. The two-alternative situation will be considered in detail first and discussion of the K-alternative situation will follow.

1. Two-Alternative Forced Choice

Suppose that of the two test items one is in fact old and one new, and that they are presented in a standard display order, such as left–right spatial positions or first–second temporal order. The S's response is designating position A_1 or A_2 as containing the old item. Let $P(A_1 \mid o_1)$ denote the probability of choice A_1 when the old item is in position 1, and $P(A_1 \mid o_2)$ the probability of choice A_1 when the old item is in position 2. These correspond to the hit rate and false alarm rate. Assume that when match scores of the two alternatives are tied, S chooses A_1 with a probability bias b that depends on the payoffs and the probability of an o_1 test trial.

Consider first the null-state interpretation. If x components are retained in the trace, then the match score for the old (correct) alternative will be x, and for the new (incorrect) alternative will be binomially distributed over the values from 0 to x. In case $M_n < x$, the correct alternative will be chosen. In case $M_n = x$, a tie results and the response bias is used. From these considerations, the following expression describes the probability of response A_1 given an o_1 trial:

$$P(A_1 \mid o_1) = \sum_{x=0}^{N} P(R = x)[1 - (1 - d)^x] + b \sum_{x=0}^{N} P(R = x)(1 - d)^x,$$

$$= 1 - (1 - b)(1 - rd)^N. \tag{13}$$

The probability of an A_1 response on an o_2 trial is just the second sum in the first line of Eq. 13, or

$$P(A_1 \mid o_2) = b(1 - rd)^N. \tag{14}$$

These probabilities depend on all four parameters, the bias, the retention, the distractor dissimilarity, and the size of the unit.

The MOC curve in this case can be obtained by eliminating b in Eqs. 13 and 14, yielding

$$P(A_1 \mid o_1) = P(A_1 \mid o_2) + 1 - (1 - rd)^N. \tag{15}$$

Equation 15 describes MOC curves of slope 1 in the unit square. The intercept increases with r, d, and N and has a direct interpretation: it is the probability that at least one of the N components is both retained in the trace and changed in the distractor. The retention and dissimilarity parameters, r and d, enter reciprocally in determining discriminability in performance; better retention can offset increases in similarity of the distractors, and vice versa.

The empirical validity of Eq. 15 is unknown since recognition memory experiments of this type, where b is manipulated, for example, by $P(o_1)$, have not yet been done. For whatever credibility it may lend, it may be mentioned that corresponding forced-choice experiments with signal detection usually lead to ROC curves of unit slope (e.g., Atkinson, Carterette, & Kinchla, 1964a; Atkinson, Bower & Crothers, 1965, Ch. 5).

Consider briefly the random-replacement interpretation of forgetting. In this case, M_n (from Eq. 12) is not constrained by the value of M_o; in fact, M_n may exceed M_o. The probabilities of an A_1 response on o_1- and o_2-type test trials are

$$P(A_1 \mid o_1) = \sum_{x=1}^{N} P(M_o = x) \, P(M_n < x)$$
$$+ b \sum_{x=0}^{N} P(M_o = x) \, P(M_n = x),$$
$$P(A_1 \mid o_2) = \sum_{x=1}^{N} P(M_n = x) \, P(M_o < x)$$
$$+ b \sum_{x=0}^{N} P(M_o = x) \, P(M_n = x). \quad (16)$$

Elimination of the bias parameter (the second sums) from these two equations yields the MOC equation relating $P(A_1 \mid o_1)$ to $P(A_1 \mid o_2)$. It has a slope of 1 and a positive intercept given by the difference between the initial sums in the foregoing two equations. This intercept is the probability that M_o exceeds M_n (leading to correct choices) minus the probability that M_n exceeds M_o (leading to errors). In general properties then, the MOC curves implied by the null-state and random-replacement ideas in this instance are the same.

2. K-Alternative Forced Choice

In this test, $K - 1$ distractors to the correct alternative are presented; these are to be generated independently according to the usual change rule, each with parameter d. Suppose that x bits are retained so that $M_o = x$. Any distractor with an M_n score less than x is rejected. The probability that a distractor matches all x retained bits is $(1 - d)^x$. Let y_x denote the number of the $K - 1$ distractors that match all x bits; then y_x is binomially distributed with parameters

$K - 1$ and $(1 - d)^x$. If i distractors so match the correct answer, then the unbiased probability that the correct alternative is chosen is $(1 + i)^{-1}$. Thus, when x bits are retained, the probability of a correct choice is

$$P_K(C \mid R = x) = \sum_{i=0}^{K-1} \frac{P(y_x = i)}{1 + i},$$

$$= \frac{1 - [1 - (1 - d)^x]^K}{K(1 - d)^x}. \tag{17}$$

The unconditional probability of a correct choice is the sum over x of Eq. 17 multiplied by the probability that x bits are retained, namely

$$P_K(C) = \sum_{x=0}^{N} \binom{N}{x} r^x (1 - r)^{N-x} \frac{\{1 - [1 - (1 - d)^x]^K\}}{K(1 - d)^x}.$$

This sum can be simplified to the following expression.

$$P_K(C) = \frac{-1}{K} \sum_{i=1}^{K} \binom{K}{i} (-1)^i [1 - r + r(1 - d)^{i-1}]^N. \tag{18a}$$

Unfortunately, no simple closed expression exists for the latter sum. For immediate purposes of qualitative interpretations, however, the unconditional probability in Eq. 18a may be approximated by substituting the average amount retained Nr for x in Eq. 17. The approximation is

$$P_K(C) \simeq \frac{1 - [1 - (1 - d)^{Nr}]^K}{K(1 - d)^{Nr}}. \tag{18b}$$

The critical term in Eq. 18b, $(1 - d)^{Nr}$, is the probability that any given distractor will not be rejected by the Nr bits retained on average in the memory trace. It is the probability that a distractor effectively competes with the correct alternative.

In Eq. 18b, if either retention fails entirely ($r = 0$) or the distractors are the same as the correct alternative ($d = 0$), then choice probability is at the chance level of K^{-1}. One failing of the approximation in Eq. 18b is that it does not reduce to Eq. 13 exactly for $b = .5$ and $K = 2$, although Eq. 18a does. Another failing is its indeterminacy when $d = 1$, but in this case the basic theory and Eq. 18a imply that $P_K(C)$ will equal $1 - (K - 1/K)(1 - r)^N$. That is, retention of any one component of the trace suffices to reject all distractors generated with $d = 1$. The $P_K(C)$ is mainly dominated by the K in the denominator, decreasing like K^{-1}. Figure 13 shows several curves for the $P_K(C)$ of Eq. 18b, assuming different values of $(1 - d)^{Nr}$, the average probability that a distractor will pass the matching test and become an effective competitor. The curves decline with K and are ordered by the size of the "acceptance" probability of distractors. These predictions seem qualitatively in agreement with recognition results in which the number and dissimilarity of distractors are varied (e.g., Murdock, 1963b; Postman, 1950; Shepard & Chang, 1963).

Turning next to the random-replacement scheme for the multiple-choice task, $K - 1$ values of M_n are randomly selected from the distribution of Eq. 12 and compared to one value of M_o. The unbiased

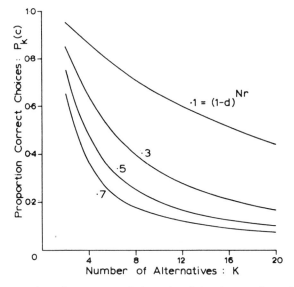

FIG. 13. Probability of a correct choice related to the number of alternatives, where $K - 1$ are distractors. The parameter is the probability that a given distractor will not be rejected by the average number of components retained in the memory tract.

probability of a correct choice is the likelihood that M_o exceeds all $K - 1$ values of M_n plus the sum over i of $(1 + i)^{-1}$ times the probability that i of the $K - 1$ values of M_n tie with M_o. The formal expression is cumbersome, of course. Computations can be substantially simplified by approximating the discrete binomial distributions by continuous normal distributions. This approximation is quite efficient for $N \geq 4$ and more so the closer the match probability (r or m) approaches $\frac{1}{2}$. Let $f_o(x)$ denote the normal density approximation to the distribution of old match scores (Eq. 9) with mean Nr and variance $Nr(1 - r)$. Similarly, let $f_n(x)$ denote the normal density approximation to the distribution of new match scores (Eq. 12) with mean Nm and variance $Nm(1-m)$. Finally, let $F_n(x)$ denote the cumulative probability that a new match score is less than x. With these concepts at hand, the probability of a correct choice in a K-alternative situation may be written as

$$P_K(C) = \int_{-\infty}^{\infty} f_o(x)(F_n(x))^{K-1}\, dx. \tag{19}$$

This is the integral over x of the likelihood that M_o equals x, whereas all $K-1$ values of M_n are less than x. The previous terms added in the discrete case for $i+1$ ties, and so on, are dropped in the continuous approximation. Equation 19 is identical to that of TSD for cases involving unequal variances and a mean difference of $N(r-m)$ (see Swets *et al.*, 1961).

3. Ranking of K Alternatives

In ranking K alternatives consisting of one old and $K-1$ distractor items, it is supposed that S orders the alternatives strictly in the order of magnitude of their match scores vis à vis the memory trace of the old item. The dependent variable is the rank assigned to the correct alternative. Let $i = 1, \ldots, K$ denote the rank, with 1 being the "most likely correct," and let $P_K(i)$ denote the probability that S assigns the correct alternative to rank i.

Consider first the null-state interpretation of forgetting. According to this view, a distractor can at best only equal (and never exceed) the match score of the correct alternative. If j distractors tie with the correct alternative, then the latter may be assigned any rank from 1 to $j+1$. The likelihood that j distractors will tie M_o given retention of x bits in the trace is binomial with parameters $K-1$ and $(1-d)^x$. No explicit expressions for $P_K(i)$, for any i and K, have been worked out; the same mathematical problems are encountered that required the approximation to $P_K(C)$ in Eq. 18. In fact, $P_K(C)$ in Eq. 18a is just the probability that the correct alternative receives a rank of 1, or $P_K(1)$ in the present notation.

To illustrate the graded test performance of the model when it is ranking, the expressions for $K = 3$ are presented.

$$P_3(1) = 1 - (1-rd)^N + \tfrac{1}{3}[r(1-d)^2 + 1 - r]^N,$$
$$P_3(2) = (1-rd)^N - \tfrac{2}{3}[r(1-d)^2 + 1 - r]^N, \tag{20}$$
$$P_3(3) = \tfrac{1}{3}[r(1-d)^2 + 1 - r]^N.$$

An important implication of these equations is that the probabilities that the correct alternative receives rank 1, 2, or 3 are graded in that order. Equalities of the three probabilities hold only when discrimination is totally absent, either because memory fails entirely ($r = 0$) or because the test stimuli are identical ($d = 0$). From these probabilities, one would expect above-chance performance when S is permitted a second guess after an incorrect first choice. The data available (e.g. Binford & Gettys, 1965; Bower, 1964; Brown, 1965) do show this excess information to be contained in second guesses following an error on the first choice.

In applying the random-replacement idea to ranking, the continuous normal approximations introduced before will be used. The probability that the correct alternative receives rank i may be written as

$$P_K(i) = \int_{-\infty}^{\infty} f_o(x) \binom{K-1}{i-1} [1 - F_n(x)]^{i-1} [F_n(x)]^{K-i} \, dx. \quad (21)$$

This is the integral over x of the probability density that M_o equals x, and that $i - 1$ of the $K - 1$ values of M_n exceed x while the remaining $K - i$ values of M_n are less than x. The final terms in the integral describe the binomial distribution with parameters $K - 1$ and $1 - F_n(x)$. This is the ranking formula for TSD. When the mean value of M_o exceeds that of M_n, then the $P_K(i)$ in Eq. 21 are ordered inversely in magnitude with the rank i. This means that graded performance is predicted by this scheme.

E. Single-Stimulus Tests

In single-stimulus tests, S is shown one item, say S_1-R_1 or S_1-R_2, and asked to make an absolute judgment regarding its familiarity to him. As noted before, this judgment may be dichotomous (accept or reject as old) or a continuous rating. Assume that the memory matching process is the same as before, and that the judgment is made on the basis of the outcome of comparing the test stimulus to the memory trace. A two-level outcome occurs for the random-replacement scheme and a three-level outcome for the null-state scheme. For the latter scheme, several alternative decision rules are plausible; for the former, only a single decision rule is plausible, so it is discussed first.

1. Random-Replacement Interpretation: MOC Curves

For the random-replacement scheme, the two-level comparison score is specified uniquely by M, the number of matches. Thus, the judgment of familiarity will be made with respect to M. Of course, M might be transformed in some way before the judgment is made. A simple transformation would take a weighted sum of the number of matches and mismatches for test stimulus i, according to

$$s_i = a \text{ (matches)} - b \text{ (mismatches)} + c,$$

$$= aM_i - b(N - M_i) + c, \tag{22}$$

$$s_i = (a + b)M_i + c'_N.$$

Here, a and b are positive weighting coefficients for matches and mismatches. However, since the M_i are binomially distributed, so will be the s_i (for new and old items); Eq. 22 simply shifts the location and spread of the M_o and M_n distributions without changing the MOC curve implied by them. Thus, decisions on the s_i axis are equivalent to decisions on the M_i axis. In fact, if $\phi(M_i)$ is any order-preserving (positive monotone) transformation of M_i, then M_i and $\phi(Mi)$ are isomorphic decision axes in the sense of implying the same MOC curve.

If M_o and M_n are approximated by continuous normal distributions, the MOC curves are the same as those derived from TSD. The MOC is obtained in theory by sliding a cutoff point C along the axis and plotting values of $P(M_o \geq C)$ against $P(M_n \geq C)$. Some examples of such MOC curves derived from the theory are shown in Figs. 14a and 14b. In Fig. 14a, $r = .7$ and the dissimilarity parameter d is varied; in Fig. 14b, $d = .3$ and the retention parameter r is varied. These MOC curves were obtained from the binomial distributions of M_o and M_n assuming that N equals 20. For such large N values, the MOC curves based on the binomial are indistinguishable from those that arise from normal density approximations. The straight line for $r = .20$ in Fig. 14b arises because $v = 5$ was assumed in plotting these graphs; and it can be shown (cf. Eq. 23 following) that $r = m$ whenever $r = 1/v = g$. The theoretical MOC curves in Figs. 14a and 14b have the same general shape as the empirical curves for recognition memory reported by Bernbach (1964), Egan (1958), Murdock (1965), and Pollack et al. (1965). With freedom to choose the three parameters N, r, and m, the theory will fit the empirical curves fairly well. Such good fits, of course, are only a minimal requirement for any reasonable theory, and do not provide a very stringent test.

In experimental practice, the MOC curve is estimated by plotting the cumulative probabilities that the rating of old versus new items exceeds rating R_i. From an n-point rating scale, $n - 1$ points of the MOC are obtained. Using normal approximations to the binomial distributions, two parameters determine, and thus can be estimated from, the empirical MOC curve (cf. Swets et al., 1961). These estimates are obtained

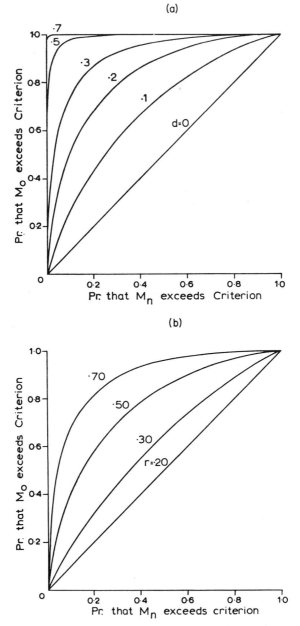

Fɪɢ. 14. Memory-operating characteristics for the random-replacement model. In (a) the dissimilarity of the distractors (new items) is varied, with discrimination increasing as d increases; in (b) the average retention of the memory trace is varied. The straight line is obtained when $r = m = g$.

by fitting a straight line to the inverse-normal transformation of the MOC points. The intercept of the straight line estimates the mean difference scaled with respect to one of the standard deviations, such as that of M_o, namely,

$$\theta_1 = \frac{E(M_o) - E(M_n)}{\sigma(M_o)} = \frac{d(r - g)}{1 - g}\left[\frac{N}{r(1 - r)}\right]^{1/2} = K\left[\frac{N}{r(1 - r)}\right]^{1/2}. \quad (23)$$

where $g = v^{-1}$ and $K = d(r - g)(1 - g)^{-1}$. This parameter corresponds to the d' measure of TSD. It determines how far the MOC curve deviates toward the upper left-hand corner at $(0, 1)$, away from the diagonal line. The slope of the fitted straight line in normal-normal coordinates is an estimate of the ratio of the standard deviations, that is,

$$\theta_2 = \frac{\sigma(M_n)}{\sigma(M_o)} = \left[\frac{m(1 - m)}{r(1 - r)}\right]^{1/2} = \left[\frac{(r - K)(1 - r + K)}{r(1 - r)}\right]^{1/2}. \quad (24)$$

This ratio controls the symmetry of the MOC curve about the anti-diagonal line from $(1, 0)$ to $(0, 1)$. The MOC curve is symmetric when $\theta_2 = 1$; humped below the antidiagonal line when $\theta_2 < 1$; and humped above when $\theta_2 > 1$. Theoretically, the symmetry depends on the sign of $2K(r - .5 - .5K)$. If this sign is positive, $\theta_2 > 1$; if negative, $\theta_2 < 1$; if zero, $\theta_2 = 1$. Since K depends on the size of $r - g$, it is expected to be positive; so the MOC curve may be expected to be humped above $(\theta_2 > 1)$ when retention is high $[r > .5(1 + K)]$, and humped below when retention is low $[r < .5(1 + K)]$. If curves of one type of asymmetry were consistently obtained regardless of retention probability, such evidence would discredit this model. Obviously with three theoretical unknowns (N, r, K) and only two estimated numbers, θ_1 and θ_2, the theoretical parameters cannot be estimated uniquely on the basis of the MOC curve.

a. *The Optimal Setting of the Criterion.* The MOC curve is derived from category rating data where the category boundaries correspond in theory to different judgment criteria established by S. In the dichotomous experiment, only a single criterion is set. If S were to set his criterion so as to maximize the expected value of the trial outcomes over the experiment, it is easy to show (cf. Swets *et al.*, 1961) that the optimal criterion would be that value C where

$$\frac{P(o)}{P(n)}\frac{P(M_o = C)}{P(M_n = C)} = \frac{W_n - L_n}{W_o - L_o}. \quad (25)$$

In Eq. 25, $P(o)$ and $P(n)$ are the probabilities that the test item is in fact old and new, W_o and W_n are the utilities of the winnings earned by a correct response to old and new items, and L_o and L_n are the utilities of the penalties incurred for an error on old and new items, respectively. The sense of Eq. 25 is that the criterion should be so set that the relative likelihood of a match score of C arising from an old versus a new item equals the payoff differential for new versus old items. If the M_i are interpreted as discrete-valued variables, then C may lie in an interval between two integers; if the continuous normal approximation to the M_i is used, then Eq. 25 determines a unique value of C. The extent to which Ss will approximate in practice this ideal criterion is not known; clearly, their criterion will vary roughly in the manner summarized by Eq. 25. At present it appears difficult to determine how well Ss approximate the criterion in Eq. 25 because the parameters of the M_o and M_n distributions must be estimated before Eq. 25 can be tested. But earlier it was mentioned that a single point or even the entire MOC curve does not suffice to estimate all the parameters of the theory.

   b. *Alternative Method for Setting Criterion.* Parks (1966) has suggested an alternative rule by which Ss set their criterion in dichotomous (yes-no) recognition tasks. The proposal is that S sets his criterion so that his over-all probability of saying "Old" is proportional to the actual proportion of old items in the test series. Letting k denote the proportionality constant and p_o denote the proportion of old test items, the proposal is that C is so chosen as to satisfy the following equality.

$$p_o P(M_o \geq C) + (1 - p_o) P(M_n \geq C) = k p_o.$$

The proportionality constant k is presumed to vary with the payoffs. It is easily estimated, for example, by the sum of hit and false alarm rates on a $p_o = .50$ condition (any other p_o between 0 and 1 would serve as well). Given assumptions about normality and equal variances of M_o and M_n, the same data will also serve to estimate d', the scaled mean separation between M_o and M_n. Having thus estimated k and d', the relation just proposed specifies a unique C for any new p_o schedule, thereby allowing predictions of the hit rate and false alarm rate on this new p_o schedule. Parks reported several sets of recognition memory data in which such predictions were quite accurate. This supports his proposal for how S sets his criterion in the dichotomous recognition task.

2. Null-State Interpretation and Absolute Judgments

   Recall that the null-state model of the memory trace yields a three-level comparison score consisting in general of M_i matches, $R_i - M_i$ mismatches, and $N - R_i$ unknowns or question marks. It will be assumed that the decision axis is formed by a linear combination of these three scores. Letting s_i denote the score for test stimuli of type i (old or new), the assumption is that the decision axis is

$$s_i = AM_i - B(R_i - M_i) - C(N - R_i) + D. \qquad (26)$$

In this score, A, B, and C are weighting coefficients. For old items in memory $M_o = R_o$, so the second term vanishes, yielding

$$s_o = (A + C)M_o + D'_N. \qquad (27)$$

Since M_o is binomially distributed, so will be s_o; Eq. 27 just shifts the mean and spread of M_o. For new (distractor) items $M_n \leq R_n$; thus all terms of Eq. 26 may exist and the full distribution of s_n is given by Eq. 10; that is,

$$P[s_n = (A + C)x - By + D'_N] = P(M_n = x \ \& \ R_n - M_n = y),$$

$$= \binom{N}{x}\binom{N-x}{y}[r(1 - d)]^x (rd)^y (1 - r)^{N-x-y}, \qquad (28)$$

for $0 \leq x, y \leq N$, and $x + y \leq N$. This distribution of s_n is inconvenient to work with, and the general shape of MOC curves implied by Eqs. 27 and 28 are unknown. This question should be investigated.

A particularly simple scheme arises if, in Eq. 26, B is set equal to zero. When information about mismatches is ignored, the theory leads to a one-dimensional decision axis similar to that of TSD. That is, the decision axis is the match score and M_o and M_n have binomial distributions given by Eqs. 9 and 11, respectively. Using continuous normal approximations to the binomials, the two parameters of the MOC curve will be

$$\theta_1 = \frac{E(M_o) - E(M_n)}{\sigma(M_o)} = d\left(\frac{Nr}{1 - r}\right)^{1/2},$$

and

$$\theta_2 = \frac{\sigma(M_n)}{\sigma(M_o)} = \left[\frac{(1 - d)(1 - r + rd)}{(1 - r)}\right]^{1/2}. \qquad (29)$$

The value of θ_2 determines the symmetry of the MOC curve, and it depends on the sign of the quantity $1 - r(2 - d)$. If this sign is positive, then $\text{Var}(M_o)$ exceeds $\text{Var}(M_n)$, $\theta_2 < 1$, and the MOC curve is humped below the antidiagonal; if the sign is negative, then $\theta_2 > 1$ and the MOC is humped above the diagonal; if the quantity is zero, then $\theta_2 = 1$ and the MOC is symmetric. When retention is less than .5, then $\theta_2 < 1$ regardless of d; when retention is greater than .5, the sign depends on d.

Some MOC curves based on the null-state model are shown in Figs. 15a and 15b, wherein d and r are separately varied. The curves are very similar to those for the random-replacement model.

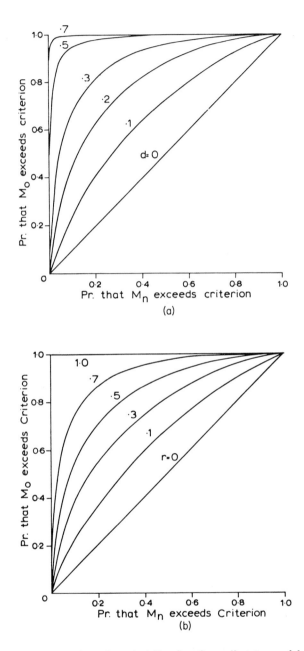

Fig. 15. Memory-operating characteristics for the null-state model. In (a) the dissimilarity of the distractors is varied; in (b) the average retention of the memory trace is varied.

3. *Category Discrimination and a Posteriori Probabilities*

Before leaving the topic of MOC curves based on rating data, it may be mentioned that the degree to which the various rating categories are used discriminately by S can be estimated by the a posteriori probabilities (see Norman & Wickelgren, 1965). This is the likelihood that an item assigned rating C_i is in fact old. Suppose that there are 7 categories, $N > 7$, and that S sets the six boundaries $B_1, B_2, \ldots, B_6$, as shown in Fig. 16a. The probability of a rating of C_i given an old or

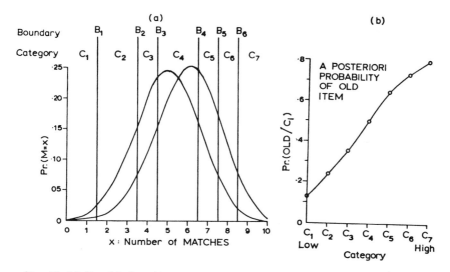

Fig. 16. (a) Possible locations of six boundaries B_i partitioning the M scores into seven categories C_i. (b) The a posteriori probability that the item is old given that a rating of C_i occurs.

new item is just the area of $f_o(x)$ or $f_n(x)$ between boundaries B_i and B_{i-1}. Letting $F_o(B_i)$ and $F_n(B_i)$ denote the cumulative probability that f_o and f_n, respectively, are less than B_i, then the equations for the a posteriori probabilities are

$$P(\text{old} \mid C_i) = \frac{F_o(B_i) - F_o(B_{i-1})}{F_o(B_i) - F_o(B_{i-1}) + F_n(B_i) - F_n(B_{i-1})} \qquad (30)$$

For C_1, we interpret $B_o = -\infty$, and for C_7 we interpret B_7 as $+\infty$. Plots of Eq. 30 are shown in Fig. 16b for the boundaries in Fig. 16a. The important point about $P(\text{old} \mid C_i)$ is that in theory it increases monotonically with the rating C_i. This monotonicity property should hold so long as N exceeds the number of categories, whatever the spacing between the category boundaries.

The theoretical expression for the a posteriori probabilities is easily derived, but its relation to the observed curve (derived from category ratings) must be interpreted with caution. The likelihood that an item is old given that it yields a match score of x is

$$P(\text{old} \mid M = x) = \frac{p_o P(M_o = x)}{p_o P(M_o = x) + (1 - p_o) P(M_n = x)}.$$

For example, using the expressions for the null-state model, a logistic or S-shaped curve is implied, namely,

$$P(\text{old} \mid M = x) = (1 + Ab^x)^{-1},$$

where
$$A = (1 - p_o) \left(1 + \frac{rd}{1 - r}\right)^N p_o^{-1}$$

and $b = 1 - d(1 - r + rd)^{-1}$. The logistic increases monotonically with x, of course, thus establishing that property of the expected data. It should be noted, however, that the theoretical curve for $P(\text{old} \mid M = x)$ cannot be directly compared to the observed proportions $P(\text{old} \mid C_i)$ obtained from category ratings. It suffices to note that the independent variables differ for the two functions, the first depending on the unknown M values, and the second on unknown intervals on the M scale (that is, the category boundaries). In principle the observed curve is obtained from the theoretical curve by segmenting or chunking the M scale into n category divisions, and then plotting for each category the value of $P(\text{old } M = x)$ averaged over all x values within that interval or chunk. But unfortunately, the theory does not predict the locations of the category boundaries, so detailed fitting of the theoretical to the observed curve is precluded. Since at best it can be assumed only that the category boundaries are arranged in increasing order on the M scale, the strongest predictions possible are that the observed a posteriori probabilities (a) will have a minimum no less than $P(\text{old} \mid M = 0)$ and a maximum no greater than $P(\text{old} \mid M = N)$, and (b) will increase monotonically with the category rating C_i.

4. The Effect of Too Many Rating Categories

Mention must be made of one complication to the preceding discussion of MOC curves and a posteriori probabilities derived from rating data. Recall that M is a discrete-valued variable ranging over the integers from 0 to N. A complication can arise if the number of rating categories S is requested to use exceeds N, the number of components in the memory trace. This would occur, for example, if $N = 6$ and S were asked to use 10 rating categories, as was done in experiments by Norman and Wickelgren (1965) and Murdock (1965). If such were the case, S would have the choice of either not using some categories at all or else using several indiscriminately. Since instructions are usually interpreted by S to mean that he should use all the categories (cf. Parducci, 1965), he would tend in such a case to use several categories indiscriminately.

There are many idiosyncratic variations on how the categories could be assigned in such cases, but to show the possible effects of this excess of categories, a simple scheme will be used. Suppose that $N = 6$, S is asked to use 10 categories, and he decides to assign M scores to the categories as follows: $M = x$ is assigned uniquely to category C_{4+x}, except that $M = 1$ and $M = 0$ are assigned randomly to categories C_1 through C_5. Figures 17a and 17b show the MOC and a posteriori probability curves that can arise in this case. For these curves, retention is assumed to be generally poor ($r = .26$) and $d = .62$.

As Fig. 17a shows, the MOC curve based on such category assignments yields straight-line segments over that portion of the rating scale that is used indiscriminately. And as Fig. 17b shows, the lower five categories contain no differential information in the sense of giving different a posteriori probabilities. Both curves are similar, in fact, to several re-

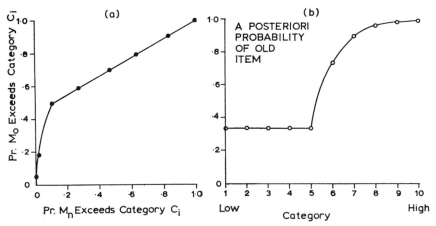

FIG. 17. Possible distortions produced when the number of rating categories (10) exceeds the number of information components in the memory trace (6). In (a) the MOC has a straight-line segment over that portion of the rating scale used indiscriminately. In (b) the aposteriori probabilities are the same for the lower five categories, which are used indiscriminately.

ported by Norman and Wickelgren (1965) for poorly retained material.

The point to be emphasized here is that knowledge or memory of an item is not infinitely divisible, but rather is limited. By simply increasing the number of rating categories, we cannot increase S's resolving power beyond certain limits; if you will, S has a definite "channel capacity" for the amount of information he can transmit about these items by using the category responses. An essentially similar conclusion has been reached about information transmitted by category responses to psychophysical stimuli (cf. Garner, 1962, pp. 87–90).

V. Related Aspects of Recall Performance

The theory will now be used to interpret several features of recall performance. The topics to be discussed in this section include the amount of information transmitted in recall, confidence ratings of the correctness of a recalled response, effects of a possible threshold for recall, the operation of proactive biases in recall, and response latencies. For all topics except the first, the discussion is sensible only in terms of the null-state interpretation of component forgetting since in these cases the model has to "be aware" of how much information has been retained and how much forgotten from a memory trace and, as mentioned earlier, the random-replacement interpretation of forgetting provides no basis for discriminating how much has been retained.

A. The Information Transmitted in Recall

Pollack (1953), Miller (1956), and others have reported data indicating that the amount of information transmitted in recall increases directly with the formal uncertainty of the ensemble of items used as memory materials. The measure of transmitted information is formally derived from the complete matrix of inputs versus outputs (see Garner, 1962, Ch. 3). For present purposes, the input will be the correct response given to the memory system, and the output will be the response recalled by the system. To distinguish these two usages of response, let A_i denote input of alternative i of some ensemble, and R_j denote recall of alternative j of that same ensemble. The data matrix consists of entries $p(A_i, R_j)$ denoting the joint proportion of study-test trials when A_i was "sent" and R_j was "received." In the following, the aim is to derive from the theory the expected information transmission, so as to compare this to some of Pollack's results. The equations used are given by Garner (1962, pp. 56–59).

The transmitted information, or contingent uncertainty, between R and A is defined as

$$U(R : A) = U(R) - U_A(R), \tag{31}$$

where

$$U(R) = -\sum_j p(R_j) \ln_2 p(R_j)$$

is the uncertainty in the over-all response recall distribution, and

$$U_A(R) = -\sum_i p(A_i) \sum_j p(R_j \mid A_i) \ln_2 p(R_j \mid A_i)$$

is the conditional uncertainty in R when A is known.

Suppose that 2^N response alternatives are used, with memory vectors encoded into N binary components. Let these alternatives be used as correct responses equally often, so that $p(A_i) = 2^{-N}$, and suppose that the various responses are, over-all trials, recalled equally often. Without specific response biases, $p(R_j) = 2^{-N}$. With this structure, it follows that

$$U(R) = -\sum_{j=1}^{2^N} 2^{-N} \ln 2^{-N} = N$$

and

$$U_A(R) = -\sum_{j=1}^{2^N} p(R_j \mid A) \ln p(R_j \mid A). \tag{32}$$

The task now is to characterize theoretically the probability distribution over the R_j given that a particular A_i is sent. With no output biases, all the distributions turn out to be the "same" in a sense to be defined now. For any given A_i sent, the 2^N possible responses to be recalled can be partitioned into $N + 1$ subsets, denoted $S_0, S_1, \ldots, S_N$, where each member of a given subset has an identical probability of occurrence. The number of response members in subset S_i is $\binom{N}{i}$, and the common response probability for each member of subset S_i is

$$p(R_i \mid A) = [.5(1 - r)]^i [.5(1 + r)]^{N-i} = c^i (1 - c)^{N-i}.$$

Derivation of these statements from the independent-loss model is lengthy and cannot be given here. The input A_i determines which responses belong to which subsets, but the over-all numerical pattern remains the same in theory regardless of the specific input. This partitioning accounts for all the recall possibilities since, summing elements of the subsets,

$$\sum_{i=0}^{N} \binom{N}{i} = 2^N.$$

Also the sum of probabilities of all recall responses is unity since

$$\sum_{i=0}^{N} \binom{N}{i} c^i (1 - c)^{N-i} = 1.$$

Consider a single element of subset S_i, and define U_i^* as the uncertainty associated with recall of this response. It is

$$U_i^* = -p \ln p = -c^i(1 - c)^{N-i}[i \ln c + (N - i) \ln (1 - c)].$$

Since uncertainty measures are additive, the uncertainty of the $\binom{N}{i}$ members of subset S_i is

$$U_i = \binom{N}{i} U_i^*.$$

Finally, the total uncertainty $U_A(R)$ may be obtained by summing U_i over the $N + 1$ subsets to obtain

$$U_A(R) = \sum_{i=0}^{N} \binom{N}{i} U_i^*,$$

$$= \sum_{i=0}^{N} \binom{N}{i} [i \ln c + (N - i) \ln (1 - c)] c^i (1 - c)^{N-i}.$$

But this sum just involves constants times the mean of a binomial distribution. Summing, substituting $c = .5(1 - r)$, and then simplifying, we obtain

$$U_A(R) = N - \frac{N}{2} [(1 - r) \ln (1 - r) + (1 + r) \ln (1 + r)].$$

Using this in Eq. 31 along with Eq. 32, we get the end result

$$U(R : A) = N(.5)[(1 - r) \ln (1 - r) + (1 + r) \ln (1 + r)],$$
$$= Nb. \tag{33}$$

The information transmitted in recall is thus proportional to N, the information contained in the ensemble of correct responses ("messages") sent into the memory system. The proportionality constant b depends on the retention parameter r and behaves sensibly; that is, when $r = 0$ and there is no remembering, responses are completely random and the information transmitted from input to output is zero ($b = 0$); when $r = 1$, the output perfectly maps onto the input and $b = 1$; for $0 < r < 1$, b takes on intermediate values.

Figure 18 shows the fit of Eq. 33 to Pollack's (1953) memory data as summarized in a figure published by Miller (1956). The graph relates the information transmitted in recall to the information characterizing the ensemble of materials used as memory items. The least-squares estimate of b was .64. The straight-line relation provides an adequate description of the data.

B. Confidence Ratings of Recalled Responses

Several investigations (e.g., Atkinson & Shiffrin, 1965; Bower & Hintzman, 1963) have indicated that Ss can give accurate confidence judgments regarding whether the response they have recalled is in fact correct. For example, Fig. 19, taken from the report by Atkinson and Shiffrin (1965), shows an exponential function relating the probability that a recalled response was correct to its confidence rating of either 1 (certain correct), 2, 3, or 4 (very uncertain). The proportion correct in this instance is approximately equal to the reciprocal of the confidence rating. The result indicates the accuracy of S's judgment of the likelihood that his response is correct.

To apply the theory to confidence ratings, begin by supposing that S retains x of N components in the memory trace and responds correctly with probability g^{N-x}. Assume that x and N are known to the decision-maker and a confidence judgment is made on the basis of these numbers. The rule transforming x and N into a confidence judgment will

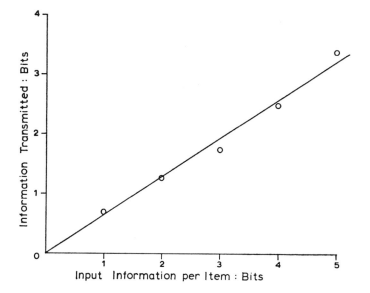

Fig. 18. The amount of information transmitted in recall as a function of the information per item of the materials to be memorized. The open dots are the observed values and the straight line is the theoretical prediction. Data from Pollack (1953) as summarized in a graph by Miller (1956).

depend on the instructed form of the rating scale for S—for example, whether high confidence is to be associated with a high or low number. For example, for the Atkinson and Shiffrin data shown in Fig. 19, the transformation would be something like $z = 1 + A(N - x)$, where z is the confidence rating and A is the weighting coefficient for the number of forgotten components.

Fig. 19. Proportion correct for those recalled responses assigned a confidence rating of 1, 2, 3, or 4. Based on Fig. 10 from Atkinson and Shiffrin (1965).

Suppose generally that the confidence rating is some monotonic function $f(x)$ of x, the amount retained. It then follows that the probability of a correct response is related to the confidence rating z according to

$$C(z) = g^{N - f^{-1}(z)} = k a^{f^{-1}(z)}.$$

Different choices of $f(x)$ then lead to different $C(z)$ functions. For example, if f is linear, then $C(z)$ is an exponential function; if f is a power function, then $C(z)$ is a Gompertz function: if f is an exponential function, then $C(z)$ is a power function. All of these are more or less reasonable $f(x)$ and $C(z)$ functions.

The important point is not the specific equations derived in this discussion, since they depend on an arbitrary assumption relating confidence judgments to x. Rather the point is that the theory provides a natural means for interpreting such confidence data and indicates, in general, the basis for the fact that Ss judgments about the correctness of a recalled response can be very accurate.

Clarke, Birdsall, and Tanner (1959) have suggested that the distributions of confidence ratings for correct versus incorrect responses can be used to construct what they called the Type-2 operating characteristic. To illustrate, suppose that S is permitted five gradations of confidence in the correctness of his answers, with 5 meaning very high and 1 very low. Then the point for rating C on the Type-2 ROC is obtained by plotting the conditional probability that the confidence ratings exceed C given that the response was correct against the similar likelihood given that the response was incorrect. From an n-point confidence scale, $n - 1$ points of the Type-2 curve can be estimated. Clarke et al. point out that the Type-2 curve tells us how discriminating are S's confidence ratings, although they admit that theoretical interpretations of such curves are somewhat obscure.

Our reason for raising the point here is because Murdock (1966) has used this method for analyzing a memory (recall) experiment. In his study, Ss were exposed to many blocks of five S-R pairs and after each block were tested for recall on one of the five pairs and required to state their confidence in the correctness of the response they gave. The percentage of correct recalls for the five pairs varied over a large range according to a typical serial position curve. The remarkable result, however, was that the Type-2 operating characteristics were very similar for the five items despite variations in their percentage correct. Roughly speaking, the accuracy of the confidence judgments was almost independent of whether an item on the average was remembered well or ill.

Such Type-2 operating characteristics are easily derived from the multicomponent model for recall. Two conditional probability distributions are involved: the first, denoted $p(x_c)$, is the probability that x bits are retained given a correct response; the second, denoted $p(x_e)$, is the probability of retaining x bits given an incorrect recall. Letting C denote the over-all proportion of correct recalls, the expressions for these conditional distributions are

$$p(x_c) = C^{-1} P(R = x)g^{N-x},$$
$$p(x_e) = (1 - C)^{-1} P(R = x)(1 - g^{N-x}).$$

The first expression weights $P(R = x)$ by the likelihood of a correct recall given x and the second weights it by the likelihood of an error given x. These conditional distributions are skewed away from the binomial from which they derive, but they are unimodal.

If confidence boundaries are aligned in increasing order with the amount retained x, the operating characteristic can be plotted from these two conditional distributions by methods illustrated previously (cf. Figs. 12 and 16a). The foregoing expressions for the conditional distributions imply the following expression for the Type-2 operating characteristic.

$$CP(x_c \geq j) + (1 - C) \, P(x_e \geq j) = P(R \geq j).$$

The Type-2 curves obtained in theory are asymmetric and are similar in form to those reported by Murdock (1966). However, contrary to Murdock's finding, the theoretical Type-2 curve changes with variations in the retention parameter r. To show this, we may calculate the d' measure of the two distributions, defined here as the mean difference scaled with respect to $\sigma(x_c)$. The relevant quantities are found to be

$$E(x_c) = Nrb, \qquad \text{Var}(x_c) = Nr(1 - r)gb^2,$$

$$E(x_e) = Nr(1 - C)^{-1} (1 - Cb),$$

and

$$d' = \frac{E(x_c) - E(x_e)}{\sigma(x_c)} = K(1 - C)^{-1}\sqrt{r(1 - r)},$$

where $b = (r + g - gr)^{-1}$, $C = b^{-N}$, and $K = (1 - g)(N/g)^{1/2}$. The value of d' increases with r under most circumstances (that is, N and g values); however, the increase in d' appears generally to be of small magnitude relative to the associated increases in C, the probability of correct recall. It is not implausible to suppose that the small increase expected in d' may not appear in empirical estimates provided by a single experiment, as it did not in Murdock's study. It is admittedly a weak defense of a theory to explain away results by appeal to sampling variability, but no better alternative comes to mind in this case. Rather than discard the entire theory on the basis of this one result, it would appear wiser to await replications and clearer elaboration of the conceptual significance of Type-2 operating characteristics.

C. The Recall Threshold

We now examine some implications of supposing that a recall threshold exists. The basic idea is that S will not attempt recall unless the amount retained in the memory trace equals or exceeds some threshold number of remembered components. Such a threshold, or criterion, would be operative in recall from very large or poorly defined response ensembles, but it will be shown how a threshold can be introduced, if desired, into recall performance from smaller ensembles. Let T denote the recall threshold; it is to be conceived of as an adjustable criterion that S sets depending on motivational and payoff conditions for recall.

1. *The Effect on Recall Probabilities*

Since the number of bits retained R is binomial, the probability that a recall will be attempted is $P(R \geq T)$, which is the area at and above the threshold T in the tail of the binomial distribution. The unconditional probability of a correct recall is

$$C(T) = \sum_{x=T}^{N} \binom{N}{x} r^x [g(1 - r)]^{N-x},$$

and this decreases as T increases since fewer recalls will be attempted. The conditional probability of a correct response, given that recall is attempted, is $C(T)[P(R \geq T)]^{-1}$, and this increases directly with T. Several examples of the effect of the threshold upon $C(T)$ and $P(C \mid \text{recall})$ are shown in Fig. 20. The latter relation is similar to that between probability of correct recall and confidence; that is, T measures the "internal confidence" S requires of his memory before he will overtly respond.

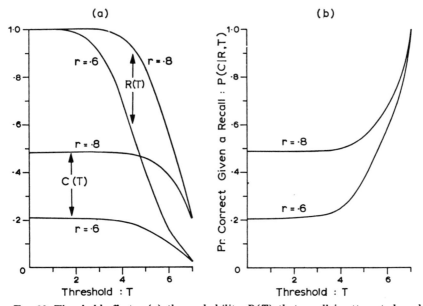

Fig. 20. Threshold effects: (a) the probability $R(T)$ that recall is attempted, and the probability $C(T)$ of a correct recall, plotted as a function of the recall threshold T; (b) the conditional probability of a correct response given that recall is attempted when the threshold is T. The parameter in each set of curves is r, the average retention probability of each component.

2. *The Optimal Criterion*

The optimal setting of the recall criterion will clearly depend on the payoffs for not responding and for responding right or wrong, and on the probability of guessing correctly given particular amounts of retention. Let W denote the utility of the payoff for a correct recall, L the utility of the payoff for an overt error, and u the utility occasioned by not responding at all. Since only the differences in these utilities are important, suppose that they have been so scaled that they all are positive numbers. If S retains x of N components and recalls by guessing on the forgotten components, the probability of a correct recall is g^{N-x}. The expected utility of the payoffs encountered for recalling when x of N bits are retained is

$$EU(\text{recall} \mid R = x) = Wg^{N-x} + L(1 - g^{N-x}),$$

$$= (W - L)g^{N-x} + L.$$

Contrariwise, if S fails to recall at all, his utility is u for certain. If S were to maximize his expected utility, he would attempt recall whenever x is such that $EU(\text{recall} \mid R = x)$ is larger than u, and otherwise would not recall. Thus the threshold should be set at that value T which satisfies the relation

$$(W - L)g^{N-T} + L = u. \tag{34}$$

Solving for T yields the value

$$T = N - \frac{\log (u - L/W - L)}{\log g}. \tag{35}$$

A value of $R \geq T$ should lead to recall; any other should not. Adoption of this recall criterion maximizes the expected utility.

If the utilities of the payoffs are strictly ordered as $W > u > L$, then $T < N$ and some recall will occur. If there is no gain in recalling (that is, $u \geq W$), then $T > N$ and no recall should occur. If u is less than L (a greater penalty for not responding than for overt errors), then Eq. 34 has no solution, but obviously in this case the optimum is at $T = 0$ and S should always attempt recall.

To briefly illustrate the relation between T and the payoffs, consider an example where $N = 4$, $g = .50$, $L = -1$ and $u = 0$; the relation between T and the payoff W for correct recalls is desired. Using Eq. 34 directly,

$$(W + 1)(.5)^{4-T} - 1 = 0,$$

or

$$W = 2^{4-T} - 1.$$

Thus, to force the threshold to be 4 (never recall) requires zero or negative payoff, $W \leq 0$; for $T = 3$ requires $W = 1$; for $T = 2$ requires $W = 3$; for $T = 1$ requires $W = 7$; and for $T = 0$ (always recall) requires $W \geq 15$. Thus, by appropriate choice of the win payoff the optimal setting of the criterion can be varied. Whether Ss in fact set their recall criterion in this optimal fashion is a question for empirical investigation; but Ss probably will approximate it to some extent.

3. Recognition of Unrecalled Items

The existence of a recall threshold implies that S frequently has information in storage that does not appear in recall. Indeed we may suppose that it is just this unused information that is tapped when S chooses the correct item on a recognition test although he was unable previously to recall it. Landauer (1962) and others have reported such results. Of course, the recognition probability for such unrecalled items will be considerably less than for recalled items, but it nonetheless can be considerably better than chance. How much better than chance it is will depend on how high was the recall threshold (which the memory trace failed to pass) and the similarity of the distractors to the correct item on the recognition test.

A particular case will illustrate the influence of the recall threshold upon subsequent recognition of unrecalled items. The probability distribution of R for unrecalled items, when the threshold is T, is given by

$$P(R = x \mid x < T) = \frac{\binom{N}{x} r^x (1 - r)^{N-x}}{\sum_{x=0}^{T-1} \binom{N}{x} r^x (1 - r)^{N-x}}, \qquad \text{for } 0 \leq x \leq T - 1.$$

Suppose the recognition test is an unbiased forced choice between two alternatives, with the distractors generated with dissimilarity d. Then the probability of a correct choice on the recognition test for unrecalled items is

$$P(T) = \sum_{x=0}^{T-1} P(R = x \mid x < T)[1 - .5(1 - d)^x],$$

$$= 1 - .5 \frac{\sum_{x=0}^{T-1} \binom{N}{x} [r(1 - d)]^x (1 - r)^{N-x}}{\sum_{x=0}^{T-1} \binom{N}{x} r^x (1 - r)^{N-x}}. \tag{36}$$

Some curves of this function are drawn in Fig. 21 for different values of the recall threshold T and different retention parameters. The other parameters are $N = 6$ and $d = .5$. The point to be established about Fig. 21 is that the recognition probability increases sharply with the threshold value that prevented recall, reaching higher asymptotes as r increases. High recall thresholds bury more information beneath them than do low thresholds, and this difference appears in recognition tests.

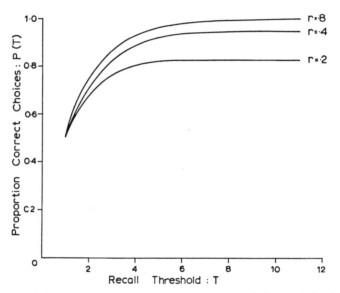

Fɪɢ. 21. Probability of correct recognition on a two-choice test for items not recalled when the recall threshold was T. The retention parameter r varies among the curves.

A further point of interest may be mentioned here. Suppose that S has some subjective measure or "awareness" of the size of R even when it is below his threshold for recall. If this subjective measure is proportional to R, then it constitutes available information helping S to predict whether he could recognize the item he is presently unable to recall. A recent experiment by Hart (1965) is relevant to this suggestion. He had his Ss estimate their "feeling of knowing" on items they could not recall. Later multiple-choice recognition tests on the unrecalled items showed that Ss chose correctly more frequently for items they felt they knew (but could not recall) than for items they felt they did not know. In terms of the theory, Ss demonstrated some ability to discriminate among R values falling below the recall threshold. In later experiments, Hart tried various means to induce Ss to try harder, or to make more guesses on the recall test; in our terms, T was lowered. This tended to cause a shrinkage in the differential recognition probability of unrecalled items that S felt he knew versus those he felt he did not know. This shrinkage is expected by the theory (cf. Eq. 36 and Fig. 21).

D. Proactive Biases in Recall

In the previous discussion, it was assumed that in recall the motor-output unit treated null-state components as instances requiring a guess by randomly selecting one of the v values to fill in at that component. But suppose, on the contrary, that the assignment of values to unknown (forgotten) components is biased by the past history of the memory machine. In principle, there are two ways this nonrandomness could be introduced. One way is based upon an accumulation of experience (memories) in which components within the vector become highly inter-correlated (see the later discussion of redundancy). For instance, if the values of components i and j are x_{in} and x_{jn}, then the value of component k over the past history has usually been x_{kn}. It is easy to imagine that such intercorrelations would be used in recalling from a trace in which component k has been forgotten whereas components i and j have been retained. The other method of introducing bias would have the value of a null-state component assigned according to its relative frequency of occurrence in past usage, independent of possible correlations of the value of this component to the values of other components in the encoding system. This notion is similar to the "spew" hypothesis of Underwood and Schulz (1960), where the output of a structure is seen as more or less matching the statistical distribution of inputs to it.

By either method, the bias in component-value assignments will tend to produce leveling or "commonizing" in the recall of the system. The recall of the system would tend to move in the direction of popular stereotypes, away from any uniqueness of the memory trace of the original event. This aspect of the system reminds us of the research on memory distortions carried out by Bartlett (1932) on stories, by Allport and Postman (1948) on rumors, and by Wulf (1922) and many successors on recall of outlined drawings. Riley (1962) gives a fine review of the later work.

Wulf's hypothesis was that the memory of simple outlined figures would tend over time to be autonomously reorganized in the direction of making a "good Gestalt" figure. Thus, local irregularities, small gaps, and slight asymmetries in the original figure would tend to be regularized in recall. Riley's review summarizes the evidence critical to this hypothesis, which is not generally favorable. Of the distortions that do occur in recall, Riley indicates two potent factors determining their direction: first, the way in which S encodes, describes, or labels the stimulus figure upon his initial viewing of it; and second, the proactive influence of similar common figures (popular stereotypes) upon recall of a unique figure, resulting in a commonizing in recall of the unique figure. These same factors are regarded in the present system as important in determining the type of distortions obtained in recall.

If the trace is successively recalled, with long time intervals between successive recalls, what is retained each time is some increasing fraction of the components recalled on the previous occasion. If the forgotten components are filled in by using the bias in a way consistent with the remembered components, the recalled pattern will change progressively over the recall series. Thus, some aspects of the figure may be leveled while other aspects may be "sharpened." The latter case could arise if some unique component is retained and several related forgotten components are assigned values consistent (correlated in the past) with the unique component retained.

These are only qualitative implications of the memory system, and to make them more exact would require more elaboration of the system and its input than can be pursued at present. The important point of this discussion, however, is to show that the system has the potential flexibility to deal with meaningful as well as random distortions in remembering.

E. Response Latencies in Recall

The system delivers reasonable predictions about recall latencies if some elementary hypotheses about processing times in the motor-output unit are adopted. The memory vector retrieved and fed into the motor-output unit consists of, say, x retained components and $N - x$ forgotten components with null values. Suppose that in constructing (or locating) a response to recall, the motor-output unit has to process each of these N components, and each processing takes a variable (small) amount of time. Suppose that the time taken to process a null-state component has probability density function $f_n(t)$ and that the time to process a retained (nonnull) component has density function $f_r(t)$. So much of the structure is relatively innocuous. The crucial assumption, having several important implications, is that the mean processing time is shorter for a retained component than for a null-state component, since in the latter case the motor-output unit has to make an additional (random) decision about what value to assign to the forgotten component. Two immediately obvious predictions from this scheme are that as learning proceeds and more bits are retained, the average response latencies become shorter, and that at any given stage of learning the average latency of correct recalls will be shorter than the average latency of erroneous recalls.

There are several options to filling in details of this system. One option concerns the choice of the elementary processing-time distributions. In the following we make the customary assumption (e.g., McGill, 1963) that $f_n(t)$ and $f_r(t)$ are exponential density functions with rate parameters u_n and u_r, respectively. A second option concerns whether the motor-output unit is viewed as operating by serial or parallel processing of the N-component vector. A serial device would examine the components one at a time in serial order, and the time to respond would be the sum of the separate processing times of the N components. A parallel device would examine all N components simultaneously and the response would finally be initiated only after all N components had completed processing; for such a device the time to respond is determined by the slowest of the N processes. A few features of each system will be derived using exponential density functions for the underlying distributions of f_n and f_r. These latency systems are similar to those investigated by Christie and Luce (1956). The difference is that they assumed that the unit processing time was the same for all units, whereas we must deal with a binomial mixture of two unit-processing distributions.

1. Serial Processing

The time to respond with a serial device is the sum of the N separate processing times. Assuming that x components are retained and $N - x$ forgotten, then the total time is the sum of x samples from $f_r(t)$ and $N - x$ samples from $f_n(t)$. Let $M_r(\theta)$ and $M_n(\theta)$ denote the moment-generating functions (mgf) for $f_r(t)$ and $f_n(t)$, respectively. Because independent random variables are being summed, the moment-generating function for the total time in this case is

$$M(\theta \mid R = x) = (M_r(\theta))^x (M_n(\theta))^{N-x}. \tag{37}$$

To obtain the unconditional moment-generating function for the total time, Eq. 37 is multiplied by the binomial probability that $R = x$ and then summed over x, yielding

$$M(\theta) = \sum_{x=0}^{N} M(\theta \mid R = x) \, P(R = x),$$

$$= [rM_r(\theta) + (1 - r)M_n(\theta)]^N. \tag{38}$$

Equation 38 expresses the mgf of the total time in terms of the mgfs of the elementary distributions and the memory parameters r and N.

An exponential density with rate u has mgf of $(1 - (\theta/u))^{-1}$. Substituting these into Eq. 38 yields

$$M(\theta) = \left[r\left(1 - \frac{\theta}{u_r}\right)^{-1} + (1 - r)\left(1 - \frac{\theta}{u_n}\right)^{-1} \right]^N. \qquad (39)$$

By evaluating the first two derivatives of $M(\theta)$ at $\theta = 0$, the first two moments are found to be

$$E(t) = N[ru_r^{-1} + (1 - r)u_n^{-1}],$$

$$\text{Var}(t) = N[ru_r^{-2} + (1 - r)u_n^{-2}] + Nr(1 - r)(u_r^{-1} - u_n^{-1})^2. \qquad (40)$$

The probability density function corresponding to the mgf in Eq. 39 is not presently known since inversion proves difficult. However, the mean in Eq. 40 gives the conjectured information. Since u_r^{-1} is smaller than u_n^{-1} by assumption, $E(t)$ decreases as the retention probability r increases. Also, since correct responses are more likely to occur when R is high, and high R scores produce faster response times, the conditional mean latency will be less for correct recalls than for errors.

2. Parallel Processing

The cumulative density function (cdf) is easily derived in this case, but little else can be obtained without substantial effort. Suppose there are x samples from $f_r(t)$ and $N - x$ samples from $f_n(t)$, and we seek the cdf of the maximal (largest) element of the two samples considered together. Let $F_r(t)$ and $F_n(t)$ denote the cdfs of the elementary densities $f_r(t)$ and $f_n(t)$. Since all N processes are carried out independently, when x is given the cdf of the time to the last of all N events is

$$F(t \mid R = x) = (F_r(t))^x (F_n(t))^{N-x}.$$

The unconditional cdf is obtained by multiplying the foregoing by $P(R = x)$ and summing, yielding

$$F(t) = \sum_{x=0}^{N} F(t \mid R = x) \, P(R = x),$$

$$= [rF_r(t) + (1 - r)F_n(t)]^N. \qquad (41)$$

If an elementary distribution is exponential with rate u, then its cdf is $1 - e^{-ut}$. Such may be substituted into Eq. 41 using the rates u_r and u_n. Differentiating Eq. 41 then gives the probability density function for the total times.

Calculation of even the expected value of t for the cdf in Eq. 41 has proved difficult. It is known to be bounded in the interval

$$u_r^{-1} \sum_{i=1}^{N} \frac{1}{i} \leq E(t) \leq u_n^{-1} \sum_{i=1}^{N} \frac{1}{i}.$$

The upper bound is obtained when all N samples come from the slow f_n density function and the lower bound when all come from the fast f_r density. Each is the mean for a "pure death" process (see McGill, 1963), giving the time until the slowest component has completed its processing. Intuitively, $E(t)$ will be something like r times the lower bound plus $1 - r$ times the upper bound. If so, then the same qualitative implications hold for this system as for the serial processor; that is, response latency decreases as retention increases, and correct responses occur faster on average than do errors in recall.

The times just derived describe only the processing time in the motor-output unit. To these times must be added constants representing stimulus-encoding time, trace-retrieval time, plus apparatus constants. These have not been explicitly mentioned before since they are the same whether the response recalled is correct or incorrect. Differences in retention affect only the processing time of the motor-output system, which is the system under study in the foregoing discussion.

The purpose of this discussion has been to show how the general system makes contact with data concerning recall latencies. The particular assumptions used here (for example, that densities for unit processes are exponential) are to be considered as illustrative. The qualitative implications of the system agree with the findings of several investigations of latency in short-term recall (e.g., Atkinson, Hansen & Bernbach, 1964b; Izawa & Estes, 1965).

3. Reaction Time and Memory

For this system, the time to react to a stimulus will consist of the following components: the time for the stimulus-analyzers to encode the input stimulus, the time to retrieve the response trace to this stimulus from memory and send it to the motor-output unit, the time for the motor-output unit to decode the response vector, all plus a constant that depends on physical characteristics of the effectors used and the apparatus. To illustrate a few properties of this system, the serial processing device discussed earlier will be used. For such devices, the processing time is proportional to N, the number of components that are to be processed.

Adding the times for the components just listed, the equation for reaction time T is

$$T = (ET) + (RT) + (DT) + C,$$

where ET, RT, and DT are encoding, retrieval, and decoding times, respectively. If all three processes are carried out by serial devices, each process takes an average time proportional to N. Hence, the average reaction time may be expressed as

$$T = AN + C, \tag{42}$$

where A is the sum of constants representing rates of encoding, retrieval, and decoding.

The relevance of this reaction-time equation to memory is that correct recall probability, when retrieval and decoding are delayed until some time after input, is also a function of N, namely,

$$P(C) = (u)^N.$$

If N is expressed in terms of the mean reaction time in Eq. 42 the relation between percentage correct recall and T is

$$P(C) = (u)^{T-C/A} = a\phi^T, \tag{43}$$

where $0 < \phi \leq 1$. Hence, the longer the average time required to identify (name or react to) an incoming stimulus, the poorer should be recall of such units in a memory experiment.

Experiments supporting this conjecture have been reported by Mackworth (1963; 1964). She used different types of input materials, including letters, digits, colors, and geometric shapes, and measured average "reading time" (time for S to rapidly name the members of a series) as well as immediate memory span for each set of materials. It seems reasonable to suppose that the average time to read off k symbols of a given set is proportional to the average reaction time to the individual symbols. Hence, the time taken to read a fixed number of symbols is proportional to T in Eq. 43. Consistent with Eq. 43, Mackworth found that the probability of correct recall of elements of a string of k symbols decreased with their average reading time. Mackworth measured memory span, and the complexities of that measure preclude an exact relation to the $P(C)$ in Eq. 43, which is the retention probability for an individual symbol with a particular lag between its input and recall. However, expected span would clearly be a monotone increasing function of $P(C)$. Hence, Mackworth's data, showing longer memory spans for materials that could be read faster, provides qualitative confirmation of Eq. 43.

In passing, it may be mentioned that the reaction time Eq. 42 is consistent with results reported by Hick (1952), Hyman (1953), and several others investigating multiple-choice reaction time. The finding is that mean T increases with the number of equiprobable response alternatives K approximately as log K. To apply the theory to this situation, assume that N is chosen by S so as to provide a reasonably efficient coding of the K alternative stimuli and responses. That is, K is to be expressed as

$$K = Bv^{N_k}$$

where B is a proportionality constant representing the efficiency of the coding system, $v = g^{-1}$, and N_k is selected by S. For any coding system employing N_k components, the mean reaction time T_k in Eq. 42 is a linear function of N_k. Hence K may be written as

$$K = Bv^{(T_k-C)/A}$$

By taking logarithms of both sides, we find that

$$T_k = b + b' \log K,$$

where b and b' are nonnegative constants. Thus, mean reaction time with K alternatives increases linearly with the logarithm of K. This is approximately the result reported by Hick and Hyman.

The relation just derived follows only if it is likely that the conditions force S to modify his "natural" coding system to deal more efficiently with the set of stimuli and responses actually used in the experiment. Natural coding system here refers to that used and over-learned throughout S's past history in dealing with the entire ensemble of events of which the experimental presentation-set may compose only a small fraction.

VI. Repetition and Redundancy in Trace Formation

A. ALTERNATIVE REPRESENTATIONS OF TRACE REDUNDANCY

Various information theorists have pointed out that sensory events contain much more information than is required to specify the initiating stimulus uniquely from a known ensemble. In fact, the sensory transmission system is often described (e.g., Attneave, 1954; Barlow, 1959) as a filter that makes use of redundancies to discard part of the sensory inflow of information. And Brown (1959) has suggested that a memory trace of an event will, at least initially, contain some of this redundant or excess information. To the extent that redundant information is stored in a memory trace, accurate recall of that trace will be facilitated.

Within the proposed system there are basically two ways to represent information redundancy in an individual memory trace. Possibly both operate together, but they will be presented as independent methods.

One representation of redundancy supposes that more information components are encoded and stored in the memory trace than are minimally required to select the initiating event from its appropriate ensemble. This will be called the *excess components* idea. The other idea is to represent redundancy in terms of intercorrelations among the component values of a trace; thus, if components i and j are highly intercorrelated, then retention of either one will suffice for recall of both. This will be called the *intercorrelation* idea.

1. *Excess Components*

Here it is supposed that S initially encodes an event and stores it in memory in terms of $N + K$ information components, although in fact only N components are required to reconstruct or select the item from the test ensemble. The number of excess components K is then a measure of the initial redundancy of this individual trace. For simplicity in the following, it is assumed that the $N + K$ components are "interchangeable" in the sense of providing equal information toward selection of the correct response.

If the components are forgotten at the same independent rate, the number of components retained is distributed as

$$P(R = x) = \binom{N + K}{x} r^x (1 - r)^{N+K-x}. \tag{44}$$

One crucial influence of the excess components is that they modify the response rule. Using the null-state interpretation of forgetting, suppose that if N or more components are retained, then the null states are ignored in constructing a response. This means that recall will be perfect until more than K components have been forgotten. Formally, the response function when x components are retained is

$$P(C \mid R = x) = \begin{cases} 1 & \text{if } N \leq x \leq N + K, \\ g^{N-x} & \text{if } 0 \leq x \leq N. \end{cases}$$

Using this response function in conjunction with the retention distribution in Eq. 44, we find that the expression for the unconditional probability of a correct recall is

$$P(C) = \sum_{x=0}^{N+K} P(C \mid R = x) P(R = x),$$

$$= \sum_{x=0}^{N} \binom{N + K}{x} r^x (1 - r)^{N+K-x} g^{N-x}$$

$$+ \sum_{x=N+1}^{N+K} \binom{N + K}{x} r^x (1 - r)^{N+K-x}. \tag{45}$$

This expression cannot be appreciably simplified. The second sum is the probability above N in the upper tail of the binomial. The first sum can be rearranged so that it is a constant times one minus the tail of a different binomial distribution.

Some graphs of Eq. 45 are shown in Fig. 22a and 22b. The theoretical

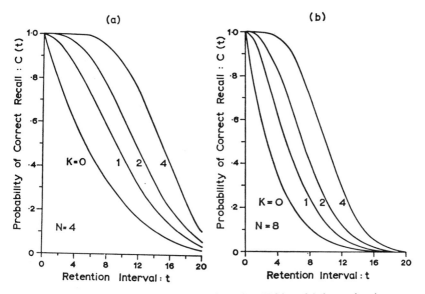

(a)   **(b)**

FIG. 22. The effect on recall probability of storing K bits of information in excess of the N required to specify the response. The $r(t)$ function is a linear descent to zero at $t = 20$. The curves differ in N and K.

values for the curves are $r(t) = 1 - .04t$, $g = .25$, $N = 4$ or 8, and the parameter varying between curves is K, the redundancy or number of excess bits. The average recall probability increases with K. Of more interest is the fact that as K increases, the recall function approaches an S-shaped curve. The initial plateau of the S curve becomes longer as K increases, since K is the number of excess components that can be forgotten before recall begins to fail. The S curves in Fig. 22a and 22b are of interest because such curves have been obtained in several investigations of short-term memory (e.g., Hellyer, 1962; Peterson, 1963).

No detailed discussion of the implications of this redundancy scheme for performance on recognition tests will be given. It is clear that an increase in K will improve recognition generally. This is obvious from Eq. 29, which shows that the scaled mean difference between the match scores of old and new items increases directly with the square root of N, the number of components in the memory trace.

2. *Intercorrelated Components*

An alternative representation of redundancy supposes that some of the components in the memory trace are highly intercorrelated. Two components are said to be correlated (or redundant) if knowledge of the value of one component enables one to predict the value of the other. The advantage of this correlation for memory performance is that both components can be produced if either one is retained. Whereas two independent components have probability r^2 of being both retained, two perfectly correlated components have probability $1 - (1 - r)^2 = 2r - r^2$ of being both retained. Thus, the presence of intercorrelations among the components will increase the amount recalled, and to an extent depending on the number and pattern of intercorrelations.

Although this general approach appears attractive, we confess an inability to develop it to any great extent. There are several decisions to be made in any formal representation. These include the questions of whether nonunity correlations are to be permitted; whether all correlations are symmetric (go in both directions); whether multiple or only pairwise correlations of elements are admitted; and so forth. Even the simplest assumptions—pairwise, symmetric correlations of unity—encounter the basic problem of how to represent conveniently the over-all pattern of intercorrelations existing in a trace. Recall performance will depend on this precise pattern, and a simple index, such as the number or proportion of component pairs correlated, has no unique relationship to recall. The analytic problem is of a kind encountered in graph theory (Harary, Norman, & Cartwright, 1965), where k intercorrelation lines are distributed at random among N points. The connectivity or clustering of the points determines recall when some (random) components are forgotten. Particular cases (patterns) can be enumerated and consequences worked out, but this is neither an elegant nor illuminating attack upon the general problem. The most general statement possible is that such intercorrelations will increase the average retention probability r in some complicated way depending on the amount of redundancy present.

Adding to this analytic difficulty, a possible conceptual difficulty of this approach may be mentioned. An intercorrelation between two components would seem itself to require a memory trace. That is, the correlation represents knowledge derived (remembered) from past experience with a particular population of stimuli, and it seems that such correlative knowledge should be explained rather than taken as a primitive postulate in a theory of the memory trace. Possibly this objection can be sidestepped by supposing that the correlative knowledge does not "reside" in the individual memory trace, but rather is added to it (at forgotten components) when it passes through the motor-output unit. This unit could bias the assignment of values to forgotten components of a trace by reference to the statistical distribution of that component value in other traces it holds in its memory store.

B. The Effects of Repetition

It is well known that repeated study trials on an item increase its retention. To mention just one illustration, in an experiment by Hellyer (1962), S saw either 1, 2, 4, or 8 successive presentations of a verbal item before he began an interpolated activity filling a retention interval of from 3 to 27 sec. Hellyer found that repetitions slowed the rate of decay of recall probability and increased the apparent asymptote of the recall curves. A similar effect can be produced by increasing the duration of a single study interval on an item before interpolated activity begins.

Such effects may be interpreted in the system by supposing that repetitions increase the effective retention parameter. Two general hypotheses may be suggested to account for this increase. One is that repetitions increase the internal redundancy of the memory trace, the notion just discussed. Such increases in internal redundancy would elevate the average retention. However, as was noted before, no specific consequences have been derived from this type of hypothesis.

An alternative and more tractable hypothesis supposes that repetitions or increases in study time result in *multiplexing* of the trace, by which we mean that the whole trace or components of it are copied several times in the memory banks. Suppose that the initial study time or the number of uninterrupted presentations (as in Hellyer's experiment) is such as to allow z copies of a given component to be recorded. If all components are so copied, then the trace system would be best represented as a z by N matrix with identical rows. Assume that the several copies of a component fade out randomly and independently with retention probability r, and that a component's value will be assigned correctly if any one copy of it is retained; then, the more copies made, the greater the probability that at least one is retained, leading to the assignment of the correct value to that component. Let p_z denote the probability that a component represented by z copies is retained; it is

$$p_z = 1 - (1 - r)^z. \tag{46}$$

There are several schemes for generating the z's. A simple and general scheme that contains several special cases of interest is the following binomial process: during the study time available after input of an

N-bit vector, the system makes k attempts to copy each component, each attempt producing a successful copy with probability c. Thus, the total copies available at the end of this period is one (the original input vector) plus $z - 1$ excess copies, where $z - 1$ is binomially distributed with parameters k and c.

The N components will probably be copied differing numbers of times, and for each z value Eq. 46 gives the retention probability of that component. By a derivation too lengthy to include here it may be proved that the distribution of the number of retained components is given by

$$P(R = x)$$
$$= \binom{N}{x}\left[\sum_{z-1=0}^{k} P(E = z - 1)p_z\right]^x\left[\sum_{z-1=0}^{k}(E = z - 1)(1 - p_z)\right]^{N-x} \quad (47)$$

In this expression, $P(E = z - 1)$ is the binomial probability that $z - 1$ excess copies are made, where $z - 1$ ranges in value from 0 to k. The terms inside the two brackets sum to one. Since each forgotten component is guessed correctly with probability g, the recall probability will be

$$P(C) = \sum_{x=0}^{N} g^{N-x} P(R = x),$$

$$= \{\Sigma P(E = z - 1)[g + (1 - g)p_z]\}^N. \quad (48)$$

Substituting into Eq. 48 the expression for p_z and the binomial probabilities and simplifying, we obtain the desired final result, namely,

$$P(C) = [1 - (1 - r)(1 - g)(1 - cr)^k]^N. \quad (49)$$

The parameters k and c represent the rate and efficiency, respectively, of the multiplexing system. If either $k = 0$ or $c = 0$, then no excess copies are made and Eq. 49 reduces to the former expression for recall of a single input copy.

For $c = 1$, each component is copied exactly k times and the forgetting probability is $(1 - r)^{k+1}$. Some hypothetical curves of Eq. 49 with $c = 1$ are shown in Fig. 23a and 23b. In Fig. 23a, the retention parameter $r(t)$ is assumed to decline linearly to zero according to $1 - .04t$. The other parameters are $N = 6$, $g = .25$, and the amount of multiplexing k increases from 0 to 4 across the various curves. The quantity k would be expected to increase with study time or with the number of uninterrupted presentations. The recall functions in Fig. 23a increase with k and become positively accelerated with longer initial plateaus the larger k is. The functions in Fig. 23a asymptote near zero because the $r(t)$

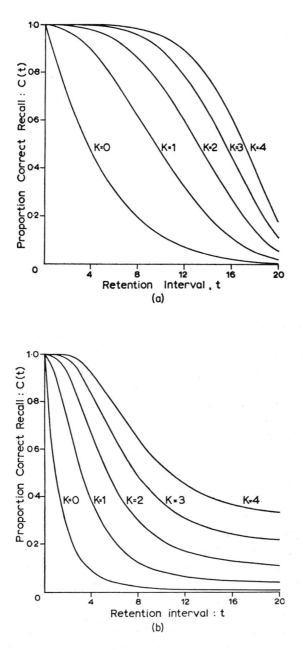

Fɪɢ. 23. The effect on recall probability of multiplexing the trace K times. In (a) the retention function is $1 - .04t$, asymptoting at zero when $t = 25$; in (b) the retention function is $.25 + .75(.8)^t$.

519

function is assumed to go to zero. Figure 23b shows curves for an $r(t)$ function that has a nonzero asymptote; that is, $r(t) = .25 + .75(.80)^t$. In this case, the asymptote of $C(t)$ increases in approximately exponential fashion with k, the amount of multiplexing. These curves are similar to those reported by Hellyer.

If this scheme were applied to spaced repetitions of an item with interpolated activity between successive presentations, then k would be assumed to be proportional to the number of presentations and c would be interpreted as the probability that a given copy is retained between successive presentations. In fact, c would either equal r or be some simple function of r. By making k (the number of trials) large enough, the probability of correct recall in Eq. 49 can be brought arbitrarily close to unity. Such a system also provides an interpretation of the beneficial effect on retention of overtraining provided after response probability has reached unity. If the intertrial interval is relatively short, then r will be high, and a few copies will suffice to keep short-term recall probability near unity. However, the benefit of extra copies induced by overtraining would appear upon testing at a long retention interval, when r has a lower value.

This multiplexing scheme has been developed because it is a simple way for a memory device to improve its component memory (p_z) without changing the reliability of its single memory units (the copies). That is, by multiplexing and pooling many unreliable memory units, the entire system can become very reliable. The simplest alternative to this scheme is to suppose that the parameters of the single unit change in a direct manner with repetition. For example, in Eq. 6 for $r(t)$, it would be supposed that the asymptote J increases directly with repetition. But auxiliary assumptions would be required to describe such changes.

VII. Perceptual Recognition of Degraded Stimuli

A. Similarity of Memory to Recognition of Noisy Stimuli

In the following, some possible contacts between this model of memory and results concerning immediate perceptual recognition of stimuli embedded in noise backgrounds are suggested. In the foregoing discussion of memory it was assumed that the input event was faithfully encoded and then was degraded by forgetting. Metaphorically, forgetting introduces "noise" into delayed recognition of the original faithful recording of the input event. A model of perceptual recognition in noise may perhaps be found by analogous reasoning: a particular signal or message is sent over a noisy channel to the N stimulus-analyzers to be encoded, but while in the channel the signal is degraded to various degrees so that what is finally encoded by S bears only a probabilistic resemblance to what was sent.

Several alternative models can be developed along these lines; a promising one, based on a random-replacement interpretation of degradation, will be illustrated. It will be supposed that when sent over a perfectly noiseless channel the signals are encoded into N (say, binary) components. The set of analyzers that actually perform these conversions can, of course, be quite complicated. For example, in speech recognition the input signal is actually a time-varying frequency-amplitude spectrum of very complex nature, and it is a difficult (and as yet, only partially solved) scientific problem to design a system of analyzers that can extract from a population of such signals the relevant phonetic parameters and exclude various irrelevant aspects (such as the speed and intonation of speech). However, available models of speech recognition (e.g., Forgie & Forgie, 1959; Halle & Stevens, 1964; Stevens, 1960) do propose a set of analyzers whose function is to perform by one or another means this conversion of a continuous time-varying spectrum into a discrete listing of the phonetic parameters of the input. Our concern here is not with the nature of the analyzers themselves, but rather with their joint output, considered as a list or vector of N binary components.

When a signal is sent over a noisy channel and then encoded, it will be assumed that some components are faithfully (correctly) recorded, whereas other components are distorted and incorrectly recorded. Let h denote the probability that the component value sent is encoded correctly, and $1 - h$ the probability that the encoded value differs from the one sent. If the encoded representation were to be matched component by component to the item sent (or rather, to what would be the encoding if $h = 1$ and there were no distortions due to noise), the number of matches would be binomially distributed with parameters N and h. In this system, h is a measure of the fidelity of the channel, decreasing as the signal-to-noise ratio is decreased. The h parameter plays the same role as r, the retention parameter of the memory system. The reasonable bounds on h are $.5 \leq h \leq 1$, the lower bound being obtained only when the signal : noise ratio is so low that no information whatever is conveyed by the signal.

Three aspects of this system will be considered. The first concerns the effect on recognition accuracy of the number of alternative signals, wherein selection of a response is from the entire ensemble of possible inputs. The second concerns the effect of experimentally restricting the set of response alternatives after the signal has been received; this restriction has a large effect on the percentage of correct choices (recognition accuracy) almost independently of the size of the ensemble of signals that could have been sent. Finally, the information transmitted by the response will be related to the information contained in the stimulus ensemble. The following discussion will be clarified if a particular experimental situation is taken as a referent. These purposes are served by an experiment on auditory recognition by Pollack (1959): an S with earphones monitors a channel into which white (Gaussian) noise is continuously introduced and at discrete intervals, or trials, a warning signal comes on and is shortly followed by a spondee (a two-syllable word like "backbone," "doorstep," or "hothouse") spoken into the channel by E. The S then selects what he thought he heard from a list of alternatives provided to him.

B. RECOGNITION ACCURACY AND THE SIZE OF THE S-R ENSEMBLE

Consider first the accuracy of immediate recognition responses when selection occurs from all possible alternatives. Suppose there are 2^N possible input signals and that E has provided S with a unique identification function relating the correct response to the signal sent, that is, there are 2^N response alternatives. The identification function is in fact a list of paired associates in memory, relating the encoded stimulus to its correct response. The stimulus is encoded by the perceptual system as a vector of N binary components; call this the image for convenient reference. The image may be distorted somewhat from the correct representation of the signal sent. The likelihood that the image is completely accurate is h^N. If it is inaccurate in one or more details and the response alternative corresponding to this inaccurate image is available on the choice test, then it will be chosen and the response identifying the signal sent will not be chosen. Hence the probability of a correct response from an ensemble of 2^N alternatives is just

$$C_N = h^N. \tag{50}$$

Thus, accuracy of recognition declines with the number of alternatives, and declines at a rate depending on the signal-to-noise ratio. This is true; the decline in accuracy with increasing numbers of alternative signals is one of the best-documented facts about perceptual recognition (e.g., Garner, 1962).

C. RESTRICTIONS ON THE RESPONSE SET

Consider first the effect of restricting the response alternatives to just two. That is, one of 2^N possible signals is sent, but on the test S is to choose only between this one and a second (distractor), chosen by E at random from the remaining $2^N - 1$ alternatives. It is supposed that the image is matched component by component to the two test alternatives. That alternative yielding the higher match score is chosen; if the match scores of the two alternatives tie, then a random choice is made.

The match score of the image to the signal sent is binomially distributed with parameters N and h. The match score of the image to the distractor depends on the particular distractor chosen as well as the number of changes occurring in the image. Depending on these variables, some distractors may be always chosen in preference to the correct alternative, others never, and still others half the time. For the Pollack (1959) experiment, the distractor used was selected at random from the remaining $2^N - 1$ alternatives, and the percentage of correct choices was averaged over the various tests.

To show the calculations from the theory for this experiment, suppose there are four alternative signals $(N = 2)$ and the binary states of each component are labeled 1 and 2. Suppose that the signal sent is (1 1). The four possible images are shown in the first column of Table II; the second column gives the probabilities that each of these images is received when (1 1) is sent. The entries in the next three columns represent the probability that the correct alternative (1 1) is chosen, given that the test distractor is as indicated at the top of the column. Tests involving these three distractors occur equally often, with probability $\frac{1}{3}$. The final column gives the average probability of a correct choice given that a particular image is received, assuming that the distractor is randomly chosen.

TABLE II

PROBABILITY OF CORRECT CHOICE RELATED TO
IMAGE RECEIVED AND TEST DISTRACTOR[a]

Image received	Probability	Test distractor			Average probability of correct choice
		1 2	2 1	2 2	
1 1	h^2	1	1	1	1
1 2	$h(1 - h)$	0	1	.5	.5
2 1	$h(1 - h)$	1	0	.5	.5
2 2	$(1 - h)^2$	0	0	0	0

[a] The correct coding of the stimulus sent is 1 1.

For this case, the over-all probability of a correct choice is seen to be

$$p_2 = h^2 + h(1 - h).5 + h(1 - h).5 = h.$$

Now h is also the probability of correct recognition when the stimulus ensemble consists of only two possibilities. Hence, we conclude that when the response set is restricted to two members, the probability of correct recognition is the same (namely, h) whether the stimulus sent is one of 2 or 4 possibilities.

It would be convenient if this result held for any N, but this unfortunately is not the case. By enumerating the possibilities in tables similar to Table II but for $N = 3$ and $N = 4$, the probability of a correct choice on the binary test is found to be

$$p_3 = \frac{6h}{7} + \frac{h^2}{7} (3 - 2h),$$

$$p_4 = \frac{2h}{3} + \frac{h^2}{3} (3 - 2h).$$

Cases for higher N's have not been enumerated because of the excessive labor involved, so no basis for inducing a general formula is provided.

The important feature to be noticed is that p_3 and p_4 give values that are practically equal to h in the range from .5 to 1.0. They are greater than h by only about 2 or 3 percentage points even at their maximal discrepancy. In practice, such small differences cannot be discriminated experimentally. Hence, to a first approximation we have

$$p_N \simeq h. \tag{51}$$

That is, the probability of a correct identification on a two-choice test is approximately independent of the size of the stimulus ensemble.

Tests of Eqs. 50 and 51 from Pollack's (1959) data are shown in Figs. 24a and 24b for two different signal : noise ratios (different h values). The graph for signal-to-noise (S/N) $= -15$ db is the average of two such conditions run by Pollack (panels 1 and 3 of his Fig. 7). The open circles are the proportion of correct identifications on two-choice tests; their relation to the size of the possible message set is well described by the horizontal line at the mean value. This is the implication of Eq. 51. The black circles depict the proportion correct when the choice is from all 2^N alternatives, and these are well described by the h^N function of Eq. 49. The h parameter was estimated from the mean value of the two-choice points (the horizontal lines in Figs. 24a and 24b); as expected, the h estimate is lower for the lower signal : noise ratio.

The case just discussed involved restriction of test responses to only two of the 2^N possible response alternatives. To a first approximation, the percentage of correct choices was found to be h, relatively independent of the size of the ensemble of possible stimuli. But suppose that 2^i alternatives are present on the test, corresponding to the message sent plus $2^i - 1$ distractors chosen at random from the remaining $2^N - 1$ possibilities. Although exact equations have not been worked

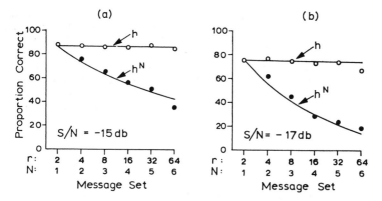

FIG. 24. Probability of correct identification related to the size of the message set r (2, 4, ..., 64) or the number of bits in the message set N(1, 2, ..., 6). In each case, the horizontal line and open dots represent the predicted and observed values, respectively, when the choice is restricted to two alternatives. The decreasing curve and black dots are the predicted and observed values when choice is from all 2^N alternatives. The signal : noise ratio (S/N) is indicated on the two figures. Graphs adapted from Fig. 7 of Pollack (1959).

out for the general case, it seems intuitively clear that the theoretical percentage correct will be of the approximate magnitude of h^i when the choice set is restricted to 2^i alternatives. This relation is exact for $N = 2$. The fit of this approximation equation to some of Pollack's (1959) data is shown in Fig. 25. The size of the message set varied from 2 to 64 and, independently, the size of the set of response alternatives was varied from 2 up to the number of possible messages. In general, accuracy decreases with the size of the response set but, holding constant the size of the response set, accuracy is relatively unaffected by the size of the message set. The mean values for each response set (drawn from the middle panel of Pollack's Fig. 2) are indicated by horizontal lines. The value predicted for 2^i response alternatives comes from the formula h^i. With the exception of the 64-response data, the function h^i provides a satisfactory fit to the mean accuracy scores. Pollack mentioned that half of the words in the 64 set were new and relatively unfamiliar to the Ss, so performance to this full set may not be completely comparable to that obtained from subsets of the other (familiar) set of 32 words. That is, in Fig. 25 the experimental points for the 64-message set are usually lower than predicted.

From Pollack's results in Figs. 24 and 25, it is clear that the largest effect is that due to the number of alternative responses and not the number of possible stimuli. In discussing these and similar data, Garner writes:

But one thing does seem very certain, and this is that some sort of matching operation goes on, and that the larger the number of categories to be matched against, the greater the possibility for error or apparently faulty perception. We can say that the perceptual confusions among the set of possible responses increase as we increase the number of such responses, and that these confusions contribute to errors of recognition. We are, in other words, not dealing with relations between stimuli which are present and those which are not—rather we are dealing with relations between responses all of which are present and must be chosen from (Garner, 1962, p. 38).

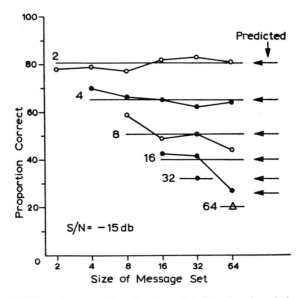

Fig. 25. Probability of correct identification related to the size of the message set. The number beside each horizontal line is the number of response alternatives on the choice test and the flat line is the average of the values for that size of response set. The arrows indicate the predictions of the mean values. Graph adapted from the middle panel of Fig. 2 of Pollack (1959).

The model presented here seems to be an appropriate formalization of Garner's ideas. That is, S is viewed as matching his image (percept) to the image appropriate to each of the available response categories, and selecting that response category whose image best matches the percept. And as the number of response alternatives increases, there is increasing likelihood that some distractor will match the percept better than does the correct alternative.

D. Information Transmitted by Immediate Recognition

To complete this discussion, the theoretical relation between input information and transmitted information will be derived, where choice is from the entire ensemble of 2^N alternatives. The derivation follows lines similar to that for the memory model with the exception that a null-state interpretation of degradation was used there, whereas the present development uses a random-replacement interpretation. As before, when any stimulus A_i is sent, the 2^N response alternatives may be partitioned into $N + 1$ subsets, S_i for $i = 0, 1, \ldots, N$, where each of the $\binom{N}{i}$ members of S_i have the identical probability $h^i(1 - h)^{N-i}$. Following through the derivations as before, we find the contingent uncertainty to be

$$
\begin{aligned}
U(R : A) &= N[1 - h \ln h - (1 - h) \ln (1 - h)], \\
&= NJ.
\end{aligned}
\tag{52}
$$

Thus transmitted information is proportional to the input information. The coefficient J depends on the fidelity parameter h in a reasonable way: when $h = 1$, $J = 1$; when h attains its lower bound of .5, $J = 0$; and for intermediate values of h between .5 and 1, J is likewise of intermediate value between 0 and 1. To check the validity of Eq. 52, a study on the intelligibility of words spoken over a noisy channel may be considered. Using intelligibility (recognition accuracy) data from an experiment by Miller, Heise, and Lichten (1951), Garner (1962, p. 80) calculated contingent uncertainty scores and plotted them against information input (the logarithm of the size of the message set). The information transmitted increased linearly up to some limit, then leveled off. The slope of the line was lower with lower signal : noise ratios (lower h values in Eq. 52). The leveling off of the functions may be interpreted as reflecting a limiting channel capacity—in our terms, a limiting value of N, N_{max}—for this particular kind of ensemble. Equation 52 implies that the asymptote of transmitted information is JN_{max}, which is lower for smaller signal : noise ratios. This was true for the data plotted by Garner.

The preceding discussion illustrates how the general multicomponent model can be developed to deal with perceptual recognition experiments. The particular model presented requires considerably more exploration and thought. For example, one of its obvious failings is that it cannot handle confidence-rating data when all 2^N alternatives are available on the test. Moreover, it supposes that each feature (component) is recorded faithfully with the same probability h, thus leading to symmetric confusion matrices, but this is a gross approximation sufficient only for certain limited purposes. However, more elaborate alternative models can doubtless be developed along the same general lines. The purpose in carrying through this analysis was to show that a multicomponent theory views memorial and perceptual distortions caused by noise as being characterized by similar principles.

This paper began with the assumption that memory and perception are closely related. The relation of memory to perception was illustrated by Conrad's (1964) experiments showing that recall confusions are similar in manner and distribution to perceptual confusions about a noisy (degraded) stimulus. In this section of the paper, we have returned to and developed that point by treating perceptual recognition in theoretical terms that were first used to describe memory.

VIII. Commentary

A. RELATED WORK

A variety of consequences of the multicomponent representation has now been explored; the general idea seems indeed to have a diversity of implications. To place the theory in somewhat better perspective, recent similar or related work will be briefly discussed. Essentially the same hypothesis about memory has been proposed and researched by Bregman (cf. Bregman & Chambers, 1966). In his experiments, done with explicitly "dimensionalized" geometric figures varying in shape, color, and so on, Ss were shown particular patterns and told to remember the attribute-values conjoined in each pattern. Later tests of memory via reconstruction of the patterns, with additional guesses following errors, established presumptive evidence that S remembered and forgot single attributes of a pattern in an all-or-none manner. Memory test performance to a multidimensional pattern appeared graded, of course, because it was composed of several all-or-none units that could be remembered independently.

The relation of the multicomponent theory to the "one-element" model for associative learning (Bower, 1961a; Estes, 1961) is clear: the one-element model is a special case (namely, $N = 1$) of the multicomponent model. From a survey of research on the one-element model (Bower, 1964), it is clear that it fits learning data best only when there are two response alternatives. With more than two response alternatives, the data typically show "increments," or partial learning that goes on before a learning criterion is reached. Such a pattern of results is the outcome expected by the multicomponent theory.

The multicomponent theory is formally similar to models used by Crothers (1964) and Bower (1961b; 1964) to handle what they called "compound response learning." To illustrate, in one experiment by Bower (1964), Ss learned a 20-item paired-associate list in which the four response members were A1, A2, B1, and B2, consisting of two ordered binary components. Backward learning curves and other analyses of precriterion responses gave presumptive evidence that the (A, B) and (1, 2) components were separately learned and retained in an all-or-none fashion. The precriterion increments in the probability of the correct compound response were apparently related to the learning of one response component before the other. In that experiment, the encoding of the response ensemble was sufficiently obvious to permit a direct decomposition of the total response into elementary components that were being learned and retained in all all-or-none fashion. As for the general multicomponent model, the probability of a correct compound response was equal to the product of the probabilities that the separate components were recalled correctly.

The relation of the multicomponent theory to the stimulus fluctuation theory of forgetting proposed by Estes (1955) and modified by Izawa and Estes (1965) may be noted. Estes proposed that the N_s stimulus elements available when a reinforcement occurs become conditioned to the reinforced response, but during a retention interval any element in the available set may be interchanged with one of the N'_s elements that was not present at the time of the reinforcement. If these intruding elements from the N'_s set have not previously been conditioned, they will tend to lead to the correct response with only a "guessing" probability g. Letting $r(t)$ denote the probability that an element available at the time of reinforcement is still available at time t later, we can write the probability of the correct response at time t as

$$C(t) = r(t) + g(1 - r(t)). \tag{53}$$

This is obtained by averaging over the N_s elements currently available, of which a number $N_s r(t)$ were available and conditioned at the time of the previous reinforcement and a number $N_s(1 - r(t))$ were unavailable then but have intruded during the retention interval.

The $C(t)$ function in Eq. 53 is the same as the $u(t)$ function of the multicomponent theory in Eq. 7. Moreover, the $r(t)$ function that Estes (1955) derived from stimulus fluctuation theory is the same as Eq. 6 derived earlier from different considerations. Whereas stimulus sampling theory expresses $C(t)$ as an *average* over the N_s available elements of their probabilities of correct association, the multicomponent theory expresses $C(t)$ as the *product* of the N component probabilities. The response rules are the same when $N = 1$, but not otherwise. For the multicomponent theory, g is a constant and $r(t)$ increases with successive repetitions; for the fluctuation theory, $r(t)$ is a constant and the effective g in Eq. 53 increases with repetitions. But since $r(t)$ and g enter Eq. 53 in exactly the same way, these alternate descriptions are indistinguishable mathematically. Thus it would appear that predictions of *average* response probabilities for the multicomponent theory with $N = 1$ can be made identical to those of fluctuation theory. They will differ, however, in predictions of conditional probabilities of responses over several tests (that is, the RTT paradigm of Estes, 1960).

Finally, the multicomponent model may be compared to the "continuous-strength" model for recognition memory suggested by Egan (1958), Murdock (1965), Norman and Wickelgren (1965), Parks (1966), and developed more formally and extensively in a paper by Wickelgren and Norman (1966). The common approach of these investigators has been to apply to recognition memory essentially the same concepts as used in TSD, the theory of signal detectability (Swets *et al.*, 1961). In terms of specific assumptions, it is supposed that putting an item into the memory store establishes a trace characterized by a numerical "strength" that decreases with forgetting. Whenever this trace is retrieved on a test trial, its strength is subjected to random variations due to noise in the system. These noise variations are presumed to be continuous and the strengths of memory traces so varied are presumed to be normally distributed. Moreover, it is presumed that new items, not previously put into memory, nonetheless have, because of stimulus generalization, a memory trace existing at a certain strength, and these are assumed to be normally distributed. Finally, the average separation between the distributions of strengths of new and old items is assumed to vary with the amount of retention and the dissimilarity of the two sets of items. By such postulations, TSD is carried over for application to recognition memory—specifically, to account for MOC curves.

The main difference between the continuous-strength approach and the theory proposed here is one of strategy. The continuous-strength theory simply postulates a particular decision structure (corresponding to TSD) for recognition memory. In contrast, the multicomponent theory provides a rationale for deriving this decision structure from more elementary assumptions. Because of their wider range of application, these elementary assumptions obtain evidential support from other sources besides the shape of MOC curves for recognition. Also, in providing a rationale for TSD in recognition memory, the multicomponent theory eliminates some of the awkward or inelegant postulations required by the continuous-strength approach.

B. SOME CRITICISMS

In developing a theory, the alternate role of a critic of the developments must also be adopted. There are a variety of criticisms that can be lodged against the specific theory outlined here. Many concern the incompleteness inherent in any initial formulation, or indicate the need to admit further complications to the first simple representation explored (for example, the components may be forgotten at different rates or have different guessing probabilities). Incompleteness or even ambiguity in certain respects is to be expected here since, as mentioned at the outset, the proposal deals with really only one aspect of the memory problem, namely, representing a possible logical structure of the memory trace. But to say that a preliminary theory is incomplete, idealized, or even occasionally ambiguous is not to say that it is dead wrong, but rather than it requires further thought and elaboration. Of the several incompletenesses of the present formulation, two particularly vexing ones will be discussed.

The first concerns the parameter N, the number of information components encoded by the stimulus-analyzers and stored in memory. For a given population of stimulus materials (such as nonsense syllables), what approximately is N? Is N a fixed constant determined by the past perceptual learning of S in dealing with materials of a given type, or is it an elastic variable that can be adjusted on the spot to efficiently encode the limited ensemble of materials that happen to be selected for experimental use? For a given item in a constant ensemble, does N remain stable or does it change systematically over the course of learning? What, if any, difference in N exists for encoding integrated versus nonintegrated strings of symbols (such as DOG versus OGD)?

Such questions cannot be answered now with any definiteness or assurance. They are really questions concerning the operation of the pattern-recognition machine in Fig. 1—whether and how its operations can be modified by knowledge in the memory stores. It will be recalled that at the outset of this paper the operation of the pattern recognizer was left deliberately vague; this vagueness is necessary because no completely adequate model of pattern recognition is known (cf. Gyr, Brown, Willey, & Zivan, 1966, and Uhr, 1965, for a review). The only assumption made about the pattern recognizer was that its output could be characterized as a list of features or information components.

More specific assumptions about its operation can be explored for their consequences in the memory system. For example, a likely assumption is that the pattern recognizer groups or segregates the experimental stimulus materials into elementary functional units (such as alphabetic letters of a trigram), which it treats as the units for encoding and identification. According to this view, presentation of the visual trigram OGD would initiate three separate identification and storage operations. An O would be identified in position 1, leading to storage of the trace (P1, C(O)), where C(O) would be a list of the distinctive phonetic features of saying O to oneself; G and D would be similarly identified and stored in association with markers for positions 2 and 3. Thus, the compound trace system storing OGD would be represented as [(P1, C(O)), (P2, C(G)), (P3, C(D))], where C(O), C(G), and C(D) are vectors describing phonetic features of saying O, G, and D, respectively.

The problem with this naive approach is that the elementary units for storage will change as the material goes from nonsense to meaningful words. Thus, the grapheme DOG, although initially identified in terms of its letters, would be given a secondary phonetic coding, the distinctive features of saying "DAHG," and this shorter secondary code would be stored. Because this code is shorter than the three-letter code, forgetting is less and learning faster. This view agrees with the finding (Underwood & Schulz, 1960) that the pronounceability of a trigram corelates highly with its rate of being learned. However, this view simply assumes that the encoding units change without really explaining why. It does not dispose of the *deus* in the perceptual *machina*. The conceptual problem remains and probably will continue thus until more substantial progress is made on theories of pattern recognition.

C. Possible Retrieval Schemes

1. *Stimulus Confusion Errors*

The second incompleteness of the theory that requires mention regards retrieval of the memory trace. The derivations have proceeded on the naive view that the retrieval mechanism (whatever it is) operates perfectly, always pulling out the appropriate memory trace for recall or comparison to a test stimulus. Moreover, only cued retention tests (such as paired associates with distinctive stimulus members) have been explicitly considered. These simplifications were introduced into the initial formulation to see what types of retention data were explicable in part by assumptions only about the structure of the memory trace. A more complicated but realistic retrieval mechanism for cued retention tests can be elaborated (cf. Bower, 1964). Given storage of the pairs S_1-R_1, S_2-R_2, and so on in terms of compound encoded vectors (CS_1, CR_1), (CS_2, CR_2), and so on, retrieval of the trace to test stimulus S_i is determined by a "similarity" principle. That is, the test stimulus S_i, encoded as CS_i, is matched successively or in parallel to the encoded stimulus members of the traces located in the relevant parts of the storage system. That trace whose encoded stimulus best matches CS_i is retrieved (provided the match score exceeds a criterion) and the response vector of this trace is sent to the motor-output unit.

Suppose that this were indeed the retrieval process. If the information in the encoded stimulus CS_1 is perfectly retained, then stimulus S_1 always will retrieve the (CS_1, CR_1) trace. But retrieval errors will occur if the components of the stimulus members are themselves subject to forgetting. In this case, the encoded test stimulus CS_1 would be compared to the degraded forms of CS_1, CS_2, . . . , and a better match may possibly result for an incorrect stimulus. In such cases, the trace that S retrieves would lead to a response best described as a "stimulus generalization" error. The over-all retrieval process when K traces are effective in the relevant memory bank (through which the search is done) is identical in form to the process described in Section IV,D, for multiple-choice recognition tests with K alternatives, except that in the latter case the comparison and matching operations are carried out on the response rather than the stimulus members of the pairs. The likelihood of retrieving the correct trace will vary with (a) the number of alternative traces to be compared, (b) the rate of forgetting stimulus information, and (c) the similarity of the encoded representations of the various stimuli. Let $w(K, t)$ denote the probability that the correct trace, as degraded at time t, is retrieved out of a store holding K traces, and let q denote the probability of correct recall when a trace with an incorrect stimulus member is erroneously retrieved; then the modified recall probability would be

$$C'(t) = w(K, t)C(t) + [1 - w(K, t)]q \qquad (54)$$

In this expression, $C(t)$ is the previous value calculated when retrieval was assumed to be perfect (that is, Eq. 4), $w(K, t)$ is the retrieval probability, comparable to Eq. 18, and $C'(t)$ is the correct response probability when retrieval effects are considered.

Two immediate consequences of Eq. 54 may be mentioned. First, over the course of a short-term memory experiment, K will begin at or near zero and increase as more items are introduced, arriving at some stable asymptote dependent on the net forgetting rate; correspondingly, the correct retrieval probability $w(K, t)$ will decline, and so will $C'(t)$ as a consequence. Thus, immediate recall of the first item in the experiment should be highest, with progressively poorer immediate recall of the second, third, and so forth, item in the series, until K reaches its equilibrium value. Such changes in $C'(t)$ over the experiment have been reported by Keppel and Underwood (1962) and Loess (1964). Second, an abrupt change, in mid-experiment, in the nature of the items to be remembered (as, to a different set of letters) will increase the effective d in Eq. 18, causing an abrupt increase in the correct retrieval probability in Eq. 54. Thus, the first few items after the shift in materials would have higher retrieval and recall probabilities. This effect has been reported by Wickens, Born, and Allen (1963). Both of these effects were interpreted by the experimenters in terms of the accumulation and release of proactive interference; they are interpreted here in terms of changes in the probability of retrieving the correct memory trace. Although the vocabulary used differs, there is in fact very little difference between the two interpretations (proactive interference versus retrieval difficulty) in this instance.

2. *Item Recognition*

This simple matching scheme may be applied also to the item recognition task introduced by Shepard and Teghtsoonian (1961). In their experiment, S viewed a long series of items (three-digit numbers), half of which were repetitions of items presented earlier. For each item S judged whether or not it had occurred previously (was "old"). Conceived in terms of the present model, the successive items $I_1, I_2, \ldots ,$ would be encoded and stored as compound vector traces, denoted $CI_1,$ $CI_2, \ldots ,$ and these traces would decay as previously assumed. For S to decide whether a freshly presented item is old or new, it would be supposed that its encoded representation would be matched successively to the CI_j's in the memory store, and the comparator would report back the maximal match score so obtained. The probability distribution of the maximal match scores would be difficult to derive, but its mean value would clearly be greater for old than for new items, and would also be greater the larger the number of active traces in the store. To make a decision, the maximal match score obtained in a given scan of the memory store would be compared to an adjustable criterion, with the "old" decision arising if the score exceeded the criterion. Such a system would show a decline in recognition rate with time (or intervening items) since a target item was put into it. The system would also show an increasing false alarm rate as the experimental series proceeds, since the more traces in the memory store to be compared to the current (new) item, the greater on the average will be the maximal match score obtained, thus leading to a (false) positive judgment with appreciable probability. Such were the results reported by Shepard and Teghtsoonian (1961). Furthermore, once steady state has been reached (that is, once the average number of effective traces reaches equilibrium), if an item is falsely called old upon its first presentation, it is more likely to be called old on its second presentation than would be an item called new on its first presentation. That is, the similarities between the former item and other items in the store that caused it to be called old upon its first presentation are likely to persist and boost the probability of its being called old again the second time, even though its encoded representation in memory may be forgotten. Such conditional effects of the first response upon the second response to an item have been found in experiments by Melton (cited in Bernbach, 1964). Detailed mathematical investigations of the proposals for this task have not been undertaken, but simulation by Monte Carlo runs could easily be carried through.

3. Noncued Recall

Finally, consider noncued recall tasks, which can be either restricted or unrestricted in order of recall. Examples of the first would be a digit-span test or the single-trigram recall procedure of Peterson and Peterson (1959); an example of the second is free verbal recall of a list of words (Murdock, 1962), where the words may be recalled in any order. Since many different lists and tests are given successively in the typical experiment, it is clear that in retrieval S must be guided by temporal cues, essentially selecting only items from the most recent list. It is clear that Ss can make such temporal discriminations with fair accuracy (see Yntema & Trask, 1963), but the present theory must be expanded before it can account for such phenomena.

Such temporal discrimination among memory traces could be carried out by several methods. One approach would assume that an "arrival-time tag" of some sort is one of the pieces of information stored along with a memory trace. Temporal discrimination among traces would then use only the information provided by this time-tag component. An alternative hypothesis is to suppose that the storage system itself has an inherent means for keeping track of the order of arrival of incoming information.

An example of a simple device that preserves temporal order of item arrivals is a "push-down list," wherein a newly arriving item is placed on the top of a memory list and is the first encountered. A familiar analog is the spring-loaded plate holder commonly found in cafeterias, which operates on a "last in, first out" principle. Consider using such a device to represent storage of temporal recency and spatial-order information in the Peterson and Peterson (1959) task. The S is presented with a series of nonsense trigrams, counting backward and recalling each one after it is presented. The representation would consist in three push-down lists, one for each of the three letter positions. The notion of using a separate list to store the letter in each position is essentially the hypothesis Conrad (1965) proposed to deal with confusions and misorderings in serial recall from short-term memory. To illustrate these concepts, suppose the first four trigrams presented (and then recalled) are XYZ, FLP, DUX, and MLS, in that order. Then the push-down list in memory after presentation of the fourth trigram could be represented as in the accompanying tabular array.

	Letter position		
	1	2	3
Top (last in):	C(M)	C(L)	C(S)
	C(D)	C(U)	C(X)
	C(F)	C(L)	C(P)
	C(X)	C(Y)	C(Z)
	.	.	.
	.	.	.

The C(X) notation denotes the encoded vector of information corresponding to X. Since forgetting degrades the memory vectors to an extent depending on their time in memory, the vectors lower down on the list will usually contain less information than those higher up.

Recall of the most recently presented item is provided by retrieving the top "plate" of the stack. Its integrity for aiding recall would depend on how much degradation of this vector had occurred during the counting-backward activity that followed its input. Such a device could also perform in recalling items at a constant lag back in time; for example, upon presentation of item n, store it, then recall item $n - j$. The processor would simply count down j deep into the stack, retrieve that vector, and output whatever was possible (if anything) on the basis of its degraded information. Recall accuracy, of course, would decline rapidly with the lag j and with the size (complexity) of the experimental items. Slight errors in the count backward would produce recall of items adjacent to the one j back. Such results were reported by Mackworth (1959) and have been repeated in unpublished experiments by the author. Furthermore, if two previously presented items were shown on a test trial, the device could do a creditable job at recognizing which item had occurred more recently in the past. This could be done by its noting the location on the list at which each test item obtained its maximal match score, and then choosing as more recent that one higher up on the list. Forgetting, causing loss of information, would introduce error into locating the items in question, and more so the more components forgotten. Thus, accuracy of judging the more recent of two items would decline as the items grew older in memory. Such results seem qualitatively in line with those reported by Yntema and Trask (1963) for recency discrimination. Again, Monte

Carlo simulations would be needed to investigate further implications of the system.

Turning finally to free recall, the evident complexities of that process prevents any simple hypotheses. Various potent factors have been identified in determining whether a word will be recalled and in what order; such factors include list length, study time, serial position, inter-item associations, word clustering, and approximation of word order to English text. Moreover, over successive practice trials in recalling the same list of words, it is clear that Ss subjectively organize the items into idiosyncratic patterns, presumably using clusters that facilitate carrying out a systematic search through memory that will retrieve most of the items (Tulving, 1962). We are unable to suggest any sensible retrieval scheme that, in conjunction with the present memory system, would begin to make contact with the complexities of free recall data. The obvious candidate—simply sampling traces from the store and "dumping" them out in recall—gives a gross approximation for some purposes (such as serial position curves, cf. Atkinson & Shiffrin, 1965; Bower, 1964), but it ignores too many of the potent determinants of such recall.

ACKNOWLEDGMENT

Many of the themes developed in this paper were stimulated by attendance at a 1965 summer institute on Mathematical Models for Memory at Cambridge, Massachusetts, sponsored by The Center for Advanced Study in the Behavioral Sciences. The author wishes to express his gratitude to the conference participants for their encouragement and stimulation.

REFERENCES

Allport, G. W., & Postman, L. *The psychology of rumor.* New York: Holt, 1948.

Atkinson, R. C., Bower, G. H., & Crothers, E. J. *An introduction to mathematical learning theory.* New York: Wiley, 1965.

Atkinson, R. C., Carterette, E. C., & Kinchla, R. A. The effect of information feedback upon psychophysical judgments. *Psychon., Sci.,* 1964, **1**, 83–84 (a)

Atkinson, R. C., Hansen, D. N., & Bernbach, H. A. Short-term memory with young children. *Psychon. Sci.,* 1964, **1**, 255–256. (b)

Atkinson, R. C., & Shiffrin, R. M. Mathematical models for memory and learning. Tech. Rep. No. 79, Institute for Mathematical Studies in the Social Sciences, Stanford Univer., 1965.

Attneave, F. Some informational aspects of visual perception. *Psychol. Rev.,* 1954, **61**, 183–193.

Barlow, H. B. Sensory mechanisms, the reduction of redundancy, and intelligence. In *Mechanization of thought processes.* Vol. II. London: H. M. Stationery Office, 1959. Pp. 535–561.

Bartlett, F. C. *Remembering.* London and New York: Cambridge Univer. Press, 1932.

Bernbach, H. A. A decision and forgetting model for recognition memory. Tech. Rep. No. 64–4, Univer. of Michigan, Math. Psychol. Program, Ann Arbor, 1964.

Binford, J. R., & Gettys, C. Nonstationarity in paired-associate learning as indicated by a second guess procedure. *J. math. Psychol.,* 1965, **2,** 190–195.

Bower, G. H. Application of a model to paired associate learning. *Psychometrika,* 1961, **26,** 255–280. (a)

Bower, G. H. Application of the all-or-none conditioning model to the learning of compound responses. Tech Rep. No. 37, Institute for Mathematical Studies in the Social Sciences, Stanford Univer., 1961. (b)

Bower, G. H. Notes on a descriptive theory of memory. Paper read at second conference on learning, remembering, and forgetting. Princeton, 1964. To appear in D. P. Kimble (Ed.), *Learning, remembering, and forgetting,* Vol. 2. New York: N.Y. Acad. Sci., in press.

Bower, G. H., & Hintzman, D. L. Confidence ratings during paired associate learning. Unpublished manuscript, 1963.

Bregman, A. S., & Chambers, D. W. All-or-none learning of attributes. *J. exp. Psychol.,* 1966, **71,** 785–793.

Broadbent, D. E. A mechanical model for human attention and immediate memory. *Psychol. Rev.,* 1957, **64,** 205–215.

Broadbent, D. E. *Perception and communication.* Oxford: Pergamon Press, 1958.

Brown, J. Information, redundancy and decay of the memory trace. In *The mechanisation of thought processes.* Natl. Phys. Lab. Sympos. No. 10. London: H. M. Stationery Office, 1959.

Brown, J. A comparison of recognition and recall by a multiple-response method. *J. verb. Learn. verb. Behav.,* 1965, **4,** 401–408.

Christie, L. S., & Luce, R. D. Decision structure and time relations in simple choice behavior. *Bull. math. Biophysics,* 1956, **18,** 89–112.

Clarke, F. R., Birdsall, T. G., & Tanner, W. P., Jr. Two types of ROC curves and definition of parameters. *J. acoust. Soc. Amer.,* 1959, **31,** 629–630.

Conrad, R. Acoustic confusions in immediate memory. *Brit. J. Psychol.,* 1964, **55,** 75–84.

Conrad, R. Order errors in immediate recall of sequences. *J. verb. Learn. verb. Behav.,* 1965, **4,** 161–169.

Craik, K. J. *The nature of explanation.* London and New York: Cambridge Univer. Press, 1943.

Crossman, E. R. F. W. Information processes in human skill. *Brit. Med. Bull.,* 1964, **20,** 32–37. (Issue on *Exp. Psychol.*)

Crothers, E. J. All-or-none learning with compound responses. In R. C. Atkinson (Ed.), *Studies in mathematical psychology.* Stanford: Stanford Univer. Press, 1964. Pp. 95–115.

Deutsch, J. A. *The structural basis of behavior.* Chicago: Univer. of Chicago Press, 1960.

Egan, J. P. Recognition memory and the operating characteristic. AFCRC TN 58–51, AD 152650, Hearing and Communication Laboratory, Indiana Univer., June, 1958.

Estes, W. K. Statistical theory of spontaneous recovery and regression. *Psychol. Rev.,* 1955, **62,** 145–154.

Estes, W. K. Learning theory and the new mental chemistry. *Psychol. Rev.,* 1960, **67,** 207–223.

Estes, W. K. New developments in statistical behavior theory: Differential tests of axioms for associative learning. *Psychometrika,* 1961, **26,** 73–84.

Forgie, J. W., & Forgie, C. D. Results obtained from an auditory-recognition computer program. *J. acoust. Soc. Amer.*, 1959, **31**, 1480–1484.

Garner, W. R. *Uncertainty and structure as psychological concepts.* New York: Wiley, 1962.

Gomulicki, B. R. The development and present status of the trace theory of memory. *Brit. J. Psychol. Monogr.*, 1953, Suppl. 29, 1–94.

Gyr, J. W., Brown, J. S., Willey, R., & Zivan, A. Computer simulation and psychological theories of perception. *Psychol. Bull.*, 1966, **65**, 174–192.

Halle, M., & Stevens, K. N. Speech recognition: A model and a program for research. In J. A. Foder and J. J. Katz (Eds.), *The structure of language.* Englewood Cliffs, New Jersey: Prentice-Hall, 1964. Pp. 604–612.

Harary, F., Norman, R. Z., & Cartwright, D. *Structural models: An introduction to the theory of directed graphs.* New York: Wiley, 1965.

Hart, J. T. Memory and the feeling-of-knowing experience. *J. educ. Psychol.* 1965, **56**, 208–216.

Hellyer, S. Frequency of stimulus presentation and short-term decrement in recall. *J. exp. Psychol.*, 1962, **64**, 650.

Hick, W. E. On the rate of gain of information. *Quart. J. exp. Psychol.*, 1952, **4**, 11–26.

Hyman, R. Stimulus information as a determinant of reaction time. *J. exp. Psychol.*, 1953, **45**, 188–196.

Izawa, C., & Estes, W. K. Reinforcement-test sequences in paired-associate learning. Tech. Rep. No. 76, Psychol. Ser. Institute for Mathematical Studies in the Social Sciences, Stanford Univer., 1965.

Keppel, G. Problems of method in the study of short-term memory. *Psychol. Bull.*, 1965, **63**, 1–13.

Keppel, G., & Underwood, B. J. Proactive inhibition in short-term retention of single items. *J. verb. Learn. verb. Behav.*, 1962, **3**, 153–161.

Landauer, T. K. Two states of paired-associate learning. *Psychol. Rep.*, 1962, **11**, 387–389.

Loess, H. Proactive inhibition in short-term memory. *J. verb. Learn. verb Behav.*, 1964, **3**, 362–368.

McGill, W. J. Stochastic latency mechanisms. In R. D. Luce, R. R. Bush, & E. Galanter (Eds.), *Handbook of mathematical psychology.* Vol. I. New York: Wiley, 1963. Pp. 309–360.

MacKay, D. M. Towards an information-flow model of human behavior. *Brit. J. Psychol.*, 1956, **47**, 30–43.

Mackworth, J. F. Paced memorizing in a continuous task. *J. exp. Psychol.*, 1959, **58**, 206–211.

Mackworth, J. F. The relation between the visual image and post-perceptual immediate memory. *J. verb. Learn. verb. Behav.*, 1963, **2**, 75–85.

Mackworth, J. F. Interference and decay in short-term memory. *J. verb. Learn. verb. Behav.*, 1964, **3**, 300–308.

Melton, A. W. Implications of short-term memory for a general theory of memory. *J. verb. Learn. verb. Behav.*, 1963, **2**, 1–21.

Miller, G. A. The magical number seven, plus or minus two: Some limits on our capacity for processing information. *Psychol. Rev.*, 1956, **63**, 81–97.

Miller, G. A., Galanter, E., & Pribram, K. *Plans and the structure of behavior.* New York: Holt, 1960.

Miller, G. A., Heise, G. A., & Lichten, W. The intelligibility of speech as a function of the context of the test materials. *J. exp. Psychol.*, 1951, **41**, 329–335.

Murdock, B. B., Jr. The serial position effect in free recall. *J. exp. Psychol.*, 1962, **64**, 482–488.

Murdock, B. B., Jr. Short-term retention of single paired associates. *J. exp. Psychol.*, 1963, **65**, 433–443. (a)

Murdock, B. B., Jr. An analysis of the recognition process. In C. N. Cofer & B. S. Musgrave (Eds.), *Verbal behavior and learning.* New York: McGraw-Hill, 1963. Pp. 10–22. (b)

Murdock, B. B., Jr. Signal-detection theory and short-term memory. *J. exp. Psychol.*, 1965, **70**, 443–447.

Murdock, B. B. Jr. The criterion problem in short-term memory. *J. exp. Psychol.*, 1966, **72**, 317–324.

Nilsson, N. J. *Learning machines.* New York: McGraw-Hill, 1965.

Norman, D. A., & Wickelgren, W. A. Short-term recognition memory for single digits and pairs of digits. *J. exp. Psychol.*, 1965, **70**, 479–489.

Parducci, A. Category judgment: A range-frequency model. *Psychol. Rev.*, 1965, **72**, 497–418.

Parks, T. E. Signal-detectability theory of recognition-memory performance. *Psychol. Rev.*, 1966, **73**, 44–58.

Peterson, L. R. Immediate memory: Data and theory. In C. N. Cofer & B. S. Musgrave (Eds.), *Verbal behavior and learning.* New York: McGraw-Hill, 1963. Pp. 336–353.

Peterson, L. R., & Peterson, M. Short-term retention of individual verbal items. *J. exp. Psychol.*, 1959, **58**, 193–198.

Peterson, L. R., & Peterson, M. J. Minimal paired-associate learning. *J. exp. Psychol.*, 1962, **63**, 521–527.

Pollack, I. Assimilation of sequentially encoded information. *Amer. J. Psychol.*, 1953, **66**, 421–435.

Pollack, I. Message uncertainty and message reception. *J. acoust. Soc. Amer.*, 1959, **31**, 1500–1508.

Pollack, I., Norman, D. A., & Galanter, E. An efficient non-parametric analysis of recognition memory. *Psychon. Sci.*, 1965, **1**, 327–328.

Posner, M. I. Immediate memory in sequential tasks. *Psychol. Bull.*, 1963, **60**, 333–349.

Postman, L. Choice behavior and the process of recognition. *Amer. J. Psychol.*, 1950, **63**, 576–583.

Postman, L. Short-term memory and incidental learning. In A. W. Melton (Ed.), *Categories of human learning.* New York: Academic Press, 1964.

Riley, D. A. Memory for form. In L. Postman (Ed.) *Psychology in the making: Histories of selected research problems.* New York: Knopf, 1962. Pp. 402–465.

Shepard, R. N., & Chang, J. J. Forced-choice tests of recognition memory under steady-state conditions. *J. verb. Learn. verb. Behav.*, 1963, **2**, 93–101.

Shepard, R. N., & Teghtsoonian, M. Retention of information under conditions approaching a steady-state. *J. exp. Psychol.*, 1961, **62**, 302–309.

Stevens, K. N. Toward a model for speech recognition. *J. acoust. Soc. Amer.*, 1960, **32**, 47–51.

Swets, J. A., Tanner, W. P., Jr. & Birdsall, T. G. Decision processes in perception. *Psychol. Rev.*, 1961, **68**, 301–340.

Tulving, E. Subjective organization in free recall of "unrelated" words. *Psychol. Rev.*, 1962, **69**, 344–354.

Uhr, L. Pattern recognition computers as models for form perception. *Psychol. Bull.*, 1963, **60**, 40–73.

Uhr, L. (Ed.) *Pattern recognition: Theory, experiment, computer simulations, and dynamic models of form perception and discovery.* New York: Wiley, 1965.

Underwood, B. J., & Schulz, R. W. *Meaningfulness and verbal learning.* Philadelphia: Lippincott, 1960.

Waugh, N. C., & Norman, D. A. Primary memory. *Psychol. Rev.,* 1965, **72,** 89:104.

Wickelgren, W. A., & Norman, D. A. Strength models and serial position in short-term recognition memory. *J. math. Psychol.,* 1966, **3,** 316–347.

Wickens, D. D., Born, D. G., & Allen, C. K. Proactive inhibition and item similarity in short-term memory. *J. verb. Learn. verb. Behav.,* 1963, **2,** 440:445.

Wulf, F. Uber die Veränderung von Vorstellungen. *Psych. Forsch.,* 1922, **1,** 333:373.

Yntema, D. B., & Trask, F. P. Recall as a search process. *J. verb. Learn. verb Behav.,* 1963, **2,** 65–74.

INDEX

543